How to Do *Everything* with Your

Genealogy

How to Do *Everything* with Your Genealogy

George G. Morgan

McGraw-Hill/Osborne

New York   Chicago   San Francisco   Lisbon
London   Madrid   Mexico City   Milan   New Delhi
San Juan   Seoul   Singapore   Sydney   Toronto

McGraw-Hill/Osborne
2100 Powell Street, 10th Floor
Emeryville, California 94608
U.S.A.

To arrange bulk purchase discounts for sales promotions, premiums, or fund-raisers, please contact **McGraw-Hill**/Osborne at the above address. For information on translations or book distributors outside the U.S.A., please see the International Contact Information page immediately following the index of this book.

How to Do Everything with Your Genealogy

890 FGR FGR 0198

ISBN 0-07-223170-X

Publisher	Brandon A. Nordin
Vice President &	
Associate Publisher	Scott Rogers
Acquisitions Editor	Megg Morin
Project Editor	Mark Karmendy
Acquisitions Coordinator	Athena Honore
Technical Editor	Drew Smith
Copy Editor	Claire Splan
Proofreader	Susie Elkind
Indexer	Rebecca Plunkett
Composition	International Typesetting & Composition
Illustrators	Melinda Lytle, Kathleen Edwards
Cover Series Design	Dodie Shoemaker
Cover Illustration	Tom Willis

This book was composed with Corel VENTURA™ Publisher.

Dedication

To my brother and best friend,
Carey Thomas Morgan.
Your constant love and support are living proof that family *is* forever.

About the Author

George G. Morgan is the internationally recognized author of the award-winning weekly online column "Along Those Lines" for Ancestry.com, and the author of several books about genealogy. He is currently the president of the International Society of Family History Writers and Editors (ISFHWE). His countless articles on genealogy have appeared in journals, magazines, and online venues in the United States, Canada, the United Kingdom, and Singapore.

A professional educator and lecturer, he is the president of Aha! Seminars, Inc., a company specializing in providing continuing education seminars for library professionals. He is a popular, featured speaker at local, state, and national genealogical conferences, and was program chair for the 2003 Federation of Genealogical Societies Conference. He is a member of the Association of Professional Genealogists (APG), the Genealogical Speakers Guild (GSG), the International Society of Family History Writers and Editors (ISFHWE), and of more than a dozen genealogical societies at all levels. He lives in a suburb of Tampa, Florida.

Contents

Acknowledgments

Writing of any sort, I've always found, is a cathartic experience. It forces me to draw from my personal knowledge and experiences and somehow translate it all into words that will evoke a comprehensible image on the part of my readers. I also know and sincerely appreciate the fact that no writer can do it all alone. The help and support of many people and organizations contribute to any successful publication, and this book is certainly no exception.

I would like to thank the following people for their graciousness in providing sample documents and images for use as illustrations in this book: Gillian Anderson, Carl F. Johansson, Ingrid H. Johansson, Jody Johnson, Sheena Maguire, Jim Powell, June Roth, Karen Roth, Drew Smith, Jeff Smith, Carey Morgan, Veronica Vinson, and Sherrie Williams. The book is so much better because of your help!

I'd also like to thank the following organizations and people for help in providing their gracious permission to use document images, screen shots, and other materials in the book: Aha! Seminars, Inc.; The General Register Office for Scotland; The National Archives in the United Kingdom; The National Archives and Records Administration; Dan Rencricca of Battery Park Software; Simon Orde of Calico Pie, Ltd.; Bill Woodruff and Michele Mosteller of the Church of Jesus Christ of Latter-day Saints; Bruce Buzbee of FormalSoft, Inc.; Doug Gordon of GHCS Software; Jake Gehring of HeritageQuest/ProQuest; Gaylon Findlay of Incline Software, LC; Deb Stuller of Leister Productions, Inc.; Loretto "Lou" Szucs and David Farnsworth of MyFamily.com, Inc. and Ancestry.com, Inc.; Kevin Phillips of Northern Hills Software; Clive Henry and Kim Harrison of Otherdays.com and Irish Origins Media; Lisa Wagner of the Tampa-Hillsborough County Public Library; and Thomas Ward of Tapperware.

I am especially grateful to the people who worked so hard planning and editing the book. They could see the proverbial forest for the trees when I couldn't, and their dedication to excellence make the book a better read for everyone. Megg Morin, Athena Honore, and Mark Karmendy, the McGraw-Hill/Osborne Media staff who so expertly managed this book project, are my heroes. They listened, provided guidance, and lent support at every step of the process and I am in their debt. Drew Smith's technical editing, advice, and reference assistance helped make the book more accurate.

Claire Splan's copy editing polished the rough edges, making sometimes complex ideas read better. I can't applaud these people's efforts enough. Thank you, TEAM!

And finally, I have to express my love and gratitude to the two people who gave me the most support and encouragement during this long, arduous project. Carey Morgan and Drew Smith were always there when I needed them, giving moral support and advice along the path to completing the book. A million thanks!

George G. Morgan
March 2004

Introduction

Family is forever! That is a lesson I learned at a young age when my aunt and grandmother exposed me to their pride in their family history. Their stories and enthusiasm sparked an interest in me to explore and learn more on my own. From that day forward, history and geography were no longer just names, dates, and places. They became the world stage on which my ancestors and family members actively participated, observed, and/or were affected. That perspective has served me well over time because it encouraged me to always try to place my family into context with the places, periods, and events of their lives and to view them as *real* people.

The title of this book, *How to Do Everything with Your Genealogy* is, perhaps, something of a misnomer. My first reaction when this project was being discussed was, "Well, volume one of the work will be 15,000 pages long." No one laughed. Those of us who have been working on our genealogy for a while, however, know that the amount of information and resources available to us is nearly incomprehensible and that a work covering literally "everything" would probably occupy an entire bookcase. Still, I believe you will find in these pages a well-balanced foundation for your family history research.

As researchers, we must become methodical detectives who investigate every clue and carefully weigh the evidence we uncover. There are logical processes we can follow and strategies we can employ to help achieve success, even getting past many of the inevitable "brick walls" we encounter. I have included scores of illustrations to help you visualize the documents and Web sites discussed in the text. Many of these are actual documents and images from my own research collection, while others have been loaned or supplied to me for use in the book. There also are screen shots of Web pages and representative screens from a variety of online databases and genealogical software programs that will help you visualize what the providers have to offer.

This book will provide you with a solid foundation for beginning and continuing your family history research. It covers the major record types available in the United States, Canada, and the United Kingdom, as well as research strategies for successfully locating and evaluating them. The fact that all three geographies and more are addressed makes this book unique.

You will find that the book is organized in a logical progression to help you build and expand your knowledge. Regardless of your level of experience and expertise, I think you will find something helpful at every turn. You will learn the basic rules of genealogical evidence and how to use your "critical thinking skills" in evaluating the source materials you find. Along the way, you will learn successful research methods and strategies, including tips and techniques for effectively using the fastest-growing segment of genealogical research tools: the Internet. In addition, an often little- or poorly-utilized facility, the online catalog of libraries and archives, is discussed in detail and should substantially help your research. The document images, photographs, screen shots, and tables will provide you with visual references to help understand the material discussed in the text.

Gathering information wherever you go is a given, but many people simply show up unprepared and wander aimlessly in their research. Advance preparation and organization for a genealogical research trip are the keys to success, regardless of whether you're planning a visit to your local public library or making a once-in-a-lifetime trip to a foreign country in search of records of your family's origins there. I've therefore included an entire chapter covering planning and making a successful genealogical research trip that I'm sure will help you conduct research like a professional.

Modern genealogists depend on computers and peripheral equipment for processing, storing, evaluating, and documenting all types of text and multimedia materials. I've therefore included two chapters that provide guidance for assessing and selecting computer hardware (desktop, notebook, PDA, printer, scanner) and software. This includes how to choose the "right" genealogical database program for your needs, as well as available genealogical software for your PDA that allows you to take your entire database wherever you go. No other book on the market today combines such a full range of research guidance and data processing/storage topics from a genealogist's perspective. This really *is* a balanced "how to do everything" book that genealogists have been waiting for.

You are embarking on a fascinating genealogical research odyssey that may last your entire lifetime. Along the way, you will meet many wonderful people and will come to know your ancestors and their families as real people—and as close personal friends. It is my fervent hope that your research will be successful and that your family tree will prove to be a fruitful source of information to help you better understand your family origins.

Happy hunting!
George G. Morgan

Part I

Begin Your Family History Odyssey

Chapter 1

Why Explore Your Genealogy?

How to...

- Start at the beginning with yourself and work backward
- Discover sources of information in your own home
- Understand what types of records and materials can help you learn more
- Interview *all* your relatives
- Begin to organize what you find

We are living in fast-paced times, and sometimes it feels as if we are transients without a sense of place. Jobs, marriage, and a wide variety of circumstances draw us away from the places where we were born and raised and separate us from our family members. It isn't unusual at some point to feel the need to reconnect in some way, and often with that need comes the desire to learn more about our family origins. It therefore should be no surprise that researching genealogy, or family history, is the second most popular hobby in the English-speaking world, following online auctions. It also is estimated to be the third most popular use of the Internet after the use of e-mail and reading news sites.

The terms *genealogy* and *family history* are often used interchangeably. While they may seem similar, there actually is a distinction between them.

- Genealogy is the scholarly study of a family's line of descent from its ancestors, during which one develops an understanding of the family's historical context and documents its history and traditions.
- Family history is the study of a family's history and traditions over an extended period of time and may involve documenting some or all of the facts.

A family historian may seek to trace and document specific family members or a branch of the family, and to perhaps write a family history. A genealogist, on the other hand, typically has a much broader view of the family. He or she will trace an entire or extended family structure, including brothers, sisters, aunts, uncles, cousins. This will include both their antecedents (the persons from whom they are descended) and their descendents. The genealogist will actively seek documentary evidence of many types to prove and verify facts about the family. In addition, the genealogist seeks to place family members and ancestors into geographical, historical, and social context in order to better understand their lives.

We *are* the product of our ancestry in many different ways. Certainly genetics play a critical part in our physical makeup, determining our physical characteristics and potential susceptibility to medical and mental conditions. However, the circumstances of place, time, education, economics, experiences, family group dynamics, and interactions with the personalities of our family members and friends also distinctly influence our development. They all contribute to the overall person that we become. The family stories and traditions that we have observed and that have been passed from generation to generation contribute to our sense of kinship and belonging. It is no wonder that we want to explore, maintain, document, and preserve these factors.

There are many motivations for genealogical research. Some people trace their family to help understand their place in it. Others study and document a family's direct line of descent in order to link to some famous personage. Often this is done in order to join one or more of the lineage or heritage societies, such as the Daughters of the American Revolution, the Mayflower Descendants, or the First Fleet Fellowship. Still others may research their family's history for reasons such as medical history, trying to locate their natural parents, document a family's or community's history, or to help locate heirs. Whatever *your* reasons for tracing and investigating your own family's history, your search will lead you on an interesting and exciting journey of discovery. Don't be surprised if your quest lasts a lifetime.

Start at the Beginning: Yourself and Your Family

My genealogical research began on a cold, snowy January day in my North Carolina hometown when I was ten years old. While snowfall was not unusual, a six-inch accumulation was rare indeed. There was no school scheduled for several days, and I spent the days at the home of my aunt, Mary Allen Morgan, and my Grandmother Morgan while my parents worked. Both women had a strong sense of family and history, especially my grandmother. She was the daughter and granddaughter of prominent physicians, as well as the great-great-granddaughter of two North Carolina Revolutionary War patriots. One of these was John McKnitt Alexander, the secretary of the group of citizens in Mecklenburg County who formed the provincial committee that crafted and signed the Mecklenburg Declaration of Independence on 20 May 1775. The other was Major John Davidson, a Revolutionary War military leader after whom Davidson College was named.

On that snowy day, the three of us gathered at a drop-leaf table dating back to the 1740s and these ladies proceeded to educate me about our family history. Using a roll of brown parcel paper, a ruler, and pencils, we began drawing a family tree. Fortunately for me, my grandmother was a packrat and had saved generations worth of materials. We used family bibles, one of which dates to 1692 in Edinburgh, Scotland; family letters, postcards, and Christmas cards dating back to the late 1930s; a group of old deeds and wills; and a "History of Mecklenburg County" by J. B. Alexander, published in 1902, to construct our family tree. During the process, my ninety-year-old grandmother related family stories and anecdotal information dating back to her own childhood in the 1870s. Needless to say, I was hooked, and subsequent visits involved my appeal of "Tell me about when you were a little girl." I have since spent more than four decades in my own quest for more and more information about all branches of my family's origins and history.

You will want to start your own genealogical odyssey with yourself and what you know, and then work your way backwards. Along the way you will want to collect documentation to verify every fact *and* keep track of where and when you obtained every piece of evidence. (We will discuss types of evidentiary documents and the process of documentation in more detail in Chapter 2.)

A typical research path for you to follow would begin with the following information:

- **Yourself** Obtain a copy of your own birth certificate. This document will provide you with the date, time, and location of your birth, and often information about your physical characteristics at birth, such as weight, length, and hair and eye color. It also will indicate the names of your parents, their race or nationality, their ages at the time of the event, the name of the physician attending the birth, and possibly additional details. The content of a birth certificate will vary depending on when and where the document was created. Later certificates may contain more information.

  - Birth certificates can be obtained in the United States from county health departments, state bureaus of statistics, or other governmental agencies.

  - In England and Wales, general registration of births, marriages, and deaths began in 1837, and a central copy of all registrations is held by the General Register Office (GRO), a part of the Office for National Statistics. Their Web site is located at **http://www.statistics.gov.uk/nsbase/registration/certificates.asp.** A central index is held at the Family Records Centre (FRC) in London. Local offices hold copies of their records registered since 1837.

  - The General Register Office for Scotland (GROS) is located in Edinburgh and is the contact point for birth, marriage, and death certificates. You may check their Web site at **http://www.gro-scotland.gov.uk/grosweb/grosweb.nsf/pages/home** for more information.

  - The General Register Office of Ireland in Dublin is the depository for many vital records documents. You will want to visit their Web site at **http://www.groireland.ie** and click the link to Research.

  - In Canada, the responsibility for the civil registration of births, marriages, and deaths lies with the province or territory. The National Archives of Canada Web site at **http://www.archives.ca/01/01_e.html** provides links to a vast collection of Canadian genealogical resources grouped into categories, including links to provincial and territorial archives, libraries, and other repositories.

  - Like Canada, responsibility for civil registration in Australia lies with the territory or state. The Society of Australian Genealogists has produced an excellent Web page concerning Australian civil registration at **http://www.sag.org.au/ozsources/civil.htm.**

  - If you are researching vital records or civil registration in other countries, you may want to use your favorite Internet search engine and enter the type of document and the name of the country. As an example, I entered the phrase **"death certificate" + singapore** and was rewarded with a link to the Immigrant & Checkpoints Authority (ICA) and its Web page at **http://app.ica.gov.sg/serv_citizen/birth_death_reg/death_registration.asp** concerning Death Registration and the Death Extract Application.

■ **Your Parents**   Learn as much about your parents as possible. Obtain copies of their birth certificates, their marriage license, and any other documents possible. Your mother's maiden name will appear on these documents and will be an essential part of your research. Ask questions to learn where they grew up, where they went to school, where they lived at every point in their lives, what religious affiliation they have had, and the names and addresses of the religious institutions they attended, what jobs they may have had, what their hobbies and interests are, and anything else you can learn. Take copious notes along the way because this may be the only opportunity you have to gather these important family details. Obtain a copy of the death certificate if a parent is deceased.

■ **Siblings**   Obtain a copy of the birth certificate for each of your brothers and sisters. In addition, obtain any other documents that may have been created for them. Your lives are inextricably linked and the information you learn about them may reveal other research paths for you.

■ **Aunts and Uncles**   Your research will extend to your parents' siblings as well. You will want to learn as much about their family groups as you can. After all, the family structure and dynamics can be important in learning more about the factors that influenced your life.

■ **Cousins**   Regardless of the family relationship with your cousins, close or distant, try to learn as much about them as possible. They are tangible extensions of your family's line too.

■ **Grandparents**   Obtain copies of documents for your parents' parents too. You are tracing a line of descent from these people and want to know as much as possible about them.

Continue expanding outward as far as you can to learn about other family members, their spouses, parents, and children. Don't worry if you can't locate information or obtain all the documents on everyone. This is an ongoing process and, as you progress through this book, you will learn more about how to extend your research reach and locate more and more information. Part of what we, as genealogists, do is fill in gaps in the informational puzzle in order to create a larger picture.

Discover Sources of Information in Your Own Home

Your quest for family information should begin in familiar territory. Start with what you know and work backwards. It is probable that you have any number of resources in your own home or in the homes of your parents, grandparents, and other family members that can help you document the family. Take time to consider the following list of home source materials that you might find around your home and what information they may provide.

Vital Records

Vital records are those documents that record milestone life events. They include birth certificates, marriage licenses and certificates, divorce decrees, and death certificates issued by government agencies. Examples of a birth certificate and a death certificate are shown in Figures 1-1 and 1-2.

The vital records documents issued by governmental entities may or may not contain completely accurate information. A death certificate, for example, will provide the details of an individual's

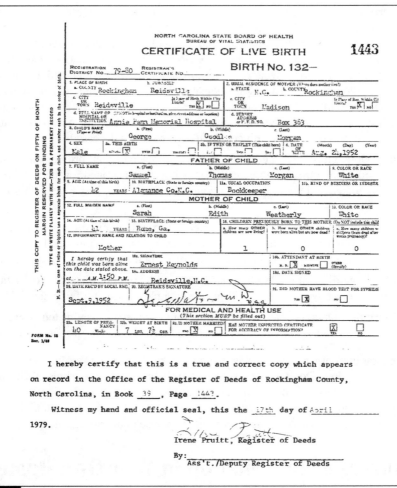

FIGURE 1-1   Birth certificates provide essential clues for date and location of birth, names of parents, and other facts (From the author's collection).

death such as name, gender, date, cause of death, and the location where the death occurred. This data may or may not be 100 percent correct; however, it is considered to be the official record of the death. Likewise, a coroner's report or the report of an inquest will provide what is deemed the official report on the death.

Other information found on a death certificate, such as the individual's date of birth, parents' names, occupation, and other personal data unrelated to the death, may or may not be correct. This information is typically provided to the official completing the form by a family member or another person, and that informant may or may not have the accurate details. In addition, the person completing the form may make errors in recording or transcribing the information provided. As a result, the details unrelated to the individual's death should be viewed with some skepticism until

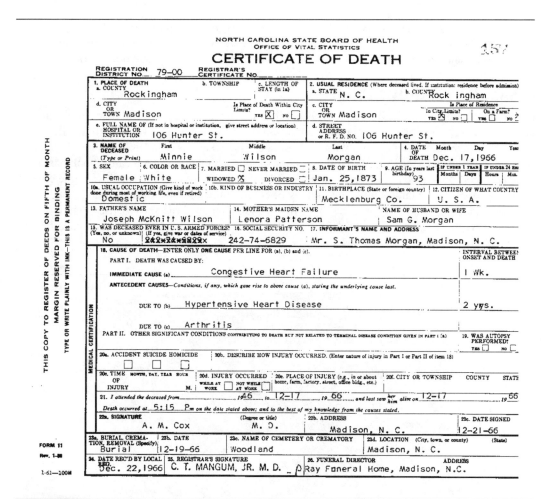

FIGURE 1-2   A death certificate provides information about a person's death (From the author's collection).

you have verified them with other independently created sources. We will discuss this in greater detail in Chapter 2.

Religious Records

Ecclesiastical records are often found in the home. Certificates of baptism, christening, confirmation, or records of *bar mitzvah* or *bat mitzvah* may be found among family papers. Documents of marriage issued by the church, as opposed to a government-issued marriage license or certificate, may be among the family's treasured documents. Look also for church programs or bulletins issued at the time of and/or commemorating the occasion as these may contain names of relatives and other information. These also may be recorded in the religious organization's files or archives, along with more detailed accounts of the events and participants. Other congregation publications might include a commemorative congregational history, photographs, newsletters, and other periodicals.

Personal or Family Bible

Pages containing birth, marriage, death, christening, confirmation, baptism, and other events are commonly included in Bibles. Your ancestors or family members may have entered detailed information themselves. You also may find other materials tucked inside a Bible, such as letters, postcards, greeting cards, newspaper clippings, photographs, obituaries, funeral cards, bookmarks, and other items considered special or important to the owner. These may provide invaluable clues to other locations where family information may be found. In one family Bible, I found a page listing the wedding guests at my grandmother's first wedding on 2 February 1898. (See Figure 1-3.) Two pages revealed a listing of the bridegroom's death just five months later of "that dreaded disease typhoid fever." (See Figure 1-4.)

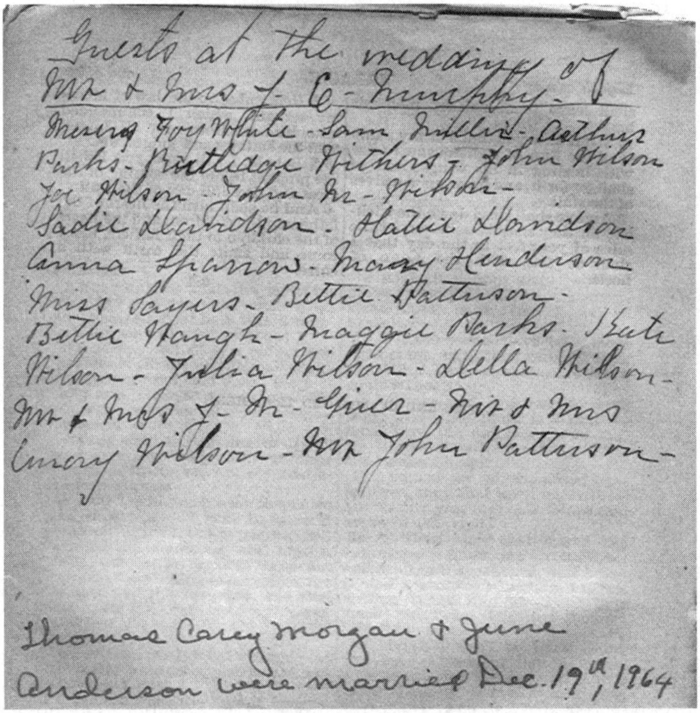

Guests at the wedding of
Mr & Mrs J. E. Murphy.
Messrs Foy White - Sam Miller - Arthur
Parks - Rutledge Withers - John Wilson
Joe Wilson - John M. Wilson -
Sadie Davidson. Hattie Davidson
Anna Sparrow. Mary Henderson
Miss Sayers. Bettie Patterson.
Bettie Haugh - Maggie Parks. Kate
Wilson - Julia Wilson - Della Wilson -
Mr & Mrs J. M. Greer - Mr & Mrs
Emory Wilson - Mr John Patterson -

Thomas Carey Morgan & June
Anderson were married Dec. 19th, 1964

FIGURE 1-3 A personal Bible may include interesting information, such as this example in which guests at the wedding of Mr. and Mrs. J. E. Murphy are listed (From the author's collection).

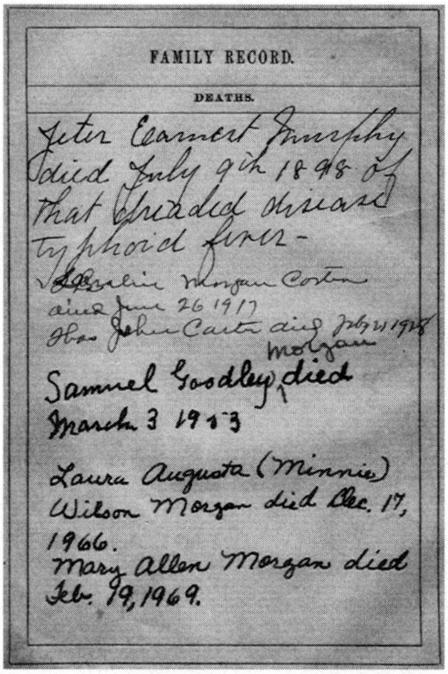

FIGURE 1-4   Jeter Earnest Murphy, the bridegroom at the marriage documented in Figure 1-3, died of typhoid fever just five months and one week after his wedding. The Bible entry is probably the only record of the cause of his death (From the author's collection).

Photograph Albums

Family albums may contain photographs and other family memorabilia. If you are very fortunate, photos will be labeled with the name(s) of the subject(s), the location, and the date. If not, be prepared to spend time with other family members and try to identify and label the pictures. This can be an enjoyable experience for everyone and especially rewarding for you as a genealogist. Photographs are keys to understanding your family's history and can be used to help place them in geographical, social, and historical context.

Scrapbooks

A scrapbook often presents a chronicle of life events for an individual or for an entire family group. Newspaper clippings can point you to additional sources for more information and documents. Programs of recitals, plays, sports events, and other occasions may reveal a family member's talents or interests. Obituaries, such as the one shown in Figure 1-5, are full of family history pointers and are often included in scrapbooks or memory books. While an obituary may be undated and the newspaper in which it was published is unknown, the value of the clues found in the obituary can be enormous.

MRS. MAY WRENN MORGAN

New York, N. Y., June 29.—M₁ May Wrenn Morgan of 25 Fif Avenue, New York City, N. Y., wi of John Allen Morgan, retir₁ economist for the Guaranty Tru Company, died today in Lenox Ho pital after an illness of sever₁ months. She was a native of Sil₁ City, N. C., and her husband is native of Prospect Hill, N. C.

Mrs. Morgan was a graduate ₁ Duke University where she was member of Alpha Delta Pi Sororit₁ Long active in sorority and pan hellenic circles, she served in man official capacities, and at the tim of her death was a member of th₁ Board of Directors of the Panhel lenic House Association. She wa₁ also a member of Chapter G. o P.E.O Especially interested in chilc welfare work, Mrs. Morgan served with a child placement bureau and the "Save the Children Federation." In recent years she has been on the staff of Christ Church (Method-ist), of which Dr. Ralph W. Sock-man is minister.

Funeral services will be held from Christ Church, New York City, N. Y., at 3 P. M. Thursday. Interment will be in the Wrenn family cemetery near Siler City, N. C. Friday at 4 P. M.

FIGURE 1-5   Obituaries, such as this one, are often found in scrapbooks (From the author's collection).

Letters

Family correspondence is an important chronicle of life events. They may provide first-hand accounts of births, graduations, weddings, funerals, and other family occasions. You may uncover details about a person's everyday life, trips they made, their problems and concerns, and news about other family members. Here you may learn more about personal characteristics and family relationships than anywhere else. A return address in the body of a letter, such as in the example shown in Figure 1-6, on the original envelope, or on a postcard may provide an invaluable clue to locating other records about these family members at the time the communiqué was mailed.

Diaries and Journals

Everyday life events and often an individual's innermost thoughts are to be found in diaries and journals. Our ancestors often spent more time recording the details of their lives than we do today, and these cherished volumes can be real treasure troves for the family historian.

Accounting journals for a family farm or business may paint a detailed picture of the lifestyle of the family at the time, the crops and livestock they raised, the costs of supplies and clothing,

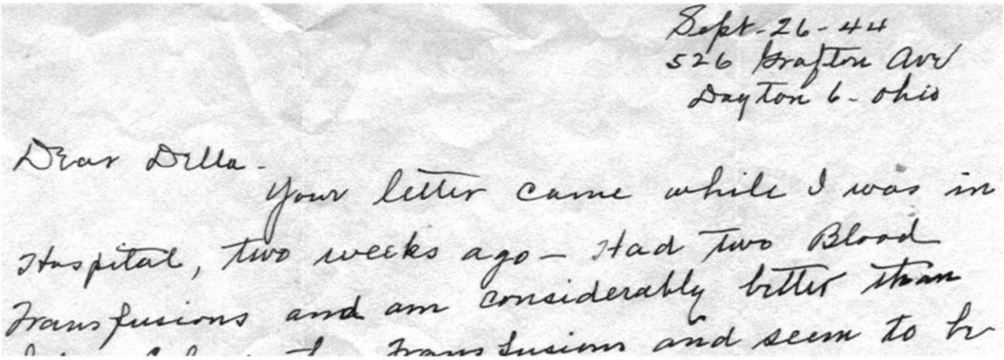

> *Sept.-26-44*
> *526 Brafton Ave*
> *Dayton 6.-Ohio*
>
> *Dear Dilla.*
> *Your letter came while I was in*
> *Hospital, two weeks ago — Had Two Blood*
> *Transfusions and am considerably better than*
> *... — ... transfusion and seem to h*

FIGURE 1-6   A return address on a letter or postcard from a family member may point to a geographical area where other documents may be found (From the author's collection).

and weather patterns, to name a few. During the time of slavery in the United States and elsewhere, the names of slaves may be listed, along with information about their births, deaths, and other events.

Family Histories

An ancestor or another member of the family may already have prepared a historical account of a portion of the family's history. That doesn't mean that the work is already done for you. It merely means that you have a ready-made path to follow and to re-prove the facts and hypotheses already set forth by the other researcher.

Local Histories

Don't overlook books, pamphlets, and other publications that focus on the area where your ancestors and family members have lived. These may be in the family collection because of the area and also because information about the family may be included. In the book *The History of Mecklenburg County from 1740 to 1900* by J. B. Alexander, published in Charlotte, North Carolina, in 1902, I was rewarded not only with a biographical sketch of my great-great-grandfather, Isaac Wilson, M.D., but also with the only surviving photographic image of the man. Figure 1-7 shows two facing pages from that book.

Baby Books

The joy of the arrival of a child is recorded in baby books in great detail by parents, guardians, grandparents, and others. You may find that photographs such as the one shown in Figure 1-8, copies of birth documents, and clues to other materials and their location are included in these little books.

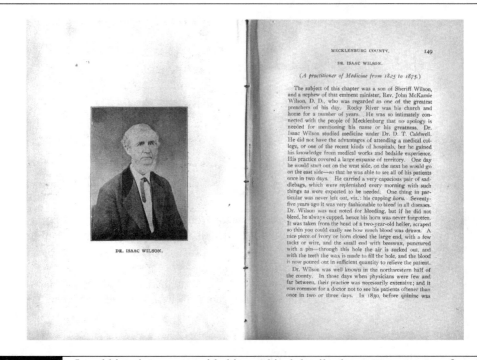

MECKLENBURG COUNTY. 149

DR. ISAAC WILSON.

(A practitioner of Medicine from 1825 to 1875.)

The subject of this chapter was a son of Sheriff Wilson, and a nephew of that eminent minister, Rev. John McKamie Wilson, D. D., who was regarded as one of the greatest preachers of his day. Rocky River was his church and home for a number of years. He was so intimately connected with the people of Mecklenburg that no apology is needed for mentioning his name or his greatness. Dr. Isaac Wilson studied medicine under Dr. D. T. Caldwell. He did not have the advantages of attending a medical college, or one of the recent kinds of hospitals, but he gained his knowledge from medical works and bedside experience. His practice covered a large expanse of territory. One day he would start out on the west side, on the next he would go on the east side—so that he was able to see all of his patients once in two days. He carried a very capacious pair of saddlebags, which were replenished every morning with such things as were expected to be needed. One thing in particular was never left out, viz.: his cupping horn. Seventy-five years ago it was very fashionable to bleed in all diseases. Dr. Wilson was not noted for bleeding, but if he did not bleed, he always cupped, hence his horn was never forgotten. It was taken from the head of a two-year-old heifer, scraped so thin you could easily see how much blood was drawn. A nice piece of ivory or horn closed the large end, with a few tacks or wire, and the small end with beeswax, punctured with a pin—through this hole the air is sucked out, and with the teeth the wax is made to fill the hole, and the blood is now poured out in sufficient quantity to relieve the patient.

Dr. Wilson was well known in the northwestern half of the county. In those days when physicians were few and far between, their practice was necessarily extensive; and it was common for a doctor not to see his patients oftener than once in two or three days. In 1830, before quinine was

DR. ISAAC WILSON.

FIGURE 1-7 Local histories may provide biographical details about your ancestors found nowhere else (From the author's collection).

FIGURE 1-8 Baby books contain photographs such as this one, along with other important details (From the author's collection).

Marriage Books

A wedding presents an occasion for the gathering of families and for the creation of often vivid records. Matrimonial registers signed by attendees, photograph albums, wedding gift lists, and other records may provide excellent resources for your further research. You also may find copies of a marriage license or certificate, and copies of documents from the couple's religious institution(s) to help document the event. These can often lead you to religious membership rolls, and these can sometimes be used to trace family movements from place to place.

Funeral Books and Memorial Cards

Mortuaries and funeral homes have long provided families of the deceased with a funeral or memory book. These can be rich in untapped detail. The name of the deceased and the dates of birth and death are included, as well as the date and place of any services, and the place of interment. Copies of obituaries may be included. The register of persons who attended the visitation or wake will include family members' names and signatures, confirming their presence at the time. An examination of the register may help you reveal the married names of female relatives. In addition, the list of active and honorary pallbearers, as shown in Figure 1-9, should be studied to determine if family members were tapped to participate.

Bearers

Rahn Boyer	Lee Lauten
Frank Lauten	Bobby Steele
Wayne Tilley	Otis Bullins
Gordon Tucker	Dick Anderson

Honorary Bearers

FIGURE 1-9   A page from a funeral book showing names of pallbearers (From the author's collection)

Cards such as the one shown in Figure 1-10 are often distributed at funerals and memorial services. They may commemorate the vital dates of the deceased and/or provide the text for a prayer to be read in unison by participants in the service.

Identification Documents

A number of documents may be found that can be used as evidence in your research. A driver's license or passport will confirm date of birth, age, physical characteristics, and residence. A Social Security card in the United States can provide an account number and can be used to obtain a copy of the person's SS-5 application for a Social Security number. A health service card, an insurance card, and other identity papers from a variety of sources can provide leads to their issuers for potentially informative data.

Immigration Papers

On admission to a new country, an immigrant is typically issued some piece of documentation to prove his or her identity. Depending on the country and the historical time period, this may have been as simple as a letter or as formal as a visa, passport, alien registration card, or another document.

IN LOVING MEMORY OF

Mabel Christine Pollock

August 31, 1899
August 23, 1989

The Lord is my shepherd; I shall not want.
He maketh me to lie down in green pastures:
He leadeth me beside the still waters.
He restoreth my soul: He leadeth me in the
paths of righteousness for His name's sake.
Yea, though I walk through the valley of the
shadow of death, I will fear no evil:
for thou art with me; thy rod and
thy staff they comfort me.
Thou preparest a table before me in the
presence of mine enemies:
thou anointest my head with oil;
my cup runneth over.
Surely goodness and mercy shall follow
me all the days of my life:
and I will dwell in the house
of the Lord for ever.

Heeney-Sundquist Funeral Home
Farmington, Michigan

FIGURE 1-10 A memorial or prayer card (From the author's collection)

In addition, vaccination records may also be located among immigration papers that point to the place of vaccination in the previous country of residence.

Naturalization Papers

Many immigrants took the necessary steps to renounce their original citizenship to become citizens of their new country. Some countries have required multiple documents to facilitate the process. In the United States, for example, an immigrant would swear an oath renouncing any allegiance to any foreign "power, sovereign, or potentate" and then sign a Declaration of Intent document. This was done at a courthouse and was the first step in the process to indicate his or her plan to seek citizenship. After a five-year waiting period, the person would file a Petition for Naturalization to initiate the paperwork to verify his or her good record and to request to become a naturalized citizen. While the process and the names of the documents vary in different countries, the process is similar.

The applicant or petitioner usually maintains copies of each document associated with their naturalization process and, finally, of the citizenship document. Figure 1-11 shows a United States

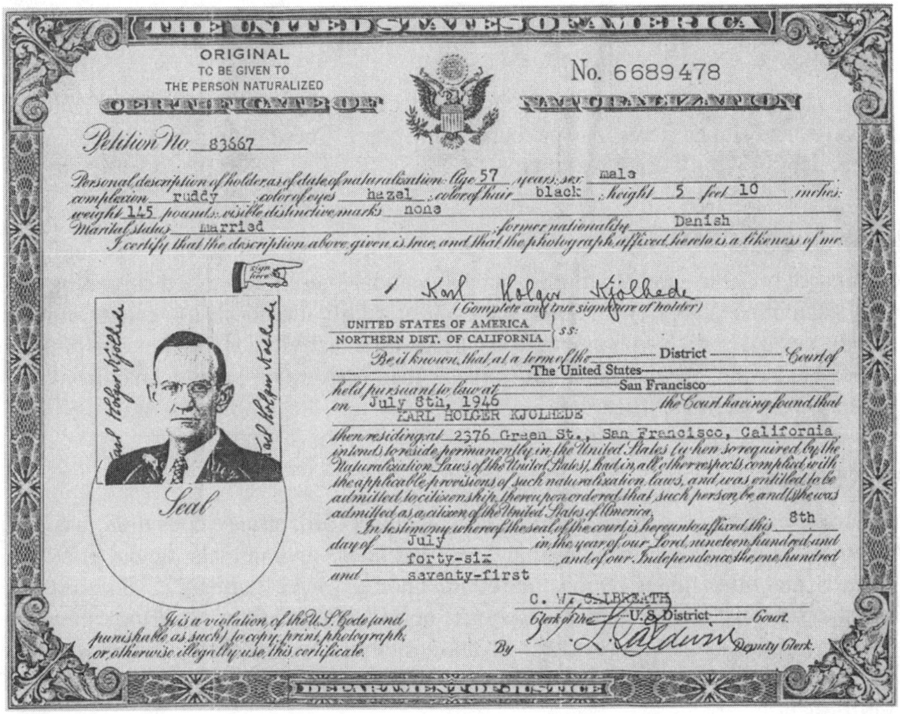
THE UNITED STATES OF AMERICA

ORIGINAL
TO BE GIVEN TO
THE PERSON NATURALIZED

No. 6689478

CERTIFICATE OF NATURALIZATION

Petition No. 83667

Personal description of holder as of date of naturalization: Age 57 years; sex male
complexion ruddy ; color of eyes hazel ; color of hair black ; height 5 feet 10 inches;
weight 145 pounds; visible distinctive marks none
Marital status Married ; former nationality Danish
I certify that the description above given is true, and that the photograph affixed hereto is a likeness of me.

Karl Holger Kjolhede
(Complete and true signature of holder)

UNITED STATES OF AMERICA
NORTHERN DIST. OF CALIFORNIA } SS:

Be it known, that at a term of the District Court of The United States held pursuant to law at San Francisco on July 8th, 1946 the Court having found that KARL HOLGER KJOLHEDE then residing at 2376 Green St., San Francisco, California intends to reside permanently in the United States (when so required by the Naturalization Laws of the United States), had in all other respects complied with the applicable provisions of such naturalization laws, and was entitled to be admitted to citizenship, thereupon ordered that such person be and (s)he was admitted as a citizen of the United States of America.

In testimony whereof the seal of the court is hereunto affixed this 8th day of July in the year of our Lord nineteen hundred and forty-six and of our Independence the one hundred and seventy-first

Seal

C. W. CALBREATH
Clerk of the U.S. District Court.
By Deputy Clerk.

It is a violation of the U.S. Code (and punishable as such) to copy, print, photograph, or otherwise illegally use this certificate.

DEPARTMENT OF JUSTICE

FIGURE 1-11 Certificate of Naturalization for Karl Holger Kjolhede, dated 9 July 1946 (Courtesy of Jody Johnson)

Certificate of Naturalization. Not only are these treasured documents, they also provide evidence of citizenship that entitles the person to citizenship privileges such as the right to vote in elections.

Land Records

Land and property records provide evidence of land ownership and residence. These are among the most numerous and yet the least used documents available for genealogical research. They include land grants, deeds, mortgages, agreements of sale, leases, mortgages, abstracts of title, land contracts, bonds, tax notices, tax bills, homestead documents, liens, legal judgments, dower releases, easements and releases, surveys, and other documents.

Military Records

These documents come in a wide range of record types and formats. Military service statements, disability certificates, discharge papers, separation papers, and pension records are common. Commendations, medals, ribbons, decorations, uniforms, swords, firearms, and other weapons are more tangible evidence of military service. Military regimental histories may also be in the family possession, as may be correspondence between the service person and his or her military branch and with other friends from service.

Directories

City directories, telephone directories, professional directories, alumni lists, personal telephone and address books, and similar items may be found in the home. These may include names, addresses, ages, and other details about family members.

Religious Publications

Newsletters, church bulletins, and other religious publications present a detailed chronology of the congregation's activities. You may find your ancestor or family member's life events announced there, as well as news of their involvement in congregational activities. However, the presence of family members' names in these publications suggests that there are probably membership records available in the congregation's offices.

School Records

Enrollment forms, homework papers/reports/projects, report cards, transcripts, diplomas, honor rolls, fraternity and sorority documents and jewelry, yearbooks and annuals, school photographic portraits, awards, and other materials may be found at home. (See Figure 1-12.) They represent information about family members from a specific period of time. Don't overlook these great resources and the insights they may provide. In addition, alumni directories and other correspondence may provide names and addresses of administrative offices that you may potentially contact for additional information.

A college yearbook, such as Peace Institute's 1925 *Lotus,* may yield important biographical information about your ancestor's participation in school activities (From the author's collection).

Employment Records

Employers may be reluctant to release records concerning their employees. However, around the home you may locate materials such as résumés, apprentice agreements, indentures of servitude, pay vouchers, paycheck stubs, union documents, life and health insurance policies, severance papers, retirement or pension documents, a Social Security (or Railroad Retirement Board) card, a medical care or prescription benefit card, a National Health Service identification card, or other employment-related materials.

Search for the Less-Than-Obvious Items

In addition to all of the items listed above, don't overlook household items that may contain important clues. Engraved jewelry and silverware may speak volumes to you. For example, an 18-karat gold locket holding tiny photographs of an elderly couple and engraved with the dates "1856-1906" provided the clue I needed to identify them as one set of my great-grandparents.

These are the only known surviving pictures of these ancestors. Embroidered samplers, needlework, and quilts often include names and dates. Plaques, coats of arms, and personalized souvenirs offer other information. And don't overlook heirloom furniture and pictures because you never know what may be incorporated into the design or concealed inside or underneath them.

It is important to investigate *all* the materials at home that may provide information or clues to your family's history. Search through books, letters, papers, trunks, suitcases, boxes, drawers, chests, attics, basements, garages, and everywhere else you can imagine. As you discover each new piece of evidence, keep track of where and when you located it. While that may seem unimportant now, it is definitely a worthwhile part of your documentation. Consider temporarily placing each document in an archival quality envelope or polypropylene sheet protector sleeve along with a note concerning the name(s) of the person(s) about whom the item concerns, the date you located it, and where you located it. (We will discuss the importance of documenting your source materials in more detail in Chapter 2.)

Interview *All* Your Relatives

You never know where you will find that next piece of information. It could be as close as the family member sitting right beside you or it could be a distant cousin with whom you've never spoken. Your job is to learn as much as you can—*now*! Many a genealogist or family historian has lamented having waited too late to talk with parents and grandparents. However, it is never too late to make contacts with uncles and aunts, cousins, and family friends to learn as much as you can. You also may find that the "missing" family Bible isn't really lost; it may be in the possession of another relative after all.

Genealogy is a lot like journalism. You are seeking information from a variety of sources, asking questions, gathering facts and speculation alike, researching your sources, evaluating what you find, and producing hypotheses. If you do your job in a scholarly manner, you may be rewarded with factual proof as well as a better understanding of your family's story.

A good researcher learns how to ask questions, both of himself or herself and of others. Good interviewing skills are an essential part of your research, and it takes time to become an expert. There is an art to successfully conducting an interview with another family member but, with a little advance preparation and organization, you can become a pro in no time.

An interview need not be an "interrogation" so much as a friendly discussion. You will ask open-ended questions that require more elaboration than just a "yes" or "no" response. You want to get your relative to share knowledge and experiences in a friendly, non-threatening environment. A two-way conversation can be a mutually satisfying experience, blazing a trail for a stronger relationship—and more information—in the future.

Examples of some open-ended questions might include

- Where and when were you born?
- What was it like growing up during the Great Depression?
- Tell me about your first date.
- What kind of trips did you take when you were younger, and which was your favorite?
- What can you tell me about your aunts and uncles?

It is important to realize that there may be sensitive issues in the family that people are uncomfortable about and prefer not to discuss. Scandal, shame, secrets, lies, embarrassment, humiliation, and disgrace are all reasons for reluctance or refusal to discuss a person, place, time, or event. The two most powerful emotions are perhaps pride and the desire to protect the family reputation. Let me give you four examples involving refusals of family members to talk about the past.

- Both of my grandmothers were concerned that no one be aware of their ages. One refused to tell anyone the year of her birth and left instructions in her will that only her date of death be inscribed on her gravestone. The other shaved years from her age at each census until, in 1930, she had 'lost' 16 years.

- A woman of Native American descent refused to discuss her parents. She was ashamed that she was an Indian and had inherited the desire to mask her origin from her mother.

- One woman was shocked to learn that the woman she thought was her older sister was, in fact, her mother and that she had been born out of wedlock. When asked about this by the family genealogist, she not only refused to discuss the matter but made the genealogist swear never to repeat the scandalous information to anyone else in the family. She wanted to protect her own children and other family members from the scandal of illegitimacy.

- Imagine the surprise of the genealogist who discovered that her grandmother had made the family fortune in a most unusual way. Granny always said she didn't want to talk about her husband, and that he was a worthless man who left her before her daughter was born. The genealogist located Granny in the 1910 United States census in Chicago listed as a boarder in the home of two sisters, Minna and Ada Everleigh. Further research revealed that the Everleigh sisters were the proprietors of one of the most famous bordellos in Chicago and that Granny had been an "employee" there.

As you can see, there may be many reasons why family members are reluctant to discuss the past and other family members. However, don't leap to any conclusions. Some people are just not the talkative type.

Consider Several Types of Interview

Most people think of an interview as a face-to-face encounter between two or more individuals. An interview, however, can take one of several forms. In fact, some of the best interviews I've ever conducted with relatives have been done by telephone, and in multiple sessions. Consider the following types of interviews as possibilities for obtaining information from your family members:

- **Face-to-Face Interview**   This technique involves setting a time and place that is convenient to everyone involved.

- **Family Gatherings**   A family reunion, a holiday dinner, a graduation, a wedding or funeral, or just a simple visit with other relatives can stimulate informal conversations from which stories and important family details can be learned.

■ **Telephone Conversations**   The telephone can be used to schedule and conduct either a casual or a more formal, in-depth interview. Use a "phone visit" as an occasion to ask one or two questions at a time. By establishing ongoing telephone communications with a relative, you not only build and strengthen the relationship between you, but can continue asking questions about details over time as you proceed with your research.

■ **Written Questionnaires**   Use postal mail or e-mail to gather family information. Some researchers prepare open-ended questions in document form and send these to relatives. Beware of sending a lengthy questionnaire, though. Few people are willing to spend a lot of time responding to dozens of questions. A few shorter sets of questions posed over an extended period of time often yield a better response rate. If you choose to use postal mail for your survey, be sure to enclose a self-addressed, stamped envelope (SASE) to encourage replies.

■ **Requests for Corrections**   Two effective tools used by genealogists to gather information are the family tree chart, commonly referred to as a pedigree chart, and the family group sheet. We will discuss these in more detail in Chapter 2. However, these are the documents genealogists prepare to organize their family data and present it in report format. You may choose to send a copy of the documents to relatives, along with a SASE. Request that they add to and/or make corrections to the information you have compiled. Be sure to ask for photocopies of any documents they may have that corroborate the facts they provide, and always offer to reimburse them for the cost of their copying, postage, and mileage. Be sure to follow-up by sending them a thank you note and an updated copy of the forms.

When preparing your list of questions, leave plenty of space in between them for responses. You will appreciate this when you are conducting an oral interview, and mail and e-mail respondents are encouraged to fill in the blank space with their commentary.

You may be surprised at the information gleaned during the oral interview process. I've located family Bibles, marriage certificates, deeds, letters, journals, and a host of other documents this way. Most important, however, have been the wealth of stories I've heard. These tales help bring the family members and their experiences to life. A first cousin related a story to me that her mother told her about two of our retired great-aunts and a train trip they made to Savannah, Georgia, to buy fresh crabs. They made the trip by day, purchased a bucket of live crabs, and then returned to the train station to take a sleeper train back home, booking an upper and a lower berth. During the night, one aunt awoke to use the bathroom. When she returned to her berth, she decided to reach up and pinch her sister's behind. Her sister burst from her berth yelling, "Good heavens! The crabs are loose!" Other passengers were awakened by the racket and peered out of their berths, only to see a woman race to the end of the train car and pull the emergency brake to stop the train. Not only is this a hilarious story, but it provides some insight for me into the relationship of the two sisters and one's love of practical jokes.

Schedule Interviews for Best Results

It is important to respect your relative's time. It is inconsiderate and rude to show up unannounced to ask a lot of questions for which your relative is unprepared, especially if he or she has another commitment. Your best course of action, regardless of whether you would like to conduct a face-to-face or telephone interview, is to make contact in advance and schedule a mutually convenient time for your encounter. Be prepared for the question, "Well, what is it you want to know?" Before you even make the appointment, you should have decided what information you hope to learn and the questions you want to use to elicit the information.

By knowing the areas about which you want to know and letting the family member know in advance, he or she can mentally prepare for your visit or telephone call. The person also might like to gather together photographs, Bibles, papers, and other items to share with you. By contacting an elderly first cousin in advance and telling her I was interested in her parents and grandparents, I was rewarded with an opportunity to see my great-grandparents' Bible, letters they had written during their courtship, and pieces of heirloom furniture I had not known existed.

If you would like to audiotape or videotape the interview, be sure to ask permission in advance. Remember that recording devices can be intimidating and distracting, and can make your subject self-conscious and nervous. If you detect any reluctance on the part of your subject, either in advance or at the time of the interview, don't record. Be prepared instead to take notes of the conversation.

Ask the Right Questions

Know something about the person you plan to interview *before* you make the appointment and *before* you arrive or call to conduct the interview. The last thing you want to do is waste anyone's time, and you want to make the most of the time you have together. That means understanding the person's place in the family structure, where they were geographically located, what other family members he or she would likely have known, and what materials might have come into their possession. Your primary goal should be to learn about the people and their lives. If there are materials that might document their life events, it is a bonus to be able to see them. It is most important, however, to learn *about* the people and their lives so that you can place them into geographical, historical, and sociological context. This will help you anticipate what records might exist to document their lives, where they were created, and where they may be found today.

Your family's origins and background certainly will determine the questions that you will ask. There are many, many places on the Internet where suggested lists of interview questions have been published. The following are a few links I think you will enjoy:

- "Interview Questions" by Juliana Smith
  http://www.ancestry.com/library/view/news/articles/3425.asp

- "Asking the Right Question" by George G. Morgan
  http://www.ancestry.com/library/view/columns/george/7041.asp

- "Sparking Family Memories" by Juliana Smith
  http://www.ancestry.com/library/view/columns/compass/2935.asp

- "Interviewing Grandma" by Michael John Neill
  http://www.ancestry.com/library/view/news/articles/7206.asp

- "Interview Absolutely Everyone!" by George G. Morgan
  http://www.ancestry.com/columns/george/04-03-98.htm

Use the Right Equipment for Your Interviews

You should be properly prepared to capture the information you are about to receive. Here are some basic pieces of equipment you will want to take with you to the interview:

- Paper and pencils or pens
- Tape recorder or video recorder
- Extra tapes
- Camera
- Extra film
- Extra batteries

If you obtained permission in advance to tape the interview, you will want to have checked the operation of the recorder in advance. The smaller the recording device, the less intrusive it will be. Be sure you know how to use it and that it is in good working condition before you leave home. When you arrive for the interview, ask again if it is okay to record. If not, move the equipment out of the interview area so that it is not a distraction. If your relative agrees to recording, though, you will be prepared to quickly and efficiently set up the equipment. Perform a sound check on the recording volume before you start, and place the microphone closer to your subject than to yourself. You want a clear recording of the responses and, even though you may not be able to hear all your questions and comments, you should be able to easily relate your subject's responses to your original questions.

Take one or two family items with you to help encourage conversation. I often use an old family photograph as a prop. I ask questions such as "Can you tell me where and when this picture was taken, and can you help me identify all the people in it?" This single question may be the icebreaker you need and the catalyst to open the floodgates of recollection. It literally *can* be worth the proverbial thousand words.

If you own or can borrow a laptop computer and a portable scanner, consider taking them with you as well. Family members may have Bibles, documents, photographs, and other items which can be copied on-site. You will find that most of your relatives, regardless of how close they feel to you, are reluctant to let the family treasures out of their possession for any period of time. Some items can be photographed clearly enough using a digital camera to provide a clear and legible image. However, a scanner will always provide the best quality image for your records. (The books *How to Do Everything with Your Digital Camera* by Dave Johnson (McGraw-Hill/Osborne, 2001) and *How to Do Everything with Your Scanner* by Jill Gilbert (McGraw-Hill/Osborne, 2003) offer excellent training for maximizing your use of these tools.)

Set the Tone of the Interview

It is important in a face-to-face interview especially, but also in a telephone interview, to establish a comfort level for your relative and for yourself. Make sure that there is plenty of time available and that it is a pleasant environment. Interruptions should be kept to a minimum if possible. A third person sitting in on an interview can be a distraction and may prevent the person you are interviewing from opening up to you. Your interviewee may feel uncomfortable or reluctant to discuss people, events, and personal topics with another person present.

Start the interview with a few minutes of lighthearted conversation to set the tone of your time together. Share something with your relative about your life, news of the family, or some other item that might be of mutual interest. It helps break the ice and make your subject feel more at ease. When you begin the actual interview, however, make a tangible transition to that part of the session. In a face-to-face interview, you can do this by straightening yourself in your chair, opening your notebook, setting up a tape recorder (if your subject has already agreed to taping), or some other visible transition. If conducting a telephone interview, make the shift with a comment such as, "Well, I don't want to take up a lot of your time, so why don't we get started?" Use your common sense and tact about what is the right method of transitioning with each relative.

Think of yourself as a friendly, non-threatening journalist. Ask open-ended questions that require a response. "Where were you born and when?" is a good starter. You want to learn names, places, and dates, but you also want to know about the people in your relative's life: parents, brothers, sisters, grandparents, aunts, uncles, cousins, nephews, nieces, friends, teachers, ministers, librarians, and anyone else who may have influenced his or her family and life.

There may be topics that are sensitive and uncomfortable to discuss. Don't press the issue. Move on to the next question. The answer to the question may come up in another way, at another time, and perhaps from another relative but, for the present, let the subject drop. Being pushy and insistent can raise barriers between you and your relative that may interfere with the remainder of the interview and with the relationship between you as well.

Keep the interview short, no longer than one or two hours. Be alert to signs of fatigue. If you notice that your subject is beginning to tire, especially older relatives, be considerate and suggest that you continue later. A break may be sufficient but scheduling another session may be a better option. In the interim, both you and your relative will have time to digest what you have already discussed. You may revise your list of questions as a result, and your relative will have time to regroup and perhaps locate photographs and other materials he or she feels will be of interest to you.

Don't Forget the "Thank You"

After the interview, be sure to thank your relative for the time together and for sharing so much wonderful family history with you. Make another appointment, if appropriate, to meet again and talk. After you return home, consider sending a thank you note expressing your appreciation. Building these personal relationships in small ways like this is important. The connections you make are personally gratifying for both of you, and you never know what genealogical dividends they will pay in the future.

Begin to Organize What You Find

As you collect documents, photographs, family artifacts, and the exciting information gleaned from interviewing your relatives, you soon may feel overwhelmed at the volume of materials you are compiling. You're probably wondering what you're going to actually do with all this "stuff."

It is important to keep track of where and when you actually obtained the information and materials, and that will become part of the documentation process we'll explore in Chapter 2. It also is a good idea to develop a filing system early in your research process. We'll discuss that in detail in Chapter 11 but, in the meantime, consider creating a large file folder or three-ring binder for each family surname (last name) you identify. Start with your own surname, moving on to your father's surname if it differs from yours, and then your mother's maiden surname. Continue on to the surnames of each of your four grandparents, your twelve great-grandparents, and so on. You may also be interested in setting up files for the spouses of your brothers and sisters, aunts and uncles, cousins, and on and on. My filing system uses binders, and I file all the records for a surname (such as Morgan) in one binder. Within that binder, I file documents by given name (first name) of each person, and then I file the documents for each of these individuals in chronological sequence. I also file each document in an archival-safe, polypropylene sheet protector. These protective sleeves are available at every office supply store and will help preserve the condition of the documents you obtain.

This is a starting point in your organization process, and your own filing system will be customized to your own research and reference needs. We will discuss organization and preservation in extensive detail, as I said, in Chapter 11. In the meantime, you can get started so that the job won't seem so overwhelming when we get there.

Summary

The starting point for your genealogical research begins with yourself and moves backwards to your parents and beyond, as well as to your siblings and their families. Start with what you know and then move on to the unknown territory, actively seeking information and documentation along the way. The more data you obtain and the better you get to know about your family members' lives, the better prepared you are to venture further and learn more. Step by step, you will work your way further back in time and learn more about your ancestry. Placing your ancestors into context with the places and time periods in which they lived, and understanding the social and historical factors that influenced them, will bring these people to life for you. You are, after all, a direct product of these people, their genetic makeup, their circumstances, and the life decisions they made. As you learn more, you will become more self-aware of why you are the person you are, and you'll find yourself wanting to learn even more. Few things are more thrilling than touching a marriage certificate signed by your ancestors 150 years ago or holding an old Bible that was lovingly used by an ancestor. It won't be long before you have joined the tens of millions of other family historians around the world and are involved in the thrill of the research chase and the excitement of discovery.

Chapter 2

Create Your Family Tree

How to...

- Evaluate primary vs. secondary sources
- Recognize and evaluate original vs. derivative materials
- Apply critical thinking skills to your genealogical research
- Place your ancestors into context
- Format names, dates, and locations correctly
- Work with pedigree charts
- Work with family group sheets
- Create source citations for your data
- Select a family tree format

Gathering your family information is fun and exciting. I like to think of family history as a large tapestry made up of many colorful threads that, when woven together, present a vivid story. You should recognize, too, that it is important to organize the materials you find in your genealogical quest in order to document and better understand the big picture.

In later chapters, we'll discuss how to go about selecting the genealogy database software program that best suits your needs and how to organize and file your data. Before you make those decisions, though, there are some essential concepts that form the foundation for everything else you do. In this chapter, you will learn about the essential methodologies for identifying and properly analyzing the evidence you discover, whether that be documents, books, photographs, microfilm, cemetery markers, or oral stories. The goal is to help you understand these points and to prepare you to dive right into the investigative research process.

Evaluate Primary vs. Secondary Sources

One of the most important considerations in your research is adhering to the basic rules of genealogical evidence. You will quickly learn that not every source of information is equal and that some materials are more reliable than others. That means that you will evaluate every piece of evidence, regardless of the source, and analyze its strength and value.

In many cases, a piece of documentary evidence is generated as the result of some event: birth, marriage, death, sale of property, voting, taxation, court action, probate process, or some other occasion. Sometimes, though, a record is made before the fact, as in the case of marriage bonds or marriage licenses issued where the marriage never took place, tombstones created for an individual who was never buried in the plot, and agreements of sale that were never executed. Are these valid pieces of evidence too? Of course they are, because they were created to represent intent. And even if the intended action never occurred, the piece of evidence places the person(s) involved in a certain place at a specific point in time and tells you something about his or her life. It may lead you to another clue or source of information.

When evaluating the records of your ancestors' lives, you must always consider the source of the information. Why was it created? When was it created? Who created it? Is it truthful? Source materials can be grouped into two categories: *primary* and *secondary sources*. There are distinct differences.

Primary sources were created at or very near the actual event being recorded and are therefore more likely to be accurate. Secondary sources were typically created after the fact and, because of the lapse of time and memory, tend to be less reliable than primary sources.

Birth Certificates

An example of a primary source would be an original or photocopy of a birth certificate. The information on this document was provided at or just after the time of birth and was completed for the purpose of recording the event. An amended birth certificate, such as one issued later that changes the information recorded at the time of the birth, may have been intended to provide more accurate or complete information than that which was entered on the original document. However, there may indeed be other, less correct information placed on that document just because it was done later. A delayed birth certificate, though, which is one issued years after the event—probably for someone born before birth certificates were issued, born at home with the benefit of a midwife, or whose records were destroyed in a courthouse or other repository—is a secondary source.

Marriage Certificates

Another example of a primary source would be a certificate. Prior to a marriage, the couple usually must have obtained a license to marry, and a license was typically issued by a government office. When the marriage was performed, the person officiating at the ceremony signed and dated the license to indicate that the marriage had been completed according to law. The signed license was then returned to the government office for issuance of the official marriage certificate. The signed license is commonly referred to as a "marriage return," and the information on this document was transcribed by a clerk into a marriage book. When the marriage book was filled, it was usually alphabetically indexed in two sequences: by the groom's name and by the bride's name. One of marriage returns transcribed into a marriage book, such as the one shown in Figure 2-1, would be considered a secondary source even though the information was copied into the book shortly after the event. That is because it has been transcribed, or copied by hand, and there is the possibility that the clerk made a transcription error. The entry of an incorrect maiden name on my great-grandparents' marriage record caused me to spend years searching for the possibility that my great-grandmother had been married before.

Can something be *both* a primary *and* a secondary source? You bet! A death certificate is considered a primary source for information related to the person's death but is a secondary source for all other information, such as date of birth of the decedent, his or her birthplace, names of the parents and spouse, occupation, and other information. That is because the person who provided the information to the individual who completed the death certificate may not have had adequate knowledge of these details or accurate facts. Sometimes you may even see a death certificate on which some data fields are left blank or are marked "unknown."

STATE OF GEORGIA, FLOYD COUNTY.

TO ANY JUDGE, JUSTICE OF THE PEACE, OR MINISTER OF THE GOSPEL:

YOU ARE HEREBY AUTHORIZED TO JOIN

Luther Moffett Holder _____ *and Miss Mary Choice Omberg* _____

in the Holy State of Matrimony, according to the laws of this State, if they are such persons as are by law authorized t.
marry, and for so doing this shall be your license.

    Given under my hand and official seal, this __17__ *day of* _Nov._ , 190_3_

                                      John P. Davis ____(Seal
                                                      Ordinary.

    I hereby certify that on the __18__ *day of* _November_ , 190_3_

Luther Moffett Holder _____ *and Miss Mary Choice Omberg*

were lawfully joined in the Holy State of Matrimony by me.   *G. G. Sydnor, M. G.*

    Recorded by me this __4__ *day of* _Dec._ , 190_3_   *John P. Davis,* ____Ordinar.

FIGURE 2-1	A marriage license can be a good primary source of information (From the author's collection).

    Every piece of information that does not directly relate to the event for which the source document was prepared should be considered a secondary source. You certainly can use secondary material as a clue or pointer to other primary materials that verify or refute what is on that death certificate.

    Let's examine three examples of secondary sources which might contain erroneous information.

Obituaries

An obituary is a written notice of the death of an individual. It typically includes the name of the person, where they lived, the date of death, and information about any planned funeral or memorial service. An obituary may also include biographical information provided by family members or friends, as well as the names of surviving family members. There are a number of places where errors may be introduced in an obituary, starting with the informant who provided the information to the writer of the notice. He or she may provide incorrect information. The person taking down the information, such as a funeral home clerk or a newspaper copy desk clerk, may omit a word, alter a fact, or introduce spelling or punctuation errors. The publisher may create errors in the typesetting process, or an editor may either miss catching an error or introduce a mistake. Each person handling the information may potentially contribute to the possibility of errors. The result may be a severe error that might lead you on a wild goose chase. In Figure 2-2, my father's obituary contained an error in my place of residence. Instead of indicating "Chicago, Ill.," the obituary stated that I lived in "Fargo, Ill." The error originated with the funeral home clerk who, when taking down the information, abbreviated Chicago as "Ch'go" and the newspaper interpreted the clerk's handwriting to be "Fargo."

2

SAMUEL THOMAS MORGAN

Funeral services for Samuel Thomas Morgan, 70, of Rt. 2, Madison, were held at 11 a.m. Monday at Ray Funeral Home with Dr. Larry Bennett officiating. Burial was in Woodland cemetery. Mr. Morgan died Friday at Annie Penn Memorial Hospital in Reidsville.

He was a native of Alamance County and a retired industrial engineer with Gem-Dandy Inc. He was was a member of the Madison Presbyterian Church. He joined the Madison Lions Club in 1952 and was a member for 28 years, with perfect attendance 26 years, was secretary from 1956-57; treasurer of the Agricultural Fair Association from 1967-1978, received a Quarter Century award in 1977; 25 years Monarch Award in 1977; Outstanding Award for Lion of the Year in 1966.

Surviving are wife, Mrs. Edith Weatherly Morgan; sons, Carey Morgan of Greensboro, and George Morgan of Fargo, Ill.

FIGURE 2-2 Obituary with error introduced by newspaper (From the author's collection).

As you can imagine, this error might send a genealogical researcher seeking information about me in a location where I never lived. Worse yet, the researcher might waste time looking for a non-existent location.

Cemetery Markers

Tombstones, grave markers, and memorial plaques placed in cemeteries, mausoleums, and elsewhere may provide clues to primary and/or secondary sources of information. Some are simple and others are more elaborate and may contain great quantities of information. The name and dates on a marker can lead you to search for documents such as birth and death certificates, church or religious records, military records, obituaries, and other materials.

Some markers may even be adorned with medallions commemorating military rank or membership in some organization, such as the example in Figure 2-3, which indicates that Olin Talley McIntosh was a member of the Society of the Cincinnati. This medallion would encourage you to look for a local chapter of the Society and to obtain copies of the member's records.

FIGURE 2-3   This grave marker indicates the person's membership in an organization (From the author's collection).

More elaborate markers, like the one shown in Figure 2-4, may provide more information. This stone indicates that Harry was the youngest son of "Benj. & Isabella Green." His date of death is shown as "Oct. 10, A.D. 1871" and his age as "8 years and 6 months." This detailed information provides a link to the parents' information and would encourage you to seek details concerning the child's date of birth and the cause of his death.

Like obituaries, though, gravestones and plaques are created based on information provided to the creator of the marker and may contain erroneous information. It is not unknown for a stone carver to make a mistake. For example, the surname on one gravestone in an old cemetery in downtown Tampa, Florida, is misspelled. Instead of replacing the stone, however, someone returned to carve a slash mark through the incorrect letter and inscribe the corrected letter above. Remember that the stone carver is only inscribing what was provided and that he or she, too, can introduce errors.

Another problem with tombstones is that, unless you were involved with the purchase or placement of a marker on a grave, you may have no idea when the stone was created or installed. During the Great Depression of the 1930s, families could not always afford a marker for a grave. As a result, it may have been years or decades before a stone was ordered and installed. While the information you see is "set in stone," always seek corroboration elsewhere of the facts engraved there.

TIP   *I wrote an article for Ancestry.com some time ago that will provide you with additional information on this subject. It is titled "Tombstones Are Secondary Sources" and can be found at **http://www.ancestry.com/library/view/columns/george/2840.asp**.*

FIGURE 2-4   Elaborate marker for Harry Green at Bonaventure Cemetery, Savannah, Georgia
(From the author's collection)

Bible Entries

It is a natural assumption for all of us to make that what is entered in the family Bible is correct, but these entries can be misleading as well. Remember that birth, marriage, death, and other information could have been made at any time. There are several things to look for when examining entries made in a Bible that may indicate that they are not primary sources.

- *Always check the publication date of the Bible.*   If the date of any entry predates the publication date, you know that it was added later and is therefore secondary material.

- *Examine the handwriting carefully.*   The fact that the handwriting is identical doesn't mean much, especially if this was a personal or family Bible. One person may have been the family scribe. However, if you can identify the owner of the handwriting for the entries and can determine that entries were made prior to that person's birth *or* for a logical period when he or she could not have made the entry, you may conclude that the information is secondary in nature.

- *Examine the ink used in the entries.*   If all the entries appear to have been made with the same pen and ink, it is possible that someone added a group of entries at one time and not as they occurred. Another tip-off is if any entries for events with dates that precede 1945 are made using a ballpoint pen, they are definitely secondary sources. Why? Because the ballpoint pen was not invented until 1938, was introduced during World War II for military use, and was not sold commercially until 1945.

Recognize and Evaluate Original vs. Derivative Sources

Another consideration in your research is whether the evidence you find is an *original* or *derivative* source. By that, I mean that the material is either an original document *or* that the information has been taken (derived) from some other source. Derivative material might be such things as word-of-mouth accounts, information that was transcribed from other materials, extracted or abstracted from the original materials, or anything else that is not the genuine, original source.

The original sources you use are indeed the actual documents or other materials created for the purpose of recording something. A marriage certificate would certainly be an original source document. So, too, would be an exact photocopy, a microfilm image, or a scanned document image. Anything that is an accurate and exact image of the original document can be considered an original source.

Derivative materials are a different story. As we've already discussed, anytime someone copies or transcribes something, there is a possibility that an error may be introduced. In the course of your genealogical research, you will work with many different materials. Sometimes it is impossible to obtain a photocopy or an exact image of the material. As a result, you will spend time copying information by hand. What you are doing is "deriving" information from the original material, regardless of whether it is a document, a tombstone, an engraved piece of jewelry, or another original source item.

Genealogists know that there are three types of derivative sources: a transcription, an extract, and an abstract. Let's discuss the attributes of each of these materials.

Transcription

A transcription is an exact written copy of an original source material. The operative word here is "exact." That means that you are working from the original and are copying its content exactly, word for word, and preserving the spelling and punctuation precisely as it appears in the source document. Since it is possible for you to make transcription errors, it is important that you carefully check your work to ensure that you don't omit or introduce any additional words or characters, and that you don't make any alteration to the content or intent. If you must make a personal notation in the transcription for clarity, you would enclose it in square brackets and precede your text with the Latin word *sic*. For example, if you encountered a name spelled as Lizzy and you know that it was spelled differently, you might notate it as follows: [*sic,* Elizabeth].

Consider the situation in which a will for a certain man included a list of his six children. The list included "John, Paul, Edward, Polly, Ann, and Elizabeth." If you transcribed these names and omitted the comma between John and Paul, you or a subsequent researcher might read your transcription and conclude that there were only five children instead of six. A conclusion might be drawn that the first name was 'John Paul' rather than the two names, John *and* Paul. This could be confusing for you and for other researchers reading your supposedly accurate transcription.

Extract

In the case of a lengthy document, you might decide only to copy portions of the original that pertain specifically to an individual you are researching. An extract is similar to a transcription except that, instead of copying the entire document, you would be excerpting portions of the original.

You would still copy the content of the section(s) in which you are interested, word for word, and preserve the spelling and punctuation as it appears in the source document. However, you will omit portions that you feel are unimportant to your research.

Extracting from original source materials is a common practice. It also is a source of many errors. An index of names and other information created from original documents can really be an extract or an abstract. People sometimes, in their haste to gather information, make transcription errors or omit important details, which may adversely impact their work and that of other researchers who access and use it. You can protect the integrity of your own research by using extracts, such as indices, to direct you to the original source material. It is always good to obtain a copy of the entire source document, if at all possible. You can evaluate its contents yourself, and you may find at a later date that you would like to refer to the original to reconfirm your work, provide a copy to another researcher, or to look for additional details that may have seemed irrelevant to your earlier research.

Published extracts can be especially problematic in some cases. Remember, when an extract is prepared, much material is left behind. The loss of details, language, and spelling can adversely impact your or someone else's research. In the case of African-American research, for example, an extract of a slaveholder's will may ignore the names of slaves bequeathed, sold, or freed under the terms of the will. Those details may be unimportant to one of the slaveholder's descendants. However, descendents of the slaves could be very interested in the existence of their antecedents' names in the will. As a result, the extract would be useless to the African-American researcher unless he or she traced the genealogy of the slaveholder and personally examined the original of the will.

Abstract

Another type of derivative work is the abstract. Unlike the transcription or extraction, an abstract does not seek to preserve the content of the original source. Instead, an abstract merely describes the content of the original source. It contains far less detail than even an extract and may only list what the researcher feels is pertinent to his or her research. An abstract represents the researcher's interpretation of the original material. An abstract of the slaveholder's will discussed in the previous section might consist of only the family and heirs of the slaveholder, and might omit altogether any mention of the slaves.

Depending on the knowledge, insight, and skill of the researcher, the information derived from the original and documented in the abstract may contain errors. His or her interpretation, hypothesis, and/or conclusion may be correct but, then again, it may be flawed as a result of taking information out of its original documentary context.

As you can see, there potentially are problems with each of these forms of derivative materials. If errors are introduced at any point by the researcher, these often are disseminated to other researchers. As a result, an error may be perpetuated and, because it appears again and again in many researchers' work, may come to be considered "fact." You therefore want to use extreme caution when you encounter other people's transcription, extraction, and abstraction work. Try to obtain a copy of the original source material so that you can examine it yourself. Your hypotheses and conclusions may differ from those of another researcher. By personally reviewing and analyzing the original document, you can apply your own knowledge and insight into your own ancestry in arriving at your own conclusions.

You will certainly do your own share of derivative work, and fortunately there are some excellent forms available on the Internet. Among the absolute best are those at Ancestry.com at **http://www. ancestry.com/trees/charts/researchext.aspx.** Here you will find a Research Extract form, Census forms for all of the United States federal censuses, 1790–1930, and the 1891 U.K. census. Genealogy. com also offers an excellent selection of census forms at **http://www.genealogy.com/00000061.html.** You can also find any number of forms for extracting and abstracting wills, deeds, property descriptions, and other documents by searching on the Internet.

Apply Critical Thinking Skills to Your Genealogical Research

As you have seen, the examination of source materials can tell you a great deal. Personal analysis is a key activity in determining the strength of the evidence you discover. You are acting like an investigative journalist, investigating the scene, the events, the people, and the story. You should always ask about the *who, when, where, what, how,* and *why* of your ancestor's life events. In addition to merely reporting the story, you will analyze information and evidence, and develop realistic hypotheses. Like the journalist, you have equipment, knowledge, skills, and a structured methodology to apply to your investigation. Your job is to bring all of these factors together for the purpose of identifying, classifying, and analyzing the evidence you find.

One thing you will do in your genealogical research is employ your critical thinking skills to the evaluation of the evidence you find. This is an imperative in your work because you must determine what material you have and its quality. There are five basic evaluation criteria you will use, and these should be applied to everything you evaluate, from printed resources to electronic and Internet materials to physical objects and heirlooms.

A component of your critical thinking skills is what you have learned throughout your life, coupled with a healthy dose of common sense. Another piece is the knowledge you will acquire as you continue encountering and working with new and different types of genealogical source materials. You cannot take anything for granted, but should instead measure the evidence by the five criteria listed here.

- **Origin** You must always question where the material originated, when it was created, who created it, and why. Determine if you are working with an original piece of evidence or an exact facsimile, such as a photocopy, microfilm, or scanned image. If you have a piece of derivative source material, you must determine whether it is a transcription, an extract, or an abstract of the original.

- **Quality and Accuracy** The origin of the source material goes a long way toward determining the accuracy of the material. However, recognize that mistakes can be made even in original materials. For example, a census taker could misspell a name on the form he or she is completing. Ask yourself whether the information can be verified (or refuted) by other evidence and, if so, by what other types of evidence and how good (or bad) is that material.

■ **Authority**   Is the creator or author of the material an authority or expert? How do you know? Have you checked his or her credentials or reputation? Is the information hearsay or is it fact? Is the information you are examining a hypothesis or a proven truth? Again, it is important to consider whether the material being analyzed is original or derivative and primary or secondary material.

■ **Bias**   Is there any possibility that what you are evaluating is influenced by any bias? Does the creator or author have another agenda? It is possible that you are dealing with partial truth in some instances, especially where individuals' accounts of events are concerned. There may be a reason to lie or to mask the truth. Examples might include a child born out of wedlock; a person misrepresenting his or her age due to vanity or a desire to legally marry, or to qualify for or avoid military service; or the perception of being descended from a particular ethnic or religious group. How do you know that you have not discovered purposely bogus information?

■ **Sources**   Evaluate the sources from which you have obtained the information. This relates back to origin, quality and accuracy, authority, and bias. However, if you obtain information from another researcher, carefully examine the sources he or she cites, and be prepared to verify everything that person has cited.

With all of this in mind, you should maintain a healthy skepticism in your investigation. Be wary of information that seems too good to be true. You can expect to encounter some brick walls in your research. This book will teach you ways of approaching apparent dead ends and circumventing brick walls in your research, and how to use alternative research strategies and substitute record types in the process.

Place Your Ancestors into Context

English poet John Donne is famous for his *Meditation XVII,* in which he states, "No man is an island, entire of itself…" He asserts that all of mankind is interconnected, and all a part of one another's history and activities. This is as true in our genealogical research of the past generations as it is of today. Our ancestors lived in places and times, and they witnessed and participated in events and activities as surely as we ourselves do.

It is essential during your research process to learn as much about your ancestors' lives and times as possible so that you can better understand them. That means learning about the geography of the places where they lived, including where the jurisdictional boundaries of their state, province, country, or territories were drawn. You also must become a student of the history of the places and times in which your ancestors lived. This will help you understand what their lives were like and perhaps the motivations for some of their actions. Major cataclysms as well as ordinary events shaped the lives of our ancestors. Consider, for example, the Potato Famine in Ireland in the 1840s, which, according to some sources, caused more than 1.5 million starving Irish citizens to migrate to North America. Or perhaps the rule of *primogeniture,* under which the oldest son inherited the land of his father and may have forced one or more younger sons to leave home to make his own way in the world. Your investigation of the place, history, culture, and climate where your ancestors lived—and where they may have migrated—will serve you well in understanding their lives, what records may have been created by and about them, and where these materials may now be located.

Format Names, Dates, and Locations Correctly

Gathering information about your family is one thing; recording it in a format that can be understood and used by others is quite another. Genealogists use a number of standardized forms for this purpose, and genealogy database software programs (which we will discuss in Chapter 13) can produce printed versions of these forms as a result of data entered into and stored in their programs. Let it suffice to say that genealogists have standards for the entry of data. Let's discuss each type of data and the standards that are universally used. Figure 2-5 demonstrates how information should be properly formatted.

Record Names

People's names are entered using their first name (also referred to as a given name or forename), full middle name(s), and surname (last name). A woman's name is always recorded with her first name, her middle name, and her maiden surname. While it is not mandatory to do so, a great many genealogists capitalize the entire surname, as in the following examples.

Green Berry HOLDER
Laura Augusta WILSON

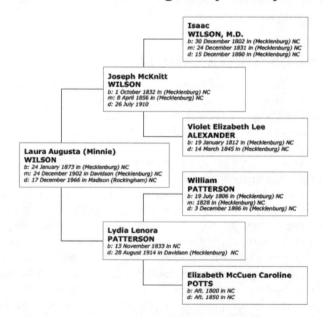

Ancestors of Laura Augusta (Minnie) Wilson

FIGURE 2-5   Chart showing properly formatted names, dates, and locations

Capitalization of surnames is especially effective in written correspondence, such as letters, e-mails, online message boards, mail list postings, and other communiqués because it causes the surnames to be easily seen. If someone is scanning a written document, the capitalized surname jumps out at them.

Record Dates

The United States uses a different format for dates than most parts of the world. You will find that while most Americans might write a date such as June 14, 1905, in their documents and correspondence, most of the rest of the world will write it as 14 June 1905. From a consistency standpoint, you always want to use the DD MONTH YYYY format for all of your genealogical work. You will find that using this standard will make communicating with other genealogists worldwide easier.

Record Locations

When conducting your research, you will find that boundaries, place names, and political/ governmental jurisdictions have changed throughout time, sometimes more than once. It is important for you to seek records in the correct place. That means learning what governmental or other official entity had jurisdiction over a place at the time your ancestor lived there and at the time a specific record was created. It also means working with both contemporary and historical maps. For example, some of my early Morgan ancestors settled in the mid-1750s in what was then Orange County, North Carolina. Today, the exact area in which they settled is divided into Caswell and Person Counties.

The way you record locations in your research should reflect the name of the place, the county, parish, or other geopolitical area in which it was located, and the state, province, or country. You can record them with the county, for instance, enclosed in parentheses or separated by commas. Here are some examples:

Location	Record It As
Madison, North Carolina	Madison (Rockingham) NC
Rome, Georgia	Rome (Floyd) GA
Montreal, Canada	Montreal (Québec) Canada
Barkham in Berkshire, England	Barkham (Berkshire) England

Certainly be careful to record the correct geopolitical entity for the location *at the time the event occurred*. This is essential because that is the place where the records will have been recorded and where they are probably still stored. For example, if I wanted to record the marriage of one ancestor in that area in Yanceyville, North Carolina, in 1761, I would record the birth location in the following manner:

Reuben MORGAN   24 August 1761   Yanceyville (Orange) NC

The marriage date of his son, which occurred in the same community after the formation of Caswell County in 1777, would be recorded as follows:

William MORGAN   22 December 1783   Yanceyville (Caswell) NC

The difference in the county name distinguishes the fact that the event occurred under a different governmental jurisdiction. Therefore, if I want to obtain a copy of Reuben's marriage record, I would contact or visit the Orange County courthouse in Hillsborough, whereas I would visit the Caswell County courthouse in Yanceyville for William's marriage record. Suffice it to say that it is important to properly identify the right location *and* to record it as part of your records.

Work with Pedigree Charts

Now that you know how to collect, evaluate, and analyze evidence, and know how data is to be formatted, it's time to learn about the forms that genealogists use to enter their data.

One of these forms is known as a pedigree chart, and is sometimes known by other names, such as "ancestral chart" or "family tree chart." These forms come in a variety of styles and typically represent three or more generations. Let's begin our discussion by looking at some examples. Ancestry.com provides their Ancestral Chart at **http://c.ancestry.com/pdf/trees/charts/anchart.pdf** (see Figure 2-6). The Public Broadcasting System, as part of its *Ancestors* television series,

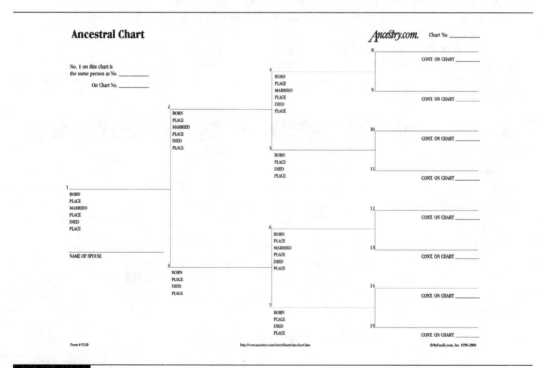

FIGURE 2-6   Ancestry.com's ancestral chart (Used by permission of MyFamily.com, Inc.)

has made a number of genealogical forms available, including a pedigree chart, which you will find at **http://www.pbs.org/kbyu/ancestors/charts/pdf/pedigree.pdf.** You will want to download a copy of each of these as references for this section of the chapter.

Pedigree charts are used to represent multiple generations of direct descent. Both of the downloadable charts I cited above can be used to represent four generations. Others you might locate through retail stores or on the Internet may represent three or more generations. Some versions may be used to represent as many as ten, twelve, sixteen, or more generations. These latter specimens are usually intended for showy displays, but some genealogists will use the larger format as a working document in order to have their family lineage shown on a single sheet.

Let's use your own family as an example and use the Ancestry.com Ancestral Chart form as a worksheet. Remember we said you should start with yourself? That's what you do here. You will note that lines are numbered 1 through 15. Fill in *your name* on line 1 and enter your surname in all capital letters (uppercase). If you have a spouse, you may fill in his or her name on the line below. Remember that you should enter a woman's maiden name as her surname. Under your name on line 1, enter your date of birth (in the format of DD MONTH YYYY such as 10 July 1911), the place of your birth (in the format of City (County) State or similar format), the date of your marriage to the person listed below you, and the place of the marriage. We will assume that you are not yet deceased, of course, so you can leave the areas for date of death and location blank.

The next pair of lines is numbered 2 and 3. Line number 2 represents your father and line number 3 represents your mother. (Even numbers are always male and odd numbers are always female on pedigree charts, with the exception of the individual 1, which may be either male or female.) Enter your father's name with his surname in all capital letters. Enter his birth, marriage, and (if applicable) death dates and locations. Please note that marriage information is always listed on pedigree charts under the male. Enter your mother's name on line 3—this time with her first, middle, and maiden names, and enter her maiden name in capital letters. Enter her birth and, if applicable, death dates and locations. You may not yet have all the names or other information yet. That's the purpose of genealogical research. Enter as much as you have and enter it in pencil so you can change it later as needed.

The next column consists of lines numbered 4, 5, 6, and 7. Line number 4 represents your father's father and line 5 represents your father's mother. Line 6 represents your mother's father and line 7 represents your mother's mother. Fill in these people's names and any vital information you know.

The next column contains lines numbered 8 through 15. These represent the names and information about your great-grandparents. Please fill in as many names, dates, and locations as you can.

You have probably discovered already that you have gaps in your family knowledge. You may also be unsure about some of the information you entered. That's okay, though. That's why we enter the data in pencil, so that we can change or correct it as we locate evidence of the true facts.

Next, you will notice that there are places for chart numbers to be entered. This provides a way for you to organize and cross-reference charts. For example, you may have obtained information on your great-grandparents' (line numbers 8 and 9 on this chart) parents and grandparents. Since you don't have enough room on this chart to represent them, you will need a new pedigree chart for persons numbered 8 and 9. Let's say you start a new chart for your great-grandfather (#8). On the new chart, his name will be listed on line number 1. His parents' (your great-great-grandparents) names will then be entered on lines 2 and 3, and so on. You may label this as **Chart 2.** Label the first chart you completed **Chart 1.** Now, cross-reference them as follows:

- Under Line #8 on Chart 1, on the line labeled "CONT. ON CHART _____", enter the number **2** (for Chart 2).

- In the upper-left corner of Chart 2, where it is labeled "No. 1 on this chart is the same person as No. _____ on Chart No. _____", enter the person number as **8** and the chart number as **1.**

You have now cross-referenced the charts for easy navigation back and forth. You will want to create a binder to hold your pedigree charts. We'll discuss organization in detail later in the book but, for now, start by filing the charts in a generational sequence. File your generation on top, followed by other generations in sequence.

Work with Family Group Sheets

While the pedigree or ancestral chart represents a single thread of descent, a *Family Group Sheet* is a representation of a complete family unit: father, mother, and all children. You potentially will prepare a family group sheet for every family unit you document. An example of Ancestry.com's Family Group Record document is shown in Figure 2-7, and a free downloadable version is available at Ancestry.com at **http://www.ancestry.com/trees/charts/familysheet.aspx.** Some family group forms include space for recording the sources of the information that you have found. The Source Summary for Family Information from Ancestry.com at **http://www.ancestry.com/trees/charts/sourcesum.aspx** can be used in conjunction with their Family Group Record document to keep track of the origin of the evidence you use to document the facts. Please take a few minutes to download and print copies of these sheets now.

The family group sheet begins by asking for the name of the preparer and his or her address. In the event you share a copy of this form with another person, he or she will be able to contact you with questions or to share their research with you. You also have a place at the top of the form to cross-reference this sheet to a pedigree chart.

This form contains space for substantially more information than the pedigree chart, but the sources and types of information are pretty self-explanatory. You will note, though, two interesting columns for the children. The first is one with an asterisk (*) at the top, representing whether or not the father and mother are direct ancestors. Remember, some children in a family unit may be from another marriage and may have been adopted by the new spouse. The other column is for Computer ID. You may decide to cross-reference this chart with entries in a computer program, and this column can facilitate that effort.

The Public Broadcasting System has produced a two-page Family Group Record, which can be accessed at **http://www.pbs.org/kbyu/ancestors/charts/pdf/familygroup1.pdf** (page 1) and **http://www.pbs.org/kbyu/ancestors/charts/pdf/familygroup2.pdf** (page 2). Download and print these two pages and compare them with the forms from Ancestry.com.

What if you have the name of one person and not the name of his or her spouse? What if you only know a wife's first name and not her maiden name? What if you know there was a child

Family Group Record

Ancestry.com.

Prepared By _____   Relationship to Preparer _____

Address _____   Date _____   Ancestral Chart # _____   Family Unit # _____

Husband	Occupation(s)				Religion

	Date —Day, Month, Year	City	County	State or Country	
Born					
Christened					Name of Church
Married					Name of Church
Died					Cause of Death
Buried	Cem/Place				Date Will Written/Proved
Father	Other Wives				
Mother					

Wife maiden name	Occupation(s)				Religion

Born					
Christened					Name of Church
Died					Cause of Death
Buried	Cem/Place				Date Will Written/Proved
Father	Other Husbands				
Mother					

*	Sex M/F	Children Given Names	Birth Day	Month	Year	Birthplace City	County	St./Ctry.	Date of first marriage/Place Name of Spouse	Date of Death/Cause City	County	State/Country	Computer I.D. #
		1											
		2											
		3											
		4											
		5											
		6											
		7											
		8											
		9											
		10											
		11											
		12											

NOTE: *=Direct Ancestor   Form # F106   http://www.ancestry.com/save/charts/familysheet.htm   ©MyFamily.com, Inc. 1998-2000

FIGURE 2-7   Sample of a Family Group Record form (Used with permission of MyFamily.com, Inc.)

but not his or her name? Leave the information blank, or add a question mark, backslashes (//), or some other notation to indicate missing data. You can always return to enter it when you locate it.

Take a few minutes to complete a family group sheet for your parents' family unit, and include information about your siblings and yourself. Any facts you don't know can be left blank for now. You can come back to complete them later when you have located documentation of the facts.

How to Handle Multiple Family Units with a Common Spouse

What do you do when a spouse died or a couple divorced and a spouse remarried? How do you represent that? The answer is that you create a new family group sheet for the new family couple and for their family unit. Children produced from this union are included on this separate sheet.

How to Handle Non-traditional Family Units

There have always been family units operating without the benefit of marriage. Whatever the arrangement and whoever the people are, it is important to record the family unit "as is." Therefore, when you record two individuals in a relationship, portray it on a family group sheet. If there was no marriage, indicate it as NONE. Most genealogy database programs today now allow you to represent a relationship status with such codes as "friends," "married," "partners," "single," "private," "other," or "unknown." You should be honest about relationships where known unless the publication of such knowledge would be detrimental in some way. If there are children produced from a non-traditional pairing, show them as you normally would, as issue from the union.

How to Handle Adopted Children

A common question is how to handle adopted children on a family group sheet. Should you include them? The answer is, of course, an emphatic yes. Adopted children are part of the family unit, regardless of the identities of their birth parents. The adopted child's birth parents, if known, can be recorded in the notes section of your family group sheet or elsewhere. However, the adoption formalizes the legal relationship between the child and his or her adoptive parents and should become the primary family relationship represented in your records.

Most genealogy database software programs allow for the identification of a child's relationship to the parents. The Family Tree Maker program, for example, provides values of Natural, Adopted, Foster, Unknown, Step, Family Member, and Private.

Remember that adoption may be a sensitive topic for the adoptee, his or her parents, or some other family members. Therefore, you will want to be considerate about publishing the information outside the family circle. That does not mean you shouldn't record it in your records. However, many of the genealogy database programs allow for the omission of the parent-child relationship information when reports are produced or data files are created.

Create Source Citations for Your Data

When you were in school and preparing term papers, you were probably required to prepare a bibliography of your source materials. You may also have used footnotes and endnotes for individual fact or quotation references. This is the scholarly way to document research because it provides details for the reader or subsequent researcher to retrace your work.

As you collect information, evidence, documents, and other materials for your family history research, it is essential to record where you found them. You want to provide a record for yourself and any other genealogical researcher so that he or she can retrace your steps, locate the material you used, and personally examine it. Your interpretation of data may be different from someone else's. The fact that you may actually be looking for different information may influence what you search for, what you believe is important, and the way you interpret it in your family's application. One seemingly insignificant name to you in an ancestor's will may be just the "missing link" that another researcher has been seeking for years.

Your source citations will generally follow standard bibliographic citation standards for books, magazines, journals, and other printed sources. Students and researchers know that there are several citation formats, but typically the style used by genealogists resembles the standards of the Modern Language Association (MLA) or *Chicago Manual of Style*. The structure of your source citations should contain all essential information that will help another researcher identify and locate the source material you used. However, the citation format may not necessarily adhere precisely to either of these styles. The following are examples of some of the more common source materials.

Book

Mills, Elizabeth Shown. *Evidence! Citation & Analysis for the Family Historian.*
    Baltimore, MD: Genealogical Publishing Co., 1997.

Magazine Article

Morgan, George G. *"A Path of No Returns."* Genealogical Computing, Volume 23.2,
    (October/November/December 2003).

Newspaper Article

Gussow, Dave and Jules Allen. "On the Road, Smartly." *St. Petersburg (FL) Times,*
    6 October 2003: C2.

Newspaper Article on the Internet

Gussow, Dave and Jules Allen. "On the Road, Smartly." *St. Petersburg Times,* 6 October
    2003. <http://www.sptimes.com/2003/10/06/Technology/On_the_road__smartly.shtml>
    Accessed 10 October 2003.

Family Bible (One-of-a-Kind)

Family data, Morgan Family Bible, *The Holy Bible,* new edition (New York, NY: Christian Book
    Publishers, Inc., 1921); original owned in 2003 by George G. Morgan (229 N. Dalton Street,
    Anytown, FL 33333).

Print materials make up a sizeable portion of reference material for genealogists. However, we work with an amazing array of materials, including letters, postcards, journals, diaries, deeds, census records, birth certificates, marriage licenses, christening and baptismal records, *bar* and *bat mitzvah* records, wills, probate packets, obituaries, ships passenger lists, naturalization records, medical records, tombstones, jewelry, furniture, embroidered samplers, and much, much more. We work with all types of media as well: paper, microfilm, microfiche, CD-ROMs, computer files, databases, photographs and slides, scanned images, and records found on the Internet or exchanged electronically in such media as e-mail and in data files.

As you can imagine, no citation style guide can anticipate every possible source used by genealogical researchers. The MLA standard, however, provides the most appropriate general framework for genealogical source citations.

The essential components of every citation are the name of the author or creator, a title or description of the source, where and who published it, and the date of creation or publication. In addition, if the source is a rare or one-of-a-kind item, it is important to include the place where it resides and/or where you accessed it. Here are examples of some sources unique to genealogical research and appropriate citation formats for them.

Cemetery Marker (Large Cemetery)

Green Berry Holder tombstone; section New Front Addition, Terrace 1, Lot #1, Myrtle Hill. Cemetery, Rome (Floyd County) Georgia; transcribed by the writer on 14 July 1998.

Cemetery Marker (Small Rural Cemetery)

Caroline Alice Whitefield Morgan Carter tombstone, Cooper Cemetery, Caswell County, North Carolina (Ridgeville township, Latitude 36° 17' 15" North, Longitude 079° 12' 02" West) photographed by George G. Morgan on 14 July 1998.

Microfilm of U.S. Federal Census

Green B. Holder household, 1870 U.S. census, Subdivision 141, Floyd County, Georgia, page 102, line 22; National Archives micropublication M593, roll 149.

E-mail Message

Mary A. Morgan, "Your Great-grandmother Patterson," e-mail message from <mam@auntmary190505.com> (106 E. Hunter Street, Madison, NC 27025) to author, 14 June 2003.

Web Site

Matthews, Elizabeth. "Matthews Family Genealogy Page," online <http://www.matthews.org>. Elmer Watson data downloaded 19 December 2002.

The amount of information included varies with the type of source material you use, what it provides, and in some cases where it is physically located. You will want to learn all about citing your sources so that you do a scholarly job. The best genealogical source citation reference book on the market today is Elizabeth Shown Mills' definitive book *Evidence! Citation & Analysis for the Family Historian,* published by Genealogical Publishing Company. (You'll note that I used this work above as a representative source citation example for a book.) It is an excellent resource for the serious genealogist, and I heartily recommend it as a part of your core personal reference library.

The more information you locate, the more important it is to have clearly documented the sources. You will soon learn from personal experience that it is often impossible to recall the origin of a particular piece of information. Source citations are invaluable when retracing your own research and are essential as documentation for other researchers' use in trying to retrace and verify your work.

You will always want to perform effective and scholarly research on your family history. That means identifying and using the best possible source materials you can locate, analyzing them carefully, weighing the evidence, formulating reasonable hypotheses, and drawing realistic conclusions. It combines all the skills discussed so far in this chapter, and these comprise the basic rules of genealogical evidence.

Select a Family Tree Format

Throughout this chapter, I've discussed the mechanics of collecting, analyzing, recording, and citing sources for your family history data. Now is the time to start considering just how to record and display your data.

As you read the header of this section, you probably are thinking, "How can there be more than *one* format of a family tree?" Actually, there are a number of different ways to view family data and each one can help you analyze what you have discovered in perhaps a different way. Genealogists also have their own preferences about which display format they use. For example, you should know that there are two major family tree display formats: the *standard chart* format and the *fan chart* format. The standard format shown in Figure 2-8 presents a vertical, linear view two of generations. The double, parallel lines linking individuals indicates their marriage or union.

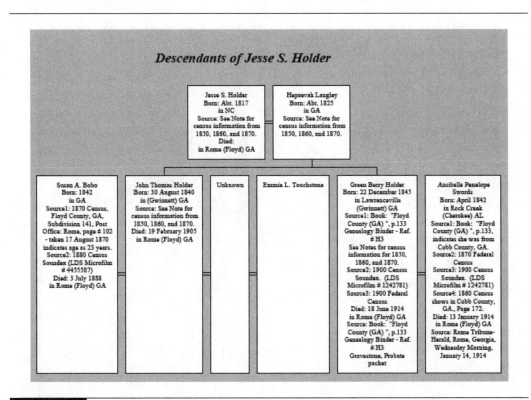

FIGURE 2-8   Sample of a descendants chart in standard format

The same data can be displayed in a fan format, as shown in Figure 2-9, starting with the focus individual and his or her spouse, and additional generations' information extending in semi-circular bands by generation.

As you are working with your family genealogy, you will find it useful to be able to create both ancestor and descendant tree views. An ancestor chart starts with one individual as its focal point and presents a picture of that person's ancestors. A descendant chart starts with an individual and shows his or her descendants. The number of generations represented on any chart is your option. In the examples shown in Figures 2-8 and 2-9, only two generations are represented. You also can choose to include as much or as little information as you like. At the very minimum, however, you should include each individual's name, date of birth, date of marriage, and date of death. The location of each of these events is important, and you may want to include that data as well.

In addition to the standard and fan formats of the ancestor and descendant chart formats, there are some other formats as well. An *hourglass tree* combines the features of both the ancestor and descendent tree views. In Figure 2-10, my great-grandfather, Rainey B. Morgan, is the focal individual, with his wife, Caroline A. Whitfield, shown at his side and their union being indicated

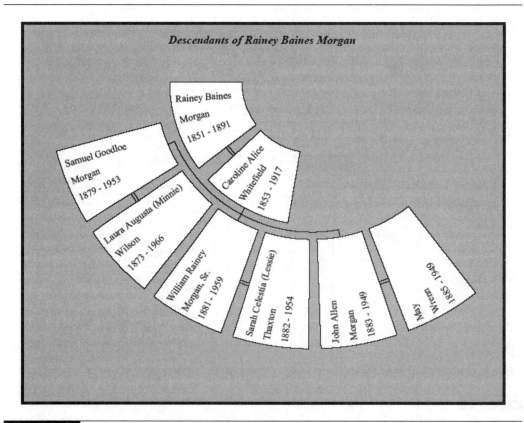

FIGURE 2-9   Sample of a descendants chart in fan format

Hourglass Tree of Rainey Baines Morgan

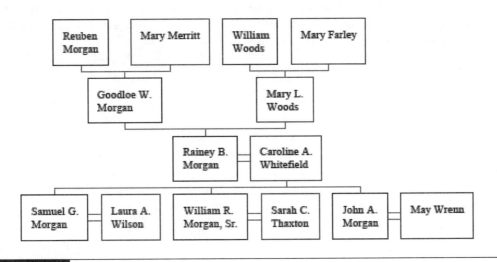

FIGURE 2-10   An hourglass tree format

with the double lines linking them. Rainey's parents, Goodloe W. Morgan and Mary L. Woods, and his two sets of grandparents, Reuben Morgan and Mary Merritt, and William Woods and Mary Farley, are shown above him as his ancestors. Rainey's three sons, Samuel G. Morgan, William R. Morgan, Sr., and John A. Morgan, are shown as descendants, and their respective wives are shown beside them, again with the unions represented by double lines.

All of the tree formats discussed above really are just that: tree formats. They are called trees because they begin somewhere with a root individual and branch out from there. The format that you will encounter most for representing lineal family relationships is the pedigree chart that we discussed earlier in the chapter. It is an ancestral tree representation, but is by far the most commonly used representation in day-to-day genealogy work.

Blank pedigree charts, as you have seen, can be downloaded from the Internet. They also can be purchased in many formats and range from as few as three generations to as many as twelve or even more. Genealogy database software programs can also produce pedigree charts whose contents and formats you can customize.

You will want to experiment with the various formats to determine which one you like best and/or which one best represents your family data. It is time-consuming to complete a family tree chart by hand, however many people do just that. Sometimes they create a display-quality tree using graphics, photographs, and calligraphic text. These can be framed and displayed as family heirlooms.

On the other hand, you will find that there are a number of genealogy database software programs available. You enter your data and source citations, even photographs, and can produce a variety of customized computer-generated reports. Those reports include pedigree charts, family group sheets, and family trees in the standard, fan, hourglass, and other formats. Some of these databases also facilitate writing and publishing a quality family history, while others can produce HTML files containing your family data for Web pages. We'll discuss a variety of software packages in Chapter 13. However, for now, it is important for you to know what is available.

With all this foundation work under your belt now, let's proceed into the wealth of record types and what they can tell us. Let's move on now to Chapter 3.

Chapter 3

Place Your Ancestors into Context and Locate Vital Records

How to...

- Place your ancestors into context
- Become a student of history
- Establish your ancestor's location at different times
- Use maps to locate the *right* place to research
- Locate birth, marriage, and death records
- Create an ancestor profile

The most basic record types for establishing an ancestor's locations and life events are birth, marriage, and death records. Government census records can verify his or her location at regular intervals. The use of these records forms a framework for other research of an individual's life. Once you establish an ancestor's location in a specific place at a given point in his or her life, you can pursue your search for other documents and evidence to expand your knowledge and understanding of that person.

This chapter focuses on how to place your ancestors into historical and geographical context so you can be most effective in understanding and using records about their lives. A simple yet extremely effective methodology for the proper use of maps and gazetteers to help locate records is presented. We also will discuss the most basic of genealogical records, the vital records: birth certificates, marriage licenses and certificates, and death certificates. Examples of documents from the United States, the United Kingdom (like the one shown in Figure 3-1), and Canada are included to provide a better understanding of what these documents can offer.

Chapter 4 will continue the discussion of how to place your ancestor into context with a detailed discussion of census records. For now, though, let's concentrate on methodologies for placing your ancestors' lives into context and get started locating these records.

Place Your Ancestors into Context

Our ancestors were real people. They lived in particular locations and were influenced by other people and events, just as we are today. Their curiosity and interest in the world around them was keen. Like the people shown in Figure 3-2, they actively sought out the news of the day, sometimes traveling considerable distances to even obtain a newspaper. They lived in a community and interacted with their family members, friends, neighbors, and other people in the area. Climate influenced their lifestyle, and the social, political, and economic environment most certainly played a part in their lives. The type of government, its organization, leadership, and regulations imposed a structure under which they lived as well. All of these factors contributed to the types of records that may have been created for and about your ancestors.

An ancestor who was a farmer was dependent on weather and a market for his crop in order for him to survive and prosper. Another who was conscripted for military service received special training and was assigned duties in a specific area; he may have traveled a great deal and been involved in armed conflict.

Consider, for example, an Irish family in the mid-1840s who was impacted by the Potato Famine. Starving and economically devastated, the father may have sought relief for himself and his family by emigrating to America. By studying the history of Ireland in that period, you can understand the factors that motivated someone to want to emigrate elsewhere. Also studying the history of America at that time, and the specific area to which the family immigrated, you can gain an appreciation for what drew the family there: jobs, opportunity, cost of living, and climate, to name but a few.

As you can see, it is impossible to research your ancestors in a vacuum. It is important to place them into geographical and historical context, and that means studying history, geography, and all sorts of materials that may provide you with insights into their lives and their motivation for making some of the decisions they made.

Become a Student of History

The study of your family's story also becomes a study of history at all levels. I've found that making the connection between my ancestors and the history of the places and times in which they lived has brought history to life. My ancestors came alive for me beginning on the snowy day spent with my aunt and grandmother long ago, and my interest in and appreciation for history, geography, and my family heritage were sparked forever. No longer are historical facts merely a memorization of places, dates, and famous people's names. My exploration of *my* family's history makes me place *them* at a particular place, and I give consideration to what the impact of events in the area at the time might have had on them. I reflect on what their participation in those events, and that of their contemporaries, might have been. It is vivid and exciting!

Consider the circumstances of one of your ancestors who might have lived in Pennsylvania on 1 July 1863 near a little town called Gettysburg. Even if no one in that family was actively involved in military service, imagine the terror your ancestor must have felt at being near the site of the epic Battle of Gettysburg. He or she, and probably the entire family, fled the area to escape the approaching armies and the impending destruction. What impact would the estimated 569 tons of ammunition used, and the deaths of more than 50,000 soldiers and 5,000 horses have had on the community and on your ancestor? That place and every person there was forever changed during and by the three days of intense conflict and horror.

Your research will take you into many interesting places where you will discover a wealth of information. There's no doubt that you will be fascinated with contemplating what your ancestors' lives must have been like as you read and learn more about history.

Family Histories

It is possible that someone else has written a history of your family or one that includes details about your family. Unless one of your ancestors was an eminently famous person whose biography would be of interest to a wide audience, you will find that most family histories are either self-published by the author or privately published. Sometimes the author only generates a few copies of the family chronicle and perhaps donates a copy to the local public library. These gems can be invaluable resources and point you to all sorts of information. However, it is important to use your critical thinking skills to evaluate the content and the source materials. Don't accept any "fact" at face value, even if the family history was compiled and written by Uncle Al or Cousin Becky.

Research and verify everything for yourself. You may find that all of their information is correct, well-researched, and the sources are meticulously cited. However, there is no substitute for examining the source materials yourself and forming your own conclusions.

County and Local Histories

Histories written about a limited area, such as a town, county, or parish, can provide important details in your research. *The History of Mecklenburg County, 1740-1900* by J. B. Alexander, originally published in 1902 by the Observer Press, proved a goldmine in my family research. I learned a great deal about the history of Charlotte, North Carolina, and the surrounding area, which a number of my ancestors helped settle. Included were articles concerning agriculture, commerce, and economics through the years that helped me visualize my ancestors' environment. Other articles discussed individual churches, their histories, and their congregations. Modes of travel, clothing, and medical treatments were described. However, of special interest to me were biographical sketches of several of my ancestors, including my great-great-grandfather, Dr. Isaac Wilson, M.D., for whom a photograph was included. (See Figure 3-3.) To my knowledge, this is the only surviving photograph of my ancestor who was born on 30 December 1802 and died on 15 December 1880. Imagine my excitement at learning specific details about him, such as the fact that he was a "progressive physician" who practiced between 1825 and 1875. I learned that he eschewed the practice of cupping, in which a cupping glass was used to increase the blood supply to an area of the skin.

My great-great-grandfather organized and participated in both shooting matches and fox hunts. I also learned that he was a Justice of the Peace and officiated at many weddings. This was the first

DR. ISAAC WILSON.

FIGURE 3-3   This photograph of the author's great-grandfather, perhaps the only surviving picture, was located in a county history published in 1902 (From the author's collection).

place I learned that he was married three times. Based on what I gleaned from this book, I set off on research to verify the information using other records and found it to be extremely accurate.

County heritage books have become popular in the United States and elsewhere over the years. These are primarily compilations of information about places, events, and families whose roots have been based in that county. Organizers solicit articles from citizens and descendants. Recognize that a great deal of this information may be hearsay or family myth, and written by persons who are not researchers or historians. Every fact should therefore be scrutinized for accuracy.

There are a variety of places where you can locate local histories. Towns and cities celebrating centennials, sesquicentennials, bicentennials, and other milestone anniversaries often publish booklets commemorating the extended history of the area. Articles and photographs may include your ancestors and other family members. In addition, local newspaper and magazine coverage may include similar genealogical treasures. Don't overlook these resources in your search for family information.

Churches and synagogues preserve many types of records and also can be a source of local historical information. Commemorative books and albums are common and include names, photographs, and other details that may be useful.

The local or county genealogical and historical societies are essential research resources. They may have unique photographic and documentary materials relating to your family found nowhere else. In addition, these groups undertake transcription and preservation projects. These may involve compiling materials, creating indexes, generating reports or articles for their newsletter or journal. Such projects might include compiling histories of local businesses, canvassing and indexing cemeteries, and transcribing tax rolls and jury lists. They also may possess diaries, journals, photographs, and correspondence files of local residents. You never know what they have until you ask.

The local public library and nearby academic libraries may have originals or copies of information of local historical value. Besides the privately published family histories mentioned earlier, they may also have file cabinets with miscellaneous documents such as correspondence and obituaries. Some libraries' special collections have acquired unusual sets of records. The University of South Florida in Tampa has acquired the records of several local mortuaries/funeral homes that have gone out of business. The Special Collections department of the Clayton Library in Houston, Texas, owns an impressive collection of microfilm materials, including manuscripts concerning New England, the Mid-Atlantic States, the Midwest, the Old South, and the New South, described at **http://www.hpl.lib.tx.us/clayton/cla_c10.html**.

State and Provincial Histories

Learning about local history is important, but be sure to learn about state and provincial histories as well. These provide a broader perspective of the historical role played by a town or county. This can lead to a better understanding of the events and influences in your ancestor's life.

Again, historical and genealogical societies can potentially provide excellent resources for your research. Libraries of all types hold books about state or provincial history, particularly state libraries and archives. One of my favorite Web sites is LibrarySpot.com at **http://www.libraryspot.com**.

3

Here you will find links to all types of libraries in the United States, links to national libraries in more than 40 countries, and many reference resource links. The UK Public Libraries Page at **http://dspace.dial.pipex.com/town/square/ac940/weblibs.html** provides a compilation of links to libraries in the British Isles, while the National Library of Canada has created a Web page of Canadian library Web sites and catalogs at **http://www.nlc-bnc.ca/canlib/eindex.htm.**

State, provincial, and national libraries and archives provide extensive materials about history. Many of these facilities also house and preserve original materials, as well as printed, microfilmed, and scanned images. Such collections include

- U.S. National Archives and Records Administration (NARA) at **http://www.archives.gov/**
- Library of Congress at **http://www.loc.gov**
- National Library of Canada at **http://www.nlc-bnc.ca/index-e.html**
- U.K. National Archives at **http://www.nationalarchives.gov.uk**
- National Archives of Australia at **http://www.naa.gov.au**

Many more such national sites can be located using your favorite search engine and entering terms such as "national library" or "national archive" and the name of the country. For example, you might enter the following search string of words:

"national archive" singapore

You will notice that I used the singular of the word "archive" rather than the plural. Be sure to consult the Help or Tips & Tricks information of *your* favorite Web browser to determine what search format is appropriate for your searches in order to obtain the most accurate results. For example, by searching for a singular form of the word "archive" rather than the plural of "archives," some search engines will present you with search results whose pages contain both forms of the word. This is referred to as *word stemming,* and not all search engines support this approach. The popular Google search engine does not support the use of word stemming. Therefore, in order to obtain search results for both "national archive" *and* "national archives" in my search results, I would need to use the Advanced Search facility of Google and specify that I want Web pages presented that include either "national archive" *or* "national archives" in their content.

Another feature supported by some but not all search engines is the wildcard search. A *wildcard* is simply a unique character that represents one or more characters of which you are unsure. If I am searching for Web pages in which I am seeking the color "grey" or "gray," and am not sure how the word is spelled on Web pages, I could substitute the search engine's wildcard character and type **gr*y,** using an asterisk wildcard and this would provide me with search results with either spelling. Wildcard characters do vary from search engine to search engine. Again, Google is one of the search engines that does not use a wildcard character. As a result, I would have to use the Advanced Search facility of Google and specify that I want Web pages that include either "grey" *or* "gray" in their content.

National and World History

The influences of national and international events were important factors in the lives of our ancestors, their families, and their communities. The perspective of history gives us the opportunity to better understand our forebears' place in it. You may think events in France in the late 1700s had little impact on the American continents, but you would be incorrect. On the contrary, following its devastating defeat in the Seven Years War against Britain (1756–63), France was eager for revenge against the British. When the American Revolution erupted, statesman Benjamin Franklin traveled to Paris, met with French government officials, and the two countries entered into a treaty on 6 February 1779. Franklin met with King Louis XVI and Queen Marie Antoinette on 20 March 1779 to confirm that treaty, and with that the French entered into an agreement to provide aid and support to the American Colonies. Following the American Revolution, the French helped broker the signing of the Treaty of Paris at Versailles on 3 September 1783, in which Great Britain recognized the independence of the United States of America. (See Figure 3-4.)

In another treaty, signed on 30 April 1803, the United States successfully completed the negotiations for the Louisiana Purchase from France at a price of 60 million francs, or about $15 million. The area comprised more than 800,000 square miles extending from the Mississippi River in the east to the Rocky Mountains on the west.

In addition to this impact on North America, the French also occupied Spain in the early 19th century. The occupation cut off commerce between Spain and its colonies in Central and South America. Between 1808 and 1826, all of Latin America with the exception of Cuba and Puerto Rico were lost by the Spanish. Emulating the example of their neighbors to the north in the new United States, the Spanish colonies rebelled and ultimately claimed their independence.

Another important event in France in the late 1780s was the formation of a group, the Friends of the Negro, who met in Paris in early 1788 to campaign against the French slave trade. On 4 February 1794, slavery was abolished in the French colonies. The news spread across the Atlantic and slaves were freed in the French colonies. The action did not go unnoticed in the United States. By 1807, the slave trade to all British colonies was abolished and that same year the United States Congress passed legislation prohibiting the importation of slaves into the country and its territories. Slave smuggling persisted through 1862, and President Abraham Lincoln's *Emancipation Proclamation* abolished all forms of slavery in the Southern states, effective on 1 January 1863. The 13th Amendment to the United States Constitution was passed by Congress on 31 January 1865 and ratified on 6 December of that year, ending slavery and involuntary servitude in the United States and greatly expanding the civil rights of Americans.

As you can see, events on a national level had far-reaching and enduring impacts elsewhere. That is why it is important to study history and to consider how the events may have impacted your ancestors and their contemporaries. The French actions described above can be applied to persons of French, Spanish, English, and North American, South American, and African descent. You will find that it is imperative to learn something about the history of both the place where your ancestors originally lived *and* about the places to which they migrated. There definitely is a push-pull influence involved that, if you take the time to explore it, may provide a much clearer understanding and appreciation of your heritage.

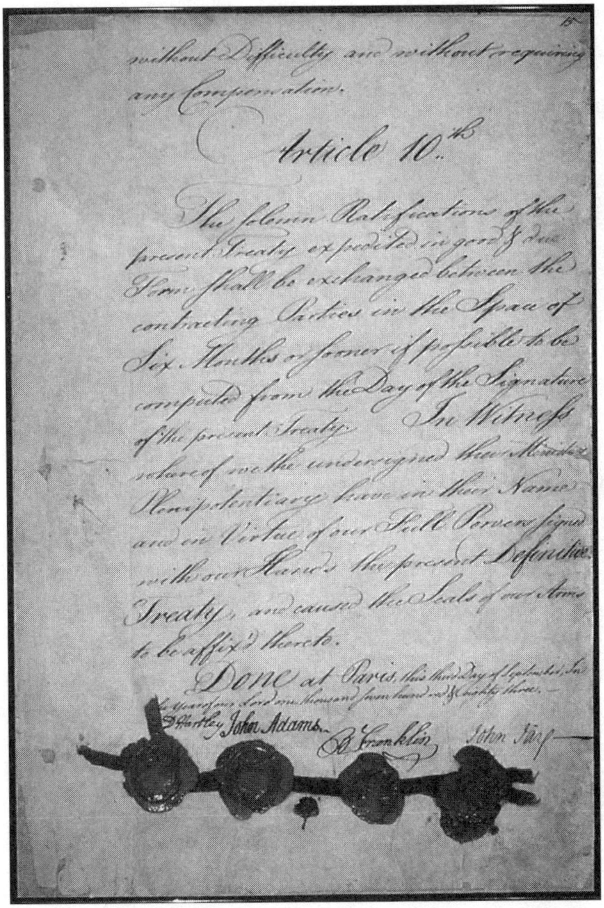

without Difficulty and without requiring any Compensation.

Article 10th.

The solemn Ratifications of the present Treaty expedited in good & due Form shall be exchanged between the contracting Parties in the Space of Six Months or sooner if possible to be computed from the Day of the Signature of the present Treaty. In Witness whereof we the undersigned their Ministers Plenipotentiary have in their Name and in Virtue of our Full Powers signed with our Hands the present Definitive Treaty, and caused the Seals of our Arms to be affix'd thereto.

Done at Paris, this third Day of September, In the Year of our Lord one thousand seven hundred and eighty three.

D Hartley John Adams B Franklin John Jay

FIGURE 3-4 Signatures on one of two original copies of the Treaty of Paris—3 September 1783 (From the National Archives and Records Administration collection)

Use Maps to Locate the *Right* Place to Research

Maps, like the one shown in Figure 3-5, are an essential part of our everyday life. We consult them to plot travel routes as we move from place to place, check them to determine correct postal codes, and use them in a wide variety of other ways. We find maps today printed on paper, on the Internet, in computer software programs, and the use of Global Positioning System (GPS) technology is becoming more widespread.

Throughout history, maps have changed again and again. Country and county boundaries moved, towns have come under different jurisdictions, place names have changed, and some places have ceased to exist for innumerable reasons. For this reason, we cannot simply use contemporary maps as references for locating records. We must use a number of types of historical maps in our genealogical research. In order to determine the *right* place to look for records and other evidence,

FIGURE 3-5   Map of Sydney, Australia—1922 (Library of Congress Geography and Map Division)

it is essential to understand the geographical history of an area. Many genealogists hit "dead ends" and waste inordinate amounts of time because they either fail to understand the importance of properly using maps in their research or they don't possess the skills to use them.

Avoid Wasted Time and Energy

Imagine the frustration of having planned a vacation that included research at a courthouse in a particular area, only to discover when you arrived that the information you were seeking was actually located in another county's courthouse. It happens all too frequently, especially when a person fails to determine beforehand where his or her ancestors lived and which county had jurisdiction over the area at that time.

Perhaps expending the time and expense of a research trip is an extreme example, but it does happen. However, there are many other ways we can waste time and money, researching the wrong materials. You want to avoid the following types of errors:

- Researching in the wrong books
- Checking the wrong census areas
- Using the wrong finding aids and indices
- Ordering and researching on the wrong microfilm reels
- Writing to the wrong courthouse
- Traveling to the wrong location

Worse yet, you could actually be researching the wrong ancestors! When your family has a common name and there are people of the same name in the area, it is possible to latch onto the records of an individual whose details seem "almost right." You might then spend a great deal of time tracing that person's records until you encounter names, places, dates, and other evidence that definitively tells you that you've been on a wild goose chase. Don't think it can't happen to you; it happens to the best of us. In my own search for records concerning my great-great-grandfather, Jesse Holder, a few years ago, I located one in Laurens County, South Carolina, at about the same time period. I thought, "Well, I don't know his birth date for certain, but this fellow is about the right age." After researching this Jesse Holder for a while, I discovered that he married twice and died there in South Carolina. I had evidence, however, that my great-great-grandfather had lived in two Georgia counties and was listed in censuses with a wife and their two sons (one being my great-grandfather) subsequent to the date of death of the South Carolina Jesse. Remember, proving that someone is *not* your ancestor can be valuable too—if that had been your intent in the first place. In my case, I wasted time with the wrong Jesse.

Use Maps for Multiple Purposes

Maps are a necessity in our genealogical research. They help us locate landmarks, waterways, roads and streets, towns, cities, counties, parishes, states, provinces, territories, countries, oceans, continents, islands, and more. Contemporary and historical maps, such as the one shown in Figure 3-6, help us determine the geopolitical jurisdictions in place at a specific time. They provide a visual representation of the geographic spatial relationships between physical locations, and can help us place our ancestors' physical location into perspective. This can help us better understand where they might have been in relationship to events occurring around them.

I happen to use historical maps of and from the 16th to 18th centuries to plot the possible migration paths followed by my own ancestors in the American Colonies. This means having studied the history of migration routes north and south as well as across the Appalachian Mountains. The investment in that research has allowed me to plot the potential migration routes for ancestors between two points and to anticipate what their journey entailed. Then, using colored markers, I draw the probable routes(s) on a map and begin researching the interim stops they may have made and the records that may have been created and left behind. The process has been remarkably successful, and I'd like to share it with you.

FIGURE 3-6   Map of Massachusetts—1879 (Library of Congress Geography and Map Division)

Use a Methodology that Works

I have worked with maps for many years and have found a practical methodology for working with maps and other related resources that can improve your success at locating the *right* place to search for records.

Step 1: Start with a Contemporary Map

Obtain a good current map of the area where you believe your ancestors lived in the past. There are any number of excellent map resources available, including bound atlases, printed individual maps for areas, and maps available from motoring associations such as the American Automobile Association (AAA). In addition, highway department maps at a local, county, or other administrative area level provide excellent detail including secondary and tertiary roads, natural landmarks, churches and cemeteries, and other features. Whatever maps you use should include contemporary boundary lines.

You probably won't want to use cheap maps and atlases because they seldom contain as much detail as you would like, and they sometimes contain errors or omit important features. Maps on the Internet services also are sometimes less than accurate, and seldom contain the detail you need, especially boundaries. Beware of driving directions from these sites, and always compare two sets of driving instructions for conflicting information. Consider the creator of the map, their authority and expertise, the purpose of the map, and the accuracy.

On your good contemporary map, follow this progression and make notes as you proceed.

1. Locate the place you seek.

2. Note the name of the specific county or province in which it is located today.

3. Make specific note of the location within the contemporary boundaries.

4. Note surrounding towns or cities and their direction from your site.

5. Make note of other surrounding geographic features such as waterways, mountains, and shorelines, and their physical position in relation to the place you located.

It is possible that the place you are searching for isn't listed on the map. Perhaps it is too small, is an unincorporated area, or perhaps the place has been renamed or no longer exists. What do you do? Never fear, there are other resources available to you. Local histories are invaluable in helping locate these places. However, one of the best tools you can use is a *gazetteer,* also referred to as a *place name dictionary*. There are many of these available for different parts of the world, both printed and Web-based. For United States research, I have become addicted to using the book *American Place Names of Long Ago* by Gilbert S. Bahn. The work is based on a portion of Cram's World Atlas, published in 1895, and whose U.S. information was based on the 1890 U.S. federal census returns.

Among the best Internet-based gazetteers are the following:

- United States Geological Survey Geographic Names Information System (also referred to as the USGS GNIS), a massive searchable database of United States national mapping information. Located at **http://geonames.usgs.gov/pls/gnis/web_query.gnis_web_query_ form,** the GNIS allows you to search by name and location and to narrow your search to specific feature type. I often find this facility indispensable in locating somewhat obscure cemeteries. The results include latitude and longitude, as well as links to a number of map images, most helpful of which is the U.S. Census Bureau's Tiger Map Server. Figure 3-7 shows an image from this server.

- The University of California's Alexandria Digital Library Gazetteer Server, located at **http://www.alexandria.ucsb.edu/clients/gazetteer,** also provides similar detail at a global level. It incorporates data from multiple online cartographic information servers.

- The Atlas of Canada, located at **http://atlas.gc.ca/site/english/data_services/gazetteer.html,** provides access to the Gazetteer Map Service and allows you to search for place and feature names. You can narrow your search to a specific province and territory and/or feature type. In addition, however, the site contains links to collections of different maps, including a large number of historical maps covering the history of Canada, outline maps, and an archive of images from various editions of the *Atlas of Canada,* going back to the first edition published in 1906.

- The Geoscience Australia gazetteer's Place Name Search facility, hosted by the Australian government and located at **http://www.ga.gov.au/map/names/,** is a compilation of more than 297,000 geographic names provided by members of the Committee for Geographic Names in Australasia.

■ The Gazetteer for Scotland at **http://www.geo.ed.ac.uk/scotgaz/gaztitle.html** is an excellent resource for locating towns and features in Scotland.

■ The GENUKI at **http://www.genuki.org.uk/** has compiled a wealth of helpful resources, and its collection of links beginning with the page at **http://www.genuki.org.uk/big/** includes maps of administrative regions, both contemporary and historical, and other online gazetteer materials.

■ The HGS: German Gazetteers site, located at **http://www.horlacher.org/germany/ gazetteer/,** provides access to collections of links including a historical atlas/gazetteer with downloadable maps and genealogical gazetteers for most provinces.

If you are seeking an online gazetteer facility for another country or locale, you can always use your favorite Web browser and enter search terms like the one shown here:

gazetteer "insert country/province name here"

and you will be rewarded with search results that you can explore.

You should also consider using the reference resources available to you in libraries of all sorts. Reference librarians at public and academic libraries are trained to conduct expert research for inquiries from patrons. State and national libraries and archives are another resource and many of them handle reference question requests via telephone and e-mail.

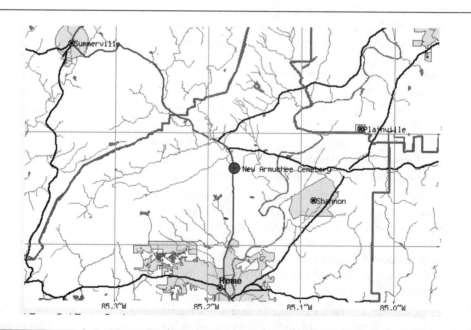

FIGURE 3-7   New Armuchee Cemetery outside Rome, Georgia, was located in the USGS GNIS and the map was produced by the U.S. Census Bureau's Tiger Map Server.

Step 2: Locate and Examine Historical Maps

Your next step is to determine the time period when your ancestors lived in the area. Locate an historical map of that area from that time period. (See Figure 3-8.) If you are researching your ancestors in the United States, you might want to consult the *Map Guide to the U.S. Federal Censuses, 1790-1920* by William Thorndale and William Dollarhide. This book provides maps of every state for every one of the decennial censuses taken between 1790 and 1920. Each map shows the current counties and their boundaries and the counties in existence at the time of the census and their boundaries. This is an excellent tool for a high-level comparison between the contemporary and historical geopolitical boundaries. You can follow up with a search for and consultation of a detailed historical map of the period. This is the procedure you should follow for other countries and locales as well.

Locate the place you found on your contemporary map in Step 1. Compare it to historical maps from before and after the dates in which your ancestors lived in the area. Make note of the surrounding towns and landmarks you found on your contemporary map and locate these on the historical map. This can be crucial when you are looking for places that changed names or disappeared. More important, though, is to carefully note the administrative boundaries, such as state, parish, or province. If the place you are researching was located in another county at the time your ancestors were there, for instance, you will be seeking to locate records in *that* governmental

FIGURE 3-8   Historical map of Washington, D.C.—1822 (Library of Congress Geography and Map Division)

division's records and not in that of the current governmental unit's repositories. There are some rare cases in which records are transferred to new jurisdictions, such as when new counties are created. It is therefore important to keep this in mind when asking about the availability of records in and from the original government offices.

Step 3: Fine-tune Your Search Location

The examination of maps is an important factor in locating the *right* place to research records, but there is another step you should perform. While the *Map Guide to the U.S. Federal Censuses, 1790-1920* is an excellent reference, it only provides detail at the ten-year intervals at which time the federal censuses were taken. You may need to determine a more concise date when the administrative area was formed. Let's look at two examples.

The Pennsylvania county of Wyoming (see Figure 3-9), for instance, was formed in 1842 from Luzerne County. If you were looking for marriage records of your ancestors from 1840, you would

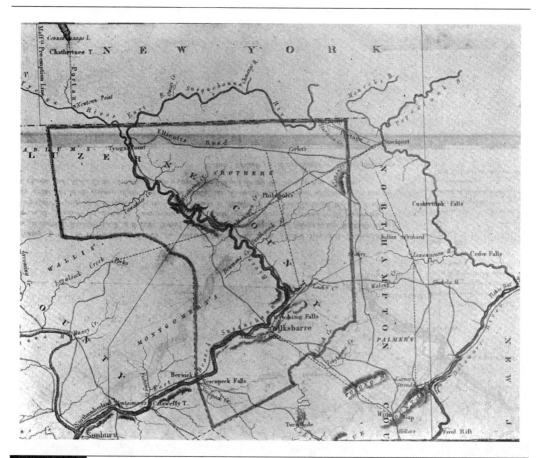

FIGURE 3-9   Historical map of Wyoming County, Pennsylvania—1791 (Library of Congress Geography and Map Division)

seek them in Luzerne County, while if they were married in 1843, you would look in Wyoming County. I was able to determine the county formation dates through use of *Ancestry's Red Book,* published by Ancestry.com, Inc., and *The Handybook for Genealogists,* published by Everton Publishers. I might also search the Internet for information concerning the formation of Wyoming County and its parent county.

Geopolitical boundaries across Europe have changed time and time again. Poland provides an excellent example of this. It was partitioned between Austria, Prussia, and Russia in 1772 and each country annexed a portion of Poland. In 1793, Russia and Prussia signed a Second Partition Treaty and more of Poland was seized. In 1795, Russia effected yet a third partition and obtained part of the remainder of Poland. While some of the records from these periods may still exist in Polish archives, others would have been created by the three other national governments. And, since the Kingdom of Prussia no longer exists, what would have happened to all of those records? Jumping forward to 20th century Poland, the invasion by the German army on 1 September 1939 began yet another period of division. The Germans and the Russians partitioned and divided Poland yet again. As you can see, your research of Polish ancestral records would be dependent on the historical time period, the partitioning of the country, and the government in control at the time, as well as a number of other factors.

Step 4: Identify the Records Created and Their Current Location

It is important to read about the types of records created at the time and their purpose. You also will need to determine if they still exist and where they are located. The type of record often dictates its ultimate fate. Some records are of such a temporary nature that, once they have served their purpose, they are discarded or destroyed. Others are of such perpetual importance that they are maintained permanently or for an extended period of time.

Ancestry's Red Book gives detailed descriptions of record types created in each state, the dates when record-keeping for various records began, and where these records are most likely to be housed. I say "most likely" because there is the possibility that records may have been relocated for any of a number of reasons.

When researching in England, you will want to learn about the National Archives in Kew, Richmond, Surrey, and at **http://www.nationalarchives.gov.uk.** The General Register Office for Scotland (GRO) in Edinburgh and at **http://www.gro-scotland.gov.uk/** is your starting point to learn what is available there, while the General Register Office in Dublin, and at **http://www.groireland.ie,** is the equivalent in Ireland. The combined National Library of Canada and National Archives of Canada site, at **http://www.archives.ca/,** is accessible in both English and French. It offers excellent, well-organized information about available records. The National Archives of Australia site at **http://www.naa.gov.au/** likewise presents information about its record-keeping and details about available resources.

In addition to all of the places mentioned above, The Church of Jesus Christ of Latter-Day Saints (LDS), sometimes also referred to as the Mormon Church, has the largest genealogical library in the world. Their Web site at **http://www.familysearch.org** is filled with interesting resources, but one of your best references for locating records is their collection of Research Guides located at **http://www.familysearch.org/Eng/Search/RG/frameset_rg.asp.**

Step 5: Contact the Repository to Obtain Copies of Records

Once you have determined the *right* place to search for records, make contact with the facility. *Ancestry's Red Book* and the *Handybook for Genealogists* both provide excellent contact information for state and county/parish records. So, too, do the LDS Research Guides mentioned earlier. However, don't assume that they are always correct. Materials are sometimes relocated, stored off-site in another location, have limited or prohibited access due to legislation or government restrictions, or sometimes records are lost or destroyed. It is therefore a good idea to make contact with the repository of record to determine what they really have, how accessible the materials are, and how to access or obtain copies. This is especially important if you are planning a research visit. You will want to learn the days and hours of operation, what personal access is permitted, and costs. If records are off-site in storage, you will want to determine how you can gain access to them.

Whenever you make contact with a facility, you can avoid some dead-ends by being prepared and by asking open-ended questions. Over the years, I've found that preparing a written set of the questions I want to ask is a way to make certain that I cover everything necessary and all the contingencies. You can try this method yourself and I'm certain you will find it helpful.

Begin by performing some advance research and know the names of the persons for whom you are seeking records, what type of records you want, and the correct time period. You should include nicknames and any other names by which a person may have been known, and be certain to use the maiden name of a woman if you are seeking marriage records or other documents created before her wedding date. One distant cousin I always knew to be called "Sudie" actually was born Susan Elizabeth Wilson. It was under her nickname that I found her in some records, and under her birth name that I found her in others.

Open-ended questions are those that require more than a "yes" or "no" answer. For example, if you ask a clerk if their facility has the marriage records from 1902 and he or she responds in the negative, what do you do? Your next question should be, "Can you tell me if the records exist and, if so, where I would be able to locate them?" Otherwise, the clerk may or may not volunteer that information.

Maps Can Equal Success

Libraries, archives, courthouses, records offices, government offices, museums, churches, other physical repositories, and the Internet can all be used to obtain maps. This methodology for effectively locating and using maps will substantially improve your chances for success in locating the *right* place for finding your ancestors' records and other evidence. With this in mind, let's proceed to learn about locating some official documents.

Locate Birth, Marriage, and Death Records

The most basic and yet most important records you can locate for your ancestors are ones that record their birth, marriage, and death (see Figure 3-10). These are generally referred to as "vital records" because they record the vital life events. One of my English friends refers to these as the "hatch, match, and dispatch" records. What makes these records so important is that they not only confirm your ancestor or family member in a specific place at a given point in time, but they potentially connect the person to other family members.

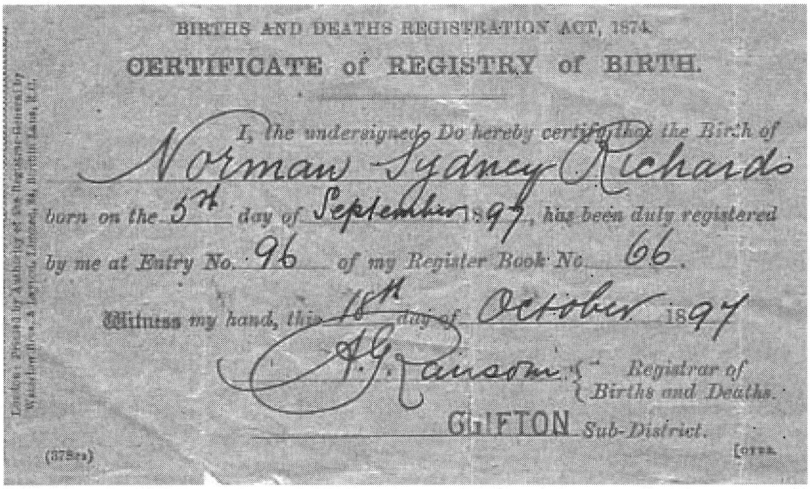

BIRTHS AND DEATHS REGISTRATION ACT, 1874.

CERTIFICATE of REGISTRY of BIRTH.

I, the undersigned, Do hereby certify that the Birth of

Norman Sydney Richards

born on the 5th day of September 1897, has been duly registered by me at Entry No. 96 of my Register Book No. 66.

Witness my hand, this 18th day of October 1897

A. G. Ransom.   { Registrar of
                  { Births and Deaths.

CLIFTON Sub-District.

FIGURE 3-10   Certificate of Registry of Birth from the U.K.—1897 (Used by permission of the National Archives, U.K.)

The originals or copies of these records may be in your family's possession, and you just need to ask family members for access to them. However, in many instances and especially in cases of births, marriages, and deaths, you will have to determine if the records were commonly created at the time and, if so, where they are located. You then will have to expend effort to obtain copies of them, either by mail, e-mail, telephone, or personal visit to the repository where they are held. It is important to recognize right away that you may not be able to obtain copies of some of these records. A birth certificate, for example, may not have been required to be created at the time your ancestor was born. In the United States, for instance, you may find that some of the counties in a particular state began creating official birth records earlier than others. Kentucky counties, for instance, created birth records dating from 1852. In contrast, the North Carolina legislature did not pass legislation requiring counties to create birth and death records until 10 March 1913, and it was not until 1920 that all counties were in full compliance with the law.

In other cases, access to copies of birth records may be limited to the individual for whose birth the document was created and/or his or her parents. Since the terrorist attacks in the United States on 11 September 2001, many state legislatures have limited access to these and other records in consideration of the possibility of identity theft. Certain information on death certificates may also be masked when copies are created in order to preserve the privacy of the surviving family members and to prevent the release of information that might be used to steal an identity.

Keep in mind that these three types of records—birth, marriage, and death records—can be used to establish the location of your ancestor or family member at a specific place at a point in time. By extension, that helps you begin locating other records created in the same vicinity, which can expand your knowledge of that person and his or her extended family. When official birth, marriage, and death records are not available for whatever reason, you will need to consider locating alternative record sources to establish the same or similar information. We will discuss this later in the chapter.

Locate the Birth Certificate

All of us were born somewhere and at some time, and the first document created for many people was a birth certificate such as the one shown in Figure 3-11. We all have had parents and the vast majority of us were probably born with the benefit of some medical attention. And typically there was a record made of the birth in the form of a birth certificate and/or a hospital or other medical record. A birth certificate is an important document because it is used to verify identity. From a genealogist's perspective, it can be the basis for beginning research in a specific geographic area for other family members and a wide variety of other records.

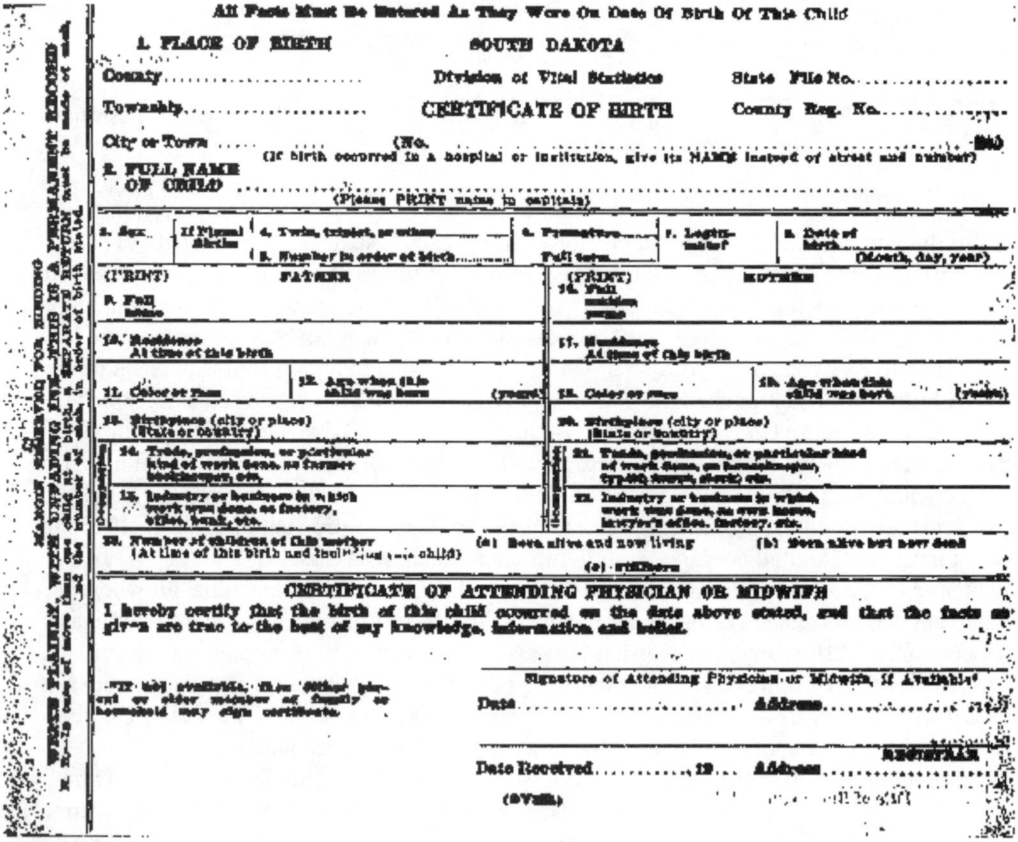

All Facts Must Be Entered As They Were On Date Of Birth Of This Child

1. PLACE OF BIRTH — SOUTH DAKOTA

County .... Division of Vital Statistics — State File No. ....

Township .... CERTIFICATE OF BIRTH — County Reg. No. ....

City or Town .... (No. .... St.)
(If birth occurred in a hospital or institution, give its NAME instead of street and number)

2. FULL NAME OF CHILD ....
(Please PRINT name in capitals)

3. Sex — If Plural Births — 4. Twin, triplet, or other — 5. Number in order of birth — 6. Premature — Full term — 7. Legitimate? — 8. Date of birth (Month, day, year)

(PRINT) FATHER — (PRINT) MOTHER

9. Full name — 16. Full maiden name

10. Residence At time of this birth — 17. Residence At time of this birth

11. Color or Race — 12. Age when this child was born (years) — 18. Color or race — 19. Age when this child was born (years)

13. Birthplace (city or place) (State or country) — 20. Birthplace (city or place) (State or country)

14. Trade, profession, or particular kind of work done, as farmer, bookkeeper, etc. — 21. Trade, profession, or particular kind of work done, as housekeeper, typist, nurse, clerk, etc.

15. Industry or business in which work was done, as factory, office, bank, etc. — 22. Industry or business in which work was done, as own home, lawyer's office, factory, etc.

23. Number of children of this mother (At time of this birth and including this child) — (a) Born alive and now living — (b) Born alive but now dead — (c) Stillborn

CERTIFICATE OF ATTENDING PHYSICIAN OR MIDWIFE

I hereby certify that the birth of this child occurred on the date above stated, and that the facts as given are true to the best of my knowledge, information and belief.

*If not available, then either parent or older member of family or household may sign certificate.

Signature of Attending Physician or Midwife, if Available*

Date .... Address ....

REGISTRAR

Date Received ...., 19... Address ....

(OVER)

MARGIN RESERVED FOR BINDING — WRITE PLAINLY, WITH UNFADING INK—THIS IS A PERMANENT RECORD — N.B.—In case of more than one child at a birth, a SEPARATE RETURN must be made of each, and the number of each, in order of birth stated.

FIGURE 3-11 Blank South Dakota birth certificate form

You will need to determine *where* the person was born in order to determine if there is a birth certificate from that time. The methodology for using maps to locate the *right* place to search for records is especially helpful.

Ancestry's Red Book, for example, can be used to determine, state by state and county by county, when official birth records began to be kept by the government offices in the United States, as well as where to seek them.

Birth certificates come in many formats, with different titles, and contain different amounts of information. At a minimum, you would expect to find the name of the child, the parents' names, the child's date of birth, gender, the location where the birth occurred (or was registered), the name of the attending physician or midwife, and the signature of the registrar. Other information likely to be found on birth records may include the child's birth weight and length, and the precise time of birth, as well as the parents' racial or ethnic background and occupations. More recent birth certificates may include the child's footprints and perhaps even a photograph. You will find a number of examples of birth certificates in the graphics throughout this chapter. Figure 3-12, for example, shows a certificate issued by a government office in 1942 that confirms a birth entry in the official files dating to 1875. Birth records in different parts of the world may look different and contain different levels of detail, but their intent was to formally record a birth. The Dutch birth certificate shown in Figure 3-13 is a good example of this.

You may come across an amended birth certificate from time to time. These are used to change or correct information entered on the original birth certificate. A typical reason for the issuance

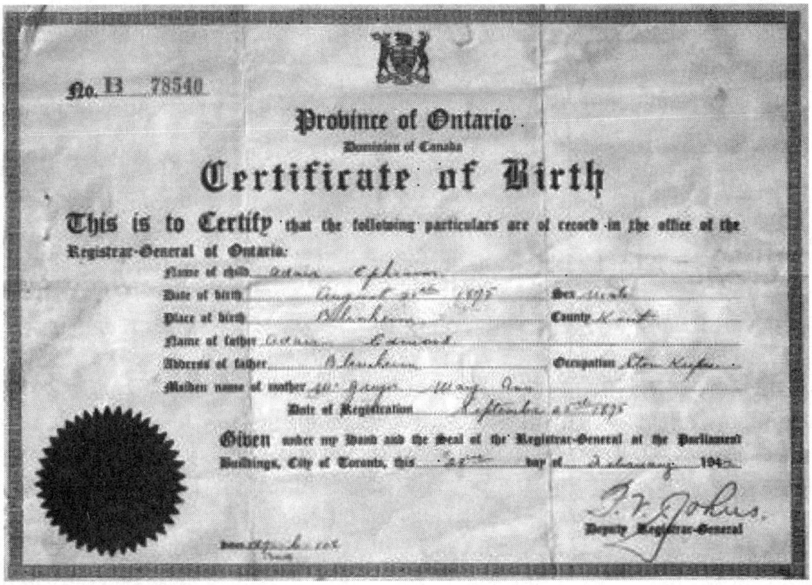

No. B 78540

Province of Ontario.

Dominion of Canada

Certificate of Birth

This is to Certify that the following particulars are of record in the office of the Registrar-General of Ontario:

Name of child

Date of birth Sex

Place of birth County

Name of father

Address of father Occupation

Maiden name of mother

Date of Registration

Given under my Hand and the Seal of the Registrar-General at the Parliament Buildings, City of Toronto, this day of 194

Deputy Registrar-General

FIGURE 3-12 Certificate issued in 1942 attesting to a Canadian birth entry in Ontario in 1875 (From the author's collection)

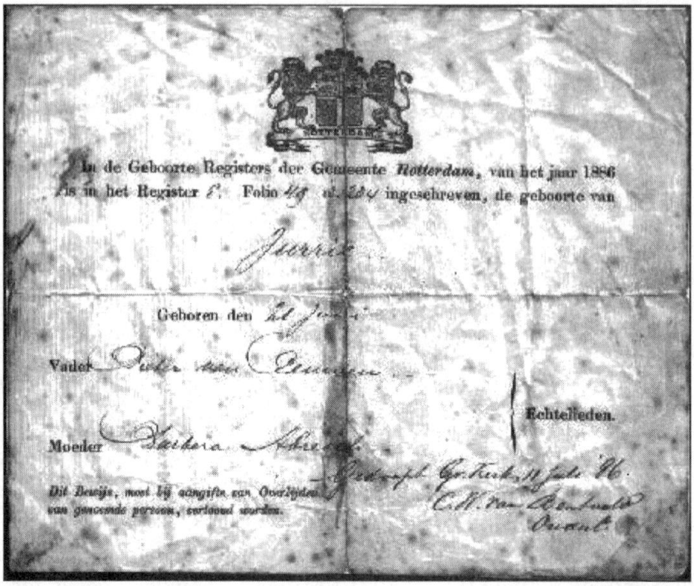
In de Geboorte Registers der Gemeente Rotterdam, van het jaar 1886
is in het Register Folio ingeschreven, de geboorte van

Geboren den

Vader

Echtelieden.

Moeder

Dit Bewijs, moet bij aangifte van Overlijden van genoemde persoon, overlegd worden.

FIGURE 3-13 An original Dutch birth certificate—1886 (Library of Congress collection)

of an amended certificate is to change or correct the name of the child or its parents. Amended birth certificates are also used in cases of adoption. At the time of the legal adoption, particularly that of an infant or small child, a magistrate will order the creation of an amended birth certificate. This document will include the names of the adopting parents and will replace the original birth certificate in all file locations. The original, which lists the natural or birth parents, is removed and placed in a court file with the adoption records. In most cases, these records are sealed by the court and require a judicial order to access them. The amended birth certificate is clearly marked to indicate that it is amended and, in the case of adoption, that there was an adoption that caused its creation.

Delayed birth certificates are not uncommon. They are issued by governments in lieu of an original birth certificate. In cases in which birth records were not created at the time of a person's birth, or where the original records have been lost or destroyed, the governmental office will issue a substitute document. Typically, the applicant needs proof of birth for identification purposes in order to obtain a passport, a visa, or some other document to prove identity or to apply for pension benefits. The person completes an application and presents himself or herself in a governmental facility, and supplies several alternative forms of proof. These might include a family Bible, school enrollment records, church records, military service records, employment records, and affidavits from other people who were alive at the time of the applicant's birth and can confirm that the applicant is indeed the correct person. These alternative proofs, all of which are usually secondary sources, are reviewed. If they are deemed sufficient, a Delayed Birth Certificate is issued and is considered the equivalent of an original birth record. An example of a delayed birth certificate is shown in Figure 3-14.

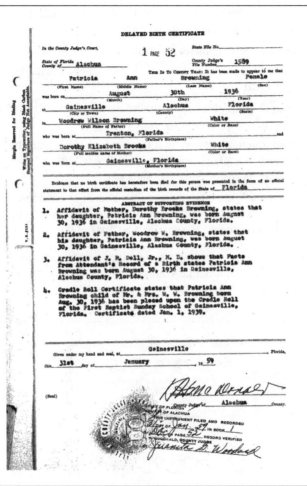

FIGURE 3-14 A delayed birth certificate is issued when no original was created. Alternate proofs of age are presented to the government (Courtesy of Jim Powell).

Alternative records can, of course, be used as evidence of the birth. Remember that you must use your critical thinking skills to evaluate these materials and determine whether they are primary or secondary, or original vs. derivative sources. You will determine that these may be sufficient to prove the fact in question, in this case, a birth. Some of the many types of alternative records you might be able to use might include the following:

■ Baby books created by the parents of other family members that document information about the birth.

■ Christening or baptismal records, such as the one shown in Figure 3-15, may be found in family documents or obtained from a church, and these contain the child's name, date of birth, parents' names, and sometimes names of other family members and godparents.

- A birth announcement published in a newspaper or church publication can provide clues to the date and location of primary birth records.
- The family Bible may contain entries recording names and dates of birth.
- Letters, journals, and diaries of members of the immediate or extended family may contain information about a birth.
- Affidavits from witnesses at or near the time of the event are useful in obtaining delayed birth certificates but may be helpful to you as well.
- Medical records, although not generally released to persons other than the patient and his or her immediate family members, may provide a date of birth. Medical practitioners often maintained their own records of deliveries they performed.
- School enrollment records are a good secondary source of birth information. Data may be obtained by making a request of the school administration officials, who may provide photocopies or written responses to specific questions.

Another part of your investigative process also involves using your knowledge of history, geography, and your family and coupling that with your creative thinking to consider what other types of record types and materials might provide evidence of the event.

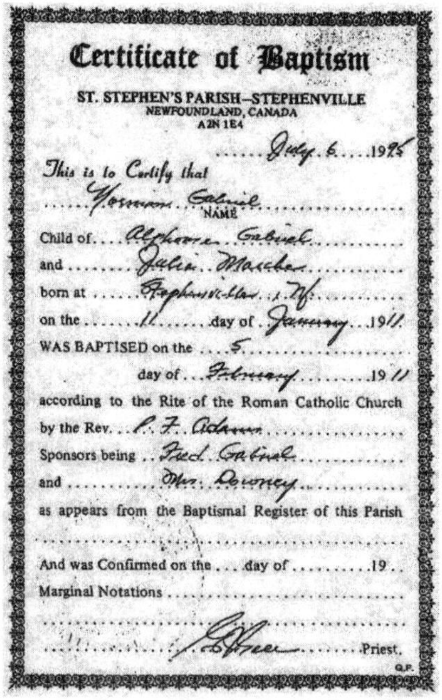

Certificate of Baptism

ST. STEPHEN'S PARISH—STEPHENVILLE
NEWFOUNDLAND, CANADA
A2N 1E4

July 6 1995

This is to Certify that

Norman Gabriel
NAME

Child of Alphonse Gabriel

and Julia Marche

born at Stephenville, Nf.

on the 11 day of January 1911

WAS BAPTISED on the 5

day of February 1911

according to the Rite of the Roman Catholic Church

by the Rev. P. F. Adams

Sponsors being Fred Gabriel

and Mrs. Downey

as appears from the Baptismal Register of this Parish

And was Confirmed on the ... day of .... 19..

Marginal Notations

Priest.

Q.P.

FIGURE 3-15 Certificate of baptism from Newfoundland, Canada (From the author's collection)

Find Marriage Licenses and Certificates

Marriage records are among the oldest records kept. The earliest ones are found in religious institutions, but others are to be found among the many places where civil registration records are located. They are often indexed for easy reference, both in groom and bride sequence by surname and then given name.

In some places, such as United States courthouses, you will find large ledgers containing copies of marriage license or marriage certificate documents, maintained in chronological sequence. The older ones are handwritten entries made by a clerk (who may also have been known by the title of "ordinary") that indicate the authorization of a couple to be married. The actual license or certificate was then taken to a member of the clergy, a judge, or a justice of the peace, and the ceremony was performed. The original document was then returned to the courthouse where the clerk transcribed information about the date of the wedding and the name of the officiating individual. As a result, these entries are often referred to as marriage returns. Figure 3-16 shows an example of a marriage return from the State of Indiana.

In other places, there are civil offices or civil registration offices at which the license to wed was issued. There you often may find the original documents, or you may obtain a copy of the document or a certified document, such as the one shown in Figure 3-17, attesting to the content of the marriage entry.

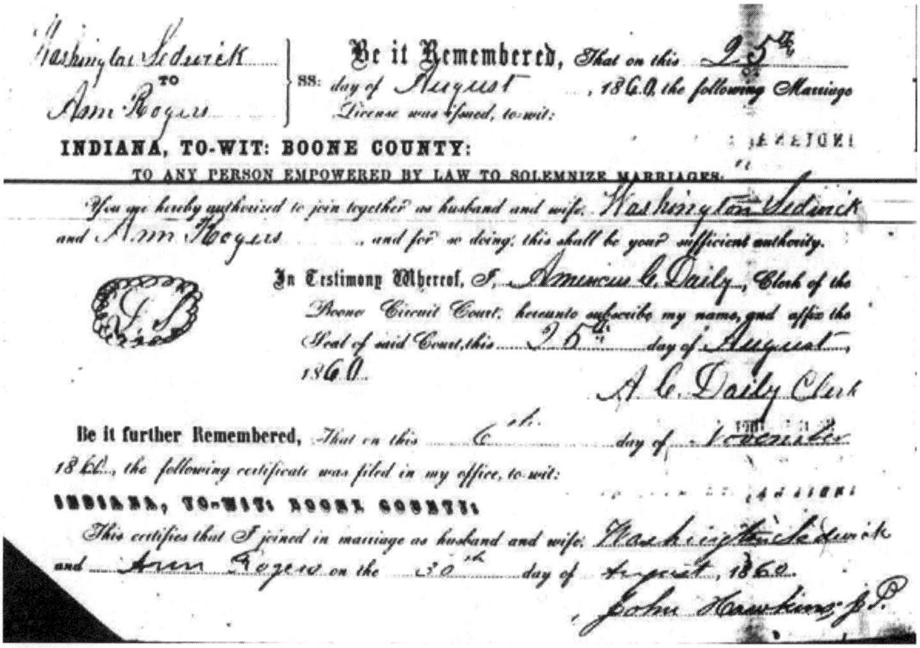

Washington Sedwick TO Ann Rogers } SS: Be it Remembered, That on this 25th day of August, 1860 the following Marriage License was issued, to-wit:

INDIANA, TO-WIT: BOONE COUNTY:

TO ANY PERSON EMPOWERED BY LAW TO SOLEMNIZE MARRIAGES.

You are hereby authorized to join together as husband and wife Washington Sedwick and Ann Rogers, and for so doing, this shall be your sufficient authority.

In Testimony Whereof, I, Americus C. Daily, Clerk of the Boone Circuit Court, hereunto subscribe my name, and affix the Seal of said Court, this 25th day of August, 1860.

A. C. Daily Clerk

Be it further Remembered, That on this 6th day of November 1860, the following certificate was filed in my office, to-wit:

INDIANA, TO-WIT: BOONE COUNTY:

This certifies that I joined in marriage as husband and wife Washington Sedwick and Ann Rogers on the 30th day of August, 1860.

John Hawkins J.P.

FIGURE 3-16 This 1860 marriage license from Indiana was returned to the county clerk for registration and filing (From the National Archives and Records Administration collection).

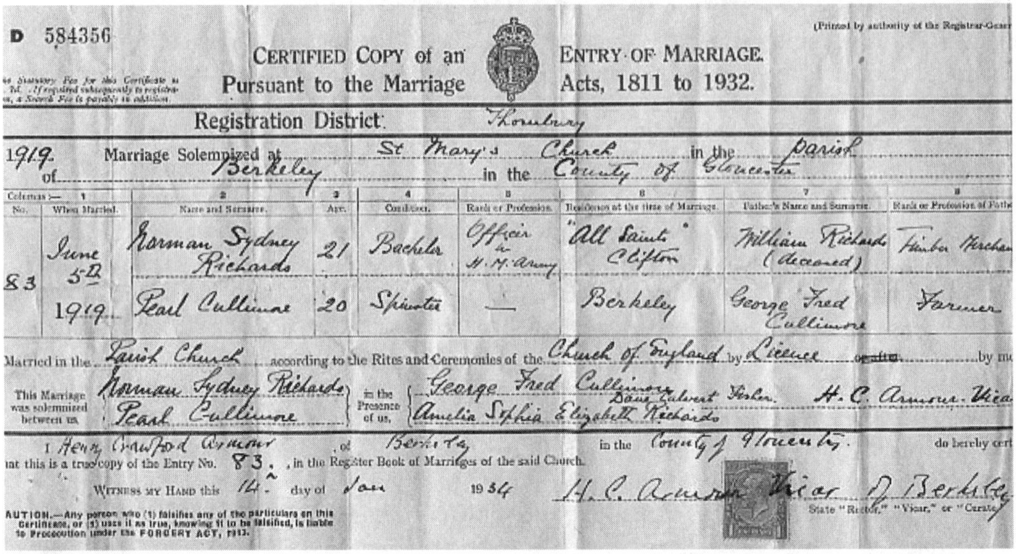

D 584356

(Printed by authority of the Registrar-General)

CERTIFIED COPY of an ENTRY OF MARRIAGE.
Pursuant to the Marriage Acts, 1811 to 1932.

Registration District: Thornbury

1919. Marriage Solemnized at St Mary's Church in the parish of Berkeley in the County of Gloucester

No.	When Married.	Name and Surname.	Age.	Condition.	Rank or Profession.	Residence at the time of Marriage.	Father's Name and Surname.	Rank or Profession of Father.
83	June 5th 1919	Norman Sydney Richards	21	Bachelor	Officer in H. M. Army	"All Saints" Clifton	William Richards (deceased)	Timber Merchant
		Pearl Cullimore	20	Spinster	—	Berkeley	George Fred Cullimore	Farmer

Married in the Parish Church according to the Rites and Ceremonies of the Church of England by Licence by me,

This Marriage was solemnized between us, Norman Sydney Richards, Pearl Cullimore

in the Presence of us, George Fred Cullimore, Amelia Sophia Elizabeth Richards, Dora Calvert Fowler. H. C. Armour. Vicar

I Henry Crawford Armour of Berkeley in the County of Gloucester do hereby certify that this is a true copy of the Entry No. 83, in the Register Book of Marriages of the said Church.

Witness my Hand this 14th day of Jan 1934 H. C. Armour Vicar of Berkeley

State "Rector," "Vicar," or "Curate."

CAUTION.—Any person who (1) falsifies any of the particulars on this Certificate, or (2) uses it as true, knowing it to be falsified, is liable to Prosecution under the FORGERY ACT, 1913.

FIGURE 3-17 The Certified Copy of an Entry of Marriage was issued in Gloucester in 1919 as legal documentation of the marriage (Used by permission of the National Archives, U.K.).

Marriage laws have varied over time in different places. The legal age at which an individual could enter into a marriage contract may have been sixteen, eighteen, or some other age. Exceptions to these laws may have been made with the express permission of one or both of the parents of a minor. In addition, laws dictating the permissibility of marriage between couples who shared a certain consanguinity, or blood relationship, were generally closely adhered to. For example, a person might not be permitted by law to marry his or her sibling, first cousin, uncle or aunt, or another close relative.

Marriage licenses are common across the world. What differs, however, is the format and the amount of information contained on them. The typical marriage record will include the name of the groom, the name of the bride, the date and location, the name or signature of the person who officiated, and the names or signatures of at least two witnesses. Other records may include far more details such as the ages or even the dates of birth of the bride and groom, the names of their parents, the filing date and location, and the name or signature of the clerk or ordinary. I have even seen a few with addresses of the bride and groom.

The elaborate marriage certificate shown in Figure 3-18 appears to have been issued by the church rather than by a government office as there is no registration information on it. The couple's names are Germanic and the bride's name, Adolphine M. Reeb, is followed by the notation, "geb. Kleinknecht." The "geb." is an abbreviation for the German word *geborene,* which is the feminine of the German word for *born* or, in this context, *nee*. This notation indicates that Kleinknecht was the bride's maiden name, and that she has been married before. Also note that another member of her family, Theodor (or Theador), signed the document as one of the witnesses.

FIGURE 3-18   This elaborate marriage certificate dated 20 April 1881 was probably issued by the church.

The earliest marriage documents are all handwritten and later ones used standardized forms. Still others can be found that are extremely ornate, with elaborate artwork, gold or silver leaf, wax or metallic seals, and affixed with ribbons.

There are other records that can be used to help prove a marriage or the intent to marry. The following list includes a number, but certainly not all, of the kinds of alternative record types you might use to help document a marriage.

- Marriage banns are a public announcement, read out on at least three successive occasions in a parish church, of a declaration of intent to marry. These may be documented in church minutes, bulletins, and other publications. Figure 3-19 shows a page from an English parish church's marriage banns in 1796.

- Newspaper announcements of engagements and marriages can provide clues to the date and place of a wedding that you can then follow up to locate primary documents.

- A wedding invitation is an excellent indicator of intent that you may use to help locate a primary marriage record.

- Marriage ceremonies performed in a religious institution are typically recorded in their records.
- Civil marriages performed in a city hall or other government office will be found recorded in their files.
- Bible entries may contain marriage information.
- Letters, journals, and diaries may discuss details of a wedding, the persons who attended, and other details of the occasion.
- Printed announcements, notices in church publications, or newspaper accounts of milestone anniversary celebrations, such as a 25th, 50th, or 75th wedding anniversary, are pointers back to the date and location of documentation of the original event.

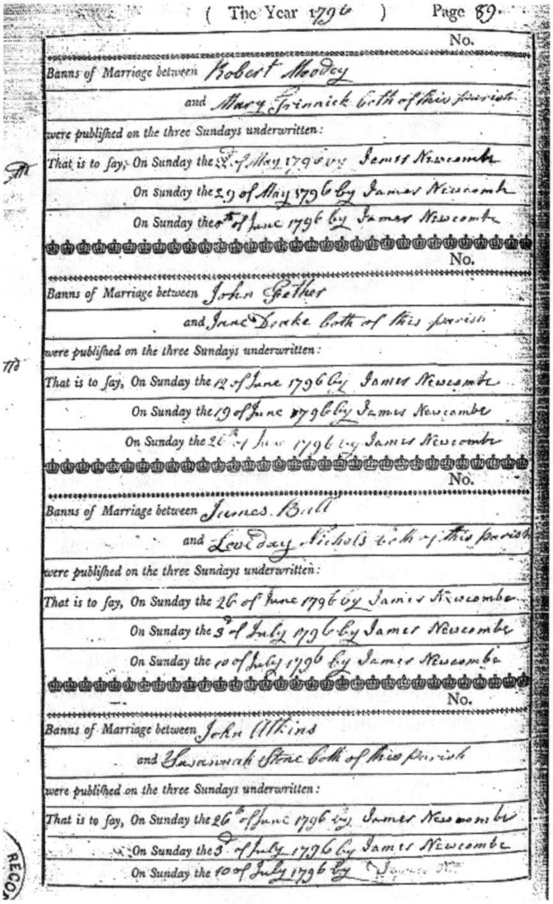

(The Year 1796) Page 89.

No.

Banns of Marriage between Robert Moodey
and Mary Grinnick both of this parish
were publiſhed on the three Sundays underwritten:
That is to ſay, On Sunday the 22 of May 1796 by James Newcombe
On Sunday the 29 of May 1796 by James Newcombe
On Sunday the 5th of June 1796 by James Newcombe

No.

Banns of Marriage between John Gether
and Jane Drake both of this parish
were publiſhed on the three Sundays underwritten:
That is to ſay, On Sunday the 12 of June 1796 by James Newcombe
On Sunday the 19 of June 1796 by James Newcombe
On Sunday the 26 of June 1796 by James Newcombe

No.

Banns of Marriage between James Bull
and Loveday Nichols both of this parish
were publiſhed on the three Sundays underwritten:
That is to ſay, On Sunday the 26 of June 1796 by James Newcombe
On Sunday the 3 of July 1796 by James Newcombe
On Sunday the 10 of July 1796 by James Newcombe

No.

Banns of Marriage between John Wilkins
and Susannah Stone both of this parish
were publiſhed on the three Sundays underwritten:
That is to ſay, On Sunday the 26th of June 1796 by James Newcombe
On Sunday the 3 of July 1796 by James Newcombe
On Sunday the 10 of July 1796 by J[illegible]

FIGURE 3-19 Marriage banns were published on three successive Sundays (Used by permission of the National Archives, U.K.).

Marriage records can be helpful in a number of ways. First, they are primary sources of evidence of the marriage. They place a couple in a specific place at a particular time. Using the name of the person officiating at the ceremony, you may be able to refer to a city directory of the time and connect him with a specific religious institution. That may take you to individual and family records for the bride and perhaps even to the groom. Membership records may then point you to previous and subsequent places of residence in the form of entries in church minutes where transfers of membership were noted. Names of parents and witnesses may connect you with other family members, friends, and collateral relatives, too. These are examples of how to use your critical thinking skills and creativity to identify other potentially helpful records.

Research Divorce Records

Records of a divorce are far less numerous than marriage records, and so you would think they would be easier to locate. Unfortunately, though, that is not always true. Some courthouses and government facilities have done an excellent job indexing the divorces by the names of the husband and wife. In other places, the divorce documentation may be filed only under the name of the plaintiff—the person who sued for divorce. Others, however, may simply have filed divorce petitions and decrees in chronological sequence. This can make your job problematic and require you to spend hours paging through sheaves of papers. Even if the courthouse or clerks have not been as organized or diligent in their filing, there are other possibilities.

Make certain, before you undertake a search for divorce records, that you determine which court would have handled the process for the period in time when the divorce likely occurred. For example, in one place and time a divorce might have been handled by a civil court, while in another place the hearings may have been held and the dissolution of the marriage may have been finalized in a family court, a high court of justice in the family division, a superior court, a chancery court, or other division. Figure 3-20 shows an example of a bill of divorce handed down by a chancery court in 1846. Knowing in advance what the laws were at the time *and* the court of law that handled marriage dissolutions at the time can be crucial to your success.

Contact the court that would have handled the divorce petition or suit before you make a trip there. If an index of documents does not exist, request a search of the minutes of the appropriate court. The minute books are well-indexed to facilitate location of pertinent documentation, reference to previous court hearings and actions, and to the expeditious handling of cases by the magistrate. You may have greater success by obtaining the dates of the filing and hearing in the court minutes, and then going directly to the records filed in chronological sequence.

Early records were handwritten and reading the clerk's penmanship may be a challenge. Later records, such as the Final Judgment of Divorce shown in Figure 3-21, are typewritten and easier to read.

Locate Death Certificates

The sheer volume of records created as a result of a contemporary individual's death can be enormous. However, you may find that records from earlier times may be nonexistent. The creation and existence of these records will depend on a number of factors. Did the government require them to be kept? Who was responsible for creating them: the government or the church? What information

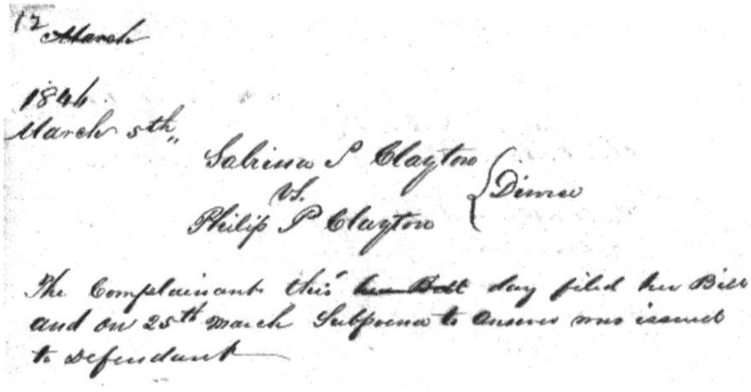

12 March

1846.
March 5th,

Sabina S Clayton
vs.
Philip P Clayton } Divorce

The Complainant this day filed her Bill and on 25th March Subpoena to Answer was issued to defendant

FIGURE 3-20 Simple bill of divorce dated 5 March 1846 found in chancery court records

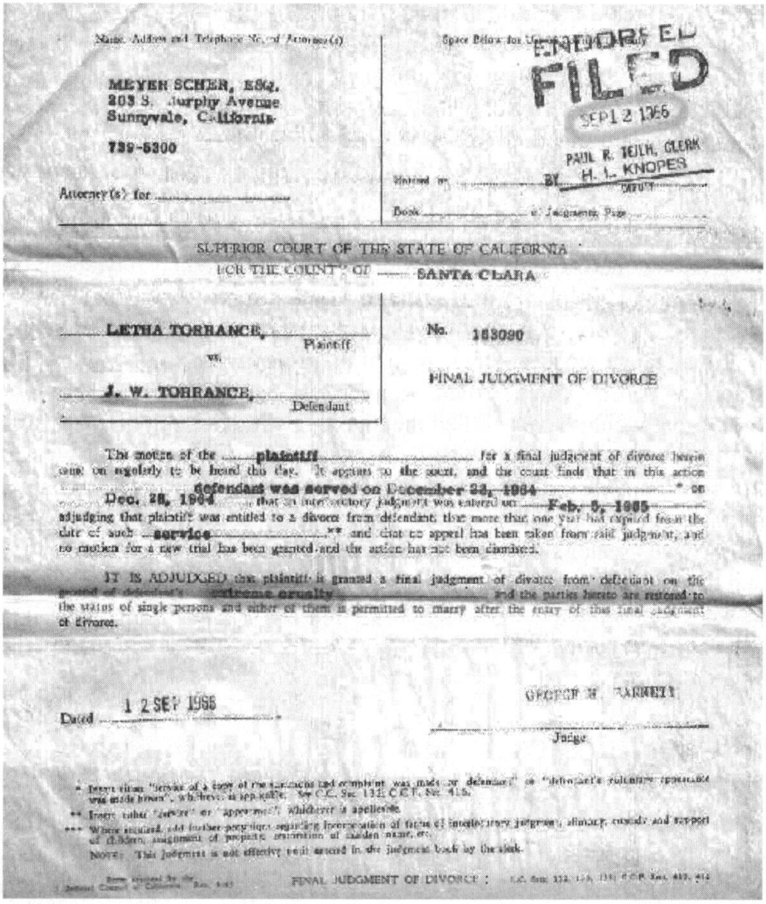

Name, Address and Telephone No. of Attorney(s)

MEYER SCHER, ESQ.
203 S. Murphy Avenue
Sunnyvale, California
739-5300

Attorney(s) for

ENDORSED FILED
SEP 12 1966
PAUL R. TEILH, CLERK
BY H. L. KNOPES
DEPUTY

Entered on ... Book ... of Judgments, Page ...

SUPERIOR COURT OF THE STATE OF CALIFORNIA
FOR THE COUNTY OF SANTA CLARA

LETHA TORRANCE, Plaintiff
vs.
J. W. TORRANCE, Defendant

No. 163090

FINAL JUDGMENT OF DIVORCE

The motion of the plaintiff for a final judgment of divorce herein came on regularly to be heard this day. It appears to the court, and the court finds that in this action defendant was served on December 23, 1964 * on Dec. 28, 1964, that an interlocutory judgment was entered on Feb. 5, 1965 adjudging that plaintiff was entitled to a divorce from defendant; that more than one year has expired from the date of such service ** and that no appeal has been taken from said judgment, and no motion for a new trial has been granted and the action has not been dismissed.

IT IS ADJUDGED that plaintiff is granted a final judgment of divorce from defendant on the ground of defendant's extreme cruelty and the parties hereto are restored to the status of single persons and either of them is permitted to marry after the entry of this final judgment of divorce.

Dated 12 SEP 1966

GEORGE H. BARNETT
Judge

FINAL JUDGMENT OF DIVORCE

FIGURE 3-21 Final Judgment of Divorce—Santa Clara County, California—1955 was to be included? Where were these records stored and for what duration? Were there natural or manmade catastrophes that caused records to be lost or destroyed? How will you find out what is and is not available?

The most common vital record is the death certificate. It, too, was not required to be used in many states until the first two decades of the 20th century. Again, *Ancestry's Red Book* or *The Handybook for Genealogists* can help you determine when records were kept in a specific state and where they may be found. Please remember that a death certificate is a *primary source* for death information but is merely a *secondary source* for birth information and other data. This other information should be corroborated with other primary evidence.

Death records come in many forms. The form familiar to most people will be the death certificate. Other documents, however, serve a similar or identical purpose for genealogists because they are, after all, official documentation of a death. These might include a coroner's report, an autopsy, the final report of an inquest into the cause of death, or a ruling on evidence of an actual or assumed death presented to a judge or jury. This latter situation would include, among others, a case in which a person has disappeared and, after some period of time, is declared dead by a court of law. You also may encounter or obtain a document that acts as a certified copy of an original death certificate or that certifies the official death entry in the government's records. Figure 3-22 shows an example of a certified copy of a death entry document.

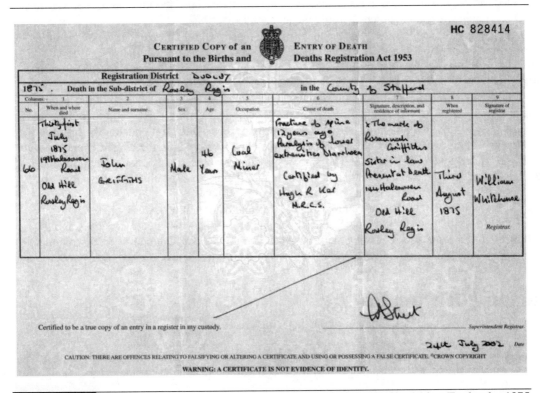

FIGURE 3-22   Certified Copy of an Entry of Death document—Staffordshire, England—1875 (Used by permission of the National Archives, U.K.)

You will remember from our discussion of sources that a death certificate can be both a primary *and* a secondary source of information. Since a death certificate is an official record of a person's death, it is usually created at or near the time of death in order to record the event. There are exceptions, of course, such as the case noted above of a disappeared person being declared dead. There also are instances of amended death certificates being issued in order to correct or add to information entered on the original document.

The veracity of the information on a death certificate will depend on where the information originated. Information about the identity of the decedent and the death itself are usually obtained from medical, law enforcement, forensic, and other professional persons. It is their job to gather and report the correct information. You would therefore place a great deal of credence in their data and, if placed on a certificate created at or very near the time of death, consider it to be good primary source information.

Other information found on a death certificate may not be as reliable as that gathered by the professionals. The other details included on a death certificate are provided by someone who supposedly knows something about the deceased. Another family member or friend is usually solicited to provide the information, and he or she is referred to as the informant. The informant may or may not know the answers to the questions that are asked and, on the spur of the moment, may provide what he or she "thinks" is correct. As a result, there are many errors entered on death certificates. Unless the informant has direct, first-hand, accurate knowledge of facts, the data provided can only be assumed to be secondary in nature. Everything should therefore be verified or corroborated with other sources before you accept it as fact.

As an example, let's examine the death certificate presented in Figure 3-23. The name of the person may or may not be correct, depending on the source of the information. The informant provided information concerning the decedent's date and place of birth, the parents' names, marital status, name of spouse, occupation, place of residence, and any other data.

When you request a copy of a death certificate, you may receive an actual copy of the original document. However, it is altogether likely that the official office from which you ordered a copy will issue a certified document attesting to be information correctly copied from the original death registration document. Figures 3-22 and 3-24 show this from both the United Kingdom and from the United States, respectively. These copies commonly contain far less information than the original document. Remember that an exact copy of the original is your better resource, and that transcription errors can be made despite all caution.

Other source materials for determining date of death and other family details include newspaper obituaries (a veritable wealth of clues!), burial permits, transit permits, medical records, family Bibles, tombstones and other cemetery markers, cemetery/sexton records, religious records, mortuary and funeral home records, and wills and probate records, just to name a few.

Create an Ancestor Profile

Now that you have a solid foundation of the genealogy research basics and some methodologies to help you, you should begin to obtain copies of the vital records documents we have discussed. Recognize that evidence comes to us out of chronological sequence and in bits and pieces. One scrap of information may be meaningless until it is connected with another. Sometimes seemingly

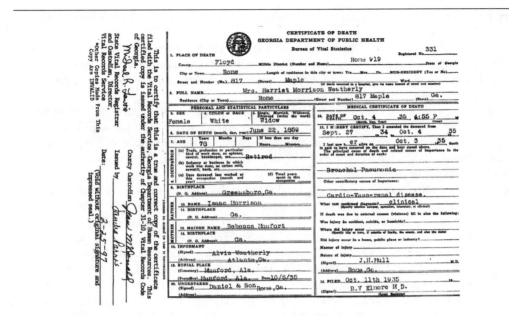

FIGURE 3-23 Death certificate from Floyd County, Georgia—1935 (From the author's collection)

FIGURE 3-24 Certified copy of a death record from New Jersey—1961 (Courtesy of Drew Smith)

unrelated pieces of evidence, when placed or considered together, can form an interlinking pattern or provide a larger story.

You will soon find that you are gathering genealogical evidence from any number of sources, such as books, magazines, periodicals, maps, letters, wills, deeds, church records, courthouses, libraries and archives, other family members, and people around the world with whom you connect via the Internet.

One means of getting to know and understand an ancestor or other family member's life is the creation of an ancestor profile. The process will clarify for you what you know and what you *don't* know, while helping you to identify gaps in your research and analyze the quality of the sources for the information that you have obtained. More important, though, is that it causes you to think chronologically about the person's life—just as they lived it.

The ancestor profile is, in effect, a biographical timeline that builds a life story. However, rather than simply compiling a list of dates, places, and factoids, the creation of an ancestor profile forces you to add information about places, historical events, social influences, and other people in the person's life that may have influenced his or her life. It is a meaningful exercise that I use on a regular basis that helps place *everything* I know about a particular person into context and perspective. By doing so, you will get to really know the person as more than just a name in a place with associated dates. The character of the person will, in effect, come to life. You will really come to know the person and his or her circumstances, and by doing so you may gain important insights that may help you anticipate decisions or actions that the person took in their life. This can lead you to develop educated hypotheses about additional records to seek and the places to look for them.

The ancestor profile is simple to create, but it requires you to examine everything you know about the person. And that means reading everything you have collected. No, that doesn't mean merely scanning a document, such as a death certificate; it means *really rereading* it as if you've never seen it before. Remember that your information comes to you in bits and pieces from a variety of sources over a long period of time. While you will have analyzed each piece at or near the time you encountered or acquired it, you probably will not have thoroughly considered it in the totality of the person's life. By rereading everything as if it were new to you, the information will take on freshness and add a new perspective for you. And by incorporating the historical events and other people's information into your ancestor profile, you will be compelled to consider these influences as well.

There are six steps to preparing an ancestor profile. Let's examine each of them.

Start with What You Know

Gather together all the documentation and evidence you have acquired on the individual and organize it in chronological sequence. In other words, place birth information first, childhood information next, marriage information, any documentation of life events, and then the death information, such as a death certificate, obituary, or tombstone inscription.

Once everything is in chronological sequence, prepare a typed listing. You can do this in a word processor or in a spreadsheet. It also may be entered into the notes of your genealogy software database program. The key is to place it into some sort of document format into which you can insert additional information and reprint from time to time. Leave a blank line or two for handwritten notes later on. Your document should include the following information for each event:

- ■ **Date**   Choose the format that makes the most sense to you. You may choose to use only the year. However, if you are using a spreadsheet and plan to sort the data in other ways, you may also want to include the month and day.

- ■ **Fact**   Enter a description of the event or information that you are recording. Provide enough useful detail so that, if you take the document with you on a research trip, it will allow you to recognize what you do and do not know about the person.

- ■ **Source**   Enter information about your source(s) of the information. If you have multiple sources for a fact, record both of those. You then will know if one is better than another, if they corroborate or contradict one another, and the quality of your citation.

That sounds pretty simple, doesn't it? It really is easy. Take a look at Figure 3-25, which shows a portion of an ancestor profile for my great-grandmother, Lydia Lenora Patterson (1833–1914). The fun part is rereading the evidence you have, analyzing it, and forming descriptions while creating the profile. You often will discover that one piece of what seemed to be inconsequential information suddenly becomes a very important key to understanding something else. Sometimes that small fact will provide a pointer to some other research opportunity for this person or for another

---

<u>Lydia Lenora PATTERSON (1833 - 1914)</u>

1833 -   Born 13 November 1833 in NC.
Source: Obituary, *Charlotte* [NC] *Observer*, 29 August 1914.
Source: Church records at the Davidson Presbyterian Church in Davidson (Mecklenburg) NC.

1835 -   Brother, John Newell Williamson Patterson, was born 5 December 1835.
Source: Tombstone, Davidson Presbyterian Church in Davidson (Mecklenburg) NC.

1840 -   Mecklenburg County, NC (Member of household of William PATTERSON and his wife, nee Elizabeth McCuen Caroline POTTS.)
Source: NARA Microfilm publication M704, Roll 365, Page 319.

1840 -   Sister, Elizabeth Patterson, was born ca. 1840.
Source: 1850 Census. Microfilm publication M432, Roll 637, Pages 33-34, Dwelling # 545, Family # 548.

1846 -   Brother, James Patterson, was born ca. 1846.
Source: 1850 Census. Microfilm publication M432, Roll 637, Pages 33-34, Dwelling # 545, Family # 548.

1849 -   Snow on 15 April 1849 killed wheat, corn and cotton crops and badly damaged fruit crops. Harvest that year was miniscule. Patterson family donated money for relief of the poor in the area.
Source: Alexander, J.B. *History of Mecklenburg County from 1740 to 1900.* Charlotte: Observer Printing House, 1902.
Source: Letter from Lydia Lenora Patterson to Joseph McKnitt Wilson dated 27 December 1855.

FIGURE 3-25   Sample segment of an ancestor profile

family member. During the preparation of the profile for my great-grandmother, the fact leapt out at me that one of her granddaughters had been born less than eight months after her parents' wedding. While that might not be considered particularly scandalous in the 21st century, it certainly was shocking among so-called good families at the time that it occurred in July 1888.

Establish the Person's Location Throughout Their Life

The vital records for birth, marriage, and death establish the ancestor or family member's location at specific times. In other chapters in this book, you will learn about many other types of records and each one of these also verify a person's whereabouts. Your ancestor profile will reflect this and therefore will present you with a roadmap, as it were, for your family member's travels.

Using other records you have located, as well as additional ones you discover over time, add this information into the profile. If there are places and events that you think you know about but that you have not confirmed with documentation, you certainly can enter them. However, be sure to add a notation indicating that verification needs to be made. The absence of a source citation for that entry in the profile should be a tip-off that you need something more, but adding a notation of what type of record or source you want to locate will visually help prompt you.

Some of the best documents for establishing a person's location are census records, letters, church and parish records, deeds, tax lists, voter registrations, licenses, and wills and probate records. These are just a few of the countless possible resources that can help substantiate geographic location of a person.

Add Other People to the Profile

Your person certainly interacted with other people throughout his or her life, and they may have influenced your ancestor or family member. It is important, therefore, to add information about those people to the profile you are creating. These would include parents, siblings, aunts and uncles, spouse(s), children and grandchildren, friends, neighbors, clergy and fellow church members, medical personnel, teachers, military personnel with whom your ancestor served, political figures, and others. As you conduct your research, you will encounter many such people in your ancestor's life. Some of these may have had enormous influence in his or her life, while others may have had little impact.

It is particularly important to understand the person's family unit. A family group sheet provides an excellent visual record of parents and their children, as you already know. Placing your person in chronological birth order helps understand group dynamics. Naming patterns, sibling interaction, and other relationships may emerge.

You don't necessarily have to insert every fact about other people's lives into your ancestor profile, simply the more important ones that probably would have been noteworthy. Figure 3-26 shows a section of my profile for Lydia into which I have inserted other's people's information. When you are considering what information to insert, it really is your judgment call. You will determine what is and is not going to be of importance when you review your ancestor's entire life's profile. However, the birth, marriage, or death of a sibling, the death of a parent, or some other event would certainly be important. Adding the destination of the honeymoon trip taken by a sibling and his or her spouse would probably not be particularly noteworthy unless it had some impact on your person. If is often better to include more information than less, but that must be your decision.

1902 – Joseph McKnitt WILSON and Lydia Lenora PATTERSON moved into their rebuilt home in Davidson (Mecklenburg) NC.

1902 – Laura Augusta (Minnie) WILSON married Samuel Goodloe MORGAN on 24 December 1902 in Davidson (Davidson) NC.
Source: Marriage license on file in North Carolina State Archives.

1905 – Grand-daughter, Mary Allen MORGAN, daughter of Samuel Goodloe MORGAN and Laura Augusta (Minnie) Wilson, was born on 14 June 1905 in Mebane (Alamance) NC.
Source: Family Bible of Laura Augusta (Minnie) WILSON. In possession of George G. Morgan on 1 January 2004.
Source: Tombstone, Woodland Cemetery, Madison (Rockingham) NC.

1909 – Joseph Patterson WILSON and Frances Lamb MIMMS were married on 5 January 1909.
Need marriage certificate to verify date and location.

FIGURE 3-26   Section of an ancestor profile showing other people's data and a note prompting for additional documentation

Update your ancestor profile by adding date, description, source(s), and notes for these other people's information. Insert them in chronological sequence, interspersing them into your own ancestor's information. What you are doing is connecting these people and their lives with one another, interweaving more of the family tapestry I mentioned in Chapter 1.

Add Historical and Social Events

My Grandmother Morgan was a prolific letter-writer and a number of her letters have survived. Before she married my grandfather in 1902, they exchanged letters on almost a daily basis. In September of 1901, United States President William McKinley was assassinated while attending the Pan-American Exposition in Buffalo, New York. One of my grandmother's letters dwells on the tragedy and discusses her emotions on hearing the news and the reactions of other family members. She described in a later letter that month the swearing-in of the new president, Theodore "Teddy" Roosevelt.

When constructing your ancestor profile, consider the historical and social events that might have influenced our ancestors. Never underestimate the power of other events, happening locally or on the other side of the globe, on our forebears. Some of the more influential ones would include war, political oppression, religious persecution, economic depression, crop failure, drought, and famine. Insert these events into your ancestor profile, again placing them in chronological sequence.

Add Personal Events

Personal experiences may have exerted some effect on your family that would cause changes. These need to be considered and inserted into the profile as well. These might include the birth of a sibling or the person's own child, a marriage, a death in the family, an accident, a fire or flood, a hurricane or tornado, a personal physical or emotional disability or one in the family, or financial problems.

Read, Review, and Revise the Profile

The final step in the process is perhaps the most enlightening one. Once you have finished entering the data you have into the profile, print a copy of the profile. Settle down in a quiet place and simply read it. Read it as if you have never seen it before, and edit it for spelling, punctuation, and transposition errors you may have made. Once you have read it through once, *reread* the profile. This time, critically read it and make notes for yourself. There are three things you are evaluating:

- *Where are the gaps in this person's life?*   You want to identify those areas that are still a void, and perhaps these are the mysterious keys to solving other problems.

- *What are my sources of information and how good are they?*   Evaluate the source citations for the information you have. Perhaps the first question will be, "Why am I missing so many sources?" That tells you that you need to either enter the source citations for the information you have or that you need to locate good primary source materials to verify (or contradict) what you think you know.

- *What else do I need to find?*   Ask yourself, for every entry, what additional material do you need or want to locate. Make notations on the profile of what it is you want to know, what type of document or other evidence you think might provide the answer, and where you would try to locate that material.

When you finish this review, go back to your document and enter the corrections and additional notations you have made. Print the document again and edit it for accuracy one more time. Make any more revisions you think are necessary and print this version of the document.

What you have now is a detailed outline of your research of this individual. It is a chronological outline of a life that establishes the person at every point in life, documents their life events, and places them in family, social, and historical perspective. In other words, you have created a biographical outline. You can use this profile as a take-along tool for research trips. However, you also have the beginning of a well-structured biographical sketch or for a full-scale biography.

The point of the exercise is to cause you to "think chronologically" about your ancestor or family member and to provide some organization to the materials you have collected. It provides a structured approach to your research that should lead you to fill in the gaps and perform a more detailed evaluation of evidence. The review process forces you to review the sources of your information and evaluate the quality of your citations. However, the ancestor profile is an excellent tool to encourage you to develop a better understanding of your ancestor's circumstances and to develop more knowledgeable hypotheses about their decisions and actions.

And, of course, if you are planning on producing a written family history, developing one or more ancestor profiles will assist you in preparing a well-researched, well-organized biographical outline.

We've covered a great deal of territory in this chapter. By now, you have a well-grounded feel for how to conduct scholarly research and some excellent methodologies to help ensure your success. Chapter 4 will take you into a thorough examination of census records and they, in turn, can lead you to a wealth of other records.

Chapter 4

Use Census Schedules and Records to Locate Your Ancestors

How to...

■ Use census schedules and related documents

■ Understand and work effectively with United States census materials

■ Understand and use the Soundex indexing system to locate family members in the census

■ Discover the history of the census in the British Isles

■ Learn more about the census in Canada

■ Locate information about censuses in other places

■ Gain access to census records

Learn About Population Census Records

Among the most important records that exist for confirming the presence of an ancestor at a particular place at a specific point in time are census records. A *census* is defined as an official count of a population carried out at regular intervals. Censuses have been taken for many centuries. The Babylonians and Chinese enumerated their populations in ancient times for purposes of taxation and military service. You also will recall that the Bible recounts that censuses were taken by Rome. Over the centuries, censuses were taken for purposes of taxation, to determine legislation representation, to analyze trends in population growth and movement, and for planning purposes.

Census records are the most-used records by genealogists in the United States and their use here and in other countries continues to accelerate and grow. This is especially true with the availability and expansion of Internet-based databases containing scanned census document images and searchable indices.

We are going to focus on the available census records in the United States, the British Isles, and Canada in this chapter. Unfortunately, early Australian census records have been destroyed by the government and no known copies exist.

Certainly other countries have taken censuses at various times and, if you are interested in learning more about them and accessing extant records, you can use your Web browser to search for the word "census" and the name of the place. If you were looking for information about a census in Russia, for example, you could enter one of the following searches:

census russia
census russian

In addition, you might use your favorite Internet search engine that supports image searches, such as Google, AltaVista, AlltheWeb, or others, to look for specific images. For example, the image of the 1867 Russian census for Mednyi Island shown in Figure 4-1 was located at the Web site for the Library of Congress in Washington, D.C., using a Google image search and *census Russian*.

You will not find entire countries' historical census record images on the Internet. You will need to search Web sites, particularly those of national archives and libraries, to locate what holdings they may have and learn how and where to access them.

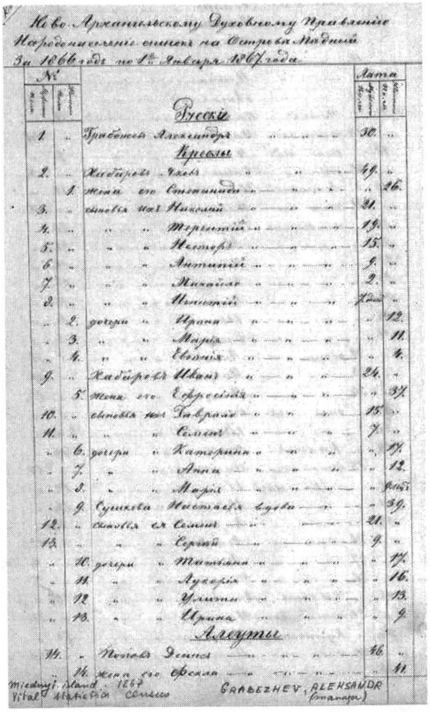

4

FIGURE 4-1 Russian census document from 1867 located through a Web search (From the National Archives and Records Administration collection)

As we discuss census records, be aware that they are a primary source of information to help establish a person's location in a specific place at a certain point in time. Even that is suspect at times, as you will see. All other information on a census document should definitely be considered secondary source material, and should be verified and corroborated with other sources whenever possible.

Understand and Work with United States Census Records

In the United States, there have been censuses taken by the federal government every ten years, beginning in 1790 and continuing to the present. A number of state censuses also have been taken periodically and these can supplement your use of federal census records in American research. Prior to 1790, a few of the original 13 colonies performed partial or complete enumerations of citizens for their own purposes. Some of these records still exist and, in order to locate them, it is a good idea to contact the respective state archive or state library to determine what might have been created, might still survive, and where to locate the materials.

The United States Constitution, which took effect on 4 March 1789, established the taking of a national census on a regular basis. Article I, Section 2 specifically called for a census to be taken every ten years. Direct taxation of the population to support the federal government's operation was to be based on census information. The Constitution stated that each free person counted as a whole number, including those bound for service for a term of years, and that free males would be taxed and could vote. Indians living on treaty land were excluded from direct taxation and voting. Other, non-free persons were to be counted as three-fifths of a free person for legislative representation. An Indian who joined the white population was to be considered a "free person" and could vote. The entire text of the Constitution is available at the Library of Congress Web site at **http://memory.loc.gov/const/const.html.**

Federal decennial censuses have been taken every decade from 1790 through 2000. An official Census Day was established for enumerators to ask questions "as of" that date. The official United States Census Day for each decade is shown here:

1790	2 August
1800	4 August
1810	6 August
1820	7 August
1830 through 1900	1 June
1910	15 April
1920	1 January
1930	1 April

The enumerators were given a deadline by which time they were to accomplish their work, instructions to follow, and a set of questions to be used. Census forms for the 1850 to 2000 censuses are available at **http://www.ipums.org/usa/voliii/tEnumForm.html.** The enumerators' instructions for those years can be found at **http://www.ipums.org/usa/voliii/tEnumInstr.html.** Refer also to the Web site at **http://www.ipums.org/usa/voliii/tQuestions.html** for only the questions.

The earliest census enumerations, 1790 through 1870 (see Figure 4-2), were performed by assistant marshals of the U.S. judicial districts. At the time of the 1790 census, there were 16 federal court districts. These represented each of the original 13 states and Vermont, which was included in the first census even though it didn't become a state until 1791. The 2 additional districts comprising the 16 were due to the area of Virginia that became Kentucky and the area of Massachusetts that became Maine. These marshals performed the census enumerations in addition to their ordinary duties. They were poorly paid for their work and often bought their own paper, pens, ink, horse feed, and other supplies with their own funds. They had little incentive to do a good job. They sometimes erred in the areas in which they were assigned. When they failed to reach the state and county boundaries they were assigned to enumerate, or when they enumerated past these boundaries, the result was either omitted residents or duplication of other marshals' enumerations. During these decades, Congress provided funding for the enumeration period and a subsequent tabulation only. This funding was usually appropriated in the Congressional session prior to the enumeration year.

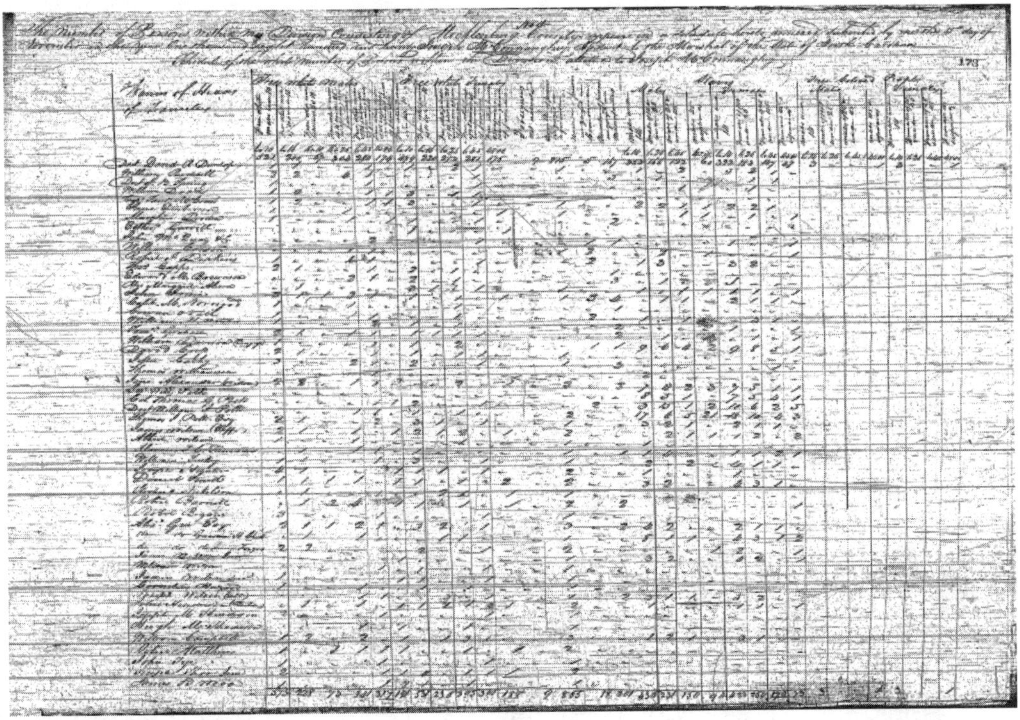

4

FIGURE 4-2 1820 U.S. federal census showing names of only heads of household (Used by permission of MyFamily.com, Inc.)

The first central Census Office established in Washington, D.C., to coordinate the taking of a decennial enumeration was opened in 1850. When the tabulation was complete, however, the office was disbanded and all census activity was discontinued until the next census. The same process was used in both 1860 and 1870.

A Congressional act established and provided funding for a permanent Census Office beginning in 1880. This year was a benchmark in the United States federal census in that, for the first time, the assistant federal marshals were removed from the process. The Census Office hired employees to conduct the actual enumerations, devised formal Enumeration District maps and descriptions, revised the enumeration instructions, and revised the census forms (or census schedules as they are called). The most common of the federal census documents is the Population Schedule, a sample of which from 1900 is shown in Figure 4-3. These and other schedule documents are discussed next.

It is important to note that the early federal census forms only contained the names of the heads of household, with the other members of the household represented numerically in categories organized by sex, age, and race. It was not until the 1850 census that the names of all persons within a household were listed. In the 1880 census, the revision of the Population Schedule format called

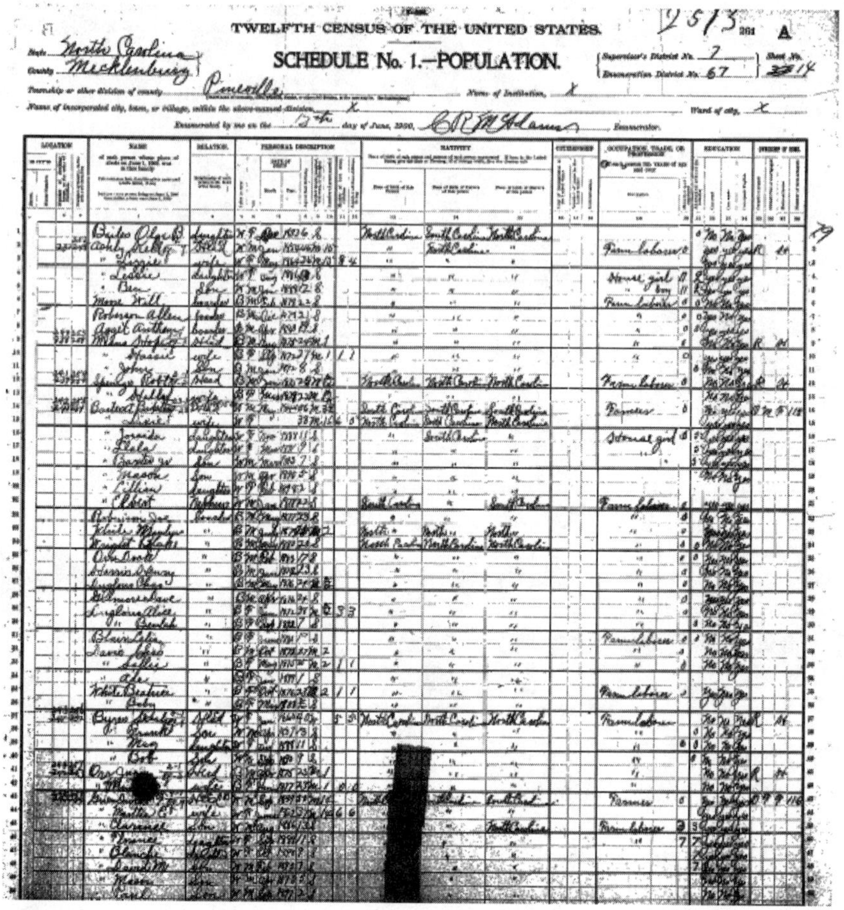

FIGURE 4-3 1900 U.S. federal census Population Schedule—Mecklenburg County, NC (Used by permission of MyFamily.com, Inc.)

for the names of all inhabitants and their relationship to the head of household to be included, and this is an important addition for genealogists. Table 4-4 at the end of this chapter defines for each federal census each of the census forms, or schedules, used for each enumeration year, and what information can be found on each schedule.

Original vs. Copies of Census Documents

There have been various numbers of copies of the original documents created as part of the census enumeration process. From 1790 through 1820, the states sent only summary data to Washington, D.C., and kept their original census documents. The summaries for 1790 through 1810 were destroyed during the War of 1812.

In 1830, Congress required the states to send all pre-1830 original documents to Washington. Some states complied while others, unfortunately, sent nothing or only partial documentation. As a result, you may find that no census materials exist for certain states for certain years, or that only partial records exist.

If you examine Table 4-1, you will notice that for census years 1830 through 1885, copies of the original census schedules for each state (not summaries) were sent to Washington, D.C., and not the original documents, which were kept by the states.

It is important to note that the census schedules that ultimately ended up in the possession of the National Archives and Records Administration (NARA) are the originals returned by the states for 1790–1820, the copies submitted between 1830 and 1885, and the originals for all subsequent enumerations. The copies are transcriptions and, by their very nature, are prone to transcription errors. In the case of the 1870 census schedules, a transcription of a transcription was actually sent. Therefore, when you work with census images on microfilm and in online databases, remember that the "copy censuses" are prone to a higher error rate than the originals.

Use Strategies to Work with Population Schedules

The census Population Schedule is the most comprehensive of the federal census documents, containing the entries for each household. The completeness and accuracy of the enumeration was, of course, dependent on the quality of the work performed by the enumerator, as well as any transcription work done to generate a copy or copies.

Certainly there are omissions in any census. This can be the result of an enumerator missing a residence for whatever reason. Perhaps the enumerator didn't exert the effort to walk all the way up the stairs to the fifth floor of a Chicago apartment building or ride to the end of a long, muddy country road through a heavy rain. Perhaps there was no one at home when the enumerator arrived to provide the information. For example, I know that my maternal grandparents lived in a particular town in 1920 and 1930 and I even know their street address. Yet, in both censuses, the houses on either side were enumerated but theirs was not. It is possible that your ancestor or a family member refused to respond to the census taker at all. There's really no way to know, but it is worth your effort to check every resource you can access.

An important strategy for every genealogist when working with census records is to locate the family you are researching in one census, and to make note of three to six other families on either side of your family. The reason you will do so is to create a reference group for researching other census years. If you find your family in one census and cannot locate them in the next, check any indexes for that census and look for the neighbors next to them in the previous census. If you can find the neighbors but your family is not there, there are four possibilities:

- The enumerator omitted or skipped your family's residence.

- Your family was not home when the enumerator called, or refused to participate.

- Your family moved.

- Your family is deceased, which is more probable when there was only one family member at that location or if the family members were up in age at the time of the previous census.

Year	Enumerator	# Copies Prepared	Sent To Washington
1790	Assistant Marshal	■ 1 original	Summary sent
1800	Assistant Marshal	■ 1 original	Summary sent
1810	Assistant Marshal	■ 1 original	Summary sent
1820	Assistant Marshal	■ 1 original	Summary sent
1830	Assistant Marshal	■ 1 original ■ 1 copy prepared by clerk	Copy sent
1840	Assistant Marshal	■ 1 original ■ 1 copy prepared by clerk	Copy sent
1850	Assistant Marshal	■ 1 original ■ "Clean copy" prepared by Assistant Marshals and sent to state secretary of state ("state copy") ■ Secretary of state prepared complete copy for federal government ("federal copy")	"Federal copy" sent
1860	Assistant Marshal	■ 1 original ■ "Clean copy" prepared by Assistant Marshals and sent to state secretary of state ("state copy") ■ Secretary of state prepared complete copy for federal government ("federal copy")	"Federal copy" sent
1870	Assistant Marshal	■ 1 original ■ "Clean copy" prepared by Assistant Marshals and sent to state secretary of state ("state copy") ■ Secretary of state prepared complete copy for federal government ("federal copy")	"Federal copy" sent
1880	Census Office	■ 1 original ■ 1 copy prepared by district supervisor	Copy sent
1885	Census Office and State Enumerators	■ 1 original for CO, FL, NE, and Dakota and New Mexico Territories ■ 1 copy	Copy sent
1890	Census Office	■ 1 original ■ No copy	Original sent (most was destroyed by fire and water)
1900	Census Office	■ 1 original ■ No copy	Original sent
1910	Census Bureau	■ 1 original ■ No copy	Original sent
1920	Census Bureau	■ 1 original ■ No copy	Original sent
1930	Census Bureau	■ 1 original ■ No copy	Original sent

TABLE 4-1   U.S. Federal Censuses, Number of Copies, and Disposition (Used by permission of Aha! Seminars, Inc.)

Another important strategic consideration is that families that lived next door or close to one another, especially in the earlier times, may have intermarried. A check of marriage records in the area may reveal a marriage between families, in which case your "missing" family member may have relocated to live with the newly married couple. I have numerous examples in my own family ancestry in which a husband died and the wife relocated to live with a son or daughter and their family. Don't be surprised to find a mother-in-law living with her daughter and son-in-law, and even buried in their cemetery plot.

Perhaps the best advice I can give you when doing your genealogical research is to learn how to *misspell* your family members' names. Heaven knows, they misspelled them and so did the other people who created records about them. Consider the many spellings of the surname of SMITH. There are SMITH, SMYTH, SMYTHE, SMIT, SCHMIT, SCHMIDT, and even extended spelling versions of the names such as SMITT, SMITTY, SMITHERS, and many more. One of my ancestors, John Swords, has military service and pension records from the Revolutionary War filed under the spellings of SWORDS, SOARDS, and SORDS, and that doesn't include several other errors in indexes other people have prepared. You can prepare yourself for your research in any type of records by considering the spelling of the surnames, and even the given names, and by preparing a list of alternate spellings and possible misspellings. Using the list, make sure you look for these spellings in census indexes and schedules, or any other records of genealogical importance. By doing so, you can avoid missing records for your own family.

Use Substitutes for the 1890 Census

The eleventh census of the United States, taken in 1890, was different from all others before or since. The Population Schedule included information on only one household per form, rather than listing multiple households and visitations on the same document. It also included a special Veterans and Widows schedule on which Union soldiers, sailors, and marines, or their surviving widows, were to be enumerated. Again, Congress only financed one copy of the census documents, as it did for all later censuses. States or counties wishing to obtain a copy for their own records would have had to pay for a transcription for their own files. There is no known request having been received for a state or county copy. All original copies of the census documents were sent to the Census Office.

The federal government, recognizing that the tabulation of the 1890 census schedules would be an enormous job, called for a competition to be held for a mechanized method of processing the data to be collected. Herman Hollerith, who had been working on such machines for a number of years, entered and won this competition. His system utilized punch cards created by use of a manual keyboard resembling a telegraph key. Clerks were able to process an average of 700 cards per day, after which tabulators tabulated an average of 2,000 to 3,000 families per day. As a result, over six million persons were counted by Hollerith's machines in a single day.

Once the census was complete, the original documents were placed in cartons and stored. In 1896 or 1897, the Census Office destroyed all but the population and Union Veterans and Widows schedules. The Population Schedules ended up in the basement of the Commerce Building in Washington, D.C., and the Veterans and Widows schedules were apparently stored on an upper floor. Around 5:00 P.M. on 10 January 1921, a fire broke out in the basement of the building. Records that had not been destroyed by flames had been inundated with water from the firefighters' efforts. The documents were relocated to another storage location but, unfortunately, no salvage was ever performed on the documents. The entire remainder of the 1890 census was destroyed in 1934 or 1935.

The 20-year gap in census records can seem, at first glance, devastating to your research. However, there are other types of records that can be used as a substitute for this lost census. You will need to use some creativity and refer to reference resources that still exist. These include:

- City directories
- Jury rolls
- Voter registration cards and lists
- Land and property records, including plat maps and tax lists
- Newspapers and journals

Ancestry.com at **http://www.ancestry.com** and other online facilities include 1890 Census Substitute materials in their subscription database collections. There also have been some printed volumes compiled by individuals and genealogical societies containing documented rosters of substitute records. While only Population Schedules for only 6,160 of 62,979,766 persons survived the 1921 fire, most of the Veterans and Widows schedules did survive and can be accessed on microfilm. Be sure that you don't make the mistake of assuming that nothing exists for the 1890 census.

Use More than Just Population Schedules

The primary type of census document used by the federal government is the Population Schedule. As we have discussed, the amount of information requested and entered on the Population Schedules varied over time. Additional schedule forms were used at various times, and these include the following types of schedules. All of these have been microfilmed and are available from NARA in Washington, D.C., and are accessible at many of their regional branches. In addition, copies of the NARA microfilm are available through the LDS Family History Library (FHL) in Salt Lake City, Utah, and the LDS Family History Centers (FHCs).

- **Slave schedules** were used in 1850 and 1860 to determine the numbers, vital statistics, and living conditions of slaves. You can cross-reference the slaveholders' names to Population Schedules on which they were listed. (See Figure 4-4.)
- **Mortality schedules** were used in the 1850 through 1885 censuses to determine how many persons died in the twelve months prior to Census Day, their vital statistics, duration of illness, and cause of death. (See Figure 4-5.)
- **Union Veterans and Widows schedule** was used in the 1890 census and was used to enumerate the Union veterans of the U.S. Civil War and widows of Union soldiers. (This is the only complete surviving fragment of the 1890 census—see Figure 4-6.)
- **Agricultural schedules** were used in the 1840 through 1910 censuses to determine what agricultural activity was being conducted (farming, ranching, forestry, mining), the value of the land and agricultural output, and production in some key products. These can be used to determine the location and size of an ancestor's land holdings, the commodities in which he was engaged in producing, and the livestock owned.

- **Industry and/or Manufacturing schedules** were used in the 1810 through 1910 censuses to determine the industrial and manufacturing activity and output, value of products, and other data. Many of these schedules have been lost or were intentionally destroyed by the federal government. Images of the surviving schedules are mostly poor quality.

- **Defective, Dependent, and Delinquent Classes schedules** were used only in the 1880 census. This was a seven-page document that was completed when the enumerator received a response about one of these types of persons on the Population Schedule. The enumerator could also, through personal observation, make an entry in one of the seven categories as defined as follows:

  - **Schedule 1**—Insane inhabitants

  - **Schedule 2**—Idiots

  - **Schedule 3**—Deaf-mutes

  - **Schedule 4**—Blind inhabitants

  - **Schedule 5**—Homeless children (in institutions)

  - **Schedule 6**—Inhabitants in prison

  - **Schedule 7**—Pauper and indigent inhabitants

- **Social Statistics schedules** were used in the 1850 through 1880 censuses. Important genealogical information can be gleaned from these schedules. They include information that can be used as a resource to locate specific types of institutions in these years, and trace any surviving records. They include

  - Cemeteries within town borders (names, addresses, descriptions, maps, and other data)

  - Churches, a brief history, affiliation, and membership statistics

  - Trade societies, clubs, lodges, and other social institutions, and statistics about their membership

- In addition to all the census schedules, beginning with the establishment of the Census Office for the 1880 census, the area to be canvassed by each enumerator was more clearly defined. The Census Office designated what were known as enumeration districts, or EDs. These were defined and represented with textual descriptions and ED maps to define the boundaries for each group of enumerators reporting to a district supervisor. Figure 4-7 shows the ED map for a portion of Detroit in the 1930 census. The enumeration districts defined on ED maps sometimes coincided with political or voting areas, but not always. These ED maps exist for federal census areas from 1880 through 1930, and are accessible on microfilm published by the National Archives and Records Administration.

In Chapter 3, I told you about the importance of maps in your research, and provided you with a strategy for using maps to find the *right* place to locate your ancestors and their records. The censuses can provide you with another opportunity to use different types of maps. An ED map is helpful if you know your ancestors' address and where in the area that address is situated. And once you know the ED in which your ancestors and family members lived, you greatly improve

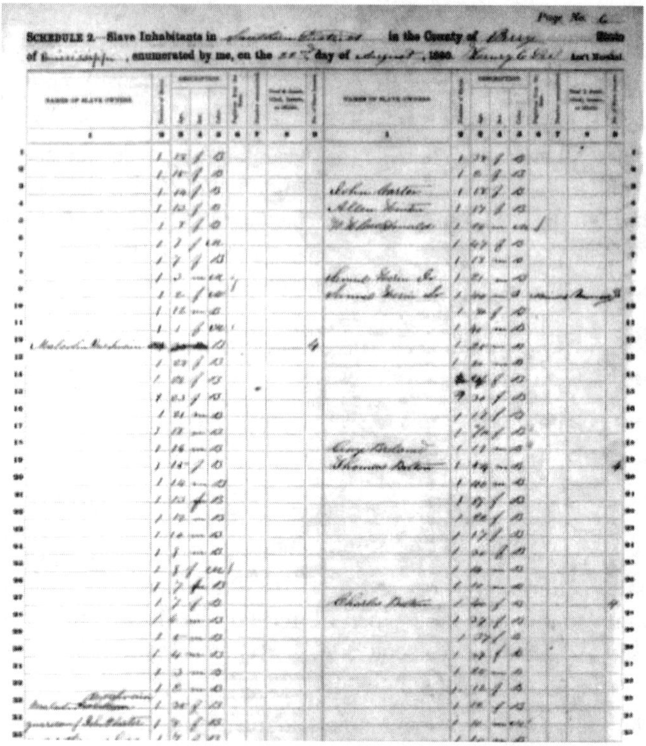

FIGURE 4-4   A Slave schedule from the 1860 federal census of North Carolina (Used by permission of MyFamily.com, Inc.)

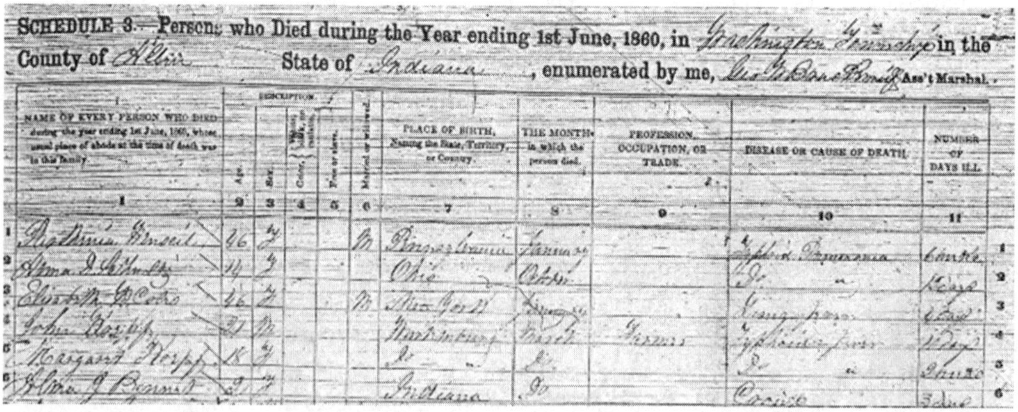

FIGURE 4-5   Portion of a Mortality schedule from the 1860 federal census of Indiana (Used by permission of MyFamily.com, Inc.)

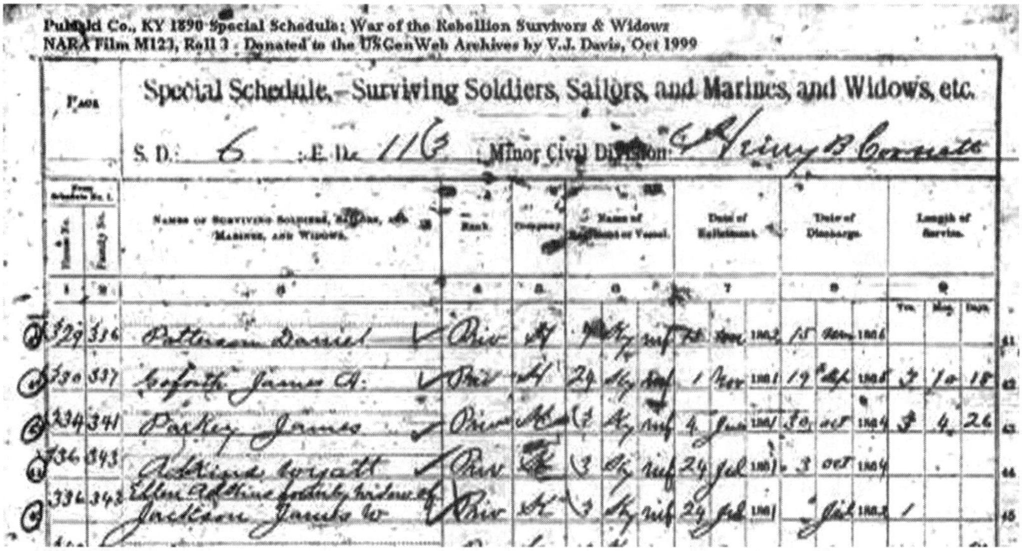

Pulaski Co., KY 1890 Special Schedule: War of the Rebellion Survivors & Widows
NARA Film M123, Roll 3 - Donated to the USGenWeb Archives by V.J. Davis, Oct 1999

Special Schedule.—Surviving Soldiers, Sailors, and Marines, and Widows, etc.

S. D.: 6 E. D.: 116 Minor Civil Division:

House No.	Family No.	Names of Surviving Soldiers, Sailors, and Marines, and Widows.	Rank.	Company.	Name of Regiment or Vessel.	Date of Enlistment.	Date of Discharge.	Length of Service.
329	336	Patterson Daniel	Priv					
330	337	Goforth James A.	Priv					
334	341	Parker James	Priv					
336	343		Priv					
336	343	Ellen Adkins formerly widow of Jackson James W	Priv					

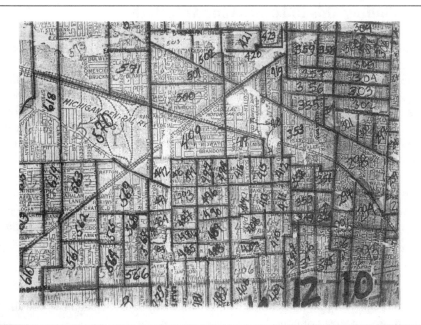

FIGURE 4-6 Portion of a Union Veterans and Widows schedule (Used by permission of MyFamily.com, Inc.)

FIGURE 4-7 1930 Enumeration District map showing an area of Detroit, Michigan (From the National Archives and Records Administration collection)

your chances of quickly locating the right census page(s) to find them, even if the surname was misspelled. There are other resources you can use to help you with this.

- **City directories** are name and address listings published on a fairly regular basis in towns and cities, and were used to help people locate one another. Some of these directories include both individual persons and businesses.

- **Telephone directories,** like city directories, can be helpful in locating addresses.

- **Land and property records,** which we will discuss in some detail later, typically include deeds, indentures, tax rolls, lien papers, and other records indexed by name for easy location by the property clerk, tax assessor, and other government officials. These can provide the names and addresses of the owners, and the governments' maps of property for taxation purposes can be compared with ED maps to help quickly establish a family member's location.

- **Sanborn Fire Insurance Maps** were used in the United States to clearly document urban areas for property and casualty insurance purposes from 1867 until about 1970. These maps provide street-by-street details concerning the buildings, the materials used in their construction, the use of the building, and other information. Additional maps of subareas provide extensive detail showing down to the actual shape of an individual building and its construction materials. You can use Sanborn maps in conjunction with directories and land and property records, and compare it against an enumeration district map in order to quickly home in on an ancestor's census records.

Use Census Finding Aids to Locate Your Ancestors

Indexes to the 1790 through 1870 federal census are available for most states in book form and can be found in many public libraries with genealogical collections and in academic libraries with genealogical and government documents collections.

Online subscription databases offering access to U.S. federal census indexes include those at the Ancestry.com Web site and through the HeritageQuest Online census database operated by ProQuest, available through many libraries. Both of these online database providers are continuing to expand their indices and provide links to actual online census document images. Ancestry.com provides additional indices for the 1885 federal census enumeration conducted in and for the five states and territories mentioned in Table 4-4 at the end of this chapter.

Use Soundex and Miracode Index Resources

Another important finding aid for locating your ancestors in the census is the sound-alike indexing system. There are two forms of this system that were used in the indexing of census schedules for 1880 through 1930. These are the Soundex and Miracode systems and were used for some states in the 1880, 1900, 1910, 1920, and 1930 censuses as follows:

- **1880**   Includes only those households with children aged 10 years and younger
- **1900**   Complete for all households with separate cards for each adult whose surname differed from the head of household

- **1910** Includes only 21 states: AL, AR, CA, FL, GA, IL, KS, KY, LA, MI, MS, MO, NC, OH, OK, PA, SC, TN, TX, VA, and WV.
- **1920** Includes all states as well as U.S. territories at the time: Alaska, Hawaii, the Canal Zone, Puerto Rico, Guam, American Samoa, the Virgin Islands, and military and naval institutions.
- **1930** Includes only 12 states: AL, AR, FL, GA, KY, LA, MS, NC, SC, TN, VA, and WV.

Soundex and Miracode are similar coding systems that use the first letter of the surname, followed by three numbers to represent the next three remaining consonants (no vowels are used in the numeric portion of the code) in the surname. This number is used to group similar sounding names—such as Smith, Smyth, Smythe, for example—together for ease of location.

The coding for Soundex and Miracode is actually pretty simple. The four-position code begins with the first letter of the surname, whatever it is. The next step is to take the remainder of the surname, discard all the vowels, and retain any consonants. If you have more than three consonants remaining, you discard those additional ones. If you have less than three consonants, don't worry. Whatever you have left at this point will be used to calculate the numeric digits. Zeroes are used to represent a "no consonant" situation. If your family surname is LEE, for example, you would have the letter "L" and no consonants remaining. Your Soundex code would be L000.

You will select a numeric code for each of the consonants you have left, using Table 4-2.

Let's take an example. My surname, MORGAN, would be coded as follows:

- Surname beginning letter is "M"
- Discard vowels "O" and "A"
- Remaining consonants are "R," "G," and "N"
- Equivalent numeric digits to represent "R," "G," and "N" are 6, 2, and 5
- Soundex code for MORGAN is therefore M625

There are some unusual exceptions for which some special rules apply. These are pretty straightforward, however, so don't let them throw you. They actually help you obtain a crisper separation.

Code #	Represents These Letters…
1	B, F, P, V
2	C, G, J, K, Q, S, X, Z
3	D, T
4	L
5	M, N
6	R
	Disregard A, E, I, O, U, H, W, and Y

TABLE 4-2 Basic Coding Scheme for Soundex and Miracode; Additional Rules Apply

- In *surnames with double letters, treat those as a single letter.* For example, the surname SOMMERS would be coded as S562. (The vowels "O" and "E" are discarded, leaving "MM," which is treated as a single "M," an "R," and an "S.")

- *In names with letters side by side that have the same Soundex code value, treat the two letters as one letter.* Here are three examples:

    - MACKEY would be coded M200. (The vowels "A" and "E are discarded, the "CK" are treated as a single letter and coded as a 2, the "Y" is disregarded and there are no other consonants, and therefore the last two of the four codes are 0 and 0.)

    - TOMCZYAK would be coded T522. (The vowels "O," "Y," and "A" are discarded, the "CZ" is treated as a single letter and coded as a 2, and the "K" is coded as a 2.)

    - PFISTER would be coded as P236. (The "P" in the double-letter of "PF" is the surname letter, and the "F" is dropped, the "S" is coded as a 2, the "T" is coded as a 3, and the "R" is coded as a 6.)

- *Names with prefixes, such as CON, DE, DI, LA, LE, LO, VAN, and VON, could have been coded either way by the personnel who created the Soundex or Miracode index.* Therefore, you should code the name both ways and check both listings. In all cases, the surnames beginning with MC or MAC are not considered to have used prefixes. These letters are considered part of the entire surname and will be a part of the code.

- *If the two successive consonants have the same Soundex code and are separated by a single vowel ("A," "E," "I," "O," "U"), the consonant to the right of the vowel is coded, and the other one is ignored.* This could be represented by the example of TOMCZYAK above. However, if two successive consonants having the same Soundex code are separated by an "H" or a "W," the consonant on the right of the "H" or "W" is not coded. For example, the surname ASHCROFT would be coded A261. (The "S" is coded as 2, the "C" is ignored, the "R" is coded as 6, the "F" is coded as 1, and the "T" is dropped.)

Try the coding system yourself. In fact, I have created a Soundex and Miracode list for myself for all the surnames for which I regularly perform research. I keep a reference card handy with the coding rules, as well as an electronic copy of the card on my handheld computer.

Special index cards, using either Soundex or Miracode, were created at the request of the Social Security Administration for the 1880, 1900, 1910, 1920, and 1930 censuses in order to help their employees verify the ages of persons applying for retirement benefits. These were created by the Works Progress Administration during the Great Depression in the United States, and they were then grouped and microfilmed by WPA personnel and by some other personnel later. The microfilm is available at many libraries with sizeable genealogical special collections or through the local LDS Family History Center in your area on loan from the main Family History Library (FHL) in Salt Lake City, Utah. Soundex and Miracode card records can point you to the exact census district and census page for the actual census entry for your ancestor or family's member.

Soundex or Miracode microfilm are organized by state, and then in code sequence. Within code, the cards are organized in alphabetical order by the spelling of the surname, and within surname by initials and/or given name of the primary person on the card.

Figure 4-8 shows a Soundex card from the 1920 federal census. For a smaller family, only the one side of the card would have been completed. In this case, however, Lucius Boddie is the head of the household and his family's Soundex card is filed under B300 and then under Boddie, and then under Lucius' name. The Lucius Boddie family consisted of himself, his wife, and seven children. Since the family was so large, the listing was continued to the back of the Soundex card, which is shown in Figure 4-9.

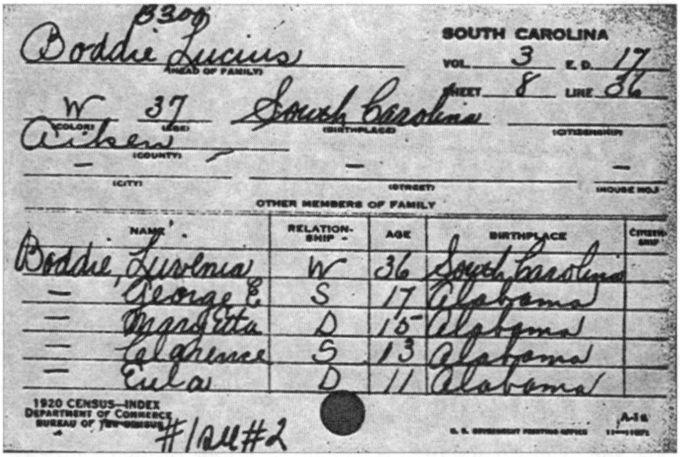

B300

Boddie Lucius (HEAD OF FAMILY)

SOUTH CAROLINA VOL. 3 E.D. 17 SHEET 8 LINE 36

W (COLOR) 37 (AGE) South Carolina (BIRTHPLACE) (CITIZENSHIP)

Aiken (COUNTY)

(CITY) (STREET) (HOUSE NO.)

OTHER MEMBERS OF FAMILY

NAME	RELATIONSHIP	AGE	BIRTHPLACE	CITIZENSHIP
Boddie, Luvenia	W	36	South Carolina	
— George E.	S	17	Alabama	
— Margretta	D	15	Alabama	
— Clarence	S	13	Alabama	
— Eula	D	11	Alabama	

1920 CENSUS—INDEX
DEPARTMENT OF COMMERCE
BUREAU OF THE CENSUS

#1 all #2

A-1a

FIGURE 4-8 Soundex card for the 1920 census (front) for Lucius Boddie family (Courtesy of Drew Smith)

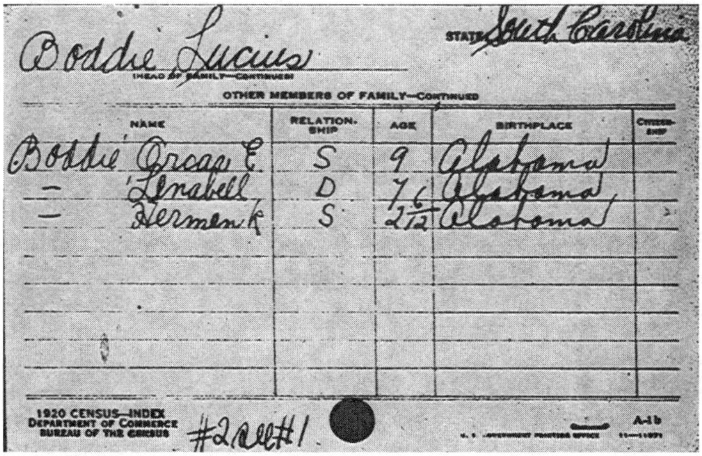

Boddie Lucius (HEAD OF FAMILY—CONTINUED)

STATE South Carolina

OTHER MEMBERS OF FAMILY—CONTINUED

NAME	RELATIONSHIP	AGE	BIRTHPLACE	CITIZENSHIP
Boddie Oscar E.	S	9	Alabama	
— Lenabell	D	7 1/6	Alabama	
— Herman K	S	2 1/12	Alabama	

1920 CENSUS—INDEX
DEPARTMENT OF COMMERCE
BUREAU OF THE CENSUS

#2 all #1

A-1b

FIGURE 4-9 Same Soundex cards (back) listing remainder of the Boddie family members (Courtesy of Drew Smith)

In other cases, a person who was not a head of household and did not have the same surname as the head had a separate Soundex card created for him or her. That card indicated the name of the head of household with whom this person had been enumerated. Figure 4-10 shows an example of this for Lottie Bodie, who was enumerated with Benjamin F. Tindall. According to the card, she was his daughter.

The Soundex and Miracode indexes were not created for all of the states for the census years mentioned above. Check with your library for more information about what is available for which states. The difference between the censuses coded using Soundex and Miracode is really only in the format of the card and the reference information it provides to the precise location in the census schedules.

The Soundex card provides reference information in the upper-right corner to the actual census volume, the Enumeration District, the sheet number (or page), and the line number on the sheet on which the person appears. The Miracode card provides the volume number, the Enumeration District, and then the Visitation #. This last number refers to the number of the dwelling that the census taker visited in the course of the enumeration. Please don't confuse this with a street address/house number.

Use Excellent U.S. Federal Census Reference Books

William Thorndale and William Dollarhide's book *Map Guide to the U.S. Federal Censuses, 1790-1920* (Genealogical Publishing Co., Inc., 1987) is an excellent resource for locating places in the correct state and county for each of the U.S. federal censuses. There were also some censuses taken in colonial times, which may have been documented and/or microfilmed by state archives. Ann S. Lainhart's book *State Census Records* (Genealogical Publishing Company, Inc., 1992) is an excellent reference on this subject. Three other excellent books regarding the U.S. federal

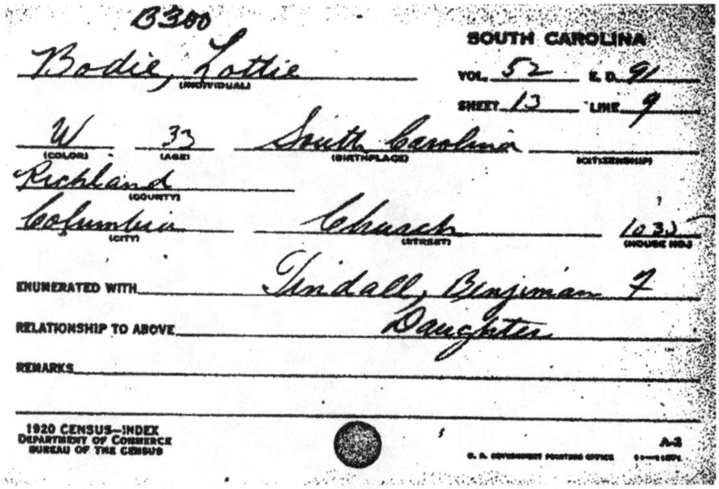

B300
SOUTH CAROLINA
Bodie, Lottie (INDIVIDUAL)
VOL. 52 E.D. 91
SHEET 13 LINE 9
W (COLOR) 33 (AGE) South Carolina (BIRTHPLACE) (CITIZENSHIP)
Richland (COUNTY)
Columbia (CITY) Church (STREET) 1031 (HOUSE NO.)
ENUMERATED WITH Tindall, Benjaman F
RELATIONSHIP TO ABOVE Daughter
REMARKS
1920 CENSUS—INDEX
DEPARTMENT OF COMMERCE
BUREAU OF THE CENSUS
A-2

FIGURE 4-10 Soundex card for the 1920 census showing a person who had been enumerated with a household of a different surname (Courtesy of Drew Smith)

censuses are William Dollarhide's *The Census Book: A Genealogist's Guide to Federal Census Facts, Schedules and Indexes* (Heritage Quest, 2000), Kathleen W. Hinckley's *Your Guide to the Federal Census for Genealogists, Researchers, and Family Historians* (Betterway Books, 2002), Loretto D. Szucs and Matthew Wright's *Finding Answers in U.S. Census Records* (Ancestry Publishing, Inc., 2001), and Thomas Jay Kemp's *American Census Handbook* (Scholarly Resources, Inc., 2001).

Access the Census Images on Microfilm and in Online Databases

Federal census records were microfilmed and are available for the years 1790 through 1930 through the National Archives and Records Administration (NARA). Your library may be able to assist you in renting film. Subsequent years' census records are protected through the Privacy Act and are not made public for 72 years. You may, however, contact the United States Census Bureau to request copies of the census records for your family for 1930 through 1990. There is a fee for this search service, and you will need to provide proof of your connection to the family.

Ancestry.com at **http://www.ancestry.com** has compiled the most complete online indices for the United States federal censuses and has digitized Population Schedules for all censuses from 1790 through 1930. These are available through a paid subscription to their Images Online collection. Figure 4-11 shows the result of a search at Ancestry.com in the 1920 census records, and you will note a link to view the actual census page for this person.

Heritage Quest has digitized many of the federal census records and these are available on CD-ROM and through access to the ProQuest databases. ProQuest is available by subscription

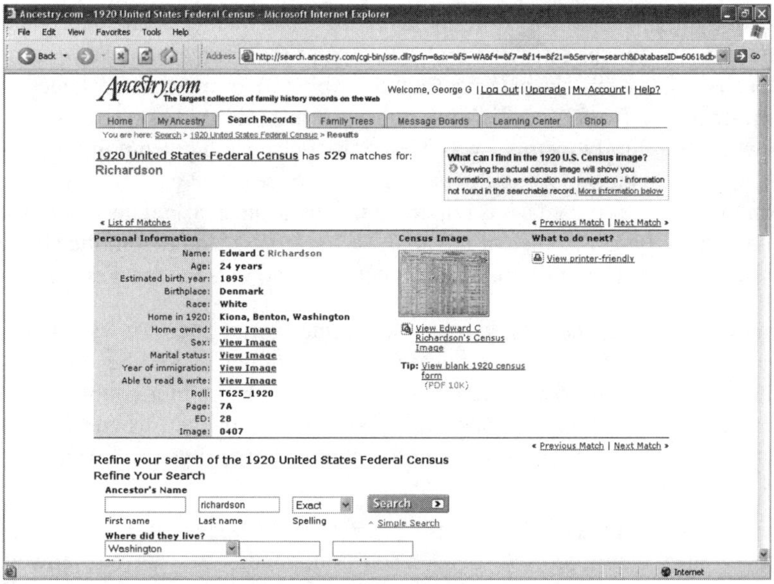

FIGURE 4-11   Census search result screen from Ancestry.com with link to census image (Used by permission of MyFamily.com, Inc.)

and you will find that public and academic libraries often have subscriptions. As a library card holder for one of those libraries, you may be able to remotely access the ProQuest/HeritageQuest databases from your home computer.

The Church of Jesus Christ of Latter-Day Saints (LDS) has indexed the 1880 U.S. federal census, and this may be accessed at **http://www.familysearch.org.** No images are available. However, the Family History Library in Salt Lake City has copies of all the NARA census microfilm, and you can access them there or through your nearest Family History Center.

You will find that some individual census indexing and transcription projects have been undertaken. Some of these have been published in print format, while others have been placed on the Internet at various sites. You can use your favorite Internet search engine to help locate these. Others are included at Web pages at the USGenWeb Project site at **http://www.usgenweb.org.**

Don't Forget to Search State Censuses

In addition to the federal censuses, at certain times a number of the individual states have conducted their own census enumerations. These typically occurred halfway between the decennial federal enumerations, in other words, at the half-decade mark. These records, many of which have been microfilmed and are stored at the respective state's archive or library, can provide evidence of the presence of your ancestor or family member in a particular location.

Ann S. Lainhart has compiled an authoritative reference titled *State Census Records,* which details which states conducted their own censuses, and in what years, whether the records have been microfilmed and/or indexed, and where the records reside.

Caveats About Census Records and How to Work with Them

Census records are by no means the most reliable records. The quality of the data is as good as the person conducting the census interviews, also known as the enumerator. The enumerator may have missed someone, made a mistake entering (or transcribing it), or may have obtained information from a neighbor rather than from the individual himself or herself. At best, census data is merely a milestone for whether a family member was present in a place at a given point in time. Always seek other corroborating evidence of their presence (or absence).

When working with census records, it is important to look at an area, and not just at your family. A good rule of thumb is to make copies of the actual census page, and record the six families on either side of your ancestors or family members. There are two reasons for doing so:

- In a prior or subsequent census, you can determine if your ancestor was present between these families. Often, if your ancestor was somehow omitted, by locating one or more of the other families in a prior or subsequent census, you can be certain you were looking in the right place. This is especially important if you consider that census enumeration districts, like county boundaries and voting precincts, changed over time. You want to make sure you are searching in the right place.

- Surrounding families may, in some cases, be related. It was not unusual for neighbors' children to marry neighbors' children. In addition, a father may have bestowed a gift of property on a married daughter, and the family with the different surname next door to your family member or ancestor may actually be the daughter and son-in-law of the family.

Always take census records with the proverbial grain of salt. Locate other records to corroborate the data you find in census records. Invest some time, too, in learning about each of the censuses and what the data in each column of the form represents.

Census extraction forms for the United States censuses can be found at the Ancestry.com Web site at the HeritageQuest Online census database marketed by ProQuest and subscribed to by a number of libraries. These forms are free for your use. They were created in Adobe Acrobat format and you must have the Adobe Acrobat Reader in order to open, read, and print them. There are forms for each of the decennial Federal Population Census years, 1790 through 1930 (except 1890) and for the 1891 U.K. census. These are excellent for understanding the types of data you will find on the census schedules themselves, and for transcribing census data when you cannot print a copy of the actual census record from microfilm or an online database.

Understand and Work with British Census Records

The first modern census in the British Isles was taken in order to determine the makeup of the population and its activities. There had been a period of poor harvests and food shortages. A substantial number of agricultural workers had joined the military services and therefore could not be involved with working the land.

The Census Act of 1800 (41 George III, cap. 15) was enacted and called for a full population enumeration of England, Wales, and Scotland beginning in 1801. The act also called for an enumeration to be conducted every ten years thereafter. A census has been performed ever since, with the exception of 1941 when, because of war, very little census work was performed.

In order to determine the livelihoods of the citizens in the 1801 census, questions were asked that elicited responses to help divide the population into three categories: those involved with agriculture, those working in manufacturing and trade, and those engaged in other types of employment. The population of England and Wales in 1801 was almost nine million, and the population of Scotland was a little over 1,600,000. No names were requested, although a few officials did include names in their documents. The questions asked in 1801 included

- How many inhabited and uninhabited houses are located within the parish, and how many families live in the inhabited houses?

- How many persons are living in the parish, and distinguish males and females of all ages? Military personnel and seamen in military service or on registered vessels were not to be included.

- How many persons are involved with agriculture, with manufacturing or trade, or handicraft, or in other types of employment?

- How many persons' baptisms and burials have there been within the parish in 1700, 1710, 1720, 1730, 1740, 1750, 1760, 1770, 1780, and in each subsequent year up through 31 December 1800, and distinguish totals by gender.

The process of conducting this first census was extensive. Standardized forms were distributed to all households and were to be completed based on persons in a residence as of the census night, 10 March 1801. (See Table 4-4.) The information was gathered by enumerators, attached to a copy of the Census Act of 1800, and the enumerator presented them to a high constable or other officer and swore an oath as to the accuracy of the information. The returns were gathered by the official, endorsed, and submitted with a list of the names of the enumerators to a town clerk or clerk of the peace. The returns were then summarized into statistical reports and these were then submitted to the Home Office by 15 May 1801.

A similar format with similar questions was used in the 1811, 1821, and 1831 enumerations. In 1811, a question was added to determine why a house was unoccupied. In 1821, a question was added to elicit ages of men in order to help determine how many men were able to bear arms. It was also in 1821 that Ireland was first included in the census, and her population at that time was calculated to be over 6,800,000. The 1831 census included more detailed questions concerning economic conditions.

The 1841 census was the first to record the names of the inhabitants, their gender, and age (rounded to the lower five years when over age 15), and it therefore is the earliest British census used by most genealogists and family historians. In addition, these census documents were sent to a central government location for tabulation and reference. For that reason, they have been preserved and images have been made.

The 1851 census included those persons living on vessels in inland waters or at sea (including the Royal Navy and merchant navy). In addition, persons serving abroad with the armed forces and those working with the East India Company were enumerated, and British subjects residing overseas were also counted.

Between 1861 and 1891, there were few changes in the format and questions asked on the census. The most important additions from a genealogical perspective, however, were the addition of questions concerning the languages spoken. This question was added for enumerations in Scotland beginning with the 1881 census and for Wales beginning with the 1891 census. It is shown in the last column on the example in Figure 4-12.

The 1901 census included questions to elicit more precise responses. A good introduction to the British census information can be found at the National Archives Web site at **http://www.pro.gov.uk/ pathways/census/events/census3.htm** where you also can view examples of 1841 and 1901 census forms.

Census records' contents are protected for a period of 100 years. The 1901 census information was released in 2001. The National Archives, previously known as the Public Records Office (PRO) is custodian of the 1901 census records for England and Wales, which also includes the Channel Islands and the Isle of Man. Separate enumerations for Scotland and Ireland were taken, and these records are in the possession of the General Record Office of Scotland (GRO) at **http://www.gro-scotland.gov.uk** and at the National Archives of Ireland at **http://www.nationalarchives.ie/ index.html,** respectively.

Work with British Census Records

Like the United States, the British government defined an "as of" date for use by the respondents and this date is referred to as the "census night." The individual household schedule was to be completed based on the persons who were in the household during the period of Sunday night to Monday morning on the dates listed in Table 4-3.

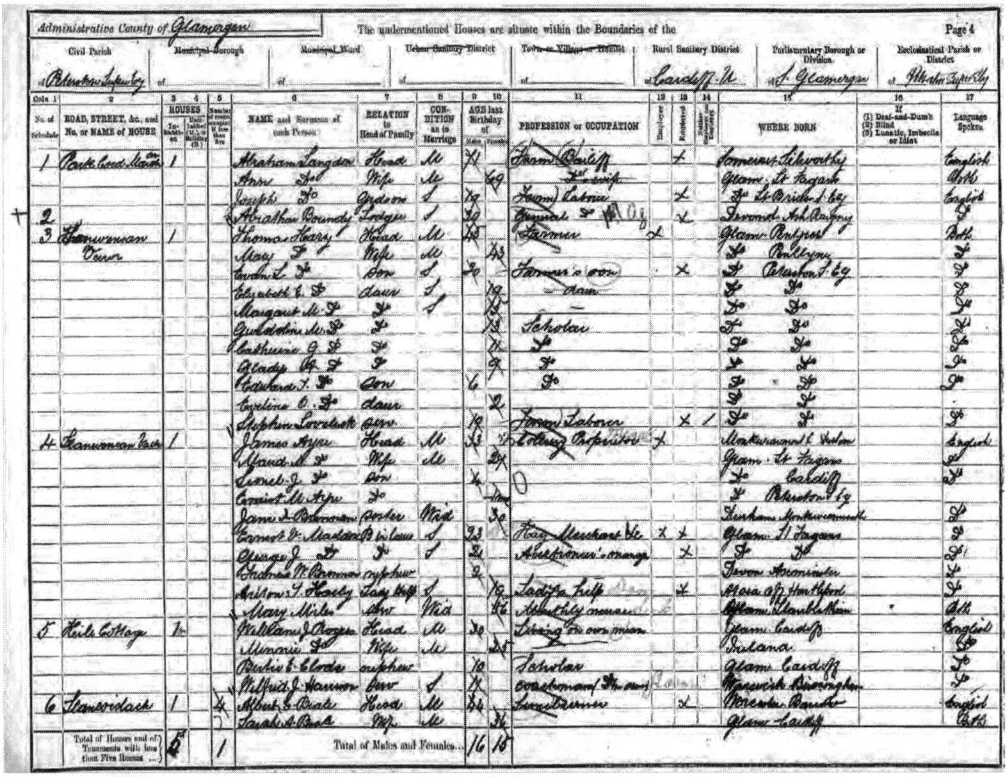

FIGURE 4-12   1891 census form created in the parish of Peterston-super-Ely in Cardiff, South Glamorgan, Wales (Used by permission of the National Archives, U.K.)

It is important that you take into consideration the "as of" date when considering the information found in a census schedule with other genealogical evidence. For example, you might wonder why a person's age is listed as 41 in the 1841 census and only as age 50 in the 1851 census. If you examine the dates in Table 4-3, you will notice that the 1851 census was taken more than a month earlier than the one the previous decade. You could hypothesize that the respondent's birthday fell after 30 March and up to and including 6 June of 1800. Based on that theory, you could then begin searching for proof of the date of birth in other records.

If the census form was not completed properly by the head of the household, the enumerator was supposed to have requested the additional information when he called at the house. If the person was illiterate, blind, or could not for some other reason complete the schedule, the enumerator was to have conducted an interview, asked the questions, and completed the document himself.

Descriptions of the enumeration districts can be extremely helpful in locating your ancestors' records. The example shown in Figure 4-13 is from the 1891 census of England and Wales and shows the registration district of Spilsby and the subdistrict of Alford in Lincolnshire.

Year	Census Date
1801	Monday, 10 March
1811	Monday, 27 May
1821	Monday, 28 May
1831	Monday, 30 May
1841	Sunday, 6 June
1851	Sunday, 30 March
1861	Sunday, 7 April
1871	Sunday, 2 April
1881	Sunday, 3 April
1891	Sunday, 5 April
1901	Sunday, 31 March

TABLE 4-3   Census Enumeration Dates for British Censuses 1801–1901

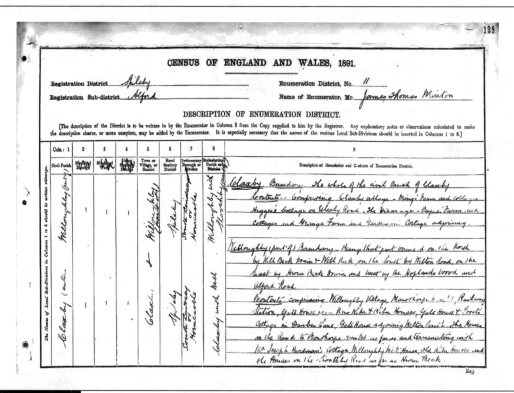

FIGURE 4-13   1891 Description of enumeration district form (Used by permission of the National Archives, U.K.)

Learn the Status of Irish Census Records

The Irish government took an independent census in 1813, and then censuses were taken every ten years from 1821 through 1911. Due to the Irish Civil War, no census was taken in 1921, but the next census was done in 1926. The next censuses were taken in 1936 and 1946. From 1946 to 1971, the census was taken every five years. Since 1971, the census has been taken every ten years.

Unfortunately, the Irish census records have not fared well over time. The 1813 census no longer exists. Most of the census information from the 1821 through 1851 censuses was destroyed in a fire in Dublin in 1922, and the censuses from 1861 and 1871 were destroyed by government order shortly after the data was compiled and summarized, and the 1881 and 1891 censuses were pulped during World War I due to the paper shortage. The surviving materials have been microfilmed by the LDS and these films can be obtained through the LDS Family History Library in Salt Lake City, Utah, and through the LDS Family History Centers worldwide.

As a result of the loss of so much of the Irish census material, census substitutes can sometimes be used as alternate evidence sources of residence, age, and other information. These include Old Age Pension Records, Tithe Appointment Books (1823-1838), Griffith's Primary Valuation (1848-1864), and other, later land and property records.

Use Quality Reference Materials When Working with British Census Records

There are excellent resources available for your reference when working with British census records. One of these is the GenDocs site on the Web, located at **http://www.gendocs.demon.co.uk/ census.html.** This link connects you with their "Census Returns for England & Wales" page, which includes a link to descriptions concerning the handling of persons not in normal households on census night. In addition, you will find an extensive list of abbreviations used in the 1841–1891 census returns.

The best written reference concerning the 1801–1901 censuses is Edward Higgs' *Making Sense of the Census: The Manuscript Returns for England and Wales, 1801-1901*, published in London by Her Majesty's Stationery Office in 1989. Unfortunately, however, it is out of print. If you can locate a copy in a library, it provides an excellent history and perspective of the enumerations of that period. More recently, however, an excellent how-to book by Susan Lumas has been released in its fourth edition, *Making Use of the Census,* one of the Public Record Office Reader's Guide series. The new edition coincided with the release of the 1901 census records and contains excellent instructions for how to access and use them.

Indexes of censuses have been prepared by a variety of organizations. One excellent starting point is the GENUKI Web site at **http://www.genuki.org.uk,** which is concerned with U.K. and Ireland genealogy. Another is the BritishIslesGenWeb Project, which is a subsidiary part of the WorldGenWeb Project (**http://www.worldgenweb.org**). The BritishIslesGenWeb Project can be accessed at **http://www.britishislesgenweb.org** and there you can visit the various county or island sites where information about and links to census resources can be found.

Access the Census Records for the British Isles

We've already mentioned a number of resources for gaining access to census records for England, Wales, Scotland, and Ireland, but let's recap:

- The England and Wales manuscript returns of the 1801 to 1901 censuses are in the possession of the National Archives (formerly known as the PRO). These have been microfilmed and are available for review at the National Archives, at larger libraries with genealogical materials, and through the LDS Family History Library and LDS Family History Centers. (You can locate the Family History Center closest to you by conducting a search through the LDS FamilySearch Web site, specifically using the search template at **http://www.familysearch.org/Eng/Library/FHC/frameset_fhc.asp.**)

- The 1901 census of England and Wales has been indexed and the images digitized, and these have been placed online at the 1901 Census Website at **http://www.census.pro.gov.uk.** You can search for names or addresses at the site and, for a fee, retrieve the actual census document image. You can then view, zoom in or out, print, or download that image. A credit card can be used to pay for images or to purchase vouchers for use at the site. Microfilm is available for access at the National Archives in Kew, Richmond, Surrey.

- Surviving Irish census records have been microfilmed. These are available through the Public Record Office of Northern Ireland (PRONI) or through the LDS as described above. You can learn more about the 19th century records at **http://proni.nics.gov.uk/records/census19.htm** and about the 1901 census at **http://proni.nics.gov.uk/records/1901cens.htm.**

- Scotland's census records are in the possession of the General Register Office for Scotland (GROS). Leaflet S-11 is available online at **http://www.gro-scotland.gov.uk/grosweb/ grosweb.nsf/pages/leaflt11** and describes in detail their digitization project for census records. Census records have been microfilmed. Microfilm can be accessed at Register House in Edinburgh, Scotland, at larger libraries with genealogical collections that have purchased the film, or through the LDS as described above. In addition, the GROS and Scotland On Line have partnered to create and maintain a pay-per-view Web site called ScotlandsPeople at **http://www.scotlandspeople.gov.uk.** The site provides a "fully searchable index of Scottish births from 1553–1902, marriages from 1553 to 1927, and deaths from 1855 to 1952. In addition, indexed census data is available from 1881 to 1901. To respect privacy of living people, Internet access has been limited to birth records over 100 years old, marriage records over 75 years, and death records over 50 years."

Understand and Work with Canadian Census Records

Canada's history is a fascinating study of many people: French, English, Aboriginal, and a mélange of religions, ethnicities, and cultures. The first census in what became Canada was conducted in 1666 by Jean Talon. This enumeration recorded the name, age, marital status, and occupation of each of the 3,215 inhabitants of New France. Between 1666 and the first official Canadian census in 1871, there were no less than 98 different colonial and regional censuses conducted, most of which were performed for purposes of taxation and military conscription. Over time, new questions were added to gather more information about building structures, livestock, crops, firearms, and churches. Religious affiliation—Catholic or Protestant—became another area of interest, and it became important to enumerate other groups, such as the Acadians, Indians (or "First People"), and Blacks. Census returns prior to 1851 are incomplete for most areas.

The Canadian census returns after 1851 used a Population Schedule form for the enumeration by name of every individual in a household, and the Population Schedule was usually accompanied by a separate agricultural schedule that included information about the acreage, land use, buildings, crops, livestock, and valuation.

The National Archives of Canada (**http://www.archives.ca**) is the repository for most of the census materials, including those from before Confederation in 1867. However, some of the original documents for New Brunswick, Nova Scotia, and Prince Edward Island prior to 1871 are still in the possession of the provincial archives or libraries.

Explore the Depth of the 1871 Census

The first official national census was conducted in 1871 and was part of the British North America Act in 1867, which created the Canadian Confederation. The Act stated, "In the general Census of the Population of Canada which is hereby required to be taken in the Year One thousand eight-hundred and seventy-one, and in every Tenth Year thereafter, the respective Populations of the Four Provinces shall be distinguished."

This first census requested a vast amount of information from the respondents and for that reason is extremely important for genealogical researchers whose ancestors and family members lived in Canada at that time. There were nine schedules used to collect information.

- **Schedule 1** Population Schedule by name of every living person
- **Schedule 2** Schedule with the name of every person who died within the previous 12 months
- **Schedule 3** A return listing all public institutions, real estate, vehicles, and implements
- **Schedule 4** Agricultural return for cultivated produce, such as crops, fruits, and plants
- **Schedule 5** Agricultural return for livestock, animal products, furs, and homemade fabrics
- **Schedule 6** Return of industrial manufacturing
- **Schedule 7** Return of products of forest resources
- **Schedule 8** Return for shipping concerns and fisheries
- **Schedule 9** Return for mining and mineral products

You can relate the information found on surviving schedules 3, 4, 5, 7, 8, and 9 to the name of a person whose name is listed on schedule 1, the Population Schedule. By doing so, you can expand your knowledge of what that person's economic livelihood entailed, the extent of the holdings, the success or failure of the operation, and you gain perspective of the lifestyle of the person or family unit.

The 1881 census eliminated the schedule of industrial manufacturing. Unfortunately, though, only the Population Schedule exists. It has, however, been microfilmed.

The 1891 census returned to nine schedules again, but only the Population Schedule survives and has been microfilmed.

By the time the 1901 census was to be conducted, Canada consisted of: British Columbia, Manitoba, Ontario, Quebec, New Brunswick, Nova Scotia, and Prince Edward Island; two territories, Yukon Territory and Northwest Territories; and the District of Keewatin. Census enumeration areas generally, but not always, corresponded to electoral districts. It is important for you to refer to enumeration area descriptions to help you home in on your family members' locations.

Enumeration was conducted by door-to-door interview, with enumerators individually visiting each house and asking the questions of the "head" of the household. Enumeration was to be completed within 30 days of 31 March 1901. The census commissioners were forced to revise the schedules, however, before being able to compile and send the completed forms to the census office. By the end of August, 98 percent of the forms had been received by the central census office in Ottawa. The original schedules for British Columbia schedules were lost when the steamer *Islander* sank on 15 August 1901. The census in British Columbia therefore had to be taken all over again, and this delayed the final tabulation of the census data.

The original documents from the 1901 census were destroyed by the Dominion Bureau of Statistics at the direction of the Public Records Committee in 1955. Fortunately, however, all of the population records (Schedule 1) and most of the buildings, land, church, and school records (Schedule 2) have all been preserved on microfilm, although the quality of the filming is uneven and some images are unreadable. Some instances of the additional schedule forms used are to be found among the microfilmed records.

The good news is that the National Archives of Canada has digitized the microfilm images and made them available at its Web site (**http://www.archives.ca/02/020122_e.html**) in a searchable database. Census districts and maps also are accessible online, which, as you've already learned, can be invaluable in helping you quickly locate your family. A search of the database for the census records for a province and then a geographical area will return a search results list with records like the one shown in Figure 4-14. It provides you with details about the specific location of the records associated with that place. It also indicates the Record Group under which the National Archives of Canada has classified and catalogued the records, as well as the reel number for use in accessing the microfilm from which the digital image was produced.

You can then use the drop-down window labeled "Associated Images" and view the total number of image pages. By clicking on one in the list, you cause the MrSID viewer to be opened on your computer for viewing the actual image. If the MrSID software is not detected on your computer when you try to view an image, you will be prompted to download and install it. You do not have to use the MrSID viewer; you can view the images without it. However, the MrSID viewer has a small menu bar that allows you to zoom in or out on the image, to pan (or move it), return to a full-image view, and some other options. You may want to save the image on your own computer and use a graphics software program to enhance the image for easier reading later on.

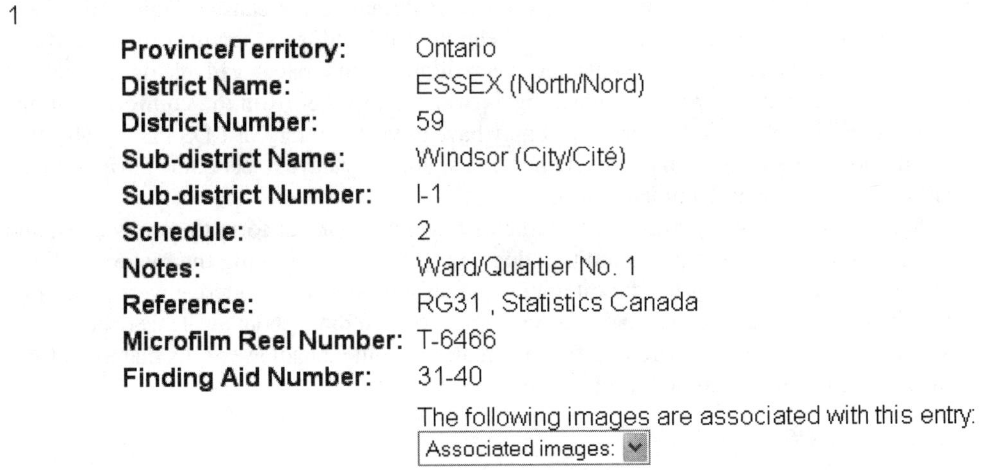

4

1

Province/Territory:	Ontario
District Name:	ESSEX (North/Nord)
District Number:	59
Sub-district Name:	Windsor (City/Cité)
Sub-district Number:	I-1
Schedule:	2
Notes:	Ward/Quartier No. 1
Reference:	RG31 , Statistics Canada
Microfilm Reel Number:	T-6466
Finding Aid Number:	31-40

The following images are associated with this entry:
Associated images: ▾

FIGURE 4-14   Search results from the online index to the 1901 census at the National Archives of Canada's Web site

In 1905, the Census and Statistics Act received Royal Assent and defined that a general census would be taken in Canada in 1911 and every ten years thereafter. It also declared that a population and agriculture census was to be taken in Manitoba, Saskatchewan, and Alberta in 1906 and every ten years thereafter. As a result, two schedules were prepared and the enumeration was conducted. The two schedules are

- Population and livestock
- Agriculture

Like the 1901 census, microfilm was created of the original records, but the original documents were destroyed in 1955. The National Archives of Canada also has digitized the microfilm images and made these available on their Web site.

Locate Additional Information on the Censuses

Census records can provide you with a huge amount of information and many clues to research. As I've mentioned before, it is important to become a student of history and to learn about the places where your ancestors and family members lived, the time period, the documents that may have been created at the time for whatever purposes, which ones have survived, where the surviving materials are located, in what format(s) they exist, and how to gain access to them.

You have seen examples in this chapter of census materials that were created for various purposes. Some have survived while others have been lost to fire or through other causes. Transcripts may have been made or original documents may have been microfilmed, and then the originals were destroyed. In some cases, census documents have been digitized and made available on the Internet. You may be able to conduct "armchair genealogy" over the Internet from the comfort of your own home to access images. In other cases, you may have to visit a library or LDS Family History Center in order to access microfilm copies. Other times, you may have to schedule a trip to visit the repository where original documents reside.

Your challenge is to actually trace the documents down in whatever form they may exist, and determine how you can access them. And that does, indeed, mean studying the history of the documents. Fortunately for all of us, the Internet provides a wealth of knowledge we can use in our quest. I often use my Web browser and a search engine to learn more about available documentary materials. As an example, when searching for information about Canadian census materials for 1906, I entered the following in the search engine:

canada census 1906

I was rewarded with a huge number of search results, not the least of which was one at the top of the list that happens to be the authoritative site on the subject: the National Archives of Canada's Web site for the Census of the Northwest Provinces, 1906, at **http://www.archives.ca/ 02/020153_e.html.**

Learn to use the Internet effectively to search and locate information that may be of historical value to your research. In addition, learn how to use online catalogs of libraries, archives, and other facilities so that you can determine what publications may be available to help in your search.

By this time, you have become very knowledgeable indeed about the process of genealogical research and about placing your ancestors into geographical and historical context. The next chapter will take you into some more advanced record types to help further trace and understand your ancestors and family members. You're on your way now with perhaps the most exciting journey you will ever make. Let's move right ahead!

4

Census Year	Type of Document	Columns for Information	Comments
1790	Population Schedule	■ Head of household ■ Number of free white males (by age range) ■ Number of free white females (by age range) ■ Other free persons and slaves	Name of the head of household was the only name listed.
1800	Population Schedule	Same as 1790 Population Schedule	
1810	Population Schedule	Same as 1790 Population Schedule	
1810	Manufacturing Schedule	■ Name of owner, agent, or manager ■ Type of business ■ Commodity produced ■ Value of output ■ Number of employees	■ These schedules may be of limited interest if family operated a manufacturing concern. ■ All 1810 schedules are lost.
1820	Population Schedule	Same as 1790 Population Schedule ■ Head of household ■ Number of free white males (by age range) ■ Number of free white females (by age range) ■ Number of slave males (by age range) ■ Number of slave females (by age range) ■ Number of free colored males (by age range) ■ Number of free colored females (by age range) ■ Aliens ■ Disabilities (deaf, dumb, blind, insane)	
1820	Manufacturing Schedule	Same as 1810 Manufacturing Schedule	Some schedules missing or lost
1830	Population Schedule	Same as 1820 Population Schedule, plus questions on Alien status	
1830	Manufacturing Schedule	Same as 1810 Manufacturing Schedule	Some schedules missing or lost

TABLE 4-4   United States Federal Census Records—1790 Through 1930 (Used by permission of Aha! Seminars, Inc.)

Census Year	Type of Document	Columns for Information	Comments
1840	Population Schedule	Same as 1830 Population Schedule, plus the following: ■ Number involved in variety of trades ■ Number in school ■ Number over 21 can read and write ■ Number insane ■ Age and name of Rev. War veterans	
1840	Agricultural Schedule	■ Name of owner, agent, or manager ■ Number of acres of improved and unimproved land ■ Detailed information about crops, timber, mining, livestock, honey, and other commodities	■ Submitted to Secretary of the Interior to catalog and evaluate the utilization of farmland. ■ Excellent insight into family life
1840	Manufacturing Schedule	Same as 1810 Manufacturing Schedule (mostly statistical information and of very limited use)	Some schedules missing or lost
1850	Population Schedule	■ Head of household ■ All names, ages and gender and race ■ Occupation ■ Real estate value ■ Place of birth ■ Married in last year ■ Literacy ■ Deaf, dumb, blind, insane	First census to include the names of every person in the household
1850	Slave Schedule	■ Name of slave holder ■ Number of slaves ■ Age, sex, and color ■ Fugitive from a state? Which state? ■ Number manumitted ■ Deaf, dumb, blind, insane or idiotic ■ Number of buildings in which housed	Slave names are seldom listed, but some are included
1850	Mortality Schedule	■ Deceased's name ■ Whether widowed ■ Sex, age, and color (white, black, mulatto) ■ Birthplace ■ Month of death ■ Occupation ■ Cause of death ■ Number of days ill	Information on those who died during 12 months prior to census day
1850	Agricultural Schedule	Same as 1840 Agricultural Schedule	

TABLE 4-4   United States Federal Census Records—1790 Through 1930 (Used by permission of Aha! Seminars, Inc.) *(Continued)*

Census Year	Type of Document	Columns for Information	Comments
1850	Industry Schedule	Same as 1810 Manufacturing Schedule, but was retitled Industry Schedule in 1850–1870	Some schedules missing or lost
1850	Social Statistics	Included: ■ Cemeteries within town borders (names, addresses, descriptions, maps, and other data) ■ Churches, a brief history, affiliation, and membership statistics ■ Trade societies, clubs, lodges, and other social institutions	Can be used as a resource to locate specific types of institutions in these years, and trace any surviving records
1860	Population Schedule	Same as 1850 Population Schedule	
1860	Slave Schedule	Same as 1850 Slave Schedule	
1860	Mortality Schedule	Same as 1850 Mortality Schedule	
1860	Agricultural Schedule	Same as 1840 Agricultural Schedule	
1860	Manufacturing Schedule	Same as 1810 Manufacturing Schedule	Some schedules missing or lost
1860	Social Statistics	Same as 1850 Social Statistics	
1870	Population Schedule	Same as 1850 Population Schedule, plus the following: ■ Whether or not parents were of foreign birth ■ Month of birth if within this year ■ Month of marriage if within year	
1870	Mortality Schedule	Same as 1850 Mortality Schedule, plus parents' places of birth	
1870	Agricultural Schedule	Same as 1840 Agricultural Schedule	
1870	Manufacturing Schedule	Same as 1810 Manufacturing Schedule	Some schedules missing or lost
1870	Social Statistics	Same as 1850 Social Statistics	
1880	Population Schedule	■ 1880 Census Contents ■ Head of household ■ All names, ages, gender, and race ■ Relationship ■ Marital status ■ Occupation ■ Deaf, dumb, blind, insane ■ Illness or disability ■ Literacy ■ Birthplaces (person & parents) ■ Month of birth if within the year	■ First census to include relationship of every resident to the head of household ■ Parents' birthplace information provides information for tracing ancestral records

TABLE 4-4   United States Federal Census Records—1790 Through 1930 (Used by permission of Aha! Seminars, Inc.) *(Continued)*

Census Year	Type of Document	Columns for Information	Comments
1880	Indian (or Native American) Schedule	■ Name of each individual in household (Indian and English) ■ Relationship to head of household ■ Age, gender ■ Marital/tribal status ■ Occupation ■ Land ownership	Native Americans were enumerated annually by the Indian Agent
1880	Mortality Schedule	Same as 1870 Mortality Schedule, plus the following: ■ Where disease was contracted ■ How long a resident of the area	
1880	Agricultural Schedule	Same as 1840 Agricultural Schedule	
1880	Manufacturing Schedule	Same as 1810 Manufacturing Schedule	Destroyed by act of Congress
1880	Social Statistics	Same as 1850 Social Statistics	
1880	Defective, Dependent and Delinquent Classes Schedules	Seven separate schedules to be compiled by the enumerator: ■ Schedule 1—Insane Inhabitants ■ Schedule 2—Idiots ■ Schedule 3—Deaf-Mutes ■ Schedule 4—Blind Inhabitants ■ Schedule 5—Homeless children (institutions) ■ Schedule 6—Inhabitants in Prison ■ Schedule 7—Pauper and Indigent Inhabitants	Includes inmates of asylums, orphanages, poor houses, almshouses, prisons, and other institutions, as well as those who the enumerator observed
1885	Population Schedule	Same as 1880 Population Schedule	Special census for which the federal government agreed to share 50 percent of the cost with any state or territory desiring another census Only five states/territories took advantage of this offer: ■ Colorado ■ Dakota Territory (only a part survives) ■ Florida (four counties missing) ■ Nebraska (two counties missing) ■ New Mexico Territory (four counties missing)

TABLE 4-4   United States Federal Census Records—1790 Through 1930 (Used by permission of Aha! Seminars, Inc.) *(Continued)*

Census Year	Type of Document	Columns for Information	Comments
1890	Population Schedule	Same as for 1880 Population Schedule, plus the following: ■ Ability to speak English ■ Rent or own home ■ Years in country, and if naturalized ■ Number of children born and number still living ■ Whether Civil War veteran or surviving spouse (in which case a separate schedule also was completed—see below)	■ Each family was listed on a single sheet. ■ Population Schedules destroyed by fire and water in fire at Commerce Building in January 1921. ■ Originals destroyed in mid-1930s.
1890	Indian (or Native American) Schedule	Same as 1880 Indian Schedule.	Destroyed in 1896 or 1897
1890	Mortality Schedule	Same as 1880 Mortality Schedule	Destroyed in 1896 or 1897
1890	Surviving Soldiers, Sailors, and Marines, and Widows, etc. Schedule	■ Name of veteran or surviving spouse ■ Age ■ Branch of service (Army, Navy, Marines) ■ Duration of service ■ Date of enlistment and discharge ■ Rank, company, regiment, and vessel ■ Disability	■ Survived the 1921 fire ■ Union veterans only, but a few Confederates are included ■ Partial returns; some counties missing ■ Originals destroyed in mid-1930s.
1890	Agricultural Schedule	Same as 1840 Agricultural Schedule	Destroyed in 1896 or 1897
1890	Manufacturing Schedule	Same as 1810 Manufacturing Schedule	Destroyed in 1896 or 1897
1900	Population Schedule	Same as 1890 Population Schedule, plus the following additional information: ■ Plus exact month and year of birth (only 1900) ■ Number of years married	This was the first census to enumerate United States citizens abroad.
1900	Indian (or Native American) Schedule	Same as 1880 Indian Schedule, plus the following: ■ Tribe of person and his/her parents ■ Degree of Indian or White blood ■ Education	Indian schedules often found at end of state or county returns.
1900	Agricultural Schedule	Same as 1840 Agricultural Schedule	
1900	Manufacturing Schedule	Same as 1810 Manufacturing Schedule	Destroyed by act of Congress

TABLE 4-4   United States Federal Census Records—1790 Through 1930 (Used by permission of Aha! Seminars, Inc.) *(Continued)*

Census Year	Type of Document	Columns for Information	Comments
1910	Population Schedule	Same as 1900 Population Schedule, plus the following additional information: ■ Year of arrival in United States ■ Whether veteran and which war (only on the 1910 census)	
1910	Indian Schedule	Same as 1900 Indian Schedule	
1910	Agricultural Schedule	Same as 1840 Agricultural Schedule	
1910	Manufacturing Schedule	Same as 1810 Manufacturing Schedule	Destroyed by act of Congress
1920	Population Schedule	Same as 1910 Population Schedule, plus the following additional information: ■ Native tongue	Note: Question regarding whether a veteran (on 1910 census) was not included.
1920	Indian Schedule	Same as 1900 Indian Schedule	
1930	Population Schedule	Same as 1920 Population Schedule plus the following additional information: ■ Whether owns a radio ■ Year of naturalization	Indians schedules often found at end of state or county returns.
1930	Indian Schedule	Same as 1900 Indian Schedule	

TABLE 4-4   United States Federal Census Records—1790 Through 1930 (Used by permission of Aha! Seminars, Inc.) *(Continued)*

Chapter 5

Further Your Research with Advanced Record Types

How to...

- Use ecclesiastical records to trace your family
- Obtain and analyze mortuary and funeral home records
- Read between the lines in obituaries
- Discover the wealth of information in cemetery records
- Get inside your ancestor's mind using wills and probate records
- Consider other institutional records

Expand Your Family's Story

You've learned a great deal about your family so far by locating and using home sources, vital records, and census resources. Along the way, you also have built a foundation for all of your future genealogical research. You now know how important it is to place your family into context, to conduct scholarly research, to analyze every piece of data you uncover, and to properly document your source materials.

You've made a lot of progress so far, but you probably have only just begun to scratch the surface of your family's rich history. There literally are hundreds of different records that may contain information of value in documenting your forebears' lives.

This chapter discusses some of the more important document types associated with your ancestor or family member's religion and those associated with the end of his or her life. They can provide a treasure trove of information and clues for you. You just need to know where to look, how to access the records, and how to properly analyze them. You will learn to apply those critical thinking skills to the evidence and formulate reasonable hypotheses, sometimes circumventing the "brick walls" that we all invariably encounter.

Use Ecclesiastical Records

Ecclesiastical records are those that relate to a church or some similar established institution. Organized religion has provided a source for scholarly philosophical and theological study and writing for many centuries. Documentation reaches far back into human history. Religious groups also have variously maintained documents concerning their operations, administration, and membership information. As a result, religious records of many types can provide rich genealogical details and clues to other records.

There are a number of challenges you will face in your search for and investigation into these ecclesiastical records. Let's discuss these first, and then we'll explore some of the types of records you might expect to find.

Locate the Right Institution

It is an easy task to contact the place of worship for yourself, your parents, and your siblings. The knowledge of the religious affiliation and where the family members attend worship services is pretty easy to come by. However, as we move backward in time, this information may become obscured. You may make the assumption that your ancestors belonged to the same religious denomination as your family does today, and you may be making a terrible error.

Not every member of a family necessarily belongs to the same church. My maternal grandmother's family is a prime example. Her father belonged to the Presbyterian Church and her mother to a Primitive Baptist congregation. Among their six sons and six daughters, I have found them to have been members of two Presbyterian, three Baptist, one Methodist, and one Christian Science churches. In addition, some of the people changed churches. Most notable was the entry I found in the First Presbyterian Church's membership roll dated 31 October 1926 for one of my great-aunts, which read, "Seen entering Christian Science Church." That clue pointed me to that church where I learned that she had formally joined and become a member of its congregation.

In some cases, prior to or upon marriage, one spouse may change his or her religious affiliation to that of the other. The Catholic and Jewish religions want to see children of a marital union raised in their faith, and formal religious instruction and conversion is common.

Determining the religion of an ancestor or other family member is an important part of your research because there may be any number of records to provide more information for your research and pointers to other records. Look for clues to the religion of a person in the name of the *clergy* who performed marriage ceremonies for the person *and* the spouse, for the person's parents, and for any siblings. Clergy names are sometimes found on marriage certificates created by churches, such as the one shown in Figure 5-1, and always on marriage licenses filed at government offices after the marriage ceremony has taken place. Look, too, at obituaries for officiating clergy at funerals and memorial services. It is often easy to determine the religious affiliation of the clergyperson and the organization to which he or she was attached in local historical records and city directories, and this can provide an important link.

The religious affiliation provides one level of information. However, your job is to determine the *right* institution to which your ancestor belonged. If the community in which he or she lived has multiple churches of the same denomination, you may have to contact or visit each one in order to determine if your person was a member. Your best strategy, however, is to start with the congregation located closest geographically to where your ancestor or family lived, and work outward. One parish or similar jurisdiction is a good place to start.

Determine What Records They Might Have Created

Once you have determined the religious affiliation of your person, it is important to learn something about the organization. Some groups are meticulous about documenting their organizational affairs and their membership information, while others are less inclined. The Catholic Church, for example, maintains thorough documentation of the church business and has created detailed documents about each member, including birth, baptism, christening, marriage, death, other

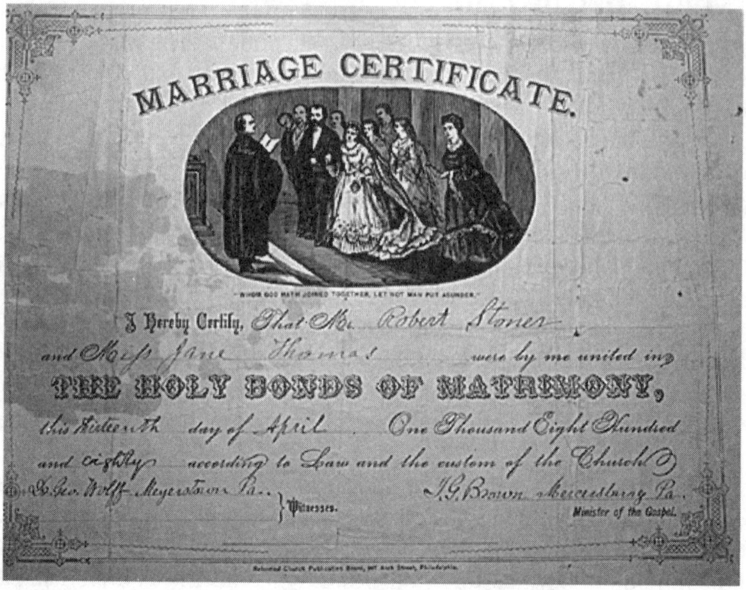

MARRIAGE CERTIFICATE.

I Hereby Certify, That Mr. Robert Stoner and Miss Jane Thomas were by me united in THE HOLY BONDS OF MATRIMONY, this Sixteenth day of April One Thousand Eight Hundred and eighty according to Law and the custom of the Church

G. Geo. Wolff Meyerstown Pa. } Witnesses.

J.G. Brown Mercersburg Pa.
Minister of the Gospel.

FIGURE 5-1 Marriage certificate issued by a church showing the name of the clergyman

sacramental and personal events, and even tithing records. I have found that Baptist records are far less detailed or revealing.

Invest some time understanding the history of the denomination and what types of records may have been created by a particular denomination to which your ancestor may have belonged. This will give you a foundation for your research. You will know what types of records to request when you make contact with the particular church or organization, where they were created and by whom, what information is likely to be contained in them, and where they were kept.

Locate the Records Today

Your most immediate consideration is where to locate the records *now*. Churches sometimes merge with one another, or a congregation finds itself no longer able to sustain itself financially and the church dissolves. What happens to the records?

Your understanding of the history and organization of the denomination can go a long way in helping you locate records. Your study will also help you identify the types of records that were created. For example, some Christian denominations may mark a person's first communion with a ceremony and issue a certificate such as the one shown in Figure 5-2, while others may only record the event in membership records. While an existing church location may have all of its records dating back to its founding, they may not necessarily be located on-site at that church. They may be stored in a rectory, parsonage, or vicarage. Records may have been moved to a central parish or diocesan office, or to a regional or national-level administrative or storage site.

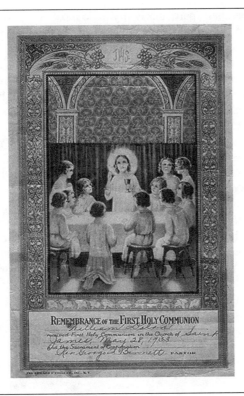

FIGURE 5-2   Certificate of first communion

A good strategy for determining the location of historical records is to contact the clergy or secretary at the specific house of worship. Having learned what records would have been created, you can ask about their availability and access to them. If the records have been moved or sent elsewhere, ask for a name and address of a contact and then follow up that lead.

If a congregation no longer exists or you can't find it, contact the local public library and any academic libraries in the area and ask the reference department to assist you in tracing the church and its records. The local, county, state, or provincial genealogical and historical societies are additional resources you should enlist in your research. Their in-depth knowledge of the area and religious groups can be invaluable. Indeed, they may have copied or transcribed indexes, and some ecclesiastical records may even have come into their possession.

Gain Access to the Records

Another challenge can be gaining access to or obtaining copies of the church records you want. Religious groups are, in effect, private organizations and have a right and an obligation to protect their privacy and that of their members. Most are willing to help you locate information about your ancestors and family members, particularly if you do most of the work. Remember that not all church office personnel are paid employees; some are simply members volunteering their time. Not all members of the office staff, and even members of the clergy, know what records they have and what is in them. The old books and papers in their offices may just be gathering dust in a closet or file cabinet. Few of these materials are indexed, such as the document shown in Figure 5-3, which was found among a sheaf of loose papers tucked into a cardboard box in a church office cabinet. It often takes a considerable effort to go through such documents and locate information that may relate to your family.

Be prepared to offer to help the person you contact in the church office. You may have to describe the types of record you are seeking and where they might look. Reluctance you encounter may be a result of the person's lack of knowledge and experience, lack of time, the cost of making and mailing copies for you, or some other reason. Be kind, patient, and friendly, and offer all the help you can. Be prepared to reimburse all the expenses and to make a donation to the congregation.

Sometimes you may be refused access outright. One woman I spoke with described a Catholic church office priest who told her that the records were sealed and that she could not obtain any information about her grandparents' membership in that church. She contacted the bishop and finally escalated her request to the archbishop of the archdiocese. He instructed the parish priest to provide what she sought. Unfortunately, though, the priest only provided photocopies of the face of a number of documents which did, in fact, also include additional data on the reverse.

The point here is to understand what may or may not be available, and be able to request access to specific materials in a knowledgeable and professional manner.

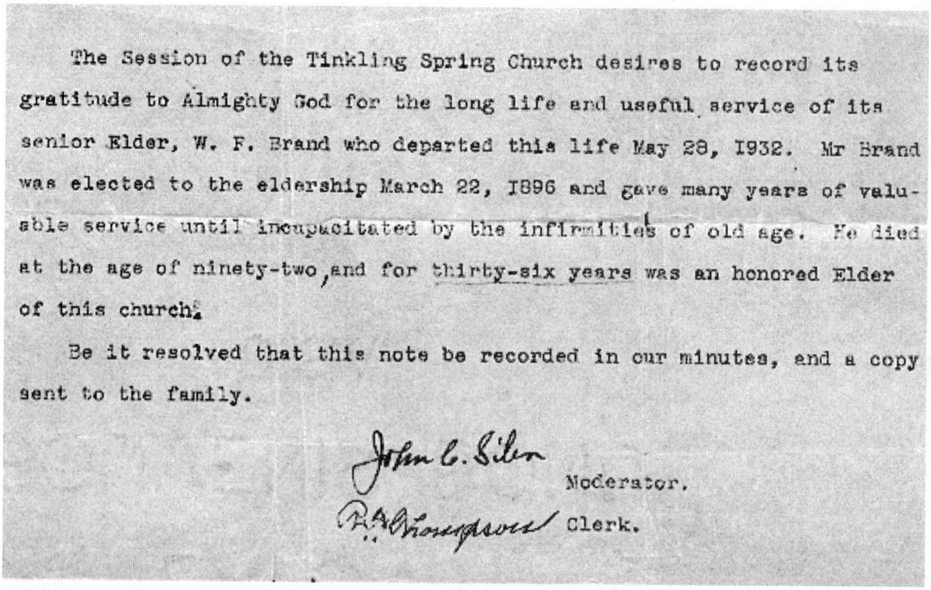

The Session of the Tinkling Spring Church desires to record its gratitude to Almighty God for the long life and useful service of its senior Elder, W. F. Brand who departed this life May 28, 1932. Mr Brand was elected to the eldership March 22, 1896 and gave many years of valuable service until incapacitated by the infirmities of old age. He died at the age of ninety-two, and for thirty-six years was an honored Elder of this church.

Be it resolved that this note be recorded in our minutes, and a copy sent to the family.

John C. Silen   Moderator.

R.A. Thompson   Clerk.

FIGURE 5-3   Loose document from the minutes of a church session commemorating the life and service of a member

Interpret, Evaluate, and Place the Records into Perspective

Once you obtain the documents you want, your next step is to read and review them. Interpretation can be a real challenge, particularly if the handwriting is poor, the copies are dim or illegible, or the document is written in a language you do not understand. Many church records are written in Latin, particularly those of the Catholic Church; however, you may encounter Jewish documents written in Hebrew, Russian documents written using the Cyrillic alphabet, and any number of foreign languages and dialects. Old English script and German Fraktur both resemble calligraphy and their character embellishments can be particularly difficult to read. Other older or archaic handwritten materials may be difficult or nearly impossible to decipher. You will want to consider obtaining books on the subject of paleography (the study of ancient writings and inscriptions) and using the skills or services of interpreters.

As with the other documentary evidence you have obtained, be prepared to evaluate the contents of the documents. Consider the information provided and use it to add to the overall chronological picture you are constructing of your ancestor or family member.

Consider a Variety of Ecclesiastical Records

Your research will present you with a vast array of potential information sources from religious organizations. The following is a list of some of the records you may encounter. Some are more common than others, and the list certainly will vary depending on denomination, time period, and the specific congregation.

Membership rolls	Certificates of membership	Records of excommunication
Meeting minutes	Committee minutes and reports	Hearings and inquiries
Birth records	Baptismal certificates	Christening records
Confirmation records	Records of *bar mitzvah* or *bat mitzvah*	First communion records
Marriage certificates	Records of divorce and annulment	Lists of elders and deacons
Clergy appointments	Office administrative records	Building plans and related documents
Missionary records	Fellowship group records	Photographs
Church bulletins	Newspapers and journals	Donation and tithing records
Death and burial records	Cemetery records	Sexton and administrator records

Any of these documents can provide clues about your ancestor or family member's life. Don't overlook the fact that membership records and meeting minutes also may record the previous place of membership for an individual. I was successful in tracing my maternal grandfather from the church in which he was a member when he died, back through three other churches in which he was a member, to the church in which he was baptized more than six decades before, all through notes of membership records. A church bulletin, such as the one shown in Figure 5-4, provided

First Baptist Church
MEBANE, N. C.

The Lord is in His holy temple,
Let all the earth keep silence before Him.
Habakkuk 2:20

L. H. Hollingsworth, Pastor
Telephones
Res. 3911—Study 3914

FIGURE 5-4 Church bulletins share news and may point to other church records (From the author's collection).

details of the election of another family member to the position of head deacon. And another church had a photograph of a grandfather at the ground-breaking ceremony for a new church building. You never know what you will find in the records of religious organizations.

Obtain and Analyze Mortuary and Funeral Home Records

Among some of the most detailed records compiled about a person are those that are created at the time of his or her death. The records of an ancestor or family member whose remains were handled by a mortuary or funeral home may hold many important clues. As with ecclesiastical records, it is important to do some research in advance to determine whether a mortuary's services were used and, if so, which mortuary it was.

A mortuary or funeral home performs a variety of functions, and someone usually selects the specific duties desired for the person who is deceased. Their activities may include providing a simple coffin or fancy casket, embalming and cosmetic preparation, clothing the corpse, arranging for or conducting services, providing transportation for the family, arranging for interment or cremation, and other more specialized services.

A mortuary or funeral home file for the handling of one person's arrangements can include many documents. You will usually find a copy of a document, such as a death certificate or coroner's report, in the file, along with an itemized accounting or invoice for all the services provided. Figure 5-5

Ray Funeral Home

119 NORTH MARKET STREET · MADISON, NC 27025 · (919) 548-9606

PAID

12-20-93

FORBIS & DICK
FUNERAL SERVICE

December 22, 1993

MR. CAREY MORGAN
3606 CALYX CT.
GREENSBORO, NC 27410

The Funeral for EDITH WEATHERLY MORGAN on November 21, 1993

We sincerely appreciate the confidence you have placed in us and
will continue to assist you in every way we can. Please feel free
to contact us if you have any questions in regard to this statement.

THE FOLLOWING IS AN ITEMIZED STATEMENT OF THE SERVICES, FACILITIES,
AUTOMOTIVE EQUIPMENT, AND MERCHANDISE THAT YOU SELECTED WHEN MAKING
THE FUNERAL ARRANGEMENTS.

SELECTED SERVICES OF FUNERAL DIRECTOR AND STAFF:
Local Removal . . . . $ 90.00
Embalming . . . . $ 300.00
Other Preparation . . . . $ 75.00
Director and Staff . . . . $ 760.00
SELECTED USE OF FACILITIES AND EQUIPMENT:
Other Use of Facilities . . . . $ 120.00
Use of Visitation Room . . . . $ 120.00
Equip. for Church Service . . . . $ 120.00
SELECTED USE OF AUTOMOTIVE EQUIPMENT:
Hearse . . . . $ 100.00
Family Vehicle . . . . $ 80.00
Utility Van . . . . $ 80.00
Service Vehicle . . . . $ 80.00

          FUNERAL HOME SERVICE CHARGES . . . . $ 1925.00

SELECTED MERCHANDISE:
Lexington Maple . . . . $ 2765.00
Continental . . . . $ 994.00
Register Books . . . . $ 25.00
Acknowledgement Cards . . . . $ 10.00
Rita Barber #6749 . . . . $ 100.00

THE COST OF OUR SERVICES, EQUIPMENT, AND MERCHANDISE
THAT YOU HAVE SELECTED. . . . . $ 5819.00

AT THE TIME FUNERAL ARRANGEMENTS WERE MADE, WE ADVANCED CERTAIN
PAYMENTS TO OTHERS AS AN ACCOMMODATION. THE FOLLOWING IS AN
ACCOUNTING FOR THOSE CHARGES.

EDITH WEATHERLY MORGAN
Page 1

FIGURE 5-5   Detail page from a funeral home invoice (From the author's collection)

shows a page of detail from a funeral home invoice. Information about the selection of a coffin or casket, the burial vault, and other commodities are often included. A mortuary is often called upon to prepare and handle placement of obituaries in newspapers and other communication media, and that information or a copy of the obituary information may be included. Look for copies of a cemetery deed and a burial permit, depending on the time period, place, and type of burial. These are the more common documents you might find in these files but occasionally you may find others, such as correspondence and photographs.

Mortuaries and funeral homes are private companies and, as such, are not required to provide copies of their business documents to genealogists. An owner or administrator may decline to provide access to you for reasons of business privacy or to protect the confidentiality of family information. They also are not required to retain and preserve records in perpetuity.

Many of these facilities have disappeared over the years, been sold, or gone out of business. Their records may have been transferred, lost, or destroyed. You may need to work with libraries, archives, and genealogical and/or historical societies to determine the disposition of their records. Some may have been preserved in the special collections of libraries, such as those of several funeral homes in Tampa, Florida, which are now residing in the University of South Florida's Tampa Library collection.

Read Between the Lines in Obituaries

We're all familiar with obituaries, those announcements of people's deaths that appear in the newspaper and other media, now including the Internet. These gems often contain a wealth of biographical information in condensed form. You can gather a lot from reading what is printed *and* from reading between the lines.

An obituary is definitely a secondary source of information. You will want to confirm and verify every piece of data listed there. The accuracy of the information included should always be considered questionable because errors can be introduced at any point in the publication process. The informant for the information may or may not be a knowledgeable family member, or the person may be under the stress of the occasion and provide inaccurate details. The newspaper or media person who takes down the information may make an error, a data entry operator may transcribe something incorrectly, and an editor may miss a typographical error.

Some of the information and clues you can look for in obituaries include the following:

- Name and age of the deceased
- Date, location, and sometimes cause of death
- Names of parents and siblings
- Names and/or numbers of children and grandchildren
- Places of residence of living relatives
- Names of and notes about deceased relatives

- Where and when deceased was born
- When deceased left his/her native land, perhaps even the port of entry and date
- Naturalization date and location
- Place(s) where deceased was educated
- Date and location of marriage, and name of spouse (sometimes maiden name)
- Religious affiliation and name of church or temple
- Military service information (branch, rank, dates served, medals, and awards)
- Place(s) of employment
- Public offices held
- Organizations to which he/she belonged
- Awards received
- Events in which he/she participated
- Name and address of funeral home or church where funeral was to occur
- Date and time of funeral
- Name(s) of officiating clergy
- List of pallbearers
- Date, place, and disposition of remains
- Statement regarding any memorial services
- Directions regarding donations or memorial gifts

I use obituaries as pointers to locate primary record sources. I certainly use them to help corroborate other sources of evidence, and to help verify names, dates, and locations of events. They may include the names and locations of other family members (and we hope they will be more accurate than that of my father), and they can identify alternative research paths to get past some of the "dead ends" I may have encountered.

One of my most successful uses of obituaries occurred when researching a great-grandmother. I had tried unsuccessfully for years to trace back and identify her parents. I finally visited the town where she lived in 1997 and was able to access the actual 1914 newspaper in which her obituary had been printed. The obituary included the names of three surviving sisters whose married names I had not known. Two of the three were dead ends, but records for the third sister and her husband were easily located. I transferred my research attention to that sister and pretty quickly was able to identify and locate the parents' records. I then used a will to "connect downward" and prove that my great-grandmother was one of their children. Suddenly the doors opened and, within a matter of months, I had traced my lineage back to a great-great-great-grandfather who fought in the American Revolution and obtained copies of his military service and pension records.

Locate and Delve into Cemetery Records

Most people's perception is that a cemetery is a lonely place, devoid of any activity other than the interment of remains and the visits by families and friends of those who have passed before. However, if you have ever participated in the process of making arrangements for a family member, spouse or partner, or a friend, you know that there can be a lot of paperwork involved. And where there is paperwork, there are pieces of potentially valuable genealogical evidence. Some of these materials are accessible to you, the researcher, and others are not. However, let's examine the processes involved with handling the death of an individual and the documentation that may have been created.

Cemeteries are much more than graveyards. They are representations in a community of the society, culture, architecture, and the sense of the community. Many genealogists and family historians arrive at a cemetery, wander around looking for gravestones, copy down the names and dates, perhaps take a few photographs, and then leave, thinking they have found all there is to be found. In many cases, they have merely drifted past what might have been a treasure trove.

It is important to know that a tombstone and other types of markers aren't necessarily the only records to be found associated with cemeteries. You also should recognize that these memorial markers are not necessarily accurate *primary sources* of evidence. That is because the markers are not always created at or near the time of death. While they may have been, you cannot always determine if that is the case. Also, understand that the information carved on a tombstone or cast in a metal marker is actually a transcription of data provided, and that one or more errors may have been made. For example, there is a rather large granite marker in an old cemetery in Tampa, Florida, on which an incorrect name was carved. Rather than replace the entire stone, the stone cutter returned to the cemetery, struck a line through the incorrect letter in the name, and carved the correct letter above the name. Perhaps it seems pretty tacky, but it is true.

Someone or some organization owns and is responsible for a cemetery. A visit to the local city government office that issues burial permits, to the office that handles land and tax records, or to the closest mortuary can usually provide you with the name of the owner or a contact individual. The next step is to make contact with the person or agency responsible for the maintenance of the cemetery. That may be an administrator or sexton, and this contact may yield important information.

Cemeteries typically consist of lots that are subdivided into plots into which persons' remains are interred. Someone owns the lot and has authorized the burials there. If a government is involved, there may have been a burial permit created to allow a grave to be opened and an individual's remains to be interred. Other documents may well have been created and all of these can potentially have been given to the cemetery administrator or sexton for inclusion in the cemetery's files. As a result, making contact with the cemetery may help you obtain copies of documents that are available nowhere else. Let me give you a few examples.

When I was searching for the burial location of my great-grandparents, Green Berry Holder and his wife, nee Penelope Swords, I knew they were buried in Rome, Georgia, in the Myrtle Hill Cemetery. I contacted the Rome city administrative offices to determine who was responsible for the cemetery's administration and maintenance. I was directed to the Rome Cemetery Department, which is responsible for all five of the municipal cemeteries. I made a call and spoke with the sexton of Myrtle Hill Cemetery. He was able to quickly pull the records for Green Berry Holder while we were on the telephone and told me the following:

- The date of the original purchase of the cemetery lot
- The identification information of the lot (lot number and location)
- The names of each person buried in the lot, their date of death, their ages, and the dates of their interments
- The date on which two plots in the lot were resold to the owner of an adjacent lot

I also asked about a great-uncle, Edward Holder, whom I believed was also buried in that cemetery. There was, in fact, a joint grave marker for him and his wife, shown in Figure 5-6, although his year of death was incomplete. I had assumed that he was buried there; however, the sexton told me that only his wife was interred in this cemetery. It turned out that my Great-uncle Ed actually was buried in another municipal cemetery on the other side of town beside another woman bearing his surname. I learned that he had a *second* marriage about which neither I nor anyone else in the family was aware.

Based on the information the sexton was able to provide, I had much better details with which to research my family members interred in both of the cemeteries. I also had information about approximate dates of death that I followed to the Floyd County Health Department to obtain copies of all the death certificates. I also headed to the county courthouse for a marriage record for my Great-uncle Ed's second marriage and to the library to work with microfilmed newspapers, looking

 FIGURE 5-6   Grave marker for my great-uncle, who is buried in another cemetery (From the author's collection)

for marriage announcements and obituaries. Had I located the obituary of the great-uncle earlier, I would have known he was buried in the other cemetery *and* that he was survived by his second wife.

These clues led me to others, including the name of the current owner of the local funeral home that handled most of the family members' funerals over the decades, and to church records, land and property records, and more.

An on-site visit to the cemetery sexton's office also provided me the opportunity to see the physical files maintained there. My great-grandmother, Penelope Swords Holder, died prior to Georgia's requirement that counties issue death certificates. However, there were copies of her obituary, a burial permit, and a note to the sexton from my great-grandfather asking that my great-grandmother be buried in a specific plot adjacent to one of their grandchildren. In addition, the sexton checked an ancient interment ledger and found recorded there the cause of death— pneumonia. This was important because of the absence of a death certificate, and it confirmed the family story of her cause of death.

There are other documents that you may find in a cemetery's office. These include requests for burial, such as the ones shown in Figures 5-7 and 5-8. A burial permit, such as the one shown in Figure 5-9, is often required in order to control and keep track of the interment, and as another source of local tax revenue.

Transit permits are used to facilitate the movement of human remains from one political jurisdiction to another. Two examples are shown in Figures 5-10 and 5-11. These documents were usually completed in multiple copies. The original document accompanied the body to the place

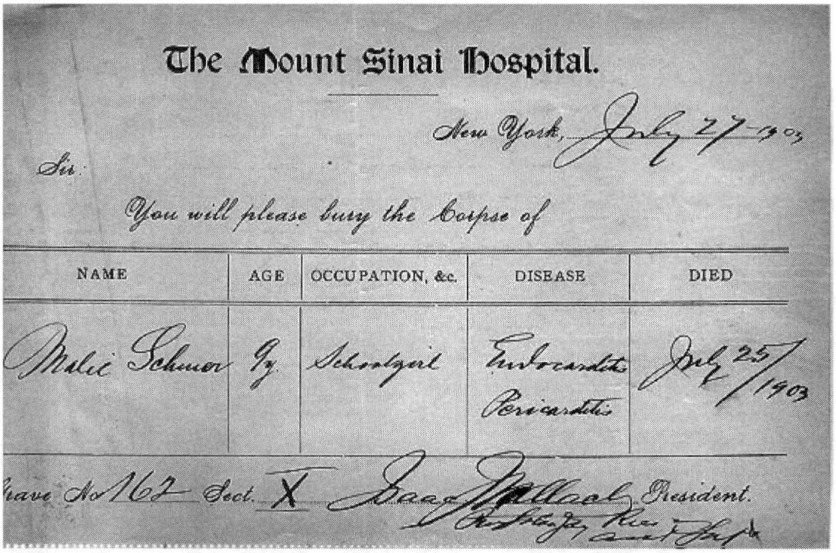

FIGURE 5-7   A request for burial found in a cemetery file (From the author's collection)

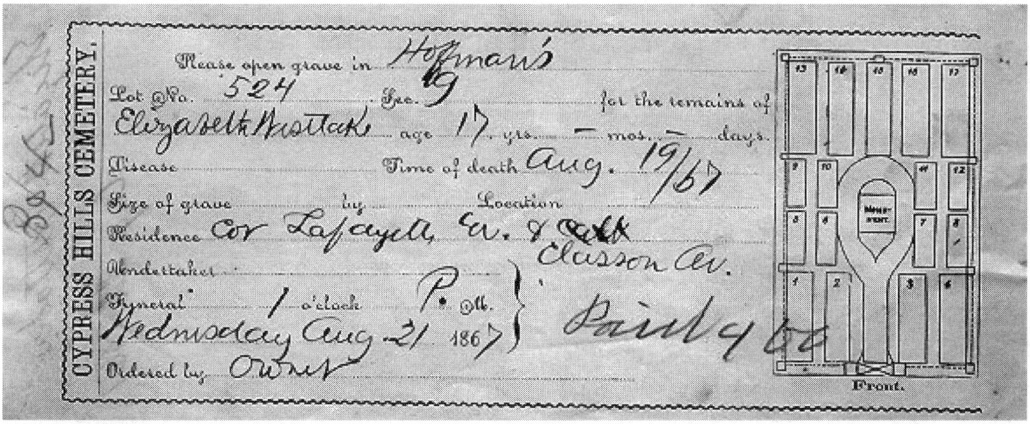

CYPRESS HILLS CEMETERY,

Please open grave in Hoffman's

Lot No. 524 Sec. 9 for the remains of

Elizabeth Westlake age 17 yrs. — mos. — days.

Disease Time of death Aug. 19/67

Size of grave by Location

Residence Cor Lafayette Av. & Classon Av.

Undertaker

Funeral 1 o'clock P. M.

Wednesday Aug 21 1867

Ordered by Owner

Paid 4 00

Front.

FIGURE 5-8 Cemetery's form requesting the opening of a grave (From the author's collection)

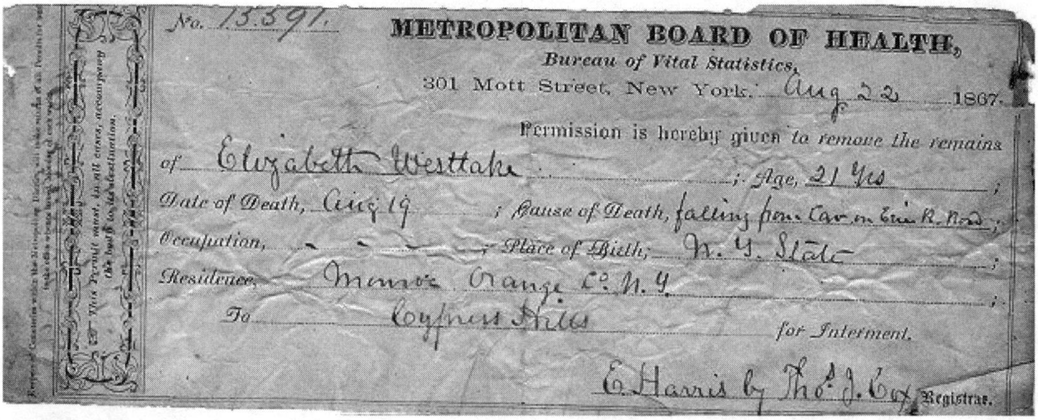

No. 13591.

METROPOLITAN BOARD OF HEALTH,

Bureau of Vital Statistics,

301 Mott Street, New York. Aug 22 1867.

Permission is hereby given *to remove the remains*

of Elizabeth Westlake *; Age,* 21 Yrs *;*

Date of Death, Aug 19 *; Cause of Death,* falling from Car on Erie R. Road *;*

Occupation, — *; Place of Birth,* N. Y. State *;*

Residence, Monroe Orange Co. N. Y. *;*

To Cypress Hills *for Interment.*

E. Harris by Thos. J. Cox Registrar.

FIGURE 5-9 A burial permit from New York, 1867 (From the author's collection)

of final interment, while one copy (or coupon) was retained by the issuing governmental office and others may have been provided to the transportation carrier(s). A transit permit, such as the one shown in Figure 5-10, may have contained a significant amount of information about the deceased, including the age, address, cause of death, the names of the physician and coroner, the name of the undertaker, and the mode of transportation.

Other transit permit formats provided very little information, such as the example shown in Figure 5-11. Transit permits were used when shipping bodies of soldiers back home from other locations, and a copy may be found in the mortuary records, in cemetery files, and in existing military personnel files.

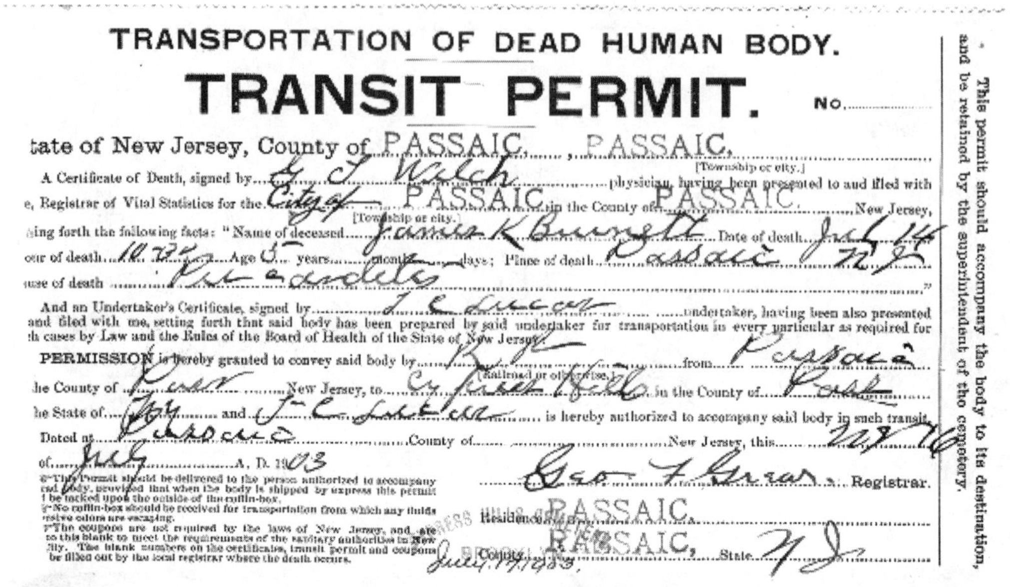

TRANSPORTATION OF DEAD HUMAN BODY.

TRANSIT PERMIT. No.......

tate of New Jersey, County of PASSAIC, PASSAIC,
[Township or city.]

A Certificate of Death, signed by E. J. Walch physician, having been presented to and filed with e, Registrar of Vital Statistics for the City of PASSAIC in the County of PASSAIC, New Jersey,
[Township or city.]
ing forth the following facts: "Name of deceased James K Burnett Date of death July 14
our of death 10 AM Age 5 years months days; Place of death Passaic N.J.
use of death

And an Undertaker's Certificate, signed by ...... undertaker, having been also presented and filed with me, setting forth that said body has been prepared by said undertaker for transportation in every particular as required for h cases by Law and the Rules of the Board of Health of the State of New Jersey,

PERMISSION is hereby granted to convey said body by ...... from Passaic
[Railroad or otherwise.]
he County of ...... New Jersey, to ...... in the County of ......
he State of ...... and ...... is hereby authorized to accompany said body in such transit.

Dated at Passaic County of ...... New Jersey, this ...... of July A. D. 1903

...... Registrar.

Residence PASSAIC.
County PASSAIC, State N.J.

This permit should be delivered to the person authorized to accompany the body, provided that when the body is shipped by express this permit be tacked upon the outside of the coffin-box.
No coffin-box should be received for transportation from which any fluids offensive odors are escaping.
The coupons are not required by the laws of New Jersey, and are to this blank to meet the requirements of the sanitary authorities in New York City. The blank numbers on the certificate, transit permit and coupons be filled out by the local registrar where the death occurs.

This permit should accompany the body to its destination, and be retained by the superintendent of the cemetery.

FIGURE 5-10 This 1903 transit permit contains many details that can be researched (From the author's collection).

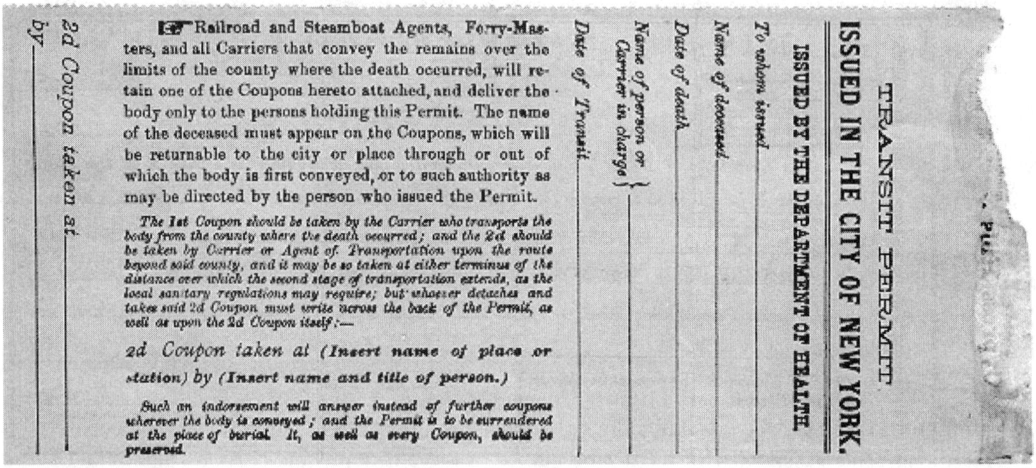

TRANSIT PERMIT

ISSUED IN THE CITY OF NEW YORK.

ISSUED BY THE DEPARTMENT OF HEALTH.

To whom issued

Name of deceased

Date of death

Name of person or Carrier in charge

Date of Transit

Railroad and Steamboat Agents, Ferry-Masters, and all Carriers that convey the remains over the limits of the county where the death occurred, will retain one of the Coupons hereto attached, and deliver the body only to the persons holding this Permit. The name of the deceased must appear on the Coupons, which will be returnable to the city or place through or out of which the body is first conveyed, or to such authority as may be directed by the person who issued the Permit.

The 1st Coupon should be taken by the Carrier who transports the body from the county where the death occurred; and the 2d should be taken by Carrier or Agent of Transportation upon the route beyond said county, and it may be so taken at either terminus of the distance over which the second stage of transportation extends, as the local sanitary regulations may require; but whoever detaches and takes said 2d Coupon must write across the back of the Permit, as well as upon the 2d Coupon itself:—

2d Coupon taken at ***(Insert name of place or station) by (Insert name and title of person.)***

Such an indorsement will answer instead of further coupons wherever the body is conveyed; and the Permit is to be surrendered at the place of burial. It, as well as every Coupon, should be preserved.

2d Coupon taken at

by

FIGURE 5-11 This City of New York transit permit provides less information, but can still provide clues to a death certificate (From the author's collection).

Search for burial and transit permit records in the county or municipal district in which the death occurred.

Search for Other Death-Related Documents

Death certificates, obituaries, and burial permits are not the only documents relating to death that you may locate that contain genealogical information. Nor are mortuaries, funeral homes, and cemeteries the only places to look for these documents.

Table 5-1 includes a number of important documents, data that they may contain, and where you may search for them.

Get Inside Your Ancestor's Mind Using Wills and Probate Records

Wills and probate packets are among the most interesting and revealing sets of records you can find for an individual. A person's last will may be one of the most honest statements about his or her relationships with other family members and friends. And the probate packet's contents can provide information and insights into the person that you may never find anywhere else.

Understand the Meaning of a Will and Testament

Let's first discuss some of the terminology. A *will* is a legal document in which a person specifies the disposition of his or her property after death. The person who makes the will is called the *testator,* and the will may also be referred to as the *last will and testament.* At the time the testator dies, he or she is referred to as the *decedent* or the *deceased.* The process of proving a will's authenticity or validity is called *probate,* taken from the Latin words *probatim* or *probare,* which means "to examine." The legal body responsible for reviewing and examining materials related to the handling of an estate is the *probate court.* The person appointed by the court to oversee or administer the affairs of the estate during the probate process is known as the *executor* or, in cases where a woman is appointed, the *executrix.*

Depending on the size of the estate and/or the amount of detail to which the testator went, a will may be a short document or a lengthy one. A will does not need to be drawn up by a lawyer or solicitor; an individual may write his or her own. It is a legal document so long as it is signed by the testator. Usually, however, it is advisable to have two or more witnesses to the signing of the document. This makes the probate process, or proving of the will, simpler because it assures that the signature or mark of the testator is genuine.

If the testator decides to change the will after it is made and signed, a new will can be drawn up, signed, and witnessed. Sometimes, if there are minor changes or if there is an expedient required (such as an interim change to a will while an entirely new one is being drawn up), a codicil can be drafted and signed. A codicil is simply a supplement to a will, usually containing an addition or a modification to the original will.

Type of Document and Description of Its Use	Cemetery-Related Information You Likely Will Find on the Document	Where You Are Likely to Locate the Document
Death Certificate—Used to document a death. It is an excellent *primary source* for death information, but a *secondary source* for all other information. Death certificates may not exist in many places prior to 1900. Consult *Ancestry's Red Book* for specifics in U.S.	▪ Date and place of death ▪ Name of mortuary or funeral home handling body ▪ Name and location of the place of interment	▪ County department of health ▪ County courthouse ▪ Government offices of health or vital statistics ▪ Mortuary or funeral home records ▪ Files of the cemetery administrator or sexton
Coroner's Report—Used to document cases of unusual, suspicious, or accidental death.	▪ Date and place of death ▪ Cause of death ▪ Name of mortuary or funeral home handling the body ▪ Name(s) of investigating officials ▪ Final determination	▪ Office of the coroner or medical examiner ▪ Courthouse with jurisdiction over location of death at the time ▪ Probate court records ▪ Other court records
Transit Permit—Used to document the movement of the deceased's remains from one political jurisdiction to another, i.e., state to state or country to country.	▪ Date and place of death ▪ Cause of death ▪ Sometimes includes the address and age of the decedent ▪ Name and location of the originating mortuary or funeral home ▪ Name and location of the destination mortuary or funeral home ▪ Sometimes includes the name and location of the place of interment	▪ Government office of the place of origin of the body's departure ▪ County department of health ▪ County courthouse ▪ State department of health or vital statistics ▪ Mortuary or funeral home records ▪ Files of the cemetery administrator or sexton
Burial Permit—Used to record the opening of a grave and allow the interment of remains. This may be issued by the government entity that had ownership and administrative control of the cemetery.	▪ Name of the deceased ▪ Date and place of death ▪ Name of cemetery ▪ Interment location (lot and plot identity, tomb or mausoleum identity, or columbarium identity) ▪ Scheduled date of interment	▪ Issuing agency, usually the owner or administrator of a municipal-, county-, state-, or federal-owned/operated cemetery ▪ Files of the mortuary or funeral home

TABLE 5-1   Other Death-Related Documents and Where to Locate Them (Table Used Courtesy of Aha! Seminars, Inc.)

Type of Document and Description of Its Use	Cemetery-Related Information You Likely Will Find on the Document	Where You Are Likely to Locate the Document
	■ Name and location of mortuary or funeral home ■ Sometimes name of the person or company authorized to open and close the grave ■ Authorizing agency, signature, and date of issue	■ Files of the cemetery administrator or sexton for the cemetery ■ For military service personnel, seek a permit for a burial in a military cemetery in the individual's military personnel file
Interment Ledger—Used in some cemeteries in older times to record interments.	■ Name of the deceased ■ Date of death ■ Sometimes includes the cause of death and location ■ Location of interment in the cemetery ■ Date of interment	■ Office of the cemetery administrator or sexton for the cemetery
Cemetery Lot Deed or Land Title—Used to record the sale of a cemetery lot and sometimes the sale of individual plots.	■ Name of purchaser ■ Name of seller ■ Date of the sale ■ Location and description of the lot (or plot) ■ Amount paid for the parcel	■ Office of the cemetery administrator or sexton for the cemetery ■ May also be recorded in county clerk's office along with other property records ■ May find a copy in the files of the mortuary or funeral home that handled the arrangements, particularly if this was the first interment in the lot
Obituary—Used to publicly announce a death, location, and date(s) of arrangements.	■ Name of deceased ■ Date and location of death ■ May contain extensive or abbreviated information about the person's life, survivors, and other personal information ■ Date and location of funeral or other services ■ Location of interment	■ Newspapers, church bulletins and newsletters (local and regional), union and fraternal organization publications, professional publications ■ Libraries and archives with microfilmed holdings of the above publications ■ Internet-based obituary transcriptions

TABLE 5-1 Other Death-Related Documents and Where to Locate Them (Table Used Courtesy of Aha! Seminars, Inc.) *(Continued)*

Type of Document and Description of Its Use	Cemetery-Related Information You Likely Will Find on the Document	Where You Are Likely to Locate the Document
Public Notices—Used to advertise a death, and both to announce the collection of debts for the estate and to request presentation of claims.	■ Name of deceased ■ Date of death and residence ■ Name of administrator ■ Sometimes place of death and place of interment are listed if different than place of residence	■ Newspapers ■ Libraries and archives with microfilmed holdings of the newspapers ■ Estate and probate packets ■ Probate court minutes
Cemetery Canvasses and Gravestone Transcription Projects—Compilations and publications to record the interments in a cemetery or other place of interment for posterity.	■ Any information inscribed or cast onto a tombstone or other grave marker ■ May or may not be all-inclusive, including epitaph ■ May or may not include photographs ■ May or may not be published	■ Genealogical societies in the area and at the state level ■ Historical societies as above ■ Libraries and archives ■ Genealogy society periodicals, which can be located using the Periodical Source Index (PERSI) online at Ancestry.com and then ordered from genealogical libraries
County and Local Histories—Used to record information of historical significance in a specific geographical area.	■ May contain a variety of information about individuals, families, ethnic groups, and other facts to help you locate religious, public, private, and family places of interment	■ Genealogical societies in the area and at the state level ■ Historical societies as above ■ Libraries and archives
Military Histories and Regimental Histories—Used to record information of historical significance relating to a specific military event or military unit.	■ May contain a variety of information about individuals serving in the military, their families, ethnic groups, and other facts to help you locate religious, public, private, family, and military places of interment	■ Genealogical societies in the area and at the state level ■ Historical societies as above ■ Libraries and archives

TABLE 5-1 Other Death-Related Documents and Where to Locate Them (Table Used Courtesy of Aha! Seminars, Inc.) *(Continued)*

Type of Document and Description of Its Use	Cemetery-Related Information You Likely Will Find on the Document	Where You Are Likely to Locate the Document
Military Service Papers—Records used to document the military service and pension information for an individual.	■ May contain a variety of information about an individual and his or her military service. May also include information about death benefits paid and interment in a military cemetery in the U.S. or abroad	■ Military service and pension files (different locations) ■ American Battle Monuments Commission Web site (for WWI, WWII, Korean War, and Vietnam War) at **http://www. abmc.gov** ■ Other Web-based sites
Funeral or Condolence Books—Provided by the mortuary or funeral home to allow persons visiting the family of the deceased to sign their name and write a message.	■ May contain a variety of information, but also may specify date and location of interment	■ Family effects
Web Sites—Many Web sites contain information related to places of interment.	■ The Internet contains a wealth of information concerning deaths and interments, and using a search engine can be of some assistance	■ Ancestry.com databases (**http://www.ancestry.com**) ■ RootsWeb databases (**http://www.rootsweb.com**) ■ USGenWeb Project (**http://www.usgenweb.org**) ■ WorldGenWeb Project (**http://www.worldgenweb.org**)

TABLE 5-1   Other Death-Related Documents and Where to Locate Them (Table Used Courtesy of Aha! Seminars, Inc.) *(Continued)*

The Probate Process Defined

The United States, Canada, and Australia are all influenced by medieval English law and legal customs. The terms "will" and "testament" originally referred to separate portions of an individual's estate, and the documents were usually separate documents handled by separate courts. A "will" was used to dispose of one's real property, or real estate, and the "testament" was used to bequeath personal property. A study of history in the British Isles will reveal that the courts used to probate an estate changed over time from ecclesiastical ones to civil courts. In Wales and England, the last will and testament became a single probated entity and this spread to other places. If you are researching wills and probate in the U.K., an understanding of the history of the process, the courts, their jurisdictions, and the documents' contents in England, Wales, Scotland, and Ireland, respectively, is essential.

In the United States, though, the use of the singular last will and testament document is generally found to be the norm. This is the case of the probate process we will explore below. Of course, there are exceptions and special circumstances as with any legal documentary process. However, in the interest of clarifying the probate process, let's focus on a rather straightforward definition.

A person's last will and testament is intended to express his or her wishes for what is to be done with their possessions after death, as illustrated in the case of Isaac Mitchell whose will is shown in Figures 5-12 and 5-13. In some cases, there are heavy religious overtones to the document. This is perhaps understandable under the circumstances because, at the time this document is written, the testator is giving careful thought, no doubt, to meeting their Maker. In many cases, a person's will may include instructions concerning the disposition of their body, funeral directions, and/or memorial instructions. A will may be revoked through the creation of a new will or through a document known as a codicil. A codicil can be used to revoke and/or amend specific sections

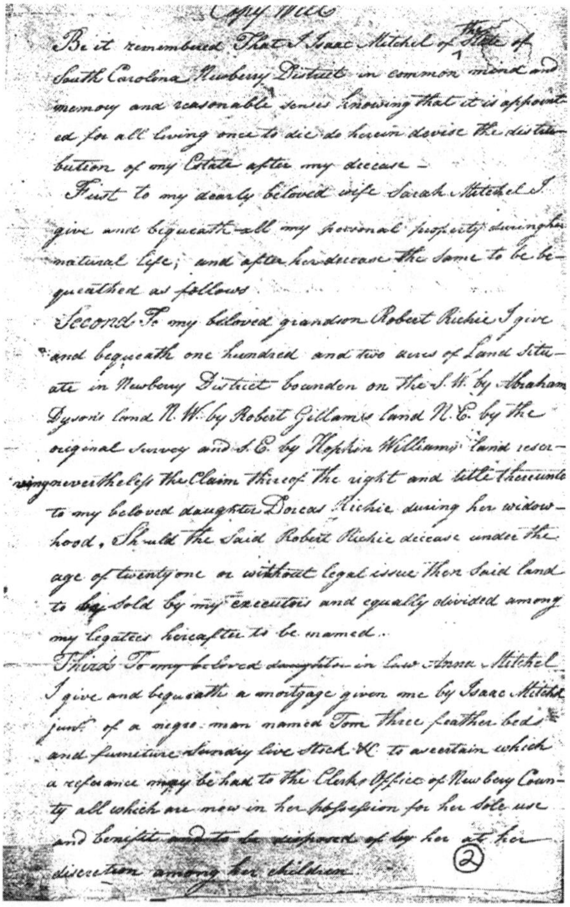
Copy Will
Be it remembered That I Isaac Mitchel of the State of
South Carolina Newberry District in common mind and
memory and reasonable senses knowing that it is appointed for all living once to die do herein devise the distribution of my Estate after my decease –
First to my dearly beloved wife Sarah Mitchel I
give and bequeath all my personal property during her
natural life; and after her decease the same to be bequeathed as follows
Second To my beloved grandson Robert Richie I give
and bequeath one hundred and two acres of Land Situate in Newberry District bounded on the S.W. by Abraham
Dyson's land N.W. by Robert Gillam's land N.E. by the
original survey and S.E. by Hopkin Williams land reserving nevertheless the Claim thereof the right and title thereunto
to my beloved daughter Dorcas Richie during her widow-
hood, Should the Said Robert Richie decease under the
age of twenty one or without legal issue then Said land
to be Sold by my executors and equally divided among
my legatees hereafter to be named..
~~Third To my beloved daughter in law Anna Mitchel~~
I give and bequeath a mortgage given me by Isaac Mitchel
jun. of a negro man named Tom three feather beds
and furniture Sundry live Stock &c to ascertain which
a reference may be had to the Clerks Office of Newberry County all which are now in her possession for her sole use
and benefit ~~and to be disposed of by her at her~~
~~discretion among her children~~ ②

FIGURE 5-12 Page one of the will of Isaac Mitchell of Newberry District, South Carolina, taken from the copy transcribed into the county will book (From the author's collection)

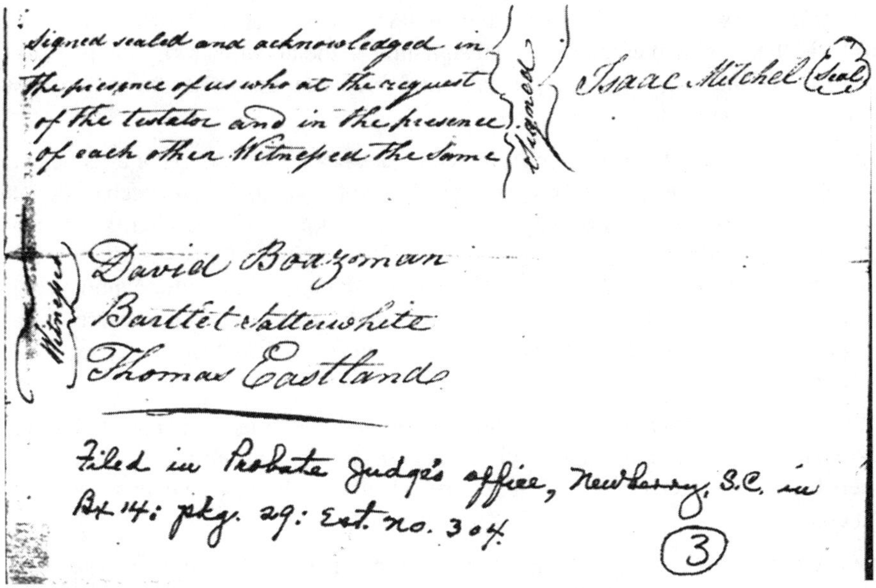
Signed sealed and acknowledged in the presence of us who at the request of the testator and in the presence of each other Witnessed the Same

Signed

Isaac Mitchel (Seal)

Witnessed

David Boazman
Bartlet Satterwhite
Thomas Eastland

Filed in Probate Judge's office, Newberry, S.C. in Bx 14: pkg. 29: Est. no. 304

(3)

FIGURE 5-13 Signature area of Isaac Mitchell's will showing names of the witnesses and the probate clerk's filing reference details (From the author's collection)

of a will without the person having to write an entirely new will. It may also be used to append additional, supplemental instructions to an existing will. In all cases, however, a will or codicil must be signed by the individual and witnessed by at least two other persons. Sometimes the document is also witnessed by a notary public.

The probate process is a legal procedure intended to certify that a person's estate is properly disposed of, and the process has changed very little over the past centuries. Where there is a will and it is presented to a court to be proved, there is usually a probate process that takes place. In cases where a person dies without having written or left a will, also known as *intestate,* a court may become involved in making sure the person's estate is correctly valued, divided, and distributed to appropriate beneficiaries.

While there may be some special conditions of a will or codicil that add additional steps to the process, here's how a simple probate process works:

1. The testator/testatrix makes his/her will and any subsequent codicil(s).
2. The testator/testatrix dies.
3. Someone involved in the testator/testatrix's legal affairs or estate presents the will/codicil(s) to a special court of law called the probate court. The probate court and its judge are concerned with the body of law devoted to processing estates. (Minutes and notes concerning the estate and any probate court proceedings related to the estate are recorded throughout the process and should not be overlooked in your research of the estate.)

4. The will/codicil(s) are recorded by the probate court. The persons who witnessed the testator/testatrix's signature are called upon to testify or attest to, in person or by sworn affidavit, that they witnessed the actual signature to the document(s). This is part of the "proving" of the will—that it is the authentic document on which the testator/testatrix signed his/her name.

5. The probate court assigns an identifying code, usually a number, to the estate and enters it into the court's records. A probate packet is created for the court into which all documents pertaining to the settlement of the estate are placed. If the will or codicil(s) named one or more persons to act as the executor/executrix and/or administrator of the estate, the probate court issues what is called Letters Testamentary. (If a named executor cannot or will not serve, the court may name another person to act in that capacity.) This document authorizes that person or persons to act on behalf of the estate in conducting business related to settling all fiduciary claims.

6. Potential beneficiaries named in the will/codicil(s) are identified and contacted. If any are deceased, evidence to that effect is obtained and, if the intent of the will indicates that others besides the deceased beneficiaries are to benefit from the estate, they are identified and contacted.

7. The executor/executrix and/or administrator publishes a series of notices, usually in the newspapers where the testator/testatrix lived, concerning the estate. Persons having claims on or owing obligations to the estate are thereby given notice that they have a specified amount of time to respond.

8. The executor/executrix and/or administrator conducts an inventory of the estate and prepares a written list of all assets, including personal property, real estate, financial items (cash, investments, loans, and other instruments), and any other materials that might be a part of the estate.

9. The executor/executrix and/or administrator will settle any debts, outstanding claims, or obligations of the estate, and then prepare an adjusted inventory of the deceased's assets. This document, along with any supporting materials, is submitted to the probate court, and becomes a permanent part of the probate packet.

10. The probate clerk reviews all the documentation for completeness and submits it to the probate judge for review. The probate court rules that the estate is now ready for distribution to beneficiaries.

11. Inheritance taxes and other death duties are paid.

12. The estate is divided and distributed and, in many cases, beneficiaries are required to sign a document confirming their receipt of their legacies.

13. Following the distribution, the executor/executrix and/or administrator prepares a final statement of account and presents it to the probate court.

14. The probate court rules that the estate has been properly processed, that all assets have been divided and distributed, and that the estate is closed.

15. The probate packet is filed in the records of the probate court.

16. The estate is closed.

Special arrangements in wills and codicils, such as trusts and long-term bequests, may involve additional steps in the process. In some cases, the final settlement of an estate may be deferred for many years until certain conditions are satisfied. A trust, for instance, may require the establishment of a separate legal entity, and the estate may not be settled until a later date. Some people leave wills that skip a generation, perhaps leaving monies to grandchildren, in which case the estate may not be settled for a generation or more and may require extended administration. In the case of any estate whose settlement extends to multiple years, the executor/executrix and/or administrator must prepare annual reports to the probate court. These are entered into the probate court record and the reports usually are placed into the probate packet.

During the process, the executor/executrix and/or administrator likely may pay to publish one or more notices in the press as a public notice that all claims against the deceased's estate should be presented and all debts owed to the estate are to be presented by a specific date. As a result, not only will you be looking in the courthouse and the probate court minutes and files, but you also should be looking in the local newspapers and other publications.

Learn What a Will Can Tell You—Literally and by Implication

Some of the most interesting insights into an individual's personality and his or her relationships with other family members can be found by looking at probate records. A wife may have been provided for through a trust. It is not unusual in older wills to see a bequest such as, "To my beloved wife, Elizabeth, I leave her the house for her use for her lifetime, after which it is to be sold and proceeds divided between my children." One of the most amusing bequests I've seen was, "I leave my wife, Addie, the bed, her clothes, the ax and the mule." What a generous husband! However, the husband actually may have, legally, owned all of his wife's clothing.

Farther back, you will find that laws sometimes dictated that the eldest son inherited all of the estate, a custom known as the law of primogeniture. Sometimes the eldest son is not listed in the will at all because this law dictated that all real property automatically came to him. In other cases, the eldest son may be named and may be given a double share of the otherwise equally divided estate.

You will often see a father leave his daughter's share of his estate to her husband. Why? Often it was because a woman was not allowed to own real property or because it was felt that she could not manage the affairs of the bequest. Sometimes, because a father may have settled a dowry on his daughter when she married, the father's bequest may be a smaller one than to other, unmarried sisters. It is also possible that a will may leave an unmarried daughter a larger amount than her sisters, in order to make them equal in their overall share of the father's estate.

A father who did not possess a large estate may have made arrangements for the placement of a son as an apprentice or indentured servant. This was a common means of guaranteeing the care and education of a son when there would not have been enough from the estate to support him. If you find such a statement in a will, investigate court records for the formalization of the arrangement. The guardian became responsible by law for the apprentice or servant.

The absence of a specific child's name may indicate that he or she is deceased. It may indicate that the child has moved elsewhere and has not been heard from for some considerable time. It might also indicate some estrangement, especially if you can determine that the child was, in fact, still alive at the time of the death. Otherwise, it is more likely that the testator would leave an equal part to that child and the court would probably have charged the executor with locating the child.

It also is possible that, before a will was prepared and signed, an individual may have personally prepared an inventory of his or her possessions or may have engaged the services of an appraiser. Such an inventory would help determine the value of items of real and personal property and therefore facilitate the decisions concerning how to divide them in an equitable fashion.

Examine the Contents of a Probate Packet

You may be amazed at what is or isn't in a probate packet. Some courts are very meticulous in their maintenance of the packets, in which case you may find vast amounts of documents. Other courts are less thorough, and documents may have been misplaced, incorrectly filed, lost, or even destroyed. It is important when examining probate packets to also review probate court minutes for details. (I once found a missing document from one ancestor's probate packet filed in the packet of another person's packet whose estate was heard the same day in court. It had been misfiled.)

- **Will** These documents are the core of a probate packet and include names of heirs and beneficiaries, and often the relationship to the deceased. Married names of daughters are great clues to tracing lines of descent, and names of other siblings may only be located in these documents.

- **Codicil** Look for these amendments to a will as part of the probate packet. They also will be noted in the minutes of the probate court, along with the judge's ruling on the validity of the will and the changes included in the codicil. Figure 5-14 shows the first codicil to the will of John Smith of Chelsea, London, making an additional bequest of £1,000 to a neighbor, revoking the bequest of an automobile to his grandson, and calling for the sale of the car and the distribution of the proceeds to a daughter.

- **Letters Testamentary** Look for a copy of this document in the probate packet. If it isn't there, look in court records. The name(s) of the actual executor/executrix and/or administrator may well be different from that named in the will. You will want to determine the actual person(s) and their relationship (if any) to the deceased. It is important to know if and why the named executor did not serve. Was the person deceased or did he or she decline to serve?

- **Inventory or appraisal of the estate** The inventory will reveal the financial state of the deceased, and this is a good indicator of his/her social status. The inventory of personal property, such as the example shown in Figure 5-15, will provide indicators to the person's lifestyle. The presence of farm equipment and livestock may indicate the person was a farmer; an anvil and metal stock might point to blacksmithing as a profession; hammers, chisels, nails, a level, and other tools may reveal carpentry. In an 18th-century estate inventory, the presence of books indicates education and literacy, and the possession of a great deal of clothing and shoes indicates an elevated social position. The inclusion of slaves, as shown in the inventory in Figure 5-16, indicates a position of some wealth. There are many indicators that may direct you to other types of records. You may even find items listed in the inventory that may confirm family stories, such as military medals.

- ■ **List of beneficiaries**   A list of persons named may differ from the list of names in the will. Beneficiaries may be deceased, they may have married and names changed, they may not be locatable, their descendants or spouses may become inheritors, and so on. This list will tell you much about the family.

- ■ **Records of an auction**   Sometimes all or part of an estate was auctioned. Assets were sometimes liquidated to pay bills or to raise money for the surviving family. Auction records will reveal much about estate contents and their value. It was common for relatives to participate as bidders/purchasers at an estate auction, and you may find people with the same surname (or maiden name) as the deceased. These may be parents, siblings, or cousins you will want to research.

- ■ **Deeds, notes, bills, invoices, and receipts**   There may be a variety of loose papers in the probate packet that point to other persons. Deed copies will point you to land and property records and tax rolls. Names appearing on other papers may connect you to relatives, neighbors, friends, and business associates whose records may open doors for you.

- ■ **Guardianship documents**   Letters and other documents relating to the guardianship and/or custody of widows and minor children are common in probate packets. These can point you to family court documents and minutes that formally document the legal appointment of guardian(s). Figure 5-17 shows a petition for the appointment of a guardian for minor children, and Figure 5-18 shows a combination petition for and granting of guardianship from probate court records in 1911.

- ■ **Accounting reports**   Reports filed with the probate records can provide names of claimants and entities holding estate debts, including names of relatives.

- ■ **Final disposition or distribution of the estate**   A final estate distribution report is of vital importance. You may find the names and addresses of all the beneficiaries, and what they received from the estate. This will ultimately point you to the locations where you will find other records for these persons.

Watch for Clues and Pointers in the Probate Packet

You almost always find clues and pointers in wills and probate packet documents that point to other types of records. As such, you will soon come to recognize that you must work these documents in tandem with other documents. Let's discuss some of these.

A will or probate file may contain information about land and property—including personal property. These references will point you to other areas of the courthouse. You may go into land records, tax rolls, court records, and other areas. If any of the assets of the estate were auctioned, check the auction records. These are generally a part of the probate packet too, and may have been entered into the court minutes. Here you may find connections to other relatives of the same surname who came to purchase items.

Guardians are appointed to protect the interests of children and, in some cases, young widows. Remember that in many states, if the father dies and leaves a widow and minor children, the children are considered to be "orphans." Most often, the guardians appointed by the court are relatives of the deceased or of the spouse. A different surname of a guardian may be a clue to the maiden

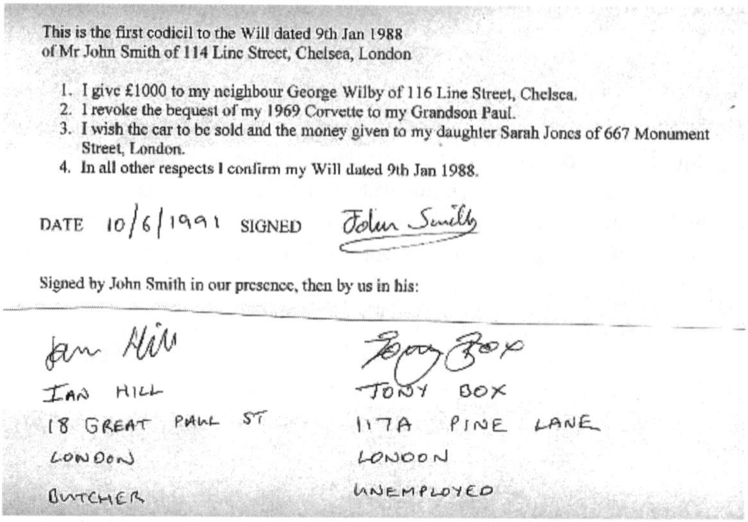

This is the first codicil to the Will dated 9th Jan 1988
of Mr John Smith of 114 Line Street, Chelsea, London

1. I give £1000 to my neighbour George Wilby of 116 Line Street, Chelsea.
2. I revoke the bequest of my 1969 Corvette to my Grandson Paul.
3. I wish the car to be sold and the money given to my daughter Sarah Jones of 667 Monument Street, London.
4. In all other respects I confirm my Will dated 9th Jan 1988.

DATE 10/6/1991 SIGNED *John Smith*

Signed by John Smith in our presence, then by us in his:

IAN HILL   TONY BOX
18 GREAT PAUL ST   117A PINE LANE
LONDON   LONDON
BUTCHER   UNEMPLOYED

FIGURE 5-14   Codicil of John Smith

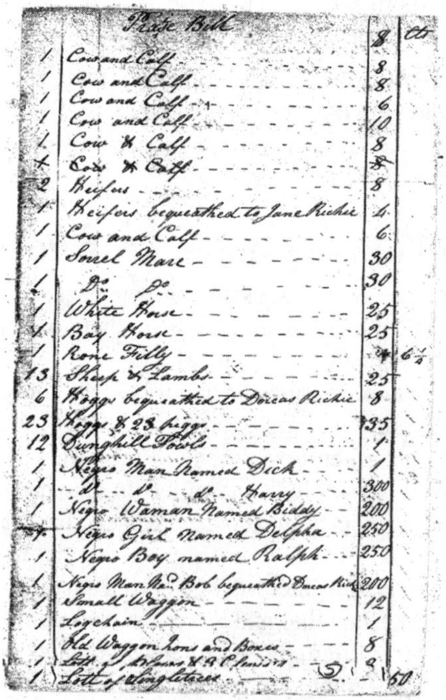

FIGURE 5-15   Inventory appraisal of a wealthy of Southern man (From the author's collection)

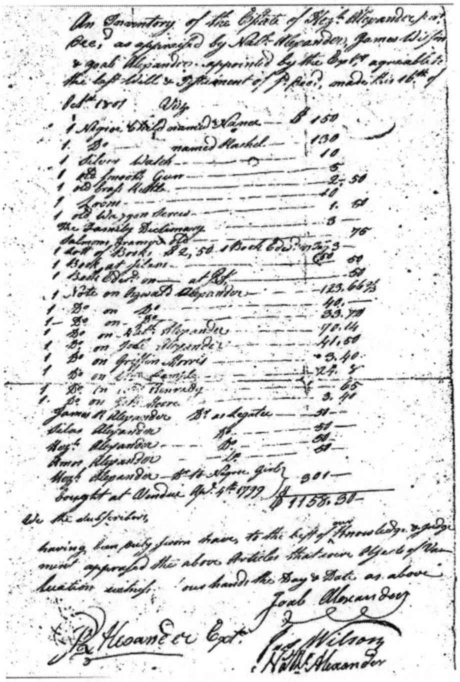

FIGURE 5-16 Estate inventory dated 1801 that includes names of slaves (From the author's collection)

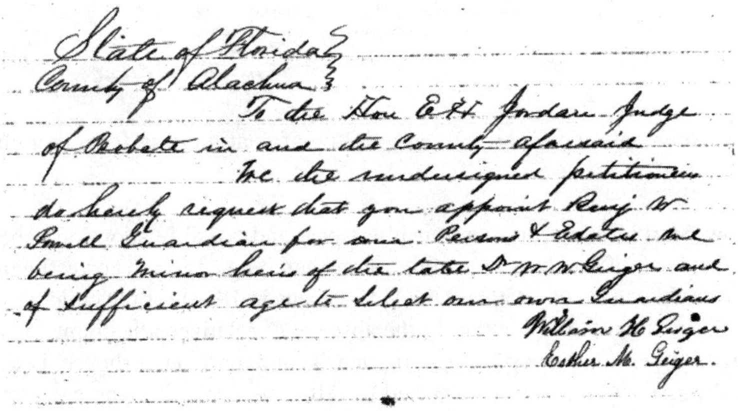

State of Florida }
County of Alachua }
To the Hon E H Jordan Judge
of Probate in and the County aforesaid
We the undersigned petitioners
do hereby request that you appoint Benj W.
Powell Guardian for our Persons & Estates we
being minor heirs of the late Dr W. W. Geiger and
of sufficient age to select our own Guardians
William H Geiger
Esther M. Geiger

FIGURE 5-17 Petition to the court for the appointment of a guardian for minor children (Courtesy of Jim Powell)

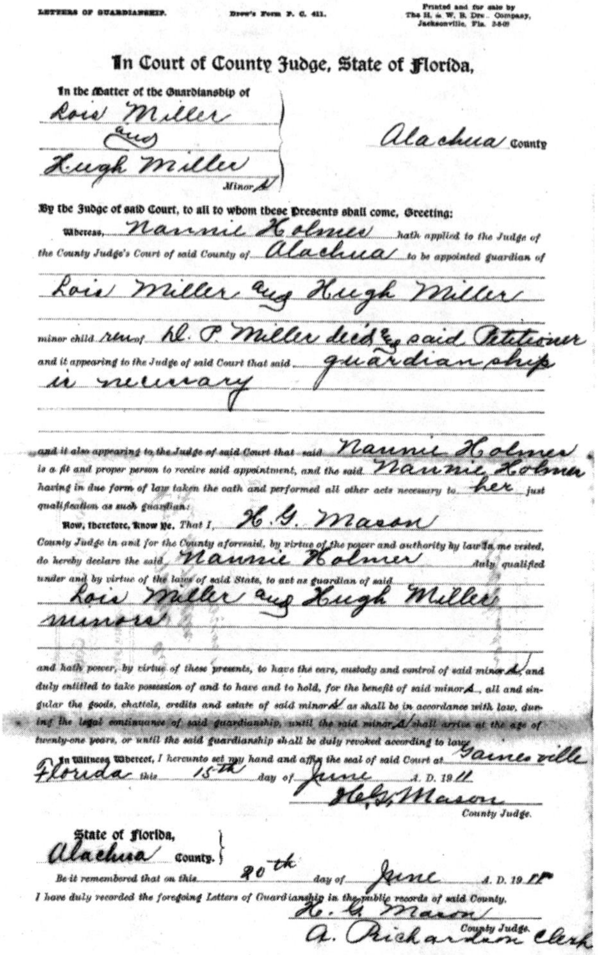
LETTERS OF GUARDIANSHIP. Drew's Form P. C. 411. Printed and for sale by The H. & W. B. Drew Company, Jacksonville, Fla.

In Court of County Judge, State of Florida,

In the Matter of the Guardianship of Lois Miller and Hugh Miller Minors — Alachua County

By the Judge of said Court, to all to whom these Presents shall come, Greeting:

Whereas, Nannie Holmes hath applied to the Judge of the County Judge's Court of said County of Alachua to be appointed guardian of Lois Miller and Hugh Miller minor children of W. P. Miller dec'd & said Petitioner and it appearing to the Judge of said Court that said guardianship is necessary

and it also appearing to the Judge of said Court that said Nannie Holmes is a fit and proper person to receive said appointment, and the said Nannie Holmes having in due form of law taken the oath and performed all other acts necessary to her just qualification as such guardian:

Now, therefore, Know Ye, That I, H. G. Mason County Judge in and for the County aforesaid, by virtue of the power and authority by law in me vested, do hereby declare the said Nannie Holmes duly qualified under and by virtue of the laws of said State, to act as guardian of said Lois Miller and Hugh Miller minors

and hath power, by virtue of these presents, to have the care, custody and control of said minors and duly entitled to take possession of and to have and to hold, for the benefit of said minors, all and singular the goods, chattels, credits and estate of said minors as shall be in accordance with law, during the legal continuance of said guardianship, until the said minors shall arrive at the age of twenty-one years, or until the said guardianship shall be duly revoked according to law.

In Witness Whereof, I hereunto set my hand and affix the seal of said Court at Gainesville Florida this 15th day of June A. D. 1911.

H. G. Mason County Judge.

State of Florida, Alachua County.

Be it remembered that on this 20th day of June A. D. 1911 I have duly recorded the foregoing Letters of Guardianship in the public records of said County.

H. G. Mason County Judge. A. Richardson Clerk

FIGURE 5-18 Combination petition for and granting of guardianship for minor children

name of the widow. Start looking for guardianship papers and possibly adoption papers. If you "lose" a child at the death of one or both parents, start searching census records (beginning with the United States federal census of 1850 and the U.K. census in 1851) for the child being in another residence, particularly in a relative's home. In the absence of relatives, the county, parish, or state may have committed the child to an orphanage, orphan asylum, or to a poorhouse. Leave no stone unturned. Check the respective court minutes and files for the year following a parent's death for any evidence of legal actions regarding a child. You'll be surprised at what you may locate.

Witnesses are important. By law, they cannot inherit in a will; however, they may be relatives of the deceased. It is not uncommon to find an in-law as a witness. Bondsmen involved in the settlement of an estate may also be relatives. If the wife of the testator is the executrix of the estate, the bondsmen are usually her relatives. (If you do not know the maiden name of the wife, check the surnames of the bondsmen carefully because one of them may be her brother.)

You will almost always find an inventory of the estate in the probate packet. The executor (or executrix) or administrator(s) of the estate is first charged by the court to determine the assets, the debts, and the receivables of an estate in order to properly determine what needs to be done in order to divide or dispose of it. The inventory often paints a colorful picture of the way of life of the deceased. The type of furniture, the presence or absence of books, farm equipment, livestock, real and personal property listed all tell us what type of life and what social status the person enjoyed—or did *not* enjoy.

Obviously, there are many things to consider when reviewing wills and probate packet contents. The location, the laws in effect at the time, the religious affiliation of the testator, the size of the estate, the presence or absence of a spouse, children, brothers, sisters, and parents—these are just a few.

You *Really* Want to Examine Documents Yourself

There are many ways to obtain information about a will or probate packet. Since most of us cannot afford to travel to all the places where our ancestors lived, we may need to do some "mail order" business, writing for copies of courthouse records.

One of the problems with will and probate documentation published in books, magazines, periodicals, and on the Internet is that someone *else* has looked at the documents. Since these are not their ancestors, they may not have the family perspective and insight that you might have. If they have transcribed the document *verbatim,* it might be correctly done, but you can't be sure unless you review it yourself. Even worse, materials that have been extracted or abstracted will often contain omissions of details that might be of significant importance to your research. As an example, one will listed nine children's names, some of which were double-barrel names, such as Billy Ray and Nita Beth. The insertion of extra commas in the transcription, extract, or abstract of these two children's names could easily turn these two children's names into *four* children—and wouldn't you play havoc trying to straighten that out?

Watch wills carefully for names of children. Don't make any assumptions. One of my friends researched her great-great-grandfather's family and was convinced that there were seven children in the family. That was until she studied the actual will of the great-great-father. In the will, the names Elizabeth and Mary had no comma between them. This led her to suspect that there was one daughter named Elizabeth Mary, rather than two daughters. Further investigation of marriage records in the county contradicted the one-daughter theory because she found that there were individual marriage records for two daughters, one married a year after her father's death and the other two years later. Further, Elizabeth and Mary and their respective spouses settled on land that was part of their father's holdings and appeared on census records thereafter.

Locate and Obtain Copies of Wills and Probate Documents

Wills, testaments, codicils, and other probate documents can be found in a variety of places. It is important to start in the area in which the person lived and make contact with the courts that had jurisdiction at that time, if they still exist.

In England, this may be difficult for older wills that at one time were handled by different levels of ecclesiastical courts that no longer exist. From the 13th century until 1858, church courts handled all the probate process. Their jurisdictions sometimes overlapped and their administrative powers were not always clear. In addition, English wills that required the probate of an estate containing multiple pieces of land could be complicated if the parcels were in multiple church administrative districts. In those cases, the probate process was handled by a level of ecclesiastical court whose administrative level included *all* of the districts in which the lands were located. It is important to understand this structure before undertaking a search for your English ancestor's will. It was not until 1858 that civil courts began handling probate and a more standard approach was imposed.

Probate documents may be encountered in many forms. The original documents may still exist and may be filed with the records of the court that handled the process. Look for court minutes and other evidence of the proceedings. Many courts and administrative offices have microfilmed their court records. Microfilm provides for compact storage of these voluminous records while preserving the originals. Microfilm also allows for the economic duplication of the records for access and use in multiple locations, and makes printing and copying simple and inexpensive.

You may also find that some original probate documents have been digitized and made available on the Internet. The Scottish Archive Network has made more than half a million Scottish wills and testaments dating from 1500 to 1901 accessible in digital format at **http://www.scottishdocuments. com.** Individual counties, municipalities, and courts also have digitized records. A particularly impressive effort has been accomplished in Alachua County, Florida, with the ongoing digitization of the county's Ancient Records Archives. This collection of indexed and, in some cases, transcribed documents can be seen at **http://www.clerk-alachua-fl.org/Archive/default.cfm.**

Obtain Information from the Social Security Administration and Railroad Retirement Board

The Social Security Administration was established by an act of Congress in 1935, in the depth of the Great Depression. President Franklin D. Roosevelt's administration was hard at work trying to help the U.S. recover economically through a number of social and financial programs. One area that required attention was that of old-age pensions. Older Americans were at significant risk of disaster during the Depression, and previously the only old-age pensions were available from some state and local governments. Many of those pension programs were faltering or had collapsed, and Congress was under pressure from the administration and from the public to take action.

The Social Security Act of 1935 established a national program for Americans over the age of 65 to receive benefits, and set up the structure and criteria for participation of those people in the work force and their employers to contribute to their retirement security. The program would not begin for several years and credit would not be given for any service prior to 1937.

In the meantime, railroad employees clamored for a program that would provide credit for prior service *and* an unemployment compensation program. Legislation passed in 1934, 1935, and 1937 established the Railroad Retirement program for employees of the United States railroads. More about that later.

At the beginning, in order to determine which persons would immediately be eligible to receive unemployment benefits, the Social Security Administration (SSA) used the 1880 U.S. federal census as a reference to help verify the age of recipients. The SSA formed a special branch called the Age Search group to handle this function. That branch still exists today to perform the same function. The Age Search group quickly determined that searching the 1880 census population schedules for a single person's enumeration listing was a highly laborious process. The SSA therefore commissioned the creation of an indexing system to assist in the search process. It was at that time that the Soundex coding system was developed for this program, and the first index was created for the 1880 census. Index cards were prepared by a group of WPA employees, and these cards were only created for households in which there were children aged 10 and under. After the 1880 census was Soundexed, indexes were prepared for entire households in the 1900, 1910, 1920, and 1930 censuses. This is the same Soundex and Miracode coding scheme described in Chapter 4.

In order to pay retirement pension benefits, the SSA required that an applicant must prove his or her age eligibility. While the Soundex system was used by the Age Search group, the person applying for benefits had to a) have applied for and been assigned a Social Security number (SSN), b) prove his or her identity, and c) provide evidence of his or her age. (Persons with disabilities who could not work also later became eligible for Social Security benefits, and the requirements were the same for them.)

SSNs were assigned by offices in each state and territory, with each geographical division (state and territory) having been assigned a block of numbers. The number consists of three groups of digits: the first group of three digits represents the place of assignment, the second group of two digits is used as check digits to identify fraudulent numbers, and the last group of four digits is randomly assigned. These numbers were assigned at the time that the SS-5 application form, such as the one shown in Figure 5-19, was completed to obtain the SSN. The *first* group of three represents where the applicant's SSN was assigned, and not necessarily where the person was born. This is an important distinction, and a source of confusion and misunderstanding among many genealogical researchers. In order for an individual to receive a SSN, an application form (known as the SS-5) was completed.

When a beneficiary dies, it is a legal requirement that the SSA be notified so that payments are immediately stopped. A benefit check for the last partial month of the person's life usually must be returned, and the SSA has a procedure for handling the final payment. The SSA does not require a copy of a death certificate or other form of written proof of death. In some cases, a simple telephone call or the return of the check with a notation that the person is deceased is sufficient for the SSA to update its database.

The SSA's records were maintained on paper until the late 1950s. At that time, data from the SS-5 forms of all known living persons with SSNs (along with the last known address) and information from all new applicants' SS-5 forms were entered into a computer database. In addition, the SSA began maintaining benefit information by computer and entering death information as notifications of the deaths of recipients were received. Beginning in 1962, the Social Security

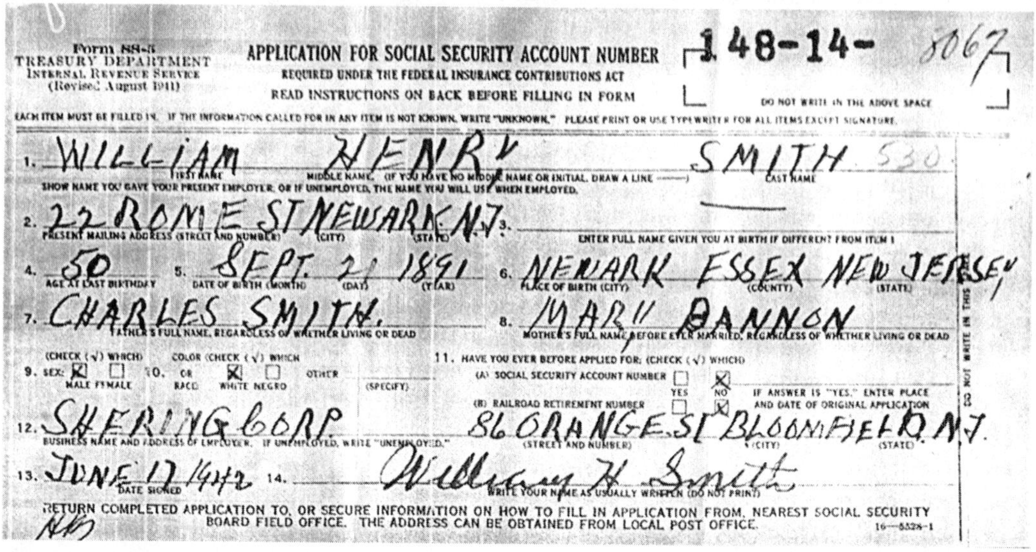

Form SS-5
TREASURY DEPARTMENT
INTERNAL REVENUE SERVICE
(Revised August 1941)

APPLICATION FOR SOCIAL SECURITY ACCOUNT NUMBER
REQUIRED UNDER THE FEDERAL INSURANCE CONTRIBUTIONS ACT
READ INSTRUCTIONS ON BACK BEFORE FILLING IN FORM

148-14-8067
DO NOT WRITE IN THE ABOVE SPACE

EACH ITEM MUST BE FILLED IN. IF THE INFORMATION CALLED FOR IN ANY ITEM IS NOT KNOWN, WRITE "UNKNOWN." PLEASE PRINT OR USE TYPEWRITER FOR ALL ITEMS EXCEPT SIGNATURE.

1. WILLIAM (FIRST NAME) HENRY (MIDDLE NAME. (IF YOU HAVE NO MIDDLE NAME OR INITIAL, DRAW A LINE ——)) SMITH (LAST NAME) 530
SHOW NAME YOU GAVE YOUR PRESENT EMPLOYER, OR IF UNEMPLOYED, THE NAME YOU WILL USE WHEN EMPLOYED.

2. 22 ROME ST NEWARK N.J. (PRESENT MAILING ADDRESS (STREET AND NUMBER) (CITY) (STATE))
3. —— (ENTER FULL NAME GIVEN YOU AT BIRTH IF DIFFERENT FROM ITEM 1)

4. 50 (AGE AT LAST BIRTHDAY)
5. SEPT. 21 1891 (DATE OF BIRTH (MONTH) (DAY) (YEAR))
6. NEWARK ESSEX NEW JERSEY (PLACE OF BIRTH (CITY) (COUNTY) (STATE))

7. CHARLES SMITH. (FATHER'S FULL NAME, REGARDLESS OF WHETHER LIVING OR DEAD)
8. MARY DANNON (MOTHER'S FULL NAME BEFORE EVER MARRIED, REGARDLESS OF WHETHER LIVING OR DEAD)

9. SEX: (CHECK (√) WHICH) [X] MALE [ ] FEMALE
10. COLOR OR RACE: (CHECK (√) WHICH) [X] WHITE [ ] NEGRO OTHER (SPECIFY)
11. HAVE YOU EVER BEFORE APPLIED FOR: (CHECK (√) WHICH)
(A) SOCIAL SECURITY ACCOUNT NUMBER [ ] YES [X] NO
(B) RAILROAD RETIREMENT NUMBER [ ] YES [X] NO
IF ANSWER IS "YES," ENTER PLACE AND DATE OF ORIGINAL APPLICATION

12. SHERING CORP. 86 ORANGE ST BLOOMFIELD N.J. (BUSINESS NAME AND ADDRESS OF EMPLOYER. IF UNEMPLOYED, WRITE "UNEMPLOYED." (STREET AND NUMBER) (CITY) (STATE))

13. JUNE 17 1942 (DATE SIGNED)
14. William H. Smith (WRITE YOUR NAME AS USUALLY WRITTEN (DO NOT PRINT))

DO NOT WRITE IN THIS SPACE

RETURN COMPLETED APPLICATION TO, OR SECURE INFORMATION ON HOW TO FILL IN APPLICATION FROM, NEAREST SOCIAL SECURITY BOARD FIELD OFFICE. THE ADDRESS CAN BE OBTAINED FROM LOCAL POST OFFICE.
16—5528-1

FIGURE 5-19 A photocopy of the SS-5 application form from the Social Security Administration (Courtesy of Drew Smith)

Death Master File began to be produced electronically on a regular basis. Initially, it contained only about 17 percent of the reported deaths, but that increased to more than 92 percent in 1980. The percentage of completeness has varied up and down since then, and will never be 100 percent complete. The file has since come to be known as the Social Security Death Index, or SSDI. Genealogists with family members in the United States have used this valuable tool to locate the place of last residence or benefit payment in order to locate other records.

It is important to understand that the SSDI contains only information about deceased individuals, in compliance with both the Privacy Act, which protects individuals' information for 72 years, and the Freedom of Information Act, which makes information available to the public. There are four criteria for a person's information to be included in the SSDI:

- The person must be deceased.
- The person must have had a Social Security number assigned to him or her.
- The person must have applied for and received a Social Security benefit payment.
- The person's death must have been reported to the Social Security Administration.

If a person was assigned a SSN and is deceased, but never received a benefit of any sort, he or she will not be found in the SSDI. For these persons and for those persons who died prior to the computerization of the SSA records, you can still obtain a copy of their SS-5 application form from the SSA. All you need to do is write the SSA Freedom of Information Officer, provide the full name, address, and birth date of the individual, and request the SS-5. If you can provide the person's SSN, the cost of obtaining an SS-5 at this writing is $27; without the SSN, the cost is $29. In addition, you can request a copy of a printout from the SSDI database known as a Numident. The Numident is nothing more than the data entered into the SSA database. The price of this document is $16 but is only available when you can provide the person's SSN. Requests for SS-5 forms and Numident printouts should be directed to:

Social Security Administration
Office of Earnings Operations
FOIA Workgroup
300 N. Greene Street
P.O. Box 33022
Baltimore, Maryland 21290

Your request to the SSA for a copy of the application (SS-5) for a person who never received a benefit and for whom the SSA wasn't notified of the death may be denied. However, if you can supply evidence of the person's death, such as a copy of a death certificate, you can appeal the decision and, in fact, then receive the copy of their SS-5 form.

The SSDI is available online at a number of Web sites, including Ancestry.com (**http://www.ancestry.com**) and RootsWeb (**http:///www.rootsweb.com**) and these provide the ability to automatically produce a request letter for you.

The Railroad Retirement Board (RRB) is the administrative body for the railroad workers' retirement pension benefits system. The Railroad Retirement program is similar to Social Security but has been administered by the Railroad Retirement Board (RRB) in Chicago, Illinois. Up until 1963, persons who worked for a railroad in the U.S. at the time they applied for a SSN were assigned a number between 700 and 728. Therefore, if you locate any document that lists a SSN whose first three digits are in that numbering range, you will know that the person worked for the railroad industry at the time he or she was assigned the number. You also will know to check first with the RRB for records.

A person who worked exclusively in the railroad industry will apply for and receive old-age pension benefits from Railroad Retirement. An individual who worked for both the railroad industry and elsewhere would have contributed to both a Railroad Retirement pension account and to Social Security during his or her working career. At the time of retirement, the person had to apply for a retirement pension benefit from either one or the other, but not both plans.

The RRB records you obtain may be more detailed, including earnings reports, copies of designation of beneficiary forms, and perhaps more. The address to which you would send your request, along with a check for $27 made payable to the Railroad Retirement Board, is

Office of Public Affairs
Railroad Retirement Board
844 North Rush Street
Chicago, Illinois 60611-2092

5

For more information about the RRB, visit their Web site at **http://www.rrb.gov** and specifically their genealogy Web page at **http://www.rrb.gov/geneal.html.**

Consider Other Institutional Record Types

You can see now how the investigative work you are doing and the scholarly methodologies you are using can begin to pay big dividends. In many of the examples I've shown in this chapter, I have tried to convey the ways that one record may provide clues and pointers to others.

As you encounter new sources of information, use your critical thinking skills to read between the lines. Consider the other institutional records that might add to your knowledge. These could include employment records, union memberships, schools, professional organizations, civic and social club memberships, and veterans groups, just to name a few. Just as with cemetery offices, you never know what information might be in these organizations' files.

Chapter 6

Use Records of Military Service and Land Documents

How to...

- ■ Expand your knowledge of the military services
- ■ Identify possible sources for military records
- ■ Learn from military pension records
- ■ Understand and use land and property records
- ■ Place your ancestors into context with property records
- ■ Find sources of land and property records in different places

Consider Military and Property Records

In the previous chapters you have learned the importance of building a firm foundation on your ancestors' and family members' records of many types. We discussed census records in Chapter 4, and you saw that there are cases in which a census document may have included information about someone's military service record. The United States federal census of 1840 was the first to call for the name and age of Revolutionary War veterans, and the 1890 census included a separate census schedule specifically for Civil War veterans and their widows. In Great Britain, the 1851 census included those persons living on vessels in inland waters or at sea, including members of the Royal Navy and the Merchant Navy. In addition, persons serving abroad with the armed forces and those working with the East India Company were enumerated. As you can see, census materials may provide information about an ancestor that can spur you to search for military records. Even if you are unsure whether or not your ancestor or a family member served in the armed forces of a particular country, it is wise to invest some amount of time researching the official rosters and/or indexes to see if a familiar name appears there. You would be surprised how often people make the discovery of a military ancestor when they didn't know or think there was one. Military service and pension records can, indeed, provide more detailed insight into a person's life than you could imagine. In addition, census records often show information about a person's or family's land and property holdings.

You're probably wondering why I decided to combine two apparently quite different record types, military records and land and property records, together in a single chapter. While there are certainly plenty of things I could write separately about each group of records, there is sometimes a link between them. For example, the United States federal government compensated some military personnel with land rather than or in addition to paying them cash. These "bounty lands" were granted to persons in reward for their military service or for rendering goods and services to the government and/or troops.

Other sources you may encounter may refer or point to military records or to property records. Some examples of these are obituaries, wills and probate records, tombstones, divorce documents, dowry records, jury lists, voter registration records, naturalization records, legal judgments, settlements, tax delinquencies, court-order auctions, guardianship records, indentures of servitude where land was awarded at the end of the term of service, homestead documentation, court records of many types, newspaper notices of land transactions, and many other resources.

I often find references to a person's military service in death-related records, and military documents have often been used as a form of identification and/or to apply for some benefit such as a voter's registration, naturalization without having to file a Declaration of Intent document, educational benefit (such as the G.I. Bill), a housing subsidy, low-interest loans, retirement pension, medical assistance, and death benefit for the surviving spouse and family.

Court records in the British Isles, as you will see, can be quite complex to locate and work with, but they also can contain exceptionally detailed history. The clues you find that point to an individual's military service or to the holding or rental of property should always be followed to locate the source evidence. Often these slightly divergent research paths will reward you with a rich bounty yourself. For example, there are numerous examples of land patent files in the possession of the United States Bureau of Land Management (BLM) that contained more that just the basic documentation. In addition to the original homesteader's application and the federal grant, the applicant had to fulfill a continuous residency on and make improvements to the property for a period of years. Not only do the files contain these documents and the sworn affidavits of the applicant and other witnesses concerning the meeting of the residency requirements, some files may also contain surprising documents. Occasionally, an original marriage certificate was submitted to provide proof of the marriage of a couple applying for the land and was never returned to the applicant. These marriage certificates have lain undiscovered and undisturbed for generations and, when a genealogist requests copies of the contents of a BLM file, he or she may be astonished to find a marriage document in the file. Original marriage certificates are also sometimes found in military pension files, submitted by a widow as proof of her entitlement to the continuation of her husband's military pension.

It is important for you to understand that land and property are among the most numerous documents in existence, extending back hundreds of years. The Domesday Book, for example, is one of the oldest official documents in existence in England. It was commissioned in 1085 by King William I, previously known as William the Conqueror, who invaded England in 1066. The first draft of the book was completed in August of 1086 and contained records for settlements in England south of the Scottish border at that time. (Visit the Domesday Book online Web site at **http://www. domesdaybook.co.uk** for more extensive information.) Even though land and property records exist in abundance, they are perhaps the least used records by genealogists. One reason for this is that the majority of family historians neither understand the various types of records and their organization nor do they take the time to study this area.

Likewise, many genealogists fail to follow through with a search for military service records and pension files. The reason for these omissions or oversights can generally be attributed to a lack of understanding of the history of the area where their ancestors and family members lived, the military history of which might have played a very significant role in their lives. However, another contributing factor is that military records are not always located together. Sometimes the military service records are in one archive, the pension files in another, and perhaps other pertinent records are in the possession of another governmental office. This can be confusing if you haven't taken the time to determine what records were created at a particular time, what part of the government or military used them, what they were used for, and what was done with those records when they were no longer needed. Context is important!

6

With all of this in mind, let's set out to become experts in the research of these areas. First we will discuss military records, and then we will move to land and property records. I think you will find that these are both fascinating types of records, and that they provide insights into history you never imagined.

Expand Your Knowledge of the Military Services

Military service is a job and, as such, can produce a vast amount of written documentation. Census records provide information at ten-year intervals and that is a huge span of time between milestones. Military records, on the other hand, provide a more regular form of documentation, at shorter intervals, than a census. From the date of registration, conscription, or enlistment, there will have been official military records maintained. These may include the following record types:

Draft registration cards	Draft notices
Enlistment forms and related documentation	Medical records
Quartermaster or provisions records	Educational testing and training reports/diplomas
Duty assignments	Muster rolls
Payroll records and pay stubs	Announcements/postings of promotions
Records of the awarding of medals and awards, such as the one shown in Figure 6-1	Casualty reports
Service files or dossiers	Discharge papers
Records of courts martial	Pension applications
Pension files containing affidavits, correspondence, payment records, and other documents	Pension payment vouchers
Veterans records	Veteran's life insurance certificate
Benefits records	Death and burial records

That is an impressive list. It is important to note that not every country generated or maintained this broad a range of documents, and that fewer types of records were created the farther back in history you research. Specific personnel units, too, may have required the use of additional or unique records. Still, the sheer volume of military documentation of a soldier's daily, monthly, or annual affairs can present you with a detailed insight into his or her life at that time. Remember, too, that military assignments take a person to many locations and expose him or her to a wide range of experiences. That exposure may influence the decisions made later in life to select a particular profession, to relocate to another area, or to take some other course of action.

In addition to the official file contents listed above, you may find items among materials in the home that can further your research, such as uniforms, dog tags, insignia, patches, badges, medals, ribbons, certificates and awards, correspondence, and photographs. Each of these can provide clues and pointers to other military records.

FIGURE 6-1   The Congressional Medal of Honor, the United States' highest military award

Investigate Military History for the Appropriate Time Period

Every time I visit a library or a bookstore, I am impressed at the number of books and periodicals available on the subject of military history. There are books available about armies, navies, and other military branches. Innumerable historical accounts and analyses of military units, engagements, and strategies from the present and extending back to ancient times have been published in books, magazines, journals, and in other media. There are specialty book and magazine titles that discuss the uses of horses, wagons, tanks, jeeps, ships, airplanes, helicopters, land-sea transports, landing vehicles, and other transportation modes in warfare. Every manner of weapon you can imagine is documented in intricate detail, from swords, scimitars, cutlasses, spears, lances, maces, sabers, knives, and bayonets to pistols, rifles, cannon, mortars, bazookas, flamethrowers, and other types of armaments.

You already know the importance of placing your ancestors and family members into geographical, historical, and social context. This is also emphatically true when it comes to researching the history of someone who may have performed some military service. You will benefit from the study of the history of the country in which your ancestor lived and particularly about the military establishment there at the time, military service requirements, and the military conflicts in which the country was engaged. This information can help you better understand what records you might expect to find. In a time of war, you could expect to find that a government would impose conscription or impressments to force enrollment of personnel in the military service.

In the United States in 1917 and 1918, a series of draft calls were made by the United States federal government to quickly build the armed forces for involvement in "The Great War" in Europe. Men in certain age ranges, such as 19-year-old Charles Ray Morrison shown in Figure 6-2, were required to present themselves at the office of their local draft board to complete a draft registration card. Knowing that every male between certain ages was required to complete a card will prompt you to attempt to obtain a copy of the record for your research. Likewise, if you had a male ancestor living in Prussia in 1816, it is important to know that compulsory military service had been imposed, even in peacetime. You might therefore want to investigate the existence of military service records that documented his date and place of birth and other details that might be included about him.

Sometimes you will find that individual records may no longer exist, in which case you will need to seek out alternate sources of information. State, county, parish, and local histories can be beneficial in that regard because they frequently include sections about military units that originated from the area and rosters of the people who served in them. Even if your ancestor or other family member is not listed by name, identifying the military unit(s) from that area can be important clues to lead you to other materials.

Military unit histories are abundant. Following the United States Civil War and throughout the remaining decades of the 19th century, former officers and veterans penned exhaustive memoirs and historical accounts of their experiences. These narratives often contain complete rosters of the people serving with them and anecdotal materials about them. In some cases, these stories may contain the only surviving details about the fates of individual soldiers lost in battle or to disease.

 FIGURE 6-2   Charles Ray Morrison, born in 1899, was enrolled in the United States' Third Draft Registration on 12 September 1918 (From the author's collection).

Historians also have chronicled military units' histories and their engagements, compiling official records and personal accounts to re-create a chronological account of events. Military-related heritage societies also organized to honor the veterans, their families, and their descendants, and to perpetuate the history of their service. Organizations such as the Daughters of the American Revolution, the Sons of the American Revolution, the United Daughters of the Confederacy, and the Sons of Confederate Veterans foster education, caretaking activities for historical materials, maintenance of cemeteries, and publication of information relating to their respective group. There are other organizations whose members may or may not be descendents of veterans of specific military personnel but who are interested in preserving information and materials and encouraging the study of a specific area or period. Examples of these groups would include the English Civil War Society (**http://english-civil-war-society.org**), the Indian Military Historical Society (**http://members.ozemail.com.au/~clday/imhs.htm**), the Scottish Military Historical Society (**http://www.btinternet.com/~james.mckay/dispatch.htm**), and the United Empire Loyalists' Association of Canada (**http://www.uelac.org**).

In addition, there are many magazines with military and historical themes, among them *World War II, Military History, Civil War Times, America's Civil War, History Magazine, Naval History, The Beaver: Canada's History Magazine, Canadian Journal of History, BBC History Magazine* (not available for subscription in the U.S.), and *Living History* (U.K.). You may want to purchase a copy of a magazine at the newsstand to determine if it contains information of interest or help to you. You can then subscribe to one or more publications that will contribute to your growing knowledge of the subject.

You can expect to locate vast amounts of military unit information both in book and magazine form, and also on the Internet. Whenever you begin to research an ancestor who was or may have been in the military service, do some preliminary investigative work into the history of the area and time period, and into the records that may have been created for the military command and the personnel. Once you know what was created, you can then begin tracking down the locations where those materials may be stored and the procedures for accessing them.

Identify Possible Sources for Military Records

Military records are government documents. You will find that for a particular country or government they may well be distributed across a number of document depositories. This is a primary reason why it is important to study history. In the United States, military records may be held by either the National Archives and Records Administration (**http://www.archives.gov**) or by the National Personnel Records Center in St. Louis, Missouri. In Canada, most of the military service records are held by the Library and Archives Canada (**http://www.archives.ca**). In the United Kingdom, a significant collection of military records, including service and pension records, are held by the National Archives (**http://www.nationalarchives.gov.uk**). Others, however, may still be in the possession of the Ministry of Defence. Please note that, if your ancestor served in the military forces in other than his or her native country, the records for that service will be in the other country's possession. Let's examine each of these governments' records in detail.

Many indexes, transcripts, and abstracts of military records have been prepared. These include summary personnel records, muster rolls, casualty lists, medical reports, and many other types of records. These can point you in the direction of original, primary source documents and you will want to obtain copies for your own review.

Locate Military Records in the United States

The United States, as a comparatively young nation, has a considerable military history and a vast collection of military records from colonial times still exist. You will find that the earlier the era, however, the less complete the military records will be. Documents may have been lost or destroyed, or they may simply have deteriorated before they were gathered together for archiving and preservation.

The earliest recorded military conflicts are perhaps those that occurred at Jamestown in the colony of Virginia. The Indian attack on the settlement in March of 1622 killed more than 300 settlers and almost destroyed it. The English retaliated and, over the next 22 years, almost decimated the Indians in the area. Documents in the form of correspondence and historical accounts do exist from these years, both among the documents in the United Kingdom and the United States and Virginia archives.

Other conflicts between the English and French colonies of what are now the United States and Canada and against the Indians are numerous. However, no appreciable military documents *per se* exist. Rather, correspondence and anecdotal accounts form what historical materials exist, and these are in the hands of various archives in the United Kingdom, Canada, the United States, and some of the states' libraries or archives.

Military forces serving in what is now the United States during the colonial era consisted primarily of European military personnel from the countries controlling specific respective areas. The Spanish governed Florida on multiple occasions, California, and some southern areas. The English governed the eastern colonies and Florida for a time. And the French governed the Louisiana Territory.

The American colonists supplemented the British troops with local military units and militia. It was not until the mid-1700s that the colonies began to actively oppose the government of the British Crown. The American Revolution was the first really organized armed conflict by the Americans themselves, and there are unique military-related documents that were generated as a result of the conflict. There are three major sources for discovering who actually served during that war. First, there are lists of veterans that were compiled by each state early in the 19th century. Next are the pension applications filed by veterans or their surviving spouses and family members that are stored at the federal and/or state levels. And finally, there are the records of the Daughters of the American Revolution (DAR), which may include detailed documentation, both official documents and personal materials, of the military record of members' ancestors. However, these are not the only resources you might expect to find. Let's look at one excellent example.

Let's say that you are looking for an ancestor's records relating to his military service during the period of 1775 to 1783 in what is now the United States. You will be seeking records relating to the American Revolution, and you will be looking in a number of places. It is important to know the state from which he served. For our example, let's choose North Carolina.

Next, you need to know whether your ancestor served in the local regulators, the state militia, and/or the Continental Army. You therefore are going to be dealing with records originally created at the local/county, state, or national level, and this makes a great deal of difference in how you approach locating any surviving records. If your ancestor served with the local regulators, for example, he was probably in effect policing and protecting the area in which he lived. If he served in the state militia, the records relating to his military service *and* his military pension, if any, would have been created and maintained at the state level. And if he served in the Continental Army, his military service and pension records, if any, would have been generated at a higher level and would be among the records maintained at the national level today.

Records of regulators and state militia are most likely to be found in the state archive, state library, or state historical society in the state from which your ancestor served. That is assuming, of course, that he enlisted in the state in which he lived. And yes, there are exceptions. Records for the Continental Army would be found among the records at the National Archives and Records Administration (NARA).

There are, however, exceptional situations you should consider. Your ancestor may have begun service in regulators, for example, and then enlisted in the state militia or the Continental Army. Similarly, he may have served his term in the state militia and then enlisted in the Continental Army. It is not impossible that he may have served in one or more military units at all three levels, in which case your research might reveal records in multiple places. You may find, as I did, that your ancestor collected a federal Revolutionary War pension and, upon its termination, he applied for and was granted a state military pension for his service on behalf of the state in the Revolutionary War. What's more, all of these documents will be unique, created at different times by different government, military, or judicial officials and therefore will contain different documents and potentially more information about your ancestor's service.

Military records of different eras also may be located in different places. Military service records in the United States are located at NARA for the period from 1775 to 1916. The United States' World War I draft registration cards were created during several calls for registration in 1917 and 1918, as shown in Table 6-1. These cards are in the possession of NARA at its Southeast Region Branch in Atlanta, Georgia. Understanding the history of the World War I draft registration process helped me determine that Charles Ray Morrison, shown in Figure 6-2, who was born in Munford, Talladega County, Alabama, on 27 March 1899, was not required to register until the Third Registration Day on 12 September 1918. I was able to locate his registration card and obtained additional personal details about him from that record. This is one example of how understanding the historical background of the period for a specific area can help locate records that can further your research.

Registration Call & Date	Ages at that Time	Persons Born Between These Dates
First Registration Day 5 June 1917	All males between the ages of 21 to 31	5 June 1886 and 5 June 1896
Second Registration Day 5 June 1918	Males who reached the age of 21 since 5 June 1917	6 June 1896 and 5 June 1897
Supplemental Second Registration Day 24 August 1918	Males who reached the age of 21 since 5 June 1918	6 June 1897 and 24 August 1897
Third Registration Day 12 September 1918	All males aged 18 to 20 and 31 to 45 who had not previously registered	12 September 1872 and 12 September 1900

TABLE 6-1   United States World War I Draft Registration Calls and Age Ranges of Eligible Registrants (Used with permission of Aha! Seminars, Inc.)

You can request copies of the military service records held by NARA by completing NATF Form 86. You may request copies of military pension file records by completing NATF Form 85, or by submitting a request via the Internet. You can learn about and obtain the forms, and complete the online pension file request, at the NARA Order Forms Web page at **http://www.archives.gov/ research_room/obtain_copies/military_and_genealogy_order_forms.html.**

NARA has produced tens of thousands of rolls of microfilmed military records. Their *Military Service Records: A Select Catalog of National Archives Microfilm Publications* is available in printed form but is also available in its entirety online. Visit their Publications Web page at **http://www.archives.gov/publications/microfilm_catalogs.html.** These microfilmed records are accessible at their facilities, a complete listing of which can be found at **http://www.archives.gov/ facilities/facilities_by_state.html.** (Be sure to check this site and contact the branch in advance to verify their microfilm holdings as not all branches maintain a complete collection of the microfilm materials.) In addition, contact or visit your nearest LDS Family History Center to determine if they can obtain the microfilm from the Family History Library in Salt Lake City, Utah, for your research use.

United States military service records for circa 1917 to present are maintained by the National Personnel Records Center (NPRC) at 9700 Page Avenue, St. Louis, Missouri, 63132. Unfortunately, though, a fire on 12 July 1973 at the NPRC destroyed an estimated 16 to 18 million military personnel files. Approximately 80 percent of the U.S. Army personnel records for persons discharged between 1 November 1 1912 and 1 January 1960 were destroyed. An estimated 75 percent of U.S. Air Force personnel records were lost for persons discharged between 25 September 1947 and 1 January 1964. There were no duplicates or microfilm records of these records. Some of these records in files were damaged but not destroyed, and these have been refiled. The NPRC, on receipt of a veteran's or surviving family member's request, will attempt to reconstruct a destroyed service record for an individual using other sources when possible.

As you can see, there was some overlap between the military records held by NARA and by the NPRC. Again, by doing some advance research in advance of making requests for documents, you can avoid the expense and disappointment of coming up empty-handed because you requested material from the wrong place.

You can obtain copies of surviving military personnel records from 1917 and later if you are the veteran or the next-of-kin by either completing and submitting Standard Form 180 to the St. Louis address, or by completing an online request document at the eVetRecs Web site at **http://www. archives.gov/research_room/vetrecs,** signing it, and mailing or faxing the form within 20 days. If you are not a next-of-kin relative, you can still complete and request the Standard Form 180. However, your request may be denied or you may be provided with a limited amount of information. Detailed guidelines are accessible online at **http://www.archives.gov/facilities/mo/st_louis/military_ personnel_records.html.**

This might be confusing if you don't take the time to understand the historical background of the period in which your ancestor lived, the military service at the time, the years and military conflicts in which he or she might have been serving, the branch of the military, the types of records created, and where they might be stored. For United States military records, the best book currently available is James C. Neagles' *U.S. Military Records: A Guide to Federal and State Sources—Colonial America to Present*. Published by Ancestry, Incorporated, in 1994, this book provides excellent descriptions of the records created and where they are located. There are no Internet addresses in the book and, since its publication, some government departments have been renamed and their addresses and telephone numbers may have changed. However, you can use your Internet search skills to locate current contact information.

Locate Canadian Military Records

Canada is a fascinating combination of French, British, and aboriginal cultures and a study of strength and courage of individuals carving life out of a rich but often harsh wilderness. It is interesting to read and learn about military conflicts between all of these groups, plus the clashes with the Americans to the south. In addition, Canadians have participated in both world wars and in other military conflicts around the world. If you are researching your Canadian ancestors, written histories may provide information to the portrait of those individuals and their families.

Early Records

The National Archives of Canada (NAC) is the primary source for the majority of the military records that exist, and NAC has done an excellent job of indexing materials for ease of location. The earliest materials in the NAC's Colonial Archives relate to records of the French Regime, records concerning British regiments that were stationed in Canada, and a variety of United Empire Loyalists resources from the time of the American Revolution (1775–1783). The latter group also includes some petitions to the Crown as reward for their loyalty and service. These collections are generally broken up into two sections, Upper Canada and Lower Canada. You can learn more about the Loyalist records at **http://www.archives.ca/02/020202/02020218_e.html.**

Unfortunately, however, few military records of any genealogical value exist for the period prior to World War I, with the exception of records for the South African (or "Boer") War, which lasted from 1899 until 1902. Earlier records consist of little more than muster rolls and pay lists and these contain very little information other than the name of the soldier. Most of these records also have not been indexed, which means that you will need to know the regimental unit in which he may have served.

The NAC collection of British military and naval records includes materials with references to the British army units in Canada, Loyalist regiments during the period of the American Revolution, the War of 1812, Canadian militia records, and some other materials. The index to this collection and the collection itself are available through the inter-institutional loan. The index includes a short description of the document, the date, the volume number in the collection, and the page number.

The military service personnel records for soldiers who served in the South African War are in the possession of the NAC. They have been organized in alphabetical order and have been microfilmed.

Records from World War I

The NAC's online ArchiviaNet, accessible from the main page at **http://www.archives.ca,** is an excellent research tool to locate information about the 600,000 Canadians who enlisted in the Canadian Expeditionary Forces (CEF) during World War I and to access the CEF's units' War Diaries from that period. The database of Soldiers of the First World War (1914–1918) is searchable by name, and results for an individual provide the regimental number and the specific location in the NAC for the person's original service records. A link takes you to a Web page with information about ordering copies of documents. In some cases, images of documents are accessible through the NAC Web site.

Each CEF unit was required to maintain a daily account of its field activities from the beginning of World War I. These accounts were known as "War Diaries" and are actually detailed unit histories. They include reports, maps, copies of orders, casualty listings, and other documents. Many of the War Diaries have been digitized and placed on ArchiviaNet, and are searchable by unit name and date. When you locate one that you wish to view, enter the collection and you will find the contents' images listed in chronological sequence by date and page. Click on the link and the document, or facing pages, will be displayed. Some images will be displayed at full size. Others may be resized by your browser to fit in its display window. If your browser has resized the image and it can be enlarged, there is a simple way to zoom in for easier reading. To zoom in on the image, move your mouse cursor to the lower right-hand corner of the image and pause. If it can be enlarged, a small orange box with blue arrows pointing outward from the four corners will pop up. Click on that box and the image will be expanded to full size. While the contents of these War Diaries have not been indexed to make then searchable by keyword or phrase, you will find the details of your ancestor's or family member's unit's activities will provide a clear picture of day-to-day life.

You might also want to visit the Veterans Affairs Canada (VAC) Web site at **http://www. vac-acc.gc.ca** for some of the best historical material about Canada's recent military past. Visit its Canada Remembers page where you can search the Canadian Virtual War Memorial, a registry of more than 116,000 names of Canadians and Newfoundlanders with information about their graves and memorials. The site provides access to a searchable database of personnel information, which includes the soldier's name, date of death, service number, branch, regiment, and unit. The cemetery name, location, directions to it, and the precise burial location are included. Another Web site you will want to visit is the Commonwealth War Graves Commission at **http://www.cwgc.org.** Here, too, you can search by name for an individual. At this site, which represents war memorials for the whole British Commonwealth, there is even more information, including rank and nationality, as well as a link to provide details about the cemetery of interment.

The VAC also maintains the Canadian Merchant Navy War Dead Database at **http://www. vac-acc.gc.ca/remembers/sub.cfm?source=history/secondwar/atlantic/merchant_search.** This database can be used to search for the names of sailors killed while serving in Canada's Merchant Marines. It can also be used to search for the names of Canadian Merchant Navy vessels. You can enter the name of the Canadian Merchant Navy war dead, the vessel they served on, or both.

Some but by no means all of the Canadian military records are available on microfilm through the LDS Family History Centers. Microfilmed records are available for research at the NAC or through inter-institutional loan arrangements.

Military Records after 1918

The NAC holds personnel for more than 5.5 million former military personnel of the Canadian Armed Forces and civilian employees of the Federal Public Service. You can request copies of records from the NAC in writing, using their Application for Military Service Information form, an Access to Information Request Form, or by letter. All requests are subject to the conditions of Canada's Access to Information Act and the Privacy Act. More information can be found at **http://www.archives.ca/02/020203/02020302_e.html.**

For information about documents not held by the NAC, visit their Web page at **http://www. archives.ca/02/020203/02020305_e.html.**

Locate Military Records in the United Kingdom

Military records are of great interest in the United Kingdom because they are inextricably linked with documenting the history of the British Isles going back as far as William the Conqueror. You will find during your research that literally hundreds of books have been written about military conflicts that have involved the British Isles and their residents. The authors have used manuscripts and historical accounts of the military units and individuals, and have worked with the wealth of records that have been preserved. The Naval & Military Press, for example, is one of the largest independent booksellers in Britain, and their focus is on specialized titles concerning military conflicts. You can visit their Web site at **http://www.naval-military-press.com** to view or search for specific titles and subjects.

Understand the Historical Background

It is important with any research in the British Isles to spend time understanding the historical background of the area where your ancestors lived. This is especially true when seeking military records because understanding the military structure at that time can help you determine what might be available and where any existing records may be located.

The English Civil War (1642–1649) is an important milestone in your military research. Prior to that period, there were no standing armies in England and Wales. Armed forces were raised as needed to fight in specific wars or special circumstances. Parliament raised the New Model Army, an organization of professional soldiers, in February of 1645 in order to more effectively fight the forces of King Charles I. This really was the first real army in England. The Union of 1707 brought England and Scotland together and Scottish regiments became part of the English armed forces after that period.

A significant number of army documents exist from about 1660, and some fragmentary military records from slightly earlier can also be found. However, it is not until you begin researching military units dating from the early 1700s that you will find that large numbers of military documents have survived and have been preserved. Still, the records from these periods are records of organizations and not for specific individuals.

King Henry VIII's reign saw the formation of the first permanent British navy. A few naval records exist from approximately 1617; however, the majority of the surviving records date from the about 1660, the same era as those of the army.

Soldiers were organized into specific units that were known by various designations depending on the function of the organization. It helps to know that infantry troops were organized into regiments, and that subdivisions of these regiments were battalions and companies. Cavalry regiments were subdivided into squadrons, while the artillery units were subdivided into batteries. The subdivision distinctions were typically named in earlier times after their commanding officers, and it was not until the 1700s that numeric designations and a description were used to distinguish one from another. That does not mean that commanders' names were no longer used in references to the units, because you still might encounter a reference to a numeric designation along with a reference to a specific commander's group. Other designations you will find for military units on active duty include armies, corps, divisions, brigades, and others. If your ancestor was an officer, there may be specific records concerning his service and command. However, if he was not an officer, it may be more difficult to locate specific records for him unless you know the unit in which he served, especially in the military records prior to the 20th century, which may not have been well organized and indexed.

If all of this seems confusing to you, don't feel that you are alone. The designations and names that were used have changed over time, and this just serves to illustrate the importance of learning more about your ancestor's origins and the military history of the era *and unit* in which he may have served. This can be especially important if your ancestor did not serve in the government's army but instead served in a volunteer militia.

Locate the Repositories Where Records Are Held

The National Archives in Kew, Richmond, Surrey, is the best starting point for your military research. The National Archives was formed in April 2003 from the Public Record Office (also known as the PRO) and the Historical Manuscripts Commission (HMC). Movement of the holdings of the HMC to Kew was completed in the autumn of 2003, and everything is now housed and accessible at one location. When you are reading reference materials that refer to the PRO or the HMC, remember that these now refer to the holdings of the National Archives whose Web site is at **http://www.nationalarchives.gov.uk.**

Military documents at the National Archives have been organized, stored, and cataloged in groups for ease of access, and a majority of these records have been microfilmed. Therefore, the National Archives' holdings form a huge body of reference material that can help you learn more and more successfully locate military documents for your ancestor. In addition, you will find that specific governmental and civilian organizations can provide information and reference assistance.

Army Records   Army records prior to 1914 are held at the National Archives. Officers' records from 1914–1920 have been transferred from the Army Records Centre (ARC) to the National Archives, and those from 1920 and later remain at the ARC. Records of enlisted personnel from 1914 and later remain at the ARC.

You will want to visit the Army Museums Ogilby Trust Web site's "Ancestor Tracing" pages at **http://www.armymuseums.org.uk/ancestor.htm** to determine what is in their holdings and what may have been transferred to the National Archives, especially as this situation changes over time. You also will want to visit their Useful Addresses page at **http://www.armymuseums.org.uk/ addr.htm** for postal, e-mail, and Web site addresses that may supplement your research.

Navy Records   Naval records can be a bit more problematic to locate. Royal Navy records prior to 1914 are held at the National Archives, while post-1914 records are retained by the Ministry of Defence in Whitehall, London. The location of records, however, is subject to change periodically. Some good references for the location and accessibility of naval records are found at the Web site of the Mariners Mailing List at **http://www.mariners-l.co.uk/UKRNPersonnel.html** and **http://www.mariners-l.co.uk/UK20thCSeamen.html.** In addition, be sure to check the United Kingdom Maritime Collections Strategy Web site at **http://www.ukmcs.org.uk** for links and access to specific sites holding maritime materials that may be of help in your research.

Ministry of Defence   The Ministry of Defence's Veterans Agency is the place to begin your inquiry for personnel service records and pension information for those who served in the armed forces from World War II and later. The Web site at **http://www.veteransagency.mod.uk/servicerecs/ servrecs.htm** contains links for Service Records, Medals, Remembrance, and for specific information for the Royal Navy, the Army, the Royal Air Force, and for non-U.K. and Commonwealth Service Personnel.

Military Museums of Note   Military museums hold fascinating collections of historical military materials that may be useful in your research. The following list highlights some of the best of these resources:

Imperial War Museum—**http://www.iwm.org.uk**

National Army Museum—**http://www.national-army-museum.ac.uk**

National Maritime Museum—**http://www.nmm.ac.uk**

Royal Air Force Museum—**http://www.rafmuseum.org.uk**

Royal Marines Museum—**http://www.royalmarinesmuseum.co.uk**

Royal Naval Museum—**http://www.royalnavalmuseum.org**

Royal Navy Submarine Museum—**http://www.rnsubmus.co.uk**

Other Helpful Resources   Don't overlook the resources of local public and academic libraries in the area in which your ancestors lived or from which they may have served. Other helpful resources in locating military records and historical materials include the following organizations:

■ Federation of Family History Societies (FFHS)
  http://www.ffhs.org.uk

Gazettes Online (London, Belfast, and Edinburgh)
  http://www.gazettes-online.co.uk

GENUKI—British Military Records page
  http://www.genuki.org.uk/big/BritMilRecs.html

Types of Military Records in the United Kingdom

Military records may vary across the different branches of service. There are document types that you may expect to locate, especially among the more modern era.

Attestation Form   Attestation forms were completed by most recruits when they applied to be admitted for service in the military. This is the equivalent of an enlistment form in other military organizations, such as the United States armed forces. The attestation form usually asked for the person's name, date and place of birth, place of residence, occupation and/or skills, and physical description. Later forms asked for parents' names and other information.

Muster Rolls and Pay Lists   Military units tracked the physical presence of troops and their attendance using muster rolls. Regular assembly of troops included roll calls and reports of persons missing. These rolls exist by unit and can be used to verify your ancestor's presence or status in a specific location at a precise point in time. Pay records exist in various forms ranging from payroll lists to individuals' payment stubs and/or receipts.

- **Personnel Records** These, too, vary in their existence and content over time.

- **Casualty Lists and Returns** As a result of muster calls, observations, reports, and medical information, casualty lists were created for the military unit. Depending on the time period, individual forms may have been created to document a person's injuries or death. These can take the shape of a letter or form, and there may also be copies of correspondence in an individual's personnel or service file and/or in the military unit's files.

- **Medical Records** Medical records may be included in an individual's personnel file, in the records of the military unit or the appropriate echelon, or may still exist in the archives of the medical facility in which the individual was treated. Summary reports were often sent to the military unit for its records, while sometimes the records are quite extensive. Figure 6-3 shows a single page from a lengthy medical summary for an English soldier wounded by shrapnel in World War II and who underwent several years' treatment for his wounds.

- **Records of Deserters** Military life was difficult at the best of times, and harsh conditions induced some individuals to desert. Military units maintained lists of deserters and records were included in the individual's records. In addition, the British military published lists of deserters in public newspapers and in the *Police Gazette*. You will find that these records may be helpful if your ancestor "disappeared" from the military at a particular time.

- **Records of Courts Martial** Military discipline was notoriously harsh, and a great deal was made of conducting and publicizing the court martial of personnel. Military court and tribunal records include records of hearings and trials, and detailed records are to be found in unit records and in an individual's service records. In addition, accounts of a high-profile person's court martial may sometimes be found in newspapers of the period.

- **Discharge Papers** Discharge papers vary greatly from different periods. The earliest ones are nothing more than handwritten statements confirming the name, dates, and regiment in which the individual served, signed either by an officer or clerk in the organization. Later there were forms used that provided space for the name, rank, military unit, dates of service, places where the individual served and campaigns in which he had participated, any wounds suffered, physical condition at the time of discharge, and statements concerning the individual's character and performance. Later versions of the forms used included inoculation records and other data.

- **Pension Files** Veterans and/or their surviving spouse and/or family members were entitled to certain pension benefits. In order to obtain a benefit, a person had to make an application. This might take the form of a written petition or an appearance before a court or hearing board. Documentation is therefore likely to exist in one or more places. You may find pension records and related documents in the possession of the National Archives or through a specific veterans' organization. Veterans' groups and organizations formed to assist veterans in obtaining benefits may be particularly helpful to your research. The Ministry of Defence's Veterans Agency maintains a page of Web links to ex-service organizations. You can access that Web site at **http://www.veteransagency.mod.uk/links/exservice.htm.**

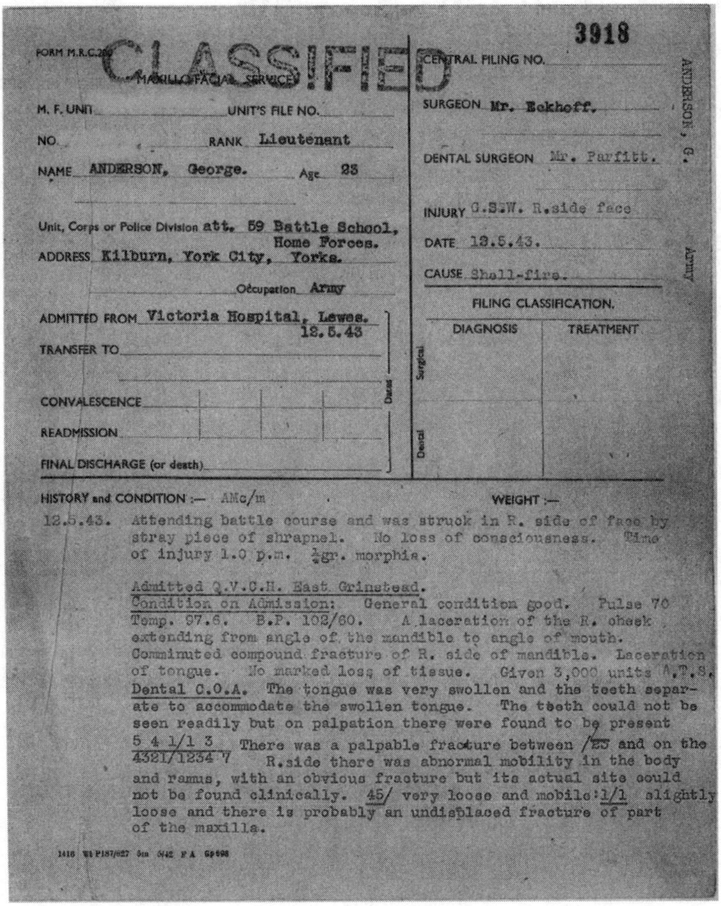

3918

FORM M.R.C.20 CLASSIFIED

MAXILLO-FACIAL SERVICE

M. F. UNIT ______ UNIT'S FILE NO. ______

NO. ______ RANK Lieutenant

NAME ANDERSON, George. Age 23

Unit, Corps or Police Division att. 59 Battle School, Home Forces.

ADDRESS Kilburn, York City, Yorks.

Occupation Army

ADMITTED FROM Victoria Hospital, Lewes. 12.5.43

TRANSFER TO ______

CONVALESCENCE ______

READMISSION ______

FINAL DISCHARGE (or death) ______

Dates

CENTRAL FILING NO. ______

SURGEON Mr. Eckhoff.

DENTAL SURGEON Mr. Parfitt.

INJURY G.S.W. R.side face

DATE 12.5.43.

CAUSE Shell-fire.

FILING CLASSIFICATION.

	DIAGNOSIS	TREATMENT
Surgical		
Dental		

ANDERSON, G. Army

HISTORY and CONDITION :— AMc/m WEIGHT :—

12.5.43. Attending battle course and was struck in R. side of face by stray piece of shrapnel. No loss of consciousness. Time of injury 1.0 p.m. ¼gr. morphia.

Admitted Q.V.C.H. East Grinstead.
Condition on Admission: General condition good. Pulse 70 Temp. 97.6. B.P. 102/60. A laceration of the R. cheek extending from angle of the mandible to angle of mouth. Comminuted compound fracture of R. side of mandible. Laceration of tongue. No marked loss of tissue. Given 3,000 units A.T.S. Dental C.O.A. The tongue was very swollen and the teeth separate to accommodate the swollen tongue. The teeth could not be seen readily but on palpation there were found to be present 5 4 1/1 3 / 4321/1234 7 There was a palpable fracture between /23 and on the R.side there was abnormal mobility in the body and ramus, with an obvious fracture but its actual site could not be found clinically. 45/ very loose and mobile: 1/1 slightly loose and there is probably an undisplaced fracture of part of the maxilla.

1416 Wt P187/627 5m 5/42 F A G$698

FIGURE 6-3 Page from medical records of a wounded English soldier in World War II (Courtesy of Gillian M. Anderson)

Military Records for Ireland

Military records for Ireland and its citizens who served in the military during the time that it was under the British government will be found among those records at the National Archives. Ireland has its own army, navy, and air corps forces, and those more modern records will be in the possession of the Irish government. An excellent Web site to begin your research for more contemporary Irish military history and records is the Defence Forces site located at **http://www.military.ie.**

As you can see, there are many, many avenues of research available for your search for military records in the British Isles. It is therefore important to conduct your preliminary historical research in advance so that you are better informed concerning what records may or may not be available and where to search for them.

Examine Samples of Military Records

I find that one helpful strategy in investigating military records is to examine specific representative examples of records created during the period I am researching. Army, navy, marine, and air force records created during World War II in the United States all contain similar if not identical information. Military records from the same period in the United Kingdom will all contain information of a similar type as defined and required by the central government organization. Examining these materials can provide insight into just what types of data *were* recorded, and this helps me focus my search on those records as well as other locations where identical or similar data were collected. Therefore, if I am unable to locate the information in one place, I can investigate alternate research paths to possibly locate it elsewhere.

There are many reference books available that can help you learn more about military records and their contents. James C. Neagles' books, *U. S. Military Records: A Guide to Federal and State Sources, Colonial America to the Present* and *Confederate Research Sources: A Guide to Archive Collections,* are both excellent American references. Mark D. Herber's book, *Ancestral Trails: The Complete Guide to British Genealogy and Family History,* contains an exhaustive study of available military records for that area. Other books, such as John J. Newman's about United States World War I draft registrations, titled *Uncle, We are Ready! Registering America's Men, 1917-1918,* provide comprehensive, definitive information to help you research specialized topic areas and record types. You will find that these and other reference works can help you significantly with your research. You just need to start investigating what is available.

Your research into military records can provide you with many details about the individual. Let's look at a number of specific examples of military records from the United States. These are not arranged in chronological sequence by when these records were created, but rather in something of a logical order in which they might occur in the career of a serviceperson.

Enlistment and Draft Registration Records

Some of the most detailed and descriptive records you will find are those relating to the enlistment or conscription of personnel. They contain name and address, date and location of birth, parents' names, a personal physical description, and other information, depending on the era. Bear in mind, however, that the information supplied on these documents should be corroborated with other sources. For example, it is not unusual for a minor to lie about his or her age in order to enlist in the military. It was not until well into the 20th century when formal birth certificates were created that a person was required to present such official proof of his age.

Figures 6-4 and 6-5 show both sides of a sample World War II draft registration card from the files at NARA. On the front are spaces for a serial number for the registration, the registrant's name, residential and mailing addresses, telephone number, date and place of birth, the name and address of a person who will always know the applicant's address, the employer's name and address, and the signature of the registrant.

The back of the card provides boxes to indicate race and to enter physical characteristics: height, weight, skin complexion, and any other distinguishing features or marks. In this case, the man had a scar on his left thumb. Birth marks, moles, and scars were the most common features listed.

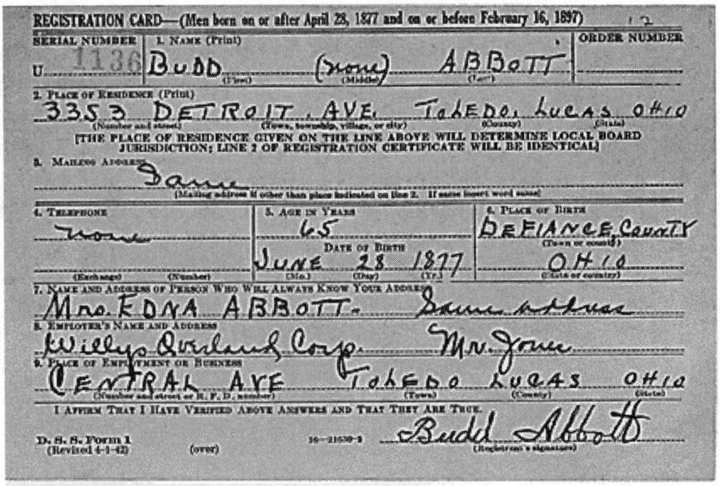

FIGURE 6-4 Front of a World War II draft registration card (National Archives and Records Administration collection)

FIGURE 6-5 Back of a World War II draft registration card (National Archives and Records Administration collection)

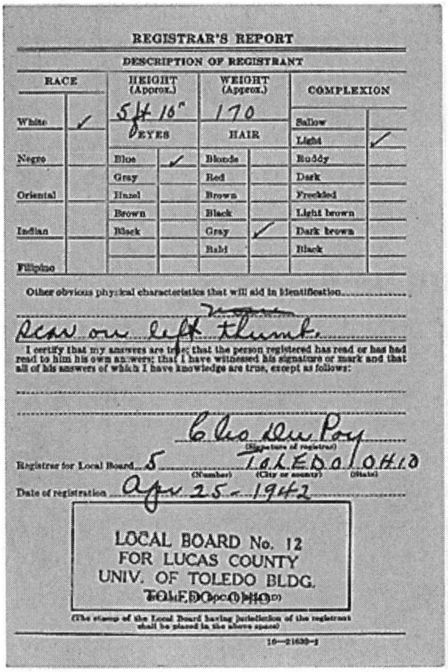

The card was then signed by the person who took the registration information indicating that the registrant has read or has had read to him all of the answers listed and has signed the card in the registrar's presence. The registrar indicated the local draft board to which he or she was attached and its location, and dated the registration. The stamp of the local draft board that had jurisdiction over the area in which the applicant lived was also applied. You will note in this example that the registrar was attached to local board 5 but that the stamp indicates local board 12. It was not unusual for registrars to move between board offices as needed.

The information on this draft card may point you to city directory listings, a voter registration, driver's license, land and property records, religious congregations in the area, employment records, and other records. The name of the person who would always know the applicant's address is most often that of a family member or other relative, which provides yet another research lead for you. In this case, Mrs. Edna Abbott may be the registrant's mother, aunt, or a sister-in-law, and you might look for census records, city and telephone directories, land and property records, death certificate, a will and probate record, obituaries, and other evidence to link the two persons together and to learn more about them.

Military Muster Rolls and Pay Records

Military units regularly muster their troops to verify attendance, issue orders, make announcements, drill, and perform other functions. Muster roll records for a military unit and muster cards for individual soldiers can be found in many United States military service files from the colonial period forward. In addition, unit payroll records and payment stubs or receipts can provide important information to help place your ancestor at a specific place and time. The pay stub shown in Figure 6-6 for my ancestor, John Sords [sic, Swords] indicates that he was paid "Three pounds, five Shill', & eight Pence half Penny Sterling" for 43 days of military duty in 1782. Coupled with other military records, such as his sworn affidavit of service found in his Revolutionary War pension file, it is possible to link John Swords with a particular military command at that date. Further, by researching military history for that unit, I can determine where he traveled and what military action he saw.

Educational and Training Records

Military personnel are trained to perform their jobs at an optimal level. We are all familiar with the idea of infantry troops going through their drills of marching, combat assault, hand-to-hand combat, rifle practice and marksmanship, use of artillery equipment, bivouac, flight training, seamanship, and a wide range of operations training. Military service records can contain information about the education testing and evaluation of an individual's skills and any specialized education or training provided. The records you may encounter in an individual's personnel files and/or the service files may include test scores, correspondence documenting successful completion of training, certificates, and diplomas. Figure 6-7 is an example of a certificate of completion of an Air Force medical training course.

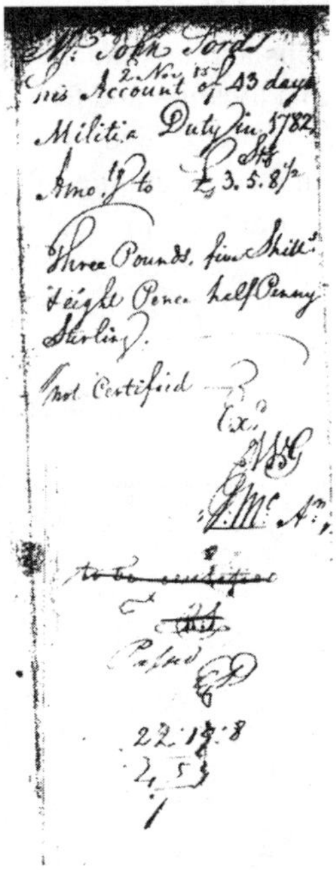
Mr. John Sords
his Account of 43 days
Militia Duty in 1782
Amo'g to £3.5.8½ Stg
Three Pounds, five Shills
& eight Pence half Penny
Sterling
Not Certified
Ex'd

FIGURE 6-6 Revolutionary War pay record for John Swords' military service in 1782 from a NARA pension file (From the author's collection)

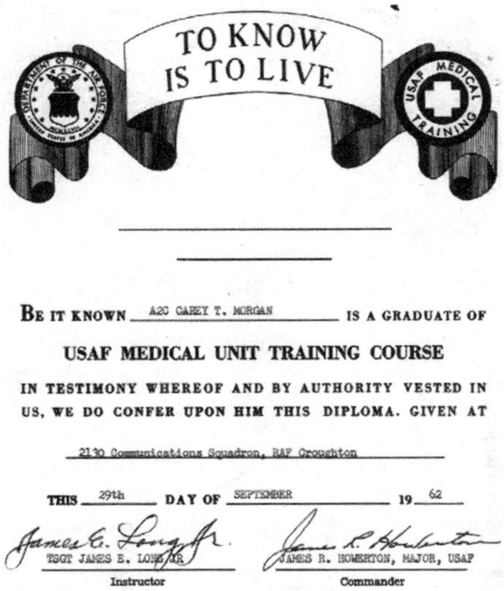

BE IT KNOWN A2C CAREY T. MORGAN IS A GRADUATE OF

USAF MEDICAL UNIT TRAINING COURSE

IN TESTIMONY WHEREOF AND BY AUTHORITY VESTED IN US, WE DO CONFER UPON HIM THIS DIPLOMA. GIVEN AT

2130 Communications Squadron, RAF Croughton

THIS 29th DAY OF SEPTEMBER 19 62

TSGT JAMES E. LONG JR. — Instructor

JAMES R. HOMERTON, MAJOR, USAF — Commander

FIGURE 6-7 Certificate of completion of a medical training course (Courtesy of Carey T. Morgan)

Station and Duty Assignment Orders

Personnel are assigned to specific locations and are attached to specific units. Documents are created to order the individual to report to a location and to perform explicit duties or functions. These documents are often referred to as "orders," and the individual is typically charged with delivering his or her orders to the new unit's commanding officer or clerk. A copy of the orders is retained in the individual's service file. Figure 6-8 shows an example of a Permanent Change of Station Order. Again, the information in this document can be used to verify the movement of an individual from one place to another and to help relate his or her service to the activities of the military unit at that time.

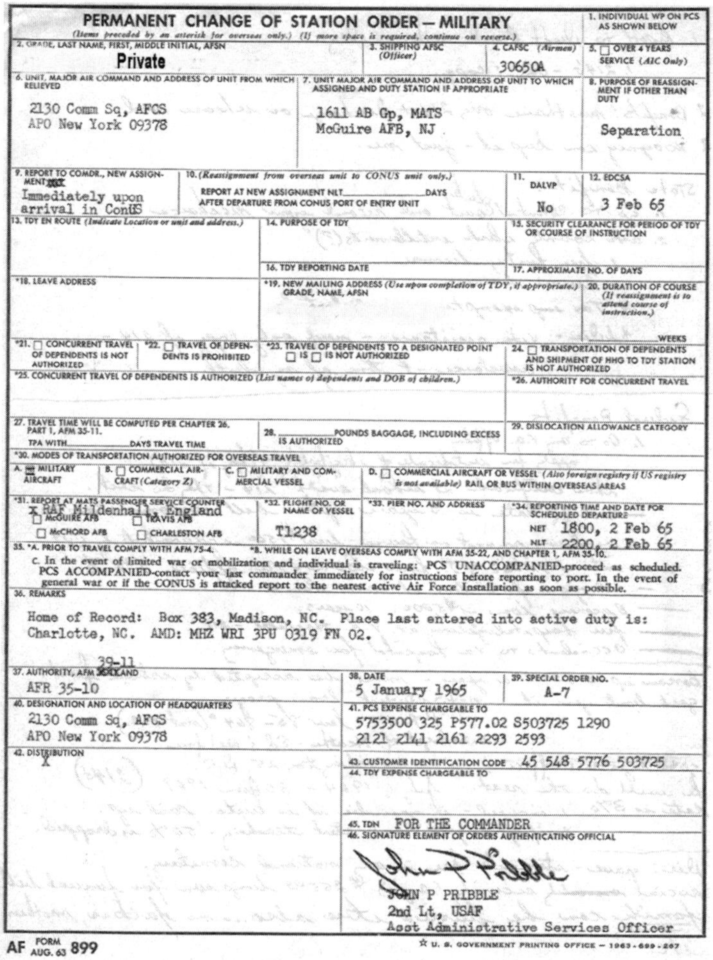
PERMANENT CHANGE OF STATION ORDER — MILITARY
(Items preceded by an asterisk for overseas only.) (If more space is required, continue on reverse.)

1. INDIVIDUAL WP ON PCS AS SHOWN BELOW
2. GRADE, LAST NAME, FIRST, MIDDLE INITIAL, AFSN: Private
3. SHIPPING AFSC (Officer)
4. CAFSC (Airmen): 30650A
5. ☐ OVER 4 YEARS SERVICE (AIC Only)
6. UNIT, MAJOR AIR COMMAND AND ADDRESS OF UNIT FROM WHICH RELIEVED: 2130 Comm Sq, AFCS APO New York 09378
7. UNIT MAJOR AIR COMMAND AND ADDRESS OF UNIT TO WHICH ASSIGNED AND DUTY STATION IF APPROPRIATE: 1611 AB Gp, MATS McGuire AFB, NJ
8. PURPOSE OF REASSIGNMENT IF OTHER THAN DUTY: Separation
9. REPORT TO COMDR., NEW ASSIGNMENT: Immediately upon arrival in ConUS
10. (Reassignment from overseas unit to CONUS unit only.) REPORT AT NEW ASSIGNMENT NLT ____ DAYS AFTER DEPARTURE FROM CONUS PORT OF ENTRY UNIT
11. DALVP: No
12. EDCSA: 3 Feb 65
13. TDY EN ROUTE (Indicate Location or unit and address.)
14. PURPOSE OF TDY
15. SECURITY CLEARANCE FOR PERIOD OF TDY OR COURSE OF INSTRUCTION
16. TDY REPORTING DATE
17. APPROXIMATE NO. OF DAYS
*18. LEAVE ADDRESS
*19. NEW MAILING ADDRESS (Use upon completion of TDY, if appropriate.) GRADE, NAME, AFSN
20. DURATION OF COURSE (If reassignment is to attend course of instruction.) ____ WEEKS
*21. ☐ CONCURRENT TRAVEL OF DEPENDENTS IS NOT AUTHORIZED
*22. ☐ TRAVEL OF DEPENDENTS IS PROHIBITED
*23. TRAVEL OF DEPENDENTS TO A DESIGNATED POINT ☐ IS ☐ IS NOT AUTHORIZED
24. ☐ TRANSPORTATION OF DEPENDENTS AND SHIPMENT OF HHG TO TDY STATION IS NOT AUTHORIZED
*25. CONCURRENT TRAVEL OF DEPENDENTS IS AUTHORIZED (List names of dependents and DOB of children.)
*26. AUTHORITY FOR CONCURRENT TRAVEL
27. TRAVEL TIME WILL BE COMPUTED PER CHAPTER 26, PART 1, AFM 35-11. TPA WITH ____ DAYS TRAVEL TIME
28. ____ POUNDS BAGGAGE, INCLUDING EXCESS IS AUTHORIZED
29. DISLOCATION ALLOWANCE CATEGORY
*30. MODES OF TRANSPORTATION AUTHORIZED FOR OVERSEAS TRAVEL
A. ☒ MILITARY AIRCRAFT B. ☐ COMMERCIAL AIRCRAFT (Category Z) C. ☐ MILITARY AND COMMERCIAL VESSEL D. ☐ COMMERCIAL AIRCRAFT OR VESSEL (Also foreign registry if US registry is not available) RAIL OR BUS WITHIN OVERSEAS AREAS
*31. REPORT AT MATS PASSENGER SERVICE COUNTER: x RAF Mildenhall, England ☐ McGUIRE AFB ☐ TRAVIS AFB ☐ McCHORD AFB ☐ CHARLESTON AFB
*32. FLIGHT NO. OR NAME OF VESSEL: T1238
*33. PIER NO. AND ADDRESS
*34. REPORTING TIME AND DATE FOR SCHEDULED DEPARTURE: NET 1800, 2 Feb 65 NLT 2200, 2 Feb 65
35. *A. PRIOR TO TRAVEL COMPLY WITH AFM 75-4. *B. WHILE ON LEAVE OVERSEAS COMPLY WITH AFM 35-22, AND CHAPTER 1, AFM 35-10.
C. In the event of limited war or mobilization and individual is traveling: PCS UNACCOMPANIED-proceed as scheduled. PCS ACCOMPANIED-contact your last commander immediately for instructions before reporting to port. In the event of general war or if the CONUS is attacked report to the nearest active Air Force Installation as soon as possible.
36. REMARKS: Home of Record: Box 383, Madison, NC. Place last entered into active duty is: Charlotte, NC. AMD: MHZ WRI 3PU 0319 FN 02.
37. AUTHORITY, AFM 39-11 AND: AFR 35-10
38. DATE: 5 January 1965
39. SPECIAL ORDER NO.: A-7
40. DESIGNATION AND LOCATION OF HEADQUARTERS: 2130 Comm Sq, AFCS APO New York 09378
41. PCS EXPENSE CHARGEABLE TO: 5753500 325 P577.02 S503725 1290 2121 2141 2161 2293 2593
42. DISTRIBUTION: X
43. CUSTOMER IDENTIFICATION CODE: 45 548 5776 503725
44. TDY EXPENSE CHARGEABLE TO
45. TDN: FOR THE COMMANDER
46. SIGNATURE ELEMENT OF ORDERS AUTHENTICATING OFFICIAL: JOHN P PRIBBLE 2nd Lt, USAF Asst Administrative Services Officer

AF FORM AUG. 63 899
☆ U. S. GOVERNMENT PRINTING OFFICE — 1963-699-267

FIGURE 6-8 Permanent Change of Station Order (From the author's collection)

Promotions and Commissions

A successful individual may, in the course of his or her military service, be promoted to higher levels of authority and greater responsibility. In the United States armed forces, there is a distinction made between recruits, non-commissioned officers (also known as NCOs), and commissioned officers. You can learn more about the various ranks by researching the individual branches of the military service and their history at the time your ancestor or family member served. There are typically several documents associated with a personnel promotion or a commission.

A promotion of a non-commissioned officer is usually documented with a written notice to the serviceperson, a copy to the every level of command under which the person serves, a copy to the person's file, and a notice posted in a unit's communication media, i.e., on a bulletin board, in a newsletter, or in some other venue.

An officer's commission is more formal. A congratulatory letter is delivered to the individual formally announcing the commissioning. The notification processes throughout the echelon are similar. In addition to the letter, an example of which is shown in Figure 6-9, a formal certificate like the one shown in Figure 6-10 commemorating the new appointment is created and presented to the individual.

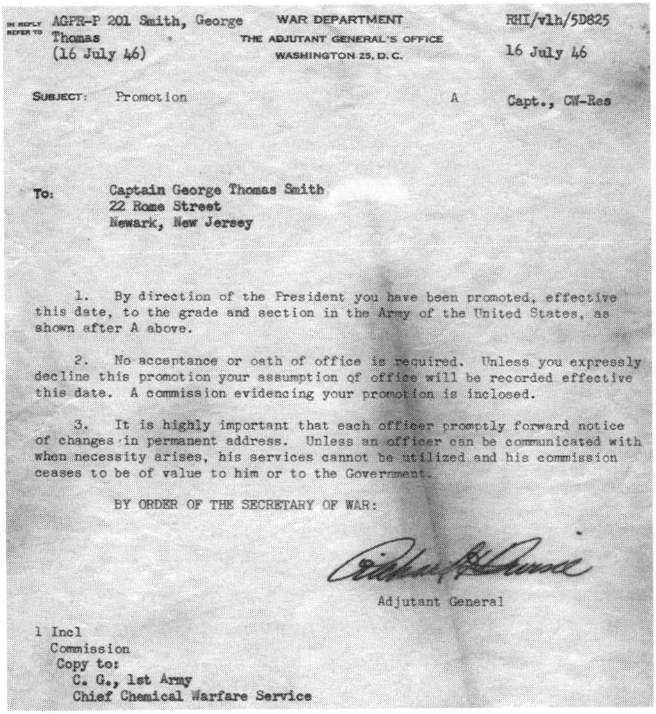

IN REPLY REFER TO AGPR-P 201 Smith, George Thomas (16 July 46)

WAR DEPARTMENT
THE ADJUTANT GENERAL'S OFFICE
WASHINGTON 25, D. C.

RHI/vlh/5D825
16 July 46

SUBJECT: Promotion A Capt., CW-Res

To: Captain George Thomas Smith
22 Rome Street
Newark, New Jersey

1. By direction of the President you have been promoted, effective this date, to the grade and section in the Army of the United States, as shown after A above.

2. No acceptance or oath of office is required. Unless you expressly decline this promotion your assumption of office will be recorded effective this date. A commission evidencing your promotion is inclosed.

3. It is highly important that each officer promptly forward notice of changes in permanent address. Unless an officer can be communicated with when necessity arises, his services cannot be utilized and his commission ceases to be of value to him or to the Government.

BY ORDER OF THE SECRETARY OF WAR:

Adjutant General

1 Incl
Commission
Copy to:
C. G., 1st Army
Chief Chemical Warfare Service

FIGURE 6-9 Letter notifying George Thomas Smith of his promotion to Captain (Courtesy of Jeff Smith)

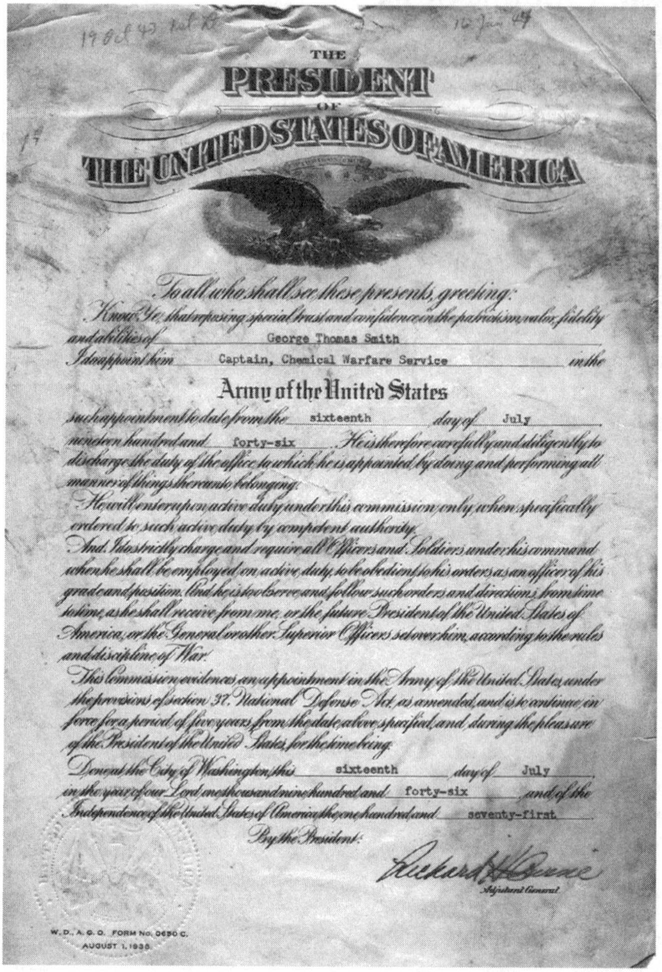

THE
PRESIDENT
OF
THE UNITED STATES OF AMERICA

To all who shall see these presents, greeting:

Know Ye, that reposing special trust and confidence in the patriotism, valor, fidelity and abilities of George Thomas Smith I do appoint him Captain, Chemical Warfare Service in the

Army of the United States

such appointment to date from the sixteenth day of July nineteen hundred and forty-six. He is therefore carefully and diligently to discharge the duty of the office to which he is appointed by doing and performing all manner of things thereunto belonging.

He will enter upon active duty under this commission only when specifically ordered to such active duty by competent authority.

And I do strictly charge and require all Officers and Soldiers under his command when he shall be employed on active duty, to be obedient to his orders as an officer of his grade and position. And he is to observe and follow such orders and directions, from time to time, as he shall receive from me, or the future President of the United States of America, or the General or other Superior Officers set over him, according to the rules and discipline of War.

This Commission evidences an appointment in the Army of the United States under the provisions of section 37, National Defense Act, as amended, and is to continue in force for a period of five years from the date above specified, and during the pleasure of the President of the United States, for the time being.

Done at the City of Washington, this sixteenth day of July in the year of our Lord one thousand nine hundred and forty-six, and of the Independence of the United States of America the one hundred and seventy-first.

By the President:

Adjutant General

W. D., A. G. O. FORM No. 0650 C.
AUGUST 1, 1938

FIGURE 6-10 Certificate commissioning George Thomas Smith to Captain (Courtesy of Jeff Smith)

A promotion or commissioning, the awarding of medals, ribbons, clusters, and special insignia, and the awarding of a commendations and other recognition to the unit or to an individual is a ceremonial occasion. The ceremony may be as simple as an announcement made at a unit formation or a more formal occasion at which dress uniforms are worn, a military band performs, troops march in formation, rifle salutes are fired, and high-ranking officers and other dignitaries speak. In any case, records are created and become part of the military record for the individual and for the military unit.

Discharge and Separation Records

You will find that the normal conclusion of an individual's military service generates a significant number of important documents. A document detailing the permanent change of duty assignment or station order may be created, along with other internal administrative documentation that may or may not be included in an individual's personnel file. There will be, however, some record of discharge or separation. These documents vary depending on the time period. Let's examine three examples.

World War I

Emil I. Hoffman's Honorable Discharge from the United States Army, dated 9 June 1919, is shown in Figure 6-11. This document is important for a number of reasons. It states that he was born in Smorgan, Russia, and that "he was thirty years of age and by occupation a Salesman" when he enlisted. Further, it describes him physically as being 5 feet 4 ¾ inches in height with brown eyes, brown hair, and a ruddy complexion.

On the reverse side of the Honorable Discharge certificate is his enlistment record, shown in Figure 6-12. This document is filled with great information, starting with the date of his enlistment

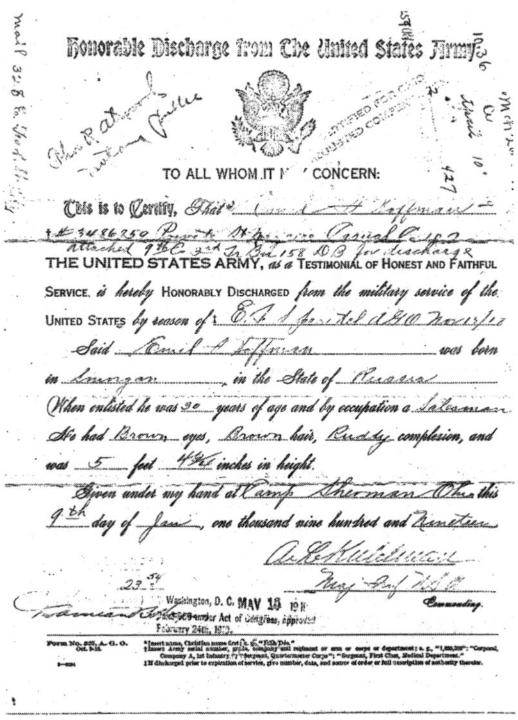

Honorable Discharge from The United States Army

TO ALL WHOM IT MAY CONCERN:

This is to Certify, That* Emil I Hoffman

† #3486250 Private

THE UNITED STATES ARMY, as a TESTIMONIAL OF HONEST AND FAITHFUL SERVICE, is hereby HONORABLY DISCHARGED from the military service of the UNITED STATES by reason of ‡

Said Emil I Hoffman was born in Smorgan, in the State of Russia

When enlisted he was 30 years of age and by occupation a Salesman

He had Brown eyes, Brown hair, Ruddy complexion, and was 5 feet 4¾ inches in height.

Given under my hand at Camp Sherman Ohio this 9th day of June, one thousand nine hundred and Nineteen.

Commanding.

Washington, D. C. MAY 15 1919

Act of Congress, approved February 24th, 1919.

FIGURE 6-11 WWI Honorable Discharge from the U.S. Army for Emil I. Hoffman (Courtesy of June H. Roth)

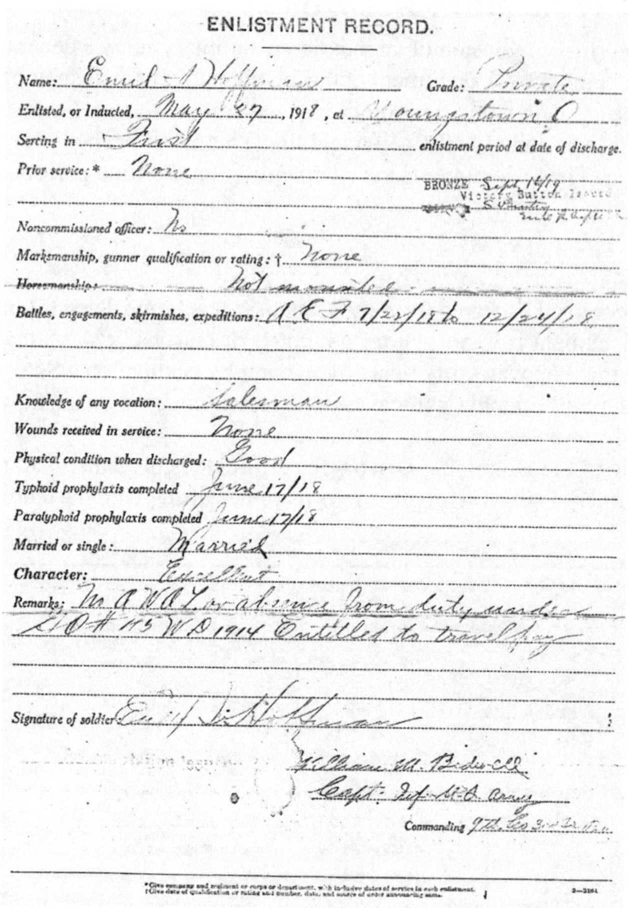

ENLISTMENT RECORD.

Name: Emil A Hoffman Grade: Private

Enlisted, or Inducted, May 27, 1918, at Youngstown O

Serving in First enlistment period at date of discharge.

Prior service: * None

BRONZE Sept 16/19 Victory Button Issued

Noncommissioned officer: No

Marksmanship, gunner qualification or rating: † None

Horsemanship: not mounted

Battles, engagements, skirmishes, expeditions: A E F 7/22/18 to 12/24/18

Knowledge of any vocation: Salesman

Wounds received in service: None

Physical condition when discharged: Good

Typhoid prophylaxis completed June 17/18

Paratyphoid prophylaxis completed June 17/18

Married or single: Married

Character: Excellent

Remarks: No A W O L or absence from duty under G O # 45 W D 1914 Entitled to travel pay

Signature of soldier: Emil A Hoffman

William M. Bidwell

Capt. Inf U.S. Army

Commanding

FIGURE 6-12 WWI Enlistment Record for Emil Hoffman (Courtesy of June H. Roth)

on 27 May 1918 at Youngstown, Ohio. He was not an NCO, and he served with the AEF (Allied Expeditionary Forces) from 22 July 1918 until 24 December 1918. He was married and deemed to be of excellent character. He was vaccinated against typhoid fever and was in good health when he was discharged. A stamp in the upper-right corner and a notation indicates that he received a bronze Victory Lapel Pin on 16 September 1919. The remarks indicate that there was no A.W.O.L. or absence from duty. He also was entitled to travel pay.

World War II

The documentation changed somewhat by the time of the Second World War. In fact, there are even more documents that comprise the military service record and the certificates awarded to the individual.

The Honorable Discharge document and Enlistment Record for George Thomas Smith, which occupy the front and back of a single sheet and which are shown in Figures 6-13 and 6-14, are very similar to those from World War I.

In addition to those records, the separate Honorable Discharge certificate on heavy paper stock, shown in Figure 6-15, was presented to the individual.

Another two-sided document was created and given to the individual at the time of separation. The Certificate of Service shown in Figure 6-16 was another form of honorable discharge documentation. However, on the reverse side is the detailed Military Record and Report of Separation, which is shown in Figure 6-17.

The Military Record and Report of Separation contains name, rank, serial number, military organization and occupation, permanent civilian address, date and place of birth, race, physical description, and marital status. The detailed military history includes the locations where the individual served, decorations and citations, education and training schools attended while enlisted, areas of service outside the United States, and information about continuation of insurance. The right thumb print was applied as another form of identification.

One additional document of interest was awarded to the individual, the Army Air Forces Certificate of Appreciation for War Service, shown in Figure 6-18. I find this document particularly

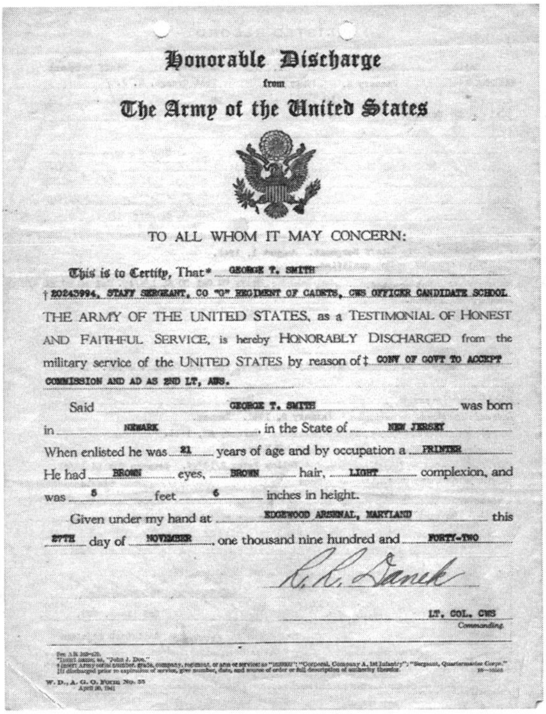

Honorable Discharge
from
The Army of the United States

TO ALL WHOM IT MAY CONCERN:

This is to Certify, That* GEORGE T. SMITH
† 20243994, STAFF SERGEANT, CO "G" REGIMENT OF CADETS, CWS OFFICER CANDIDATE SCHOOL
THE ARMY OF THE UNITED STATES, as a TESTIMONIAL OF HONEST AND FAITHFUL SERVICE, is hereby HONORABLY DISCHARGED from the military service of the UNITED STATES by reason of ‡ CONV OF GOVT TO ACCEPT COMMISSION AND AD AS 2ND LT, AUS.

Said GEORGE T. SMITH was born in NEWARK, in the State of NEW JERSEY
When enlisted he was 21 years of age and by occupation a PRINTER
He had BROWN eyes, BROWN hair, LIGHT complexion, and was 5 feet 6 inches in height.

Given under my hand at EDGEWOOD ARSENAL, MARYLAND this 27TH day of NOVEMBER, one thousand nine hundred and FORTY-TWO

LT. COL. CWS
Commanding

W. D., A. G. O. Form No. 55
April 30, 1941

FIGURE 6-13 WWII Honorable Discharge from the U.S. Army for George Thomas Smith (Courtesy of Jeff Smith)

LISTED RECORD
OF

Smith (Last name) George (First name) T. (Middle initial), 20243994 (Army Serial No.), Staff Sergeant (Grade)
inducted[1] January 6, 1941, at West Orange, N. J.
Completed 1 years, 10 months, 22 days service for longevity pay.
Prior service:[2] None.

Office of the Finance Officer,
Date NOV 28 1942
Paid in Full $ 78.55
G. F. Fischer, 1st Lt., F.D.
Assistant Finance Officer

Noncommissioned officer: Staff Sergeant. August 1, 1942.
Qualification in arms:[3] Not qualified.
Horsemanship: Not mounted. Army specialty: Heavy MG Cal 30 EX 1/6/42. Cal 50 MG EX 6/5/42
Attendance at: None.
Battles, engagements, skirmishes, expeditions: None.
Decorations, service medals citations: Favorably considered for Good Conduct Medal.
Wounds received in service: None.
Date and result of smallpox vaccination:[4] January 8, 1941. Immune.
Date of completion of all typhoid-paratyphoid vaccinations:[4] January 27, 1941.
Date and result of diphtheria immunity test (Schick):[4] None.
Date of other vaccinations (specify vaccine used):[4] Yellow Fever 2/18/42. Tetanus Toxoid 10/41.
Physical condition when discharged: Good Married or single: Single
Character: Excellent
Remarks:[5] No time lost under AW 107. Soldier not entitled to travel allowances.

Print of Right Thumb
Signature of soldier: George T. Smith
2nd Lieut, CWS,
Assistant Adjutant

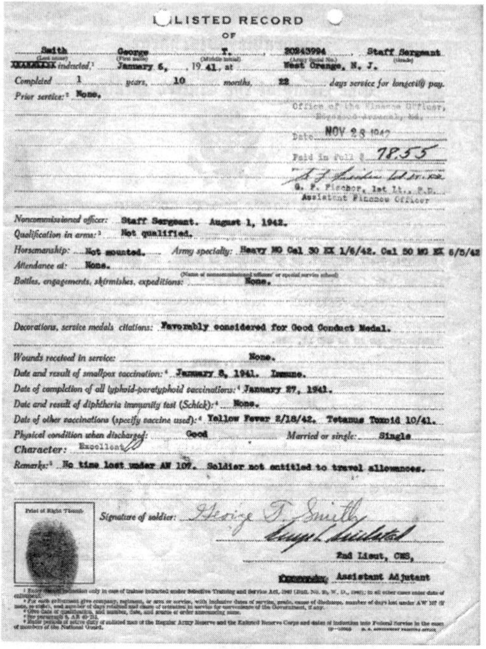

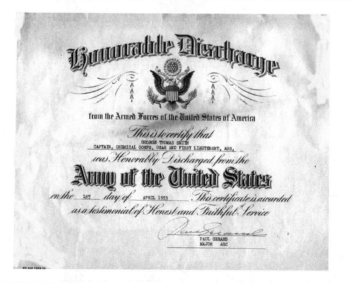

FIGURE 6-14 WWII Enlistment Record for George Thomas Smith (Courtesy of Jeff Smith)

Honorable Discharge
from the Armed Forces of the United States of America
This is to certify that
GEORGE THOMAS SMITH
CAPTAIN, CHEMICAL CORPS, USAR AND FIRST LIEUTENANT, AUS,
was Honorably Discharged from the
Army of the United States
on the 1ST day of APRIL 1953 This certificate is awarded
as a testimonial of Honest and Faithful Service
PAUL GERARD
MAJOR AGC

FIGURE 6-15 Honorable Discharge certificate for George Thomas Smith (Courtesy of Jeff Smith)

Army of the United States

CERTIFICATE OF SERVICE

This is to certify that

FIRST LIEUTENANT GEORGE T SMITH CHEMICAL WARFARE SERVICE
803RD CHEMICAL COMPANY AIR OPERATIONS
BUCKLEY FIELD COLORADO

honorably served in active Federal Service in the Army of the United States from

28 NOVEMBER 1942 to 27 DECEMBER 1945

Given at SEPARATION CENTER FORT DIX NEW JERSEY

on the 27TH day of DECEMBER 19 45

FOR THE COMMANDING OFFICER

C H TALL LT COL INF

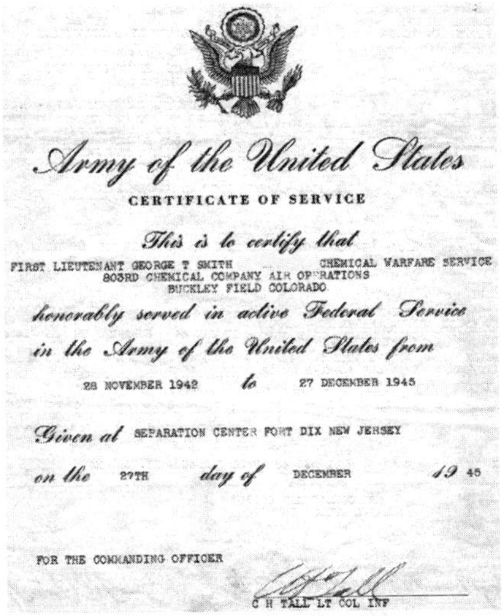

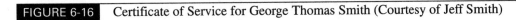

FIGURE 6-16 Certificate of Service for George Thomas Smith (Courtesy of Jeff Smith)

CF 14A 17

MILITARY RECORD AND REPORT OF SEPARATION

CERTIFICATE OF SERVICE

SMITH GEORGE T
Private
1ST LT CWS
AUS
803RD CHEMICAL COMPANY AIR OPERATIONS
BUCKLEY FIELD COLORADO
27 DEC 45
SEPARATION CENTER, FORT DIX NEW JERSEY
22 HOME STREET
NEWARK NEW JERSEY
8 NOV 17
NEWARK NEW JERSEY
SEE 9
BLUE BROWN 5'6" 130 1
X X X
ROTOGRAVURE PRESSMAN 4-48.060

MILITARY HISTORY

X
305 BOULEVARD HASBROUCK HEIGHT NEW JERSEY
28 NOV 42
CHEMICAL WARFARE UNIT COMMANDER 1413
NONE
EUROPEAN AFRICAN MIDDLE EASTERN THEATER CAMPAIGN RIBBON AMERICAN DEFENSE SERVICE MEDAL
NONE
CHEMICAL WARFARE SCHOOL EDGEWOOD ARSENAL MARYLAND AIRFORCE MUNITIONS SCHOOL LEICESTER ENGLAND
17 JAN 44 EUROPEAN TH 28 JAN 44
RELIEF FROM ACTIVE DUTY TWX AAF PDC TF2/REK/2741 25 SEP 45RR1-5 DEMOB
7 AUG 45 U S A 20 AUG 45
1 5 26 1 7 3 8 4 0

INSURANCE NOTICE

X X 31 DEC 45 31 JAN 46 13.75 X

ASR SCORE(2 SEP 45)75
LAPEL BUTTON ISSUED

F P PORTER
2ND LT SIG C ASST ADJ

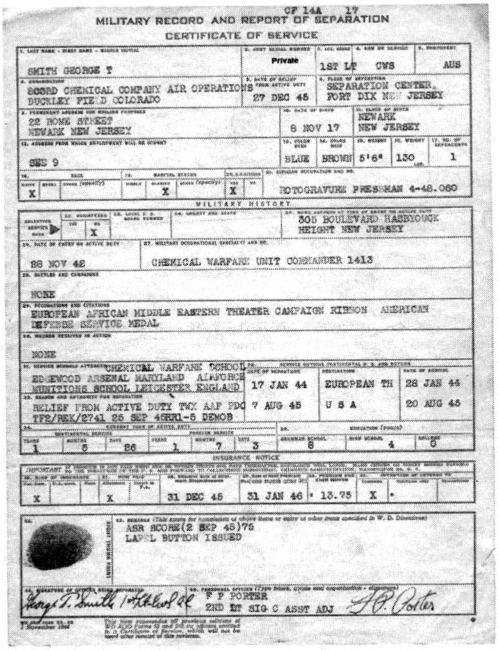

FIGURE 6-17 The Military Record and Report of Separation for George Thomas Smith (Courtesy of Jeff Smith)

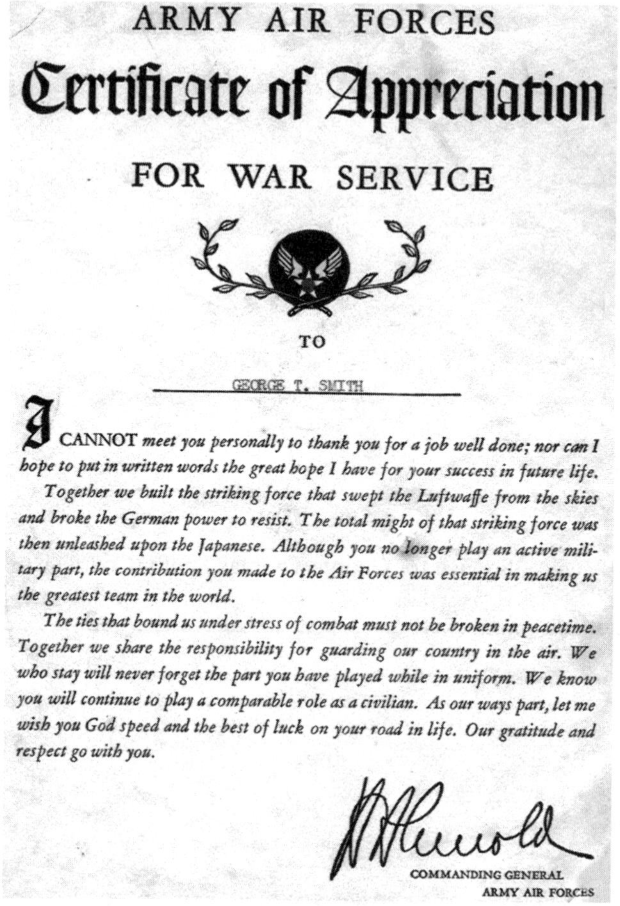

ARMY AIR FORCES
Certificate of Appreciation
FOR WAR SERVICE

TO

GEORGE T. SMITH

I CANNOT meet you personally to thank you for a job well done; nor can I hope to put in written words the great hope I have for your success in future life.

Together we built the striking force that swept the Luftwaffe from the skies and broke the German power to resist. The total might of that striking force was then unleashed upon the Japanese. Although you no longer play an active military part, the contribution you made to the Air Forces was essential in making us the greatest team in the world.

The ties that bound us under stress of combat must not be broken in peacetime. Together we share the responsibility for guarding our country in the air. We who stay will never forget the part you have played while in uniform. We know you will continue to play a comparable role as a civilian. As our ways part, let me wish you God speed and the best of luck on your road in life. Our gratitude and respect go with you.

COMMANDING GENERAL
ARMY AIR FORCES

FIGURE 6-18   Certificate of Appreciation for War Service (Courtesy of Jeff Smith)

interesting in terms of the patriotic text that appears in the second paragraph: "Together we built the striking force that swept the Luftwaffe from the skies and broke the German power to resist. The total might of that striking force was then unleashed upon the Japanese."

Post-World War II

The mix of military documents changed somewhat following World War II. In 1952, a new document, the Report of Transfer or Discharge, was introduced. It was used to facilitate the transfer of personnel between branches of the armed services and to provide document for separation and discharge. The document has become most commonly known and referred to by its form number, DD214, and an example is shown in Figure 6-19. In addition, a certificate of Honorable Discharge was issued.

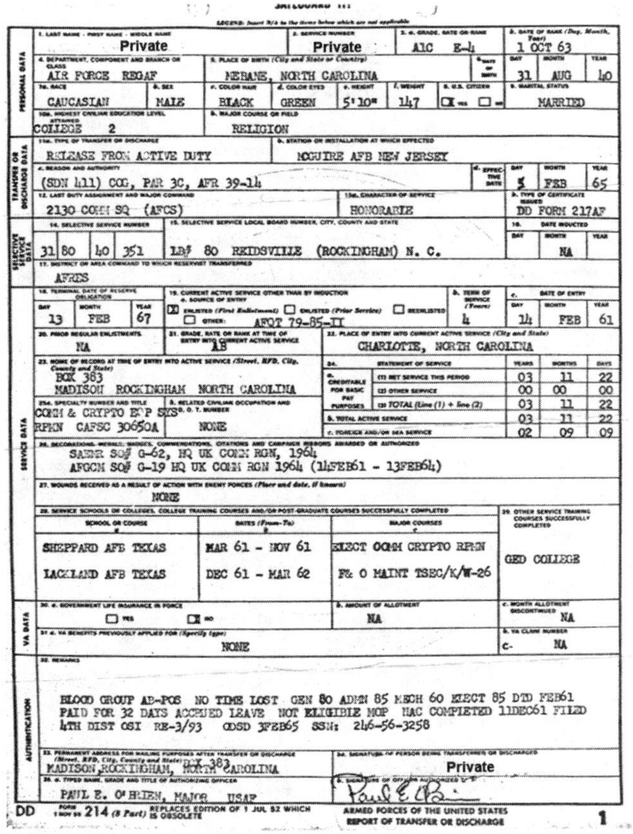

Private | Private | A1C E-4 | 1 OCT 63
AIR FORCE REGAF | MEBANE, NORTH CAROLINA | 31 AUG 40
CAUCASIAN | MALE | BLACK | GREEN | 5'10" | 147 | MARRIED
COLLEGE 2 | RELIGION

RELEASE FROM ACTIVE DUTY | MCGUIRE AFB NEW JERSEY
(SDN 411) COG, PAR 3C, AFR 39-14 | 5 FEB 65
2130 COMM SQ (AFCS) | HONORABLE | DD FORM 217AF

31 80 40 351 | LB# 80 REIDSVILLE (ROCKINGHAM) N. C. | NA
AFRES

13 FEB 67 | AFQT 79-85-II | 4 | 14 FEB 61
NA | AB | CHARLOTTE, NORTH CAROLINA
BOX 383
MADISON ROCKINGHAM NORTH CAROLINA

Statement of Service	Years	Months	Days
(1) Net service this period	03	11	22
(2) Other service	00	00	00
(3) Total (Line (1) + line (2))	03	11	22
b. Total active service	03	11	22
c. Foreign and/or sea service	02	09	09

COMM & CRYPTO EQP SYS RPMN CAFSC 30650A | NONE
SAEMR SO# G-62, HQ UK COMM RGN, 1964
AFGCM SO# G-19 HQ UK COMM RGN 1964 (14FEB61 - 13FEB64)
NONE

School or Course	Dates (From-To)	Major Courses
SHEPPARD AFB TEXAS	MAR 61 - NOV 61	ELECT COMM CRYPTO RPMN
LACKLAND AFB TEXAS	DEC 61 - MAR 62	F& O MAINT TSEC/K/W-26

GED COLLEGE
NA | NA
NONE | C- NA

BLOOD GROUP AB-POS NO TIME LOST GEN 80 ADMN 85 MECH 60 ELECT 85 DTD FEB61
PAID FOR 32 DAYS ACCRUED LEAVE NOT ELIGIBLE MOP NAC COMPLETED 11DEC61 FILED
4TH DIST OSI RE-3/93 CDSD 3FEB65 SSN: 246-56-3258

BOX 383 MADISON, ROCKINGHAM, NORTH CAROLINA | Private
PAUL E. O'BRIEN, MAJOR USAF

DD FORM 214 (8 Part) REPLACES EDITION OF 1 JUL 52 WHICH IS OBSOLETE
ARMED FORCES OF THE UNITED STATES REPORT OF TRANSFER OR DISCHARGE 1

FIGURE 6-19 Report of Transfer or Discharge, also known as the DD214 (From the author's collection)

Death and Burial Records

An inevitable consequence of military service for some is the loss of life. The United States military is meticulous in its communications with surviving family members and in offering support. When military personnel were killed overseas in World War II, they were interred in military cemeteries and families were contacted to determine whether to return the remains to the United States for burial. I have recently reviewed the case of 1st Lieutenant William J. Smith who died in England in 1943. (He was the brother of George Thomas Smith, whose records are included above.) William J. Smith was initially interred in the military cemetery at Brookwood, England. After a series of detailed written communications, the family decided that his remains should stay in England, and the U.S. War Department arranged for permanent interment in the U.S. Military Cemetery in Cambridge, England. Figure 6-20 shows the letter received from the War Department.

WAR DEPARTMENT
OFFICE OF THE QUARTERMASTER GENERAL
WASHINGTON 25, D. C.

5 January 1949

1st Lt William J. Smith, ASN O 661 675
Plot B, Row 7, Grave 25
Headstone: Cross
Cambridge U. S. Military Cemetery

Mr. William H. Smith
22 Rome Street
Newark, New York

Dear Mr. Smith:

This is to inform you that the remains of your loved one have been permanently interred, as recorded above, side by side with comrades who also gave their lives for their country. Customary military funeral services were conducted over the grave at the time of burial.

After the Department of the Army has completed all final interments, the cemetery will be transferred, as authorized by the Congress, to the care and supervision of the American Battle Monuments Commission. The Commission also will have the responsibility for permanent construction and beautification of the cemetery, including erection of the permanent headstone. The headstone will be inscribed with the name exactly as recorded above, the rank or rating where appropriate, organization, State, and date of death. Any inquiries relative to the type of headstone or the spelling of the name to be inscribed thereon, should be addressed to the American Battle Monuments Commission, the central address of which is Room 713, 1712 "G" Street, N. W., Washington 25, D. C. Your letter should include the full name, rank, serial number, grave location, and name of the cemetery.

While interment activities are in progress, the cemetery will not be open to visitors. However, upon completion thereof, due notice will be carried by the press.

You may rest assured that this final interment was conducted with fitting dignity and solemnity and that the grave-site will be carefully and conscientiously maintained in perpetuity by the United States Government.

Sincerely yours,

Thomas B Larkin

THOMAS B. LARKIN
Major General
The Quartermaster General

FIGURE 6-20 Letter from the War Department concerning final interment of 1st Lieutenant William J. Smith (Courtesy of Jeff Smith)

The American Battle Monuments Commission was established by Congress at the request of General John J. Pershing to honor the accomplishments of the American Armed Forces where they have served since World War I. The Commission is responsible for the establishment and maintenance of war memorials and cemeteries in foreign countries. Their Web site at **http://www.abmc.gov** provides access to databases of World War I, World War II, Korean War, and Vietnam War casualties buried overseas. The site provides detailed information about the name, rank, unit, date and place of death, cemetery where the individual is interred, and information about services that the ABMC can provide to help honor and commemorate individuals buried in these places.

Learn from Military Pension Records

Military pension records can be tremendously informative. In order to qualify for benefits, a veteran or surviving spouse or family member must present evidence of identity and proof of military service. As you have seen, the military records from the 20th century that veterans received at the time of separation are easily sufficient to document an application for pension benefits. However, it has not always been so easy.

Individuals who fought in the American Revolution, for example, had to swear an affidavit in a court of law concerning their military service. In addition, they had to bring forward witnesses who served with them and/or who were personally familiar with the service of the individual. The witnesses also had to swear oaths or affidavits concerning their knowledge.

The sworn statements of the veteran typically include details about the dates and places of service, the units in which they served, the names of commanding officers, and details concerning the engagements in which they had participated. Some of these accounts are vivid with details. If the widow of a man who served applied for survivor pension benefits, she was required to swear an oath and provide some evidence of her marriage to the deceased. It is not surprising that sometimes the pension files contain original marriage certificates or pages taken from the center of the family Bible on which marriages, births, and deaths were recorded. Figure 6-21 shows one of several pages from a family Bible that are included as part of the Revolutionary War pension file for my ancestor, John Swords, at the South Carolina State Archives & History Center. These documents were worth more when submitted as evidence to collect monetary benefits than as family documentation.

FIGURE 6-21   Page from the Swords family Bible that was included in the pension file (From the author's collection)

In addition, pension files may include receipts or payment stubs that document annuity payments. These and correspondence in the file may document the life events, medical conditions, and death of the veteran and/or the surviving spouse and other family members. The example shown in Figure 6-22 is a payment document for John Swords. This single document indicates that he served in the army for three years from South Carolina, and that he died on 28 September 1834. It also tells me that his wife collected pension benefits, that she is deceased, and lists the names of all the surviving children as of 13 August 1851.

Pension files for the Revolutionary War, the War of 1812, and for Union veterans Civil War in the United States can be found at NARA. You can order these from NARA using NATF Form 85 and electronically. Visit the NARA Web site for forms at **http://www.archives.gov/research_room/obtain_copies/military_and_genealogy_order_forms.html** to order copies of NATF Form 85 or to initiate an order online.

You may also find that military pensions were paid by both the federal *and* state governments, as I did with John SWORDS. I obtained a Revolutionary War pension file from NARA with more than 20 pages of copies of microfilmed documents. A number of years later, I was researching at the South Carolina State Archive and discovered another, different pension file with more extensive records. In fact, his sworn statement in that file provided details of his capture and imprisonment by the British at the Battle of Savannah. Those details were not included in the statement in the NARA file, and I therefore gained more information and insight into his life.

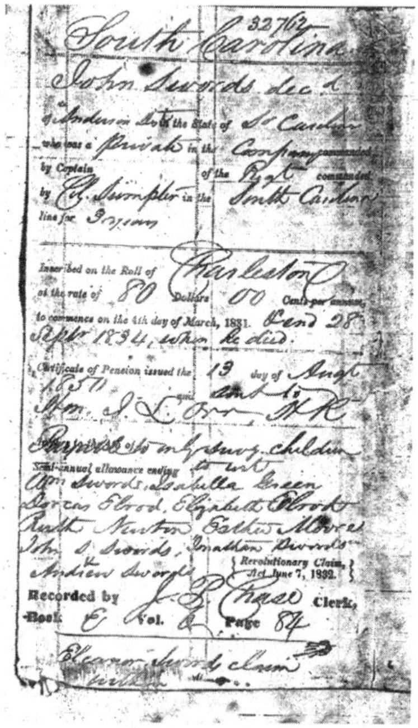

South Carolina 32762

John Swords dec'd

of Anderson Dist the State of So Carolina

who was a Private in the Company commanded

by Captain of the Regt commanded

by Col. Sumpter in the South Carolina

line for 3 years

Inscribed on the Roll of Charleston

at the rate of 80 Dollars 00 Cents per annum,

to commence on the 4th day of March, 1831. and 28 Sept 1834, when he died.

Certificate of Pension issued the 13 day of Augt 1851 and sent to

Hon. J. L. Orr H.R.

Payable to only surv. children

Semi-annual allowance ending to wit

Wm Swords, Isabella Green

Dorcas Elrod, Elizabeth Elrod

Ruth Newton Esther Moore

John S. Swords, Jonathan Swords

Andrew Swords

Revolutionary Claim, Act June 7, 1832.

Recorded by J. B. Chase Clerk,

Book E Vol. 6 Page 84

Eleanor Swords claim

FIGURE 6-22 Record of payment to the widow of John Swords that lists the names of his surviving children (From the author's collection)

Military records, as you have seen, can be a goldmine of detail if you know where to look. Your investment in the study of the history of the area where your ancestors and family members lived and from where they may have served in the military can prepare you for locating records more effectively.

Understand and Use Land and Property Records

Land and property records are among the most numerous records in existence. However, they also are some of the most poorly understood and less used resources by genealogical researchers. There are the perceptions that a) they are cryptic and unfathomable, and b) they contain little of genealogical value.

Like military records, land and property records require some advance research into the history of the geographical area and the types of records that were created at specific periods. In addition, the methods used to define boundaries and register the ownership and transfer of property also need to be understood. However, this is not an insurmountable problem, and once you have invested the time to learn about land and property records, you will find that they are a tremendous source of information. And yes, they *can and do* contain vast amounts of genealogical information to help further your research.

There are many excellent books and reference materials available to help you understand these records in various locations, such as libraries, bookstores, and on the Internet. However, as a beginning, let's explore the basics of land and property records in the United States, Canada, and the United Kingdom. These overviews should provide you with some basic knowledge to get started in locating your ancestors' records in those places, and give you ideas on how to approach similar research in other countries in which your ancestors lived and may have owned property.

Land and Property Records in the United States

The United States' history is a colorful combination of Spanish, English, French, and Mexican influences. Every American schoolchild is taught that Christopher Columbus discovered America in 1492 and, although the place that Columbus "discovered" was not exactly a part of what we know to be the United States of today, this definitely was the beginning of centuries of colonization, conflict, and amazing expansion.

The history of the United States makes for a fascinating study and its settlement parallels that of Canada in many ways. You will find in the course of your genealogical research in both the United States and Canada that land and property records development is similar because of the efforts of both France and England to colonize vast areas of the North American continent. The influence of the Spanish in Florida and the southeast, in California and the west, and in other areas brought Spain's form of government, its religion, all of its governmental processes, and its forms of record-keeping with it. Each time there was a change in government, the land and property records process was impacted from the perspectives of documentation and taxation. However, this could be said for many areas of what is now the United States.

Consider for a moment the Spanish possession of Florida in the 1500s. Spain's Catholic and Jesuit priests spent decades trying to make Christians of the Native Americans in that area. It was a bloody conflict from the outset but the Spanish continued to colonize and settle the area. In fact, the oldest permanent European settlement in the United States is in St. Augustine, Florida, which was established in 1565. The Spanish divided Florida into two administrative regions, east and west. This action continues to influence the state to this day as its capital, Tallahassee, was in the panhandle of the state and the panhandle was a much more populous area than the lower portion of the peninsula. As a result, Tallahassee became and has remained the capital despite the explosive population growth to its southeast. Britain gained possession of what was primarily east Florida in 1763 and ruled there until 1783 when the Spanish once again gained control. During the period of British rule of Florida, residents sought proof from Spain of their ownership of land. The documents created are referred to as "memorials," and these really were petitions for proof of ownership. These are written in Spanish and are among some of the earliest land documents that exist in that area.

Spain and France also struggled for what we know as the Louisiana Territory, with both struggling to colonize and control this vast area. In 1800, Spain signed a secretly negotiated treaty in which it signed over its control of the entire territory to France. When the United States government learned in 1802 that France, and not Spain, had authority over the area, it began negotiations to acquire the territory for itself. This culminated in 1803 with the Louisiana Purchase.

Spanish rule continued in Florida until 1821 when the United States government obtained possession of the area under a reparations treaty negotiated in 1819. At that time, Florida became and remained a territory of the United States until March of 1845 when it became a state. At about the same time, Mexico claimed independence from Spain and, in effect, this ended Spanish rule in what today is the United States.

This short "thumbnail" history is only one example of the kind of historical research that is important to understand as part of your preparation to conduct effective research, especially in the area of land and property records from these early periods. You will want to study the history for the areas and historical periods during which your ancestors lived there to learn more about the government(s) having jurisdiction, the records that were created, and the ultimate disposition of those particular records.

Learn About the Organization of State and Federal Lands

Land and property research in the United States can yield vast amounts of genealogical information if you understand the organization of the materials and where to search. There are two distinct types of what I'll call "land organization" in the United States: State-Land States and Federal-Land States. Understanding the distinction between them is important because the way they are measured and recorded differs. The descriptions provided in this chapter are intended only as an introduction for you. There are many books on the subject of land records in the United States and I would refer you to them for a more detailed study. Perhaps the best of these is E. Wade Hone's book *Land and Property Research in the United States* (Ancestry, Incorporated, 1997).

State-Land States

The term "State-Land States" refers to the fact that the land was originally controlled by the state and sold or distributed by the state itself. Any subsequent land transactions were conducted between private individuals and are therefore often referred to as "private lands." If you examine the list below, it is immediately apparent that many of the State-Land States were part of the original 13 colonies under the control of the British Crown. Others, such as West Virginia, were derived from an original colony. And still others, such as Texas and Hawaii, were controlled by other foreign governments. The State-Land States are

Connecticut	Delaware	Georgia	Hawaii
Kentucky	Maine	Maryland	Massachusetts
New Hampshire	New Jersey	New York	North Carolina
Pennsylvania	Rhode Island	South Carolina	Tennessee
Texas	Vermont	Virginia	West Virginia

6

Following the Revolutionary War, some of the original colonies claimed extensive westward territories as part of their jurisdictions. However, with the formation of the United States federal government and based on individual negotiations with the states, most of the land outside what are the current state boundaries was ceded to the federal government. These lands and other territorial acquisitions by the federal government became what were used to create Federal-Land States.

State-Lands Survey Methods

The common method of land measurement in the State-Land States is referred to as "metes and bounds." This scheme is based on the use of physical natural features such as rocks, trees, and waterways as reference points and the surveyor's chain as a unit of measure. Table 6-2 shows a high-level conversion from surveyor's measurements to feet and inches. You will want to refer to a complete surveyor's conversion table in another reference work.

Surveyor's Measure	Equivalent
1 link	7.92 inches
25 links	1 rod, 1 pole, or 1 perch
100 links	1 chain (also referred to as a Gunter's chain)
1 chain	66 feet
80 chains	1 mile
625 square links	1 square rod
16 square rods	1 square chain
10 square chains	1 square acre

TABLE 6-2   Surveyor's Measurement Conversion

The metes and bounds surveying method dates back to the earliest colonial days and you will find that, as a result, there are some very strange shapes of land parcels. Some surveys included the placement of stakes for use in later surveys. However, since a stake could be physically moved, a parcel of land always had to be completely resurveyed to verify the accuracy of the land holding. You will therefore find, in many surveys and land description records, references to physical features, stakes, and other people's property, as well as the use of standard surveyor's measurements. The surveyor used compass directions stated as north, south, east, west, or combinations, a compass direction in degrees, and a distance measured in surveyors' units, such as chains.

Figure 6-23 shows a surveyor's report prepared for the estate of one Eli JONES who owned property in Caswell County, North Carolina. The report includes representations of roads and waterways, and incorporates references to roads, stakes, pointers, sweet gum trees, and other persons' properties. It uses surveyor's chain measurements to illustrate and describe the property. You will also note that, at the upper end of the drawing of the parcel, there are references to "Dower" and "Dower line." This indicates that the property cited was property owned by the wife, perhaps even brought to the marriage by the bride.

Figure 6-24 shows a detailed section from another survey report that includes a detailed metes and bounds description of the parcel of property.

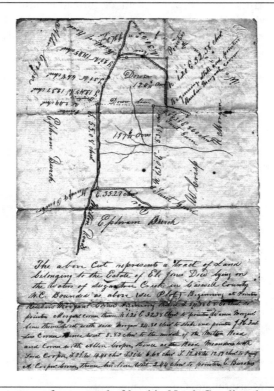

FIGURE 6-23   Survey report for a parcel of land in North Carolina that used the metes and bounds survey method (From the author's collection)

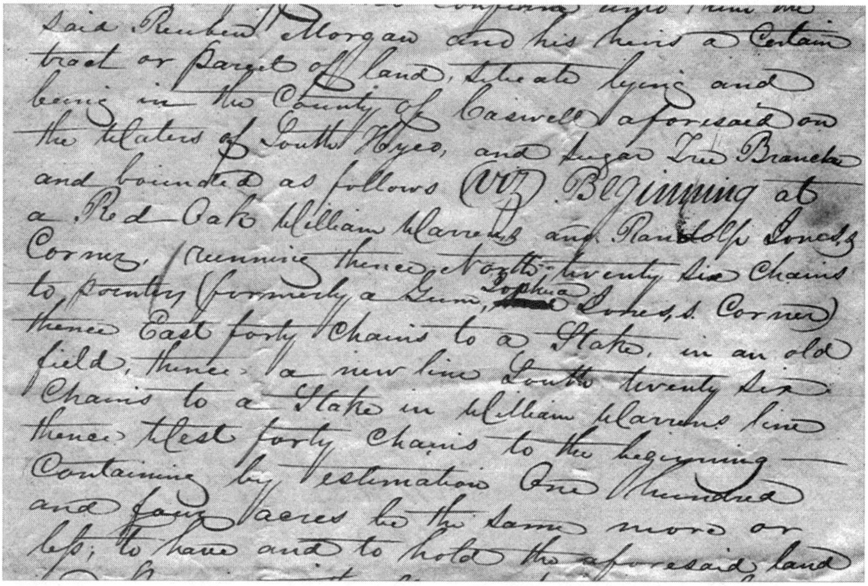
said Reuben Morgan and his heirs a Certain
tract or Parcel of land, situate lying and
being in the County of Caswell aforesaid on
the waters of South Hyco, and Sugar Tree Branch
and bounded as follows (viz) Beginning at
a Red Oak William Warren's and Randolph Jones's
Corner, running thence North twenty six Chains
to pointers (formerly a Gum, Sophia Jones's Corner)
thence East forty Chains to a Stake, in an old
field, thence a new line South twenty six
Chains to a Stake in William Warren's line
thence West forty Chains to the beginning
Containing by estimation One Hundred
and four acres be the same more or
less; to have and to hold the aforesaid land

FIGURE 6-24 Detail of a metes and bounds property description from a land survey (From the author's collection)

A separate system of measurement was used in the Federal-Land States and is commonly referred to as the "Township" system. We'll discuss that in the "Federal-Land States Records" section later in this chapter. However, be aware that a combination of metes and bounds and township systems, along with some other less widely used schemes, has been used in some areas. In Texas, for example, the Spanish land measurement method of "leagues and labors" was used in some areas, while the French method "River Lot System" of slender lots laid out perpendicular to waterways, was used in others.

State-Land States Records

You will find a wealth of varied and interesting land records in use in State-Land States. The original process of acquiring land began with a land grant. The grant simply defined the terms under which the land would be made available by the grantor to the grantee. The terms "grantor" and "grantee" continue to be used to this day in land transactions. In order to obtain an original grant, an individual (or organization) was required to make an application. A successful application resulted in the issue of a land warrant. A land warrant is nothing more than an order for a survey to be performed. The survey was conducted and returned to the appropriate land office where it was recorded. At this point, a patent was prepared. The patent is a title document signifying that the entire acquisition process has been conducted, including the exchange of any money or other consideration. The land patent is then recorded and the title process is complete.

You will find that the subsequent land transfer process typically was continued, as property ownership moved from person to person, with the use of indentures (or agreements), a property survey, and various sale transaction documents, ultimately resulting in the preparation and recording of a deed. Figures 6-25 and 6-26 show both sides of a copy of an indenture for the purchase of a piece of property in Caswell County, North Carolina, dating from 1792. (This document is a transcription prepared by the Register of Deeds on 7 November 1838 from the Deed Book in his office, as indicated by the clerk's statement at the bottom of the second page.)

During the American Revolution, there was no federal government and therefore no treasury. Soldiers were paid as possible, but some were rewarded for their service with what was known

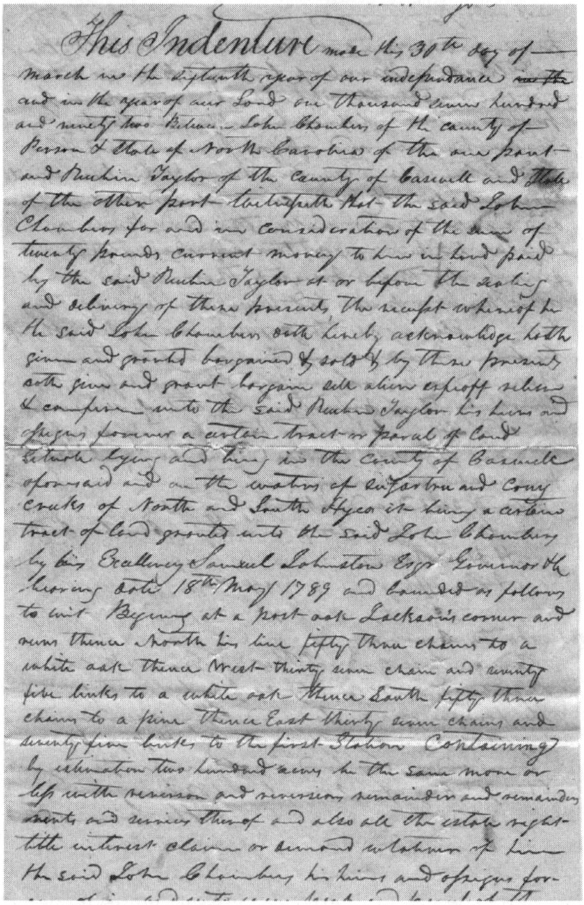

This Indenture made this 30th day of March in the sixteenth year of our independance and in the year of our Lord one thousand seven hundred and ninety two Between John Chambers of the county of Person & State of North Carolina of the one part and Reuben Taylor of the County of Caswell and State of the other part witnesseth that the said John Chambers for and in consideration of the sum of twenty pounds current money to him in hand paid by the said Reuben Taylor at or before the sealing and delivery of these presents the receipt whereof he the said John Chambers doth hereby acknowledge hath given and granted bargained & sold & by these presents doth give and grant bargain sell alien enfeoff release & confirm unto the said Reuben Taylor his heirs and assigns forever a certain tract or parcel of land situate lying and being in the County of Caswell aforesaid and on the waters of [illegible] and Cowy creeks of North and South Hyco it being a certain tract of land granted unto the said John Chambers by his Excellency Samuel Johnston Esqr Governor the bearing date 18th May 1789 and bounded as follows to wit Beginning at a post oak Jackson's corner and runs thence North his line fifty three chains to a white oak thence West thirty seven chains and seventy five links to a white oak thence South fifty three chains to a pine thence East thirty seven chains and seventy five links to the first Station Containing by estimation two hundred acres be the same more or less with reversion and reversions remainder and remainders rents and services thereof and also all the estate right title interest claim or demand whatever of him the said John Chambers his heirs and assigns for-

FIGURE 6-25 Face page of an indenture for the purchase of land in 1792 (From the author's collection)

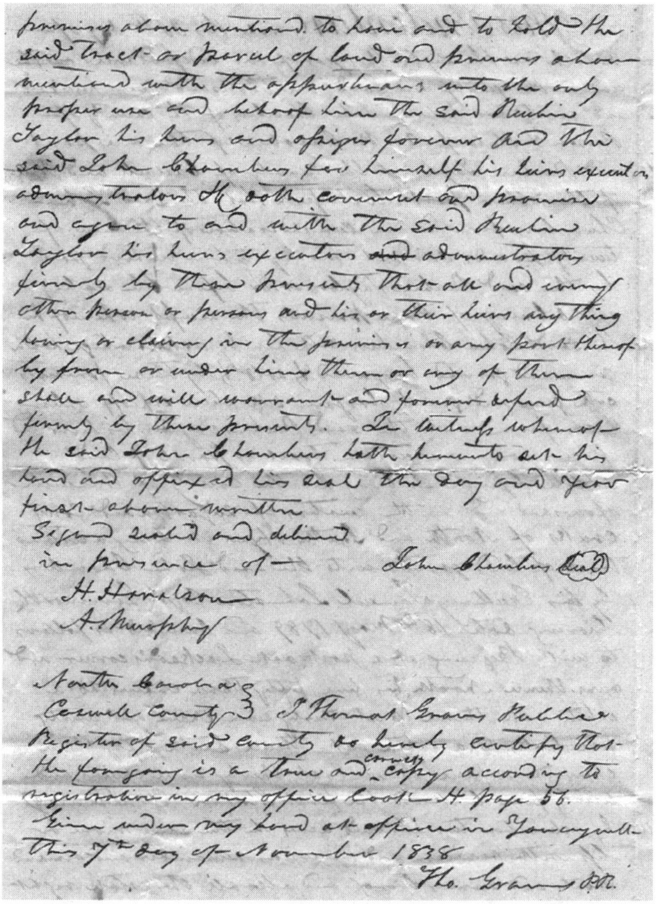

premises above mentioned. To have and to hold the
said tract or parcel of land and premises above
mentioned with the appurtenances unto the only
proper use and behoof him the said Reuben
Taylor his heirs and assigns forever And the
said John Chambers for himself his heirs executors
administrators &c doth covenant and promise
and agree to and with the said Reuben
Taylor his heirs executors ~~and~~ administrators
firmly by these presents That all and every
other person or persons and his or their heirs any thing
having or claiming in the premises or any part thereof
by from or under him them or any of them
shall and will warrant and forever defend
firmly by these presents. In testimony whereof
the said John Chambers hath hereunto set his
hand and affixed his seal the day and year
first above written
Signed sealed and delivered
in presence of — John Chambers (Seal)
H. Haralson
A. Murphy

North Carolina }
Caswell County } I Thomas Graves Public
Register of said County do hereby certify that
the foregoing is a true and correct copy according to
registration in my office Book H page 56.
Given under my hand at office in Yanceyville
This 7th day of November 1838
Tho. Graves PR.

FIGURE 6-26 Second page of the same indenture showing the clerk's notation of his transcription made in 1838 (From the author's collection)

as "bounty land." There were both federal and state bounty land warrants. States which produced their own bounty-land warrants to compensate its citizens for service were Georgia, Maryland, Massachusetts, North Carolina, Pennsylvania, South Carolina, and Virginia. In order to obtain bounty land, an individual had to make application and go through a documentation process to prove eligibility to receive the land. The number of acres granted depended on the person's rank and service. Bounty land documents may be found in county records, state land offices, and/or in state archives.

As you can see, there are some interesting and diverse land survey schemes used in the State-Land States that have their origins in their colonial past. You will want to do some preliminary research into the state and area in which your ancestors lived and owned property in order to learn what system(s) might have been in use at that time.

Measurements for Federal-Land/Public-Land States

Following the American Revolution, the new federal government instituted several processes to control territorial land it acquired. There were several reasons for this. First, the government wanted to raise revenue to build its reserves and pay off debts incurred as a result of the Revolutionary War. Second, it wanted to compensate soldiers and other supporters from the war with land rather than pay money. Finally, with all this new territory, the government wanted to encourage westward migration and settlement. As a result, documentation dating from this period is some of the richest genealogical evidence you will find.

In order to organize these Federal-Land areas, also known as Public-Land or Public Domain States, the federal government had to define a system of measurement so that parcels could be defined. Rather than using the older metes and bounds system, the government decided to use a cartographic reference system using meridians. A *meridian* is an imaginary north-south line running from the North Pole to the South Pole. Additional imaginary north-south lines are defined as guide meridians, and these are located 24 miles to the east and to the west of the meridians. A horizontal line running east to west and intersecting the meridians and guide meridians is referred to as a *base line*. It is used to measure distances from north to south. These imaginary reference lines are used to facilitate a quick reference for locating a physical location.

Meridian regions are divided into tracts, each of which is approximately 24 miles wide. Each tract is subdivided into 16 townships, each of which is approximately six miles square.

You also will encounter the term "range" in your research of townships. Ranges are imaginary north-south lines within a meridian that are set six miles apart. Remember that six miles is the width of a township. A count of the number of ranges to the east or west of a meridian and to the north or south of a base line indicates a specific township. For example, if you encounter a description that indicates "T2S and R2E," this indicates that the township being defined or described is two townships south of the base line and two townships east of the range line.

Let's further subdivide the township to gain a more finite means of locating a specific piece of property. Each township is subdivided into sections. There are 36 square sections in a township, each of which comprises approximately 640 acres. Sections are numbered from 1 to 36, with the position of the numbers being dependent on whether the township is north or south of a baseline or east or west of a range line.

A section is most often subdivided into a variety of different-sized parcels. (There are exceptions to this, particularly in Ohio and other states in which the township, range, and section scheme was not clearly in place at the time of the initial surveys or where specific governments dictated other methods.) These subdivisions of sections are typically square or rectangular in shape. That is not to say that different parcels of land might not be subdivided and shaped differently. However, land descriptions you will encounter in Federal-Land States usually refer to townships, ranges, and sections to help define the location and size of a parcel.

There are 30 Federal-Land States:

Alabama	Alaska	Arizona	Arkansas	California
Colorado	Florida	Idaho	Illinois	Indiana
Iowa	Kansas	Louisiana	Michigan	Minnesota
Mississippi	Missouri	Montana	Nebraska	Nevada
New Mexico	North Dakota	Ohio	Oklahoma	Oregon
South Dakota	Utah	Washington	Wisconsin	Wyoming

Federal-Land States Records

The Public Lands in the Federal-Land States were distributed in a variety of ways over different time periods. Others were auctioned or sold by lottery. Initial sales of land were conducted by auction with the land going to the highest bidder. Land offices opened and did the proverbial "booming business" in selling land to individuals wishing to settle on undeveloped properties to the west.

There were a number of transactions used for transferring ownership from the federal government to an individual (or organization). In order to purchase a parcel of land, an individual had to be a native-born citizen of the United States or must have filed a Declaration of Intent document to initiate the naturalization process. The exception to this requirement was in the case of bounty-land warrants.

The process of acquiring property usually began with the individual filing an application for a desired parcel of land. The person had to pay cash or present evidence of some form of credit. At that time, a warrant for survey was issued to accurately define the property description and to ensure that the property was not already owned by someone else. A completed survey report was submitted to the government and was recorded in a township plat book. The plat book consisted of a map of the township and a listing of the parcels. The surveys recorded here also included descriptions of the physical characteristics of the property, such as rocks, streams, forests, and other features.

Next, the information about the transaction was recorded in the tract book. You can use the tract books' contents to point to specific townships to locate individual landowners' records. All of the paperwork created and documentation supplied so far was then gathered together and sent to the General Land Office. The materials were placed in what are commonly known as land-entry case files and these files were reviewed. There should be a case file for every application processed, regardless of whether it was approved or rejected. At this time, a document referred to as a "final certificate" was issued to the applicant. It indicated that all of the required steps had been taken and that a land patent for the parcel had been approved. The actual land patents were generated by the General Land Office and were sent to the local land office where the applicant could then exchange the final certificate for the actual land patent. Figure 6-27 shows the land patent for my great-great-grandfather, John N. Swords, dated 10 August 1849, for a parcel of land in the area of Lebanon, Alabama.

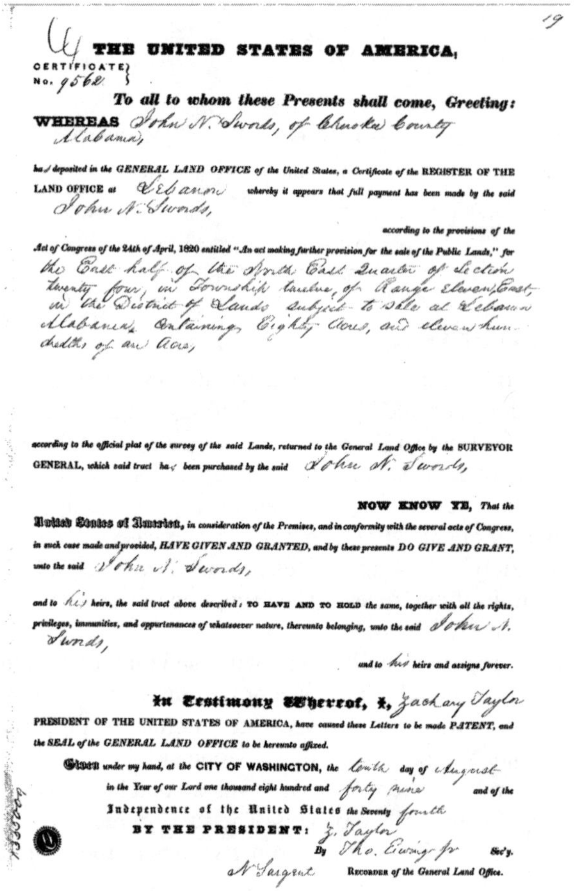

19

THE UNITED STATES OF AMERICA,

CERTIFICATE No. 9562

To all to whom these Presents shall come, Greeting:

WHEREAS John N. Swords, of Chucka County Alabama,

has deposited in the GENERAL LAND OFFICE of the United States, a Certificate of the REGISTER OF THE LAND OFFICE at Lebanon whereby it appears that full payment has been made by the said John N. Swords, according to the provisions of the Act of Congress of the 24th of April, 1820 entitled "An act making further provision for the sale of the Public Lands," for the East half of the North East Quarter of Section twenty four, in Township twelve, of Range Eleven, East, in the District of Lands subject to sale at Lebanon Alabama, containing Eighty Acres, and eleven hundredths of an Acre,

according to the official plat of the survey of the said Lands, returned to the General Land Office by the SURVEYOR GENERAL, which said tract has been purchased by the said John N. Swords,

NOW KNOW YE, That the United States of America, in consideration of the Premises, and in conformity with the several acts of Congress, in such case made and provided, HAVE GIVEN AND GRANTED, and by these presents DO GIVE AND GRANT, unto the said John N. Swords,

and to his heirs, the said tract above described: TO HAVE AND TO HOLD the same, together with all the rights, privileges, immunities, and appurtenances of whatsoever nature, thereunto belonging, unto the said John N. Swords,

and to his heirs and assigns forever.

In Testimony Whereof, I, Zachary Taylor PRESIDENT OF THE UNITED STATES OF AMERICA, have caused these Letters to be made PATENT, and the SEAL of the GENERAL LAND OFFICE to be hereunto affixed.

Given under my hand, at the CITY OF WASHINGTON, the tenth day of August in the Year of our Lord one thousand eight hundred and forty nine and of the Independence of the United States the Seventy fourth

BY THE PRESIDENT: Z. Taylor

By Tho. Ewing Jr Sec'y.

N Sargent Recorder of the General Land Office.

FIGURE 6-27 Land patent for John N. Swords dated 10 August 1849 (From the author's collection)

The land patents have been digitized and indexed by the United States Bureau of Land Management General Land Office (BLM-GLO). These can be searched in a database at **http://www.glorecords.blm.gov,** viewed, and printed. You also can order a certified copy of the document from that agency.

Places to Locate Land and Property Records

Subsequent sales and transfers of titles occurred as private transactions without the participation of the federal government unless a question of original patent or title arose. Agreements of sale, indentures, mortgages, surveys, receipts, and deeds are probably the most common documents found.

Land and property documents may be located almost anywhere. Some documents will be in the possession of the individual or family, while others will be found in courthouses, recorders of deeds offices, registrars' offices, tax assessors' offices, county offices, state archives, NARA, the BLM-GLO, and all sorts of places. Remember that city directories, voter registration lists, jury lists, and many other records may provide clues to property ownership and associated records.

Deeds are used to transfer title of property from the grantor to the grantee. Deeds are perhaps the most common document you will find in your property research, and they can contain extensive genealogical information. In the case of a piece of property owned by someone who has died, the transfer of property as part of an estate in probate may contain a great deal of information. The name of the deceased and his or her date of death are often shown to designate the reason for the transfer of ownership. The names and relationships of the devisees/heirs can be a goldmine in your research. However, this information also serves as a pointer to other records, such as a will and probate packet or marriage documents.

Another important piece of genealogical information that appears in land records is that of "dower release." In referencing Figure 6-23 earlier in this chapter, I called attention to the "Dower line" shown on that particular survey report. When a woman had an interest in the ownership of property, laws in earlier times required that the woman sign a dower release in order to allow the sale of the property. Usually, a woman was interviewed separately from her husband and was asked if she voluntarily exercised her right to relinquish ownership or interest in the property to allow for its sale or transfer. Figure 6-28 shows a copy of a deed recorded in the deed books of Alachua County, Florida, dated 7 June 1873. At the bottom of the document is a record of Priscilla McCall's dower release for that piece of property.

Warranty deeds are those instruments used in property transactions in which the grantor fully warrants good clear title to the property. A warranty deed offers the greatest protection of any deed and you will find references to and copies of these among the land and property records you research. Figure 6-29 shows an example of a cover page of a warranty deed. The remainder of the text of the warranty deed is virtually identical to other deeds but, in this case, proof of title has been presented at the time of transfer to ensure the veracity of the title.

Another type of deed is a "deed of gift" in which one person transfers ownership of property to another person without benefit of any compensation or remuneration. Figure 6-30 shows the original deed of gift from my great-great-grandfather, Goodlow W. Morgan, to his son, my great-grandfather, Rainey B. Morgan, dated 17 December 1885. This deed transfers ownership of the home tract of land to Rainey but reserves Goodlow's right of use and control for the remainder of his life. The deed is registered in a deed book in Caswell County, North Carolina.

There are other documents associated with land and property ownership in the United States that you may find helpful to your research. Particularly useful are those documents that point you to the original land records. These include property tax bills such as the example shown in Figure 6-31.

Other documents might include tax liens, court judgments, and auction records, to name just a few. As you can see, the wide range of documents and the possible contents may provide you with a great many clues. It should be obvious to you by now, though, that there is a lot to learn about United States property records. You will want to learn more about the records available in the areas

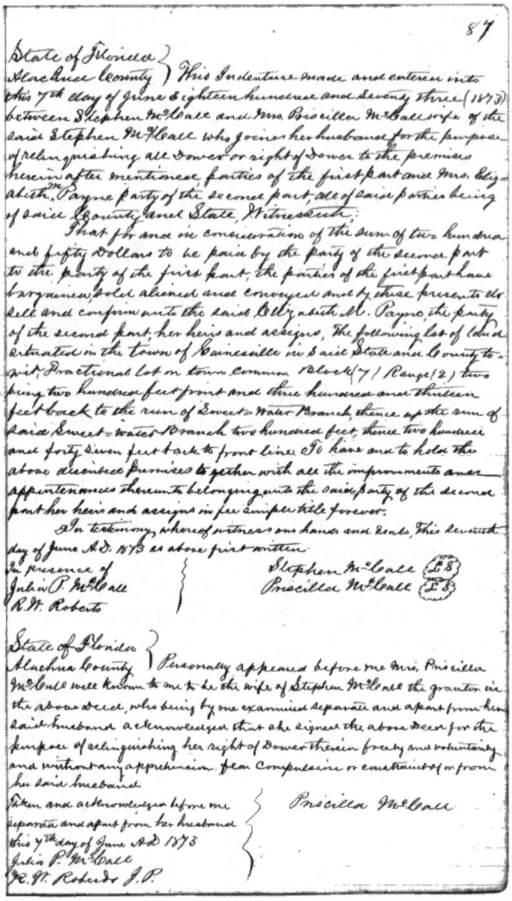

87

State of Florida }
Alachua County } This Indenture made and entered into this 7th day of June Eighteen hundred and Seventy three (1873) between Stephen McCall and Mrs Priscilla McCall wife of the said Stephen McCall who joins her husband for the purpose of relinquishing all Dower or right of Dower to the premises hereinafter mentioned, parties of the first part and Mrs. Elizabeth M. Payne party of the second part, all of said parties being of said County and State, Witnesseth;

That for and in consideration of the sum of two hundred and fifty Dollars to be paid by the party of the second part to the party of the first part, the parties of the first part have bargained, sold aliened and conveyed and by these presents do sell and confirm unto the said Elizabeth M. Payne, the party of the second part, her heirs and assigns, The following lot of land situated in the town of Gainesville in said State and County to-wit, Fractional lot on town common Block (7) Range (2) two being two hundred feet front and three hundred and thirteen feet back to the run of Sweet-Water Branch, thence up the run of said Sweet-water Branch two hundred feet, thence two hundred and forty seven feet back to front line. To have and to hold the above described premises together with all the improvements and appurtenances thereunto belonging unto the said party of the second part her heirs and assigns in fee simple title forever.

In testimony, whereof witness our hands and Seals, This Seventh day of June A.D. 1873 as above first written

In presence of
Julia P. McCall
R.W. Roberts

Stephen McCall (L.S.)
Priscilla McCall (L.S.)

State of Florida }
Alachua County } Personally appeared before me Mrs. Priscilla McCall well known to me to be the wife of Stephen McCall the grantor in the above deed, who being by me examined separate and apart from her said husband acknowledged that she signed the above deed for the purpose of relinquishing her right of Dower therein freely and voluntarily and without any apprehension, fear Compulsion or constraint of or from her said husband

Taken and acknowledged before me separate and apart from her husband this 7th day of June A.D. 1873
Julia P. McCall
R.W. Roberts J.P.

Priscilla McCall

FIGURE 6-28 This deed includes a record of the wife's dower release (Courtesy of Jim Powell)

where your ancestors lived at the times they were there and, by doing so, you can begin to tap these marvelous resources.

Land and Property Records in Canada

Canada was an attractive destination for both French and British citizens. Over the centuries, people were drawn to immigrate by the availability of land. In fact, both governments recruited people to settle there and there are examples of advertisements in the holdings of the archives of both France and England. In addition, many parcels of land were granted in payment for military service. Additionally, people migrated northward from the 13 American colonies and the United States, as well as from other areas across Europe.

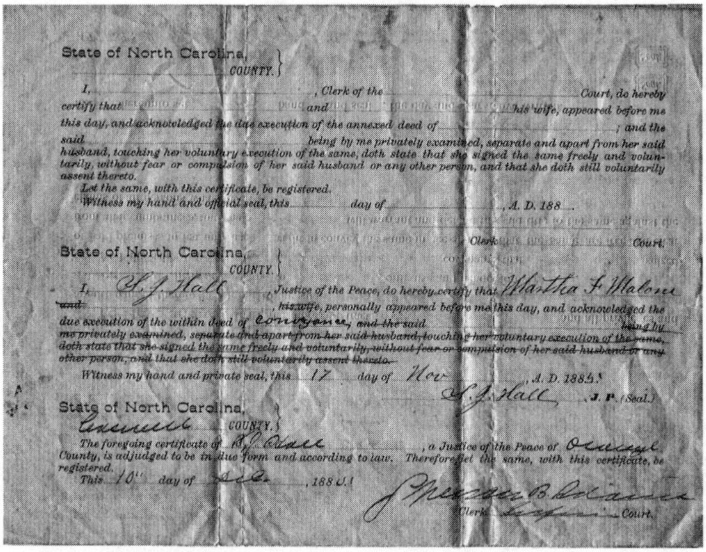

State of North Carolina, COUNTY.

I, ______, Clerk of the ______ Court, do hereby certify that ______ and ______ his wife, appeared before me this day, and acknowledged the due execution of the annexed deed of ______; and the said ______ being by me privately examined, separate and apart from her said husband, touching her voluntary execution of the same, doth state that she signed the same freely and voluntarily, without fear or compulsion of her said husband or any other person, and that she doth still voluntarily assent thereto.

Let the same, with this certificate, be registered.

Witness my hand and official seal, this ______ day of ______, A. D. 188__.

Clerk ______ Court.

State of North Carolina, COUNTY.

I, S. J. Hall, Justice of the Peace, do hereby certify that Martha F. Malone ~~and~~ ______, ~~his wife~~, personally appeared before me this day, and acknowledged the due execution of the within deed of conveyance, ~~and the said ______ being by me privately examined, separate and apart from her said husband, touching her voluntary execution of the same, doth state that she signed the same freely and voluntarily, without fear or compulsion of her said husband or any other person, and that she doth still voluntarily assent thereto.~~

Witness my hand and private seal, this 17 day of Nov, A. D. 1885.

S. J. Hall, J. P. (Seal.)

State of North Carolina, ______ COUNTY.

The foregoing certificate of S. J. Hall, a Justice of the Peace of ______ County, is adjudged to be in due form and according to law. Therefore let the same, with this certificate, be registered.

This 10th day of Dec, 1885.

______ Clerk ______ Court.

FIGURE 6-29 Cover page of a warranty deed (From the author's collection)

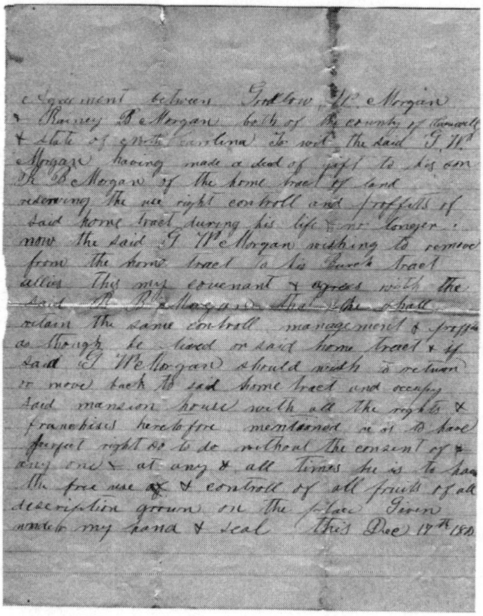

Agreement between Gorham W. Morgan & Rainey B. Morgan both of the county of ______ & State of North Carolina To wit the said G. W. Morgan having made a deed of gift to his son R. B. Morgan of the home tract of land reserving the use right controll and proffits of said home tract during his life & no longer; now the said G. W. Morgan wishing to remove from the home tract to his ______ tract allies This my covenant & agrees with the said R. B. Morgan that he shall retain the same controll management & proffits as though he lived on said home tract & if said G. W. Morgan should wish to return or move back to said home tract and occupy said mansion house with all the rights & franchises heretofore mentioned is to have perfect right so to do without the consent of any one & at any & all times he is to have the free use & controll of all fruits of all description grown on the place Given under my hand & seal This Dec 17th 188_

FIGURE 6-30 Deed of gift from the author's great-great-grandfather giving ownership of the home property to the author's great-grandfather (From the author's collection)

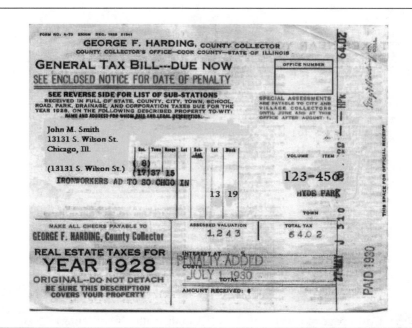

FIGURE 6-31   Sample of a tax bill, which can direct you to the address of a specific piece of property and confirm the name(s) of the owner(s) of record (Courtesy of Carl Johansson)

Among the first records that exist in many areas are land records as people settled and migrated westward. In many cases, land records will be the only records available that document people who lived in the area. What is interesting is the high percentage of early settlers who did own land. While this is encouraging, remember that these records may be handwritten in French or English by persons whose literacy and knowledge of legal affairs were not always the highest. As a result, you may find that some records are particularly challenging to read and use.

Since settlement began in the eastern area and spread westward, you can expect to find the oldest records among the surviving documentation in those areas. Most formal land records in eastern Canada, however, date from the late 1700s. Land records in New France were based on the feudal system of *seigneuries,* which were landed estates. In Canada, the holder of a *seigneurie* was referred to as a *seigneur,* as in a member of the landed gentry.

These include land petitions, conveyances, warrants and fiats (permissions), which authorized the granting of land in payment for a service, land grants and patents, Loyalist land grants, deeds, indentures, quit-claim deeds, titles, transfer documents, leases, mortgages, liens, and a variety of other land instruments. The documents that are available for research will vary based on the time period, the government having jurisdiction at the time, and the laws of the period.

Transcriptions of the documents were recorded in the government land offices in the various areas where the transactions occurred. Records of legal claims and actions may also be found in court records.

Land Measurement

As you work with property records in Canada, you will undoubtedly encounter the use of surveyors' measurements, just as in the State-Land States in the United States. Surveyors used units of measurement based on the length of a surveyor's chain. Refer again to Table 6-2 for a brief overview of conversions from surveyors' measurements to feet and inches.

Land Systems Used in Canada

Various land systems have been used in Canada throughout the centuries. In the course of your research, you may encounter these and will need to understand a little about them in order to successfully work with the land records. There are four organizational systems you are likely to encounter:

6

- **Dominion Land System**   This is by far the most common organizational system used in Canada. It is based on the system used by the American public land system and began being used in Canada in 1870. The basis of this system is the use of townships and sections. A township consists of 36 square miles and is subdivided into 36 sections, which are one mile square. Each section is subdivided into four 160-acre areas referred to as quarter-sections. This is the smallest unit of this land system. A parcel of land is typically described in its deed or other document as lying in a particular township, section, and quarter-section.

- **Patchwork System**   This system used natural land features such as rocks, rivers and streams, and trees, to indicate the beginning and end of a specific boundary. For example, a boundary might be described as "beginning at the large oak near the edge of Twenty-Mile Creek and traveling west, ending at the eastern edge of the creek." Canada is not unique in its use of such descriptive land measurements; this system also was used in areas of the United States for many years and you will find later physical features noted, along with surveyors' measurements, to more fully describe a piece of property. This system was widely used in Newfoundland, Nova Scotia, and in the Maritime Provinces.

- **River Lot System**   The use of this system is generally attributed to the land holding system developed and used in New France. Lands along rivers and streams were defined as long, relatively slender lots running perpendicular to the waterway.

- **Rectangular Lot System**   This system uses a Township or Parish system, which should not be confused with the designation of the use of township, section, and quarter-section used in the Dominion Land System described above. Used primarily in Ontario, Québec, and the Maritimes, this system employs the use of a formal Township or Parish as its largest unit, and then individual parcels were subdivided into individual lots of a uniform size and rectangular in shape. The size of the lot might range from 100 acres on up, and common sizes were 100 or 200 acres.

The land office with which you are working can help you with understanding and locating specific parcels of property. They typically have produced information sheets or leaflets that describe the system(s) in use in their records and will provide them to you on request. In addition, they will also have detailed land maps of the area going back a long way and, using a property description found on a document, can help you pinpoint its precise physical location.

Don't Forget Taxation and Duty Records

Throughout your research for the land records themselves, don't overlook the taxation and duty records associated with the land. Property taxes and duty records associated with land transactions can provide another source of information for you. In addition, those records may include names and references to military service, land descriptions, previous and subsequent residences, wills and estates, and other clues that can further your research.

Locate the Land Records

The most logical place to start your land and property research is in the area where you think your ancestor lived. That means making contact with the National Archives of Canada (NAC) to determine what they may have in their possession. Start at their Web site at **http://www.archives.ca.**

Next, you will want to make contact with the appropriate provincial or territorial archives to determine what records are in their possession, or for recommendations of additional contacts in their area. The NAC maintains a complete list of addresses and Web links to the provincial and territorial archives, and to major genealogical societies in those areas, at the Web page located at **http://www.archives.ca/02/020202/02020212_e.html.**

Be sure to use your local public and academic libraries as reference resources, and visit the nearest LDS Family History Center for help determining what materials you can access.

Land and Property Records in the United Kingdom

Some of the more complicated land and property records, from the perspective of organization, are those in the British Isles. The manorial system in use in England dates back to before the Domesday Book, which was commissioned in 1085. The manorial system is an amalgamation of an agricultural estate system and the feudal system of military tenures. In effect, the king owned all the land. A tenant-in-chief received his ability to "hold" the large piece of land from the king. The tenant-in-chief could grant the privilege of "holding" to those persons who might be his retainers or valued representatives. These retainers are also referred to as *mesne lords*. The mesne lord could also grant "holdings" to his persons. Throughout the structure, however, each of these persons could and did create their own manorial area, complete with tenants, servants, and other lower persons.

A lord and his manor at any level owed his existence to the person from whom he received his holding, and his tenants and other residents of the manor owed their service and existence to the lord of the manor. That included fields for farming and the raising of livestock, forests for hunting, cottages, the church, and common necessary services such as mills and smithies. Not only did tenants, both free and unfree, and other residents provide service to the lord, but they also contributed a portion of the produce of the labor to support the lord and the manor. The lord, in turn, paid taxes and tribute to the king and provided men, materials, and service to the monarch as required. These services were originally called "tenures" and there were multiple types of these, including the lowliest of the tenants, the free tenures and unfree tenures. These persons were also known as serfs, bondsmen, or *villeins*.

Tenures were slowly replaced by monetary payments, known as *scotage,* and military tenures were abolished in 1660.

How Many Manors Were There?

You might be surprised to learn that there were tens of thousands of manors in England in medieval times. By some calculations, there may have been as many as 25,000 to 65,000 manors. There were approximately 11,000 parishes in the 1500s and 1600s. There were manors of various sizes and with varying numbers of people affiliated with each one. Some parishes had more than one manor associated with them.

One aspect of confusion with English land records concerns the fact that manorial lords were often more than simply landlords. In many cases they acted as the administrative and judicial authority, hearing and ruling on all types of claims and complaints. Further, some of the lords also claimed jurisdiction to rule on and administer the wills and estates of their tenants. Beginning in the 14th century, however, the responsibilities of the manorial courts were transferred to other bodies. These included church courts, secular courts, ecclesiastical parish authorities, and finally to the local authorities. Manorial courts still operated, however, into the 19th century for the purpose of handling property transactions on the manor itself.

There really were three types of manorial court. The Court Leet was the most common court, established by the lord of the manor. Its purpose was to assist in the administration of activities in the manor, and its functions included acting as a court of minor law and, in some cases, monitoring the quality of the produce of the manor. The Court Customary dealt with feudal matters, and particularly with disputes and other matters between the unfree tenants, or villeins. The Court Baron dealt with matters of tenure, feudal services, feudal dues, and disputes between free tenants. Obviously, there was more to these courts than this, and their functions varied from manor to manor, in different places, and at different periods. However, this should give you a brief idea of their purposes.

Manorial Records

The good news is that many manorial records have survived for centuries, going as far back as the 13th and 14th centuries. These manorial rolls consist primarily of the minutes of the courts dealing with a vast array of issues. The bad news, however, is that the earliest of these records are written in Latin. With the exception of some records dating from 1653–1660, it was not until the early 1730s that manorial court records began being written in English, albeit they include many Latin abbreviations and subsidiary notations.

All that said, however, manorial records can contain a great deal of important and helpful genealogical information. The National Archives (and the former Historical Manuscripts Commission (HMC)) maintains the Manorial Documents Register and Manorial Lordships.

The Manorial Documents Register (MDR) was established in 1922 as a result of the abolishment of the use of "copyhold" in British property law. Proof of property ownership, however, was often contained in the original books and rolls of the manorial courts, and it was imperative that references to the original copyhold entries be easily locatable in order to expedite the handling of land and property transactions. The MDR is maintained by the National Archives on behalf of the Master of the Rolls. It maintains a record of the locations of all manorial records, excluding title deeds, throughout England and Wales. Manorial records survive today in many national and local record offices and in some cases in private hands. The MDR, therefore, is an essential tool for locating the records you might be seeking.

Some of the MDR is available online through the HMC link at **http://www.hmc.gov.uk/mdr/searchMDR.htm.** A detailed description of the MDR and Manorial Lordships records is available at **http://www.hmc.gov.uk/sheets/manorial.htm.** However, you may (at the time of this writing) search the MDR for Wales and for Hampshire, Isle of Wight, Norfolk, and the three Ridings of Yorkshire. A search of the database will provide you with information about the number and types of available manorial records and where they are located.

Your research into British land and property records will require you to do some historical research into the locations and periods in which your ancestors lived. There are many excellent reference works available concerning manorial records and other land records. Among the best is Mark D. Herber's *Ancestral Trails* (Sutton Publishing, 2003). In addition, the best presentations I've ever heard on this topic were delivered at the Federation of Genealogical Societies 2003 Conference in Orlando, Florida. The first presentation was delivered by Paul Blake, and was titled "British Property and Land Records: An Introduction to Sources." The second was delivered by Peter B. Park and was titled "The Manor, Its Records, and Its People." Recordings of both lectures are available on audiocassette from Repeat Performances at their Web site at **http://www.audiotapes. com.** These tapes sell for $8.50 U.S./£4.74 U.K. and provide excellent detailed discussions of these records.

Locate Land and Property Records Online

More and more materials are being made available on the Internet each month. The MDR is one example of land and property reference materials that may be found online. However, there are numerous free and subscription databases that can help further your research.

Otherdays.com is a subscription database that focuses on Ireland and Irish genealogical resources. Its impressive collections include maps, gazetteers, and other materials. Perhaps the most valuable resource for Irish property research between 1847 and 1864 is Griffith's Valuation of Ireland. Griffith's Valuation is a comprehensive listing of persons who rented land and property throughout Ireland in the 1850s. These persons are recorded as "occupiers," however it also includes the names of those persons from whom the land or property was rented. Not only is Griffith's Valuation an excellent tool for land and property research, it also serves as an excellent substitute for census records of the period that were destroyed. A page from Griffith's Valuation for the Parish of Killian is shown in Figure 6-32.

In addition, you will want to visit Cyndi's List at **http://www.cyndislist.com** and review the resources under England, Wales, Scotland, and Ireland for links to land and property records and related materials online.

VALUATION OF TENEMENTS.

PARISH OF KILLIAN.

No. and Letters of Reference to Map.	Names.		Description of Tenement.	Area.	Rateable Annual Valuation.		Total Annual Valuation of Rateable Property.
	Townlands and Occupiers.	Immediate Lessors.			Land.	Buildings.	
	CLOONSHIVNA (KELLY)—continued. MEELICK—con.			A. R. P.	£ s. d.	£ s. d.	£ s. d.
— b	Michael Hannan,	Daniel Ward,	House and office,		—	0 8 0	0 8 0
11	William Ward,	Denis H. Kelly,	House, offices, and land,	11 2 8	3 0 0	0 15 0	3 15 0
12	Matthew Hannan,	Same,	House, offices, and land,	24 2 5	13 10 0	0 15 0	14 5 0
13 A	Michael Garrick,	Same,	House and land,	4 2 16	2 15 0	0 10 0	
— B			Land,	2 0 10	0 5 0	—	3 10 0
	DOOLEY'S VILLAGE.						
	a James Hannan,		House and land,		2 0 0	0 10 0	2 10 0
	b Bartholomew Quinn,		House and land,		2 0 0	0 5 0	2 5 0
14	c Michael Fenerin,	Denis H. Kelly,	House, office, & land,	71 1 33	5 10 0	0 10 0	6 0 0
	d Michael Dooley,		House, office, & land,		2 10 0	0 10 0	3 0 0
	e John Dooley,		House, office, & land,		2 10 0	0 10 0	3 0 0
	f Michael Crehan,		House, office, & land,		5 10 0	0 15 0	6 5 0
	Total,			283 2 34	61 5 0	9 8 0	70 13 0
	CREEVEROE (DAVIES). (Ord. S. 32.)						
	a John Crehan,		House, office, & land,		7 15 0	0 10 0	8 5 0
	b Augustin Conneely,		House, office, & land,		4 0 0	0 10 0	4 10 0
	c James Conneely,		House, office, & land,		4 0 0	0 10 0	4 10 0
	d Bridget Egan,		House, office, & land,		2 0 6	0 10 0	2 10 0
1	e Patrick Crehan, jun.,	Matthew Cornwall,	House and land,	127 1 35	12 0 0	0 15 0	12 15 0
	f Matthew Crehan,		Ho., office, & land,			0 15 0	3 7 0
	g John Crehan,		Ho., office, & land,		7 16 0	0 15 0	3 7 0
	h Patrick Conneely,		Ho., office, & land,			0 15 0	3 7 0
	i Patrick Crehan,		House, offices, & land,		9 5 0	0 15 0	10 0 0
	— Matthew Cornwall,	In fee,	Land,		7 15 0	—	7 15 0
	j Mary Mockler,	Hon. Martin Ffrench,	House and garden,	0 1 20	0 5 0	0 5 0	0 10 0
	Total,			127 3 15	54 16 0	6 0 0	60 16 0
	CREEVEROE (FFRENCH). (Ord. S. 32.)						
1	Hon. Martin Ffrench,	In fee,	Bog,	55 3 4	0 15 0	—	0 15 0
2	Patrick Dowd,	Hon. Martin Ffrench,	Land,	4 1 8	0 15 0	—	0 15 0
3 a	Patrick Dowd,	Same,	House and land,	3 3 33	1 5 0	0 15 0	2 0 0
b	Thomas Kelly,	Same,	Land,		1 5 0	—	1 5 0
4 a	Thomas Kelly,	Same,	Land,	6 2 2	1 5 0	—	1 5 0
b			Land,	5 1 30	1 0 0	—	
5 A	John Cunningham,	Same,	House and land,	9 2 37	4 0 0	0 10 0	5 10 0
— B			Land,	2 3 1	0 10 0	—	
6 A	a Patrick Tormy,	Same,	Land,	0 2 25	0 10 0	—	4 5 0
— B			House, offices, and land,	5 1 10	2 5 0	1 0 0	
7 A	Patrick Martin,	Same,	Land,	0 15 0	0 15 0	—	
— B			Land,	3 3 10	1 5 0	—	3 12 0
6 A b			Land,	5 3 4	2 5 0	—	
	Bridget Quinn,	Same,	Land,	0 3 10	0 12 0	—	
8 A			Land,	4 3 12	1 0 0	—	3 15 0
— B			House, office, and land,	5 1 19	2 5 0	0 10 0	
9 A	Matthew Manion,	Same,	Land,	4 3 20	1 0 0	—	3 10 0
— B			Land,	5 3 38	2 10 0	—	
	Bridget Quinn (Healy),	Same,	Land,	9 2 26	1 10 0	—	1 10 0
10	Patrick Manion,	Same,	Land,		1 10 0	—	1 10 0
11	Bridget Quinn (Healy),	Same,	House, office, and land,	5 1 27	2 10 0	0 15 0	3 5 0
12	Patrick Manion,	Same,	House, office, and land,	5 1 28	2 10 0	0 15 0	3 5 0
13	William Quinn,	Same,	Land,	9 0 0	2 0 0	—	2 0 0
	John Quinn,	Same,	Land,		0 15 0	—	0 15 0
14 a	William Quinn,	Same,	House, offices, & land,	12 1 38	5 10 0	1 0 0	6 10 0
b	John Quinn,		House, offices, & land,		1 15 0	1 0 0	2 15 0
15	John Quinn,	Same,	House, office, and land,	11 2 24	4 5 0	1 0 0	5 5 0
16	Patrick Turley,	Same,	House, office, and land,	16 3 0	6 0 0	1 0 0	7 0 0
17 A	Edmund Kelly,	Same,	Land,	5 2 27	1 15 0	—	4 15 0
— B			House, office, and land,	4 3 21	2 10 0	0 10 0	
18 A	Michael Kelly,	Same,	Land,	4 1 29	1 15 0	—	5 5 0
— B			House and land,	6 1 0	3 0 0	0 10 0	

FIGURE 6-32   A page from Griffith's Valuation for the Parish of Killian (Used by permission of Otherdays.com)

Place Your Ancestors into Context with Property Records

Land and property records can most emphatically be used to place your ancestors and family members into geographical and historical context. While a census record may establish an individual's presence in a location at one point every decade, property tax records created on an annual basis can reconfirm the presence (or absence) of an ancestor. When you determine that an ancestor is no longer paying a property tax, you may then direct your research towards deed and property indexes, wills and probate documents, city directories, and other research paths to determine if the property changed hands and the reason for the change. In addition, when other government documents are lost or destroyed, property records are almost always re-created in some manner. It is essential for a government to quickly reconstruct these records in order to establish property ownership and to continue the taxation that is a primary source of its revenue.

There are numerous types of land and property records that you may encounter. As I mentioned at the beginning of the chapter, some of these may be linked to military service. They might include bounty land warrants, homestead and other tax exemptions, military pension loan programs such as the United States' G.I. Bill, and others. You also can link property records with other documents, such as wills and probate records, jury lists, voter registration, divorce settlements, lawsuits, census enumeration districts, and more.

The wide range of documents attached to the purchase, ownership, sale, and transfer of land records is extensive. And while they may at first glance seem complicated or convoluted, the processes employed and the documentation created actually are quite logical. Now that you have an understanding of the types of land and property records that are used and where they might be found, you are prepared to begin searching for those that have been created for your ancestors and their families. Combine your study of history and geography with your genealogical research skills and you really can expand the chronicle of your family's history in a given area.

Chapter 7

Locate and Use Immigration and Naturalization Records

How to…

- Understand the reasons for migration
- Identify, locate, and study migration routes
- Expand your family's story by tracing their migrations
- Locate and use immigration records
- Understand the naturalization process and work with those documents

Expand Your Family's Story

You've learned a great deal about your family so far by locating and using home sources, vital records, and census resources. Along the way, you also have built a foundation for all of your future genealogical research. You now know how important it is to place your family into context, to conduct scholarly research, to analyze every piece of data you uncover, and to properly document your source materials.

You've made a lot of progress so far, but you probably have only just begun to scratch the surface of your family's rich history. There literally are hundreds of different records that may contain information of value in documenting your forebears' lives. This chapter discusses some of the more important document types and successful methodologies for locating and evaluating them. Working with these documents will help you learn much more about the details of your family members' lives and come to know them more intimately.

A variety of other, less commonly used materials will also be referenced in this chapter, along with recommendations for where to locate them and how to incorporate their information into your family research and documentation. Remember that almost any type of document created by, for, or about one of your ancestors or family members may indeed provide information to help in your quest for clues. You will exercise everything you've learned so far about placing people into geographical and historical context, and about which documents were created at the time and their purpose. Apply your critical thinking skills to the evidence and you can formulate reasonable hypotheses, sometimes circumventing the "brick walls" that we all invariably encounter.

Why Do People Migrate?

Since the dawn of time, it is a natural state of affairs for all creatures to migrate from place to place in order to survive and to make a better existence for themselves. It is the natural order of things and humankind is no different. People moved from one place to another for a variety of reasons, sometime moving multiple times until they found a place that suited them. While there are many reasons for moving from one place to another, the following are some of the primary motivations.

- **Natural Disasters** Drought, floods, earthquakes, volcanoes, fires, hurricanes, and other natural disasters were life-altering catastrophes that caused people to leave one place and move to another. Floods in Germany in 1816 and 1830, for example, displaced thousands of people.

- **Drought, Crop Failure, and Famine** Drought and plant diseases are common natural causes of famine; wars, land mismanagement, and other human-caused disasters also result in famine. Famine in Ireland in 1816–17 and the potato famines in 1822, 1838, and between the years 1845 and 1850 caused tens of millions of people to emigrate, particularly to the United States and Canada. Famines in France in 1750, 1774, and 1790 and then the general famine across Europe in 1848 caused French, German, Italian, Dutch, and Scandinavians to immigrate to the United States.

- **Economic Problems** The economic problems of an area can cause people to migrate. Consider the mass migrations resulting from the Great Depression of the 1930s when people relocated to any place they could find work.

- **Political Turmoil or Oppression** Millions of people have emigrated from their native lands in search of asylum in another place in order to avoid political instability, conflict, persecution, violation of personal rights or freedoms, and other problems.

- **War** War is undoubtedly the greatest catalyst of change. Military conflicts and the destruction they cause have long been the primary reason for migration, relocation, and evacuation.

- **Accompanying or Following Family and Friends** Many people accompanied or followed other family members or friends who had already moved somewhere else. The lure of employment opportunities, better living conditions, and political and religious freedom was often irresistible.

- **Adoption** Adoption forces the movement of the adoptee from one place to another without his or her control. Single-child and multiple sibling adoptions have been common, especially when one or both parents died. The Orphan Trains carried children from cities across North America and placed as many as 150,000 to 200,000 children in new homes in 47 states, Canada, and South America. Orphaned and indigent children were transported from the British Isles to Canada and Australia for adoption at various times. And during World War II, children from Britain, Holland, Belgium, and other countries were often evacuated to relatives or through social agencies to help protect them.

- **Religious or Ethnic Persecution** One of the most overwhelming reasons for migration by our ancestors was their desire to live in freedom, to practice their religious beliefs without persecution, or to pursue the lifestyle of their ethnic group. The Pilgrims are an excellent example of the early settlers who emigrated from England to the American colonies. In the 20th century, the emigration of Jews and other persecuted peoples from Europe to Britain, the United States, Australia, South America, and Israel provide vivid examples of persons fleeing persecution.

7

■ **Slavery**   This odious institution was responsible for destroying families and entire communities, and for the forced relocation of hundreds of thousands of persons over the ages. The sale or exchange of human beings removed people from Africa to the New World, and then from place to place as a result of sale, barter, kidnapping, and theft.

■ **Forced Relocation of Native Americans**   Native Americans were seen as an imminent danger to settlers and an impediment to progress. Armed conflicts between the Indians and white settlers, and later the United States army, ultimately resulted in treaties calling for the ceding of Native American lands and permanent relocation of the Indians to parcels referred to as reservations. Many died in the relocation marches, such as the "Trail of Tears."

■ **Criminal Incarceration/Deportment**   Criminals, debtors, and political dissidents were transported to colonial settlements to eliminate them from society and serve sentences of hard labor. Others were offered the option of relocating to a colony rather than face prolonged imprisonment in their homeland.

■ **Primogenitor or Ultimogenitor**   It was common in the Middle Ages (and later) for the eldest son to inherit most or all property on the death of his father. Known as the "rule of primogenitor," the eldest son could then allow his mother and other siblings to remain or could force them to leave. In some places, a separate custom called Borough English or ultimogeniture, required that the youngest son inherit all the land. In either case, sisters were usually married off, and other brothers were encouraged to leave and fend for themselves.

These reasons cannot possibly encompass the universe of factors that influenced our ancestors to make a move. However, placing your own ancestors into context goes a long way toward understanding their motivations. One of my favorite reference Web sites for a chronological representation of natural disasters that affected humans over time is Gary Sharp's site at **http://sharpgary.org/Jan1_2001_Present.html.** Click on the links to the various time periods for chronological listings of events to help place natural history's influences on human history into perspective. An historical complement to this is the Timelines of History Web site at **http://timelines.ws.**

Locate and Use Immigration and Naturalization Records

The desire to trace one's ancestors back to the place of origin is one of the primary motivations for family history researchers. Many of us will spend our entire genealogical research career investigating family members in the country in which they settled, and that is also commonly the same one in which we live and with which we are familiar. However, the impetus to continue the quest backwards to our ancestors' native land(s) will take many of us on another, more rigorous research trek.

Placing your ancestor in geographical and historical context becomes a research imperative when you begin retracing his or her migration path across an ocean and back to the place of birth. It is essential that you consider the country and place of origin *and* the destination country, their geographies, the social and historical environments at the time, and the motivations for both leaving the old country *and* going to a particular location in the new country. For a great many of us, the knowledge of the place of our family's origin has been lost to time and we will have to use all sorts of clues to reconnect a migration path backward. The pointers we'll use may include letters, photographs, books, family stories or traditions, immigration records, naturalization documents, census records, passports and visas, and a host of other primary and secondary evidence. This may seem a daunting task, but it is certainly one of the most rewarding and insightful experiences you can imagine.

Earlier we discussed some of the motivating factors that compelled our ancestors and family members to migrate to a new place. Deciding to undertake a move of this magnitude was no small matter; it took a great deal of courage and planning and often meant leaving family, friends, and everything familiar forever. Our ancestors were literally risking everything, including their lives. Under extreme circumstances, some people fled their homes with little preparation. However, a majority of the emigrants left their ancestral home place for another part of the world with some plan for where they would go and what they would do to survive when they arrived. These people were courageous and endured terrible conditions in order to make a new life for themselves and their families.

Our Ancestors Came on Ships

For most of us, our ancestors traveled in ships. One of the most familiar images to many immigrants or first-generation Americans is that of the immigration processing station Ellis Island. Millions of people like those shown in Figure 7-1 arrived there between 1892 and 1954. These immigrants

  Immigrants arriving at Ellis Island from Italy, ca. 1911 (Library of Congress collection)

may have left their hometowns on foot, in wagons and carts, and even on trains, but ultimately they had to cross an ocean. Millions upon millions of people did so in ships and, depending on the time period, the type of ships on which they traveled determined the duration of the voyage and the living conditions in which they traveled. It was not until well into the 20th century that people emigrated via airplane and, when they began doing so, many of the records we seek were no longer created—in particular, the ships' passenger lists and manifests.

You will find that immigration and naturalization are inexorably linked together, not just because one event occurred before the other but because in order to become naturalized citizens in the new country proof of when, where, and how your ancestors arrived there was required. We're going to concentrate on immigration to the United States and the naturalization process to become an American citizen. However, we also will explore the wealth of records concerning immigration to Canada and Australia from the British Isles and resources for tracing ships from other countries to these destinations as well.

There are many, many migration routes, depending on the location you are researching, the time period, the method of transportation from place to place, and the destination. There are many excellent Web sites for your review, depending on your area of interest. They include the following:

- German emigration to the United States at
  http://www.spartacus.schoolnet.co.uk/USAMgermany.htm

- Irish emigration to the United States at
  http://www.spartacus.schoolnet.co.uk/USAEireland.htm

- Italian emigration to the United States at
  http://www.spartacus.schoolnet.co.uk/USAEitaly.htm

- Swedish emigration to the United States at
  http://www.spartacus.schoolnet.co.uk/USAEsweden.htm

- Emigrants to Canada at **http://ist.uwaterloo.ca/~marj/genealogy/thevoyage.html**

- Immigration Museum, to Victoria [Australia] Timeline at
  http://immigration.museum.vic.gov.au/timeline.

In the United States, I have two favorite collections of historical maps online. The first is the Perry-Castañeda Library Map Collection at the University of Texas at Austin, located at **http://www.lib.utexas.edu/maps.** Once at that site, click on the link labeled "Maps of the United States including National Parks and Monuments," and then click on the link labeled "Historical Maps of the United States." You will find the two sets of maps on this page, "Exploration and Settlement" and "U.S. Territorial Growth," to be excellent references for migration routes. Also on that page, under the section labeled "Later Historical Maps," a number of maps compiled from the 1870 U.S. census showing concentrations of population settlements of German, English and Welsh, British American, Irish, Swedish and Norwegian, and Chinese people.

My other favorite is the David Rumsey Map Collection at **http://www.davidrumsey.com.** You have a choice of viewers of the maps, and the better of them is the in*sight*™ Java Client, which requires a free download of software that installs on your computer. This collection is searchable in a variety of ways and the images are wonderful. (You must turn off any pop-up stopper software on your computer in order to use the viewer to access the map images.)

Learn About the History of Ships' Passenger Lists

Passenger lists, also referred to as "passenger manifests," will vary in format and content, depending on who created them, why they were created, the time period, and other factors. For example, persons transported in bondage, that is, prisoners transported to another colony for punishment or to permanently get rid of them, may be documented in court records and on a prisoner ship's records. In other places, there may be no immigration lists available at the destination location but there may well be emigration lists and/or ships' manifests at the point of departure.

In addition, and perhaps most important of all, it is absolutely imperative to remember that you must always look for both the obvious records *and,* in the event that you can't find those, investigate the possibilities that there may be alternative record types that can help document the migration. For example, if there are no ship's passenger lists, look for immigration records to document the arrival. Also, in the United States, you can use the decennial federal census records to help document and trace your immigrant ancestors. For example, the 1880 census asked for the place of birth of each person as well as of his/her father and mother. The 1900, 1910, 1920, and 1930 federal censuses all asked for the year of immigration and the year of naturalization. Census Population Schedules also may include the language spoken or "mother tongue" and that can help lead you to the place of origin. These records can therefore be the bonanza you need in the way of pointers to other records and/or can be used as alternative, supplemental, and corroborative evidence and documentation.

Let's look at the United States and ships' passenger arrival lists that you may want to research and examine. In order to understand what is available, we need to briefly examine the history of these records.

A Chronology of Ships' Passenger Lists in the United States

Prior to the Revolutionary War, there really was no formal attempt to require passenger arrival lists. Indeed, any requirements were instituted by the colonies themselves as they had control over their own affairs. Since the 13 colonies were, in fact, British, and close to 80 percent of the white immigrants arriving before 1790 had come from England or British-governed countries, there was little or no need to record the arrivals. Any documentation was created or maintained by the ships' owners and operators, and any information concerning shipping commerce was maintained by the colonial government. Their primary concern was the taxation on incoming and outgoing goods, and they had little interest in passenger arrivals other than those of Crown prisoners and indentured servants.

If you are seeking information about an early arrival, it will be important to look for alternative records, as mentioned before, such as "lists of departure" in the original country. Some of these are in national archives there or in the collections of libraries and archives, or in local government record repositories near the port of departure. (In Spain and Portugal, there are extensive archival holdings relating to shipping and passenger movements that trace back in many cases into the 1300s, and hence we have a solid historical record of much of the global exploration from those periods.)

There are, as I mentioned above, a few exceptions to the pre-Federal period's lack of passenger arrival lists. In Pennsylvania, for instance, beginning in 1727 that colony required that non-British immigrants be identified. The persons identified in the listings that were created were primarily of German nationality. There were essentially three lists compiled, consisting of: 1) the ship captain's list made on board ship of names from the manifest; 2) lists of oaths of allegiance to the British king that were signed by all males over the age of 16 who could march to the local magistrate at the port of arrival; and 3) lists of the signers of the oath of fidelity and abjuration, which was a renunciation of any claims to the throne of England by "pretenders," also signed by males over the age of 16 who could walk to the courthouse. One estimate is that only about two-fifths of the ships' passengers actually signed these oaths, and not all of the ledgers and documents have survived. Still, these are a source of considerable interest to researchers with German ancestors who went to Pennsylvania in that time period. These documents are in the possession of the Pennsylvania Archives.

The year 1820 is a bellwether for genealogists from an emigration/immigration perspective. In that year, Congress passed legislation calling for passenger lists to be filed by each ship's master with the customs officer in each port. These documents are referred to as the "customs passenger lists" or "customs passenger manifests." Two copies of the passenger list, like the ones shown in Figures 7-2 and 7-3, were created on board the ship and listed every passenger. Births and deaths occurring during the voyage were also to have been added to the list. Crew members' names were not required. On arrival at port, the ship's master was required to deliver both copies of the document

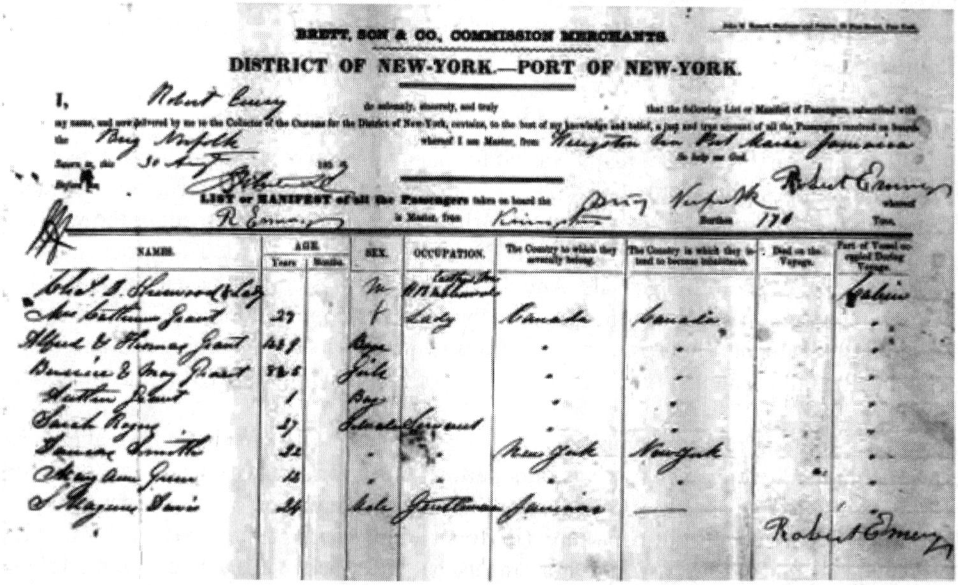

FIGURE 7-2   Passenger list of the Brig *Norfolk,* which arrived in New York on 30 August 1859 (Used with permission of MyFamily.com, Inc.)

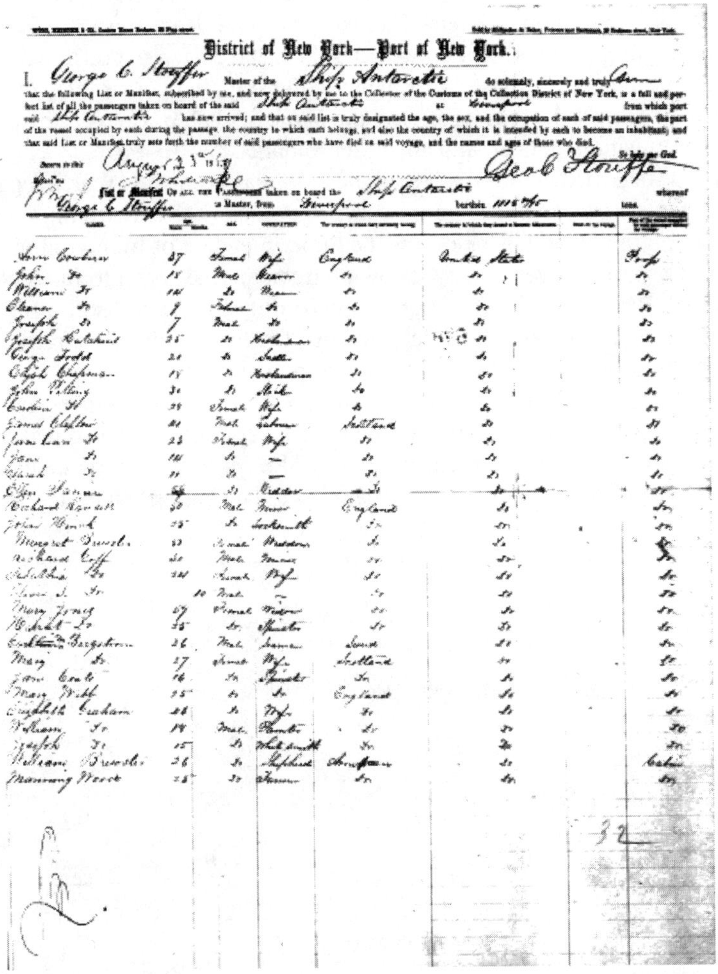
District of New York—Port of New York.

FIGURE 7-3 Manifest of the *Antarctic,* which arrived in New York on 23 August 1859 (Used with permission of MyFamily.com, Inc.)

to the customs collector. The master then swore under oath that the lists were complete and correct, and then both he and the customs officer signed the documents. One copy remained with the customs collector and the other copy was retained by the ship's master. The collectors prepared an abstract of the lists quarterly and sent it to the secretary of state in Washington. The abstract listed the name of every vessel; the port of origin; any intermediate ports of call; the date of arrival; each respective ship's master's name; and the names, gender, and ages of all passengers.

A Congressional act passed in 1882 required that all immigrants arriving in the U.S. were to be recorded by federal immigration officials. The lists produced date from 1883 for the port of Philadelphia and from 1891 for most other ports, and these have been microfilmed by NARA. These lists include the name of the master, the name of the ship, the ports of departure and arrival (including intermediate stops), the date of arrival, the name of each passenger, the place of birth, last residence, age, occupation, gender, and any other remarks.

The year 1891 is a watershed in the U.S. for a number of reasons. In that year, a separate federal governmental agency was formed whose purpose was specifically to oversee immigration. This was the Office of Immigration, and its head was the Superintendent of Immigration. For the first time, this function was strictly overseen by its own bureau and, as a result, the records created became more detailed. Between 1891 and 1906, responsibility for the collection and maintenance of the forms passed through several federal departments, finally becoming the province of the Immigration and Naturalization Service, which was formed in 1906.

Standardized forms, such as the one shown in Figure 7-4, began to be used in every embarkation port around the world and were to be prepared *before* the departure of the ship. Therefore, any changes would have been noted *prior* to entry into any U.S. port. Only births, deaths, and the discovery of a stowaway would have caused the manifest to be changed en route.

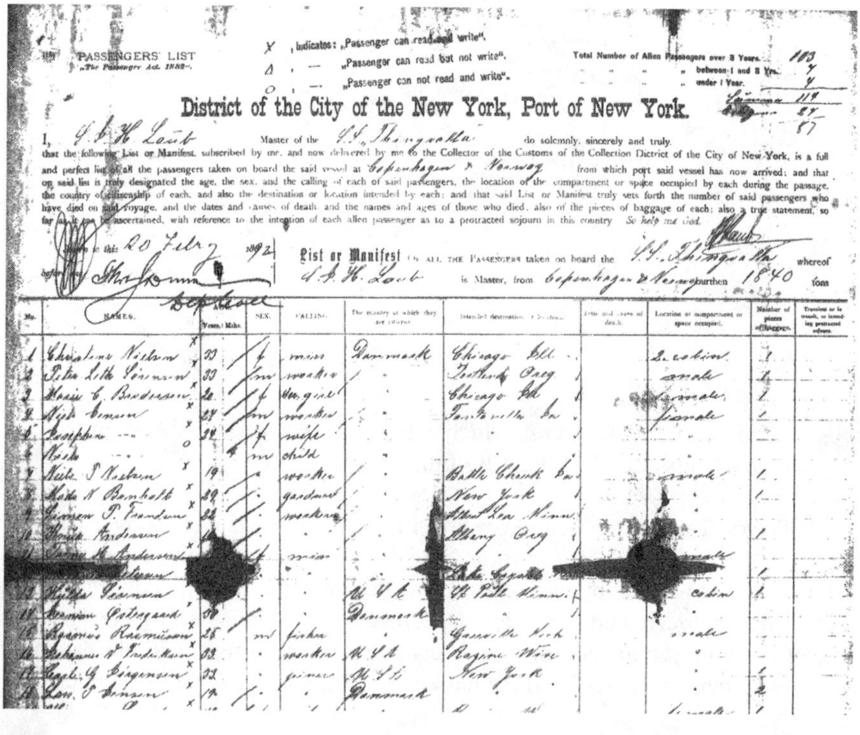
PASSENGERS' LIST „The Passenger Act, 1882".

X, indicates: „Passenger can read and write".
Δ, — „Passenger can read but not write".
O, — „Passenger can not read and write".

Total Number of Alien Passengers over 8 Years 103; between 1 and 8 Yrs. 7; under 1 Year 4

District of the City of the New York, Port of New York.

I, ________ Master of the ________ do solemnly, sincerely and truly, swear that the following List or Manifest, subscribed by me, and now delivered by me to the Collector of the Customs of the Collection District of the City of New York, is a full and perfect list of all the passengers taken on board the said vessel at ________ from which port said vessel has now arrived; and that on said list is truly designated the age, the sex, and the calling of each of said passengers, the location of the compartment or space occupied by each during the passage, the country of citizenship of each, and also the destination or location intended by each; and that said List or Manifest truly sets forth the number of said passengers who have died on said voyage, and the dates and causes of death, and the names and ages of those who died, also of the pieces of baggage of each; also a true statement, so far as it can be ascertained, with reference to the intention of each alien passenger as to a protracted sojourn in this country. So help me God.

List or Manifest of all the Passengers taken on board the ________ whereof ________ is Master, from ________ burthen ________ tons

No.	Names.	Age. Years. Mths.	Sex.	Calling.	The country of which they are citizens.	Intended destination or location.	Date and cause of death.	Location of compartment or space occupied.	Number of pieces of baggage.	Transient, or in transit, or intending protracted sojourn.

FIGURE 7-4 Detail from passenger list of the *S.S. Thingvalla,* arriving in New York on 20 February 1892 (Used with permission of MyFamily.com, Inc.)

Again, the forms were to be presented to the Customs and Immigration Service officers at the port of arrival. The forms became known as Immigration Manifests, or Immigration Passenger Lists. When these forms were introduced in the early 1890s, they required more information than ever before to be provided. (Please see Table 7-1.) Further columns were added in later years, all of which provide more information for our genealogical use.

The federal immigration department requested that all early passenger arrival records be sent to that office. Unfortunately, though, that was easier said than done. The original documents had been stored in customs houses, in courthouses, in customs collectors' homes, and in other places. Some had been damaged, destroyed, or simply lost. Fortunately, a vast majority of the original customs passenger lists from 1820 to 1905 have survived for seven U.S. ports, as have a majority of the customs collectors' abstract reports. They are in the possession of the NARA and have been microfilmed. In fact, where the original passenger list has not survived, NARA has used the customs

Time Period	Passenger List Columns/Contents
1820–1891	■ Passenger Name ■ Age ■ Gender ■ Occupation ■ Nationality
1892	■ Passenger Name ■ Age ■ Gender ■ Occupation ■ Nationality ■ Marital status ■ Last residence ■ Intended final destination in the U.S. ■ Whether ever in the U.S. before and, if so, where, when and for what duration ■ Name, address, and relationship of any relative in the U.S. which the immigrant planned to join ■ Whether able to read and write ■ Whether in possession of a train ticket to the final destination ■ Who paid the passage to America ■ Amount of money (in dollars) the immigrant was carrying ■ Whether the person was a convict, indigent, insane, or a polygamist ■ State of the immigrant's health
1903	All of the information as in 1892, plus: ■ Race or people
1906	All of the information as in 1903, plus: ■ Personal description (height, complexion, hair color, eye color, and any other identifying marks)
1907	All of the information as in 1906, plus: ■ Name and address of the closest living relative in the native country

TABLE 7-1	Required Contents for Passenger Manifests Arriving in the United States (Used by permission of Aha! Seminars, Inc.)

officers' reports as substitutes to fill in gaps in chronological sequence in the microfilmed records. While these abstracts don't contain as much detail as the original passenger manifests, they do supply some critical nominal information.

As the years passed, passenger lists were prepared with more forethought to their clarity and accuracy. Many of these documents were prepared using a typewriter, such as the example in Figure 7-5, which certainly makes for easier reading. However, because the typewritten passenger lists were likely prepared from other handwritten documents, the possibility of transcription and typographical error is increased.

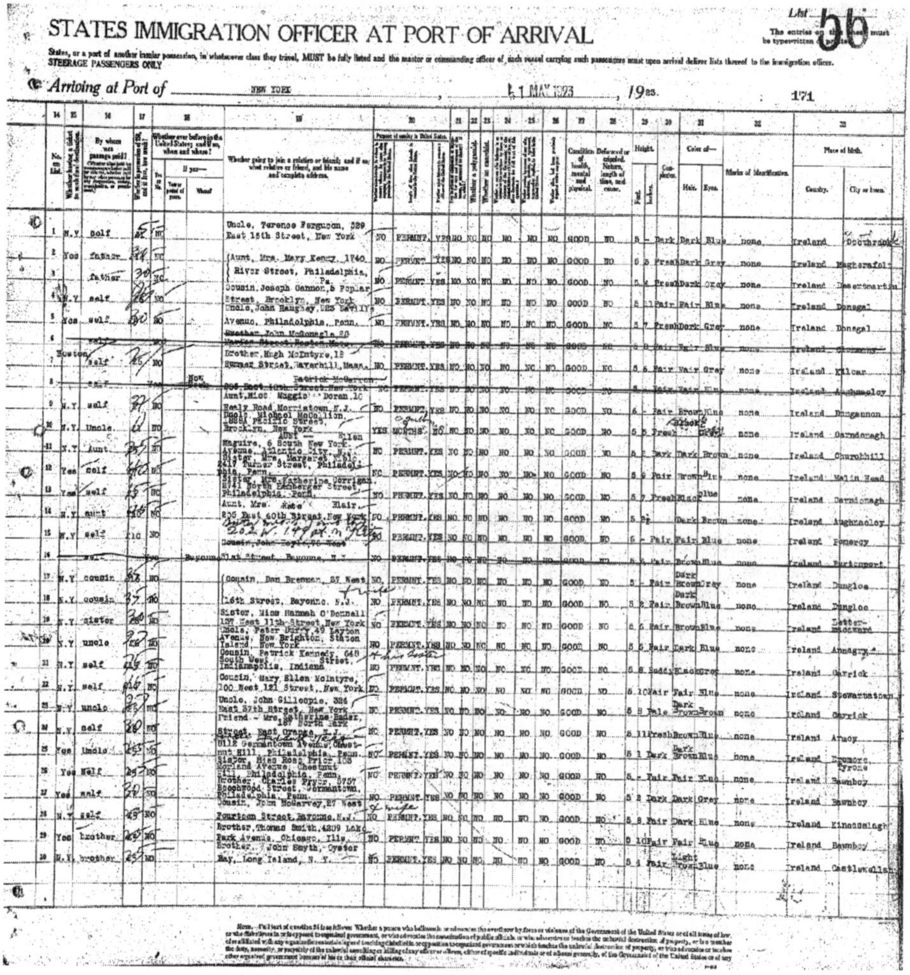

FIGURE 7-5   Page from the manifest of a ship arriving in New York on 1 May 1923 (From the author's collection)

For more extensive information about ships' passenger lists and manifests, you will want to read John Philip Colletta's definitive how-to book, *They Came in Ships* (Ancestry Incorporated, 2002), articles in Ancestry's book, *The Source* (Ancestry Incorporated, 2004), and Loretto D. Szuc's definitive reference book for immigration and naturalization reference, *They Became Americans* (Ancestry Incorporated, 1998).

There are any number of indexes and finding aids to these records, and all three of the books cited above provide excellent guidance to help you locate these indices. Perhaps the most definitive is the mammoth set of books by P. William Filby, the *Passenger and Immigration Lists Index* (Gale Research, Inc., 1985, ongoing series). These books are part of an ongoing project to index as many resources of ships' passenger information from as many sources as possible. Although Mr. Filby died in November 2002, his indexing project is continuing. The Filby index is likely to be found in libraries and archives with significant genealogical reference holdings, and is a resource you should not overlook.

Learn About the American Ports of Entry

Although passengers arrived at about 100 different ports over the years, most ports saw only infrequent traffic. Sometimes only a few ships would arrive in a given year. And during the course of these early years, most of the immigration traffic tended to be directed to one of five major ports: Boston, New York, Philadelphia, Baltimore, and New Orleans. Although Philadelphia had been the most popular of these ports during the colonial era, within the first two decades of federal immigration regulation, New York emerged as the preferred port of arrival.

By 1850, more immigrants arrived in New York than in all other ports combined. It had been the nation's largest seaport since the 1820s. By the 1850s, New York was a major railroad hub offering access to nearly every part of the country. It is no wonder that it became the primary immigration port of entry.

Because of the waves of immigrants entering the city, New York was the first port to open an immigration depot. Castle Garden, shown in Figure 7-6, was located at the Battery in lower Manhattan. It was the immigration processing center for the Port of New York prior to the opening of Ellis Island in 1892. It was a massive stone structure originally built in 1808 as a fort. It later served as an opera house until 3 August 1855 when New York State authorities transformed it into an immigration landing and processing station.

Castle Garden's primary purpose was not to inspect, but to protect new arrivals from the thieves, swindlers, confidence men, and prostitutes who prowled the piers looking for easy marks. Inside Castle Garden, immigrants could exchange money, purchase food and railway tickets, tend to baggage, and obtain information about boarding houses and employment. More buildings were erected outside the original Castle Garden to handle the additional volume of people as immigrant arrivals increased. Brick walls were constructed to enclose the large complex. On 18 April 1890, the last immigrants were processed through Castle Garden. During its lifetime, more than eight million immigrants had passed through Castle Garden.

Control over the immigration processing in New York shifted to the U.S. Superintendent of Immigration, and the Barge Office became an interim landing depot, pending the opening of a new immigrant processing center on Ellis Island on 1 January 1892.

FIGURE 7-6   View of Castle Garden in New York (From a stereoscope card in the author's collection)

Public pressures increased to regulate immigration and protect American jobs. With this pressure, a major new piece of legislation was introduced and passed, the Immigration Act of 1891. This act established the federal office of Superintendent of Immigration, which later became the Immigration Bureau. Over time, the Immigration Bureau exerted more and more control over the immigration lists and other documents, including their creation, content, distribution, processing, and retention. The Immigration Bureau was ultimately merged with the Bureau of Naturalization and became the Immigration and Naturalization Service that we have long known. It now is known as the U.S. Citizenship and Immigration Services (USCIS).

Another important milestone in 1891 was the completion of the new Ellis Island immigration processing site in New York Harbor. Ellis Island replaced Castle Garden, and opened on 1 January 1892. Immigrants such as those shown in Figure 7-7 arrived at a modern, well-organized facility where they were given physical examinations, helped with completing forms by interpreters who spoke their language, and processed efficiently through customs.

On 14 June 1897, however, fire destroyed the Ellis Island facility, and with it went the administrative records of Castle Garden (1888–1890) and Ellis Island (1890–1897). These were administrative records only and it is believed that very few passenger list documents were lost. The passenger lists that had already been handled over Ellis Island's years of operation to that date were perfectly safe and already in the custody of the Bureau of Customs and the Bureau of Immigration. The Ellis Island facility was reconstructed, this time using fireproof materials, and reopened on 15 December 1900. It served as the immigration processing site for New York

FIGURE 7-7   Immigrants arriving at Ellis Island (Library of Congress collection)

until 1954. You will want to research passenger arrivals at the Ellis Island Foundation site at **http://www.ellisisland.org.** Be aware that Steve Morse has developed an excellent Web site that can help you get past some of the limitations of the official Ellis Island Foundation site, and his site can be accessed at **http://stevemorse.org.**

New forms were instituted at different times in different ports depending upon a number of factors, most notably who was in charge of the port at the time. Some ports were immediately regulated by federal immigration officials beginning in 1891, while other ports were regulated and administered by local officers contracted by federal officials. Any lists created under the authority of the Immigration Bureau are considered and referred to as "immigration passenger lists." This distinguishes their content and handling from that of the customs collectors and the "customs passenger lists" and the associated processing used from 1820 until 1891.

Contrary to popular myth, the employees of the immigration processing centers did not arbitrarily change immigrants' names as they arrived. You may have seen photographs of immigrants queued up for interview or inspection in which a paper tag was attached to their clothing. The tag actually bore the name of the ship on which the person had arrived and the line number on the passenger manifest on which his or her name was listed. The processing stations used these tags to facilitate the expeditious processing of persons who spoke little or no English, and there was a small army of translators available to assist in the arrival and inspection process. Many immigrants actually changed their own names prior to sailing, on arrival in the new country, or later in order to become more quickly assimilated into the new environment. Versions of the same forms used in the United

States at various times have included a place to indicate the name under which the person arrived in the country.

Virtually all of the later immigration passenger lists survived and were eventually acquired by NARA after its creation. In the 1940s and 1950s, thousands of bound volumes of these lists (about 14,000 volumes of Ellis Island records alone) were microfilmed. Since the project was completed relatively early in the history of microfilming, the quality is not always good. Some estimates indicate that as much as 6 percent of the lists are difficult or impossible to read, with that number reaching as high as 15 percent for the pre-1902 lists. The passenger lists were destroyed after microfilming, though, making it impossible to create new digital images from the originals. Ancestry.com, however, embarked in the autumn of 2003 on the digitization of ships' passenger arrival records in a special subscription database. They are using the best quality images on original microfilm and digitizing these records, making every effort to produce the most readable images possible.

Locate Ships' Passenger Lists for Immigrants Arriving in the United States

The ships' passenger lists for arrivals into the United States, as I mentioned before, have been microfilmed by NARA. You can use the indexes such as those produced by William Filby, colonial, state, and local histories, and transcriptions in both print and on the Internet to locate ships whose port of origin and time period seem appropriate candidates to search.

The microfilmed records from NARA of immigration and passenger list arrivals from 1820 to 1891 are available for view at NARA locations across the U.S. (Visit the NARA site at **http://www. archives.gov/publications/microfilm_catalogs/immigrant/immigrant_passenger_arrivals.html** for information about the available materials.) In addition, you can access these microfilm records through LDS Family History Centers, which usually rent them through the Family History Library in Salt Lake City. Your local public library also may obtain the microfilm for you through the NARA Microfilm Publication Program, which charges for rental and shipment of the film to your library. (Visit the NARA site at **http://www.archives.gov/publications/microfilm_catalogs/immigrant/ immigrant_passenger_arrivals.html#pubprogram** for more information.)

Federal census schedules can be used as part of your research strategy. For example, the following years' census Population Schedules contain important clues.

- **1880**   Nativity columns ask for place of birth for the named person on the census form, as well as his or her parents.

- **1900**   Nativity information is again requested. In addition, the year of immigration is requested, as well as number of years in the U.S. and status of naturalization.

- **1910**   Nativity information is again requested. In addition, the year of immigration, whether naturalized, and language spoken if not English were included.

- **1920**   Year of immigration, naturalization status, and year of naturalization are requested. Place of birth and mother tongue are requested for the named person on the census and his or her parents.

- **1930**   Place of birth of named person on census and parents were requested, as well as language spoken in home before coming to the United States. Year of immigration and naturalization status were included.

All of these census schedules can provide pointers to dates and locations of immigration, including the language or "mother tongue" spoken. A response of Yiddish certainly points to a Jewish background, and a reply such as Polish, French, or Urdu would indicate another national or ethnic origin.

Naturalization documents, which we will discuss later in the chapter, can name the date, port of arrival, and name of the ship on which the person arrived.

If you are unsure of the ship on which your ancestor arrived, it is possible to use other clues such as language, place of birth, or spelling of the surname to narrow your search. If you have a good idea of the country of origin, you may be able to use microfilm of newspapers and read the shipping news. Ships' arrivals, name of the port of origin, intermediate ports of call, and shipping company can help you avoid having to read every entry for every ship in a given year. In addition, with the names of shipping lines arriving from your ancestor's country of origin, you may also be able to locate ships' manifests created and filed on the other side of the ocean.

The Immigrant Ships Transcribers Guild (ISTG) at **http://www.immigrantships.net** is an all-volunteer effort and is making great strides in locating, accessing, and producing accurate transcriptions of ships' passenger lists and manifests from the 1600s to the 1900s from all over the globe.

Locate and Access Canadian Immigration Records

There are many, many records available for the Canadian researcher. One important Web site with which to begin your research is inGeneas, created and maintained by genealogy professionals in Ottawa. Located at **http://www.ingeneas.com,** the site provides searchable databases, including passenger and immigration records from the 1700s to the early 1900s. Search results provide listings of matches, and following the links may present you with information about a person's age, the year of the record, and a description. You can then order transcripts of records you want more information on, or you can also order a photocopy of the original microfilmed document.

Another excellent Web site with many links is Immigrants to Canada, located at **http://www. ist.uwaterloo.ca/~marj/genealogy/thevoyage.html.** Included are scores of links, including compilations of ships for specific years, written/transcribed accounts describing the voyages, emigrant handbooks, extracts from government immigration reports of the 19th century, and many, many nationalities' emigration/immigration Web site links. Don't miss this one!

The National Archives of Canada

The Library and Archives of Canada, at **http://www.archives.ca,** provides its content in both English and French. Here you will find a wealth of information for your research, including some portraits of Immigrants and Aboriginal People of Canada, located at **http://collections.ic.gc.ca/portraits/docs/ imm/enatimm.htm.** Descriptions of the archives' immigration records information can be located at their Web site at **http://www.archives.ca/02/Passenger%20Lists%20Prior%20to%201865.** Here you will learn something about the immigration policies of the Canadian government.

First, you should know that there are no comprehensive lists of immigrant arrivals in Canada prior to 1865. Until that year, shipping companies were not required to create, retain, or supply their passenger lists to the government offices. There are apparently a few of the lists that include passenger names, and the Miscellaneous Immigration Index in the archives' reference room is accessible for locating those few records. The contents relate to immigrants from the British Isles to Québec and Ontario between the years 1800 and 1849. That information also is included in the inGeneas Web site as a result of volunteers' work to index and enter it.

Please note that records from 1 January 1936 are still in the custody of Citizenship and Immigration Canada. Privacy of individuals is protected, and certain requirements exist. Visit the web page located at **http://www.archives.ca/02/02020204_e.html#Post-1935%20Immigration %20Records** for more information.

Border Entry records also are available for immigrants arriving across the U.S./Canadian border between April 1908 and December 1935. However, not all immigrants were recorded. Some persons immigrated without being processed through ports when they were closed or where no port or governmental station existed. Others, for whom one or both parents were Canadian or who had previously resided in Canada, were considered "returning Canadians" and were not listed.

There also are registers of Chinese immigrants to Canada who arrived between 1885 and 1949.

It is important to know that the records are arranged by name of the port of arrival and the date of arrival, with the exception of the years 1923–1924 and some records from 1919 to 1922 when a separate governmental reporting Form 30A (individual manifest) was used. In addition, the Pier 21 Society of Halifax, Nova Scotia, has worked with the National Archives of Canada in inputting passenger list data from 1925–1935 and border entry record data into ArchiviaNet, the On-Line Research Tool accessible at **http://www.archives.ca/02/020118_e.html.** The search template for ArchiviaNet is shown in Figure 7-8. This database is searchable by surname, given name, year of arrival, port of arrival, and/or ship's name.

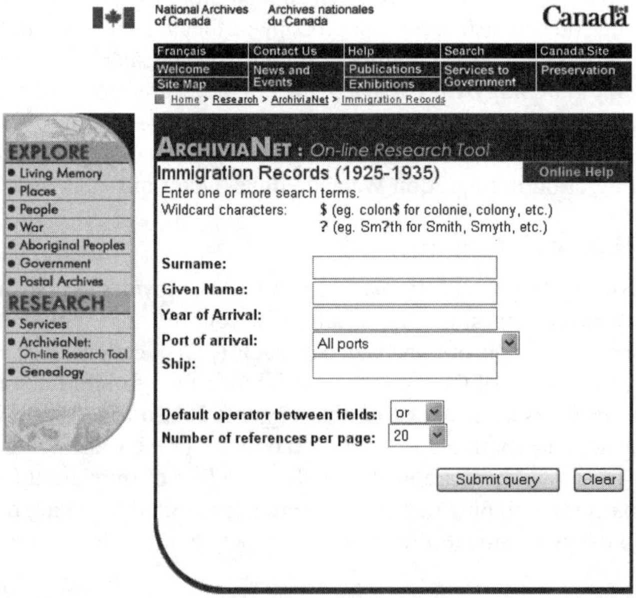

FIGURE 7-8   Search template at ArchiviaNet at the National Archives of Canada Web site

Home Children is a term used to designate the more than 100,000 children who were sent from Great Britain to Canada between the years of 1869 and the early 1930s. The intent was to supposedly provide a better, more healthy, more moral life for them. These were primarily poor or orphaned children, and rural Canadians welcomed them as cheap labor for their farms. (You may learn more about this phenomenon at the Young Immigrants to Canada Web site at **http://www.dcs.uwaterloo.ca/~marj/genealogy/homeadd.html.**) The archive contains a great deal of correspondence from sponsoring and administrative agencies for these children. Members of the British Isles Family History Society of Greater Ottawa are locating and indexing the names of these Home Children found in passenger lists in the custody of the National Archives of Canada. A searchable database of these children is accessible at **http://www.archives.ca/02/02011003_e.html.**

Passenger lists and other records from before 1865 may exist in the provincial or territorial libraries, archives, and/or at maritime museums. The passenger arrival records in the custody of the National Archives of Canada that date from 1865 and to 1935 have been microfilmed. They can be accessed in person by visiting them at 395 Wellington Street in Ottawa, Canada, through Interlibrary Loan among the Canadian libraries, and/or through the LDS Family History Center nearest you. Check the Web site at **http://www.archives.ca/02/020202/0202020401_e.html** for details about these records. (You can learn about other genealogical resources held by the National Archives of Canada at **http://www.archives.ca/02/020202_e.html.**)

An excellent strategy for researching immigrants into Canada would be to start with the Archives of Canada and then seek additional resources in the appropriate province or territory. Please note that Canada *does not* maintain records of emigrations from Canada to other countries. If you are searching for an ancestor who emigrated to the U.S., for example, you will need to refer to any U.S. immigration records.

Locate and Access Australian Immigration Records

The history of Australia is a rich one, and it is the story of two peoples: the indigenous Aboriginals and the immigrants, primarily from the British Isles. Most people know that Australia was originally a penal colony, and that most of the original, colonial settlers were, in fact, convicts who were transported from the U.K. since 1788. Nowadays it is the "in thing" to descend from a convict. In fact, Australian citizens often express the sentiment that the more convicts in the family tree, the merrier—and the more "ocker" (Australian) one becomes. So let's look at convicts first. The earlier your ancestor arrived in Australia, the greater the probability that you are descended from a convict or from member of the Crown government, an army or naval person, or a member of a ship's crew.

It is important to recognize early on that the National Archives of Australia on Queen Victoria Terrace in Canberra is the archives of the Commonwealth government. The records in that collection therefore date mostly from the Federation in 1901. The archives do not possess the records of convicts, of colonial migration, or of 19th-century Australian history concerning such periods as the early exploration, the gold rushes, or colonial administration. They also do not have information about functions administered by the state and territory governments such as births, deaths, and marriages registers, or land titles. To obtain further information on these topics, it is necessary to contact the relevant state or territory registrar.

What the National Archives of Australia does have, however, are immigration records relating to the 20th century dating primarily from 1924. They do have some older records dating to the 1850s, but most of the records will be found in the respective state and territory archives. The National Archives' Fact Sheet 38, found on the Web at **http://www.naa.gov.au/publications/fact_sheets/ fs38.html,** details their holdings. You will also want to review other fact sheets for records held in other offices of the archives as follows:

- **Fact Sheet 56**   Passenger records held in Perth (**http://www.naa.gov.au/publications/ fact_sheets/fs56.html**)

- **Fact Sheet 64**   Passenger records held in Sydney (**http://www.naa.gov.au/publications/ fact_sheets/fs64.html**)

- **Fact Sheet 172**   Passenger records held in Melbourne (**http://www.naa.gov.au/ publications/fact_sheets/fs172.html**)

- **Fact Sheet 184**   Passenger records held in Hobart (**http://www.naa.gov.au/publications/ fact_sheets/fs184.html**)

The Fact Sheet 2, located at **http://www.naa.gov.au/publications/fact_sheets/fs02.html,** is perhaps your most valuable online reference in the search for historical documents related to your genealogical research. It contains the addresses, contact information, and Web address links for all of the major Australian archival institutions.

Learn About Australian History

Many criminal offenses in England during previous centuries could be punished with extremely harsh and cruel sentences, ranging from public floggings to an appointment with the hangman, or to an executioner with an axe, if you were a "special" prisoner. During the 17th century, a more humane method of punishment was sought, and *transportation* to a distant wilderness environment was seen as an ideal solution. Thus, transportation began from the U.K. to the American colonies. Debtors' colonies and criminal settlements existed for those condemned to a penal servitude or for a term of years or for life. The outbreak of the American Revolution halted transportation of criminals and undesirables to that destination. While sentences of transportation were still passed by the courts, the convicts were remanded to prison. Before long, the prison overcrowding problem created dire conditions. The government began to acquire older, perhaps no longer seaworthy ships, which were referred to as "the hulks." These were fitted to house criminals and thousands of convicts were sentenced to terms of imprisonment in these floating jails moored in coastal waters. The deplorable living conditions in both the prisons and onboard the hulks reached a crisis stage, with rampant disease and escalating death tolls. The government sought a new penal colony as a solution. In 1787, what has been called the "First Fleet" set sail from England for Botany Bay in Australia. A number of penal colony settlements were founded and maintained over the next 70 years. Transportation as a punishment was effectively stopped in 1857, although it was not formally abolished until 1868.

As you begin your research for Australian ancestors, you will want to familiarize yourself with the history of the judicial system in the U.K. at the time in question, and about the history of the penal colonies in the various areas of Australia. You also will want to try to locate the records of the criminal proceedings against your ancestor, the details of sentencing, and to what colony he or she was transported. This will help you trace the migration path.

You also can trace the path backward, although it may be more complicated to make that leap without understanding the ancestor's circumstances and his or her offense. In either case, however, it is important to learn as much about your ancestor as possible before you begin. At a minimum, you will want to know the exact name, age, approximate date of arrival, and the port of disembarkation. Any additional information you can glean in advance may be the crucial factor in distinguishing *your* ancestor from another person bearing the same name. Again, most of these records will be in the possession of the respective state or territory to which the person was transported.

Use Strategies for Determining Your Ancestor's Ship

By now, you should have a much better idea of the types of information that are available for the various time periods and what you are likely to find at various points in time. The actual *locating* of the records is, of course, the real challenge. The following are some strategies you may consider employing in order to locate these records for your ancestors.

7

Start With What You Know

As with all effective family history and genealogical research, start with the most recent period and work your way backward. Any other approach, especially when researching back "across the pond," can be disastrous. As you proceed backward, start with what other family members may know. Look for home sources, including documentary materials that may have recorded immigration and/or naturalization details. These include Bibles, letters, naturalization papers, obituaries, and other documents. Another, older relative may even recall having heard grandpa or grandma discuss his or her trip to America, or something they recall having heard from another family member. While the intervening years may have dimmed or distorted the memory, there is likely to be a glimmer of truth or a kernel of fact with which to begin researching.

Refer to Vital Documents

Marriage and death certificates, as well as any ecclesiastical records, may provide crucial information concerning your ancestor's origins.

Don't Overlook Voter Registration Records

One important record overlooked by many researchers is the voter registration record. These records typically are maintained at the county level across the U.S. Most times they are in a list format but sometimes the original voter registration application cards still exist. In order to vote in an election, an individual had to be a citizen, and the voter registration records may include areas to indicate the place of birth, whether naturalized and when, and how may years a resident in this voting precinct/ward/etc.

Are There Passport Records?

Passports were issued as early as 1797 in the U.S. to citizens traveling to other countries. It is possible that your ancestor had to obtain a passport to return to and visit his or her homeland (and even to bring other relatives to America).

Locate and Use the U.S. Federal Census Population Schedules

Don't overlook the information included on U.S. census records from 1880 forward concerning place of birth of the individual, his or her parents, and naturalization information details. These are often direct links. However, be aware that a stated place of birth may have been in a different geopolitical jurisdiction then than it is now, and your understanding of the history and geographical boundary changes is crucial to your successful research into your ancestor's origins.

Study Published Histories

It is important to locate histories of the country and the locale from which your ancestor(s) may have come. Some of these published chronicles include the names of emigrants, their reasons for emigration, the migration paths they took, the time periods in which they relocated and, in some cases, the names of the shipping lines (and ships) used.

One category of histories which should not be overlooked is the British genealogies that mention relatives who have gone to the New World. In the 16th and 17th centuries, heralds from the College of Arms would visit the various counties and record the pedigrees of families who aspired to *armigerous* status (meaning that they would have a coat of arms). Occasionally, there would be references to younger sons who had migrated or emigrated elsewhere.

In the 18th and 19th centuries, ambitious compilers of county histories would include pedigrees of the principal families of the county. Again, there would be the occasional reference to a relative who had gone to America, or perhaps even to a specified destination.

Finally, in the 19th and 20th centuries, the various volumes of pedigrees of landed gentry, peerage, and baronetcies, published by the Burke's Peerage & Gentry (at **http://www.burkes-peerage.net**), would contain many references to American settlers.

Look for Books About Early Settlers

By the same token, the companion to the histories discussed above would be the historical publications concerning arriving immigrants at the other end of your ancestors' journey. Often these books include the names, origins, and biographical sketches of literally hundreds of persons who lived first in a particular area after their immigration from Europe.

Seek Supplemental Information on the Internet

Don't forget to conduct research for historical text, records, and other information on the Internet! Learn to use Boolean searches with your favorite browser(s) and start exploring using creative combinations of keywords and phrases. We will discuss research on the Internet in depth in Chapter 9.

Consult Indices

William Filby's indices, already mentioned here, remain a monumental reference work. However, there are many, many other indices you can use. The Soundex index of the passenger records that are in NARA's possession provide an exceptional reference. Similar indices in other locations, including in the archives of states, counties, and other entities, will be equally as helpful. And don't forget the national archives of other countries for emigration lists, criminal transportation records, shipping company records, crew lists, and other documents.

Search for Shipping News

Newspapers of the period in a location can provide important information about ships' departures and arrivals. Shipping was big business! For example, one researcher accessed microfilmed newspaper records for the port of Bremen and identified every ship sailing during a particular three-month (autumn) sailing season to the port of Boston. Armed with that narrowed-down information, she then researched the incoming shipping records in the Boston newspapers. Using the arrival dates, she then sought—and found—that there were several likely ships on which her own ancestors might have arrived. She went on to locate the passenger manifests at the state archives and more information about the ships themselves in maritime books. From those records, she was able to reconstruct her ancestors' voyage, the weather and sailing conditions, and finally located the records she sought. The picture she constructed through her research is a rich tapestry of life at the time for her emigrant/immigrant ancestors.

7

Use Other Strategies for Determining Your Ancestor's Place of Origin

By now, you should understand more clearly that there are more paths to follow than just one in the search for your ancestors' records. When the place of birth, previous residence, or other indication of native origin is conveniently and clearly marked, you can be thankful for more modern records. However, when you don't have such crystal-clear directional markers, what are you to do?

Determining your ancestral origin can be a tricky thing but it is not always impossible to ascertain. There can be a number of strategies employed, so let's look at a few. This list can never be complete because each nationality has its own nuances, but you must invest some thought and ingenuity to reach out to your ancestors' stories and traits.

Use Photographic Images

If your ancestors came to America between 1850 and present, there are strong possibilities that there are photographs of your ancestors, especially in family photographic collections. An examination of clothing, hair styles, shoes, jewelry, and other objects in the picture may be helpful. On older photographs mounted on cabinet card stock, there may even be the name of a photographer and a location. Researching these can be an interesting study as well, and it is not unusual to find a particular photographer having taken photos in a specific area or neighborhood in which a national or ethnic group lived.

Look for Letters Written in Another Language at Home

If you encounter letters written in another language among the family possessions, or Bibles and books in another language, start asking questions. These may be indicative of the nativity of members of your family or your ancestors.

Customs

Are there specific customs in your family you don't understand? One researcher wondered why the family always ate marinated herring at Christmastime, only to discover later that it was a residual custom from her maternal grandmother, whose family always ate it at their home outside Uppsala, Sweden. And are there songs in another language that are sung, such as lullabies? They might be an important clue.

Cooking

Ethnic or national cooking is always an interesting tip-off, though not always. Your grandmother's Hungarian goulash may be indicative that she is one of Zsa-Zsa Gabor and her sisters' cousins! However, don't overlook the possibility that some culinary trait might point to a particular ethnic or national heritage.

Physical Traits

One African-American friend heard a lecture at the National Genealogical Society Conference in Valley Forge, Pennsylvania, in 1997, by another African-American researcher. In that lecture, she learned that there are physical characteristics of some African peoples that may be used to trace ancestry of slave ancestors back to the geographical area and perhaps to a specific group. The physical traits in this case were the size and shape of the ear, the shape of a nose, and the physical size of the ulna. It is a very interesting approach, and it might really matter.

The point of all of these examples is to illustrate that it may be a single thing that acts as the clue to your ancestral origins, such as a document or some trait or custom, or it may be a combination of things that provide you with the pointers you need.

Be Alert to Ethnic Issues

Throughout your investigative research, you have to keep your eyes and senses open as perhaps never before. Be aware of all sorts of possibilities and exclude nothing and no one. You may be surprised to discover that you have Jewish ancestors or African-American relatives or Latin American cousins or any of a variety of other ethnic and religious links. We are an amalgam of cultures and origins, and that makes for a richer whole overall. While it may make for a more challenging research experience, it certainly expands the joy and excitement of the discovery.

Use Alternative Record Types to Identify Clues

It is important to use your creativity to identify and locate alternative records that might help you trace your ancestors to their native origins. Remember that ships' manifests are not the only possible extant records that may record that information. Consider the following record types:

- Ecclesiastical records, including letters of membership transfer
- Marriage records
- Census records
- Naturalization papers
- Death records
- Newspaper articles
- Obituaries
- Cemetery records
- Wills and probate packet documents
- Family histories
- Published local and provincial histories
- Genealogical and historical society documents
- Maritime museums and archives
- Academic libraries and archives and their special collections

Each of these is a possible source for prospecting for your immigrant ancestors' origins.

Use the Resources at the U.S. Citizenship and Immigration Services Web Site

The U.S. Citizenship and Immigration Services Web site provides some of the most important historical and reference materials for your immigration and naturalization research. The organization's History, Genealogy, and Education page at **http://uscis.gov/graphics/aboutus/history/index.htm** contains links to a variety of articles, discussions of ships' passenger lists and land arrival documents, details about naturalization, and much more relating to the former Bureau of Immigration and Naturalization Service (INS). The Web page titled "Ports of Entry and Their Records" provides a roster of the states and, within each state, you will find each port of entry, the types of records created at that port, the dates of those records, where they were originally filed, and the current National Archives microfilm publication number (if any). If a particular set of records has no NARA microfilm publication number, it means that that entry is either not yet published or its publication status was undetermined. In some cases, there are no microfilmed records, which may lead you to explore the status of those records and where they may exist today.

Understand the Naturalization Process

As our forebears began their new lives in new communities, they would strive to "fit in" and to normalize in the new environment. Many realized they would never return to their past lives, and they eagerly embraced their new circumstances. This meant renouncing their political ties to their motherland and applying to become citizens of their new country.

The naturalization process has varied in every location we will discuss here (the United States, Canada, and Australia), and has evolved over time to produce more consistent practices with more standardized and detailed records.

Naturalization in the United States, like the ships' passenger lists and manifests, has changed over the last two and a quarter centuries of the country's existence. Different methods of handling the process, different laws and requirements, different forms, and different places where the process was handled all add up to what can be a challenging research effort. There are many intricacies and exceptions and, as a result, we have to do some self-education to learn the details of the history of naturalization in the U.S. To that end, Loretto D. Szuc's book *They Became Americans: Finding Naturalization Records and Ethnic Origins* wins my applause for the best volume on the process, and is illustrated with scores of document examples.

Since 1790, the U.S. Constitution, in Article I, Section 8, has given Congress the power "To establish a uniform Rule of Naturalization, and uniform Laws on the subject of Bankruptcies throughout the United States." Congress originally vested the responsibility for conducting naturalization with the courts. This was the most convenient method of administering the process because a) the courts were closer and more accessible to the population than were the national government offices, and b) there already was a process of handling legal affairs by persons who were literate and who understood or could reasonably interpret and administer the laws.

The federal government was just forming and learning how to *be* a government, and it began its work with citizens by declaring that all persons who were citizens of the new United States were its residents. The Constitution and the Bill of Rights determined this, even though not all residents (Native Americans, African-Americans, and women) enjoyed all the privileges that free white males enjoyed. However, all in all, they were U.S. citizens.

From 1790 onward, any individual could become a naturalized citizen through any federal court. Most people, however, submitted their petition (application) to the local courts, primarily because these courts were geographically closer and the magistrates and clerks were more familiar to them.

The rules or laws governing naturalization certainly have changed over time. Your understanding of what the laws were at the time will allow you to quickly determine whether to even seek naturalization documentation for an ancestor. It is not unlike checking to see if a particular state dictated the issuance of a formal birth certificate in a particular year. If I know that North Carolina didn't require all its counties to be in full compliance of a birth certificate statute until the early 1920s, then I would know that a birth in 1909 would not be documented with a birth certificate. I know that I have to search alternate document types for evidence corroborating his birth.

In order to better understand the immigration and naturalization process, because the two activities *are* intertwined so tightly, it is essential to understand its history in the United States. There were four primary documents involved with the naturalization process:

- **Declaration of Intention** This document is signed by the immigrant, renouncing citizenship in his/her previous country and any allegiance to the country and/or its ruler or sovereign. It expresses the individual's intent to petition the United States to become a citizen after all requirements are met. Also referred to as *first papers*. The format varied over time, as you can see from the examples in Figures 7-9 and 7-10.
- **Petition for Naturalization** This document is the application that the person completes and submits to request the granting of citizenship, typically after satisfying residency requirements and after filing first papers. Also referred to as *final papers*. Figure 7-11 shows an example of this document, and Figure 7-12 shows the court document granting permission to take the oath of naturalization. Both examples originated in the Dakota Territory in 1885.
- **Oath of Allegiance** This is the document that is signed by the petitioner for citizenship at the time citizenship is granted (or restored) swearing his/her allegiance and support to the United States. This may or may not be included in the naturalization file for your ancestor.
- **Certificate of Naturalization** This is the formal document issued to the petitioner to certify that he/she has been naturalized as a citizen of the United States. Figure 7-13 shows a certificate from 1946.

7

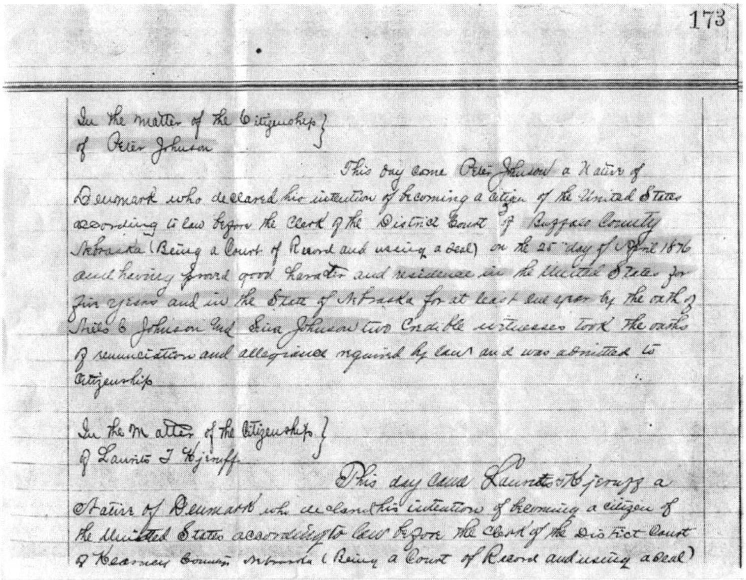
173

In the matter of the Citizenship }
of Peter Johnson }

This day come Peter Johnson a Native of Denmark who declared his intention of becoming a citizen of the United States according to law before the Clerk of the District Court of Buffalo County Nebraska (Being a Court of Record and using a Seal) on the 25 day of April 1876 and having proved good character and residence in the United States for five years and in the State of Nebraska for at least one year by the oath of Niels C Johnson and Lina Johnson two Credible witnesses took the oaths of renunciation and allegiance required by law and was admitted to Citizenship

In the matter of the Citizenship }
of Laurits T Hjeruff }

This day came Laurits T Hjeruff a Native of Denmark who declared his intention of becoming a citizen of the United States according to law before the Clerk of the District Court of Kearney County Nebraska (Being a Court of Record and using a Seal)

FIGURE 7-9 Handwritten copy of Declaration of Intent document for Peter Johnson, 25 April 1875, Buffalo County, Nebraska, from court records (Courtesy of Jody Johnson)

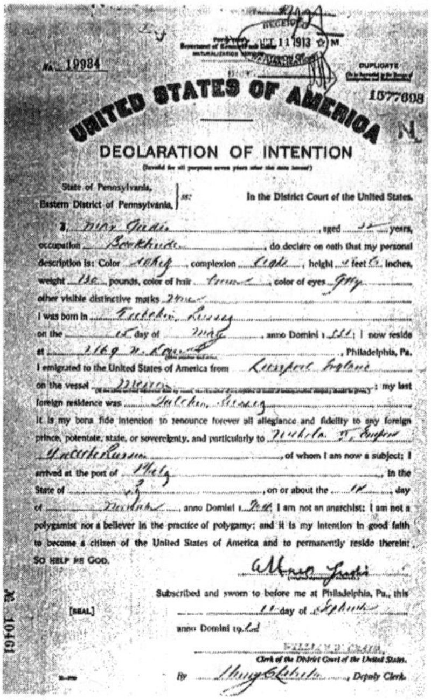

No. 19984

DUPLICATE

1577608

UNITED STATES OF AMERICA

N

DECLARATION OF INTENTION

State of Pennsylvania, Eastern District of Pennsylvania, } ss: In the District Court of the United States.

I, May Gudis, aged [illegible] years, occupation Bookbinder, do declare on oath that my personal description is: Color white, complexion light, height [illegible] feet [illegible] inches, weight 130 pounds, color of hair brown, color of eyes grey, other visible distinctive marks none

I was born in [illegible], Russia on the 15 day of May, anno Domini 1 [illegible]; I now reside at 2169 N. [illegible], Philadelphia, Pa.

I emigrated to the United States of America from Liverpool England on the vessel Merion; my last foreign residence was [illegible], Russia

It is my bona fide intention to renounce forever all allegiance and fidelity to any foreign prince, potentate, state, or sovereignty, and particularly to Nicholas II, Emperor of Russia, of whom I am now a subject; I arrived at the port of Phila in the State of Pa, on or about the 10 day of [illegible], anno Domini 1 [illegible]; I am not an anarchist; I am not a polygamist nor a believer in the practice of polygamy; and it is my intention in good faith to become a citizen of the United States of America and to permanently reside therein; SO HELP ME GOD.

May Gudis

Subscribed and sworn to before me at Philadelphia, Pa., this 11 day of September anno Domini 19 [illegible]

[SEAL]

WILLIAM W. CRAIG, Clerk of the District Court of the United States.

By [illegible], Deputy Clerk.

No. 10461

FIGURE 7-10 Declaration of Intent for May Gudis, 11 September 1913, filed in Pennsylvania (National Archives and Records Administration collection)

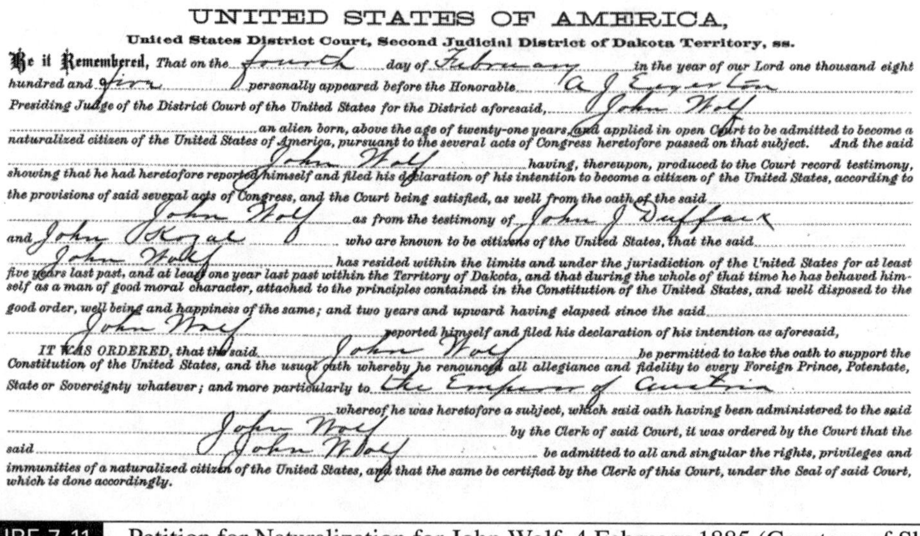

UNITED STATES OF AMERICA,

United States District Court, Second Judicial District of Dakota Territory, ss.

Be it Remembered, That on the fourth day of February in the year of our Lord one thousand eight hundred and five personally appeared before the Honorable A J Edgerton Presiding Judge of the District Court of the United States for the District aforesaid, John Wolf an alien born, above the age of twenty-one years, and applied in open Court to be admitted to become a naturalized citizen of the United States of America, pursuant to the several acts of Congress heretofore passed on that subject. And the said John Wolf having, thereupon, produced to the Court record testimony, showing that he had heretofore reported himself and filed his declaration of his intention to become a citizen of the United States, according to the provisions of said several acts of Congress, and the Court being satisfied, as well from the oath of the said John Wolf as from the testimony of John J Duffack and John Kozal who are known to be citizens of the United States, that the said John Wolf has resided within the limits and under the jurisdiction of the United States for at least five years last past, and at least one year last past within the Territory of Dakota, and that during the whole of that time he has behaved himself as a man of good moral character, attached to the principles contained in the Constitution of the United States, and well disposed to the good order, well being and happiness of the same; and two years and upward having elapsed since the said John Wolf reported himself and filed his declaration of his intention as aforesaid,

IT WAS ORDERED, that the said John Wolf be permitted to take the oath to support the Constitution of the United States, and the usual oath whereby he renounces all allegiance and fidelity to every Foreign Prince, Potentate, State or Sovereignty whatever; and more particularly to the Emperor of Austria whereof he was heretofore a subject, which said oath having been administered to the said John Wolf by the Clerk of said Court, it was ordered by the Court that the said John Wolf be admitted to all and singular the rights, privileges and immunities of a naturalized citizen of the United States, and that the same be certified by the Clerk of this Court, under the Seal of said Court, which is done accordingly.

FIGURE 7-11 Petition for Naturalization for John Wolf, 4 February 1885 (Courtesy of Sherrie Williams)

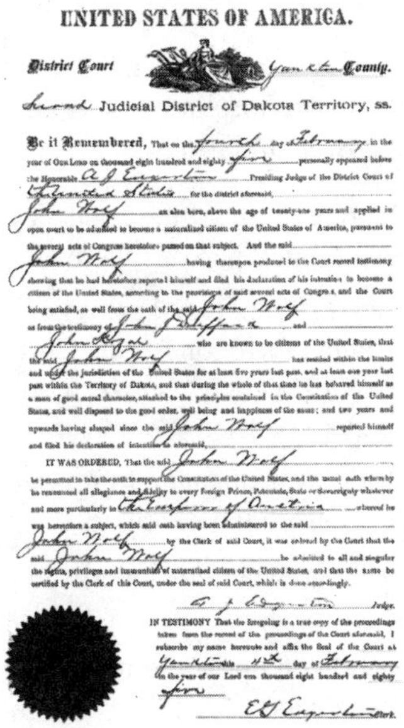

UNITED STATES OF AMERICA.

District Court Yankton County.

Second Judicial District of Dakota Territory, ss.

Be it Remembered, That on the fourth day of February in the year of Our Lord one thousand eight hundred and eighty five personally appeared before the Honorable A J Edgerton Presiding Judge of the District Court of the United States for the district aforesaid, John Wolf an alien born, above the age of twenty-one years and applied in open court to be admitted to become a naturalized citizen of the United States of America, pursuant to the several acts of Congress heretofore passed on that subject. And the said John Wolf having thereupon produced to the Court record testimony showing that he had heretofore reported himself and filed his declaration of his intention to become a citizen of the United States, according to the provisions of said several acts of Congress, and the Court being satisfied, as well from the oath of the said John Wolf as from the testimony of John J Pfeffer and John Ryan who are known to be citizens of the United States, that the said John Wolf has resided within the limits and under the jurisdiction of the United States for at least five years last past, and at least one year last past within the Territory of Dakota, and that during the whole of that time he has behaved himself as a man of good moral character, attached to the principles contained in the Constitution of the United States, and well disposed to the good order, well being and happiness of the same; and two years and upwards having elapsed since the said John Wolf reported himself and filed his declaration of intention as aforesaid,

IT WAS ORDERED, That the said John Wolf be permitted to take the oath to support the Constitution of the United States, and the usual oath whereby he renounced all allegiance and fidelity to every foreign Prince, Potentate, State or Sovereignty whatever and more particularly to the Emperor of Austria whereof he was heretofore a subject, which said oath having been administered to the said John Wolf by the Clerk of said Court, it was ordered by the Court that the said John Wolf be admitted to all and singular the rights, privileges and immunities of naturalized citizen of the United States, and that the same be certified by the Clerk of this Court, under the seal of said Court, which is done accordingly.

A J Edgerton Judge.

IN TESTIMONY That the foregoing is a true copy of the proceedings taken from the record of the proceedings of the Court aforesaid, I subscribe my name hereunto and affix the Seal of the Court at Yankton this 4th day of February in the year of our Lord one thousand eight hundred and eighty five

E G Edgerton Clerk.

FIGURE 7-12 Court document granting John Wolf's petition and authorizing him to take the oath of allegiance (Courtesy of Sherrie Williams)

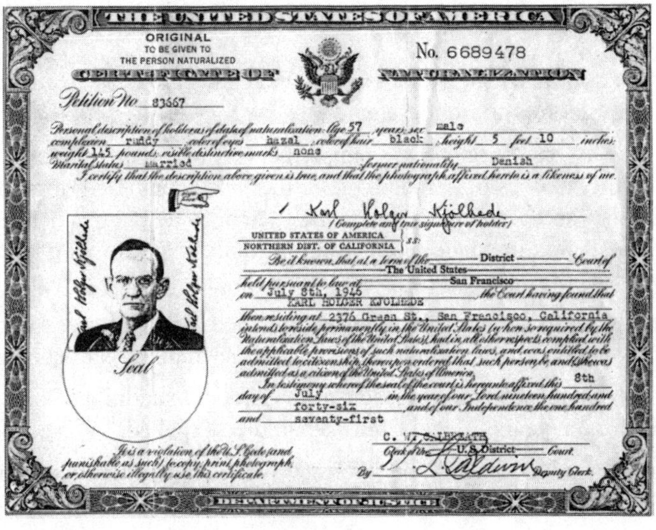

THE UNITED STATES OF AMERICA

ORIGINAL
TO BE GIVEN TO
THE PERSON NATURALIZED

No. 6689478

CERTIFICATE OF NATURALIZATION

Petition No. 83667

Personal description of holder as of date of naturalization: Age 57 years; sex male; complexion ruddy; color of eyes hazel; color of hair black; height 5 feet 10 inches; weight 145 pounds; visible distinctive marks none

Marital status married; former nationality Danish

I certify that the description above given is true, and that the photograph affixed hereto is a likeness of me.

Karl Holger Kjolhede
(Complete and true signature of holder)

UNITED STATES OF AMERICA
NORTHERN DIST. OF CALIFORNIA } SS:

Be it known, that at a term of the District Court of The United States held pursuant to law at San Francisco on July 8th, 1946 the Court having found that KARL HOLGER KJOLHEDE then residing at 2376 Green St., San Francisco, California intends to reside permanently in the United States (when so required by the Naturalization Laws of the United States), had in all other respects complied with the applicable provisions of such naturalization laws, and was entitled to be admitted to citizenship, thereupon ordered that such person be and (s)he was admitted as a citizen of the United States of America.

In testimony whereof the seal of the court is hereunto affixed this 8th day of July in the year of our Lord nineteen hundred and forty-six and of our Independence the one hundred and seventy-first

Seal

C. W. CALBREATH
Clerk of the U.S. District Court.
By L. Baldwin Deputy Clerk.

It is a violation of the U.S. Code (and punishable as such) to copy, print, photograph, or otherwise illegally use this certificate.

DEPARTMENT OF JUSTICE

FIGURE 7-13 Certificate of Naturalization for Karl Holger Kjolhede issued 8 July 1946 (Courtesy of Jody Johnson)

Understand Some Key Dates in the History of Naturalization in the United States

The following list of important dates provides a brief outline of key legislation or changes affecting the naturalization process. These dates are important because they influenced *who* would be creating the documents relating to citizenship and *when*.

- The first legislation, dated 26 March 1790, set the residency requirement for naturalization at two years, and children of naturalized persons were also to be considered citizens.

- A naturalization act of 29 January 1795 included provisions for "free white aliens" to have five years of residency in the country, with one year within the state in which they made petition. A declaration of intention to become a citizen could be filed after two years, and the petition for naturalization was to be filed three years after the declaration.

- In 1798, the residency requirement was changed to fourteen years, with the declaration of intention to be filed five years before the petition.

- In 1802, the extremes of the 1798 act were rescinded and the requirements defined in the 1795 act were reinstated.

- In 1824, alien minors were naturalized upon attaining the age of twenty-one if they had lived in the United States for five years.

- In 1855, an act was passed in which alien women married to U.S. citizens were considered to be citizens. In addition, Castle Garden was opened in New York to accommodate the massive influx of immigrants.

- In 1862, in an effort to encourage resident aliens to join the Union army, an act was passed that facilitated the naturalization process for aliens who had served in the U.S. Army and who received honorable discharges. For these people, the filing of a declaration of intention was waived.

- In 1875, immigration was denied to prostitutes and convicts. Asians were required to have residency permits in order to immigrate.

- In 1882, the Chinese exclusion law was implemented, which extensively curbed Chinese immigration. Other classes of persons, including those convicted of political offenses, "lunatics," "idiots," and persons who were likely to become public charges were banned. A head tax of $.50 was imposed on each immigrant for purposes of funding the administrative costs of running a governmental immigration department.

- In 1891, the Bureau of Immigration was established, and Congress imposed health restrictions, as well as denials of unhealthy persons, criminals, paupers, and others.

- In 1892, Ellis Island opened and replaced Castle Garden. In addition, Chinese immigration was prohibited for ten years. Illegal Chinese could be expelled.

- In 1893, Chinese residents had to apply for certificates of residence or be removed.

- In 1894, aliens who received honorable discharges from the U.S. Navy and the U.S. Marine Corps were not required to file a declaration of intention. (See the similar act in 1862 for aliens honorably discharged from the U.S. Army.)

- In 1906, the Bureau of Immigration and Naturalization was established by law on 29 June 1906 and became effective on 27 September 1906. It established uniform handling of all applications, and required the use of uniform blank forms obtained from and controlled by the Bureau of Immigration and Naturalization. Knowledge of English became a basic requirement of citizenship.

- In 1917, the Jones Act made Puerto Ricans U.S. citizens and eligible for the draft.

- In 1922, alien wives of U.S. citizens were allowed to file their Petition for Citizenship after one year of residency. Native-born American women who were married to aliens were stripped of their citizenship.

- In 1936, those women who had lost their citizenship in 1922 due to having been married to aliens were reinstated as citizens on taking oaths of allegiance to the U.S.

- In 1952, immigration quotas, security, and other regulatory rules were strengthened. The age requirement was lowered from twenty-one years of age to eighteen.

- In 1954, Ellis Island closed.

- In 1965, the old National Origins Quota System limiting numbers of immigrants from specific countries and hemispheric ceilings was abolished.

As you can see, there were some changes that affected whether a person would have filed their first papers or not, or the difference in the waiting period between the filing of first papers and the petition to become a naturalized citizen and the granting of final papers. In addition, if an individual did not consummate the citizenship process within the proscribed period, for example, within the five-year time frame, that application/petition process ended, and the person would need to begin the process again with a new declaration of intention.

Another change required by the revised statute of 1906 was the addition of a step in the process to verify the arrival/admission of the immigrant in the U.S. On the Declaration of Intention document, the individual was required to state the place from which he/she emigrated, the arrival point in the U.S., the name under which he/she arrived, the date of arrival, and the vessel on which he/she arrived. Copies of the form were forwarded to the port of arrival where clerks verified the data against the immigration manifests. If the record was found, an additional document was issued by the INS: the Certificate of Arrival, a sample of which is shown in Figure 7-14. Between its institution in 1906 and 1 July 1924, the Certificate of Arrival was an essential document to process a Petition for Citizenship. Beginning in 1924, the INS began collecting immigrant visas, and these documents ultimately replaced the need to have verification clerks search the immigration manifests. The visas were presented to an immigration inspector on arrival in the U.S., and were filed. Visas for non-immigrants were filed in the port of arrival, while visas for immigrants were forwarded to the INS in Washington, D.C., for filing and future reference.

Another important document that may possibly be of help to your research is the Alien Registration Card. Under concern for the possibility of war and relating espionage, the U.S. enacted

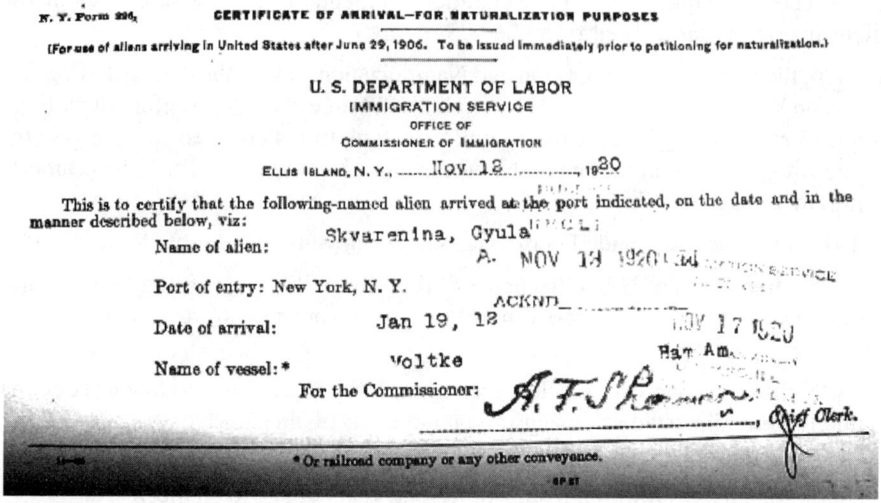

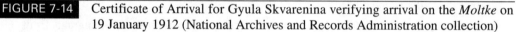

FIGURE 7-14 Certificate of Arrival for Gyula Skvarenina verifying arrival on the *Moltke* on 19 January 1912 (National Archives and Records Administration collection)

the Alien Registration Act (also known as the Smith Act) in 1940. Between 1940 and 1944, every alien was required to register as they applied for admission to the country, regardless of their origin. They completed a two-page form and were fingerprinted, and they were given an alien registration receipt card to present if asked to confirm their compliance with the law.

There are a number of other types of naturalization documents that were used during the 20th century. The scope of this book makes it impractical to list all of them here. However, Loretto Szuc provides an excellent reference list of documents issued by the INS since 1906, along with their abbreviations, on page 169 of her book *They Became Americans: Finding Naturalization Records and Ethnic Origins*.

Locate Repositories Where Naturalization and Related Documents Are Housed

Locating the original documents is your goal, and you certainly will hope to find definite data or clues as to the origins of your ancestor and how he or she traveled to America. As you conduct your research, please remember that an individual may begin the naturalization process, filing a Declaration of Intent, in one place and complete the naturalization process in another place. Therefore, the physical documents may be located in different areas altogether.

The sheer volume of naturalization indices and documents described above can be mind-boggling. You should be aware that a significant amount, but certainly not all, of the extant naturalization documents themselves that have been unearthed have been forwarded to the INS and, in turn, to the National Archives and Records Administration (NARA) for microfilming and storage. As a general rule, NARA does *not* have naturalization records created in state or local courts.

However, some county court naturalization records have been donated to the National Archives and are available as National Archives microfilm publications. For a reference to the holdings of naturalization materials at NARA, please refer to their Web site on the topic located at **http://www. archives.gov/research_room/genealogy/research_topics/naturalization_records.html.** This is essential reading for the researcher!

NARA, for example, has none of the naturalization documents for the State of Utah. These reside with the U.S. District Court for the District of Utah, and some of the older records reside with the Utah State Archives and Records Service. There certainly are many, many other exceptions.

What you will find is that the original naturalization records in NARA's possession have been stored in the National Archives Regional Archives facility, which serves the state in which the federal court is located. As an example, the NARA Southeast Regional Branch in Atlanta, Georgia, is the repository for documents relating to Alabama, Florida, Georgia, Kentucky, Mississippi, North Carolina, South Carolina, and Tennessee. It is important that you determine what NARA branch serves the state in which your ancestor would have lived at the time he or she filed the Declaration of Intent and/or Petition for Citizenship. Then you need to determine if the NARA branch does, in fact, have the documents you seek. You can begin your research by visiting the NARA Web site at **http://www.archives.gov** (formerly **http://www.nara.gov**), and then wend your way through their site to the Web page for the NARA branches (facilities). Within each one of these, you will find a link to Genealogy, and then within the resulting page, to a listing of their holdings. Not every NARA branch has genealogical records. For example, a visit to the NARA Mid-Atlantic Regional Branch Web site (Northeast Philadelphia) at **http://www.archives.gov/facilities/pa/philadelphia_ northeast.html** will reveal that genealogical records are not at the northeast Philadelphia facility but at the Center City facility. You can then click on a link to direct your browser to the NARA Mid-Atlantic Region (Center City Philadelphia) Web site at (located at **http://www.archives.gov/ facilities/pa/philadelphia_center_city.html**) where you can click on the Genealogy link and learn that the facility holds "naturalization records and indexes processed through federal courts in Delaware, Maryland, Pennsylvania, Virginia and West Virginia (dates vary by court)."

In the process of your research, it would be prudent whenever you are preparing to conduct a search for naturalization documents to visit the NARA Web site, check the holdings list of microfilm publications and/or in their online catalog, and consider making a telephone call to their reference desk. The reference staff can help you determine if the records you seek are or are not part of NARA's holdings, whether those documents have been indexed and/or microfilmed, and how to obtain copies. Be sure to check in advance of making a trip to a NARA Regional Branch facility to confirm that they do, in fact, have the microfilm and/or records you might want to view.

Don't overlook the use of your local LDS Family History Center as a resource to borrow the NARA microfilm from the Family History Library in Salt Lake City. This is an economical means of accessing and working with the materials locally, rather than traveling to a NARA facility.

In any event, inasmuch as naturalization records research can involve searching in multiple facilities and potentially working with both archives *and* court repositories, the NARA Regional Branch staff can provide excellent guidance for your research.

Work Immigration and Naturalization Records in Tandem

You will find it natural to work between the immigration and naturalization records for your ancestors and family members. Working backward, you can use the naturalization records to isolate the date of arrival, the port, and the name of the vessel. If your ancestors arrived after the implementation of the Certificate of Arrival, this document can provide a strong piece of evidence for you because the arrival date, place, and ship were researched at the time of naturalization. In addition, if the person had changed his or her name since immigration, the name under which he or she arrived would have had to have been supplied in order to verify the arrival. With naturalization information in hand, tracing the ship can be greatly simplified. You can then trace to the port of departure to determine if other documents exist. These might contain more information to help you trace your immigrant to the home town.

On the other hand, if you have already discovered the ship on which the person traveled and the port of arrival, you can begin to look for other evidence about them in that vicinity. Use the port of arrival as a central point, and seek other documents, including city directories and newspapers. Focus on other relatives or in-laws, both of the immigrant and a spouse, in the country and check census records, city directories, court records, and other documents in their areas. Your immigrant may have settled temporarily or for an extended period in that vicinity.

Using the knowledge you are already developing about genealogical record types and research methodologies, you can incorporate immigration and naturalization documents into your work. You're increasing your knowledge of each individual you study *and* you are constantly expanding the overall story of your family. As you do so, remember to apply your critical thinking skills to the evidence and formulate reasonable hypotheses.

Part II

Research Methods and Strategies

Chapter 8

Discover Where to Locate Documents About Your Family

How to...

- Determine where to look for different document types
- Use indexes, compilations, and other finding aids
- Use libraries and archives
- Use an LDS Family History Center
- Trace and locate documents that have been moved
- Deal with closed or limited access to materials
- Order document copies by snail-mail and e-mail
- Keep track of your correspondence
- Use a research log

The previous chapters have addressed the foundations of your genealogical research and discussed a broad selection of record types. By this time, you should have a pretty good idea of what you want to do with your genealogical research. You should know about a variety of common document types and how to use your critical thinking skills to evaluate and assess them.

In this chapter, we will discuss processes you can use to locate major repositories where documents or copies are held, and how to access the materials. Advance preparation is essential for your success in accessing documentary evidence, and there are many tools available to you. These include indexes, compilations, and other printed finding aides. Electronic tools include the Internet, online databases, library and archive catalogs, and CD-ROM products.

You will want to gain access to the original primary source documents whenever possible and obtain copies for your reference and documentation. Photocopies and reproductions can usually be obtained if you make an on-site visit to a facility. You also can write letters and e-mail to request copies if you cannot make a trip to the repository. If you are an active researcher, your correspondence can be extensive and it is not uncommon to lose track of the status of all of your requests for copies. A correspondence log and a little dedication to maintaining it can provide a process you can use to maintain control and to generate follow-up letters and messages.

You will visit many, many research facilities and examine literally hundreds of books, journals, periodicals, and documents in the pursuit of your family's genealogy. As a result, it is easy to forget what you have already examined and waste time and money conducting duplicate research. A research log allows me to keep track of what materials I have already researched and what I did or did not find in those sources, thus preventing an otherwise enormous duplication of time and money.

All of the topics covered in this chapter will therefore provide you with methodologies for becoming a more efficient and effective researcher. Over time, each strategy will become part of your standard operating process. However, let's explore each of these areas together.

Determine Where to Look for Different Document Types

You began your family history research in Chapter 1 when you began looking for home sources such as Bibles, letters, diaries and journals, scrapbooks, and copies of vital records. Having only one place to search is a lot easier than having to conduct research to locate places where you *can* conduct research. Yet that is what we have to do.

We can expect to find particular documents in specific places. For example, we know we can usually find *probate files* at the courthouse where the probate court conducts its business. In other cases, however, the place where document copies reside may not be where we might at first expect to find them. A birth record might be found at a county health department office, a courthouse, a state or provincial vital records or vital statistics office, or elsewhere. The challenge we face as researchers is not just evaluating the records; very often it involves tracking down the records themselves.

We have already discussed the importance of studying geography and history to place our ancestors into context. However, this can be equally as important when trying to locate the documents for our family members. The type of record, the person or organization that generated it, the reason(s) for the document's production, the place it was created, and the time period all contribute to your determining the location.

The place where a document was once stored might not be where it is stored today. The document may have been moved elsewhere, such as to another storage location. This is common when one facility exhausts its storage space or when older documents are needed infrequently for reference. They may be packed up and sent to a warehouse or other off-site storage facility.

Some documents created by one governmental entity may have been generated in one place and then sent to a central governmental archive or storage facility. For example, the United States government in 1830 requested all states to forward their 1790 to 1820 census schedules to Washington to replace the summaries that were destroyed when the British burned the city on 24 August 1814. The 1830 census documents and those for all subsequent censuses have since been sent to Washington. Additionally, in some cases there have been multiple copies of certain documents produced, possibly as exact duplicates or as supposedly exact transcriptions, and one or more copies forwarded elsewhere for someone else's use. A good example of this would be a death certificate. The original and at least one copy are typically produced. One is retained by the issuing governmental office and a copy is forwarded to a central office, such as a state or provincial vital statistics bureau. Other copies may have been provided to the undertaker, the executor or administrator of the estate, to the probate court, to the coroner, and to other persons or organizations. If you know that duplicates were produced and held by different official organizations, and you know when the process began, you can begin planning to obtain a copy of a particular document from one or the other office.

A document may have been microfilmed or digitized and the original placed in storage or destroyed. This, too, is something you will find a common practice. Let me share two examples with you.

8

■ An original and fragile document may not be able to withstand the stress of being handled. In order to preserve the original document but still make it accessible to interested parties, the library or archive may decide to produce exact facsimile copies in one of several formats. The document may be photographed, microfilmed, or electronically digitized, and images may be made available in printed format or placed in a database or on a Web page. This practice is being adopted by thousands of libraries, archives, government offices, companies, and organizations as a means of preserving ephemeral materials while still allowing people to see the original materials.

■ Returning to the United States census, the federal government determined that certain years' documents were to be organized and microfilmed by WPA personnel. This process provided exact images of the original schedules in a compact format, and the rolls of microfilm could then be replicated and copies distributed so that people could gain access to exact images of the originals. Some years after the microfilming, however, the decision was made to destroy the original census documents since their images had already been preserved. The technology for scanning and digitizing the documents had not yet been developed, and we are now using images that might have been enhanced for better viewing quality had the originals been retained.

Your study of the history of the time and place where your ancestors and family members lived will help you determine what documentary evidence might have been produced, and then you will have to track it down. Genealogical reference books can help you determine the location of primary source records and to quickly access those that you want.

Use Indexes, Compilations, and Other Finding Aids

There are many published materials to help you with your search. Some are available through traditional publishers and commercial companies, while others are published by genealogical or historical societies and individuals. Still other materials are published in the form of databases on CD-ROMs and on the Internet. Let's explore some examples of these resources.

Indexes

An index is defined as an ordered listing of people, places, topics, or other data that includes references allowing the user to quickly locate specific information. The format of the listing is dependent on the data being indexed. We're all familiar with the index found in the back of a book. This book's index is arranged alphabetically by subject, type of document, and so on, with page number references that point you to specific information. One of the plural forms of index is "indices" and you may see this term used rather than "indexes" in your research. In any case, you certainly will be grateful for genealogical indexes that have been prepared! There are at least four major categories of indexes that will be of interest to every genealogist. Let's briefly discuss each of these.

Indexes in Courthouses and Government Facilities

We've discussed a number of types of records that you will find in courthouses. This includes marriage and divorce records, wills and probate packets, judicial records of all sorts, jury lists, land and property records, property maps, taxation maps and records, voter registration records, guardianship records, poorhouse records, lunacy records, and many more. Depending on the location you are researching and the time period, the responsibilities of the government in that locality will determine what records were created at the time. As jurisdictions changed, the records usually remained in the possession of the original governmental entity. However, some of the records may have been physically transferred to (or copies made for) the new jurisdictional entity.

Most of the records are organized and filed in some manner and indexes have been prepared. An index is typically prepared at a later date than the original entries are made. You will encounter both hand-written and typed indexes. Marriages records are usually indexed twice, once in an alphabetical list of grooms' names and again in alphabetical sequence by the bride's name. Both are created in surname sequence, and then in forename or given name order. Women's surnames are entered using their maiden name for single women or surname from a previous marriage for divorced or widowed women. However, don't be surprised to find a previously married woman's maiden name sometimes listed in the bride index. That means that you should always check both possible surname entries. Land and property entries also are typically indexed in two ways, once in grantor sequence and once in grantee sequence. The indexes you find in courthouses and other governmental facilities will point you to specific places where you will find the material you want to use. Figure 8-1 shows the detail of a grantor index. If you were researching the transfer of property from Jno. W. Burroughs to Harriet C. Berrien, the grantor index indicates the transaction was filed on 16 December 1882 and that the detail can be found in an entry on page 946 of Deed Book N.

Indexes in Libraries, Archives, and Other Research Facilities

Libraries and archives are veritable goldmines for your research. Later in this chapter, I'll provide a detailed overview of how to get the most out of a library or archive. For now, however, keep in mind that these facilities may hold many unique materials in their possession, some of which may not be included in their online catalogs.

The most common items you will use in these research facilities will be the printed books, journals, periodicals, and electronic databases to which they may provide access. There are thousands of indexes that have been published to many original records. Let me provide a few examples for you, along with bibliographic citations.

Census Indexes
Gibson, Jeremy and Mervyn Medlycott. *Local Census Listings: 1522-1930: Holdings in the British Isles*. 3rd ed. Baltimore, MD: Genealogical Publishing Co., 1997.

Steuart, Bradley W., ed. *Virginia 1870 Census Index*. 4 volumes. Bountiful, UT: Precision Indexing, 1989.

Immigration Lists
Glazier, Ira A., ed. *Germans to America: Lists of Passengers Arriving at U.S. Ports*. 4 vols. to date. Wilmington, DE: Scholarly Resources, 2002– .

| GRANTORS | | | | GRANTEES | KIND OF INSTRUMENT | Date of Filing | | | Where Recorded | |
FAMILY NAMES	ABCDEFGH	IJKLMNO	PQRSTUVWXYZ			Mo.	Day	Year	Book	Page
Burge,		Louisa O.		Williams, M. D.					M	384
Buffington,			T. A.	Darby, Thos, A.					M	514
Butler,	Geo. A.			Thomas, Joseph					M	941
Burt,		James		Calhoun, Wm. L.					M	958
Buffington,			T. A.	Darby, T. A.	W D	June	25	1881	M	514
Burke,		M. A.		Tucker, Mamie W.	W D	Feb	17	1882	N	72
Bunker,		L. V.		Tison, W. O.	W D	July	19	1882	N	568
Bush,	Eliza J			Sikes, W. W.	W D	Sept	8	1882	N	692
Burroughs,		Jno. W.		Carroll, Eliza A/	W D	Oct	7	1882	N	784
Burroughs,		Jno. W.		Bevill, Francis B.	W D	Oct	9	1882	N	787
Burroughs,		Jno. W.		Berrien, Harriet C.	W D	Dec	16	1882	N	946
Burge,		L. C. extx		Mc Ewen, Chas A.	W D	Feb	21	1883	O	124

FIGURE 8-1   Detail of a grantor index to deed entries (Courtesy of Jim Powell)

Glazier, Ira A. and P. William Filby, eds. *Germans to America: Lists of Passengers Arriving at U.S. Ports.* 67 vols. to date. Wilmington, DE: Scholarly Resources, 1988– .

Marriage Index

Daniell, Anne C. *Talladega County, Alabama, Marriage Book "A-1834," 1833-1846: An Alphabetical Listing of Groom's Names with an Index to the Names of the Brides.* Anniston, AL: AlaBenton Book Shop, 1986.

Land and Property Records Indexes

Hughes, B. H. J. *Jottings and Historical Records with Index on the History of South Pembrokeshire: Manorial Accounts, 1324–33.* Pembroke Dock, Wales: Pennar Publications. 1996.

Shuck, Larry G. *Greenbrier County, (West) Virginia, Records.* 8 vols. Athens, GA: Iberian Publishing Co., 1988–1994.

Wills and Probate Records Indexes

Johnston, Ross B. *West Virginia Estate Settlements: An Index to Wills, Inventories, Appraisements, Land Grants, and Surveys to 1850.* Baltimore, MD: Genealogical Publishing Co., 1978.

Webb, Cliff, comp. *An Index of Wills Proved in the Archdeaconry Court of London, 1700–1807.*
    London, UK: Society of Genealogists, 1996.
    As you can see, there are published indexes for many types of records from around the world.

Online Database Indexes

The explosive growth of the Internet in the 1990s accelerated the already popular genealogical research to new heights. Individuals created their own Web sites to display their own genealogical data on their own Web pages and/or uploaded the contents of their databases to genealogy service providers' sites. The largest area of Internet growth for genealogists, however, has been in the area of online databases, both free and fee-based subscription services. These databases include indexes to original source records, digitized images of original documents, and other content.

A wealth of other online databases provides access to general or specific types of data. Some of these include the following:

- Ancestry.com (**http://www.ancestry.com**) has placed literally hundreds of indexed and searchable databases online, some of which are free and others available on a subscription basis. Their collections are truly international in scope and are simple to search. A search will yield a full list, such as that shown in Figure 8-2, of every database at Ancestry.com that contains that name. Among their premier subscription databases are the U.S. Census Records and Images Collection, the 1891 U.K. Census Collection, and the Historical Newspaper Collection containing hundreds of indexed, searchable newspapers dating from the 1700s to 2000 from the United States, Canada, and the United Kingdom. Ancestry.com's AncestryPlus database offering is marketed to libraries by the Gale Group, and can often be found as part of public and academic libraries' subscription database collections.

- Genealogy.com (**http://www.genealogy.com**) offers access to U.S. federal census records, international and passenger records, more than 20,000 family and local histories, and other databases.

- HeritageQuest (**http://www.heritagequest.com**), a subsidiary of ProQuest Company, is another of the major players in subscription databases. Their databases include U.S. census images and a collection of more than 25,000 indexed and fully searchable books. The ProQuest database collections can often be found as part of public and academic libraries' subscription database collections and are often accessible to registered library patrons from their home computers.

- inGeneas (**http://www.ingeneas.com**) provides a collection of database materials related to Canadian genealogy, as well as links and access to professional genealogical researchers for hire.

- Origins.net (**http://www.origins.net**), whose main Web site screen is shown in Figure 8-3, provides genealogical databases about the British Isles, including English Origins (**http://www.englishorigins.com**), Irish Origins (**http://www.irishorigins.com**), and Scots Origins (**http://www.scotsorigins.com**).

8

■ Sanborn Fire Insurance Maps were widely used in the United States by property and casualty insurance companies, underwriters, and government agencies from 1867 to 1970. Digital Sanborn Maps, a subscription database located at **http://sanborn.umi.com,** provides digital access to more than 660,000 large-scale maps of more than 12,000 American towns and cities. In electronic form, the Sanborn Maps take on much improved value over the microfilm versions of the same maps, allowing for greater flexibility of use and improved viewing possibilities. Users have the ability to easily manipulate the maps, magnify and zoom in on specific sections, and layer maps from different years. This digitized map database is part of the ProQuest collection and may be accessible through your library's subscription to the ProQuest products.

■ Otherdays.com (**http://www.otherdays.com**) is a subscription database for a wide variety of Irish genealogical materials.

■ Scottish Documents.com (**http://www.scottishdocuments.com**) is the foremost fully searchable online index for more than 500,000 Scottish wills and testaments dating from 1500 to 1901.

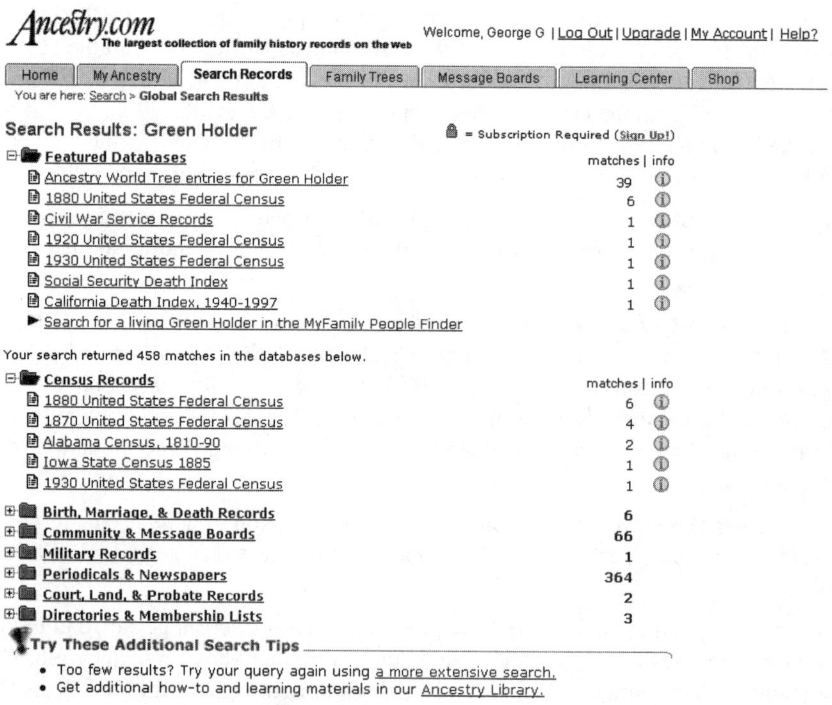

FIGURE 8-2   Sample search results list from the Ancestry.com site (Used by permission of MyFamily.com, Inc.)

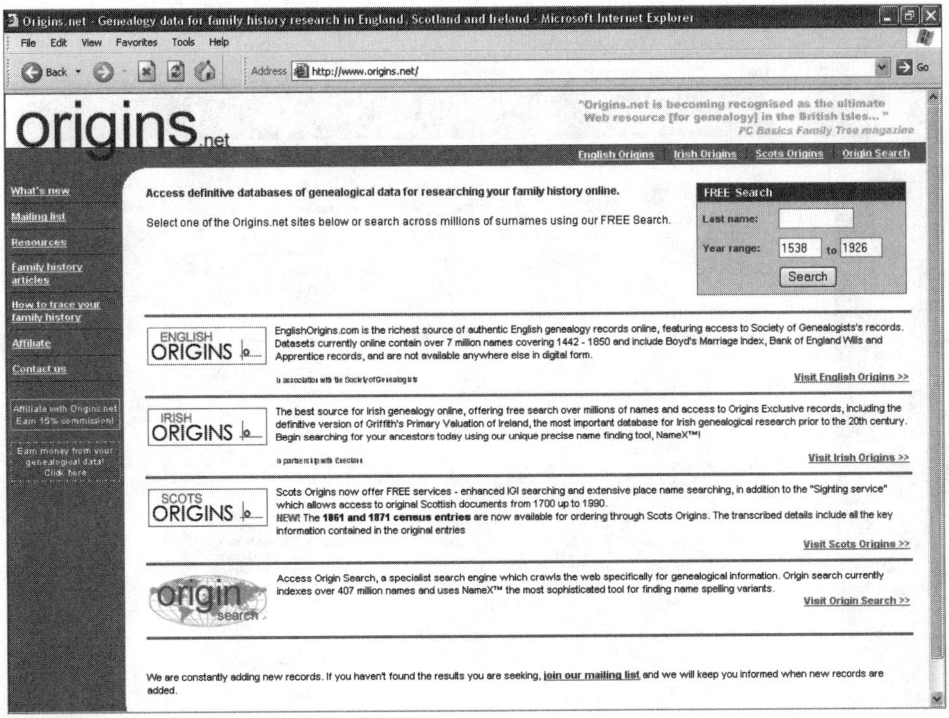

FIGURE 8-3   The main screen of the Origins.net site

Governmental agencies have also provided online databases of materials in their possession, although the concerns for individuals' privacy and identity theft have prevented making many records accessible online, either in index or image form. An excellent example of this is the Alachua County, Florida, Clerk of Court's Web site for the county archives at **http://www.clerk-alachua-fl.org/ archive.** Ancient Records Coordinator Jim Powell has scanned tens of thousands of original documents and placed them online at the Alachua County Archives Entry page shown in Figure 8-4. He also has recruited a small army of genealogical volunteers from across the United States to index the records by name and keyword and transcribe thousands of these documents. This ongoing volunteer project, sanctioned and supported by Alachua County Clerk of Court J. K. "Buddy" Irby, is an excellent model for what can be done.

Search Engines' Indexes

Whenever you use a search engine on the Internet, you are using a sophisticated index. A search engine combs the Web electronically and, when it connects to and accesses a Web page, it reads every word on the page. That includes the text, labels, and filenames of graphics on the Web page, as well as the "hidden" meta tags used in the source code of the HTML document that produces

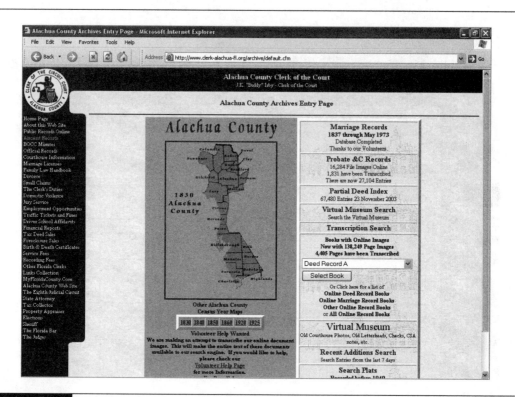

FIGURE 8-4 Alachua County, Florida, online ancient records archives Web page

the page. The search engine indexes every word and then, when you enter a word or phrase in the engine's search box or template, presents matches to your entries in the form of a search results list. Figure 8-5 shows the beginning of the search results list for the words *genealogy database georgia*. Each search engine indexes the Web differently and uses its own relevancy ranking criteria to order and display the search results. We will discuss the use of search engines and other tools to perform research on the Internet in the next chapter.

Compilations

A compilation is a gathering of information from a variety of places into a useful directory or organized listing. You could consider this book a compilation of a wide variety of information. A directory of materials on the Internet can also be considered a compilation. Perhaps the largest and best-known Web-based genealogical compilation is Cyndi's List (**http://www.cyndislist.com**), shown in Figure 8-6, which contains more than 200,000 links to other Web sites.

There are many, many excellent compilation Web sites, including the USGenWeb Project (**http://www.usgenweb.org**), the WorldGenWeb Project (**http://www.worldgenweb.org**), GENUKI

FIGURE 8-5   A search engine indexes words found on Web pages and will present a search results list.

FIGURE 8-6   Topical index at Cyndi's List

(**http://www.genuki.org.uk**), JewishGen (**http://www.jewishgen.org**), RootsWeb (**http://www. rootsweb.com**), and the Canadian Genealogy & History site (**http://www.islandnet.com/ ~jveinot/cghl/cghl.html**). You can always find resources to help your genealogy research by visiting Cyndi's List, locating the geographic or topic area you wish to pursue, and accessing the Web page resources linked there.

Other Finding Aids

The term *finding aid* shouldn't confuse you. It simply refers to any resource you can use to further your genealogical search, and includes tools such as the following.

- Maps
- Gazetteers
- Surname dictionaries by national, ethnic, or religious group
- Dictionaries of contemporary and archaic terminology
- Dictionaries of abbreviations and acronyms of different areas and time periods
- Language translation dictionaries
- Histories of geographic areas, towns and communities, different population groups, and cultural histories
- Reference works to aid in reading old handwriting
- Genealogy references, "how-to" books, and guides to working with record types
- Compilations of Internet sites related to genealogy
- Online indexes and databases as discussed previously

Anything that you can use to gain insight into your ancestral search and access to quality source materials can be considered a valid finding aid. Look around you and use your imagination and insight.

Use Libraries and Archives

Libraries, archives, and their staff are among the best resources you can have. I consider a good librarian to be a "personal information broker." While you can't expect every librarian to know everything about genealogical research and records, you can always rely on a librarian's willingness to help you and his or her ability to conduct quality research on almost any topic. A well-trained librarian or archivist understands research methods and resources of all types, and knows how to locate and access information. Furthermore, he or she is always willing to share their skills with you if you are willing to invest the time to listen and learn.

The facilities that libraries and archives provide to their users, or patrons, vary significantly depending on the content of their collection, their service population, and their stated mission.

Special collections such as genealogy and local history materials usually are not circulated but are, instead, reserved for in-house reference. There are ways, however, to gain access to the materials without physically visiting the facility and we'll discuss those shortly.

Learn to Use the Library Catalog

It has not been too many years ago that libraries had no computers. The primary finding aid for its holdings was a card catalog. There were card catalog cabinets in a central area filled with small paperboard cards, all hand-typed and filed in alphabetical sequence by author, title, and subject. Each item in the collection for which there was a card also was coded with a reference using the classification system employed by that library. Public libraries in North America and the United Kingdom typically use the Dewey Decimal Classification system, while most North American academic libraries usually use the Library of Congress classification system. Academic libraries in the United Kingdom use a variety of systems. Other archives and repositories may use another system based on the type of holdings in their collections, including one of their own devising that fits the unique needs for organizing and accessing their special collection. It is to your advantage to learn a little about the Dewey Decimal and Library of Congress systems. Understanding these systems helps you understand how any library is physically organized, and you can then quickly and effectively locate and access materials in their collections. You can learn about the Dewey Decimal Classification system at the BUBL LINK site at **http://bubl.ac.uk/link/ddc.html,** and about the Library of Congress Classification scheme at **http://www.loc.gov/catdir/cpso/lcco/lcco.html.**

Some things in libraries and archives have changed over time while others have remained static. Computers have changed information storage and retrieval expectations, and libraries understood the importance of changing their printed and typed card catalogs to computerized systems. Early online catalog systems were somewhat awkward, but what they lacked in usability they more than made up for in organization. Early on, library professionals understood that standardizing the format of library catalog computer records could and would make life as simple as the paper card catalogs had been, and they convinced the software developers as well.

Over time, standardized online catalog computer programs were developed and implemented in libraries. These programs, and the original "dumb terminals" in a closed system inside one library building on which they were used, were titled the OPAC, or the Online Public Access Computer. Soon a single OPAC could be shared by multiple libraries in an area, in a system, or in a county, through what seems now to be a painfully slow communication system.

With the growing use of modems and telecommunications, members of the general public with computers cried for dial-in access to their libraries' computers. As the Internet took hold in the early 1990s and evolved into the ubiquitous communication tool and information resource it has become, new software has been developed. Libraries have all but abandoned the old "dumb terminals" in exchange for computers—both PCs and Macintoshes—that communicate with new programs at much higher speeds. In addition, new online catalog software can be and has been integrated into libraries' Web sites and multimedia capabilities have been added. It now is not unusual for a library to have incorporated graphic and sound files of their holdings into their online catalogs, complete with links to directly access those materials. Often now the public access catalog is called the iPAC, or Internet Public Access Catalog.

Throughout all of this evolution, the principles of organization, cataloging, and standardizing catalog entries for resources have been maintained and expanded. One common denominator used in many libraries is the MARC record, which will be discussed a little later. Suffice it to say that there are standards in place within the library industry to utilize technology to its maximum, integrate as many materials as possible into the online systems as possible, and to provide excellence in customer access and customer service.

Start with What Has Already Been Done

Many of us conduct a substantial amount of our genealogical research, or pre-research, from the comfort of our homes. Perhaps you find yourself sitting in front of the computer, searching on the Internet for records concerning your ancestors. Perhaps it is three o'clock in the morning; you're there in your jammies, sipping a glass of milk, and munching on chocolate chip cookies. What a life!

Fortunately, the Internet and the online catalogs of libraries and archives are generally accessible 24 hours a day, 7 days a week, and 365 days a year. If you are conversant with the use of the catalog, you can make a tremendous amount of headway with your research into the available resources without assistance.

For a genealogist, one of the first steps in doing research is to locate any published family histories and/or local histories that may contain information about ancestors and other family members. Family histories and many local histories are not usually the type of book that you're likely to find in your neighborhood bookstore, or even in a typical online bookstore. Instead, to locate such books, you'll have to visit a library, or look in their online catalogs. The next step is to locate the indexes and other finding aids that help you find the resources you want or need. Fortunately, the Web has made that process easier.

Research, no matter what type, is often an expensive and time-consuming process. Wise researchers save money and time by first looking to see what research has already been done in the area in which they are interested. Professional researchers and those who have become astute users of the electronic online facilities often prepare for an effective research trip to a research venue by doing a substantial amount of advance work in the online catalogs. Let's look at three examples of how you can use online catalogs to your advantage.

Example 1

Let's say you are planning to visit the large genealogical collection at the New York Public Library, and you want to save yourself some time on-site. If you visit their Web site at **http://www.nypl.org,** you definitely want to know the address(es) of the facility(ies) you want to visit, the days and hours of operation, their policies for use of the facilities, and the cost of photocopies and other services.

If you enter the word **genealogy** in the search box on the main screen, you will be rewarded with a number of links to the library's collection. You would learn, by visiting the link at **http://www.nypl.org/research/chss/lhg/genea.html,** that the Irma and Paul Milstein Division of United States History, Local History and Genealogy is located at the New York Public Library, Fifth Avenue and 42nd Street, New York, NY 10018-2788, and that their telephone number is (212) 930-0828. An e-mail address is also listed. You can then read about the collection's contents, that it offers an e-mail reference inquiry service, and access to a number of electronic databases online.

More important, you can use the Catalog of the New York Public Library (known as CATNYP) to search by word/keyword, author, title, subject, call number, or other criteria. And don't forget to read their "Search Tips" section so you can optimize your use of the catalog to the fullest extent possible.

By using the online catalog from your home computer, you can certainly compile your list of materials that you want to use at the library in advance of your visit. By having read the material at **http://www.nypl.org/research/chss/lhg/research.html** in advance, you will have learned that most of the library materials are held in "closed stacks," and must be retrieved for researchers by library staff. That means that you can have your list of materials you want, organize them into a sequence to be retrieved for you, and then you can work on them in an organized fashion as opposed to just "higgledy piggledy."

Example 2

You have already learned that National Archives and Records Administration (NARA) is one of the greatest genealogical resource facilities in the United States. However, not everything is available at all the branches. By conducting research online at their Web site at **http://www.archives.gov,** you would learn that the originals of the World War I Draft Registration cards are located at the NARA Southeastern Branch in Atlanta, Georgia, but that microfilm of those cards is available at most of the NARA Branches. Perhaps you then plan a visit to Atlanta and, by learning the policies at that facility, you can prepare to make the most of your time working with the original materials at that NARA Branch.

Your advance research would provide you with the address of the facility, the days and hours of operation, and you would learn that you must have a researcher's ID card. You could learn in advance what is involved in completing an application and getting your ID right away. You also could prepare for your trip in advance by using the NARA catalog, called the Archival Research Catalog (ARC), to locate information about their holdings. If you want to use their microfilm of the World War I Draft Registration cards, you could use their Microfilm Locator to determine the microfilm publication number (M1509) and the appropriate roll for the area in which your ancestor lived at the time of the draft calls in 1917 and 1918. And if you then want to examine the actual card completed by your ancestor or family member, you can arrange at the time of your visit to have the card pulled for you.

Example 3

Let's say you were interested in the family history of the Ball Family of Virginia and you'd heard that there was an old book available about the family. If you know the library in which a copy is held, you could go to their Web site, access their catalog, and get the information. Some libraries' iPACs facilitate e-mailing a copy of the catalog record to your e-mail address, saving you time and energy.

If you did not know which library or libraries have a copy of the book, contact your reference librarian and ask for help. Libraries have access to a product called WorldCat. It is a catalog of U.S. (and some foreign) libraries' holdings, and the librarian can help you conduct a search. In some cases, having a library card may even give you access from your home computer to conduct a search in WorldCat yourself.

Once you have the information on the book in question, whose record from the John F. Germany Public Library in the Hillsborough County Public Library Cooperative based in Tampa, Florida, is shown in Figure 8-7, you now have all you need to visit the library yourself and locate the book. (You will notice in Figure 8-7 that you could add the title to a booklist, which you can later print or e-mail to yourself, and place a hold on the title to make sure it doesn't get checked out before you get there. This always requires that you have a library card with that library or that your library has a reciprocal borrowing agreement of some sort with that library.)

If you are unable to visit the library, there is another option open to you: Interlibrary Loan, also referred to as ILL in the United States and Canada. (In the United Kingdom, this is often spelled as Inter-Library Loan.) ILL is a service that allows patrons of one library to request the loan of a book from its owning library to their own. However, since most genealogy and local history collection materials are non-circulating reference materials, it is unlikely that you can actually have your library borrow the book. However, all is not lost! ILL can be used to request that photocopies be made of certain pages and sent to you or to your library for pick-up. You might want to make two ILL requests. The first will request a copy of the pages of a book's index for the surname(s) you are seeking and a second request after you've received the index pages to request copies of the text pages from the book in question. Keep in mind that, when requesting text pages, you might want to request one or two additional pages before and after the pages shown in an index. This helps alleviate the problem that arises when meaningful descriptive text begins on a previous page or continues to a subsequent page.

The Ball family of southwest Virginia : a genealogy of some of the descendants of Moses Ball of Fairfax County /

by Ball, Palmer Ray, 1900-

Cumberlandcrafters, c1933.

Subjects	• Ball family.
Description:	viii, 30 p. : map, ports. ; 29 cm.
Notes:	Cover title: The Ball family of Southwest Virginia. "George Ball, Sr., son of Moss Ball, Sr., of Fairfax County, Virginia, by Nancy Graves Ball Surface": p. 17-24.
Additional Author(s):	Surface, Nancy Graves Ball, 1871- George Ball, Sr.
COPIES:	1
HOLDS:	0

Add to booklist   Place a hold

Copy/Holding information

Library	Call #	Collection	Status
John F. Germany Library	929.2 BALL	2 West - Reference	Checked In

---

FIGURE 8-7   Catalog record for book on the Ball Family (From the Hillsborough County Public Library Cooperative catalog)

As you can see from each of the three examples, there is tremendous value to having performed advance research in an online library catalog. Let's now look at some specific library catalogs.

The Library of Congress Online Catalog

Sometimes, you'll hear about a book from a friend or other genealogist, or you may see it referred to in some publication. Unfortunately, you may find that you are missing either the author's name or the title of the book, or that one of those is incorrect or incomplete. Your first step should be to pin down the exact title of the book and the full name of the author. This will make later searching much easier and more productive.

The online catalog of the Library of Congress (LC) is often a good place to begin searching for unusual books when you don't necessarily have all of the information you need. The LC does not lend (or circulate) their materials classified as genealogy or local history. Unless you are planning a trip to Washington, D.C., in the near future, the primary purpose of your use of the LC online catalog is to obtain information about the book so that you can then look for it in a closer library.

Let's look at some examples supplied by my friend and colleague, Drew Smith. Imagine that you have been told that a woman named "Eytive" has written a book that contains information about your Bodie/Boddie ancestors. You don't know her full name and you don't know the title of the book. Your first step would be to go to the LC online catalog (located at **http://catalog.loc.gov**), and click on the Keyword button. You would then type **eytive** in the Keyword search box and click on the Search button. The system would respond by displaying a record that tells you that the author's full name is Eytive Long Evans and that the title of the book is *A documented history of the Long family,* published in 1956.

Of course, this kind of example might not work as well if the author's first name had been "Mary" instead of "Eytive." When doing a keyword search, it is best to use the most unusual word that you are fairly sure of. In that way, the number of records that you will need to work your way through will not be as large.

If you already know the author's name or the title, you can use the Subj-Name-Title-Call# button. If you know the author's name, you would first select Name Browse, type the author's name in the box, and then click on the Search button. As is the case with many library catalogs, the last name should be typed first, followed by the given name or forename. If the last name is unusual enough, you probably don't need to type the first name. In that case, all authors with the same last name will be displayed. You can then click on the one you want. In some cases, the same author might appear under different forms of his or her name, or may be listed more than once (because the LC has combined its older catalog with a newer one).

If you know the title, you would first select Title, type the title in the box, and then click on the Search button. It is important to begin with the first word of the title, but if the title begins with an article such as "a," "an," or "the" (or equivalent words in other languages), omit the article.

What if you don't know the author's name and you don't know the title? You're not completely out of luck if you can figure out the subject of the book. For example, imagine that you are looking for a book about the Boddie family. You would first select Subject Browse, type the subject word (in this case, **boddie**) in the box, and then click on the Search button. The catalog would tell you that there are three books in the LC catalog with a subject of "Boddie family." By clicking on "Boddie family" listed there, you would be shown a list of the books (author, title, and year published).

8

What Is a MARC Record and Why Do I Care?

You may or may not care what a MARC record is, but it definitely influences your success at locating materials in an online library catalog. MARC is an acronym for **Ma**chine-**R**eadable **C**ataloging record. A typical catalog record for a book (also known as a bibliographic record) contains author name, title, edition number (if applicable), its place of publication, name of the publisher, date of publication, classification number (call number), and some additional information. If you look at Figure 8-1 again, you will see there are other data there, including the measurement of the book (24 cm.). In addition, there are subject headings and keywords given to every item.

For example, a book by Michael J. O'Brien titled *The Irish in America* provides a great overview of Irish immigrants and their records. Let's look at both the regular online catalog record and the coded MARC record. Examine the data in Figure 8-8, and then locate the same information in the MARC record shown in Figure 8-9.

In the MARC record, every piece of data has a field number associated with it, as shown by the numbers in the left column. Please note in both versions of the record that there are Subjects (record code) of "Irish" and "United States." These are used in your *subject* search. However, you'll also notice the words that are highlighted in yellow in both records. These are the two words I used in the *keyword* search: "Irish" and "immigration." Examining every occurrence of the words that were highlighted can help me understand why the record was displayed.

The reason that I explain this to you is that sometimes you may be presented with a search results screen and have no idea why a particular item was included. There may be keywords that were applied to the MARC record that are not shown in the regular catalog record. Therefore, a check in the MARC record (which is usually another clicked link on the catalog record screen) may provide the answer.

One final point about MARC records. Even though libraries strive to maintain a consistency in their cataloging, there are individual catalogers who actually create the records in their library catalogs. Some of these records may be obtained from a central library group in Ohio called OCLC,

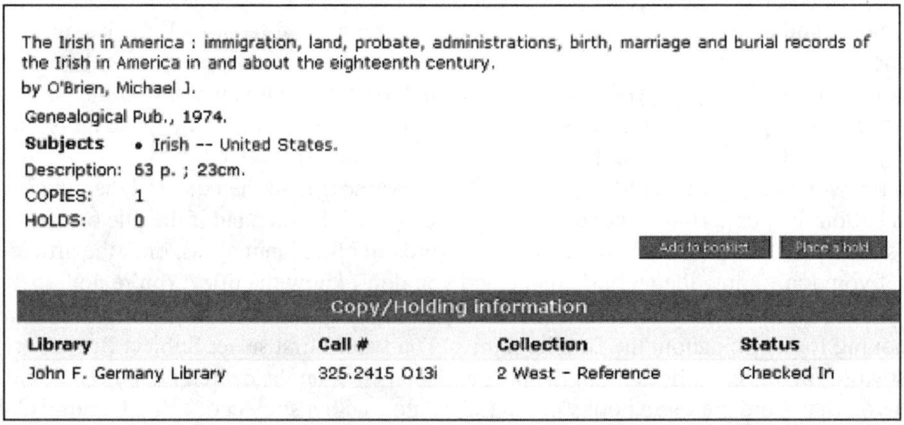

The Irish in America : immigration, land, probate, administrations, birth, marriage and burial records of the Irish in America in and about the eighteenth century.
by O'Brien, Michael J.

Genealogical Pub., 1974.

Subjects   • Irish -- United States.

Description: 63 p. ; 23cm.

COPIES: 1

HOLDS: 0

[Add to booklist]   [Place a hold]

Copy/Holding information			
Library	**Call #**	**Collection**	**Status**
John F. Germany Library	325.2415 O13i	2 West - Reference	Checked In

FIGURE 8-8   Catalog record for Michael J. O'Brien's book, *The Irish in America* (From the Hillsborough County Public Library Cooperative catalog)

Getting
past Penelope
SWORDS

My great-grandmother, Penelope SWORDS HOLDER, was an enigma, and represented perhaps my most difficult research "brick wall." I have mentioned her several times in this book because the methods I used to get past the gridlock are good examples of alternative research strategies that you will sometimes need to employ.

Defining the Problem

My childhood memories are peppered with recollections of my mother's and her three sisters' discussions of their own mother's parents, Green Berry HOLDER (1845–1914) and his wife, Penelope SWORDS (1842–1914), of Rome, Floyd County, Georgia. It was not until my early twenties that I began

Ansibelle Penelope SWORDS HOLDER (1842–1914) (From the author's collection)

to look in all seriousness at the ancestry in my maternal line. When I did, it was comparatively simple to document—first, my mother and her sisters, and second, my grandmother, Elizabeth HOLDER, and her five sisters and five of her six brothers. My great-grandfather, Green Berry HOLDER, had been a Confederate soldier, the first postmaster of two federal post offices, a farmer, a merchant, founder of the North Georgia Fertilizer Company, owner and president of the Rome Mercantile Company, board member of two banks, the elected representative to the Georgia State Legislature for two non-consecutive terms, a real estate investor, an insurance salesman, a member of the United Confederate Veterans, and a member of the Rome Presbyterian Church.

Gravestone of Penelope Swords Holder, Myrtle Hill Cemetery, Rome, Georgia (From the author's collection)

As you can imagine, there were lots of records about him and from those I was able to link him to an older brother, also in the Confederate Army, and to their parents in Lawrenceville, Gwinnett County, Georgia.

Unfortunately, though, the records for his wife were far from numerous, as was typical for women of that era. In fact, for quite a while, the only real record I had was her gravestone. My research problem was to locate information about Penelope, identify her parents, and be able to continue my research in her ancestral line. ●

Start with What You Know and Work Backward

W e've discussed the importance of beginning your research with what you know and with searches for information, sources, and evidence found at your family home or in the possession of other family members. When you hit a "brick wall" in your research, go back and review in detail all the information you have acquired. Reread everything in chronological sequence and look at the total picture of your subject's life. I personally found myself doing this again and again in the course of my research on my great-grandmother, and ultimately the pieces fell into place. Let's examine my research process in this case study.

Family Tradition

The family story (or tradition) had it that my Great-grandmother Penelope died the morning after the birth of one of my mother's sisters. My aunt, Carolyn

HOW TO DO EVERYTHING

HOW TO DO EVERYTHING

Penelope WEATHERLY, was born on 12 January 1914, in Green Berry's and Penelope's home on Broad Street in Rome, and the child was named Penelope for her grandmother. Starting with that clue, I began my search from home for records.

Look for Death-Related Records

While some Georgia counties and cities did maintain birth and death records from earlier years, it was not until 1919 that Georgia required the registration of all births and deaths in the state. Unfortunately, Floyd County and Rome did not create these records until 1919 and so there was no death certificate for Penelope SWORDS HOLDER.

I next contacted the Genealogy Department of the Sarah Hightower Regional Library in Rome to determine if they might have microfilm of the local newspapers from 1914 from which an obituary could be obtained. I was informed that their microfilm of the *Rome Herald-Tribune* was incomplete, and that 1914 was one of the years that they did not have.

Locate a Marriage Record

My next step was to contact the Floyd County Courthouse in Rome to try to obtain a marriage record for Green Berry and Penelope. I hoped the marriage license might provide the bride's parents' names, her age, and/or her place of residence. The response from the courthouse included a document that showed Greenberry [sic] HOLDER wedding Miss A. P. SANDERS (or SAUDERS) on 27 December 1866. This was a surprise. Could Penelope have been married before? I considered five possibilities:

- Penelope was supposedly born in 1842 and married Green Berry in 1866. She would have been twenty-four years old, a somewhat advanced age for a woman to be married at that time.

- The marriage occurred following the U.S. Civil War and, considering Penelope's age, it was possible that she had been married before to a man whose surname was SANDERS or SAUDERS and that she had been widowed.

- The entry from the Floyd County Marriage Book (vol. A, page 347, # 1359) clearly states *Miss* A. P. SANDERS, supposedly an unmarried woman.

- Was it possible that Green Berry married before, or could the clerk entering the record on 15 April 1868 have made an error in reading or transcribing the name?

- The couple's first child, Edward Ernest HOLDER, was born on 28 January 1868. The couple was therefore probably married before April of 1867.

Marriage record from the Floyd County, Georgia, marriage book (From the author's collection)

I contacted the Floyd County Courthouse again to determine if there was any record of another marriage for Green Berry HOLDER on file or any record of a divorce from A. P. SANDERS. I was informed that there were no such records.

Check the Census Records

Based on the information I had found so far, I decided to check in the U.S. federal census for Georgia for various years. Knowing that Green Berry married in 1867, I checked the 1870 census for his entry. I found a listing for him in Subdivision 141 of Floyd County, Georgia, along with his wife, "Ancybelle P.," and sons "Edward W.," age 2, and "Willis I.," age 3/12 years (3 months). This gave me two important clues. "Ancybelle P." certainly agreed with the "A. P." initials on the marriage record, and the age of the first son certainly agreed. The wrong middle initial for Edward did not concern me too much because the name of the second son was really William Ira HOLDER and not "Willis." These two errors, the spelling of "Ancybelle," and the fact that the original 1870 census records were transcribed

and the copy was sent to Washington all point to either enumerator spelling errors or transcription errors.

The 1880 census showed Green B. HOLDER in Enumeration District 11 of Floyd County. His wife is recorded as Ansabelle, age 24, and nine children are listed: Edward (son – 13 years old), Willie (son – 11), Scott T. (son – 9); Ida (daughter – 7), Annie (daughter – 5), Luther (son – 4), Ella (daughter – 3), Brisco (son – 1), and Emma (daughter – 4/12).

The next available federal census, in 1900, shows Green B. HOLDER in Supervisor's District 7, Enumeration District 153, Lindale District in Floyd County, with his wife, "Nancy B.," and the following children: William I (born November 1869), Ida L. (July 1872), Anna L. (April 1874), Luther M. (July 1875), Ella E. (October 1876), Emma E. (December 1879), Nita M. (June 1882), and Lizze B. (July 1885). Note that family tradition always indicated that my grandmother, Elizabeth HOLDER, was called by the nickname she gave herself as a baby, "Lizzie Bep."

The 1910 census, the last enumeration before both Green Berry and Penelope died in 1914, shows them at

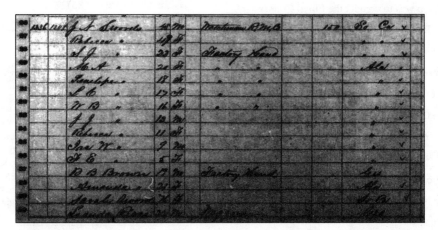

Detail from the 1860 U.S. federal census, Cobb County, Georgia (Used with permission of MyFamily.com, Inc.)

808 South Broad Street, Supervisor's District 7, Enumeration District 69, 5th Ward, the Rome Militia District. Green B. HOLDER is 65, wife "Annie" is 67, and living with them are three of their daughters: Ida (age 32), Anna (28), and Emma (26). A further clue indicates that "Annie" was born in Alabama, and that both of her parents were born in South Carolina.

It was now time to move backward from the marriage certificate to try to identify and connect Ansibelle Penelope to her parents and family. I next went looking through 1860 federal census indexes in Georgia, looking for the surname of SWORDS. I located a printed index of Cobb County, Georgia, for that year and it pointed me toward the First District, Roswell Post Office, in Cobb County. There I found the J. N. SWORDS family, including Penelope at age 18—the correct age if she was born in 1842 as indicated on her gravestone. I now had the names of her parents, J.N. and Rebecca CHAPMAN SWORDS, both of whom were born in South Carolina, and Penelope born in Alabama.

Make a Very Successful Genealogy Trip

I felt that I had done just about all I could do from the comfort of home and with the assistance of the genealogical and history collections in local libraries and archives. It was time to make a road trip. Following the procedures described in Chapter 11, I pulled all my information together about Green Berry HOLDER, Ansibelle Penelope SWORDS, and their children, organized it, and prepared a research plan. I did my preliminary research on the Internet, contacted the genealogy librarian at the Sarah Hightower Regional Library, and made contacts with the Rome Municipal Cemetery Department and the Northwest Georgia Genealogical Society for appointments to meet with

people on site. Two months later, in July 1997, I drove from my home in Tampa, Florida, to Rome, Georgia, for what would be one of the best research trips of my life.

The library in Rome proved to contain a wealth of information for my research. The genealogy librarian there at the time, Gwen Billingsly, was an outstanding help. City directories in the library's collection helped me place Green Berry and his sons at specific addresses in Rome. The papers of local historian, George Magruder Battey, contained correspondence with some of the HOLDER daughters and with others that discussed the town's history and my great-grandfather's role in the community. Local histories also helped in my quest. The microfilm collection of the *Rome Herald-Tribune* was incomplete, as I had learned before. However, Ms. Billingsly knew that the missing years' original newspapers were stored in the county school district administration's records retention facility. Apparently the library had run out of funds to microfilm all the years of publication. She contacted the administrator there and arranged for me to visit and examine these original newspapers.

When I arrived at the storage facility, I was warmly greeted and led through a warehouse to the area where the complete, leather-bound volumes of 1908, 1909, 1913, and 1914 were stored. The year 1914 was the one of most interest, since my great-grandmother died on 13 January 1914 and my great-grandfather followed her in death on 18 June 1914. It was easy to locate their obituaries and, working with the fragile newsprint and without the benefit of a photocopier, I carefully transcribed both obituaries. (These newspapers were subsequently microfilmed, by the way.) There were, of course, many clues in my great-grandmother's obituary in the *Rome Tribune-Herald*, Rome, Georgia, Wednesday

Morning, January 14, 1914, page 1, which reads as follows:

> *Mrs. G.B. Holder, aged 71 years, an old and honored resident of Rome, died Tuesday night at 11:10 at the family residence, 808 South Broad Street, after a brief illness of pneumonia.*
>
> *The deceased was born at Rock Creek, Alabama, in 1848. She married in 1867, G.B. Holder, of this city, and has since resided in Rome. Her husband is a prominent business man of the county. Mrs. Holder was a member of the Primitive Baptist church and always took an active part in the church work.*
>
> *She is survived by 11 children, five sons and six daughters. The sons are Ed Holder, Will Holder, Scott Holder, Brisco Holder and Charlie Holder. The daughters are Misses Isa [sic, Ida] Holder, Anna Holder and Emma Holder, Mrs. A.D. Starnes, Mrs. Walton Weatherly and Mrs. Wyatt Foster. She is also survived by three sisters, Mrs. Cal Menton and Mrs. Davis of Alabama, and Mrs. George Black, of Cedartown.*
>
> *The funeral services will be conducted from the residence at 3 o'clock this afternoon, the Rev. J. W. Cooper officiating. Interment will follow in Myrtle Hill cemetery.*
>
> *The following pall-bearers will meet at 2:30 o'clock at Daniels Furniture Company: Honorary, J.G. Pollock, B.F. Griffin, Capt. J. H. May, M.W. Formby, H.V. Rambo, Tom Sanford. Active: J.M. Yarbrough, G.G. Burkhalter, Sanford Moore, W.A. Long, Dr. R.M. Harbin, C.B. Geotchius.*

The most significant facts for my research beyond my great-grandmother into her siblings, parents, and other ancestors were the names of two of her surviving sisters. However, it took me a while to get past another self-imposed "brick wall."

First, I discounted "Mrs. DAVIS of Alabama" as being nearly impossible to locate. However, I did search the Alabama census records for the MENTON surname and for a man whose forename might have been Calvin, Calvert, Calbert, Calhoon, and other variations, all without success. I next did the same search with different spellings of the surname, including MINTON. It was not until I realized that the custom of the time was that a married woman used her husband's first and last names, and that a widow used her own first name and the surname of her husband. Mrs. Cal MENTON, as it turned out, was Mrs. Caroline MINTON. "Cal" was a nickname for Caroline. When I later located her, it turned out that she was the daughter listed variously as L. C. SWORDS or Lydia SWORDS; her full maiden name was Lydia Caroline SWORDS.

"Mrs. George BLACK of Cedartown," a town south of Rome in Polk County, Georgia, was easier to locate. I happened to search the probate records while at the Floyd County Courthouse in Rome for all of the HOLDERs and happened to look for BLACK, DAVIS, and SWORDS. It turned out that there was a probate packet for George S. BLACK that specifically mentioned his wife, Martha. Another marriage record in Floyd County showed George BLACK married Martha Ann SWORDS on 27 December 1866. I had another connection!

Detail from the 1850 U.S. federal census, Cobb County, Georgia (Used with permission of MyFamily.com, Inc.)

Take Another Look at Census Records

I went back to look at the census records again. In the 1860 census, two other daughters of J. N. and Rebecca SWORDS are listed: M. A. SWORDS (age 20) and L. C. SWORDS (age 17).

Next I went to the 1850 census and, based on the 1860 census and the ages of the children born in Alabama, I worked with census indexes. I found the family in the 1850 census in the 27th District, Cherokee County, Alabama. The parents were listed as John N. SWORDS and his wife, Rebecca. Among the children listed, I found a seven-year-old daughter named Lydia, an eight-year-old named Nancy, and a ten-year-old named Martha, all of whom had been born in Alabama. I'd found the right place, the right people, and the right person. The name "Nancy" in the 1850 census corresponded with the same name in the 1900 census and was certainly similar to "Ansabelle" and "Annie" in other censuses, and the names of the sisters were correct. I had the correct family and the correct individuals.

Contact Other Courthouses

I still had that burning question about the surname of SANDERS (or SAUDERS) on the Floyd County marriage document, so I considered that it was possible that Ansibelle Penelope SWORDS might have been married prior to her 1867 marriage to Green Berry. Therefore, I wrote the courthouses in the counties of Cobb and Floyd, and the counties in between—Bartow, Cherokee, Gordon, Paulding, Pickens, and Polk—to try to have a check made of bride indexes in their marriage books between 1860 and 1867 for a woman with the surname of SWORDS and a forename of Ansibelle and/or Penelope, or with the initials A. P. All the responses indicated that no such names appeared in their marriage indexes.

Other Information Discovered Along the Way

The appointment with the cemetery administrator in Rome reconfirmed dates of death and interment for Penelope Swords HOLDER in the Myrtle Hill Cemetery Interments ledger, which also listed the cause of her death as pneumonia, and for Green Berry later that year. I also learned that their daughter, Emma Dale HOLDER, sold three spaces in the family cemetery lot in 1956 to the owners of the adjacent lot, the family of George and Martha BLACK.

I obtained the marriage entries from the Floyd County Courthouse for all of Green Berry's and Penelope's children who married there, as well as copies of death certificates for eight of their children. I located the graves of all eight of those children, including Edward E. HOLDER, who was widowed and then remarried, and who was buried in a cemetery other than the one in which his original, pre-inscribed tombstone had been placed.

In the Floyd County Courthouse, a clerk's preliminary search of land and property records showed more than thirty-eight pages of entries in their deed index for G. B. HOLDER, A. P. HOLDER, Penelope HOLDER, and for their sons, Edward, William, Scott, and Luther HOLDER. I have reserved an entire future trip to study the actual land and property entries and learn what they can reveal to me.

Finally, after all of the census research, it finally dawned on me where the nickname for my great-aunt, Ella Edna HOLDER, had come from. She was called "Little Annie" after her mother because she always scurried around taking care of her siblings.

From the clues obtained along the way in my search for Ansibelle Penelope SWORDS' family, I was able to significantly expand my knowledge and documentation of the entire family unit's genealogy. However, the clue that John N. SWORDS' and his wife, Rebecca's, parents were both born in South Carolina carried me back to both their families. In addition, I've since been able to locate copious amounts of documentation about John N. SWORDS' siblings and their parents, a Revolutionary War soldier named John SWORDS, and his wife, Eleanor SWANCEY, both of whom are mentioned in other parts of the book. And my search continues for more and more information.

```
                                                                    Bib #: 185740
LD:    00602nam 2200181I 4500
001:   ocm01012088
005:   19920608110400.0
008:   740917s1974 xx 000 0 eng d
020:     $c 5.00
040:     $a MEA $c MEA $d m/c
049:     $a TNHH
092:     $a 325.2415 $b O13i
100:   1  $a O'Brien, Michael J.
245:   14 $a The Irish in America : immigration, land, probate, administrations, birth, marriage and burial
         records of the Irish in America in and about the eighteenth century.
260:     $a Baltimore : $b Genealogical Pub., $c 1974.
300:     $a 63 p. ; $c 23cm.
650:   0 $a Irish $z United States.
913:     $a OBRIIAI99
                                                         Add to booklist    Place a hold
```

| FIGURE 8-9 | MARC record for Michael J. O'Brien's book, *The Irish in America* (From the Hillsborough County Public Library Cooperative catalog) |

but other records are manually entered into the catalog. Also, there are different formats for books, microfilm, videotape, audiotape, newspapers and other serials, graphics, sound files, letters, photographs, and other materials, all of which have their own informational needs. Catalogers are the unsung heroes in the back room of the library whose work makes materials easier to find. However, they can and do occasionally make data entry errors. Also, one cataloger may enter a full book title while another enters a shorter version. Please keep this in mind as you use libraries' online catalogs. Sometimes what you want may be slightly differently cataloged than you might expect. Therefore, be prepared to search multiple ways if necessary: by author, by title, by subject, and/or by keyword. And be sure to read any online Help that might be available.

Locate Online Catalogs Worldwide

In your quest for information in libraries and archives, you will want to access every possible online resource. ILL may not be available everywhere, especially in foreign countries. However, it is always an option to be explored. And don't forget that perhaps you can make contacts on message boards and mailing lists to perform look-ups for you, make copies, and help in other ways.

You will undoubtedly want to access as many online catalogs as possible. Consider the ones discussed in this lesson and be prepared to locate catalogs elsewhere through either compiled collections of links or using your favorite, "comfortable" search engine.

There are a number of library link collections. Here are a few:

- **Libraries Online at LibrarySpot.com**   Libraries and archives in the U.S. and its territories
  http://www.libraryspot.com/librariesonline.htm
- **Berkeley Digital Library SunSITE**   Library Web sites in over 115 countries
  http://sunsite.berkeley.edu/Libweb

■ **lib-web-cats**   A directory of libraries throughout the world
http://www.librarytechnology.org/libwebcats

■ **Libdex**   An index to more than 18,000 libraries worldwide
http://www.libdex.com

If these links can't help you locate the library you seek, you can always resort to a search engine. Simply construct a search using place names as part of your keyword search. Here are some examples of searches:

"public library" tampa
"nova scotia" archive
bournemouth library

Don't overlook differences in language. Learn the words for library and archive in the language of the country in which you plan to search. You can certainly do this at the SYSTRAN Web site located at **http://www.systransoft.com.** For example, the Dutch words for *library* and *archive* are, respectively, *bibliotheek* and *archief*. Then, conducting a search for the facilities in Amsterdam I might structure my search as shown here:

Amsterdam bibliotheek
Archief Amsterdam

My search for the Dutch national archives would look like the search shown here:

Nederlands nationaal archief

When you find the Web site itself, you may find that there is an English version of the site. If not, remember that you can copy the URL and paste it into the SYSTRAN site (or into the Babel Fish translator at AltaVista) and translate the entire page. The idiom and the vernacular may not be quite right, but you can get the general idea of the site's content from the translation.

Use the LDS Family History Center

The largest collection of genealogy manuscripts, printed materials, and microfilm in the world is undoubtedly the Family History Library (FHL) in Salt Lake City, operated by the Church of Jesus Christ of Latter-day Saints. The LDS has microfilmed many family histories and local histories and, for a small rental fee, it lends them out through its system of local Family History Centers (FHCs) throughout the world. In order to identify what books it has, you would visit the FamilySearch Internet Genealogy Service, located on the Web at **http://www.familysearch.org.** Once there, you should see a link under the "Family History Library System" column entitled "Search the Family History Library Catalog for records and resources." Like the LC online catalog, the FHL catalog has a button for searching by author. Unlike the LC online catalog, the FHL catalog is designed specifically for genealogy, and so the buttons on their catalog search screen may have different labels.

For instance, let's look up the surname "Boddie" in the FHL catalog. Click on the Surname Search button, type the word **boddie** in the box, and click on the Search button. The system displays a list of books (titles and main authors) about the Boddie family. You can then click on a particular book in order to learn more about it. You can find out the names of all of the authors, some detailed notes about the book, and a list of the surnames under which the book is indexed. If the book is available in microfilm format, the View Film Notes button will appear in the top-right corner of the main screen. Clicking on the button will give you the film number, which you can use to order a copy of the microfilm from the FHL to be sent to the nearest FHC to you. If you do not know where the nearest FHC is, there is a link on the **http://www.familysearch.org** Web page that will take you to a directory so that you can locate it. If you have not visited an LDS Family History Center yet, visit the Web page at **http://www.familysearch.org/Eng/Library/FHC/frameset_fhc.asp** and search for the one nearest to you. The people who work there can help you learn how to use their materials and how to request the loan of microfilm and CD-ROMs from the FHL in Salt Lake City.

Trace and Locate Documents That Have Been Moved

Advance preparation is the key to successful research, regardless of whether you plan an on-site visit to collect information or correspond with other people. You simply cannot expect to succeed in locating information, documents, and other materials if you don't have all your facts organized. We will discuss how to plan a very successful genealogical research trip in Chapter 11. However, at this juncture, you must understand the importance of advance planning.

In Chapter 3, we discussed how to use maps to find the *right* place to conduct your research and locate records. It bears repeating here that, unless you have done your homework and verified the types of records created at the time your ancestors lived in a particular location *and* the jurisdiction of the governmental agency or other organization that created them, you risk wasting your time and resources in a fruitless search. Make certain you are researching in the correct place.

You should not only investigate the types of records created at the time your ancestors were in the area, but you also should determine where those records now reside. Earlier in this chapter, I stated that the place where a document was once stored might not be the location where it is stored today. The documents you want may have been moved elsewhere for any of the reasons I mentioned earlier. There are several strategies you can use to check the location and status of those materials before you waste time trying to research documents that aren't where you assumed they might be held. Let's examine a few of these research tactics.

Consult Reference Books

One of the best resources at your disposal will be reference books that focus on different record types and the locations of those records. Among my personal favorites for general reference are the following titles:

- *The Source: A Guidebook of American Genealogy,* edited by Alice Eicholz and published by Ancestry (new edition 2004), provides the most comprehensive reference for United States records of all types and research methodologies. Information about conducting research about specific record types, what can be found in them, and how to locate and then assess the content are discussed in detail. Used in conjunction with *Ancestry's Red Book: American State, County, and Town Sources* discussed next, this is an unbeatable reference set for United States genealogy.

- *Ancestry's Red Book: American State, County, and Town Sources,* edited by Loretto Dennis Szucs and Sandra Hargreaves Luebking and published by Ancestry (new edition 2004), provides a state-by-state reference. Historical background about the formation of each state is provided, along with descriptions of all major record types, when they began being created, and where they reside. For each state, there is a county boundary map and a table showing each county, its contact information, details about its formation, and the years when each of the following record types began being created: birth, marriage, death, land, probate, and court.

- *In Search of Your Canadian Roots: Tracing Your Family Tree in Canada,* by Angus Baxter and published by Genealogical Publishing Co., Inc., is the standard for all-Canada genealogical research. It is the most complete reference concerning all types of records created across Canada and is an invaluable aid in understanding and locating those materials.

- *French-Canadian Sources: A Guide for Genealogists,* published by Ancestry, is a compilation of scholarly chapters written by experts in French-Canadian research. The book covers the entire history of the French in Canada from establishment in 1604 of Port Royal in what is now Nova Scotia, and details the many types of records created over the centuries by the French, English, and Canadian governments. Among the elegant appendices are: a collection of French vocabulary words and phrases you are likely to encounter; charts and descriptions of Canadian census records and substitutes; and an extensive compilation of French-Canadian research addresses.

- *Ancestral Trails: The Complete Guide to British Genealogy and Family History* was written by Mark D. Herber and published by Genealogy Publishing Co, Inc., in association with the Society of Genealogists, and was updated in May of 2000. A second edition was published in 2003 by Sutton in Stroud, U.K. This is the most extensive and comprehensive guide to tracing your British heritage, presented in an orderly fashion and in easily understandable language. It provides clear descriptions of all major and many obscure records, and will help you understand the church and governmental structures employed over the centuries in creating and maintaining the records.

■ *Tracing Your Irish Ancestors: The Complete Guide,* written by John Grenham and a second edition published in 2000 by Genealogical Publishing Co., provides an excellent primer on how to begin your ancestral quest, and examines the major sources such as civil records, censuses, church records, land and property documentation, wills, emigration papers, deeds, registry sources, newspapers, and directories. A complete table of Roman Catholic parish registers' reference information is included, as are detailed materials about available research services, genealogical and historical societies, and contact information for an array of libraries and record repositories.

■ *A Genealogist's Guide to Discovering Your Scottish Ancestors,* written by Linda Jonas and Paul Milner and published by Betterway Books, is a straightforward guide for Americans tracing Scottish immigrant ancestors. Clear, concise descriptions and illustrations of many document types are complemented by step-by-step guidelines to conducting research in United States and Scottish records.

As you can see, the books listed above form a strong core of reference works for your use. You may decide to purchase some of these as components of your personal genealogical reference collection. Your local public library also may own a copy of each of these books in its own collection. However, if not, you certainly can recommend acquisition to the person responsible for the library's collection development.

Remember that any printed book can become outdated, especially in these days when Web addresses, postal and e-mail addresses, and fax and telephone numbers change quickly. My favorite book on United States military records was published as recently as 1998, but some of the military records have been relocated and at least two U.S. government departments now have different physical and mailing addresses and telephone numbers.

Locate the Repository on the Internet

Internet Web pages typically provide the most current information about a facility or document repository you might want to access. Just as libraries and archives maintain a Web presence, usually with an embedded online catalog, government agencies, companies, organizations, societies, and other entities create and maintain Web sites. If you know the Web address of the facility, you can quickly access their site and check on their holdings. If you don't know the address, you can use your favorite Internet search engine to locate the site. For example, I decided I wanted to locate information about local government offices in the area near the town of Chelmsford, located northeast of London in the United Kingdom. I entered the following in the Google search engine:

chelmsford government

I was rewarded with search results that included a number of links. The first of these was from the Google Directory, which displayed the hierarchical structure of Regional > Europe > United Kingdom > England > Essex > Chelmsford > Government. Here I accessed a direct link to the Chelmsford Borough Council's site at **http://www.chelmsfordbc. gov.uk.** Another search result was that of the LocalLife site for Chelmsford at **http://www.locallife.co.uk/chelmsford/ government.asp,** which included links to government offices' sites. I clicked on the button labeled

Local Government and another Web page was displayed showing the names of the local and county councils. None of these had hyperlinks to other Web sites, but I highlighted the Essex County Council, copied that name, and then returned to the main Google search screen and pasted it in the search box. The first item in the search results list was the Essex County Council Web site at **http://www.essexcc.gov.uk.** Here I found a number of helpful links, including one for archives and museums, one for births, marriages, and deaths, and another for lands and buildings. Each link took me to another page of frequently asked questions (often referred to as FAQs) and answers.

Researchers seeking information about vital records in the United States and its territories will want to visit the "Vital Records Information for United States" Web site at **http://www.vitalrec.com.** Also included is a link to a Web page describing how to file a consular report of the birth or death of an American citizen abroad, or a marriage ceremony abroad in which at least one party was an American citizen. Instructions for applying for a certified copy of one of these consular reports also are provided.

You certainly will use the online catalogs of libraries and archives to search their holdings for information you want to access. An excellent starting point on the Internet is the LibrarySpot Web site at **http://www.libraryspot.com.** North American libraries are organized by facility type. However, the link to Libraries Online at **http://www.libraryspot.com/libraries** provides access to three searchable directories of libraries around the world.

Contact the Repository

While we hope that the "official" Web sites of government agencies and other entities are maintained with up-to-date information, the truth is that a vast number of Web sites are less than current. The old adage of "phone first!" certainly applies here. I know of one library that closed its genealogical collection for two weeks while renovating the space. Unfortunately, a busload of genealogists arrived for a day's research to find the collection inaccessible. Their society leader had, in fact, checked the library's Web site for the hours of operation but the library had not posted an announcement of the planned closure.

Another complication that occurs is when the facility withdraws the materials temporarily for microfilming, scanning/digitization, repair, or other maintenance. By contacting the repository in advance, you can learn if the materials you want to access will, in fact, be available when you visit or if you request them through ILL, snail-mail, or e-mail.

You will frequently find that many materials of genealogical interest may not have been cataloged on the OPAC or iPAC system. You have already seen typical catalog and MARC records in this chapter and can understand the effort required to create a single catalog database record. Imagine, then, the loose documents, correspondence, maps, folders, and other materials that may be a part of a library or archive's holdings. It is expensive and labor-intensive to catalog each and every item. Sometimes there may be a single catalog entry to reference a group of related materials, such as the correspondence files of a local historian. In other cases, there may be no catalog record at all. For these and other reasons, it is important that you always ask the question of a reference professional at the library or archive, "Are there any materials of genealogical or local historical significance in your collection that have not been cataloged?" More often than not, the answer will be in the affirmative. It's then time to form a strong bond with this reference person to learn what is available, the content and scope of those holdings, and how to access the materials.

Making individual contact with the repository also allows you to confirm the location, travel directions, hours of operation, costs of printed copies of materials, and policies for security, access, and use of the materials. Obtaining that information in advance helps you plan your research more efficiently.

In addition, if you believe there are specific materials that you want to use, you can confirm that they will be available. If you find that they are unavailable, you can adjust your schedule or your research plan. If you find out that the materials you are seeking have been relocated elsewhere, you can then pursue what happened to the records and how to gain access to them now.

Seek Help from a State, Provincial, or National Library or Archive

The personnel at a local repository may be unable to tell you about specific materials of genealogical importance. The individual may not have the knowledge or training to help you, or may just be overwhelmed with his or her duties and unwilling to give that little extra something to help you make your connection with the materials you want or need. Don't overlook the use of the expert professionals who staff libraries and archives having a broader focus than local ones. Their collections are most often substantially larger, their training more intensive, and their perspective of documents, records, books, journals, microfilm, and digitized materials broader than local libraries' or county governments'.

When I have been unable to locate specific places in a particular state, I have called on the state library or state archive for assistance. Their collection of historical maps, gazetteers, and other reference materials are extensive and the staff members are well trained in effectively using these resources. In addition, I have used the telephone and e-mail reference services of academic libraries, the National Archives and Records Administration, the Library of Congress, the United States Geological Survey, and other types of facilities to answer questions and to locate materials that either were difficult to find or had been relocated.

Contact Genealogical and Historical Societies at All Levels

Genealogical and historical societies are among your best resources. They are involved with the study of history, culture, society, and documentation in their respective areas. Their business is research and, in many cases, preservation of information, documentation, and artifacts. Think of these societies as "networks" of individuals with knowledge and experience in the materials in their area. If you contact one person who does not have an answer to your question, he or she usually knows where to look or who to put you in contact with to help you. It is possible that a society may have acquired records, photographs, or artifacts that have not been accessible to researchers before. The society may be indexing or cataloging records or indexes in preparation perhaps for publishing them or donating them to a library or archive. They also may be involved with collecting and organizing information that is not yet available in any other way. There are two excellent examples that immediately come to mind in Florida. One is a genealogical society's ongoing project of indexing articles concerning individuals who lived in or passed

8

through their county in the territorial period prior to Florida statehood in 1845. The other is an ongoing project by one county's genealogical society to canvass and document every gravestone in every cemetery in the county, and to publish indexes for all of those cemeteries. The Florida State Genealogical Society is pleased to announce ongoing projects of this type at their Web site at **http://www.rootsweb.com/~flsgs/projects.htm.** Both of the societies' work products, however, may be unique and found nowhere else.

It also is not unusual for these societies' members to respond to your problem by jumping in to help you with the research. They may look up records for you, make copies, take photographs, or provide assistance in other ways.

Engage a Professional Researcher

Finally, if you are seeking records that you believe should exist somewhere but have been otherwise unable to locate them, you may want to engage the services of a professional genealogical researcher. You will want a person who has the experience and credentials to conduct a scholarly research effort for you and provide status reports and a final report with copies and fully documented source citations as the final project deliverable. There are a number of organizations that test and accredit professional researchers. Some of these are listed here:

- The Board for Certification of Genealogists (BCG) (**http://www.bcgcertification.org**)

- International Commission for the Accreditation of Professional Genealogists (ICAPGen) (**http://www.icapgen.org**)

- Accredited Genealogists who became accredited through The Church of Jesus Christ of Latter-day Saints Family History Department prior to October 2000 (**http://www.accreditedgenealogists.org**)

- Association of Professional Genealogists in Ireland (**http://indigo.ie/~apgi**)

As you can see, not all information may be up to date. You will find that using more than one of these strategic approaches can help assure a greater success rate at locating and accessing the records you need for your research.

Deal with Closed or Limited Access to Materials

Some records are not accessible to the public, or access may be restricted. Since the terrorist attacks in the United States on 11 September 2001, many legislators and government agencies around the world have taken steps to prevent access to information and records that might be used to falsify an identity or otherwise engage in illegal activities. As a result, a number of official documents previously available for research may be off-limits or require verification of your identity in order to use them. Vital records or civil records including birth certificates are highly protected because of their use in obtaining identity cards, driver's licenses, passports, and other official documents.

Some government documents are completely closed to the public and may never be opened, regardless of anything you might do. One type of these is adoption records, which, in most cases, cannot be accessed by anyone, even the adoptee or the adoptive parents, without a court order or the intervention of a judge or magistrate. Others include court-ordered, sealed files concerning some divorce settlements, civil lawsuit settlements, coroners' reports, and inquests.

Private companies and organizations also are reluctant to release any information about their clients, employees, or members for whatever reason. Some may divulge information and provide copies of records to persons who are immediate relations of an individual; however, many will refuse inquiries and requests unconditionally. As private entities, they have the right to hold information confidential and there is little you can do to circumvent their position.

Religious institutions may choose to maintain the privacy of their records and those of their members. I know a woman who requested copies of her grandparents' records from a particular Catholic church. She was seeking membership information in the form of church christening, baptism, confirmation, marriage, and death records. To her astonishment, her request was refused by the priest even though she and her parents also were members of the same church. The reason given was that the church's records and the individuals' information were private.

These brick walls can certainly seem like insurmountable problems. There are, however, several methods you may take to help gain access to otherwise restricted or closed records. Let's explore a few of these approaches.

8

Be Prepared to Provide Proof of Your Relationship

You will almost always be asked to explain the reason for requesting someone else's information, even though that person may have been deceased for some time—even decades or centuries. Your best response will be that you are researching your family and that you can provide proof of your relationship to the individual whose records you are requesting. As a good genealogist, you will already have traced your family backward from yourself and will have collected documentation of your lineage. It is important to be able to present your identification wherever you go but, if your surname is different than that of the person you are researching, you may have to present some additional proof. Be prepared by carrying a copy of a pedigree chart with you, along with copies of birth certificates, marriage licenses, death certificates, obituaries, and any other documentation that might prove your relationship. The fact that you *are* prepared to prove your relationship speaks volumes to the people from whom you make these requests. They are usually so impressed by your preparation, your openness, and the evidence that you present that they often will open access to otherwise closed or restricted materials.

Offer to Pay All the Expenses

Demonstrate your seriousness about the subject by offering to pay for the expenses associated with making copies, mailing them to you, and whatever else might be required. Be sure that the person you are dealing with knows this from the beginning. If you are working with a religious institution or a nonprofit organization, such as a genealogical or historical society, offer to make a small contribution as a gesture of appreciation and to help offset the person's time.

Provide Letters of Authorization or Permission to Access

Your relationship to the individual you are researching may not be a direct one. Perhaps you are searching for records for your grandfather's brother's children. Since you are not a direct relative, you may be challenged and blocked from access to some or all records. This can sometimes be resolved by providing a letter of authorization or affidavit from a descendant or other direct blood relative. The letter or affidavit should be signed, dated, and legalized by a registered notary public. It also helps to be able to prove your relationship to the family in the same way described previously, only this time you should be able to show your ancestral connection to this collateral, branch line of the family.

Escalate Your Request

You may need to escalate your request to a higher authority if your initial inquiry is refused. In the example of the woman whose request for copies of her grandparents' records from a particular Catholic church was refused, she chose to escalate the problem. She contacted the archdiocese and successfully petitioned the bishop's intervention on her behalf.

You sometimes will encounter situations where records have been moved to a storage facility or sent to another location. Your request for information, copies, or access may be ignored or refused because it's just too much trouble or too expensive to handle it. It is always important to obtain a reason why your request is being refused, as well as the name of the individual who refused you. Don't get angry; maintain a calm, polite demeanor. You really don't know what the person's instructions may have been. However, you certainly may ask to speak to a supervisor or superior. Ask for that person's name and, if he or she is not available, obtain an address and telephone number. Make contact with that person and make your request again. Your persistence will be noted and, if you don't obtain positive results with the supervisor, ask for the name and contact information of his or her superior. Escalate through the chain-of-command until you reach the top.

Invoke the Use of the Freedom of Information Act

In the United States, the Freedom of Information Act, also referred to as the FOIA, requires government agencies to disclose records requested in writing by any person. Certainly there are some restrictions that relate to national security, and certain privacy laws pertaining to living individuals may apply. However, it is important to recognize that the FOIA can be invoked in certain circumstances to overcome artificial obstacles and refusals by some less than cooperative clerks.

The United States Department of Justice (DOJ) maintains a Web page at its site that specifically addresses FOIA requests. You can visit that site at **http://www.usdoj.gov/04foia.** Consult their DOJ FOIA Reference Guide for specific details concerning what can and cannot be accessed and the procedures for making your request.

In addition, the American Civil Liberties Union (ACLU) has a step-by-step guide titled "Using the Freedom of Information Act," at **http://archive.aclu.org/library/foia.html** that will provide further information. The United States Department of State's online Electronic Reading Room at **http://foia.state.gov/AboutFOIA.asp** provides an overview and additional FOIA reference materials.

Obtain a Court Order

Some documents are closed or restricted to the public by governments and individuals. One effective approach is to apply to a court of law for a court order to open records or to provide copies of specific items. You must be prepared to present a convincing argument of your need to access the materials and to prove your relationship. One of the most persuasive arguments presented in contemporary court hearings of this sort is the necessity of medical information. The need to identify blood type, genetic predisposition to a disease or medical condition, or similar reason is often an effective argument for the issuance of a court order. You may or may not require a legal representative's help in preparing and presenting your request to the court. The use of a legal professional can be expensive, but the cost may be justified if this is your last resort.

Order Document Copies by Snail-mail and E-mail

Letter-writing has become something of a lost art, and people tend to forget the importance of using effective correspondence to get results. Younger genealogists also may not know what informational components are required in order to get the best results, and older genealogists may not be using modern technology to achieve success.

8

It isn't always convenient or cost-effective to make a visit to a particular place to obtain copies of documents you want or need for your research. Therefore, you will do what genealogists have done for decades: write letters and/or complete forms to obtain copies of documents. The difference between the way we handled this now and 20 years ago is that e-mail is available in addition to traditional postal mail. Since e-mail is so fast, the slower postal mail has acquired the name of "snail-mail."

Your first step, as always, is to determine the correct place to inquire about the records you want to obtain. You certainly can use the Internet and a search engine to locate the Web site of a particular facility. For example, if I was looking for the contact information for Augusta County, Virginia, governmental offices, I might enter the following into my favorite search engine:

"augusta county" virginia government

The search results list included the county government's Web site at **http://www.co.augusta. va.us.** From that page, I could navigate to other pages containing the addresses and telephone numbers of the Circuit and District Courts. I could then write a letter to the clerk of the appropriate court and mail it, along with a self-addressed, stamped envelope (SASE). The SASE is a professional gesture that encourages a response.

In another case, I decided to locate information about the court facilities in Chelmsford in the U.K. I entered a simple search with only two words: chelmsford court. The search results included a link to the Essex Magistrates' Courts at **http://www.essexmagistrates.org.uk/chelmsford_ courthouse.asp.** There I found the address at the Court House, The High, Harlow, Essex, CM20 1HH; the telephone and fax numbers; and the e-mail address. While this facility may not have many historical documents, it is still a possible source of information.

I also can obtain copies of required document request forms from some archives and libraries. The United States National Archives and Records Administration (NARA) requires you to use their preprinted, multipart forms to request searches for and copies of specific records. These can be obtained by visiting their Web site at **http://www.archives.gov,** clicking on the link labeled Search, and entering the word **genealogy** in the search box. The search results will include a link to the Genealogy Main Page. Click on that link and you will be presented with the screen shown in Figure 8-10 and there you will see a link labeled Forms to Order Records.

NARA's forms can be obtained either by sending an e-mail from their Web site or by mailing a letter to the address shown on the screen.

When generating a request to any person, organization, or institution requesting anything, use the standard business letter format. Include your complete return address and the date of your letter. The heading should include the name and complete address for the entity you are writing.

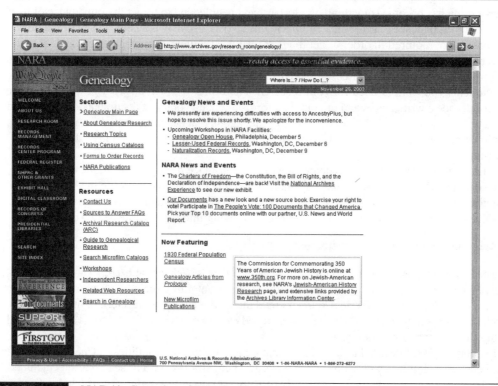

FIGURE 8-10 NARA's Genealogy Main Page

If you have the name of a specific contact individual, include that name, preceded with the title (Mr., Ms., Mrs., etc.), in the header. See the examples here:

Alamance County Offices
Attn.: Department of Vital Records
124 W. Elm Street
Graham, NC 27253

Ms. Penelope Weatherly
Clerk of Court
Alamance County Courthouse
124 W. Elm Street
Graham, NC 27253

Next comes the salutation, followed by a colon. Use the person's name and title, if you know it. If you don't know the name, use the generic salutation. Look at the following examples:

Dear Ms. Weatherly:
Dear Gentlemen and Ladies:
To whom it may concern:

The body of the letter must communicate clearly what you are seeking. Include the full name of the person whose record you want to obtain. Include any nickname and, for women, the maiden name, and define these alternative names as what they are. Here is the text from the body of a letter that I wrote concerning my paternal grandparents.

I am seeking a copy of the marriage record for my grandparents who were married on 24 December 1902 in Davidson, Mecklenburg County, North Carolina. Their names and information are as follows:

Groom: Samuel Goodloe Morgan (born 6 April 1879)

Bride: Laura Augusta (Minnie) Wilson Murphy

Laura Augusta Wilson was also known as "Minnie" and may be listed as such in the marriage records. Also, she had been previously married to a Mr. Jeter Earnest Murphy in 1898 but was widowed the same year.

I have tried to provide as much information as possible above. I hope it will be enough for you to locate this record for me. Please advise me of the cost of locating and providing me with copies of these records. I will send a check immediately or provide credit card information, whichever you prefer. I am enclosing a SASE for your reply.

If you do not have these records, please advise me if they have been transferred to another location, the state archive, to a library, or other facility so that I may continue my search there.

Thank you in advance for your invaluable help with my family quest.

You will notice that I included a paragraph asking that, if the records are no longer in that facility, the person should let me know where they may have been sent or transferred. Many clerks are overwhelmed with work and, if you don't ask the question, they may not automatically supply you with that invaluable information.

The signature block of your letter should include a complimentary closing such as "Yours" or "Sincerely." Type your full name and, if you wish, your title (Mr., Mrs., Ms.) and any professional or educational credential abbreviations that are appropriate (DDS, PhD., etc.).

Address your mailing envelope clearly so that it matches the header block of your letter, and be certain to include your return address. Enclose a clearly addressed SASE with ample postage to encourage a reply.

Another way to streamline the letter-writing process is to create a template in your word processor and save it. This can reduce the amount of typing you have to do. You might consider having a separate template document for use in requesting marriage records, one for death certificates, another for wills and probate records, and yet another for land and property records. Each template will have the specific verbiage you need to specify and obtain copies. You also might consider a mail merge document, which is one in which you can define specific fields of the letter and code them in such a way that you simply enter data into one document and then cause it to be merged into the template, creating multiple documents. Check the Help facility of your word processor program for detailed instructions for how to create document templates for these letters and/or mail merge documents. You actually could create multiple mail merge documents: Use the data entry document as the single place you type in information and then allow it to produce the letters and produce a sheet of mailing labels for envelopes. You also can create a number of SASE envelopes at one time and then only need to add the stamp and enclose it with your letters. It really is simple to automate the process. It requires a little time investment in the beginning to set everything up. However, after that, the letter-writing process itself can be a breeze.

Keep Track of Your Correspondence

My genealogy correspondence used to be a terrible mess. I would write letters to courthouses for copies of documents, send off forms to obtain copies from NARA, and shoot off e-mail messages to many other researchers. I was so busy sending things out that I wasn't really sure what I had done and what I had not. I ended up duplicating my efforts again and again, and yet never followed up on anything because I didn't keep control of it. It is particularly embarrassing when you send the same request two or three times to the same person, and it gets expensive sending money multiple times to the same courthouse or archives and receiving the same documents more than once. Yes, it *can* happen to you!

The simple solution is to maintain a correspondence log and get into the habit of entering information about all of your correspondence, including both snail-mail and e-mail. The correspondence log is merely a formatted record of what you have written to someone else about, when you wrote it, when you received a response, and what results you obtained.

Some people choose to maintain a record of their correspondence at the surname level and, by doing so, have only one place to check for every letter or e-mail sent and received for an entire family. I know other people who maintain a control log based on geography, or even surname and geography, to get a little more granular. There are a number of options for setting up and maintaining a correspondence log. You will have to choose the format and organizational scheme that works best for you and the people you are researching.

You have a number of options in terms of format. Ancestry.com provides a free downloadable Correspondence Record form at **http://c.ancestry.com/pdf/trees/charts/correc.pdf;** RootsWeb offers another format at **http://www.rootsweb.com/~cokids/forms/pics/corresp.jpg;** and Family Tree Magazine provides yet another document at **http://www.familytreemagazine.com/forms/people/correspondence.pdf.** There are other examples on the Internet that you can find by typing **genealogy forms** into your favorite search engine.

Another option is to create your own form using a word processor or spreadsheet program. You can define whatever columns you would like and format them to suit your own research needs. At a minimum, you will want to keep track of the following data fields.

- Date on which you made the request
- Name and address of the person or institution
- Type of information requested
- Type of information received
- Any money that you sent along with the request

I use a Microsoft Excel spreadsheet for my genealogy correspondence log like the one shown in Figure 8-11.

By setting up multiple columns for surname, forename/given name, and middle initial, I can sort the data in the spreadsheet into whatever sequence I like. Excel allows me to sort in ascending or descending order for every field. For example, perhaps I want to see all correspondence I've generated for all persons in alphabetical order. I could sort the surnames alphabetically as the primary sort, then by forename as the secondary sort, and middle initial as a tertiary sort. That would present a spreadsheet in all alphabetical sequence by name. I also could add another sort to place the correspondence in date sequence within person—or in surname. Perhaps I want to see what correspondence I've sent to a specific person or organization. I could sort the spreadsheet in addressee name sequence and then, if I like, I can add additional sorting within that by date and by surname. As you can see, using a spreadsheet program can provide a great deal of flexibility

Date	Addressee	Surname	Fore-name	M.I.	Info. Req.	Money Sent	Date Received	Type of Info.
1-May-02	Clerk of Court	Morgan	Samuel	T.	Birth Certificate	$10.00	17-Aug-02	Birth Certificate
14-Jun-03	N.C. State Archives	Alexander	John	M.	Probate file	$25.00	10-Nov-03	Will & probate packet copies

FIGURE 8-11   Sample correspondence log using an Excel spreadsheet

in viewing the data. That way you can generate follow-ups for correspondence for which you have received no reply.

Using a correspondence log requires a little investment in setup time and a commitment to the process of using and maintaining it. The payback, however, comes in the elimination of redundant written correspondence and in being able to maintain control over what can be an overwhelming activity.

Use a Research Log

It can be difficult to keep track of all the places and resources where you have conducted research. The danger is that you may duplicate your research and that can be a terrible waste of time and money. It is important to keep track of what resources you have investigated in the past, even those that yielded nothing of value, so that you don't duplicate your efforts. A research log or research calendar can help you record your progress. You can maintain your log by surname, by individual, by geographic area, in a combination of any of these, or in whatever organizational structure makes you most effective.

There are numerous free versions of the research log on the Internet. You can use one of the preformatted ones, such as the Research Calendar at Ancestry.com at **http://www.ancestry.aol.com/ trees/charts/researchcal.aspx,** the Research Log at the Public Broadcasting System site at **http://www.pbs.org/kbyu/ancestors/charts/pdf/researchlog.pdf,** or elsewhere. Use your favorite search engine to help you locate other examples.

As with the correspondence log, you can also create your own research log or calendar. Evaluate what information you need to track and set up columns accordingly. In my own case, I have to be careful not to make the error of using the same reference books again and again. For that reason, my research log has columns for author name (surname, forename) and title. I can sort the spreadsheet using those columns as the primary and secondary sort fields and produce an alphabetical report to use while searching online library and archive catalogs, while visiting those facilities, and while browsing in used bookstores.

Summary

All of the information discussed in this chapter will help you home in on different record types in all types of locations. In the process, the correspondence and research logs can help you identify the materials you have already used and prevent an enormous duplication of work effort and waste of money making photocopies, ordering document copies, and purchasing books.

Now that we have covered so many different record types, and discussed various printed references and finding aids, let's proceed to Chapter 9 and discuss how to locate information on the Internet about your ancestors.

Chapter 9

Locate Your Ancestors on the Internet

How to...

- Put the historical development of the Internet into perspective
- Differentiate between the three categories of genealogical resources on the Internet
- Categorize the major types of genealogical Web page resources
- Understand the concept of domain names and how to use them
- Locate Web sites that have "disappeared"
- Differentiate between directories and search engines on the Internet
- Structure effective searches to locate information
- Use online message boards to share information and collaborate with others
- Subscribe to and use genealogy mailing lists
- Write effective messages and postings that get results
- Locate and use additional Internet resources to help your research
- Access the resources of the "hidden Internet"
- Use *all* the resources at your disposal in tandem

Add Internet Resources to Your Research Toolkit

Genealogical research is one of the top uses of the Internet, and it is no surprise that so many of us are confused by all the options and overwhelmed by the information we find. Making sense of what you find on the Internet means understanding what you are looking at. Understanding the various types of Internet resources is not unlike visiting your local public library and recognizing that dictionaries are vastly different resources than fiction and nonfiction books, magazines are different than journals, and microfilm is different than the Internet. You use your critical thinking skills every time you visit the library to differentiate between materials you want to use; to recognize what is current vs. non-current information; and to discern between quality, authoritative, and unbiased information as opposed to that which is not.

The Internet didn't just appear in the 1990s; it had been around for quite a while. It may help you to understand some historical background about the development of the Internet. You can then put what you are using today into perspective and understand why it has become the ubiquitous force in communications of all sorts.

This chapter will focus on the different types of Internet resources, how to evaluate them, and how to incorporate them with the "traditional" documents, print materials, and other resources you use. Ultimately, you will work all of these sources in tandem to obtain more comprehensive results and make yourself a more effective researcher.

Categorize the Three Major Categories of Internet Resources

Many people equate "the Internet" only with Web pages. It is, however, much more than that. Certainly there are billions of Web pages, but the Internet really is a collection of a number of tools. These can be grouped into three main categories:

- Web pages
- Electronic mail (e-mail)
- Message boards and mailing lists

Within Web pages are other subsidiary contents, including text, graphics files, sound files, video files, forms for inputting data, search templates, archives of files that can be transferred or downloaded, chat rooms, and a number of other resources.

Electronic mail, which is most commonly referred to as e-mail, is the most widely used form of communication on earth today. Many billions of electronic messages are sent and received each day. Some are individual person-to-person messages while others are one-to-many messages, such as those sent to an e-mail mailing list or distribution list. E-mail has, like Web pages, become more than just textual. Messages can contain multimedia graphics, sound, and video files within the body of the message and, more commonly, as attachments.

Message boards and mailing lists are Internet tools that allow you to reach many persons at once who share an interest in a particular topic. Genealogy message boards are used by tens of thousands of persons each day to post queries concerning persons with a specific surname, questions about a geographical area, or questions concerning some other subject area. Mailing lists utilize e-mail messages to communicate to persons who have subscribed to a distribution concerning a specific surname or topic. Message boards and mailing lists are discussed in great detail later in this chapter.

Web pages, e-mail, message boards, and mailing lists are different media and are used for different purposes. If you understand their uses up front, you are better prepared for what you may and may not expect to find when you use them.

One of the best pieces of advice I can give you is to look for help on the Internet along the way with all the resources you encounter. Most Web sites and Internet resources will include a "Help" facility. This may also be titled "Tips and Tricks" or some other name. You can always become more conversant and more effective in the use of any online facility by accessing and reading the Help text area. This area will explain what is and is not available in the way of functionality. Often you will find examples of how to access content effectively and, if there is a search facility available, how to optimize your use of it. These "mini-tutorials" are intended as primers for you and usually are not long, drawn-out, dry narratives.

9

In the meantime, here is an important shortcut tip for Windows operating system users on how to find words or phrases in a lengthy Web page. Rather than read or scan the whole Web page, use the Find function in your Web browser. There are two ways to do this:

1. Go to the menu bar at the top of the screen and click Edit, and then click the Find (on This Page) choice. You'll be presented with a small window such as the one shown in Figure 9-1. Type in the Find What box the word or exact phrase you wish to locate on the page. You have other options in the search box as well, if you want to use them. Then click the button labeled Find Next. If what you typed in the box is on the Web page, the page will move and the word/phrase will be highlighted. Click again and the search will take you to the next occurrence of the word/phrase. If the word/phrase doesn't occur there, or if there are no more occurrences of it, another window will appear indicating that the Find function has "Finished searching the document." Click on the X button in the upper-right corner of these small windows to close them.

2. You can access the Find function from keyboard without going through the clicking of the Edit and Find options on the browser's menu bar. Simply press and hold the CTRL key and then press the F key. This will bring up the Find window. Press the ESC key to close the small windows.

Categorize the Major Types of Genealogical Web Page Resources

No matter whether you're just starting your genealogical odyssey on the Internet or a seasoned Web researcher, there is always something new to be discovered there. What you must remember is that Web sites change over time. New content is added, content is updated, dead links and outdated materials are removed (hopefully!), and Web sites evolve to become more user-friendly. Let's explore the major types of Web page resources you will encounter and assess what you can expect to find there.

Compilation Sites

Compilation sites are Web sites that gather significant resources together in an organized fashion. The materials are presented in a format that allows you to locate materials by reviewing the logical groupings of materials or hierarchical structures to find what you want. Some of these sites may

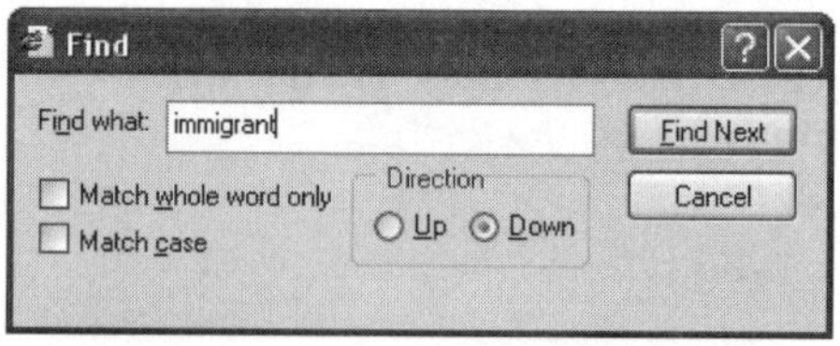

FIGURE 9-1   The Find function can be used to quickly locate text in a Web page or any other document.

include a search function that allows you to locate specific resources by keyword or phrase. Listed below are some Web site examples and suggested areas to explore.

- Ancestry.com
  http://www.ancestry.com

  Visit the main page and locate the link to Learning Center. Locate the area on the screen labeled Browse the Library and select the link labeled More. On the next screen, click on the How-to link and browse the articles in the archive. You'll also see a box labeled Search the Library where you can enter a word and search the archive. Enter the word **reunion** and see what you find.

- Canadian Genealogy & History
  http://www.islandnet.com/~jveinot/cghl/cghl.html

  Visit the main page (shown in Figure 9-2) and click on the link labeled Nunavut, and then on the link labeled Teaching & Learning about the Canadian territory of Nunavut to see a map and to learn more about this area.

- Cyndi's List
  http://www.cyndislist.com

  Look for Cyndi Howells' group of information on Wills & Probate. Scroll through the entire page to see what is there. Then, go back to the top and try the Find function to locate a listing for Delaware. Then, return to the top of the page and type **delaware** in the Search box and see what all is at her site. You can narrow the search to locate wills in Delaware by typing the two words, **delaware wills.**

- GENUKI
  http://www.genuki.org.uk

  Visit the main page and click on the link labeled Researching UK and Irish Genealogy from Abroad and, on that page, read the section about Commissioning Research.

- JewishGen
  http://www.jewishgen.org

  Visit the main page and locate the link labeled JewishGen InfoFiles, shown in Figure 9-3. Click on the link labeled Genealogical Techniques at the top of the page to move to the area on the Web page or scroll down to that area of the page. Locate the link labeled EEFAQ—Jewish Genealogical Research in Eastern Europe and learn how to conduct research for ancestors and relatives from that part of the world.

- USGenWeb Project
  http://www.usgenweb.org

  This all-volunteer effort provides access to information about all 50 states and their counties. Visit the site and click on The Project's State Pages. (There are other selections you'll want to explore as well.) Use one of the links to the map, table, or text to access the listing of states. Select Virginia and then explore what is there.

9

■ WorldGenWeb Project
http://www.worldgenweb.org/

This is the international companion site to the USGenWeb Project. Visit this site and locate Germany. Then select the link labeled States of Germany and visit the page for that.

As you can see, each of these Web sites is a compilation of many different types of information. Within some of these are "how-to" materials, databases, maps, dictionaries, and links to other sites. While Cyndi's List offers an exceptionally comprehensive collection of reference links across many subject areas across the Internet, a compilation by topic area provides an excellent focal point for your research concerning a specific topic area. The esteemed JewishGen site, for example, provides categories of general and geography-specific information and links, making it the preeminent Web site for Jewish ancestral research guidance.

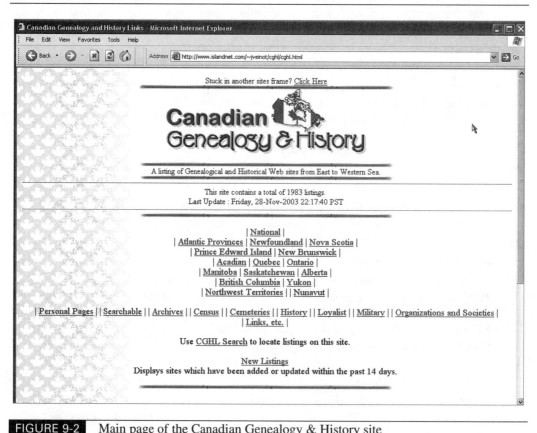

FIGURE 9-2   Main page of the Canadian Genealogy & History site

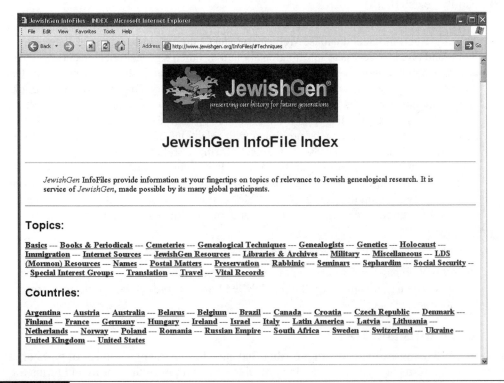

FIGURE 9-3   The main page at JewishGen is the entry point to the most comprehensive Jewish genealogical resources on the Internet.

"How-to," Educational, and Reference

This category includes "how-to" articles that provide instruction, as well as articles, columns, tips, and other online reference materials.

- ■ AfriGeneas (African Ancestored Genealogy)
  http://www.afrigeneas.com

  Visit the main screen and click on Records at the top of the page for a drop-down menu. Select Library Archives and click. Select one of the items on the page to investigate.

- ■ Family Tree Maker
  http://familytreemaker.genealogy.com/mainmenu.html

  Visit the main page and click on the box at the top labeled Learning Center. Select Genealogy How-To from the drop-down box. Choose one of the areas of interest to you on the page and visit that page.

■ Family Search (LDS)
http://www.familysearch.org

This is the genealogical database Web site of The Church of Jesus Christ of Latter-day Saints and provides access to information about the church's genealogical materials. There is a tremendous amount here. However, let's focus on excellent instructional materials. On the main Web page, click on the tab at the top labeled Library. On the next screen, click on the link under the tabs labeled Education. On the next screen, click on the link labeled Research Guidance for a list of all the locations for which research guides are available. Select Sweden. You will now be presented with selections of birth, marriage, and death categories with date ranges presented. Select "Birth—1860 to Present." You will now be presented with three tabs: Historical Background, For Beginners, and Search Strategy. Click on each one in turn. Under each is a link that you may click to be displayed as a Web page. You also may click on the link for a printable version of the document. As a resource for strategies in various areas, these are unbeatable instructional sheets for your research.

■ RootsWeb
http://www.rootsweb.com/~rwguide/

Visit this Web page and select one or more subjects that are of interest to you in your research. You might want to try the link labeled Land Records (U.S.A.) for interesting information.

Genealogy Charts and Forms

In the course of your research, you will probably find need for the use of a number of types of forms to record information you uncover. In particular, census transcription forms and forms for abstracting wills, deeds, and other documents can be great tools. You certainly can create forms for your own work style, but there also are free forms available at a number of sites.

■ Ancestry.com
http://www.ancestry.com/trees/charts/ancchart.aspx

Some of the best charts and forms are available at the Ancestry.com site. They are in the Adobe PDF file format and are downloadable here. Check out the Census Forms, the Research Abstract, and others.

■ Family Tree Magazine's Downloadable Forms
http://www.familytreemagazine.com/forms/download.html

Family Tree Magazine has perhaps the most complete collection of genealogy forms on the Internet, available in both PDF and plain text formats.

■ Genealogy.com
http://www.genealogy.com/00000061.html

There are census forms here that provide another format option to those at Ancestry.com.

■ Public Broadcasting System—*Ancestors* Television Series
http://www.pbs.org/kbyu/ancestors/charts

The Public Broadcasting System in the United States, in partnership with Brigham Young University, produced the highly successful television series *Ancestors*. These forms are a complement to the teachers' guide for the series.

These are just a few of the many places on the Internet where you can obtain free forms to download and/or print. Additional free forms can be found by entering **genealogy forms** in your favorite search engine.

Online Databases

The fastest growing area of the Internet for genealogical resources is in online databases. There are both free databases and fee-based databases. Some sites offer a combination of databases. There are a number of payment arrangements to access data at the fee-based sites. They include: access on an annual or monthly subscription basis; pay-per-day; pay-as-you-go; or pay-per-record downloaded or printed. A number of the database sites will allow you free demonstration or sample subscription. It is wise to try the site on a short-term basis before committing yourself to a lengthy subscription.

In this category of Web resources, you should consider exploring as far as you possibly can in these areas, *and* returning often to these sites for new and updated materials. Some of the best of the databases are listed below.

- Ancestry.com (free and pay databases)
  http://www.ancestry.com

  You can use the search template at the site to enter name, location, time period, and/or other data and conduct a search of all the databases. Alternatively, however, you can examine the full list of available databases at Ancestry.com. This list can be found at **http://www.ancestry.com/ search/rectype/alldblist.asp,** and you may either browse the entire list (which I strongly recommend in order to see what is there) or click on a letter of the alphabet to view titles. You will be amazed at the scope and diversity of Ancestry.com's international databases. Among their Images Online premium databases are the United States federal census population schedules (1790–1930), the Historical Newspaper Collection, the 1891 United Kingdom Census, the Civil War Pension Index, the Immigrant Ships' Passenger Lists Collection, the Pallot Marriage and Baptism Indexes (1780–1837), and the United States WWI Draft Cards. Some of these databases are in the process of being digitized and placed online, which means that you should check back often to locate additional records.

- FamilyHistoryOnline (pay-per-view databases)
  http://www.familyhistoryonline.net

  The Federation of Family History Societies in the United Kingdom provides access to more than approximately 17 million records for England and Wales at the FamilyHistoryOnline Web site shown in Figure 9-4. These records have been compiled by Family History Societies and include indexes for baptisms, marriages, burials, monument inscriptions, and census records, and some of the records include more extensive details. The site continues to expand as additional counties and records are compiled and placed online.

9

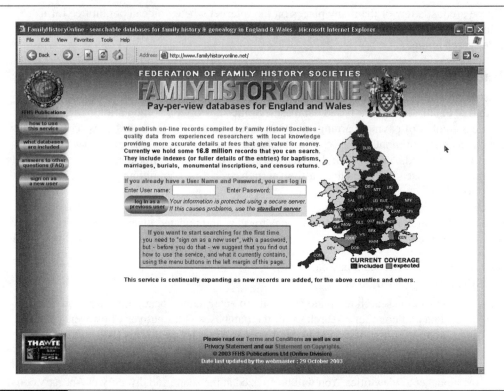

FIGURE 9-4 FamilyHistoryOnline is a pay-per-view database of records in England and Wales.

■ FamilySearch (LDS)
http://www.familysearch.org

Visit the main screen shown in Figure 9-5 and click on the area labeled Search for Ancestors. (Please note that there are various sub-links there. Run your mouse across the text on the screen to highlight the various links.) There are a number of databases here, and it is important that you know what these include. Searches of some of these will present you with a file number and/or microfilm number. These can be presented at the nearest LDS Family History Center (FHC) and the staff there can work with you to arrange to order the rental microform materials from the Family History Library (FHL) in Salt Lake City, Utah. The links include the following:

■ **Ancestral File** This data has been researched and uploaded to the LDS site by individuals. It may contain research errors.

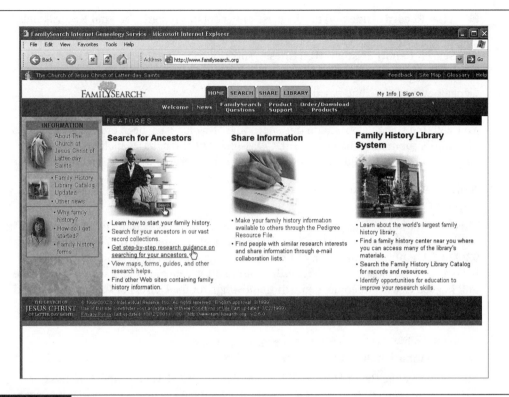

FIGURE 9-5   The main page of the LDS FamilySearch site

- **Census**   This area contains the 1880 United States, 1881 British Isles, and the 1881 Canadian Census material. This has been independently compiled and indexed by the LDS and can be ordered on microfilm.

- **The International Genealogical Index (IGI)**   This is an indexed database of materials collected and microfilmed by the LDS. There are indexing errors but this remains an excellent resource to film of the original records.

- **Pedigree Resource File**   This resource indexes the materials that have been submitted by individuals to the LDS. Many of these materials have been placed on CD-ROM and can be ordered through the LDS FHC rental program. There are errors in these materials but they can provide pointers for your research.

- **U.S. Social Security Death Index**   This resource can be found at several sites and can be an excellent finding aid.

- ■ **Vital Records Index**   This database only contains records for Vital Records Index for Mexico and Scandinavia currently.

- ■ **Search Family History Web Sites**   This is a collection of Web sites indexed by the LDS' search engine and references URLs submitted by individuals.

- ■ Genealogy.com (free and pay databases)
  http://www.genealogy.com/

  You will find some databases on this site, some of which have been created as a result of individuals submitting their own GEDCOM files. Other databases include the English Origins site, a U.K.-based pay-as-you-go facility, a newspaper database, and several others.

- ■ National Archives of Canada (free databases)
  http://www.archives.ca

  This resource was discussed in some detail in the chapter concerning census records. The National Archives of Canada has, in its online Genealogy area at **http://www.archives.ca/ 02/020202_e.html,** a collection of links to Web pages at its site describing its holdings for many of the most common records requested for genealogical research. Under the link labeled Census Records, you will find listings for the Census of Canada, 1901, and the Census of the Northwest Provinces, 1906. Both of these census returns are part of ArchiviaNet and contain digitized images of the census materials.

- ■ National Archives (U.K.) (pay U.K. census databases)
  http://www.nationalarchives.gov.uk

  The former Public Record Office (PRO) and the Historical Manuscripts Commission (HMC) were merged in April 2003 to form the National Archives. Of special interest to family history researchers are the digitized census images from the PRO collection, which may be accessed at the census Web page at **http://www.census.pro.gov.uk,** shown in Figure 9-6. You may search the database census index for free but pay to access the census page image.

- ■ Otherdays.com (Subscription databases)
  http://www.otherdays.com

  This collection of databases concentrates on Irish records. Included are Griffith's Valuations (1847–1864), which provides extensive property and residents' names; Dublin Wills and Marriages (1270–1857); books; newspaper records; maps and gazetteers; and a vast collection of other Irish resources. The main screen for this site is shown in Figure 9-7.

Genealogical Societies

Genealogical societies can offer a wealth of information to you, including reference and referrals, education, companionship, publications, and may well possess important genealogical records found nowhere else. You will want to investigate the societies at the national, regional state or provincial,

FIGURE 9-6   The 1901 Census of England and Wales home page at the PRO Web site

FIGURE 9-7   Main screen of the Otherdays.com Web site, which focuses on Irish records

county, parish, and local levels where your ancestors and family members lived. The following are some of the major ones of interest to researchers:

- Canadian Genealogical Societies
  http://www.generations.on.ca/genealogical-canadian.htm

  This Web page is a subsidiary of the Generations Web site and provides a list of links to the provincial genealogical societies' Web sites. There are, however, hundreds of genealogical societies in Canada and you may locate information for and links to a more extensive list of local societies at the provincial societies' sites.

- Federation of Family History Societies (FFHS)
  http://www.ffhs.org.uk

  This international organization, based in the United Kingdom, has more than 180,000 members worldwide. It provides education and support to individuals and to genealogical societies, and coordinates a number of national projects in order to integrate the efforts of multiple societies, publish the efforts, and publicize the results. In addition, the FFHS Publications, Inc., group publishes books and helps promote and sell the publications of member societies' publications.

- Federation of Genealogical Societies (FGS)
  http://www.fgs.org

  This organization consists primarily of United States and Canadian genealogical societies. Individual societies join FGS and it, in turn, provides a forum for society education and communications, and hosts an annual conference.

- National Genealogical Society (NGS)
  http://www.ngsgenealogy.org

  This United States organization consists of individuals and other groups forming a society focused on facilitating U.S. research. NGS provides education in the form of classes, regional lectures, and two annual conferences (the NGS Conference in the States and NGS GENTECH).

- Ancestry.com and FGS Society Hall
  http://www.familyhistory.com/societyhall/main.asp

  MyFamily.com, Inc., its subsidiary Ancestry.com, and FGS have collaborated to provide an online listing of genealogical societies in the United States and Canada with a Web presence and/or e-mail communications. The site, shown in Figure 9-8, is called "Society Hall" and is searchable by name, city, state/province, and postal code.

You also can search for a particular genealogical society by using your favorite search engine and typing the name of the area and the quotation mark-enclosed phrase **"genealogical society"** or **"genealogy society"** in the search box.

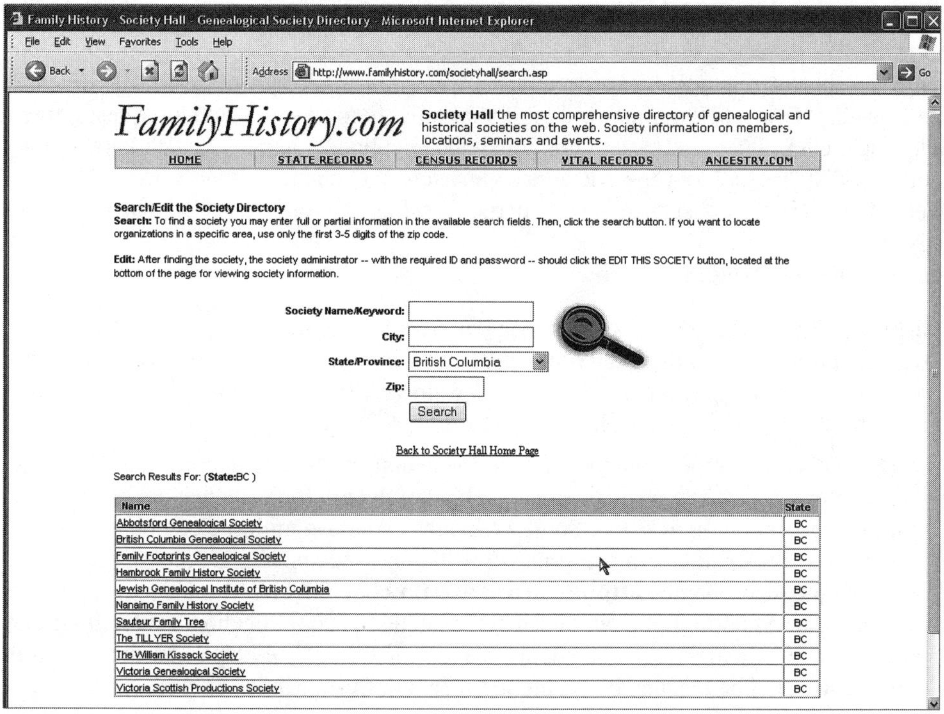

FIGURE 9-8 The Society Hall site is fully searchable for genealogical societies contact information (Used by permission of MyFamily.com, Inc.)

Understand the Concept of Internet Domain Names

We've all heard about the "dot-com" revolution as it relates to the Internet. However, it is essential to understand the concept of those "dots" in order to understand what you're getting *from* the Internet.

The World Wide Web (WWW) is built on a structure of addresses. These addresses are unique identifiers used to route electronic communications between one computer and another. Every computer has a unique address. Think of Web addresses as being like postal addresses. You send a letter to someone by addressing it to:

Mr. John T. Smith
123 Main Street
Anytown, NY 20002

You might also append to that address the indicator "U.S.A." You will also include your own return address so that Mr. Smith can respond to you. Right? You slap a stamp on the envelope and drop it into the post.

Think of the WWW in an analogous way. Instead of using the post office, though, you use your Internet Service Provider (or ISP). Somehow, someone pays for the service that moves data back and forth, like postage.

When you want to access a Web page, you type a Web address (also known as a URL, or Uniform Resource Locator). Every ISP maintains a table that tells them how to route a request going to every other main URL. It's massive, and not unlike the telephone company, which knows how to route your long-distance call to a specific area code, exchange, and telephone number.

A Web address (URL) consists of several parts. Consider the following URL: **http://www.genealogy.com**
The component pieces included here are

- **http://**   This is referred to as the *protocol indicator*. The **http://** represents "**h**yper**t**ext **t**ransfer **p**rotocol," and that really tells the computer that receives your request that you want the main Web page at the address that follows. (There are other protocols, such as **ftp://** for "file transfer protocol.")

- **www**   This really represents the name of the actual machine that stores the Web page you want to request. The **www** is actually a kind of default for a site that doesn't have more than one server computer name. Some Web sites may have multiple computers, and each one may have a separate name. For example, the message boards at Ancestry.com reside on a separate server named **http://boards.ancestry.com.** Other Web sites may have opted to omit the **www** portion of their names in the interest of simplification, especially if they only have one (or a main) server computer. An example would be **http://ahaseminars.com,** which also could be reached by typing **http://www.ahaseminars.com.**

- **.**   The next component is the period, which is known as a "dot." It is simply a delimiter that separates a portion of the URL from another.

- **genealogy**   This is the unique name applied for and assigned to Genealogy.com, Inc., and which is used in part to route communications between Internet users and the MyFamily.com, Inc., main Internet server computer.

- **.**   Here's another "dot" delimiter.

- **com**   The last piece is referred to as the top-level or high-level domain. It is a subclassification used to differentiate between different types of organizations on the Internet. We'll discuss the different top-level domains in a moment.

The combined URL of **www.genealogy.com** is what is referred to as a *domain name* and it must be unique. You also may see it referred to as a "hostname." The term *hostname* refers to the specific computer, or *host* computer, on which all the data and files associated with a domain name reside. Companies, organizations, and individuals request, purchase, and register their unique domain names, and then establish a "home" server address for their domain. When they purchase that address, the organization that administers domain name assignments will communicate the new routing address to all ISPs and servers in the world. In the United States, there are six primary top-level domains that are used. (There are others that have been approved but that are not in any widespread use.) The six top-level domains for the United States and their defined usage are as follows:

.com   These are *commercial* Web sites, used primarily by companies transacting business on the Internet.

.edu   These are *educational* organizations such as colleges, universities, teaching hospitals, etc.

.gov   These are governmental agencies and those operated by the government. Examples would include the White House at **http://www.whitehouse.gov** and the Library of Congress at **http://www.loc.gov.**

.mil   These are U.S. military organizations, such as the U.S. Navy at **http://www.navy.mil.**

.net   These are network administrative sites or noncommercial sites. This domain is a little "foggy" at the moment.

.org   These are nonprofit organizations whose purpose is noncommercial. An example would be the National Genealogical Society at **http://www.ngsgenealogy.org** or the LDS FamilySearch site at **http://www.familysearch.org.**

In the United Kingdom, the Web addresses look a little different, such as in the example of the National Archives address at **http://www.nationalarchives.gov.uk.** You will notice the use of the **.uk** at the end. This is referred to as a country-code top-level domain because it indicates the country in which the Web address is registered. (Web sites in the United States seldom use the domain name of **.us** in Web addresses.)

In the United Kingdom, there are separate domain subcategories similar to the six shown above. They are administered in the U.K. by Nominet.uk at **http://www.nic.uk** and are referred to as Second Level Domains (SLDs).

.ac.uk   This domain is used for academic establishments.

.co.uk   This is the largest SLD in the U.K. and represents commercial enterprises.

.gov.uk   This domain is used for government bodies.

.me.uk   This is used for personal domains and Web pages.

.mod.uk   This domain is used for Ministry of Defence Establishments.

.nhs.uk   This domain is used exclusively by National Health Service (NHS) sites.

.org.uk   This domain is used for nonprofit organizations.

.police.uk   This domain is used exclusively for police forces in the U.K.

.ltd.uk and **.plc.uk**   These SLDs are used only for registered company names.

.net.uk   This domain is used for Internet Service Providers.

.sch.uk   This domain is used for schools.

By understanding the *type* of Web site you are working with, using the domains listed above, you can more readily determine what type and quality of information you are likely to find there. While this is not a hard and fast rule, it is a good guideline, and we'll talk about this more later.

In addition to the domains just discussed, you should know that every country—not just the United Kingdom—has its own country-code top-level domain. By default, all Web addresses using.com, .edu, .gov, .mil, .net, and .org are United States sites. While infrequent, you may occasionally encounter Web sites that have a Web address that ends in .us and this is an indicator that it is a United States site. The following are examples of some country-code top-level domains.

Australia	.au	Greece	.gr	Poland	.pl
Belgium	.be	Iraq	.iq	Slovenia	.si
Brazil	.br	Italy	.it	South Africa	.za
Cambodia	.kh	Japan	.jp	Spain	.es
Canada	.ca	Malta	.mt	Sweden	.se
Chile	.cl	Netherlands	.nl	Switzerland	.ch
Germany	.de	Norway	.no	Yemen	.ye

An excellent Web site that lists all of the country-code top-level domains can be found at **http://www.iana.org/cctld/cctld-whois.htm.**

If you were searching for information about German genealogical resources, you certainly would be interested in those with a country-code top-level domain of .de, which is the country-code top-level domain for Germany (Deutschland). You might even limit your search to sites having that country-code top-level domain in their Web addresses.

Learn a Little More About Web Addresses

Now that you understand the concept of the Web address structure and the use of domain names, there are three more things you will want to know.

First, you may type one URL and press ENTER (or click Go) and end up at a completely different address than what you typed. That's because there are things called *aliases* that are used to reroute requests. These can be used like a letter forwarding service in the post office. Sometimes they are temporary reroutings, and at other times they are used to simplify things for you, the user.

Second, some Internet computer servers treat upper- and lowercase letters as different entities. Therefore, if you see a URL printed in upper-case or mixed-case characters, it's generally a good idea to type it that way. It usually doesn't matter whether or not the hostname part of the URL (the part right after the http://) is uppercase or lowercase. However, it usually does matter if any part of the address that appears after the hostname, if any, is uppercase or lowercase. As an example, let's imagine that you have seen a mythical URL printed in a genealogical publication whose hostname is www.aabbccddeeffgg.com. The site looks as if it may have some information of interest to your research. If the complete URL is shown as **http://www.aabbccddeeffgg.com/genealogy/ AncestorZZ.html,** the chances are good that the host computer at domain www.aabbccddeeffgg.com has a directory setup named "genealogy," and that one of the files is named AncestorZZ.html, and that the filename may be case-sensitive. If you enter a URL in your Web browser that has mixed-case letters and your browser displays an error such as "This page cannot be displayed" or "Not found," try retyping the URL, paying special attention to entering the upper- and lowercase letters exactly as they are shown.

Finally, you've certainly seen Web addresses that are longer and more involved than simply **http://www.myfamily.com.** In many cases you may have seen other structures with more information. Let's just quickly show some examples and let you know what you're seeing. Let's use the country-code top-level domain reference I provided above. Remember **http://www.iana.org/ cctld/cctld-whois.htm** from earlier? This is the Internet Assigned Numbers Assigned (IANA) Web page. It is a nonprofit organization, as indicated by the **.org** domain.

Example 1

- **http://www.iana.org**   This is the default main page for the Internet Assigned Numbers Assigned (IANA) Web page. (It could also be shown as **http://www.iana.org/** with an ending slash.) The default main page, just for your information, is most likely named **index.htm** or **index.html.**

- **http://www.iana.org/cctld**   This is a subsidiary Web page of the IANA site. It is titled the Country-Code Top-Level Domains (ccTLDs) page. The addition of the **/cctld** in the URL shown simply indicates the default main page (again, probably **index.htm** or **index.html**) within a subdirectory named cctld at the IANA Web site.

- **http://www.iana.org/cctld/cctld-whois.htm**   This is an example of, in the IANA Web site and within its subdirectory titled cctld, a specific Web page named **cctld-whois.htm.** Every Web page is a file with a filename extension of usually either **.htm** or **.html.** The three-letter extension was used by systems that could not at the outset of Web pages handle more than a three-position filename extension. Many people still use that structure, but the four-letter version, **.html,** is common as well. It is important, though, that you recognize and use the exact name as shown in order to access the page you want.

- **http://www.iana.org/cctld/cctld-whois.htm#t**   Finally, let me encourage you to go to the IANA site and to **http://www.iana.org/cctld/cctld-whois.htm.** Once there, click on the letter **T** in the alphabetical list at the top of the page. Notice that this takes you down to the beginning of the country-code top-level domain starting with that letter. Look at the URL again, and you will see the same URL but now with the addition of the characters **#t.** What you have is a situation where the author of the Web page has provided a link, in the form of an alphabetical list at the top of the page, and has embedded some hidden code in his/her document to name a specific place in the page. In this case, he/she added a named place called **t** at the top of the country-code top-level domain starting with that letter, and has allowed you to go directly there without having to have scrolled all the way down. Anytime you see a URL with a pound sign (#) followed by some other character(s), you can expect that link to take you to a particular area of a Web page that the Web page author has named. Nice work!

In addition, you may see other things in URLs. A document with the filename extension of **.pdf** is an Adobe Acrobat document, with which you are probably already familiar. Other computer application program-specific file extensions are possible too, but are seldom found in Web pages.

9

Graphic formats' filename extensions of **.jpg, .gif,** and **.bmp** are those most commonly used. The most common sound files have filename extensions of **.wav, .mid,** and **.mp3.** You may also see URLs that include **.asp** in their names, such as **http://www.medicare.gov/NHCompare/Home.asp** and some of the other examples used in this chapter. The filename extension of **.asp** refers to an "active server page" and is commonly used for interactive online applications.

As you can see, there's a lot to all this Web page "stuff," but it really isn't as complicated when you take it apart in pieces.

Strategies for Accessing Sites Whose Addresses May Have Changed

One of the problems I see with the Internet is that Web site addresses change. It's something I often call the "Here this morning, gone this afternoon" syndrome. In the course of your online research, you are certain to encounter Web sites that are no longer where they once were. Some of the sites may have been discontinued, some may have moved, and still others may have restructured their Web sites and changed the organization (and Web page names) of some or all of their resources. Typically, your browser will display an error of some sort. These may include the following:

- HTTP 404 - File not found
- Error 404 - File not found
- The page cannot be found
- You are not authorized to view this page
- Access denied

Don't despair! All is not quite lost. Here are some strategies to help you locate and access Web sites that may have "gone missing."

Strategy 1: Web Sites Whose Addresses Have Changed

A responsible Webmaster will usually make certain to leave a trail behind if the Web site moves to a completely new address. It's kind of like leaving a forwarding order with the postal service when you move. However, in the event the Web page author has not been so accommodating, you may have to do some searching.

In some cases, however, a Web address may simply have changed. This is especially applicable in cases where there is a lengthy URL that may include a directory and/or a Web page document name in its address. In that case, there's a simple methodology you can employ to try to locate the desired content again for yourself.

Let's say that we are looking for a recipe for an apple pie cheesecake in a ginger crust that we found at **http://www.thatsmyhome.com/cheesecake/applepie.html** at the That's My Home Web site at one time. (Yes, good homemade cheesecake is my weakness!) When you head to that Web site today, you'll find that it's not a valid URL. Now, we could certainly use Strategy 2, but if we didn't remember the right text to search, another approach may work better for us. There are several options available to use.

> Try typing the URL again, and delete the letter **l** in **.html.** The Webmaster may have simply changed his/her filename extension naming conventions for the site. In this case, **http://www.thatsmyhome.com/cheesecake/applepie.htm** now locates the recipe page. Yum!

> If that didn't work, start subtracting portions of the Web address, gradually heading back to the root URL. For example, entering the URL **http://www.thatsmyhome.com/cheesecake/** takes us to the cheesecake directory of the That's My Home Web site. Here we find many other recipes for cheesecakes.

> If that didn't work, subtract the directory name of **/cheesecake/** and go to the Web site's root URL at **http://www.thatsmyhome.com,** which is their site's home page.

Strategy 2: Discontinued Sites

If you think a site has been discontinued or moved without leaving a forwarding address, you may use a search engine to try to locate it. We will discuss search engines more fully a little later. However, let's say for now that you can use a search engine to locate a Web site by entering the title of the page. What you need to understand is that, in conducting searches with a search engine, the engine itself is using its own self-compiled index. There are three areas that are used by all search engines in compiling their index:

> The *title* of the Web page (the text that is seen in the blue title bar at the top of your browser)

> The invisible keyword text that a Web page author may embed in his or her Web page that is known as *meta tags*

> The text that appears anywhere in the *body* of the Web page (and this includes filenames of graphics, sounds, and other files in the page)

Therefore, when you enter a single word for a search, it may be located anywhere within these areas of the Web pages. As you'll see later, the Advanced Search facility of many search engines may allow you to specify where in the Web page the word or phrase is to be sought. However, for now, let's just say that you will use the Simple Search facility of any Web search engine to locate information that might have been in the Web page you are seeking.

Let's use one of the currently popular search engines called Google, which can be located at **http://www.google.com** or **http://www.google.co.uk.** For purposes of searching, you will enter either a single word/keyword or a phrase in the search box of the search engine.

> To enter a word, simply type it in the box.

> To enter an exact phrase (two or more words that must be contiguous to one another in the precise order you have typed them), enclose them in double quotation marks as follows:

"ansibelle penelope swords"

For our example, let's say we are searching for a Web page about genealogy for the WILSON surname and that the page may have moved. In this case, we will enter an exact phrase as follows:

"wilson genealogy web page"

You will find the two links, Wilson Lineage at **http://www.2computerguys.com/lineage/wilson.html** and Storme's Genealogy Page at **http://www.ufsia.ac.be/~estorme/genealogy.html.**

Using the Find function discussed earlier, search both of these Web pages for the text **wilson genealogy web page** we used above. (Don't include the quotation marks this time in the Find box or you won't find anything.) In the first Web page, the text appears at the bottom of the page. In the second Web page, you will find a link to the Matt Wilson Genealogy Web Page at **http://web2.airmail.net/dwidener/** and a scanned image of an obituary. (Notice the text we used is part of this link's title.)

If the text for which we were searching was only included in an otherwise non-visible meta tag in the Web page code, we could perform a Find function on the Web page and would not locate that text anywhere in the Web page. This is the primary reason why, sometimes, when you use a search engine, there appears to be no reason why a certain Web page is included in the search results list.

Both of these strategies can be used in any situation where you have a URL and the Web page isn't coming up. If the search engine you use "suggests" another Web site or URL, you can always try that as well.

Structure Effective Searches to Locate Information

The Web is an enormous place, currently consisting of billions of individual pages. In reality, we can only guess at its actual size, and it is growing at a fast pace. Because it is relatively easy for anyone to put information on the Web, there is a good possibility that somebody, somewhere, has created a Web page that contains information you might find useful for your genealogical research. The trick, then, is to locate that one useful page among the billions of pages out there.

It is important that you learn how to use, in a logical, structured way, the two primary search tools on the Internet: search engines and directories. We're going to explore each one in detail, after which you should practice, practice, and practice in order to become an expert Internet searcher.

Define the Difference Between Search Engines and Directories

Early in the development of the World Wide Web, directories were the way of the world. Before long, search engines appeared. The problem is, however, that over time the directories have added search facilities to their sites and search engines have added directories to their sites. For example, the largest of the directories, Yahoo!, now embeds a search engine that can either search within Yahoo! itself or reach out onto the Web to search millions of Web pages. Google, on the other hand, as the largest search engine currently, also has created and maintains an impressive directory. *Both* Yahoo! *and* Google include facilities to search the Web for graphics and audio files, as well as to locate news and financial information. With that in mind, let's define each of the tools and what distinguishes one from another.

A *search engine* is an index of Web pages that has been created by a mechanical contrivance known as a spider, a robot, or simply a "bot." The key here is that the index is mechanically created, with very little human intervention. You will remember that I said earlier that there are three indexed components in a Web page that a search index indexes. They are the title, the meta tags, and the body of the Web page.

You also will remember that I said that when you enter a single word for a search, it may be located anywhere within these areas of the Web pages. As you'll see later, the Advanced Search facility of many search engines may allow you to specify where in the Web page the word or phrase is to be sought.

Search engines employ the use of structured searches, using words, keywords, and phrases to match entries in their indices. Search engines offer both a simple and an advanced search facility, the second of which allows you to select criteria to narrow your search results. Others offer another kind of advanced search, using Boolean search operators, which we will discuss later.

Examples of the leading search engines today include Google (shown in Figure 9-9 and located at **http://www.google.com, http://www.google.co.uk,** and other addresses in other countries),

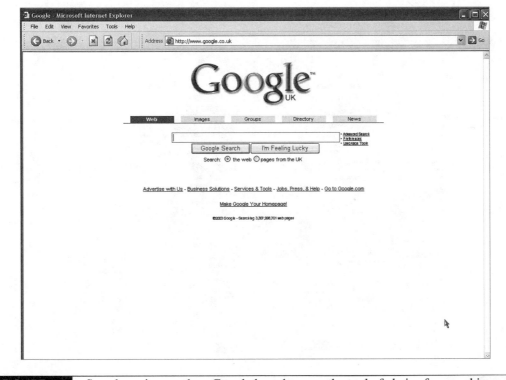

FIGURE 9-9   Search engines such as Google have become the tool of choice for searching the Web.

AltaVista (located at **http://www.altavista.com**), Teoma (at **http://www.teoma.com**), AlltheWeb (located at **http://www.alltheweb.com**), and a number of others.

A *directory* is another Internet tool that, unlike the search engine, is created entirely by human editors who look at Web pages and assign them to logical or appropriate categories. Broad categories can be broken down into narrower subcategories and sub-subcategories. This hierarchical structure can be used to browse deeper and deeper to narrow your focus and to locate materials you seek. A directory may also embed a search facility, which enables you to search in just that hierarchical category or to search the entire directory. Some hybrid directories also may allow you to expand your search onto the Web to locate non-categorized materials not included in the directory, graphic files, audio files, news wire services, and other resources.

Among the largest directories today are Yahoo! (shown in Figure 9-10 and located at **http://www.yahoo.com**), Open Directory (located at **http://dmoz.org**), LookSmart (located at **http://www.LookSmart.com**), and several others. Other important reference directories you will want to include in your Favorites list are the Librarians' Index to the Internet (located at **http://www.lii.org**) and the Internet Public Library (located at **http://www.ipl.org**). Each of these large directories has links

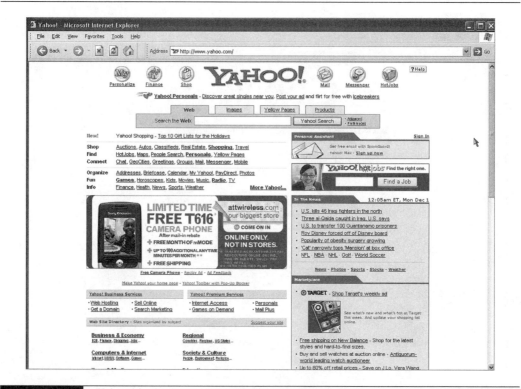

FIGURE 9-10   Yahoo! is the largest directory on the Internet, with local versions in many countries in the native language.

to several million different Web pages that have been compiled by their human editors. Because new links are added to a directory by editors, it may take some time (months, perhaps) before a new Web page will appear in a general directory.

There is one more search tool that should be mentioned: the *metasearch engine*. A metasearch engine is another hybrid creature, one which allows you to enter a search in one place and have that engine simultaneously search multiple search engines for you. Does this sound like Nirvana? Hardly! The results may be overwhelming, often coming from lightweights in the searching stratosphere of the Web, often yielding duplicate search results, and/or omitting important leads. Many experienced researchers use metasearch engines only to learn which of the individual search engines has the most or the better search results. However, a metasearch tool can save a great deal of time and can often locate higher quality results very quickly. Among the major metasearch engines in use today are Dogpile (shown in Figure 9-11 and located at **http://www.dogpile.com**), MetaCrawler (at **http://www.metacrawler.com**), Mamma (at **http://www.mamma.com**), and Vivisimo (at **http://www.vivisimo.com**).

Visit the Best Site on the Web to Learn About Search Engines and Directories

The search engines, directories, and metasearch engines described and named above only begin to scratch the surface. The very best site on the Web to learn all about search tools around the globe is SearchEngineWatch.com, located at **http://www.searchenginewatch.com** and shown in Figure 9-12. The editor, Danny Sullivan, has been reviewing, rating, and comparing search engines

9

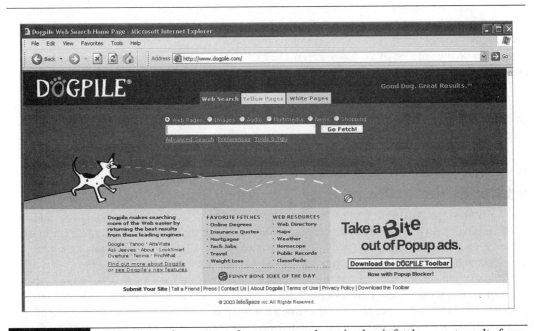

FIGURE 9-11   Dogpile is a funny name for a metasearch engine but it fetches great results from multiple resources on the Internet.

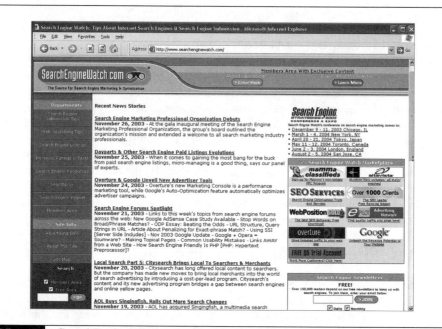

FIGURE 9-12   SearchEngineWatch.com provides unrivaled information about and comparisons of Internet search tools.

and other information tools for more than a decade and his information is the best. On the main screen at this site is a link labeled Search Engine Listings. Click there to find a categorized list of search engines. Within each category are detailed descriptions and reviews of search engines. Also on the menu on the left side of the main screen, click on Search Engine Resources for the absolute best Search Engine Tutorials anywhere. These are your very best self-instructional materials.

There is a massive amount of information on this Web site. Since search engines and directories are constantly changing their products to offer new and improved services *and* to draw new advertisers, it is important to get new information early on. For that reason, Mr. Sullivan also produces a weekly subscription e-mail newsletter to which you can subscribe.

Select a "Comfortable" Search Engine and Really Get to Know It

Once you've had the opportunity to peruse the impressive lists of available search engines, and to explore some of them for yourself, you will want to select one or two that you want to use for much or most of your Web research. Just because you've always used Google, though, don't become complacent and just decide that's the one you already know and love.

While Google's index is large and the screen is easy to use (uncluttered, in other words), that doesn't mean that it does everything. For example, if you were unsure how to spell the word "gray" or "grey," some search engines allow you to use what is called a *wildcard* character in place of the "a" or "e" in the word in order to get matches on both spellings. AltaVista does so using the asterisk (*) character and Northern Light does so with the percentage (%) character. Others do not offer it, or SearchEngineWatch was unable to confirm that it worked. (Visit the link at **http://www.searchenginewatch.com/facts/article.php/2155981** for a detailed list of Search Engine Features.)

Once you have selected the "most comfortable" search engine for you, you want to become really comfortable with it. What does that mean? It means you want to learn how to *really* use it and use it effectively—first time and every time from now on out. The way to do this is to locate its Help materials, read them, print them, try the examples provided, reread the text again, memorize it, and then place the text in a polypropylene sheet protector close to your computer for easy reference.

If you are looking for the Help material for Google, go to the main screen and then click on the Advanced Search link to the right of the search box. Then, on the Advanced Search screen, click on the link labeled "Advanced Search Tips." You'll find a link labeled "Help" on both the simple and Advanced Search screens at AltaVista, as shown in Figure 9-13. On AlltheWeb's Advanced Search screen, look for the link labeled "Query language guide." At Teoma, the help is located at the bottom of the first, simple search screen and is a link labeled "Learn How Teoma Works." And at Yahoo!, look for the ?Help icon in the upper-right corner of the main screen or the "Help" link on any other screen.

The key to your success is really getting to know the tool and getting to know its strengths (and any weaknesses). Your investment of time now will pay huge dividends later when you're heads-down seeking that research path around the ubiquitous brick wall.

9

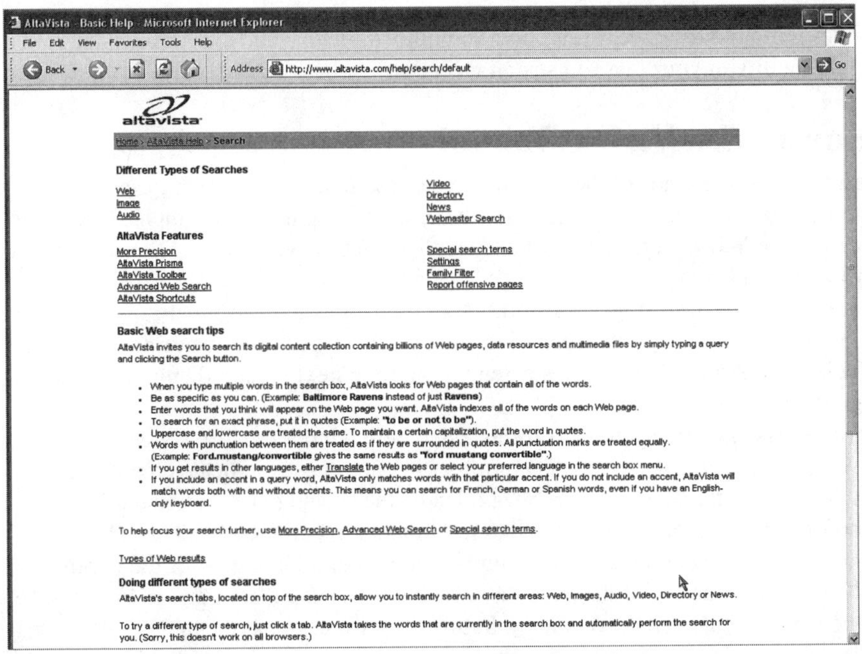

FIGURE 9-13   AltaVista provides concise guidance for all its functions in its Help area.

Structure Effective Searches to Locate Information

We now come to the crux of all this preparation. I know you thought all this foundation work above was extraneous "stuff," but now we come to the meat and potatoes of the process. Now we will *really* begin to search for real content. There are some simple rules of thumb to use in your work with searching the Web. These apply to most search engines. However, read the Help materials for your favorite engine to get the best results.

■ To enter a word, simply type it in the box—*in all lowercase letters*. (Never use uppercase or mixed-case.) Most search directories and search engines don't care, but there are a few that still differentiate between uppercase, lowercase, and mixed-case. If you use either all uppercase or mixed-case, those that recognize a difference will only return matches on Web pages that have your search term(s) typed in the exact same manner. If you type in all lowercase, however, every directory and search engine will return *all* matches, regardless of case in the original Web page.

■ Avoid the use of a plural if you can avoid it. If you are searching for matches about bluebirds, enter the word as a singular "bluebird" and most search engines will give matches for both "bluebird" and "bluebirds." When entering a surname that ends in an "s," you may want to enter it *without* the "s" in order to see what matches you will get in your search results list.

■ To enter an exact phrase in which two or more words must be contiguous to one another in the precise order you type them, make sure you enclose them in the double quotation marks to make them one entity.

These rules will hold true when searching in both a directory and a search engine, but again, check the Help facility in your favorite search tool.

Learn How to *Really* Use Yahoo!

As the largest and most respected of the Internet directories, Yahoo! occupies a special place in many people's research. To illustrate some of the points here, we need to use some graphic screen captures.

First, on the main Yahoo! screen, you should scroll down until you see the Directory area, which is shown in Figure 9-14.

The larger titles are the categories, and the smaller ones are the most popularly chosen subcategories. There can be any number of levels of subcategories, depending on the subject area. Let's select the Arts & Humanities category, and the next screen displayed looks like the one in Figure 9-15.

There are, in this case, many subcategories listed here. Under the Top Categories are some things that will be grouped By Region. The number in parentheses indicates the number of items you will find if you click there, in this case 59242. Under the heading of Additional Categories, there are many choices. Most of these have the content numbers in parentheses. The subcategory titles give you a great clue as to content, and the numbers are a good indication of the depth of content.

You will notice near the top of the page the area that looks like the picture in Figure 9-16. This shows you the hierarchical position we are in. In this case, we began at the main directory page and clicked in the Arts area. You will notice that the word Directory is underlined in blue. It is a quick

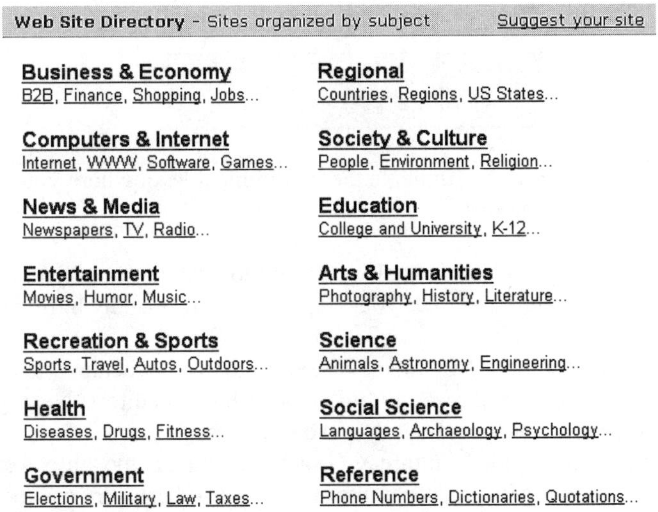

Web Site Directory - Sites organized by subject
Suggest your site
Business & Economy
B2B, Finance, Shopping, Jobs...
Regional
Countries, Regions, US States...
Computers & Internet
Internet, WWW, Software, Games...
Society & Culture
People, Environment, Religion...
News & Media
Newspapers, TV, Radio...
Education
College and University, K-12...
Entertainment
Movies, Humor, Music...
Arts & Humanities
Photography, History, Literature...
Recreation & Sports
Sports, Travel, Autos, Outdoors...
Science
Animals, Astronomy, Engineering...
Health
Diseases, Drugs, Fitness...
Social Science
Languages, Archaeology, Psychology...
Government
Elections, Military, Law, Taxes...
Reference
Phone Numbers, Dictionaries, Quotations...

FIGURE 9-14 The directory listings area on the Yahoo! site

Yahoo! Directory Arts - Microsoft Internet Explorer
Address http://dir.yahoo.com/Arts/
YAHOO! directory
Directory Home - Yahoo! - Help
Arts
Directory > Arts
Search
Advanced Search | Suggest a Site
email this category to a friend
CATEGORIES
Top Categories
By Region (59242)
Additional Categories
Art History (1592)
Art Weblogs@
Artists (1976)
Arts Therapy@
Awards (16)
Booksellers@
Censorship (12)
Chats and Forums (22)
Crafts (945)
Criticism and Theory (32)
Cultural Policy@
Cultures and Groups (326)
Design Arts (6392)
Education (639)
Employment (41)
Events (308)
Humanities (56817)
Institutes (35)
Museums, Galleries, and Centers (1043)
News and Media (248)
Organizations (311)
Performing Arts (7513)
Reference (28)
Shopping and Services@
Visual Arts (19877)
Web Directories (52)
SPONSOR RESULTS
Dick Blick Art Materials
Art Materials & Artistic Merchandise
Seized Property - Art Auction
Buy Framed Art Prints
AllPosters.com: Art Prints and Framing
See your message here...

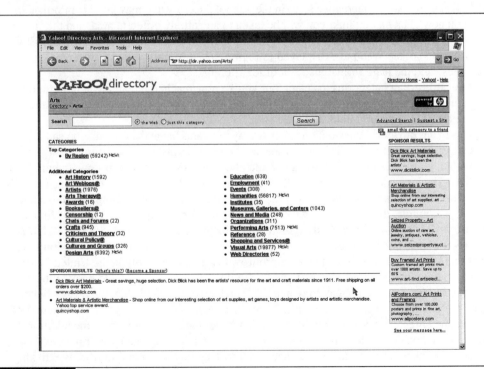

FIGURE 9-15 The Arts Category screen in the Yahoo! directory

The "thread crumbs" indicate the hierarchical level where you are located in the Yahoo! directory.

link back to the main directory. This area is also referred to as the "thread crumbs" area, and allows you (like Hansel and Gretel) to retrace your steps without repeatedly hitting your browser's Back button.

In addition, you will see the little New! icon beside some topic subcategories. These indicate that there has been new content added recently by Yahoo!'s human editors. Next, you will see the @ sign after some subcategories. More about that in a moment.

Let's click on the subcategory titled Culture & Groups. Looking at the "thread crumbs" area, you now will see that we have progressed deeper into another sub-subcategory and the new hierarchy is listed. You can click on any of these underlined links to move to that level.

On the Cultures & Groups list, you should now see a link labeled as Jewish@. That little @ sign is an indicator that, if you click on that link, you will be directed to a different hierarchical tree. It is indicative that there may be alternative areas in the Yahoo! directory that may provide information for you. If you now click on that link, you will be taken to an entirely different area, and the "thread crumbs" shown will indicate that you're now on a completely different area. Click on the Jewish@ link. When you do so, the Web page displayed in Figure 9-17 certainly shows a different set of "thread crumbs" and the page format also is a little different.

There are still further categories to select, but you've now reached the area where individual site listings are displayed. You will also note Sponsor Results in boxes at the right side of the screen; these are paid sponsors' links and messages.

If you have your browser's View option set to display the status bar at the bottom, you can move your mouse over the individual site listings and see the Web address displayed. (To turn on the display of the status bar, go to your browser's menu bar and click on View. On the pull-down menu, click on Status Bar.) The long address you see on the status bar is actually two things. First, it is Yahoo!'s internal address for this particular link. Secondly, at the end it contains the complete Web address of this site. For example, the address shown on the status bar for the American Guild of Judaic Art in Figure 9-17 is actually **http://srd.yahoo.com/S=293038:D1/CS=293038/SS=16012892/ *http://www.jewishart.org.** However, the site's real URL is simply **http://www. jewishart.org.** Looking at that URL, we can tell that it is a nonprofit Web site, and probably in the United States.

Let's look at one more important way to use Yahoo! before we move on. Go back to the main Yahoo! screen and type the word **genealogy** into the search box there, and click the Search button. You will be presented with search results from the Web, as well as the menus shown in Figure 9-18.

Note that the Directory tab is highlighted and that under the search box are some additional links. You can click on one of these links to initiate another search using that term or phrase. Also note that there are other tabs labeled Web, Images, Yellow Pages, News, and Products. By clicking

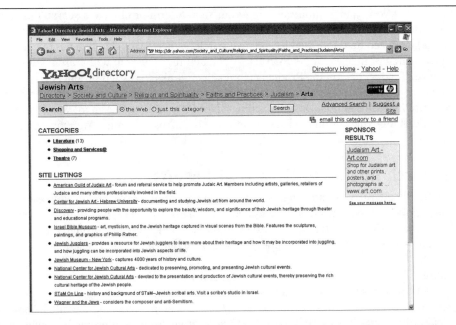

FIGURE 9-17   Clicking on Jewish@ takes you to a different hierarchical area of the Yahoo! directory.

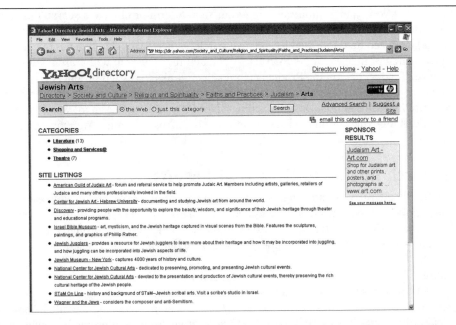

FIGURE 9-18   Search results in the Yahoo! directory

on the tab labeled Web, and without retyping your search term or phrase, a search outside of Yahoo!—on the Web—has been performed and the results are displayed. Sponsor results (paid sponsor links) are listed first, followed by the real search results. By clicking on the Images tab, you can initiate a search of images on the Internet. A click on the News tab will search news services for news stories, and a click on the Products tab results in links to related products.

As you can see, Yahoo! offers a tremendous amount of material in not only the directory area but in its flexibility with additional search facilities. Now, if you thought Yahoo! was an experience, imagine the flexibility you can find in locating information across the entire Web through a search engine!

Use a Search Engine to Get Great Results

Remember the simple rules of thumb again about using a word, multiple words, and exact phrases. These rules apply to directories and to search engines. However, a search engine is a bit more sophisticated than a directory. It really has to be in order to help you sift through all the results that it may have indexed, and to let you employ those critical thinking skills to fine-tune your searches for the very best results.

The Simple Search or Basic Search screen is typically the main screen you reach at any search engine Web site. It allows you to slap in a word or two or a phrase, and off you go. Too often, though, a researcher may believe that this is all there is to using a search engine. And while it may give you results, those results may be so massive as to be overwhelming and probably contain a whole lot of garbage. You may get a sense of all this from the first screen of your search results list. No one I know has the time to cull through 175,218 results, and I personally would be skeptical of a search result from Billy Ray Bob's Down Home Page of Genieology! (And yes, that would be misspelled, wouldn't it?) You need to narrow the field. That's where the Advanced Search screen options may help. Look at the Advanced Search screen from Google in Figure 9-19.

Don't forget to check the Advanced Search Tips (the Help text) link in the upper right-hand corner of the screen.

If you caught the options presented for the Simple Search above, consider them once again in light of the Find Results boxes shown in Figure 9-19. Consider all your options again.

- **With all the words**   Entering a single word asks for a search for all Web pages that have that word anywhere in the page. Entering multiple words asks for a search for Web pages that have *both or all* those words located anywhere in the page and in any order.

- **With the exact phrase**   Entering multiple words here will have the same effect as you would have had on the Simple Search screen had you enclosed them in double quotation marks. Here, however, you don't have to enclose them in double quotation marks. You simply enter the words you want treated as a phrase and they will be automatically enclosed in quotation marks when the search begins.

- **With at least one of the words**   Entering multiple words asks for a search for Web pages that have *any single one* of those words located anywhere in the page.

- **Without the words**   Entering one or more words here has the effect of excluding from your search results any pages in which one or more of these words might be included located anywhere in the page.

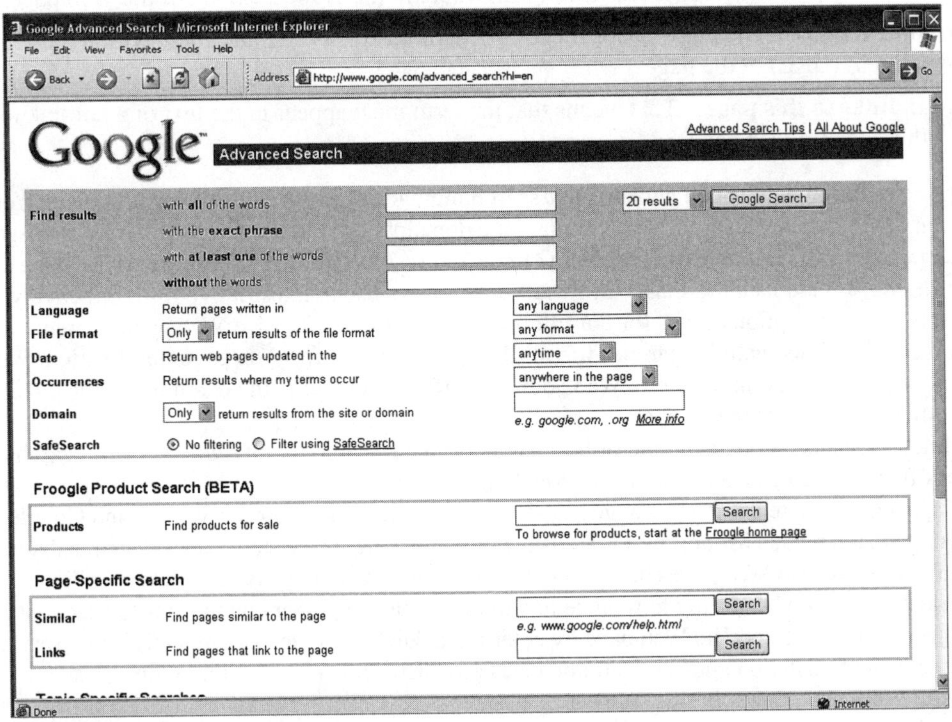

FIGURE 9-19 The Advanced Search screen of Google

The Advanced Search screen also gives you the option of narrowing your search to only Web pages written in a specific language. (You may need to download from your browser's development Web site the character set to install to display certain characters, such as Traditional Chinese, Simplified Chinese, Cyrillic, Korean, Kanji, or others.)

You may opt to have the search engine return only certain document types (or exclude Web pages with those types). These include Adobe PDF files, Adobe PostScript files, Microsoft Word, Microsoft Excel spreadsheets, Microsoft PowerPoint presentations, and Rich Text Format (.RTF) files.

You may specify how current a Web page must be in order to be returned. However, remember that many Web pages contain no date information to make this type of specification 100 percent reliable.

One very helpful feature is the Occurrences specification. Here you can designate where in the Web page the term(s)/phrase appears. This includes the following:

■ **Anywhere in the page**

■ **In the title of the page**   This means in the blue title bar at the top of your browser window.

- **In the text of the page**   This means anywhere in the viewable body of the Web page.
- **In the URL of the page**   This means the term must appear somewhere within the Web address (URL) of the page.
- **In links to this page**   This means that the term must appear in the text of a hot link to this specific Web page.

The next option, which can narrow your search dramatically, is the selection of domain. You can specify Web pages whose addresses contain the domain(s) you indicate *or* you can cause pages from certain domains not to be included in your search results. Be sure to read the Help at the search engine you are using to make sure you know how to use this restrictive filter effectively.

The SafeSearch option allows for the filtering of potentially offensive Web page content.

Two other options include searches for similar Web pages or for Web page that link to a Web page. In either case, you may enter a Web address (URL) as shown in the example on the page to locate other Web sites of these types.

While Google is a good example of how the Advanced Search facility works, other search engines offer similar or better search functionality.

Of special note here are the language translation tools available at both AltaVista and Google. AltaVista's search results list provides a Translate option. Using AltaVista's Babel Fish translator, you can easily translate Web pages between many languages. You may also translate specific text, which can be a boon when trying to write letters to recipients in another country who speak another language, or translate a specific Web page by entering its URL. Google also offers a similar service. While the exact translation and idiomatic nuances are far from perfect, you may just be able to successfully translate pages in this fashion.

Another type of search option is the Boolean Search, named after English mathematician George Boole (b. 2 November 1815 and d. 8 December 1864). Boolean comparative mathematical logic reduces otherwise complex comparisons between words and phrases to algebraic expressions. Don't be frightened off, especially if (like me) you did not excel in mathematics in school. It really is quite simple.

If you remember the old logical expressions of "*if a, then b*" and "*if $a = b$ and $c = d$ and $e \neq f$, then g*" then you are definitely on the right track here. It really *is* very simple. What Boole came up with was a way of comparing conditions, and if the comparison produced a "True" condition, then the comparison continued. As it turns out, this works beautifully with searching Web pages.

There really are four Boolean search operators, and these are used to compare words in your searches.

- **AND**   This operator joins two terms and indicates that *both* term a *and* term b must be present to satisfy the condition and return a match.
- **OR**   This operator joins two terms and indicates that *either* term a *or* term b must be present to satisfy the condition and return a match.

- **NOT** This operator indicates that the term that follows it must not be present in order to satisfy the condition and return a match.

- **NEAR** This operator is sometimes used to join two terms and to specify that they must be within a certain number of words of one another in order to satisfy the condition and return a match. The number of intervening words will vary by search engine, that is, when the search engine supports this function. Only AltaVista provides the NEAR operator, and it means that the two terms must be within ten words of each other.

So, looking at Figure 9-20, you'll see the following relationship between the Boolean operators and the data entry boxes above.

- AND is assumed in the With All The Words box
- OR is assumed in the With At Least One Of The Words box
- NOT is assumed in the Without The Words box

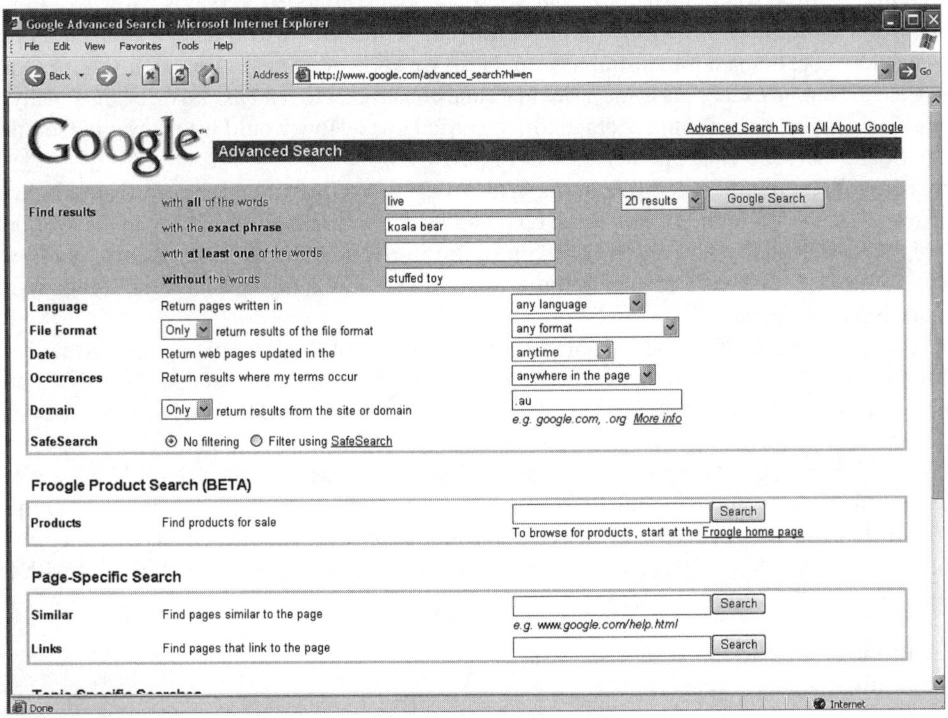

FIGURE 9-20 Use Google's Advanced Search to narrow your searches.

As an example, let's say we are searching for information on the United States Civil War Battle of Chickamauga and want to locate information about losers in the battle. (Remember our rules of thumb?) What we really want to find is Web pages that include the words "Chickamauga" and "loser" (and not the plural, "losers"). So let's enter on the Simple Search screen of Google the following:

chickamauga loser

The result is 172 search results, the first of which is a Web site at **http://ngeorgia.com/people/ rosecrans.html** that describes William S. Rosecrans as the loser of one of the most disgraceful routs for the Union Army at Chickamauga.

If you proceed now to the Advanced Search screen at Google, let's try something else. This time, enter the words **chickamauga loser** in the With All The Words box and the word **rosecrans** in the Without The Words box. Then press the button labeled Google Search. This time, the search has been narrowed somewhat to 154 results, and that is because we eliminated the Rosecrans name from the search.

Let's now try a more extended search situation. We might want information about live koala bears from their natural source, Australia, but nothing about stuffed toy versions. How would we locate it? Well, for starters, we will want to narrow our search to Australian Web sites, and the country-code top-level domain for Australia is .au. Next, we know we want information about koala bears, so we can craft an exact phrase (as a singular) and construct it to read as "koala bear." Finally, we want to include live animals and exclude toy or stuffed ones. How would we enter it in Google's Advanced Search screen? Take another look at Figure 9-20.

In this case, I entered the word **live** in the With All The Words box and the words **koala bear** (without quotes) in the With The Exact Phrase box. I added the words **stuffed** and **toy** in the Without The Words box, and finally entered the domain of **.au** in the Domain field for Australia. The result was 140 results. If I had not specified the Australian domain, my results were 3,480. What a difference a domain makes!

So far, so good. Now, let's look at some shorthand for two of the Boolean operators that can be used sometimes. You can use the plus character (+) instead of the typed-out operator AND; you also can use the minus character (–) instead of the typed-out operator NOT. Pretty simple, eh? And, of course, you can create exact phrases by enclosing them in the double quotation marks (" ").

In all search engines, entering multiple words in a sequence without the use of AND or a + character has the same effect as saying, "I want to find Web pages with both this term AND that term." You also could type the AND or the + character, but they are ignored. If I type either of the Boolean searches below in Google, though, I still get Web pages in the search results with the Rosecrans name.

chickamauga AND loser NOT rosecrans
chickamauga +loser – rosecrans

The truth is that, unless I use the Google Advanced Search facility to enter **chickamauga loser** in the With All The Words box and **rosecrans** in the Without The Words box, I will not successfully be able to narrow the search results and cull out pages with the Rosecrans reference.

When I use AltaVista, I can accomplish the elimination of the Rosecrans reference by using the Advanced Search screen shown in Figure 9-21 and typing the same terms into its search template. However, I also could search with the Boolean expression by simply typing:

chickamauga AND loser AND NOT rosecrans
or
chickamauga + loser – rosecrans

The point of this exercise is to illustrate that different search engines handle the searches differently. Likewise, the number of search results may vary because of the amount of the Web that their bots search and index, coupled with the search logic that the engine uses. Please remember, after all of this, that the SearchEngineWatch.com Web site contains a wealth of information. After you have explored searching for a while, then return to **http://www.searchenginewatch.com/facts/article.php/2155981** for a list of many features of the search engines, variations on the Boolean search operations, and other typing shortcuts that can help you become a master searcher.

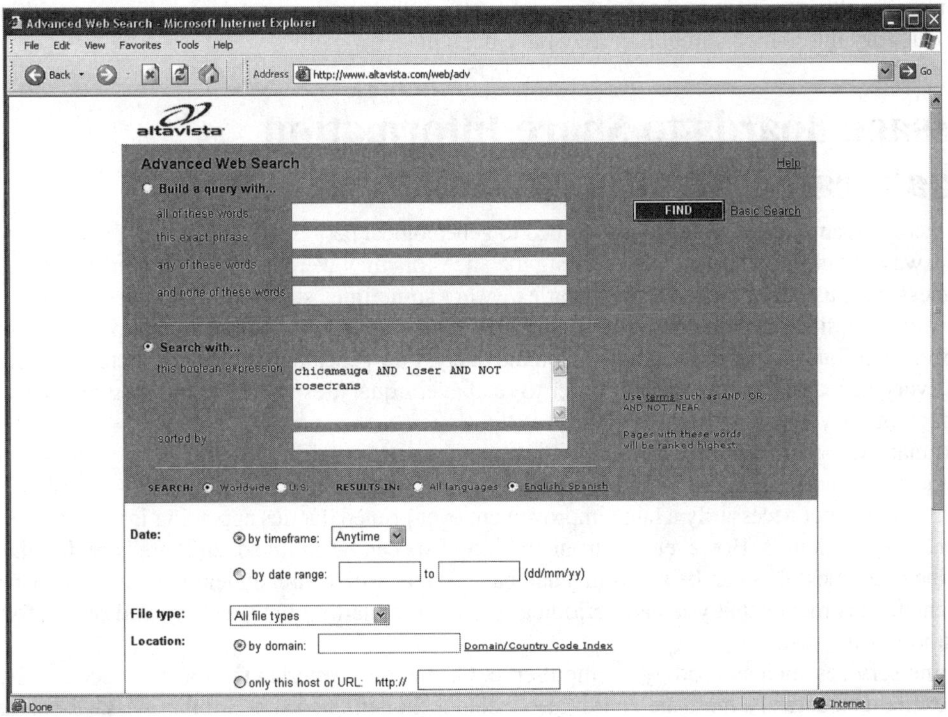

FIGURE 9-21   Sample of using the AltaVista Advanced Search with a Boolean expression

Use Other Really Helpful Search Engines

Google and AltaVista are not the only search engines around. Some of the other, newer search engines that produce interesting and helpful results are the Teoma search engine and the Vivisimo metasearch engine. You might want to try them out.

Enter your search term, exact phrase, or structured Boolean search in the Teoma engine (located at **http://www.teoma.com**), and you will be presented with a three-focus Web page. First, you will see a Results list of Relevant Web pages. To the right of the screen, you will see a Refine list, showing suggestions to help narrow your search. Click on one of these and your search is resubmitted using the new term or phrase. Please note that there may be more "refinements" listed than the ones you at first glimpsed. Finally, you will see a Resources list, which contains collections of links from other experts and enthusiasts on the subject.

Vivisimo (located at **http://vivisimo.com**) is a metasearch engine and performs its job in a little different way. It actually could be called a "clustering" metasearch engine. Enter a term and you will be presented with a search results screen that contains a list of the first batch (or cluster) of matches. On the left side of the screen are cluster results that are, in effect, categorized search results. Click on a category to display and/or expand the list of subcategories. This engine can help you narrow results into more manageable chunks, although you may sometimes disagree with the cluster category into which something may have been placed.

Use Message Boards to Share Information and Collaborate with Others

Before there was an Internet, genealogists turned to genealogical periodicals (magazines, newsletters, etc.) as a way to publish a question concerning the ancestors they were trying to learn more about. These messages, usually referred to as "queries," were sometimes successful, but even so, they usually were not, since the odds weren't usually very high that the right person (a person who knew the answer to the question) would stumble upon the query. Few genealogists would have the patience to scan every genealogy publication in order to read every query, especially a backlog of issues going back many years.

Fortunately, the Internet brought a new tool: the electronic mailing list. A query could be sent to a single e-mail address, and it would be automatically re-sent to every mailing list "subscriber." By itself, this was not necessarily a huge improvement over printed queries appearing in subscription magazines or newsletters. However, electronic mailing lists can be archived, and often are. In other words, the older messages can be saved in a database and, as we've already learned, databases can be searched. This means that you can periodically go to the mailing list's archive and search for information of interest.

Online services such as Prodigy, CompuServe, GEnie, and America Online provided another way to exchange queries: a message board (also called a "bulletin board"). Similar message boards could be found on Bulletin Board Systems (BBSs) and as part of another, older tool referred to as Usenet. Eventually, message boards devoted to genealogy were established on the Web, at such places as FamilyHistory.com (located at **http://www.familyhistory.com**), GenForum at Genealogy.com (located at **http://genforum.genealogy.com**), and Ancestry.com (a merger of the old RootsWeb message boards and the newer Ancestry.com boards, located at **http://boards.ancestry.com**).

A message board works like a cork bulletin board found in a typical office or school. Someone posts a message, and hopes that interested parties will see it (and perhaps respond appropriately to it). As with a cork bulletin board, the messages may not remain posted forever. However, as a general rule, genealogy message boards tend to keep messages posted as long as possible and then the older messages are archived elsewhere. The archived message board contents are then treated much like a database, and its data can be searched.

Just to make certain that you clearly understand the differences between a mailing list and a message board, let's explore and discuss both.

What Is a Mailing List?

A mailing list is a facility on the Internet that uses e-mail to distribute a single message to all subscribers. There literally are thousands of genealogical mailing lists to fulfill almost every interest you may have. These include the following:

9

Surnames	Geographical locations all over the world
City directories	Record types
Ethnic groups	Religious records
Fraternal groups	Immigration and naturalization
Military records	Cemeteries
Genealogical software	Search methodologies

The organization that hosts the vast majority of English language mailing lists is RootsWeb (**http://www.rootsweb.com**), and you can access their directory of available mailing lists at **http://lists.rootsweb.com.**

It is easy to subscribe to a mailing list. For example, let's say that I am researching my ancestors who lived in Rome (Floyd County), Georgia. The Floyd County mailing list would be a good place to learn more from people who also are researching there. I might learn about the history of the area, archives of records of various types, and I might even meet someone who also is researching the same surnames that I am researching.

From the RootsWeb mailing list directory (see above), I work my way to the State of Georgia, and then select Floyd County from the list of counties. Figure 9-22 shows the Web page that is displayed.

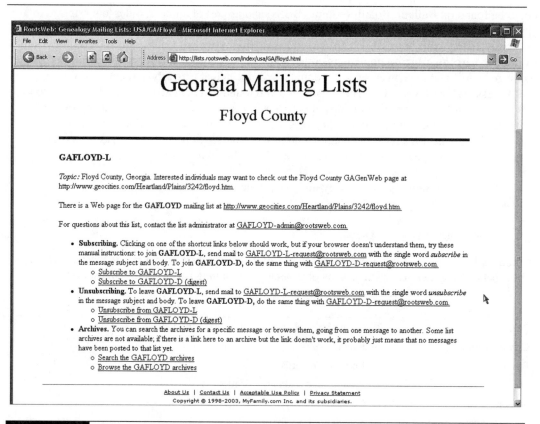

If you study Figure 9-22 for a few minutes, you will note several important pieces of information.

- ▪ The list is named GAFLOYD-L.
- ▪ There is a reference to a Web page for this county at the USGenWeb Project site that might be of interest to us.
- ▪ There are instructions for subscribing to:
    - ▪ The GAFLOYD-L mailing list (individual messages)
    - ▪ The GAFOYD-D mailing list (digest mode)
- ▪ There are instructions for unsubscribing.
- ▪ There is an archive of older messages that may be browsed or searched, using the links shown here.

The difference between the GAFLOYD-L mailing list (individual messages) and the GAFOYD-D mailing list (digest mode) is important to you as a subscriber. Subscribing to the mailing list whose name ends in –L will result in your receiving a copy of every message as an individual message. This could bury you with e-mail if this turns out to be a busy mailing list. Subscribing to the mailing list whose name ends in –D will result in your receiving a digest version. This consists of a single e-mail in which all the messages generated in a specific period will be included. There typically is a list of subject headers at the top of the message so that you can tell what types of information are in these messages, followed by the actual messages.

You will remember the Find function (which you can access by pressing the CTRL-F keys) from our previous discussion. When you subscribe to a digest version of a mailing list and receive potentially a lengthy e-mail with a number of messages inside, the Find function allows you to quickly search for surnames or specific words in which you are interested. This can be a real timesaver.

When you subscribe to a mailing list, you will receive a welcome message. Print and save this message! I personally maintain a file folder labeled "Mailing Lists" in which I keep these messages. The welcome message will provide important information to you to help you maximize your use of the mailing list:

- The purpose of the mailing list
- How to subscribe and unsubscribe
- How to contact the list administrator
- How to browse and/or search the list archives (if available)

By keeping the welcome message, you will be able to quickly locate important information about it when you need it. In particular, if you decide you want to get off the list, you will have instructions about how to unsubscribe. If there are problems with the list, including a nasty person who is abusing his/her privilege of participating, the e-mail address of the list owner is invaluable.

When you join a mailing list, it is a good idea to "lurk before you leap." In other words, watch the exchanges of information and messages for a week or two before you jump in. You may find that this isn't really the mailing list you want, and you can unsubscribe.

When you subscribe, also browse or search the archives if there is one for answers to any basic questions you have. People on mailing lists cringe when a new person (a "newbie") jumps in and asks a question that has been asked and answered a hundred times.

Last but not least, there are three important rules you should follow:

1. *Never* send an e-mail of a commercial nature unless the description of the list expressly permits it. Sending commercial e-mail on a mailing list is considered to be spamming and is offensive to subscribers.

2. *Always* be polite and patient. There are always "newbies" and your courtesy is expected and appreciated.

3. *Never* type in all capital letters. It is, in the Internet world, considered to be "shouting," not to mention that all caps are more difficult to read. The only exception is that you *should* type surnames in all caps in order to make them stand out.

What Is a Message Board?

A message board, as explained before, is a place on the Internet where people who share an interest in a topic post electronic messages. The difference between a mailing list and a message board is that, for a mailing list, people subscribe via e-mail and messages arrive in their e-mail mailbox. With a message board, the onus is on you to visit the board, to search out information, and to read the postings there yourself.

The Ancestry Message Boards at **http://boards.ancestry.com** are among the best available. They include the combined resources and archives of both Ancestry.com and RootsWeb. Figure 9-23 shows the main screen at the Ancestry Message Boards. As you can see, it is easy to locate specific surnames, localities, and topics. It also is easy, using the search template toward the top to either search *all* of the message boards for a name or text *or* to find a specific message board. Finding a message board is easy: just fill in the name and go from there. For example, I entered the name **weatherly** (no quotes) in the Find a Message Board box and was presented with the screen shown in Figure 9-24.

I simply clicked on the link and was taken to the screen displayed in Figure 9-25. If you study this screen of the Weatherly message board for a few minutes, you'll see that you can search *either*

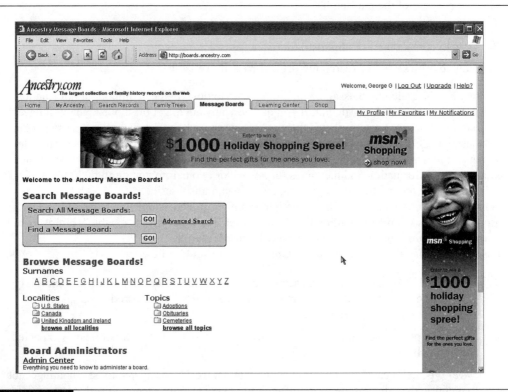

FIGURE 9-23   Main screen at the Ancestry Message Boards (Used by permission of MyFamily.com, Inc.)

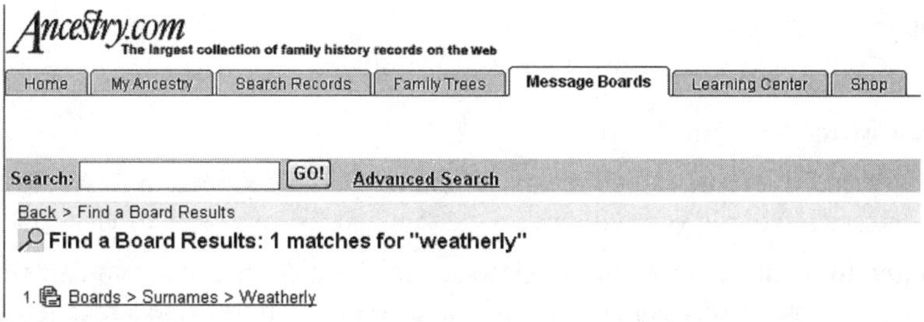

FIGURE 9-24   The search results for the Weatherly surname (Used by permission of MyFamily.com, Inc.)

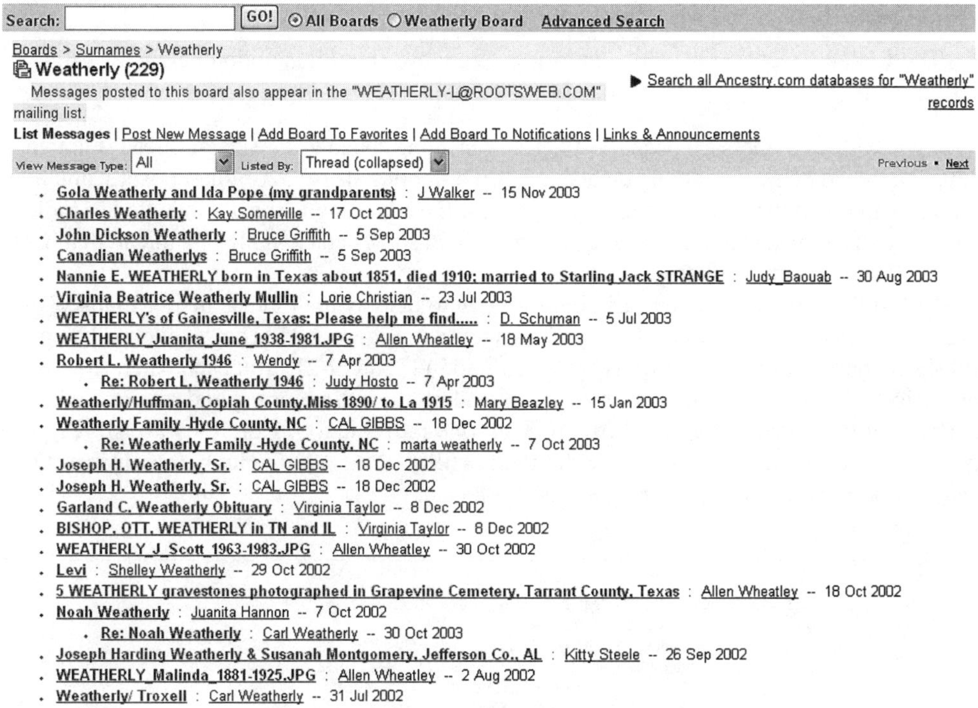

FIGURE 9-25   Listing of messages for the Weatherly surname (Used by permission of MyFamily.com, Inc.)

all the message boards *or* just this one for specific words or terms or names. Just click on the radio button you want.

You have some other options, including the following:

- **Post New Message** to this board
- **Add Board to Favorites,** which means whenever you are signed in to Ancestry and you visit the message boards you will have a customized list of places to visit.
- **Add Board to Notifications** allows you to set up a system that sends you an e-mail every time someone posts a message to this message board. You must be a registered user to use this feature.
- **Links and Announcements** will display the e-mail address of that message board administrator. It also may include a list of other Web sites and important announcements related to that message board.
- The **View Message Type** drop-down box shows various subsidiary sortings of the messages that may narrow your search.
- The **Listed By** option is worth exploring. See more about this option below regarding "threads."

What you will see in message board postings is something called a "thread." A thread is nothing more than "a thread of conversation" on a single topic. It consists of an original posting and all of the responses to it and the responses to the responses. Each posting is further indented to indicate the response in the thread chain. For example, Figure 9-26 shows an example of a thread that began 23 May 1999 and continued through a series of message postings.

The Listed By option discussed earlier allows you to display the threads in a "collapsed" way with only the subject (header) lines displayed, as shown in Figure 9.25. The "expanded" display method shows messages in their entirety, as illustrated in Figure 9-27. You can switch from one display option to the other at will, and this makes reading the entire correspondence in a whole "thread" easier than having to click through each one individually. Here they are shown on a single screen. What's more, you can use the Find facility (CTRL-F) to quickly search an entire Web page for a specific name or word you want to locate.

- Andrew WEATHERLY 1808-1887 NC>TN>AL : Ruby Nell Nicholson -- 23 May 1999
  - SIMS : Janice Mauldin Castleman -- 21 Jul 1999
  - Andrew Asenath Weatherly : Linda Matheny -- 1 Jul 2000
    - Andrew Asenath Weatherly, Hamilton, AL : Margie Cox -- 14 Feb 2001
      - Andrew and Asenath Weatherly : Linda Matheny -- 23 Feb 2001
  - Re: Gola Weatherly and Ida Pope ?? : J Walker -- 15 Nov 2003

FIGURE 9-26   A "thread" on the Weatherly message board (Used by permission of MyFamily.com, Inc.)

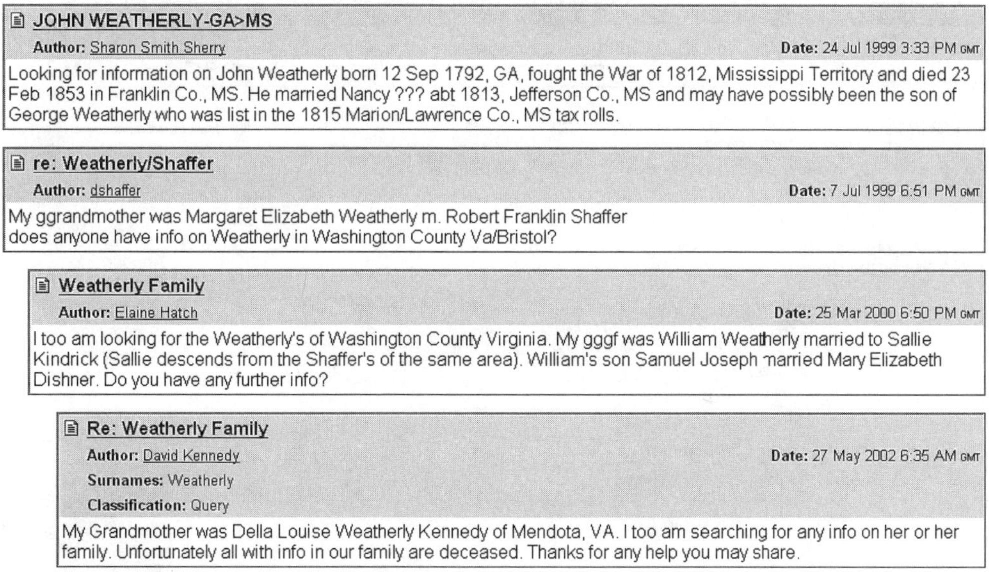

JOHN WEATHERLY-GA>MS

Author: Sharon Smith Sherry   **Date:** 24 Jul 1999 3:33 PM GMT

Looking for information on John Weatherly born 12 Sep 1792, GA, fought the War of 1812, Mississippi Territory and died 23 Feb 1853 in Franklin Co., MS. He married Nancy ??? abt 1813, Jefferson Co., MS and may have possibly been the son of George Weatherly who was list in the 1815 Marion/Lawrence Co., MS tax rolls.

re: Weatherly/Shaffer

Author: dshaffer   **Date:** 7 Jul 1999 6:51 PM GMT

My ggrandmother was Margaret Elizabeth Weatherly m. Robert Franklin Shaffer
does anyone have info on Weatherly in Washington County Va/Bristol?

Weatherly Family

Author: Elaine Hatch   **Date:** 25 Mar 2000 6:50 PM GMT

I too am looking for the Weatherly's of Washington County Virginia. My gggf was William Weatherly married to Sallie Kindrick (Sallie descends from the Shaffer's of the same area). William's son Samuel Joseph married Mary Elizabeth Dishner. Do you have any further info?

Re: Weatherly Family

Author: David Kennedy   **Date:** 27 May 2002 6:35 AM GMT
Surnames: Weatherly
Classification: Query

My Grandmother was Della Louise Weatherly Kennedy of Mendota, VA. I too am searching for any info on her or her family. Unfortunately all with info in our family are deceased. Thanks for any help you may share.

FIGURE 9-27   Messages shown in the "expanded" format make reading a "thread" simple (Used by permission of MyFamily.com, Inc.)

You also have the option to display the postings in date sequence in either the collapsed or expanded form.

When using the message boards to search for particular text, you may find the Advanced Search feature here as useful as the same function in one of the search engines or directories we have discussed. The Advanced Search template for the Ancestry Message Boards is shown in Figure 9-28.

Again, you can search either all of the Ancestry message boards or just the one for this topic, in this case, the Weatherly surname. As you can see, there are some options to help you narrow your search. At the bottom of the screen (not shown) are four additional important links.

- ■ **Request a New Board** is used if you wish to submit a request to have a new message board established when there is a surname or topic not addressed.

- ■ **Message Board Rules** contains guidelines for what is and is not a proper use of the message boards.

- ■ **Message board FAQ** contains frequently asked questions and answers.

- ■ **Message Board Help** is, as always, your best friend when you need help and guidance.

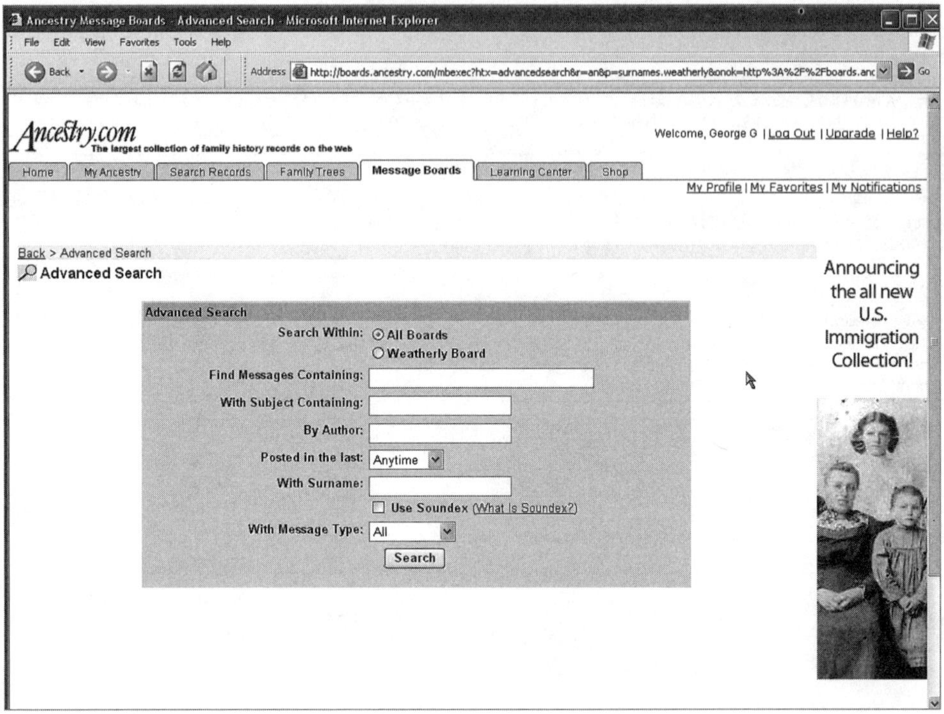

FIGURE 9-28   The Advanced Search template at the Ancestry Message Boards (Used by permission of MyFamily.com, Inc.)

Write Effective Messages and Postings That Get Results

Well-constructed, well-written messages get results. However, you need to know how to create an effective message. A great message really starts with a great subject line that captures the readers' attention. The subject line should be brief but descriptive. It should tell the reader what is inside the message and help him or her determine whether to read the message at all. The subject line content should include details such as the following.

- Name of person sought
- Location
- Time period
- All of the above or other data

Let's look at three examples of potential subject lines. The first is for Rebecca MONFORT who lived in Greene County, Georgia, and her life dates were 1819 to 1886. Please note that the surname is in all uppercase to make spotting the surname simpler. This subject line tells the reader

WHO, WHERE, and WHEN. This should be enough to help him or her decide if this is a person about whom he would like to learn more or if he/she has something to share. The reader *will* open this message.

Rebecca MONFORT—Greene Co., GA -1819-1886

The second example tells the reader that the author has or wants information concerning a church in a particular location: Madison, North Carolina, in the county of Rockingham.

Zion Baptist Church—Madison (Rockingham) NC

In the third example, the subject tells the reader a lot of information. In this case, the author is seeking information about Brisco HOLDER, who was born in 1879 and who died in the mid-1920s. Mr. Holder was in Georgia, and then moved to Alabama, and then to Kentucky, and then to some unknown place. (The greater than character (>) indicates that the person moved.) Reading just this header, you might determine (correctly) that the author is seeking to learn exactly where and when Mr. Holder died and was buried.

Brisco HOLDER—1879-ca. 1925—GA>AL>KY>?

These are all examples of good subject headers. A subject line that reads "Help!" or "Wilson Family" or "Want Grandpa's Dates" is not effective.

The body of the message is just as important as the subject line. It should be concise and should indicate the following:

- The full name (and any nickname or alias) of the individual
- The location in which the person was located
- The time period about which you are interested
- What it is specifically that you are seeking
- Any research you have already conducted or sources you have checked, regardless of whether they helped your search or not
- What else you might be willing to share with another researcher
- How someone can contact or respond to you

Let's look at an example of the body of a good message in Figure 9-29. The author wrote a subject line that clearly provided the surname and the location of her query. The body of the message indicated that she was seeking information on one Katherine Swords and family. She provided a detailed description of what she knew and this would help the reader determine what he or she might be able to share with the author.

In contrast, let's look at an example of the body of a bad message in Figure 9-30. The author posted this message with the impossible subject line of "HELP PLEASE!" on the East of London Family History Society (EoLFHS) message board. I seriously doubt that anyone read the message because of the subject line. The author has collected some facts but they are neither well organized

9

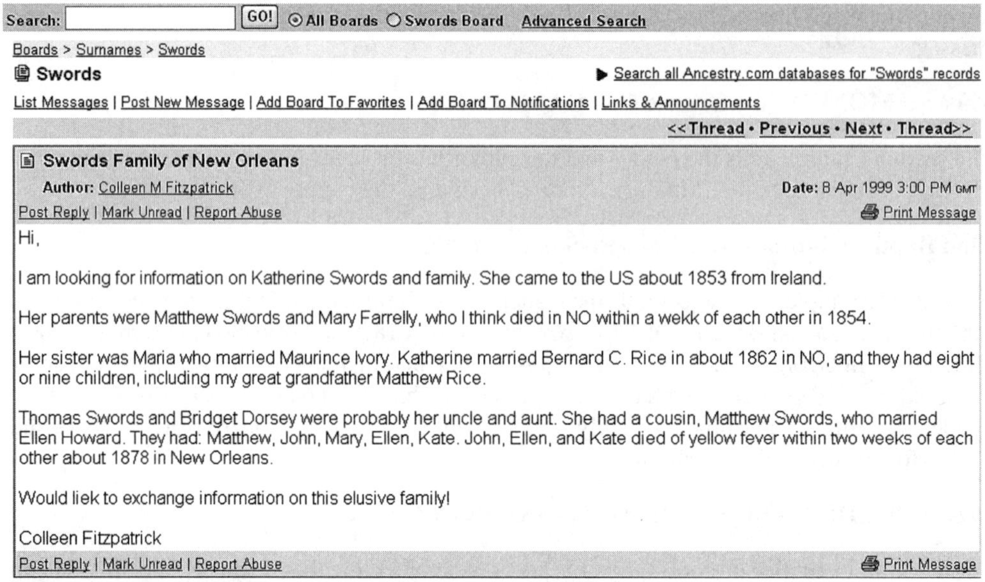

FIGURE 9-29   Example of a well-written message board posting (Used by permission of MyFamily.com, Inc.)

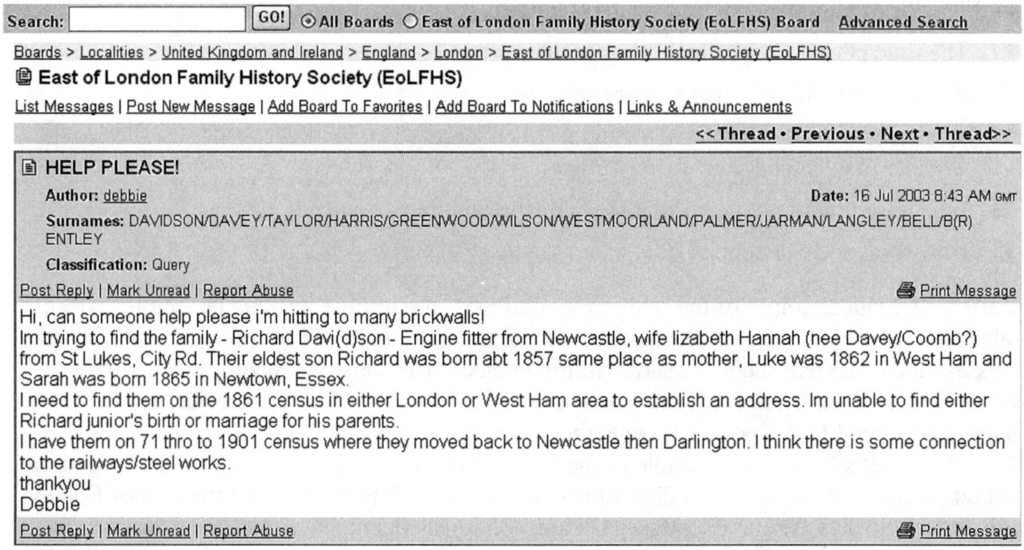

FIGURE 9-30   Example of a poorly written message board posting (Used by permission of MyFamily.com, Inc.)

nor well presented, and we don't know where she obtained them. The reader would need to dissect the message, reorganize its content, and further correspond with the author to really determine what she is seeking.

As you can see, the use of electronic mailing lists and message boards can really expand and extend your research range by providing the ability to advertise the fact that you are seeking information. You will be surprised how many other researchers, even your own cousins, are out there using these electronic queries. Whereas in our discussion of other Internet resources, now *you* have the opportunity to actively participate in requesting and sharing data *and collaborating* with others!

Locate and Use Additional Resources in Your Research

So far, we have discussed the background and structure of the Internet, the differences between primary and secondary sources, the difference between original and derivative sources, domain names on the Internet and how to use them, and the use of your critical thinking skills. We've examined many categories of Web sites to help you learn to recognize what you're looking at, how to use them, *and* to understand what you are likely to find there.

We also have compared the differences between directories and search engines, and studied how to formulate effective searches. Message boards and mailing lists were discussed and you should now have a good understanding of how to use them. And we have examined in detail the use of online catalogs for libraries and archives, why they are a vital part of your research toolkit, and how to use them.

All of these resources contribute to your understanding of how and where to locate important genealogical resources for your research. However, there are so many, many more materials available to you! Consider for a moment that you are visiting your local public library to conduct family history research. You certainly will spend time in the genealogy collection. However, you are sure to encounter material that will cause you to want to use additional library materials that are not physically located within the genealogy and local history department. You will want to consult maps and atlases, and these may be in another part of the library. Encyclopedias, biographies, dictionaries, and language translation books are also in another area. Calendar and timeline books are elsewhere, as are telephone directories and other people-finder materials. The list goes on and on. And hopefully, in the course of your library visits, you are utilizing *all* of the resources there already, and not just the genealogy books.

Let's explore a number of additional Internet-based resources that may be of help to you in your research. In the following sections, I will suggest some examples of Internet searches to help you locate materials for that genre, and will include some of my favorite sites for your review and enjoyment. Your job in all of this is to search for materials that will be of use in your own research, *and* to incorporate these tools into your search strategies.

Online Map Resources

Maps are an essential part of your research work. It is imperative that you use maps to locate precisely where your ancestors were at the time in which they lived. Political boundaries have altered tremendously over the centuries. Nations have come and gone, counties and provinces have been formed and divided into smaller, more easily governed areas, towns have been founded and disappeared, places have been renamed, and some places have simply disappeared. It is therefore important to be able to locate historical maps, atlases, and gazetteers of all types. Here are some examples of Internet searches that might be of help to you. Substitute the place name you are seeking for the one(s) shown in the following examples. Please note that Boolean search characters + and – are being used, as are the double quotation marks (" ") that form an exact phrase. You may use any search engine you like, and may want to use the Advanced Search facility to exclude some materials. For example, for the map searches, perhaps you will want to exclude commercial sources and therefore use the advanced search facility to exclude the .com sites from your results. (Remember! You've learned a lot already about how to search the Internet more effectively. Don't slip back into your old ways!) Try some of these searches to see what you can find on the Internet.

> **map + "south carolina"**
> **map persia**
> **atlas Georgia 1895**
> **gazetteer ireland 1800s -site:.com**

(This search was conducted using Google, and locates pages with the words "gazetteer," "Ireland," and "1800s," and excludes .com sites. Be sure to check the Help of your favorite search engine to verify the correct format for including and excluding specific domains and other data.)

I have a number of favorite Web sites where I find historical maps. I encourage you to try some of these terrific resources for yourself.

- Perry-Castañeda Map Collection—**http://www.lib.utexas.edu/maps**
- Library of Congress Geography and Map Division—**http://www.loc.gov/rr/geogmap**
  The Library of Congress Geography & Map Reading Room Web site, shown in Figure 9-31, is an excellent place to begin searching the facility's extensive collection. Be sure to visit the Online Map Collections from 1500 to 2003 at **http://memory.loc.gov/ammem/ gmdhtml/gmdhome.html** and view the sample map displayed in Figure 9-32.

- Institute of Historical Research: Map History/History of Cartography—**http://www. maphistory.info**
- The United States Geological Survey's Geographic Names Information System (GNIS)— **http://geonames.usgs.gov** This is a database that is searchable by name and also by *Feature Type,* such as cemetery, to locate places. The resulting list will provide you all known sites. Select one and you'll be supplied with the latitude and longitude, and if you scroll down you will see an option to click on a link titled Show Feature Location, and this will access and display a map for you from the U.S. Census Bureau's Tiger Map Server. This is a great resource for traveling, and the latitude and longitude are excellent if you plan to use a GPS unit to help locate a place.
- National Archives and Records Administration: Geographical Information Page—**http:// www.archives.gov/research_room/alic/reference_desk/geographical_links.html**

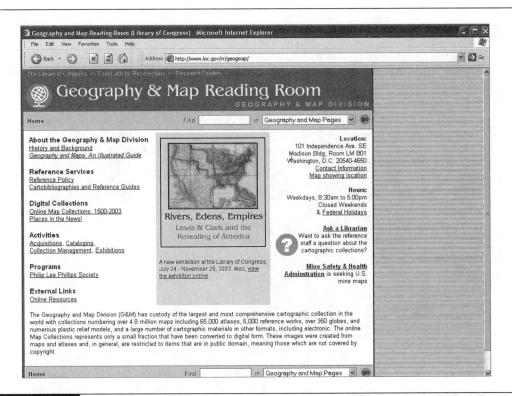

The Library of Congress Geography & Map Reading Room site is the entrance to the institution's vast collections of cartographic resources.

Dictionaries

There are hundreds of sources for dictionaries online, for English and for other languages that may be helpful for translation purposes. Some excellent sites may be found in the following directories:

- Yahoo! in the Reference category—**http://dir.yahoo.com/Reference**
- Google's Directory, under the Reference category—**http://directory.google.com/Top/ Reference**
- The Librarians' Index to the Internet, under the Ready Reference & Quick Facts category— **http://lii.org**
- The Internet Public Library, under Ready Reference—**http://www.ipl.org**

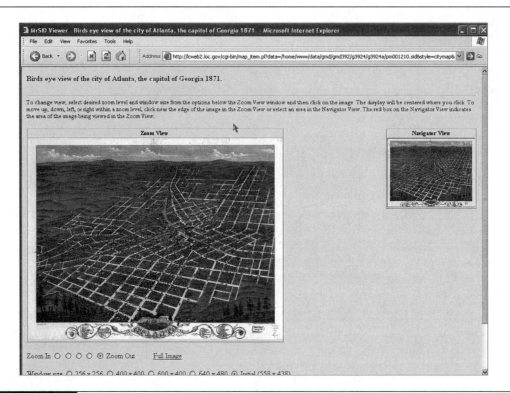

FIGURE 9-32   Sample map from the Library of Congress Online Map Collections

Language Translation

The SYSTRAN Information and Translation Technologies site (located at **http://www.
systransoft.com**) remains one of the very best resources for language-to-language translation. It
provides you with two methods you can use:

- You may type up to 150 words of text and translate it. This can be helpful when trying to
  translate foreign languages into English, or for translating into another language when
  writing letters of inquiry and for record copies.

- You may enter a Web address and it will be translated from its original language into English
  or one of a number of other languages.

The Google Language Tools page at **http://www.google.com/language_tools** includes
a language translation tool. Google uses the SYSTRAN technology, but it really is the same tool
offered at the SYSTRAN site.

Please recognize that no online translation is ever going to be perfect. The idiomatic variations and vernacular terminology may not translate well. However, the translation you obtain should be sufficient to help you gather the meaning of the text. For more precise translations, you may want to seek a professional or contact a college or university where students are learning the language. A professor may be willing to have a student assist you as a for-credit project.

Historical and Biographical Resources

Information abounds on the Internet about history and about the lives of notable or historical figures. The Ancestry.com databases include a number of important resources in this area. From the main screen at Ancestry.com, click on the tab labeled Search Records. On the next screen, on the right-hand column, locate the category titled Biography & History and click there. Here you can search the databases in one of two ways.

- Enter a name in the search template and click on the Search button.

- Search the Individual Biography & History Databases by entering a name in the search template and then clicking on one of the specific databases in the window. (One of the more prolific databases is the *American Genealogical-Biographical Index (AGBI)*.)

- You also can search, by name, in the *Slave Narratives* database and the *Biography and Genealogy Master Index (BGMI)* database.

Here are some examples of other searches you might employ using your Internet browser and a search engine.

"george Washington" biography
"george washington" genealogy
"richard ball" genealogy
pedigree "mark twain"
life "queen Victoria" –albert

Note in the last example that the minus sign (–) should be placed immediately in front of the word or phrase to be excluded.

Don't forget to also use directories, which may also have information of help to you.

Calendars

You may find good use for calendars in your research. Remember that there was a switch from the Gregorian calendar to the Julian calendar in 1752/53 in Great Britain. The changeover in other parts of the world occurred at different times. A good place to find a reference table for the 1752/1753 change is at RootsWeb's page at **http://ftp.rootsweb.com/pub/roots-l/genealog/genealog.quakerc1**. You also can search for calendar converters using the keywords **julian gregorian jewish** and others as needed.

Perhaps you want to know on what day of the week an ancestral event occurred, in which case a perpetual calendar is just what you want. There are many on the Internet, but one of the easiest to use is at **http://www.wiskit.com/calendar.html.**

People Finders and Telephone Directories

In the course of your research, you are going to want to try to locate "lost relatives" and others. There are many online telephone and people finder resources on the Internet and most are geographically specific. Be aware that there are a couple of drawbacks to using these facilities.

- People with unlisted telephone numbers are not included in the telephone number and people finder databases.
- People's cellular telephone numbers are not included in these databases.
- E-mail addresses are seldom if ever updated. Therefore, if you find an old e-mail address for someone, a message you send may not be delivered, and some e-mail service providers do not generate "postmaster" messages indicating a failed delivery attempt.

Among the most prolific of the people finder facilities for United States residents and businesses are the resources shown in the list below. You will want to search regional versions of Yahoo! and Google for other countries to locate online telephone, e-mail, and people finder services.

- Yahoo! People Search—**http://people.yahoo.com**
- Google Directory, under Reference—**http://directory.google.com/Top/Reference**
- The Ultimates—**http://www.theultimates.com**
- InfoSpace—**http://www.infospace.com**
- Internet Address Finder (IAF)—**http://www.iaf.net**
- PeopleSpot—**http://www.peoplespot.com**
- PeopleSearch.net—**http://peoplesearch.net**

Access the Resources of the "Hidden" Internet

Finally, let's discuss the so-called "hidden Internet." Among the literally billions of Web pages on the Internet, there are some that cannot be located by using search engines. There can be any number of reasons for this, including the following:

- The site is actually a database and the only way to access the information in it is to initiate a query to its computer.
- The Web site uses a firewall to protect itself from intrusion by hackers.

- The Web site uses a firewall to prevent search engines' spiders, robots, or bots from entering and indexing the site because:

  - Such activity uses a substantial amount of the site's server capacity.

  - The owner/administration does not want the content indexed by search engines.

  - A combination of the two issues above.

- The Web site is an intranet, which is a site designed to only be accessible to and used by a select group of users, such as for a company's internal employees only.

Some examples of each of these scenarios, respectively, are as follows:

- A site that is a database could be an online library catalog, or the Ancestry World Tree at Ancestry.com.

- A Web site with a firewall to prevent hackers' access would include the FBI's Web site.

- A Web site with a firewall to prevent access may include the following scenarios:

  - A small business may have a single small server that might crash if it receives too much traffic.

  - An entity that may not want its content indexed might include America Online, which makes money from its content and wants to protect its customers' data, or a university that wants to protect its faculty's and students' Web page content (which might be experimental/not finalized/under test/or other circumstance) from being accessed.

  - Both situations could exist in many situations.

- An example of a Web site that is an intranet site used only by employees might be a hospital, where there are several intranets running: one for physicians and surgeons, one for nursing staff, one for pharmacy personnel, one for administrative staff, and another for residents and students.

As you can imagine, there are many, many scenarios that exist where the content of a Web site may not be accessible. However, the most common one that you will encounter will be the first, the one in which data is inside a database and requires you to enter a data query (which is the same as a search) of the site using whatever search structure and tool(s) are built into the site.

If you want to locate some of these "hidden" databases on the Internet, the strategy has to involve some logic, a little creativity, and some search engine skill. Let's examine this and, in the process, let's start a list on a piece of paper as we progress through the next few paragraphs.

First, imagine that there is a database of material somewhere out there with information you want to locate. Perhaps the only entry way into that database is via the main screen and that is where you will enter your search terms. If the Web page designer was smart, he or she would have included the descriptive term "database" somewhere in the text on the Web page. Even if "database" was not in the Web page title (the name of the page that appears on the blue title bar at the top of your browser), it might have been included in the meta tags we discussed when we explored the use of search engines. Therefore, you could make a guess that the keyword "database" might be helpful in constructing a search. Add that to your list.

9

The word "genealogy" may or may not be helpful, and the word "genealogical" may be even less common. However, keep them on the side, and add them onto your list.

Next, consider the type of information you are seeking. Let's say we are searching for immigration information on your ancestors who came from Europe on a ship, perhaps from England. Here we have two pieces to consider: how to indicate immigration and how to indicate the origin of the ancestor. Immigration can be indicated in a search in a number of ways to obtain search results. Web pages may use keywords like "immigration," "immigrate," "immigrant," "emigration," "emigrate," or "émigré." These variants and more may be helpful in your search. Other things associated with immigration might include "manifest," "ship manifest," "ship's manifest," "ships' manifest," "ship passenger list," "ship's passenger list," or "ships' passenger list." You get the idea. Add them to your list.

How do you indicate England? Try writing some words down: "england," "britain," "great britain," "UK," or other terms. These are general enough, but also consider some ports of embarkation as alternates or search-narrowers for later: "Liverpool," "Plymouth," "Bristol," "Southampton," and others. Add these to your list. And don't forget that, in the case of the Irish emigrants, most went first to England in order to sail for America, Canada, Australia, or elsewhere.

By now, you have an extensive list of variations that may seem rather daunting. Don't despair! Start simple and see where you go. Begin by opening a search engine. In this case, I chose Teoma (located at **http://www.teoma.com**) because I personally like the way it provides me with options to refine my search. I entered the following search string:

genealogy england immigration database

The result was the screen shown in Figure 9-33. There were 30,700 search results returned, as well as some suggestions to refine my search, and some suggested resources. This is like having a mentor looking over my shoulder!

In the search results, I see the search terms highlighted in bold, and I think I want to try one or more of these terms to help make my search a little more specific. Therefore, I'm going to click on the Catalogued Cross link in the Refine list on the right. This adds those words to the search box and initiates another search. Is it helpful? Well, not really; the search results list is the same this time, but now there are Web pages concerning cataloged and cross-referenced materials moved to the top of my list. However, it tells me I may want to look for another search term. It's all in the process, and that's where some of the additional keywords we added to the list may come in handy.

Next I make a change to a slightly different search that includes the addition of the word "liverpool" to the search string to read as shown here:

genealogy database immigration Liverpool

This time my search results drops dramatically to 3,080 hits. If I insert the word "ireland" in the string as follows, I further reduce the matches to 782.

genealogy database ireland immigration Liverpool

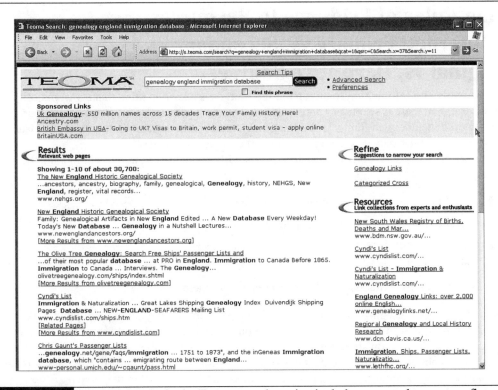

FIGURE 9-33   Search results in the Teoma search engine include suggested terms to refine your search and resource collections.

If I substitute the word "irish" for "ireland," the matches drop to 612. I further changed the search string to the following in order to *really* refine it.

genealogy database "famine irish" immigration Liverpool

In this case, I was presented with a total of only 11 matches. This doesn't mean I have what I want; I may have limited the search too much. Removing liverpool from the string expanded the number of hits to 15, and that may not be all that I want. However, you get the idea. Develop your list of possible terms, create an intelligent search string, and then explore the results you get. As you can see, playing with the terms, words, and phrases you enter can have an impact in narrowing your search results. The order in which you arrange the search terms will also influence the results, both in terms of quantity and in the order in which search results are arranged. Remember that the search engine perceives that words or phrases entered first are the more important items, and will search and rank the Web pages it finds in a relevancy ranking sequence based on your data entry order. Be sure to consult the Help facility of your search engine and the resources at SearchEngineWatch.com for specifics concerning how your engine operates.

Apply the Rules of Evidence to Resources on the Internet: Primary vs. Secondary *and* Original vs. Derivative Sources

When we work with information found on the Internet, please keep in mind that a vast majority of the information there is secondary and/or derivative source material. Primary, original source material would include such things as the Images Online at Ancestry.com in the form of census records, historical newspapers, map images, and other digitized images.

Some of the secondary, derivative materials you will encounter on the Internet include the following items:

- GEDCOM files created by other genealogists
- Message board postings by other genealogists
- Mailing list e-mail messages from other genealogists
- Indexes of all sorts
- Transcriptions, extracts, and abstracts created by others

It is important to recognize that the Internet is an excellent finding aid to point you to many types of materials. However, unless the materials you are viewing are actual digitized images of the original documents, you should maintain a healthy skepticism about what you are seeing. Always seek to obtain original document copies and examine them for yourself. Your assessment of the material may be far different than the conclusion another researcher may reach.

Use *All* the Resources at Your Disposal in Tandem

All of your reading and studying will not pay off until you apply what you learn in a practical way—*and* do it on a regular basis. Throughout this book, you have learned the foundations for research and analysis, applying your critical thinking skills to both the traditional genealogical resources and items and to electronic materials of all sorts. All types of materials can, individually, be used as important tools for your investigative work. By themselves, they are great reference materials. However, when you combine them and work them in tandem with one another, they become a powerful toolkit for your work. It is important that you recognize how important working all of these together can be. Let's look at one research scenario and what online resources might be employed to help solve its challenges.

Define the Challenge

A friend's great-grandmother, Sarah Grodovich (and the surname spelling is in question), came from Poland sometime in the last quarter of the 19th century. She married Louis Weinglass and lived in New Jersey until the time of her death on 11 August 1944. The research challenge before us is to determine when she arrived in the United States and from where.

Consider What Record Types Might Help Us

There are any number of records that might point us to the country of origin and the time of arrival in the United States. It does take some historical research of the records and of world geography to help understand and interpret the information correctly. However, in this case, here are some examples of records and online resources that may help us locate the answer.

- ■ **United States Federal Census Population Schedules**   Starting with what is available and working backwards, we start with the 1930 federal census images online at Ancestry.com or microfilm for that census. An index could refer us to the Kearny Town Enumeration District, Hudson County, New Jersey. We locate the population schedule in Enumeration District Number 9-305, Supervisor's District Number 7, as Page Number 11-b. When we locate the population schedule, a section of which is shown in Figure 9-34, it tells us, in Column 19, that she was born in Russia. Columns 20 and 21 tell us that her parents were also born there. Her mother tongue, so Column 21 reveals, is Jewish, and Column 24 indicates that she can speak English. Of special interest in solving our problem is that Column 22 indicates the year of immigration to the United States and, in Column 23, whether the individual was naturalized or was an alien The codes used by the enumerators to indicate naturalization status are "Na" for Naturalized, "Al" for Alien, and "Pa" for Papers Applied for). In this case, Sarah's entry indicates her arrival in the United States was in 1883 and that she was naturalized.

- ■ **Enumerator Instructions**   We determined the codes used for the census forms in the Enumerator Instructions at the Web site located at **http://www.ipums.org/usa/voliii/ tEnumInstr.html.**

- ■ **United States Federal Census Population Schedules**   Moving back in time, we examine the 1920 population schedule, only to find a discrepancy in the immigration date. This time, the year was listed as 1888. This will take some additional consideration; however, we know from a copy of a marriage certificate that Louis and Sarah were married in 1887 in New Jersey and that their first child was born in 1888. We therefore believe that 1888 was an error on the part of the enumerator.

- ■ **Online Library Catalogs**   It is important that we now determine what the naturalization laws were for the time for women. Did they have to apply for naturalization themselves, or were they naturalized as a result of marrying a husband who was already a U.S. citizen? We certainly could use one of the online library catalog facilities in order to locate books concerning immigration and naturalization laws over the past two centuries.

- ■ **Using a Search Engine**   The question concerning the naturalization laws regarding women's citizenship can be researched using a search engine. Using the Advanced Search screen template at Google, it was important to construct an intelligent search. So, into the With All The Words box, we entered **women 1800s** and into the With The Exact Phrase box, we entered **naturalization law.**

9

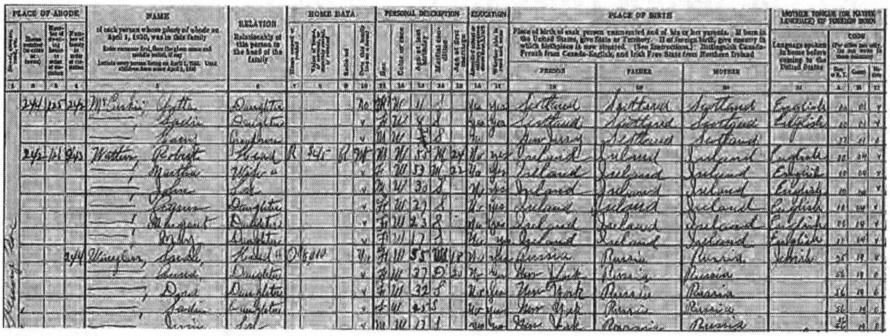

FIGURE 9-34   Portion of the 1930 census population schedule for Sarah Weinglass (Used by permission of MyFamily.com, Inc.)

The search results provided several excellent responses, including one from the NARA Web site at **http://www.archives.gov/publications/prologue/summer_1998_women_and_naturalization_1.html** and another at RootsWeb at **http://www.rootsweb.com/~nynewyo2/naturalization.** The first article indicates that the woman's citizenship at the time was derived from her marriage to her American husband. Therefore, it is highly probable that Sarah did not go through the naturalization application process herself, although it is something that we can check if only to confirm or refute the hypothesis.

■ **Mailing List Archive Search**   There is a mailing list on the subject of naturalizations that you may want to search. Go to the RootsWeb mailing lists page at **http://lists.rootsweb.com,** locate the link for Naturalizations, and from that next page, select the Naturalizations link. This will present you with the page for this topic, located at **http://lists.rootsweb.com/index/other/Immigration/USA-Naturalizations.html.** You can then choose to search or browse the archive, using the screen shown in Figure 9-35. If you do not locate information, you can subscribe to the list and post a message.

■ **Naturalization Papers**   Based on what the census records told us, we believe that Sarah (and her husband) had become naturalized citizens of the United States. It would be important to locate naturalization documents. None of these documents is online, but they are available through NARA or the United States Immigration and Naturalization Service (the INS), depending upon the time frame of the naturalization. You could therefore visit the NARA site at **http://www.archives.gov,** use the Search function on the main screen, and enter the word **naturalization.** The resulting list includes a reference to NARA | Genealogy | Naturalization records, at **http://www.archives.gov/research_room/genealogy/research_topics/naturalization.html,** and from there you can click on the link labeled Naturalization Records. This presents you with the NARA page at **http://www.archives.gov/research_room/genealogy/research_topics/naturalization.html.** From here, you can learn what records are available, what form is available to request them, and what you can expect to receive. In this case, you would probably want to complete a request form for both Louis Weinglass *and* his wife (under her full name of Sarah Grodovich Weinglass, since she would have derived citizenship through her marriage).

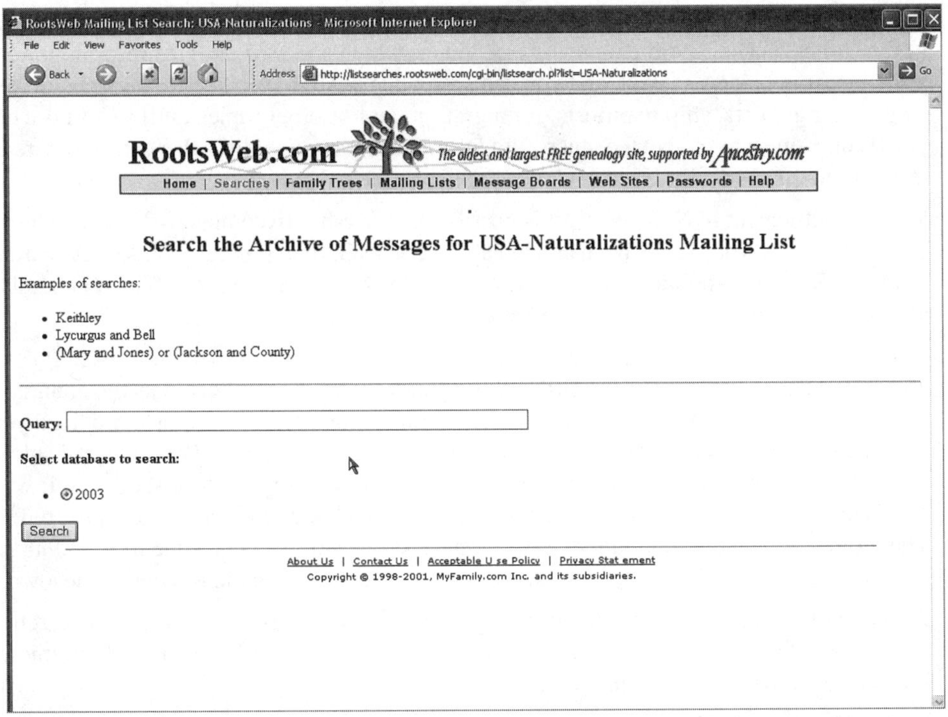

FIGURE 9-35   You can search the archive of the USA-Naturalizations mailing list at RootsWeb.

The History, Genealogy, and Education page at the U.S. Citizenship and Immigration Services Web site (**http://uscis.gov/graphics/aboutus/history/index.htm**) contains links to a variety of articles, discussions of ships' passenger lists and land arrival documents, details about naturalization, and much more relating to the Bureau of Immigration and Naturalization Service (INS). The Web page titled "Ports of Entry and Their Records" provides a roster of the states and, within each state, you will find each port of entry, the types of records created at that port, the dates of those records, where they were originally filed, and the current National Archives microfilm publication number (if any). If a particular set of records has no NARA microfilm publication number, it means that that entry is either not yet published or its publication status was undetermined. This is a very important distinction.

To order naturalization records from 1906 to 1956, you will need to complete and submit the form G-639, which is titled "The Freedom of Information Form." This form may be downloaded and printed from the Web site at **http://uscis.gov/graphics/formsfee/ forms/files/g-639.pdf,** or you may order it by calling: 1-800-870-3676. Be sure to ask for form G-639.

■ **Ship Passenger Lists**   After receiving copies of any naturalization papers, it is possible that Sarah's documents indicate her place of birth, her age, the date and place of her arrival in the United States, and the name of the ship on which she arrived. This information is available from NARA as well, and you can search the NARA Web site for information on ship passenger lists, ship manifests, immigration, and/or other topics until you find what you want. Copies of the NARA microfilm for the ship passenger lists also can be ordered through the LDS Family History Center for use at their facility.

With her settlement in New Jersey, it is possible that Sarah arrived in New York, in which case her records would have been created at the Castle Garden immigration site. A search of the NARA micro-publications catalog could help you determine the publication number and film roll number(s) you would want to research.

■ **Maps and Gazetteers**   The 1930 census enumerator instructions (referenced in Point 2 above) indicate that the place of birth for the person should be indicated as the country where it was in 1930. Your research into the naturalization records may have provided you with the name of a location in Europe at the time of her immigration and/or naturalization in the 1880s. This may have been a part of a different country in the 1880s than it was following World War I. In addition, towns may have changed names or disappeared. Therefore, it would be important to locate historical maps of the area at the time and, if the name of the town has changed, a gazetteer to help locate the old *and* new name of the town.

A search of the Internet using the words "gazetteer russia" yielded a number of search results, including the Russia page from the Global Gazetteer site of Falling Rain Genomics, Inc., at **http://www.calle.com/world.**

■ **Online Databases**   You might also want to search any of the online genealogical databases, including those at Ancestry.com (**http://www.ancestry.com**), the LDS FamilySearch site (**http://www.familysearch.org**), and others that may be applicable. In this case, since we know that Sarah was Jewish, we could visit the JewishGen site at **http://www.jewishgen.org** to access the information they have, including the Jewish Genealogy Family Finder database.

■ **Compilations**   An excellent resource to use for searching for all types of Internet resources is Cyndi's List at **http://www.cyndislist.com.**

■ **"How-To" Materials**   The Library at Ancestry.com (located at **http://www.ancestry.com** under the Learning Center tab or directly at **http://www.ancestry.com/learn/library**) can be searched for a keyword. If that search did not yield the results you want, at the bottom of the search results list is your search in a template with a drop-down box containing search criteria: any word, keyword, exact phrase, author, title, or free text.

■ **"Hidden" Databases**   There may be some "hidden" resources already on the Web. Using your favorite search engine(s), enter keywords such as **naturalization database** to start, and see if there are any additional resources that might help.

- **Message Boards**   Message boards may be helpful in making contact with other researchers seeking the Weinglass (or Wineglass) surname, immigration from Russia (or the appropriate place), or concerning naturalization.

- **People Finder Facilities**   You may decide, especially with a rather unique surname, to search the online telephone directories to see if there are persons with that surname in the United States, particularly in the area where Louis and Sarah Weinglass lived. A search in the AnyWho.com online directory at **http://www.anywho.com** for the surname Weinglass may return a number of matches. These may be their descendants, and relatives may still be living in the vicinity. You might then want to consider contacting them.

Prepare a New, Integrated Research Plan

As you can see from the case study of Internet resources outlined above, there are a lot of directions that might be taken and a great many Internet resources that might be explored. The 15 items above certainly do not comprise the complete list of Internet-based options available. It also does not include the traditional paper documents, such as marriage and death certificates, religious records, cemetery records and obituaries, wills and probate documents, land and property papers, tax lists, and such. However, the example provides an excellent illustration for starting your own Internet research.

Begin your plan, as you begin all your genealogical research, by defining what you already know. Start with a clean sheet of paper and prepare a timeline of what you know about one ancestor. Start with the birth, marriage, and death—include the locations and dates and anything else you know. Certainly these facts are gathered and verified the old-fashioned way: by writing letters or visiting courthouses and government offices to obtain copies of materials. Family Bibles, diaries, letters, journals, and other materials are useful tools as well. Remember that your research will *always* be a mixture of using the "traditional" records and methodologies as well as the more recent electronic records and associated methodologies.

Once you have your timeline started, start a list of questions for yourself like the ones below. This process is done for one reason: to define the question!

1. Who am I researching?

2. What do I already know?

3. Where were they and when?

4. What information do I want to locate or prove?

5. What types of records might answer the question I have?

6. Where might they be located?

7. In the absence of the records I want, what alternative records might also help answer the question?

8. Where do I begin looking?

9. In traditional venues? If so, where?

10. On the Internet? If so, what tools will I use?

11. How will I document my sources?

12. Where do I go from here?

Take your timeline and your questions, and start doing your homework. Integrate your new Internet knowledge and skills into your research and produce a new research strategy. Start working all the resources at your disposal in tandem—home sources, family interviews, paper documents, books, newspapers, maps and gazetteers, dictionaries, online databases, individual Web sites of compilations and "how-to" materials, message boards, mailing lists, and e-mail exchanges with individual researchers. This is the exciting part of the process: learning, sharing, and collaborating with other researchers. In the process, though, remember to employ scholarly research methods and those critical thinking skills, and don't forget to document your sources so you and others can retrace your research path.

You're really on your way now!

Chapter 10

Follow Alternative Research Paths to Locate Difficult Records

How to...

- Recognize when you have hit a "brick wall"
- Take a fresh look at old documentation
- Reevaluate the quality of your sources
- Widen the scope of your search to include new and different sources
- Use photographs
- Develop an ancestor profile/timeline
- Switch to another family member to bypass your roadblock
- Seek help from libraries, archives, and societies
- Engage the help of a professional researcher

Recognize When You Have a Hit a "Brick Wall"

It is inevitable that you will at some point be confronted with the genealogist's worst nightmare: the dreaded "brick wall." Despite all your best research efforts, your careful assessment of the documentation and facts, the quality of your source materials, and your best hypotheses, you'll find you just can't progress any farther. It happens to all of us, but the situation isn't always hopeless.

Identify the Symptoms of a Brick Wall

Sometimes the people you think are going to be the simplest to locate will become a research nightmare. Every avenue you explore seems to come to an abrupt dead end. One of the most frustrating things is not being able to locate even the most basic vital or civil records that should have been where you expected to find them. Worse, however, is the discovery that the person who you *thought* was your ancestor and in whom you've invested so much research effort actually is unrelated to you at all. You've been researching someone *else's* ancestor!

Unfortunately, it is easy to become so consumed with the "ordinary" search that you may not even realize you've hit the proverbial "brick wall." You may just think that the next record is just around the corner when, in fact, you may never find another record for the person in the place you've identified as the "correct location." Now is the time to step back, put all your knowledge and experience to the test, and employ your most creative thought processes to locate alternative sources. The work you've done to hone your critical thinking skills can provide a big payoff now.

There are several keys to solving your problem. The first thing to do is to recognize the fact that you really *do* have a brick wall, and that you haven't just made an oversight. Identify and literally describe the scope and symptoms of the problem. Write a description of your problem, including what you know to be fact and the sources of the fact. Include what you want to find out, what you have already searched, and the results you have or have not achieved. Often, just putting the facts and the actions you've already taken into words on paper can help focus your attention on the real issues. Here are examples of just a few of the more common categories of research brick walls you can expect to encounter:

- You can locate no records for your ancestor—anywhere!
- You cannot identify your ancestor's parents or cannot link him or her with people who you believe are the parents.
- Records have been lost, stolen, destroyed, or transferred elsewhere.
- Records that you want to access are private, restricted, or entirely closed to the public.

Using your written description of the problem and what you have already tried, now develop a list of alternative research paths, records, and other sources that might help resolve the problem. You may need to conduct some additional research to put your ancestor into geographical, historical, and/or social context and to determine what records might or might not exist to help you locate more information. Here are some examples of problems and possible solutions.

Problem

The person's parents cannot be identified or traced. This is perhaps the most common brick wall genealogists face. Moving backward one more generational step can be exceptionally challenging.

Possible Solutions

Search for ecclesiastical records for your person that may indicate previous membership in another congregation elsewhere. I was able to trace one of my grandfathers from the church in North Carolina in which he was a member at the time of his death back to the church in which his family were members in Georgia, then back to another church in Alabama, and finally to the church in Tennessee in which he was christened. Another possible solution, which we will discuss in further detail later in the chapter, involves researching another family member.

Problem

The person's previous place of residence cannot be identified or traced. This is perhaps the second most common brick wall genealogists face.

Possible Solutions

The ecclesiastical membership record search could work here as well. Voter registration records, school records, census indexes and population schedules, immigration and naturalization documents, land and tax records, probate packet inventories and heir lists showing property ownership and/or the residences of heirs in other locations, military service records, and obituaries are common alternative records to help locate previous places of residence.

Problem

The records you wanted or expected to find are missing. Records do disappear, sometimes through misfiling and sometimes by having been removed or stolen. Consider my dismay to find evidence of an ancestor's considerable estate documented in probate court minutes, only to find that the entire probate packet was not in the probate clerk's files. The will and the executor/administrator's documentation could have provided definitive proof of the names of my ancestor's children and whether they were living or deceased at the time of his death. It could have identified other relatives, land and property holdings, and other pointers to other documentation.

Possible Solutions

Locate all the probate court minutes for hearings concerning the estate. Some materials may have been read into evidence in the records. Seek newspaper announcements concerning the settlement of the estate. Determine the name(s) of the executor/administrator(s) of an estate through the use of probate court's minutes, and then check the probate files in the event your ancestor's packet was incorrectly filed under the executor/administrator's name rather than under your ancestor's or family member's name. In addition, it is not unheard of to find that a probate packet was removed by a lawyer or other representative and retained in that person's professional files. Investigate the possible existence of transcriptions, extracts, or abstracts of the original will in books, genealogical society publications, and elsewhere. Contact libraries, archives, and genealogical and historical societies to determine if they are aware of the existence and/or disposition of the records you are seeking.

Problem

The records you are seeking have been discarded or destroyed. Perhaps the courthouse or other government repository ran out of space and determined that records older than a certain date were no longer needed. Originals of records may have been microfilmed and then destroyed, and then the microfilm was lost. There may have been a fire, tornado, hurricane, earthquake, flood, or other calamity in which the courthouse or archive was damaged or destroyed, and records were lost.

Possible Solutions

Consider substitute records that might provide identical or similar information. Contact archives, libraries, and genealogical and historical societies that might have acquired or salvaged any records. Investigate the possible existence of transcriptions, extracts, or abstracts of the original materials made or published prior to the records' loss. Don't overlook the possibility that records could have been prepared in duplicate and sent/transferred to another agency.

Problem

Records were destroyed during a time of war. Contrary to what you may have heard, General William Tecumseh Sherman did *not* destroy every courthouse in his march through Georgia during the U.S. Civil War. (Nor did he ever conduct a similar march through Idaho!) However, some county government buildings and their records were lost. During World War II, there was so much bombing and fire damage in Antwerp, Belgium, that only a few individual ships' passenger lists survived.

Possible Solutions

Look for possible duplicate or substitute records. Investigate the possibility that the records were copied or microfilmed prior to their loss, that transcripts were published elsewhere, or that indexes survived when the actual records did not.

Problem

There is no evidence the person ever lived in that place. Your research has led you to a specific place where, no matter what type of records you investigate, there are no records that your ancestor was ever there.

Possible Solutions

Perhaps the lead you had was incorrect. Or maybe the governmental jurisdiction has changed and the records are really in another place. Stop and reexamine all of your information again to look for clues you may have missed or information that may have been incorrect.

Problem

The names and/or dates are all wrong. I was searching for the origin of one of my great-great-grandfathers, Jesse Holder. I knew he lived in Georgia after he was married, but United States federal censuses indicated he was born in North Carolina. Searches of records in North Carolina yielded nothing, and so I transferred my attention to the possibility that he may have lived in South Carolina during some period. I found a Jesse Holder in Laurens County, South Carolina. Unfortunately, his year of birth didn't seem to fit. I then determined that this Jesse Holder had married another woman and had died prior to when my great-grandfather was born in Georgia.

Possible Solutions

Retrace the research steps to determine if you are on the right track or took a wrong turn. Look also in the same area for other branches of the same family that really might be yours. Naming patterns sometimes show that children may have been named for one of the parents' parents, an aunt or uncle, or a sibling.

Problem

There is no discernable link between your ancestor and the people you think could be the parents, siblings, spouse, and/or other relatives.

Possible Solutions

Examine census records in the area in which your person lived and look for other persons in the vicinity with the same surname, and begin to research them. Examine wills, probate records, and ecclesiastical records and look for any family relationship or common denominator linking them together.

Problem

The person has just simply vanished into thin air. (I call this the "my ancestor was abducted by an alien spaceship" problem.)

Possible Solutions

Reexamine census records for your ancestor *and* for three or four neighboring families on either side of your ancestor. Locate your ancestor in the last census where you found him or her. Look, then, at the next available census for the neighbors. If they are all still in the same place and your ancestor is gone, you know you have looked in the correct place. If one or more of the neighbors also is gone, start looking for your ancestor *and* the neighbor in available census indexes in that location and surrounding parishes, counties, provinces, or states. Work in concentric circles, using a map and considering the migration routes and social trends of the time, and move outward seeking your ancestor in records that might likely have been created at the time. For example, if you know your ancestor was a Methodist, start looking at Methodist church membership records. Look for voter registration records if the period coincides with a major national election year.

Problem

Adoption records are sealed by a court and not accessible by the public.

Possible Solutions

Petition the court in whose jurisdiction the adoption took place for access to names and dates of the parties.

Problem

The records you want are the property of a private corporation and you are refused access to them.

Possible Solutions

Prepare evidence of your relationship to the person whose records you require and a solid reason for your request. Instead of access to the entire body of records, request an exact extract of the content you want to obtain. If you are refused, consider escalating your request to the headquarters and executive officer(s) of the corporation. I have used this tactic in order to access personnel records and funeral home/mortuary records of individual family members.

These examples are not, of course, comprehensive in the scope of possible alternative sources and strategies, but they will give you some ideas to contemplate. Again, it is important to understand your ancestor in context, *all* of the record types that might have been created, possible repositories, and individuals and organizations that may be of help to you.

Take a Fresh Look at Old Documentation

One strategy that I use constantly is the reexamination of documentation and other evidence that I collected previously. It amazes me how much information can be gleaned from taking a fresh look at something that I thought I knew so well. Remember that over time you will gather new evidence; learn more about history, geography, and other influences; and become acquainted with new people in your family history. Let me give you a good example of how just reexamining census population schedules could clarify my research.

My great-grandmother, Caroline Alice Whitefield, was born on 23 August 1853 to William A. Whitefield (also spelled Whitfield) and his second wife, Sophia D. Briggs. Caroline was their fourth and last child. William had fathered nine other children by his first wife, Rozella H. Moore, who died on 25 September 1841. William died on 18 September 1857 and Sophia died on 29 April 1859, both in Person County, North Carolina. Guardianship was granted in Person County in September of 1857, following her father's death, to Caroline's 35-year-old half-brother, LeGrande

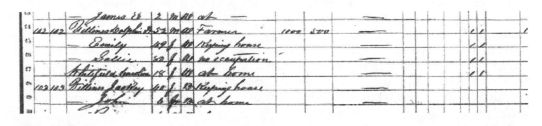

Portion of the 1870 U.S. federal census showing Caroline Whitefield in the home of her aunt and uncle (Used with permission of MyFamily.com, Inc.)

Whitefield of Montgomery County, Tennessee. I could not find Caroline with LeGrande in the 1860 census, nor could I locate her in North Carolina. However, in working my way through the United States federal census of 1870, a portion of which is shown in Figure 10-1, I found Caroline living in the home of Dolphin D. Villines (age 52) and his wife, Emily (age 49), and 80-year-old Sallie Villines, in Person County. When I first acquired the census page in 1989, I did not know why Caroline might be living with this family. It was not until 1999 when I reexamined the record that I realized that Emily Villines was, in fact, Sophia's older sister. Her maiden name had been Emily L. Briggs.

In the intervening years between examining the census population schedule, I had learned more about the family and had actually researched both of William Whitefield's wives' lineages. The connection between the Whitefield and Villines families would not have been clear unless I had reexamined the 1870 census. I now knew that, even though guardianship had been granted to LeGrande Whitefield, he did not take his half-sister to Tennessee to live with him and his wife. Instead, she remained in the area where she was born and lived with her maternal aunt and uncle.

Even though you think you are familiar with the details of all the evidence you have located for a particular ancestor or family member, look at it again. I like to organize the materials in chronological sequence and read through it all, page by page, as if it is a biography. This gives me a sense of order to the life of the individual. By approaching the person's life story sequentially as documents and other materials were produced, I begin to get to really know and understand the person better. Sometimes this is extremely helpful because, knowing their history, I may be able to anticipate a decision about migration, settlement, occupation, or some other life factor. Try it for yourself and see what you learn.

Reevaluate the Quality of Your Sources

Scholarly work is one of the foremost goals of genealogical research and we are therefore always searching for the best evidence we can find. It is certainly gratifying to locate an original marriage certificate, created at the time of the marriage and bearing the actual signatures of the bride and groom. Few things are as exciting as holding and touching a document that was handled and signed by our ancestors and that was as important to them as a marriage certificate. The next best thing, of course, is seeing a facsimile of such a document on a photocopy, on microfilm, or as a digitized image.

10

Not all of our source materials, however, can be such excellent forms of evidence. As you've learned, genealogists work with primary *and* secondary sources; with data transcribed, extracted, and abstracted from original documents; and with a vast array of published materials in all types of formats. In our quest to locate facts about our family, we often must use sources that may be one or more times removed from original source material, and often this information is less than 100 percent accurate. There is something lost in the transfer, diluted as it were, and it is for that reason that we must maintain a keen awareness of primary *vs.* secondary materials and be prepared to carefully analyze the quality of our sources.

I often tell fellow genealogists, "Two secondary sources do not a primary source make." Perhaps it sounds a little corny, but it is true. I recommend maintaining a healthy skepticism of almost any information until its authority can be proved, and evaluate the weight that it may provide to the big picture.

One major factor contributing to many of our research brick walls can be a problem with the quality of the information we may have obtained from source materials. It is important to take a giant step back from a problem and reexamine all of our evidence. I don't mean "just" the secondary sources, but everything. As I said earlier, a great way to do this is to arrange every piece of evidence you have in the chronological sequence as it may have occurred in the ancestor's life. Reread everything in order. You are sure to find gaps in what you know. In the meantime, reexamine where your information was derived. What you may think is a solid fact may be well documented by a less than excellent source. Let me give you an example.

A friend in Georgia hit a brick wall in her search to prove the identities of the parents of her grandmother and locate other documentation about them. She had a death certificate for her grandmother that documented the date of death as 4 October 1935 and indicated the place of burial was to be in Munford, Alabama. It indicated that her grandmother had been born on 22 June 1859 in Atlanta, Georgia, and that she was 78 at the time of her death. The only information my friend had about the names of her great-grandparents came from the death certificate, and she inferred from the place of birth listed on her grandmother's death certificate that her great-grandparents had lived in Atlanta.

You will remember that a death certificate can be one of those "combination" sources: a primary source for the death information and a secondary source for everything else. My friend knew that well, but still had entered the information she found on the death certificate into her genealogical database and documented the source. However, in her concentration on locating documentation on her great-grandparents, she failed to recognize that the *only* information she had about their names and the place they lived was the information on this death certificate. It turned out that the informant who provided the information for the death certificate was a nephew, and that he did not know the facts about the date and place of birth, the names of the parents, and their place of residence. One glaring error was in the age shown on the certificate. Wait a minute! When I subtract 1859 from 1935, I come up with 76, not 78! Something was amiss here. And why was she to be buried in Alabama?

My friend backed up and began her research again, this time with a fresh perspective. She knew that she had made an error in judgment and assumed that the names, dates, and locations on the death certificate were "probably correct." She now knew that she needed to search for additional source materials. Her next step was to begin again with what she really knew to be factual based on primary sources. She developed a list of document sources that might be available and that might help her solve her research problem. She did some research to determine where those documents might be located, and then began making contact with those locations to see what she could obtain by mail or e-mail. She ultimately arranged to make two short trips to conduct research on-site.

After about a year, she told me that she had solved some problems and had finally gotten around her brick wall. There were four important pieces of information she obtained from other materials that helped her.

- She located a copy of her grandmother's obituary, which indicated that she grew up in Greensboro, Georgia. It listed her age as 78, and not 76, and confirmed that burial was to occur in Munford, Alabama.

- She traveled to Alabama and located the cemetery where her grandmother was buried. Her grandmother's grave was next to that of her grandfather in his family's cemetery lot. That made sense. She also noted on her grandmother's gravestone the birth date of 22 June 1857, yet another confirmation of the age of 78 and not 76 years.

- She reexamined her grandparents' marriage certificate again and noted the marriage date of 24 November 1881 and the place of issue as Greene County, Georgia. As it was customary for a bride to be married at home or in her church, my friend believed it made sense to pursue research in Greene County, Georgia, and not in Atlanta.

- She traveled to Greensboro, Georgia, to search for records of her grandmother's family. She located microfilmed copies of the local newspaper in the public library and began searching for marriage announcements. She found the announcement in a newspaper dated Thursday, 8 September 1881, and the notice included her grandmother's name, the name of her fiancé, and the names of both sets of parents and their places of residence.

Armed with the new information, my friend continued her research in Greene County, Georgia, and located a vast amount of information about her grandmother's family. She found church records, land and property records, tax rolls, and a probate packet for her great-grandfather in which all of his children's names were listed. Knowing the correct county, she continued by working with the 1880 federal census records to verify the family's residence there, the names of the children, and their ages. Furthermore, my friend learned that her great-grandfather had been the county sheriff for many years, including at the time that her grandmother had been born in 1857. She is now trying to determine whether her grandmother really was born in Atlanta or in Greensboro, Georgia. However, that is another research story.

My friend's story is not uncommon. Even though her brick wall is a comparatively simple problem, it illustrates how a small error in judgment can result in a major blockage in a person's research. It required stepping back and the reexamination of her source material, followed with the development of an additional research plan, and some concentrated research to get around her brick wall. Since that time, she has extended her research to include other of her grandmother's siblings and has been able to identify and document her great-grandmother's parents and grandparents.

Widen the Scope of Your Search to Include New and Different Sources

One of the joys of genealogy is learning about different resources that can be used to document your family history. Discovery of these materials is exciting and invariably leads to a desire to learn more about them. I remember my excitement at learning about transit permits, those documents that are used to facilitate the transport of bodies across state or national borders to a hometown or some other place of interment. A transit permit can contain a great deal of information about the individual and, prior to the use of official death certificates, can provide details about the cause of death. In the course of my research, I have encountered transit permits in cemeteries' files for soldiers in the United States Civil War who died in battle or from disease. I found one for an uncle who died of tuberculosis en route by train from New Mexico to Georgia. I've also seen transit permits for a woman killed by a train, people killed by gunshot wounds, several suicides, and for people who died from any number of different diseases.

There are literally hundreds of documents you might never have imagined that could help document your ancestors and family members. Beyond the record types I've covered in this book, you will want to consider other sources. How do you find out about them? Well, there are all sorts of books available that can introduce you to descriptions and samples of these records. Let me share a few of my favorites.

Hidden Sources: Family History in Unlikely Places, by Laura Szucs Pfeiffer, is a compilation of more than a hundred different record types that may be of help to your personal research. Each record type is described in detail, along with information about places where it can be located and how it can be used. You will find an illustration included for each record and a bibliography for additional reading and reference. Some of the more interesting records are almshouse records, coroner's inquests, bankruptcies, Freedmen's Bureau records, name change records, orphan asylum records, passport records, school censuses, street indexes, post office guides and directories, patent records, and voter registration records.

Another excellent compilation is *Printed Sources: A Guide to Published Genealogical Records,* edited by Kory L. Meyerink. This impressive book contains authoritative chapters concerning different record categories, written by a number of eminent genealogical experts. For example, if you are looking for a more thorough understanding of United States military records, David T. Thackery's chapter, "Military Sources," is a comprehensive study of what types of records are available and a selective description of published sources for major military conflicts. Records at the federal, state, colonial, and state level are addressed in detail, histories, rosters, and important reference works are described, and a vast, definitive biography is included.

A study of English parish records requires some understanding of the structure of the parish system *and* of the social responsibilities of the parish officer. *The Compleat Parish Officer* is a reprint by the Wiltshire Family History Society of a 1734 handbook for those persons "who had to apply and interpret the increasingly complex laws enacted to deal with the various social problems as they arose, its starting point being the Great Poor Law Act of 1601 and its various amendments." This compact little book details the authorities and responsibilities of parish constables, churchwardens, overseers of the poor, surveyors of the highways and scavengers, and other officials in the parish operational hierarchy. It is an invaluable primer for genealogists and family historians in understanding the English parish environment and the records that are found documenting your ancestors.

A companion to *The Compleat Parish Officer* is Anne Cole's *An Introduction to Poor Law Documents Before 1834.* This volume describes the parish documents, explaining the reasons for each one's creation, the contents, and what can be gleaned from them. The settlement certificate, for example, was an exceptionally important document for those to whom it was issued. It provided legal proof of residence in the parish and thus, in time of need, entitled the person to financial assistance. However, more importantly, the settlement certificate was used to provide permission to persons to relocate their place of residence from one parish to another. These two books, used together, provide excellent insight for the researcher of English parish records.

Do you have an ancestor who operated or worked in an inn, a public house ("pub"), or a brewery in the British Isles? You may have thought there were no records to help you locate them or learn about their lives, but you would be wrong. *Researching Brewery and Publican Ancestors,* by Simon Fowler, is the ideal little reference for you. It recounts the history of licensing of inns and taverns, descriptions of the people's responsibilities, and records that have been maintained for reference and research.

You might be surprised to find that someone thought of taxing windows. How odd, you might think. However, as part of the land and property tax assessments in England, Scotland, and Wales, land taxes, house tax assessments, and assessed taxes based on the number of windows in the building were all used to collect revenue. *Land and Window Tax Assessments,* by Jeremy Gibson, Mervyn Medlycott, and Dennis Mills, is the definitive reference describing these types of records. More importantly, the book contains county maps showing the borough boundaries, accompanied by lists of record offices and addresses, and details of what records from what time period are housed and available there.

I don't suppose you have an ancestor who was a midwife in 17th- or 18th-century England, do you? If you do, or if you are simply interested in childbirth in this period, Joan E. Grundy's book *History's Midwives* is a fascinating read. Childbirth was a dangerous process in those times and many women died in labor. Midwifery became an important medical profession and midwives were required by law to be licensed. The documentation of their requirements and their responsibilities are documented in this book, and examples of licensing documentation are included. The author has prepared and included an index of 17th- and 18th-century midwives nomination lists from Yorkshire for those family historians who have an ancestor who was a midwife.

The examples I've provided here merely begin to scratch the surface of the wide range of record types that can be found and used for your genealogical documentation. I urge you to use the resources of library and archive catalogs, particularly the subject and title search facilities of their online catalogs, to locate books of interest for these topics. In addition, you will find that using the bibliography included in many genealogical and historical publications will lead you to more reference materials.

Use Photographs in Your Family Research

If you're like most people, you have a collection of photographs stored somewhere in your home. Many of these may be identified and labeled, but you probably have a group of unlabeled photographs that I refer to as "the unknowns." You will find that photographs can, indeed, be helpful in identifying persons and placing them in a specific place at a particular point in time.

Photographs have been around since the production of the first photographic image in June or July 1827, which is universally credited to Frenchman Joseph Nicephore Niépce. Over time, other processes and methods of mounting or displaying photographs were developed and introduced. You will find that the type of photograph and its physical attributes, the mountings used, the clothing worn by the subjects, and the background or surroundings can be used to date your photographs with surprising accuracy. It is important to understand a little history of photography first.

Learn About the Types of Photographs

Louis Daguerre's technique of capturing an image on a silver-clad copper plate was officially announced in 1839. These first commercially successful photographs were known as *Daguerreotypes* and were, at the time, quite expensive. A Daguerreotype was usually attached to a sheet of glass using a decorative frame made with a sheet of gold-colored heavy foil. The decoration was usually embossed into the foil material before enclosing the Daguerreotype and its glass. This unit was then press-fitted into a wooden case specifically designed to hold a Daguerreotype and sometimes padded with satin, silk, or velvet. The case also may have been a two-piece, hinged affair with a clasp that closed and protected the Daguerreotype.

The *calotype* was the first paper photograph, and it was made using a two-step process. The first step involved treating smooth, high-quality writing paper with a chemical wash of silver nitrate. This wash process was performed in a dim, candlelit room and the paper was then exposed to a little heat until it was almost dry. While still somewhat moist, the paper was soaked in a solution of potassium iodide for several minutes, then rinsed and gently dried. The chemical processes in effect iodized the surface of the paper to prepare it for is ultimate exposure to light. The slow drying process preserved the smooth texture of the paper, preventing wrinkling and puckering of its surface. The iodized paper could be stored for some time in a dark, dry place at a moderate temperature. The second step occurred almost immediately before the iodized paper was to be used for a photograph. The photographer mixed a solution of equal parts of silver nitrate and gallic acid that, because of its inherent instability, had to be used right away. Once again in dim candlelight, the iodized paper that had been prepared in the first step was dipped in this solution, rinsed with water, and blotted dry. It was then loaded in complete darkness into the camera and the calotype photographic image was captured. While the paper treated to the second solution could be dried and stored for use a short time later, the most reliable images were captured using paper still moist with the solution. Calotypes were made for perhaps a decade, from approximately 1845 until 1855. The main problem with them was that because the silver nitrate–gallic acid solution was not chemically stable, many of the images faded over a relatively short time. The surviving examples of many of these early calotypes appear as shadows or "ghosts" on the paper.

The *ambrotype* was introduced in 1854 and became very popular throughout the United States during the Civil War period. An ambrotype is a thin negative image bonded to a sheet of clear glass. When the negative image is mounted and displayed against a black background, the image appears as a positive. Ambrotypes were mounted in display cases much like those used for Daguerreotypes.

FIGURE 10-2   The irregular shape of this tintype is due to how it was cut from the iron sheet (From the author's collection).

Photography gained huge popularity in Great Britain when it was showcased at the Great Exhibition of 1851 in London. Both Queen Victoria and her husband, Prince Albert, were fascinated with photography and there are numerous photographs of the couple and other members of the Royal Family dating back to the 1840s. The public was introduced to several displays of photographs in various locations at the Exhibition and a subsequent increase in photographers' business in England has been attributed to the event.

The *tintype* was introduced in the early- to mid-1850s and was in use until the early 1930s. It became hugely popular in both the United States and Great Britain because it was cheap to produce and therefore accessible by almost everyone. Advertisements over time tout them as the "penny photograph," and street photographers became commonplace sights in towns, cities, and at resort areas such as Brighton, England, and Atlantic City, New Jersey, and at county fairs. Tintypes were extremely popular during the United States Civil War when soldiers wished to have a picture made of themselves in uniform with their rifle or sword to send home to loved ones. Since a tintype is an image made on metal instead of on a glass plate, it could be mailed without concern for breakage. There is no "tin" in a tintype; it actually is a thin sheet of black iron. The original name for the tintype was *melainotype,* however, the more common name is *ferrotype,* which refers to the ferrous base on which the image is recorded. It has been suggested that the term "tintype" was derived from the use of tin sheers used to cut and trim the images on the metal plates. Many tintypes will be irregular in shape, such as the one shown in Figure 10-2, because of the imprecise trimming work. It is possible to narrow the dating of tintype photographs produced during this extensive period based on a number of criteria, especially in the United States.

■ **1856–1860**   The iron plate stock used in this period is thicker than at any other time, and plates are stamped on the edge with "Neff's Melainotype Pat 19 Feb 56." They may be found in gilded frames reminiscent of those used with ambrotypes or in leather sleeves.

■ **1861–1865**   During the Civil War years, tintypes may be dated by their paper display sleeves. These "frames" may bear patriotic symbols such as stars and flags, and early ones bear the imprint of Potter's Patent. After 1863, the paper holders became fancier, with designs embossed into the paper holder rather than printed. In an effort to raise revenue to help fund the Union Army, a tax was imposed by the United States Congress on all photographs sold between 1 September 1864 and 1 August 1866. A revenue stamp was required to be adhered to the reverse side of the photograph, either on the photographic plate itself or in the case. The tax was based on the amount of the sale, and these revenue stamps are highly prized by stamp collectors. Some photographers initialed the stamps to cancel them and included the day's date and this provides a precise date for the completion of the sale of the photograph.

■ **1870–1885**   This period is referred to as the "Brown Period" because one company, the Phenix Plate Company, introduced a ferrous plate with a chocolate-tinted surface. Soon photographers across the United States were clamoring to use this new style of plate. The tintype shown in Figure 10-3 dates from this period. You should also know that photographers began using painted backgrounds reflecting a "country" look, with fences, trees, stones, and other rural images in this time period. The painted rural background in these photographs is a telltale indicator that the photograph was made after 1870.

FIGURE 10-3   Tintype photograph of the author's grandfather, Samuel Goodloe Morgan, taken circa 1880 (From the author's collection)

■ **1863–1890**   Photographer Simon Wing patented a multiplying camera that captured multiple images on a single plate. These photographs measured approximately .75" × 1" and became known and marketed as "Gem" or "Gem Galleries" photographs. These tiny portraits were typically mounted in ovals and attached to a larger mounting card. Some were even cut to fit into pieces of jewelry, such as lockets, cameo frames, cufflinks, and stickpins.

■ **Circa 1866–1906**   A new method of mounting photographs was introduced and is referred to as the "cabinet card." The photograph was adhered to a piece of cardboard stock. Early cabinet card stock is rather plain, with designs printed on the card. The type and color of the card stock and its decoration changed over the years, with embossed designs, colored inks, beveling, gilded or silvered card edges, and scalloped corners and edges being used at different periods. Photograph mountings were a point of high fashion, and you can use these distinctive traits and card sizes to date the period in which the photograph was made. The example shown in Figure 10-4 can be dated by the card stock to the period between 1880 and 1890 because the card stock is quite heavy, the front and back sides are of different colors, and the front surface is textured, rather than smooth. The woman's hairstyle indicates a bun worn high in the back. The not-so-high collar, the ornamental pleating on the shoulders of her dress and the detailed, raised embroidery along the neckline and down the front of the bodice are indicative of fashion three to five years prior to the explosive couture of the 1890s.

■ At the same time that cabinet cards were being used, other sizes and styles of photographic mountings came into use. One very popular format was a smaller mounting referred to as the *carte-de-visite,* or visiting card. These cards, like the example shown in Figure 10-5, typically measured 4 1/4" × 2 1/2" and were made of heavy, often glossy card stock. They became the rage and were used as souvenirs and, true to their name, were left as calling or visiting cards.

10

FIGURE 10-4   This photograph of the author's great-grandmother, Penelope Swords Holder, was probably made circa 1885 (From the author's collection).

FIGURE 10-5   A typical *carte-de-visite* (From the author's collection)

- Other popular styles and sizes included the Victoria (5" × 3 1/4"), the Promenade (7" × 4"), the Boudoir (8 1/2" × 5 1/4"), the Imperial, shown in Figure 10-6 (9 7/8" × 6 7/8"), the Panel (8 1/4" × 4"), and the stereograph (3" × 7").

- The stereoscope was a tremendously popular form of entertainment and education, beginning in approximately 1849 and continuing until the mid- to late-1920s. The apparatus consisted of a viewing hood with two lenses and an attached arm on which a sliding holder was mounted. It was used to view *stereographs* such as the one shown in Figure 10-7, which depicts destruction following the San Francisco earthquake of 18 April 1906. A stereograph is a card on which two almost identical photographs are mounted side by side. When viewed with the stereoscope, the effect is that of a three-dimensional view of the subject. Tens of thousands of stereographs were made for the huge consumer demand for more and more subjects. In fact, you might draw an analogy between the stereograph and a modern television/DVD setup. People could not seem to get enough of them. Subjects included Civil War battlefields and scenes, world travel photographs, public figures, expositions such as the St. Louis and Pan American Expositions, Americana, African-American subjects, children's games and antics, costumes, cemetery tours, and even series of stereographs telling a story.

FIGURE 10-6   This Imperial size cabinet card was one of the larger, more formal photograph mountings and dates from circa 1900 (From the author's collection).

- **Circa 1889 to Present**   Photography historians argue about who invented photographic film, however, an Englishman named John Carbutt, who also was an accomplished stereographer living and working in the United States, is credited with coating sheets of celluloid with a photographic emulsion while working in Philadelphia in 1888. In that same year, George Eastman introduced a new camera called the Kodak that used a roll of photographic film. The camera with the film still inside was sent to his company for processing, and the camera and a new roll of film were returned to the customer. Within a year, the Kodak name was a household world in the United States, Great Britain, Canada, France, and elsewhere, and the public was hooked on photography. People even had a choice of the way photos were printed, including as a face side for a postcard. The photograph on the postcard in Figure 10-8 was taken by my maternal grandfather and shows my grandmother. The card is dated 18 September 1908, two days after they were married in Rome, Georgia, and was taken in Washington, D.C., on their honeymoon.

- Over the years, several film base materials and a number of emulsion processes were used, each having specific attributes. You can learn more about 20th-century photography and fashions in books on the subjects and on the Internet.

Date Photographs Using Clothing and Hair Fashions

You probably never knew there was so much to learn about photographs did you? One of the best books on the subject of dating photographs is Maureen Taylor's *Uncovering Your Ancestry through Family Photographs.*

Don't overlook the fact that clothing and hair styles shown in photographs can be very important research clues. Studio photographs were often made with the subject wearing his or her very best clothing, sometimes purchased specifically for the occasion. A photograph of a woman wearing a dress with a wasp waist and balloon sleeves, mounted on a cabinet card with a buff colored,

FIGURE 10-7   Stereograph looking east from the corner of Ellis and Jones in San Francisco showing the devastation from the 1906 earthquake (From the author's collection)

FIGURE 10-8   Photographs were printed to make personalized postcards, such as this one of the author's grandmother on her honeymoon in 1908 (From the author's collection).

matte front and a dark gray back, with gold beveled edge can be dated to within a year or so of its creation date. Add a printed or embossed studio name (and location), and you are helping to narrow the focus of your genealogical search to a time and place.

Be sure to examine photographs for tiny details that might yield clues. You can do this by using a magnifying glass or you may digitize the photograph with your scanner and enlarge the image. I had an exciting experience in an online class I teach for MyFamily.com. One of my students uploaded a photograph of a boy in a school uniform to our class site's photo archive. She knew very little about the picture except that it was of her great-grandfather, and she knew very little about him. I noticed and commented on a medal of some sort on the boy's uniform. Another classmate seized the opportunity, downloaded the image, and proceeded to do some computer manipulation to enlarge and enhance that area of the photograph. He came back a few days later with a new image that showed the name of a school on the medal. The woman recognized the school as a private academy in the town where her grandparents had lived. As you can imagine, she was ecstatic and, armed with this new information, is off researching any possible leads that can be obtained from the school's archives.

There are a number of excellent books about dating photographs, costume and hair styles, and other visual history materials that can provide excellent references for you. Search the Internet for such phrases as: "history of photography"; "costume history"; or specific searches such as "Victorian clothing," "women's dresses" + 1830s, history + "men's clothing" 1860s; or other combinations of keywords and/or phrases. There is a wealth of information available to help you narrow the date and place of your photographs.

10

Develop an Ancestor Profile or Timeline

Family history information comes to us in pieces, from different places at different times. It comes from people and from courthouses and libraries. It takes the form of letters, journals and diaries, of books and magazines, public and private documents, and a range of other materials. As you collect these snippets of information, you begin to get ideas! You begin to learn more and more about your ancestor. Unfortunately, since these many pieces present themselves out of sequence, it's easy to lose sight of the big picture of your ancestor's life.

Creating a profile of your ancestor can help your research in several ways. In effect, it will become a timeline of his or her life. As a result, developing an ancestor profile can help you to:

- Identify how much information you have acquired
- Focus on the quality of your source citations
- Highlight gaps in your research
- Place your ancestor's life into a chronological sequence that can be more easily viewed and understood
- Make educated guesses about the ancestor's thought processes and motivations for making certain life decisions
- Provide the basis of a good biographical sketch or full-scale biography

Organization is the key. As you gather facts, you already know that you should be verifying and corroborating them with other sources. You should be weighing them against one another and against the "big picture" of your ancestor's life to make sure they make sense. You should be organizing all the information sequentially so that you can *clearly see* the life. In addition, you should know enough about local, state and national history to understand how historical events may have influenced your ancestor. Finally, you should study the personal events in your ancestor's life *and* the lives of the other people around your ancestor who may have exerted, influenced, or motivated certain decisions and actions.

The process is actually quite easy; it just requires compiling information into a format that allows the entry and insertion of information, editing, and revision. You might consider using a word processor, a spreadsheet, the notes section of your genealogical database program, or perhaps create a more sophisticated database using Microsoft Access or another full-feature software program. However you choose to construct your ancestor profile, remember to include the flexibility to insert other information. You'll see what I mean in a few minutes.

Start with What You Know

Gather together all the information you have obtained about a single ancestor. Arrange all the documents you have in chronological sequence as they were created. Treat all these documents and scraps of information as if they were notes you might have accumulated for writing a biographical sketch for your ancestor. Now, as I've discussed before, reread everything you have as if you have never seen it before. Don't gloss over anything. This exercise will help place you in your ancestor's life, and therefore in the right frame of mind to continue the rest of the project.

Start your document with a header that includes the name of your ancestor and his or her dates of birth and death at the top of the page. These are the starting and ending points of your timeline. Set up columns for the information you will be entering. In the example shown in Figure 10-9 for my great-grandmother, Lydia Lenora Patterson, I used two columns: YEAR and EVENT. You may choose to set up your profile with more columns, such as YEAR, EVENT, SOURCE, and COMMENTS, or in some other way.

Take each of the documents you have placed in chronological order, one at a time, and read them again. Enter information in the profile for every fact the document presents. At a minimum, enter the year, a description of the fact, and the source citation for that piece of evidence. You might also consider adding a notation for each citation to indicate whether the fact is a primary or secondary source. This can be helpful later on for items that may be of a questionable nature or strength. In Figure 10-9, my first entry represents Lydia's date of birth. My sources are her obituary

---

Lydia Lenora PATTERSON
(13 November 1833 – 28 August 1914)

YEAR	EVENT
1833 –	Born 13 November 1833 in NC.
	Source: Obituary, *Charlotte* [NC] *Observer*, 29 August 1914. (S)
	Source: Baptismal record at the Davidson Presbyterian Church in Davidson (Mecklenburg) NC. (P)
	Source: Membership record at the Davidson Presbyterian Church in Davidson (Mecklenburg) NC. (P)

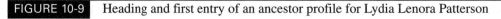

FIGURE 10-9   Heading and first entry of an ancestor profile for Lydia Lenora Patterson

and church records of her baptism and her church membership. The obituary is a secondary source, indicated with the notation (S); the church records are both strong primary records, indicated with the notation (P). I'll dispense with this scheme in future figures, but this shows you how you might indicate primary *vs.* secondary sources in your profile.

Lydia's obituary contained quite a bit of information about her life, including the names of her parents, her husband, and her children, her dates of birth and death, locations where she lived, and her church affiliation. Make special note of changes in locations as these indicate migration or changes in life situations. Emigration/immigration certainly is an important factor in your ancestor's life, as is marriage and relocation to a spouse's home. Each fact should be entered in chronological sequence in the profile, along with the source citation and an indication that the obituary is a secondary source.

As you progress through each document, enter the year, the exact date if possible, a description of the fact, source citation, and any comment that helps clarify the material. Your comment may be a reminder that you have a question about the content or need additional information, and this can prompt you to take action when you review the profile in the future.

Make every attempt to document your ancestor and to place him or her into geographical context at every point in his or her life. For example, the United States federal census did not list persons other than the head of household by name until 1850. I can surmise that Lydia lived with her parents from the time of her birth and through the 1840 census, although I cannot verify her name in the household. However, what you will want to do is list your ancestor's presence as documented in every census between the times their birth and death. You also will use other documents such as ecclesiastical records, marriage licenses or certificates, land and property records, tax documents, court records, military service and pension records, and wills and probate records of this ancestor and his or her relatives who may have bequeathed any inheritance to them. Birth and marriage announcements, news stories, obituaries, and other newspaper items can be used to add details. No document, regardless of how seemingly insignificant, should be omitted. For instance, I have in my possession the handwritten receipt shown in Figure 10-10 for the advance fee for Lydia's attendance during the 1850–1851 school term at the Salem Female Academy. This places her in a certain place at a specific time and tells me that she received an education, which at that time was something reserved for young ladies of quality.

Enter your source citation for every piece of evidence you have acquired, such as the example shown in Figure 10-11. You may find that you don't have the information required to create

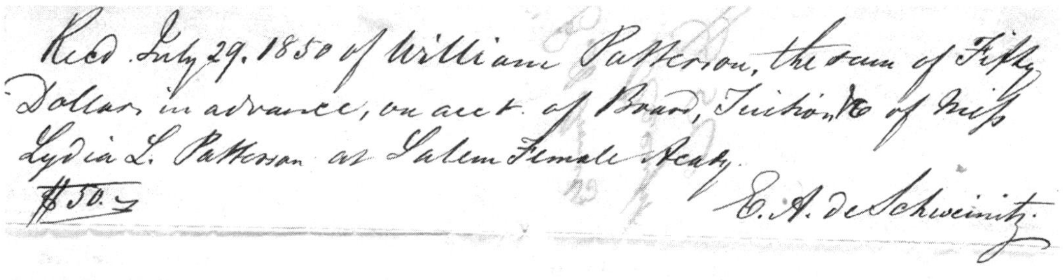

10

FIGURE 10-10   Receipt for Lydia Lenora Patterson's 1850–1851 school term at Salem Female Academy (From the author's collection)

1860 - Mecklenburg County, NC (Member of household of Joseph McKnitt WILSON.) Microfilm publication M653, Roll 906, Page 152, Dwelling # 531, Family # 580. Record shows age as 26.

FIGURE 10-11 Profile entry for the 1860 U.S. federal census including a source citation

an authoritative source citation, in which case you can add a comment to indicate that you need to obtain it.

Continue to list the date, fact, and source citation, along with any comments, until you have finished working through all your evidence. Print the profile and review it with a critical eye for misspellings, transpositions of dates, and other data entry errors. Make notation of corrections to be made later.

You will find that you may have multiple sources for the same piece of data. Some of these will be primary sources while others are secondary sources. That's fine. Enter the information and the source citations as you go along. When you review the profile, concentrate on the information and the sources at that time. Examine the fact itself as documented by each source. Ask yourself some questions.

- Does the fact appear reasonable?
- Does the fact "fit" with the overall picture, either chronologically or contextually?
- Does this fact as provided by this source agree with or contradict another source for the same fact?
- What is the source of the fact?
- Do I have an exact copy of the evidence in my possession?
- Have I created or do I have a quality, authoritative source citation that can be traced?
- Is this a primary or secondary source, or an original or derived source?
- If it is a secondary or derived source, have I obtained or can I obtain the primary or original source to examine personally?
- Is it possible that a secondary source I have for a fact is actually derived from the primary source that I have obtained?
- Is it possible that a secondary source I have for a fact is actually derived from another secondary source that I have obtained?
- What is the possibility that the source I have is incorrect, inaccurate, or otherwise flawed?
- Are there gaps in my research?
- What additional information do I want or need?
- Are there questions that I need answered before I can proceed?
- Where and how can I obtain each additional piece of evidence?
- What is my plan to obtain the additional piece of evidence?

Your review of the profile at hand will generate any number of new questions. Make notations on the profile, and then go back and make corrections and revisions. Print it again and conduct yet another review, making revisions as necessary until you are satisfied that you have a solid chronological timeline for your ancestor.

Add Personal Events to the Profile

Don't overlook the personal events that may have influenced your ancestor or those actions your ancestor may have taken that influenced other people's lives. The death of a parent, a spouse, a sibling, or a child may have had a great impact. My great-grandmother, Caroline Whitefield, became an orphan in the eyes of the law when her father died on 18 September 1857, despite the fact that her mother survived. While her older half-brother became her legal guardian, she continued to live with her mother until her mother's death on 29 April 1859. At that time, she was separated from her three natural siblings and sent to live with her aunt and uncle, the Villines family. You will remember that I found her there in the 1870 census shown in Figure 10-1.

An illness could wreak havoc on an individual or an entire family. If the head of household became ill and could no longer provide income to care for the needs of his wife and children, the entire family might collapse. Some or all of the family members could end up in an almshouse, poorhouse, home for indigents, orphanage, or completely homeless. Starvation and death were not altogether out of the range of possible fates.

Add such information about your ancestor and his or her family members to the profile when you can find it. Some personal hardships may have had little or no impact on the person or the family, while others may have been the source of overwhelming influence. You won't know for certain until you factor the information into the profile and begin examining the entire picture.

Learn About Other People in Your Ancestor's Life

An erroneous assumption that some researchers make is that they can concentrate on tracing a single family member's history without bothering to consider other people and their influence on that family member. The study of your genealogy really is the study of your *family* history, and that means focusing on the parents, brothers, sisters, aunts, uncles, cousins, children, grandchildren, and so on *and* their relationships and interactions with one another. Your job is to identify who these people were, what their relationship was to your ancestor, and how they or the events that happened to them may have influenced your ancestor. This also reaches far beyond immediate family members. You should consider neighbors, friends, members of the community, members of the same religious congregation, politicians, and any number of other persons.

The next step in developing your ancestor profile is to consider these other people and how they fit into your ancestor's life. Figure 10-12 shows more details of Lydia's profile, including the births of three of her siblings in 1835, 1840, and 1846. The impact of the birth of her brother, John Newell Williamson Patterson, when Lydia was only two years old probably would have had little impact on her life initially, but he may have played a more important role in her life later. The birth of her sister, Elizabeth Patterson, circa 1840, may have been important to Lydia because a new baby may have diverted some of her mother's attention away from her. The birth of her brother, James Patterson, circa 1846, when Lydia was eleven or twelve, however, may have placed

Lydia Lenora PATTERSON
(13 November 1833 – 28 August 1914)

YEAR	EVENT
1833 –	Born 13 November 1833 in NC. Source: Obituary, *Charlotte* [NC] *Observer*, 29 August 1914. Source: Baptismal record at the Davidson Presbyterian Church in Davidson (Mecklenburg) NC. Source: Membership record at the Davidson Presbyterian Church in Davidson (Mecklenburg) NC.
1835 –	Brother, John Newell Williamson Patterson, was born 5 December 1835. Source: Tombstone, Davidson Presbyterian Church in Davidson (Mecklenburg) NC.
1840 –	Mecklenburg County, NC (Member of household of William PATTERSON and his wife, nee Elizabeth McCuen Caroline POTTS.) Source: NARA Microfilm publication M704, Roll 365, Page 319.
1840 –	Sister, Elizabeth Patterson, was born ca. 1840. Source: 1850 Census. Microfilm publication M432, Roll 637, Pages 33-34, Dwelling # 545, Family # 548.
1846 –	Brother, James Patterson, was born ca. 1846. Source: 1850 Census. Microfilm publication M432, Roll 637, Pages 33-34, Dwelling # 545, Family # 548.

FIGURE 10-12   Add other people's information into your ancestor's profile.

more responsibility on her at the time but the age difference between the two children may have been an impediment to their becoming close.

Add information about other people into the profile of your ancestor. You may use family group sheets, pedigree charts, documentary evidence, and other materials to help you identify and enter the data. However, it is equally as important to enter the source citations for other persons' information as it was for that of your ancestor. The reason is that, when you review the expanded profile with other people's data included, you may see information that agrees with or conflicts with what you already knew. Having the source citations together in one location allows you to see and compare them on the spot without having to cull through a mountain of materials to retrace the sources. You may also notice inconsistencies you may not otherwise have spotted previously.

Figure 10-13 shows another expansion of Lydia's profile. I know that she married Joseph McKnitt Wilson on 8 April 1856 and that one their sons, Emory Lee Wilson, was born on 12 July 1865. I noted the unusual fact on Lydia's profile that her son, Emory Lee Wilson, married Dora Ester McKey on 27 November 1887. Less than eight months later, however, their first daughter, Dora Belle Wilson, was born 21 July 1888. You can be sure that I would love to know the full story behind that birth!

1873 -   Laura Augusta (Minnie) WILSON on 24 January 1873.
Source: Family Bible.

1875 -   Mecklenburg County celebrated the Mecklenburg Declaration of Independence.
Lydia Lenora Patterson Wilson participated as a member of the ladies' planning
Committee.
Source: Charlotte *Observer*, 11 May 1875.

1880 -   Mecklenburg County, NC (Member of household of Joseph McKnitt WILSON.)
Microfilm publication T9, Rolls 971/972.

1886 -   Father, William PATTERSON, died on 3 December 1886.
Source: Family Bible.
Need: Additional evidence of death date.

1887 -   Emory Lee Wilson married Dora Ester McKey on 27 November 1887.
Source: Marriage Book C, Mecklenburg County, NC, page 98.

1888 -   Grand-daughter Dora Belle Wilson, daughter of Emory Lee Wilson and Dora Ester
McKey, was born 21 July 1888.
Source: Family Bible.
Source: Baptismal record, Hopewell Presbyterian Church (Mecklenburg) NC
(**Note:** This child was born less than 8 months after the wedding of her parents.)

1890 -   Mecklenburg County, NC (Member of household of Joseph McKnitt WILSON.) No
census records available.

FIGURE 10-13   An ancestor profile sometimes reveals inconsistencies, such as the birth of
a granddaughter in 1888 less than eight months after her parents' marriage.

Add Historical Events to Your Ancestor Profile

Finally, it is important to place your ancestor into context within the place where he or she was living
and with events taking place around them. Your studies of geography, history, societal influences,
climatology, and other subjects really become important now. Add important events to your ancestor's
profile. Natural disasters are important, such as fire, flood, earthquake, tornado, hurricanes, drought,
and monsoon. Man-made catastrophes include war, political oppression, religious or ethnic
persecution, human right's violations, and other events should be considered because they may
have directly influenced your ancestor's life and possibly the decisions to migrate, settle in a particular
location, choose a particular occupation, or participate in other events.

Look at the Entire Picture—for the First Time

Print your ancestor profile again, this time with all of the components combined in chronological
sequence. Read it and edit it once again for spelling, transpositions, and other data entry errors.
Make corrections and reprint the profile.

The chances are good that you have never had a clearer view of your ancestor than you do now.
You undoubtedly will see the strengths and weaknesses in the information you have compiled about

your ancestor. You also will see gaps in your research that you will want to pursue. More important, though, you may find that you have more sources of corroborating evidence for specific facts than you might have imagined. And conflicting information and inconsistencies in facts and sources will become more apparent as well.

The preparation of an ancestor profile is a valuable favorite method of working through a brick wall problem. It forces you to organize the materials you have already located and place them into chronological sequence. It forces you to reread, classify, and reevaluate *all* of the evidence by judging the quality and authority of the information and the sources from which it came. It highlights gaps in your ancestor's timeline, in your research, and in your source citations. Moreover, the process causes you to become more intimately familiar with your ancestor as a person and with his/her family and their circumstances. This may be exactly the process that reveals where you need to focus your attention to solve your problem.

The creation of an ancestor profile helps you produce a well-organized biographical and research outline. You can then use it to formulate a biographical sketch or a full-length biography of your ancestor or of the family unit, or simply take it on a research trip as a reference. During the process, too, you will also have become a better researcher and analyst, and that is an extra dividend.

Switch to Another Family Member to Bypass Your Roadblock

Sometimes, despite all your research, analysis, and troubleshooting efforts, an ancestral brick wall will just be entirely too contrary. Every effort at direct research may be thwarted. What can you do now?

One of my favorite techniques is what I call the "Genealogy Sidestep." This move is simple to perform and involves locating another close family member and switching your research focus. There have been times when I have encountered a brick wall in my research for one person and cannot progress to the next generation. What I do then is review all I know about the person through compiling an ancestor profile. If I can identify a sibling or some other blood relative, I move to that person and begin conducting research. I have often found that, while my ancestor may not have a very good paper trail, a brother or sister may have. As a result, by researching a sibling, I sometimes have been able to trace the sibling's parents and then, from one or both parents' records, have been able to make the connection downward to my own ancestor.

If you cannot locate or identify a sibling to use in your research sidestep, look for another relative such as an aunt, uncle, cousin, and so forth. If you can find one person as a linchpin, you may just be able to blaze a research path, albeit convoluted, up, down, and across the family tree to make the connection that can then be connected downward to your own ancestor.

Seek Help from Libraries, Archives, Museums, and Societies

It may seem intuitive but I am often surprised that genealogists overlook the services that can be obtained from librarians, archivists, museums, and all types of societies. Librarians and archivists are among my favorite people. They are intelligent and have a nearly unquenchable thirst for knowledge. They love to research interesting and difficult questions and to provide help and instruction to their patrons. These unsung heroes of our communities are trained and skillful professional researchers. They may not know where my Great-grandmother Penelope Swords Holder was born, but they know how to employ their research skills, techniques, and tools to help you locate print and electronic reference materials.

If I have a particularly impossible question about the location of a place that no longer appears on any map, I certainly try to search the materials at my disposal. That includes my own collection of maps, atlases, and gazetteers; online databases and map collections; and any possible Internet resource that I can be creative enough with search terms to locate. After my own exhaustive searches, however, I have been known to contact an academic library with a good map collection, a state library or archive, and even the cartographic division of places like the Library of Congress, the National Archives and Records Administration, and the National Geographic Society. The staffs there are experts in locating this type of information and are always willing to help.

I encourage you to join genealogical societies in the places in which your ancestors lived and where you are conducting research. The cost is comparatively small but the benefits can be great. The publications of these societies, such as journals, magazines, and newsletters, often contain articles that provide contextual insight about your ancestors' lives and the events in the area. Projects the society is conducting or has completed, publications they have planned or completed, and educational seminars are detailed and documented to society members. In addition, there is the opportunity to connect with other researchers who might be researching your family or connected collateral lineages.

Genealogical *and* historical societies are excellent resources to assist in your research. Even if you are not a member, it is not unusual to make an inquiry of such a group to request information. The society can check its own collection of information and reference material and respond with information for you. Often, too, a society member will make an extra effort to help by heading to a local library, courthouse, government office, cemetery, or other facility to do a quick look-up for you. These "genealogical angels" perform extraordinarily kind services, and while it often is not expected or requested, I always offer to reimburse the person for the cost of their mileage, photocopies, postage, and other expenses. Don't overlook the National Genealogical Society (NGS) and the New England Historic Genealogical Society (NEHGS) in the United States and the Federation of Family History Societies (FFHS) in the United Kingdom as resources to help connect you to important organizations and resources in their areas.

Heritage and lineage societies are another excellent source of information. Their staff and members often maintain extensive collections of printed materials, as well as genealogical records and data submitted by members. These people are experts in genealogical problem-solving and know how to address difficult questions and help find answers to obscure facts. There are scores of different such societies, many with regional chapters, lodges, or branches. One of the best Web sites for learning about such societies around the world and their contact information is Lineages.com at **http://www.lineages.com.**

You may also determine that your ancestor or another family member was a member of a particular professional, fraternal, sororal, trade, alumni, or similar membership organization. If so, consider locating their headquarters and inquiring about any records that may exist about your ancestor, where they might be located, and how to proceed to request them. Almost all of them will have a Web site that you may locate using an Internet search engine.

All of these entities exist to serve their members and their membership operational staffs may be able to help you locate information on your ancestor. They provide yet another resource to help you locate information to get past your brick wall.

Engage the Help of a Professional Researcher

There may come a time when you simply cannot get past your most stubborn brick wall. After trying everything you can think of and following every link you can discover, you may realize that you need the help of a professional genealogical researcher. I have a few "lost souls" in my own family tree for which I've been searching for years. I also have considered engaging a professional who has expertise working with specific record types or in locating records of individuals in a certain part of the world. I love a good mystery *and* the thrill of a good genealogical chase, but I also can recognize when I can take my quest no further.

A professional genealogical researcher can help you in one of two ways. First, he or she can perform research for you on a fee basis or, second, act as a paid consultant to you and provide guidance and advice. Before engaging a professional, it is important to identify one who is qualified to provide the service(s) you wish performed, reach agreement on the scope of the work, and define the guidelines that will govern the arrangement.

Locate a Qualified Professional Genealogical Researcher

Anyone who has experience in genealogical research can assist and advise you. However, your best guidance will come from an individual who has been professionally trained and/or has successfully passed tests administered by a professional genealogy credentialing body. There are a number of organizations whose genealogical credentialing standards are held in high esteem. Let me share some of those with you, along with their Web sites at which you can learn more.

Genealogists Accredited through The Church of Jesus Christ of Latter-day Saints Historical Department Prior to October 2000

The accreditation process administered by the Historical Department of The Church of Jesus Christ of Latter-day Saints from 1964 until the transfer of its program to ICAPGen in October 2000 produced a large number of highly qualified professional researchers. These researchers' names and contact information may be accessed on the Internet at **http://www.accreditedgenealogists.org.**

Association of Professional Genealogists (USA)

The Association of Professional Genealogists (APG) is not an accreditation or credentialing body, *per se*. It is, instead, a membership organization consisting of more than 1,400 members worldwide whose primary purpose is to support professional genealogists in all phases of their work, from the amateur genealogist wishing to turn knowledge and skill into a vocation, to the experienced professional seeking to exchange ideas with colleagues and to upgrade the profession as a whole. The association also seeks to protect the interests of those engaging in the services of the professional.

Their Web site at **http://www.apgen.org** presents a good primer titled "Why Hire a Professional Genealogist?" In addition, the site contains a searchable database of all current APG members, their titles and/or certification, organizations with which they are associated, and their area(s) of expertise or specialization.

Association of Professional Genealogists in Ireland

The Association of Professional Genealogists in Ireland (APGI) acts as a regulating body to maintain high standards amongst its members and to protect the interests of clients. Its members are drawn from every part of Ireland and represent a wide variety of interests and expertise. Applicants are required to submit samples of their work in the form of a report on research conducted over a period of not less than five hours, exclusive of report preparation time. The association's Web site is located at **http://indigo.ie/~apgi.**

The Board for Certification of Genealogists

The Board for Certification of Genealogists (BCG) is an independent, internationally recognized organization that certifies qualified individuals in the field of genealogy. They define their mission as follows: "To foster public confidence in genealogy as a respected branch of history by promoting an attainable, uniform standard of competence and ethics among genealogical practitioners, and by publicly recognizing persons who meet that standard." Certification involves preparing a portfolio of materials, which is independently reviewed by a panel of three or four judges. BCG requires different materials for each certification category shown below. (The credential postnominals are shown in parentheses.)

- Certified Genealogical Records Specialist (CGRS)
- Certified Lineage Specialist (CLS)
- Certified Genealogist (CG)
- Certified Genealogical Lecturer (CGL)
- Certified Genealogical Instructor (CGI)

BCG has published the *BCG Genealogical Standards Manual,* which details the requirements for certification in each category. Certification is for a period of five years, after which time the researcher may apply for renewal of his or her certification.

The BCG Web site at **www.bcgcertification.org** maintains a current roster of certified individuals, searchable by where they are located and by special interests (Irish, English, Jewish, African-American, church records, etc.).

Genealogical Institute of the Maritimes
(Institut Généalogique des Provinces Maritimes)

The Genealogical Institute of the Maritimes is a nonprofit organization that examines and certifies persons wishing to establish their competence in the field of genealogical research. The first level of certification is that of Genealogical Record Searcher [Canada] [GRS (C)]; the second is that of certified Genealogist [Canada] [CG (C)]. By completing a preliminary application form that assigns points for education, genealogical research experience, and publication, a candidate is evaluated through a points system to determine if he or she possesses the qualifications required to apply for certification at either of these two levels. More information is available at their Web site at **http://nsgna.ednet.ns.ca/gim/index.html.**

International Commission for the Accreditation of Professional Genealogists

The International Commission for the Accreditation of Professional Genealogists (ICAPGen) is a professional credentialing organization, involved in testing an individual's competence in genealogical research. Originally established in 1964 by the Family History Department of The Church of Jesus Christ of Latter-day Saints, the program was transferred to ICAPGen in 2000. At the time of the transfer, ICAPGen was affiliated with the Utah Genealogical Society (UGA).

Each applicant for the ICAPGen Accredited Genealogist (AG) credential must demonstrate through extensive written and oral testing, and through production of high-quality, well-researched documentation, that he or she is an expert in a particular geographical or subject area. The current areas of geographical testing are the United States, the British Isles, Scandinavia, Canada, Continental Europe, Latin America, and the Pacific Area. There currently are two subject areas for which testing is administered, and these include American Indians and the records of The Church of Jesus Christ of Latter-day Saints.

The ICAPGen Web site at **http://www.icapgen.org** provides a database of accredited researchers, searchable by name, their place of residence, or area of specialization. PDF files of North American and International researchers are also available for printing.

Other Credentials

Individual genealogical researchers may have been awarded other credentials than those listed above. Some colleges and universities offer courses in genealogical studies, and there are any number of specialized genealogical lecture programs and institutes offering individual classes or immersion conferences. These all may entitle the student or attendee to receive the award of a certificate, diploma, and another document attesting to his or her successful completion of the curriculum. These may be weighed in your decision-making process to determine if an individual has the education, experience, and expertise to perform the service(s) you require.

Define the Scope of the Work to Be Performed

Once you decide which professional researcher you want to hire, he or she will likely ask you to define exactly what you are seeking. You should prepare a written report on the individual or family group for which you want research performed, and provide all the information you have gathered. Include names, dates, source materials you have located, and a description of each item's contents. Here is where an ancestor profile can really come in handy. What you are doing, in effect, is preparing a complete picture for your potential researcher of what you know.

Once that is prepared, you must decide what it is you want to know, and what you want the professional researcher to find for you. These two items may not be one and the same. For example, you may believe that identifying the parents of one ancestor may be all you need in order to continue your research beyond that point.

On the other hand, you may decide that you want the researcher to accept the commission and pursue your research farther. For example, you may have traced your ancestors back to a point at which they arrived from another country or continent, and you want the researcher to first locate the passenger arrival records in order to first determine their port of departure and then to trace your ancestors back to their native town or village.

Establish Guidelines, Goals, and Milestones

It is important to be precise in determining the goal or goals of your research. Your goal(s) will determine the scope of the work to be performed, and you should also define the scope in writing. This document complements the documentation of your research to date, that is, the ancestor profile.

The professional researcher will now be able to review your research materials and evaluate the scope of your project goals. Request a written research plan, an itemized estimate of research time and expenses, a reasonable timetable for the project, and a list of project deliverables. For example, the researcher may determine that locating your immigrant ancestors' passenger arrival may take 15 hours' work, tracing the ancestors to their native village is another 30 hours' work, and preparation of the final report will take another 5 hours' work, a total of 50 hours' work. In addition, costs of document copies, photocopies, telephone calls, postage, mileage, travel, lodging, and meals may be itemized to present an itemized grand total. A good researcher will generally offer you a list of references, and may provide a sample of a final report to give you an idea of the quality of the final product you would receive.

Take your time to review the researcher's proposal and weigh the expenses against what it might cost you in time and money to perform a similar job. Contact the references the researcher provided and discuss their experience with them. Describe at a high level to each reference what it is you want the researcher to do for you, and ask if the person believes the researcher could and would be able to satisfy your need. Take notes and prepare additional questions for your potential research candidate.

Schedule a time to talk by telephone about any questions you have. Make sure that they are all answered to your satisfaction. At that time, consider all the information you have at hand and make your decision. Investing in a professional researcher's services is much like buying an automobile. It pays to do your advance research and to shop around as necessary for the right researcher. Requesting proposals from two or more researchers is not a bad idea. This advance work may save you money and frustration as the project progresses.

Document the Relationship

Let's say that you have decided to accept the proposal of one professional researcher. The association between the two of you should be a formal employer-employee relationship. As such, it should be documented in the form of a contract. A good contract will detail the scope of the work. It also will specify the exact amount of time the researcher will spend and the precise amount of money that you authorize for the project. Be sure to establish benchmarking milestones in the project schedule. These facilitate communication of status reports from the researcher so that you know

10

what is happening. It will help alleviate surprises later on and will allow you both to determine early on whether the scope and goals of the project need to be adjusted.

The contract should include payment terms, and it is not unusual to use a graduated payment schedule. For example, you might choose to pay 25 percent of the total fee as an advance before the project commences; incremental payments payable at certain milestone points, such as written status reports or some mutually agreeable criteria; and the remainder as a final payment when the final report and documentation are delivered. Include a contract cancellation clause that protects your and the researcher's interests.

A good contract is mutually acceptable to both you and your researcher. It should be designed to provide legal protection for both of you. With the project goals and deliverables clearly defined, and the authorized expenses clearly itemized, your expectations and those of the researcher are set.

Conclude the Relationship

When the research project is completed, and you have received your final report and accompanying documentation, make time to read and study its contents. Prepare a list of any questions you have about the contents or outstanding issues. At that point, you should schedule and conduct a final recap meeting with your researcher. Discuss the report and any questions you have about it, the documentation, the source materials found, where they were located, the source citations, and any other pertinent issues. You may learn a great deal from the researcher's recounting of the research process, including information that he or she may have encountered about other individuals that is not included in the report. These may be leads you can pursue on your own at a later date.

If your experience with your professional researcher has been a positive one, you can offer to be a reference for his or her future clients' inquiries. In the event that the experience has been problematic or the researcher has not performed in a professional or ethical manner, you should consider contacting the regulating body that awarded his or her genealogical credentials and file a formal report. This action will help the organization keep track of problems and consider them when reviewing the renewal of the individual's certification or continuation of accreditation. It also helps protect other genealogists considering hiring an unsatisfactory individual.

You will find that professional genealogical researchers are eager to help you and subscribe to a code of high professional ethics and behavior. Seeking out a credentialed individual with the qualifications and experience in the field of specialization you require is a solid first step to getting what you want from a professional research experience. Carefully setting the goals and establishing the contractual relationship with your researcher is essential. You can encourage the progress of the project by establishing and following up on the milestone status reports along the way.

All of the methods and resources discussed in this chapter should make you feel more confident about the various research routes you have open to you. Difficult-to-trace ancestors will invariably show up in your family tree. However, as long as you know how to conduct scholarly research, learn about and work with all kinds of alternative records, and employ the strategies and methodologies defined here, the chances are excellent that you can knock down those brick walls and keep moving your genealogical research forward.

Chapter 11

Plan a *Very* Successful Genealogical Research Trip

How to...

- Work like a professional researcher
- Determine the scope of your trip
- Develop a research plan
- Plan your time effectively
- Pack the right materials
- Efficiently cover territory while you're traveling
- Perform a daily reassessment of your progress
- Process the materials when you return home

Work Like a Professional Researcher

You will find that it won't be long before your genealogical interest and curiosity take over and you'll find you want to start making research trips. Your genealogical research at home and through the Internet will certainly help you prepare to visit libraries and archives, courthouses, government document repositories, churches, cemeteries, and other places where you may locate information and records. You probably will even want to locate and visit the places where your ancestors and family members actually lived. The very thought of these adventures is enough to get your blood pumping, I'm sure. However, a research trip of any type cannot be undertaken with any expectations of great success unless you properly plan and prepare yourself.

Professional genealogical researchers become experts in making the most effective use of their time and resources when they conduct research for a client or for themselves. Since you typically would pay a professional researcher at an hourly rate for his or her time, you would certainly hope that they are "working smart" on your behalf, wouldn't you? Well, you want to accomplish the same result when you conduct the research for yourself. That means working the way that professional researchers do, and this chapter is sure to put you into the right frame of mind and help you organize for a *very* successful genealogical research trip.

Determine the Scope of Your Trip

The first and most important part of your work is to determine who you want to research, what information or evidence you want to locate, and in how much depth you want to go in your research. You already know that it is impractical to think you can research five entire generations in only a few days' time. It is important to set realistic goals for your trip. You have to consider where you are going to conduct your research work, what materials might be available there, and how much time you will need to invest to accomplish your goals.

When planning your research trip, select those individuals whose information provides a foundation for expanding research about them *or about other persons* later on. Perhaps you are planning an overseas trip and plan to conduct some research there. In that case, choose individuals

The author and his aunt, Mary Allen Morgan, in 1960 (From the author's collection)

to research whose information may only be obtained at the place you are visiting and in some detail. This is especially important when this may be a once-in-a-lifetime on-site research opportunity. At the time of this writing, I am planning a trip to England with my brother and a friend. My friend has ancestors with the surname of Mildmay who lived in the town of Chelmsford, Essex. While we are in England, we plan a side trip to that town so that he can visit the church, the cemetery, and the county records office to seek information about that family line. He is already compiling information about the family and determining what records are available, and where they might be found, in advance of the trip. He is working smart!

A genealogical research trip doesn't have to take you halfway around the world. Most of our research junkets are to places nearby. If you are like most genealogists, your local public and academic libraries will become something like a second home to you. However, you can maximize the use of your time and conduct highly efficient research there by defining the scope of your research in advance and setting goals for yourself. Let's look at a simple scenario.

I planned to visit the John F. Germany Public Library in Tampa, Florida, recently to conduct research to locate an ancestor in the 1900, 1910, 1920, and 1930 United States federal censuses in either North or South Carolina. I was unsure of the state in which he lived during those years, although family tradition indicated that he and his family lived in one or the other state.

In advance of my trip, I accessed the Hillsborough County Public Library Cooperative's Web site at **http://www.hcplc.org/,** and located the Web page for that specific library at **http://www. hcplc.org/hcplc/liblocales/jfg/.** There I quickly found the page for the History & Genealogy Department and their table of census microfilm holdings. I determined that the library had both the census and the census index cards (Soundex or Miracode) on microfilm in the collection. In addition, I searched the library's online catalog to find out what books, CD-ROMs, and other resources are available to help in my research. The library's catalog allows me to select titles in the search results list and add them to a facility called My Booklist, and the one I created is shown in Figure 11-1. I can print this Web page or e-mail it to myself and, as a library cardholder, I also can place a hold on any book in the circulating collection. My Booklist contains the book titles and call numbers, and I will take the printed copy with me to the library to quickly locate these books in the library's collection.

11

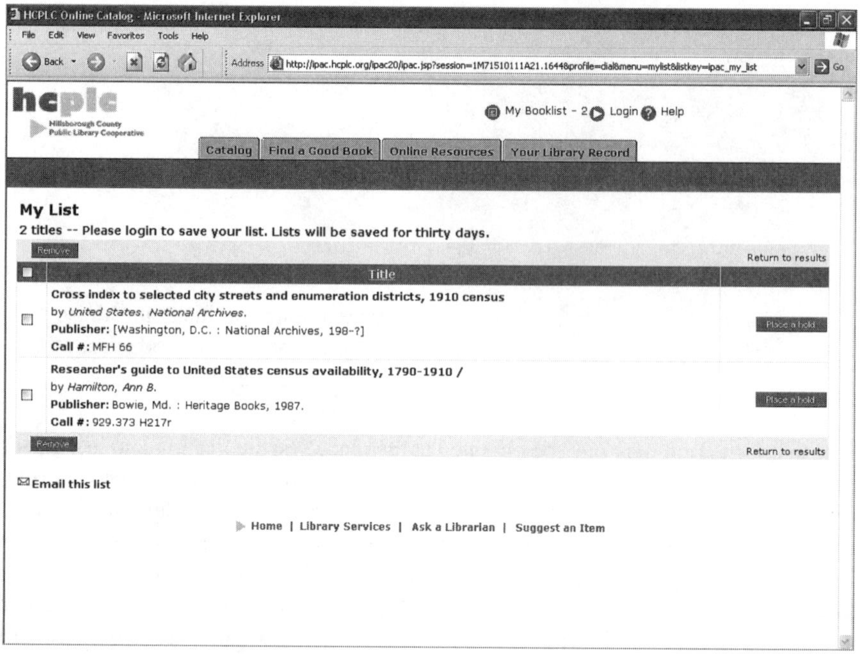

FIGURE 11-1   The My Booklist facility in one library's online catalog allows me to select and print a list of items for use when visiting the library.

By the way, I also determined while at the Web site the library's hours of operation and obtained a map and driving directions to the location. And thanks to the Internet, I was able to do all this advance work from the comfort of home at 3:00 A.M. while sitting in my pajamas!

Develop a Research Plan

A professional genealogical researcher develops a detailed research plan in advance of any trip. In the examples above, it should be apparent that both my friend in his planning for his research of the Mildmay family in Chelmsford and I in my planning for census research in the Tampa library have defined just who we want to research.

Based on the information I obtained from the online catalog, I determined that I would use both of the books I added to the My Booklist facility, and that I would be using the Soundex/Miracode and census population schedule microfilm for North Carolina and South Carolina. Since I was interested in researching records in the four census years of 1900 through 1930, I determined that I would possibly be using 16 rolls of microfilm—4 Soundex rolls and 4 population schedule rolls for each state—to locate my ancestor in the census records.

The selection of the person or persons you plan to research shouldn't be a spur-of-the-moment decision. In Chapter 10 when we discussed the option of hiring a professional researcher to help you, I told you that the researcher will ask you to be specific about what information and/or evidence you are seeking. The process I described there is the same one you need to use when you are planning to conduct the research yourself. Let's discuss each of the activities in more detail here.

Get Your Materials Organized

Before you finalize your decision about just who you will be researching, gather together everything you already have on the individual and/or the family you are considering. That includes every scrap of evidence you have accumulated, including primary and secondary sources, original and derivative materials, photocopies of books and documents you may not have yet processed, notes you have made, hypotheses you may have formulated but have not quite finalized, photographs, letters, and anything else that might be pertinent. If you're like me, you will have come across persons' names and data that don't quite fit into the family structure. I have created a file for every surname I am researching, and the notes and documents I accumulate for these people are filed appropriately. I call these my "Might Be Related" files. If you have materials on some of these people who don't quite fit, gather these together as well. You may finally be able to determine on this research trip if they really are or are not related after all.

Now is the time to review and get all these materials organized. This will likely be the most time-consuming part of your planning process. Use your critical thinking skills to read, review, and assess the information you have. You will then enter appropriate data into your genealogy database program. (We'll talk about evaluating and choosing one of these programs in Chapter 13.) Make certain that you enter your source citations so that you know where your information came from, and add any notations to indicate that a piece of information is not proved or verified, or that it is as yet merely a hypothesis.

File the Documents and Evidence You Have Collected

Next, file the documents in your filing system. My own system is arranged in three-ring binders by surname. (Women are filed under their maiden name.) Within each binder, I have filed individuals in alphabetical sequence by first name, middle name, and then Juniors, II, III, IV, etc., in successive sequence by order of descent. Finally, each document or piece of evidence is filed, by individual, in the chronological sequence in which it was originally created. Marriage documents are filed under the husband's name and a photocopy (or a cross-reference page) is filed with the wife's records under her maiden name. Evidentiary materials that are not or cannot be filed in the binder are described on cross-reference sheets. These include items such as family Bibles, jewelry that might bear an inscription, photographs, and items in other relatives' possession.

Your own filing system or method of organizing the materials you collect certainly does not have to mirror mine. On the contrary, whatever system you devise that works for you for the long-term is perfectly satisfactory. I know people who have organized their materials by geographical region or country, and then either by individual or by family group within that geography. I know others who have everything organized by family group. You also will recall our discussion in Chapter 2 of how to fill out a pedigree chart, and that we discussed the numbering system on the sheets. Some people have even organized their materials numerically to correspond with pedigree chart numbering. While the latter scheme seems overly complicated to me, it is logical and orderly for others, and it may be so for you as well.

11

Consider Who and What You Want to Research

With your materials all organized and filed, now it is time to consider which person(s) you want to include in your research trip and what you want to discover. Remember that you have a finite amount of time and that you will want to trace information on key figures whose information forms a foundation on which other work can be done later. For example, I made a visit to a courthouse in Newberry, South Carolina, to access microfilm and print a copy of the will and probate documents of Isaac Mitchell, Sr., my great-great-great-great-great-grandfather whose will is dated 29 June 1789 and was proved in court on 6 October 1789. That document indicated that he was survived by his widow, Mary, and children Ursula, Mary, Catherine, Sarah, and Isaac, Jr. The names of the children, especially Sarah, my ancestress, provided me with additional avenues of research after I returned home.

This is an ideal time to consider preparation of an ancestor profile for the individual(s) you plan to research. As you saw in Chapter 10, the process of preparing an ancestor profile helps you focus on the person's entire life. It helps clarify the strengths and weaknesses of evidence and source materials you may already have acquired and identifies areas on which you need to concentrate additional research. Based on this work, you are now prepared to develop a clear research plan.

Prepare Your List of Subjects and Evidence

Your ancestor profile will be an invaluable reference tool for you while on your research trip. Make sure you have a copy of it with you for each of the persons you plan to research. In addition, produce a pedigree chart of the person's direct ancestors and descendants. You'll remember that in Chapter 2 we discussed different styles of pedigree charts. The hourglass tree chart is a perfect tool to show ancestors and descendants.

You will also want to produce several family group sheets for every person you plan to research. It is important to have a family group sheet that represents your research subject and his or her siblings. That is because you will want to reference their vital dates of birth, marriage, and death as well as the locations, and the names of their spouses. When you are researching on site, you can never tell when you may want to check a parallel surname line, such as that of a spouse. Make sure that you have a family group sheet for your research subject and his or her spouse and children as well. I have encountered situations in which a woman was buried in the cemetery lot of a daughter-in-law's family and, unless I had had reference materials about that surname and relationship, I might never have found the woman.

This brings us to the next point. Prepare a list of *all* of the surnames of people in the area who might be related to one another. That includes the direct *and* collateral lines—those persons' families into which your relatives married. Make yourself familiar with those names before you begin your research so that they will make an impression whenever you encounter them in an index, a document, a cemetery, or elsewhere. In addition, prepare a list of possible alternate spellings—or misspellings—that might show up.

All of these documents you compile here should include the source citations so that, if necessary, you can quickly determine the origins of your evidence. In Chapter 8, we discussed the use of a research log to keep track of what information you have already researched. A professional researcher will always ask you what you have already found (or not found) and what resources you have already researched. He or she doesn't want to duplicate your work unless there is a reason to reexamine or re-verify your findings, hypotheses, or conclusions. Likewise, you don't want to duplicate your research efforts. If you have been using a research log to keep track of the source materials you used when researching a particular individual or family, you have a ready-made reference. If not, consider either preparing one for your research trip based on the materials you have compiled for your research subject or make sure you continually refer to the source citations embedded in your documentation. Few things are as frustrating as finding that you have wasted precious time and resources re-researching something.

In order to really organize what you have created, make a folder or envelope for each research subject. Include the documents listed above, and add any notes on "might be related" or "need to research" items. If you think that an image of a specific document, particularly a complex one such as a land record or a will, might be particularly helpful when you are on site, make a photocopy and include it in the appropriate folder. If such a document contains information or applicability to multiple persons you are researching, either add a note in that person's folder cross-referencing another research subject's folder where the copy is filed or make another copy for each applicable research subject's folder. Whatever you do, never take your originals with you! You can always replace a copy but an original may not be replaceable.

All of these folders or envelopes will accompany you on your trip. I find it easier to use folders than to travel with these materials in a binder. A binder is bulkier to carry everywhere than a folder. Instead, I may consolidate the files into a light-weight, portable plastic file box or into a closeable accordion file folder. Everything is still grouped together, but individual file folders can be pulled and carried into research venues only when and where they are actually needed.

Home in on the Evidence You Want

Now that you have all the evidentiary information gathered together and organized for your research trip, you should be feeling like a professional researcher. You're getting very close to having identified what you want to find.

The next step is to go through the folders and the ancestor profiles you've created and identify just what you are seeking for each individual. Prepare a list as you do so. For example, on one research trip, I determined that I wanted to locate marriage records, death certificates, and burial locations for all of my grandmother's six brothers and five sisters, if possible. In preparation, I made three lists—one for each type of record. Here is the information I included on each list:

- **Marriage records**   Full name of family member, name of spouse if known (maiden name used for women), date of marriage, and location
- **Death certificates**   Full name of family member, date of death if known, and location of death
- **Burial locations**   Full name of family member, date of death if known, location of death, name of funeral home/mortuary if known

You next need to determine where you can or will find the types of records you want to obtain. That includes the geographical location and the type of facility where the information may be stored, such as libraries and archives, courthouses, health departments, government records offices, civil registries, religious institutions, cemeteries, genealogical and historical societies, relatives, businesses, etc.

In the case of the records I was seeking, I did some preliminary research in books and on the Internet for the location where these people had lived. I determined that the indexed marriage books were to be found in the county courthouse. The death certificates were originally filed with the county health department and copies were furnished to the state bureau of vital statistics. The burial locations could be anywhere, and I knew in advance that my ability to research all of these sites would likely be dependent on information included on the death certificate. However, in advance, I determined that my resources for locating the records would include the following resources:

- The local public library's online catalog indicated that the genealogy and local history collection contained city directories for tracing residents' addresses, cemetery canvass books prepared and published by the area genealogical society, microfilm of the town's newspapers from the mid-1800s forward (a few missing years), and a published history of the town. The newspapers could be especially helpful for obtaining obituaries and funeral announcements.

- The online catalogs of the several local colleges' libraries show they own some local histories that might include information.

- The municipal cemetery department is responsible for maintenance of the town's three public cemeteries and maintains records of lot ownership and burials.

- The county clerk is responsible for issuing burial permits and transit permits and their records may include the names and places of interment for the people.

- The area genealogical society has canvassed cemeteries in the area, including the three municipal cemeteries and a number of other public, private, and religious organizations' graveyards. Some of their work has been published but some has not.

- The local historical society has a small collection of materials in a downtown storefront museum. Their collection contains correspondence and photographs.

- The local mortuaries that handled funeral and/or burial arrangements may still be in business. Their files, if they still exist, may provide information about burials.

As you can see, I put a lot of thought into the places where I might be able to locate information and records. You will need to do a similar job as well. Consider what it is you want to locate and the information or records might be found, including developing a list of likely alternative resources as I did above. In my case, I knew I had a limited amount of time to conduct my on-site research, so I needed to really organize myself for optimizing my time and resources for the trip.

Plan Your Time Effectively

Prepare a research plan far enough in advance to allow time to organize yourself properly and to do some preliminary research work. Defining the records and the places you are likely to find them is only part of the job. The other part is to refine your list of locations so that you can visit

Wedding photo of the author's maternal grandparents, Walton Carey Weatherly and Elizabeth Holder–16 September 1908 (From the author's collection)

only the facilities you really have to in order to obtain what you want. There are a number of ways you can do this, much of it involving the use of the Internet, the postal mail and e-mail, and the telephone. Let's examine the primary tools at your disposal and how to use them to your best advantage.

Obtain Information about the Area You Will Be Visiting

You certainly don't want to go into an area without having some idea of its layout, the accommodations, and what resources are available to you. Chambers of commerce and visitors bureaus are great resources for travel planning. A simple communication with a staff member is usually enough to bring packets of all sorts of information to you. Make sure to specifically request a general area map and a detailed street map, if they are available, and information about libraries, archives, and government offices. Ask for information about historical and genealogical societies in the area, museums, archives, and churches. The bureau is usually happy to compile a custom package for you.

   While you're at it, you also might request local residential telephone and business directories, or else contact the telephone company serving that area to request them. Telephone books are relatively inexpensive and the telephone company representative can usually arrange to mail you copies and bill the cost to your own telephone bill. You will find the telephone directory an invaluable research tool, both before your trip and afterward. Prior to your trip, you can learn about the area, the government offices, libraries and archives, churches, funeral homes, and even search for people who may be relatives in the area. You will use the directory to make calls in advance for appointments and as a resource for addresses when plotting your research stops while on site.

   The maps you obtain for a chamber of commerce or visitors bureau may or may not contain the finite amount of detail you might want. There certainly are other alternatives. Published atlases and travel books can be helpful for planning your trip. They might even suffice for some of your research forays into neighborhoods, suburbs, and rural regions. However, they may not contain as much detailed information. There are other options available to you. One of these would be a travel or motoring association, such as the American Automobile Association (AAA) in the United States.

11

Members enjoy the benefit of obtaining detailed maps of many types and levels of detail either for free or at a considerable savings. Other excellent maps include state highway department maps in the United States and ordnance survey maps in the United Kingdom. These are exceedingly detailed and often include finite details of landmarks such as churches, cemeteries, forts, castles, parks, and natural features such as rivers and streams, mountains, canyons, and detailed coastline features.

You can also generate maps from Web sites with mapping resources, such as: Yahoo! Maps at **http://maps.yahoo.com** (U.S.), **http://ca.maps.yahoo.com** (Canada), and **http://uk.maps.yahoo.com** (U.K.); MapQuest at **http://www.mapquest.com;** Multimap.com at **http://www.multimap.com,** and many, many others. I urge you to double-check any driving directions with more than one of the mapping sites. If the maps' directions disagree with one another, you should call ahead to verify directions.

In the United States, you might consider using the Geographic Names Information System (GNIS) of the U.S. Geological Survey at **http://geonames.usgs.gov/pls/gnis/web_query.gnis_web_query_form.** This site allows you to enter a query for a specific location, even using specific feature types such as a cemetery, a church, or a school. The result from your query can be used to produce a detailed map from the United States Census Bureau's Tiger Map Server that highlights the precise location of the feature, including the latitude and longitude of the site.

Invest time before your research trip to become familiar with the maps of the area you will be visiting. Study the maps' legends so that you don't have to use valuable on-site research time on that activity. Make note of important landmarks in the area and their directional relationships to one another. This can help keep you on the correct route or alert you to being headed in the wrong direction.

Make Hotel Reservations in Advance

I know that some people take trips and travel from one place until they feel the urge to stop at a hotel, motel, or inn. While this may be suitable in some instances, your genealogical research trip requires you to have a comfortable place to stay with space to spread your genealogical materials and do some studying, planning, and paperwork. It is therefore important to do some advance research into housing accommodations. You might find that a bed and breakfast inn is available, and the proprietors may be able to help guide you to people and places in the vicinity that will be helpful. You may, instead, prefer a full-service hotel with a restaurant, a swimming pool, an exercise room, and other amenities. When traveling abroad, consider whether you want an *en suite* accommodation, which includes a private bath, as opposed to sharing facilities with other guests.

Use the telephone directories you obtain in advance to locate possible accommodations in the area, and then use your Web browser to locate a Web site to learn more and to comparison shop. As a businessperson who travels frequently, I have found that the best room rates with national and international hotel chains can be obtained by booking rooms through their corporate Web site. These "Internet rates" almost always reflect a 10 percent or greater discount even over motoring club (AAA) or retiree (AARP) rates in the United States, and frequently are better overseas as well. I advise against the use of the so-called "bargain, last-minute discount" travel sites. My personal experience has been that the rates are not as good as Internet rates you might book yourself, and that the accommodations you obtain may not be up the standards you might expect. Do your research in advance, and *caveat emptor*!

Search the Web for Libraries and Archives

You already know how important a library or an archive can be to your research. You will want to take advantage of every opportunity to visit those collections that might hold important information to help with your research. Therefore, it is important to locate these facilities in advance of your trip and do some preliminary research about them.

You can find links for many of these facilities at the LibrarySpot.com Web site located at **http://www.libraryspot.com.** StartSpot Mediaworks, Inc., is the company that has created this excellent site. From the site's main page, click on the link labeled "Public Libraries" and the screen shown in Figure 11-2 will be displayed. You can then locate public libraries in the United States,

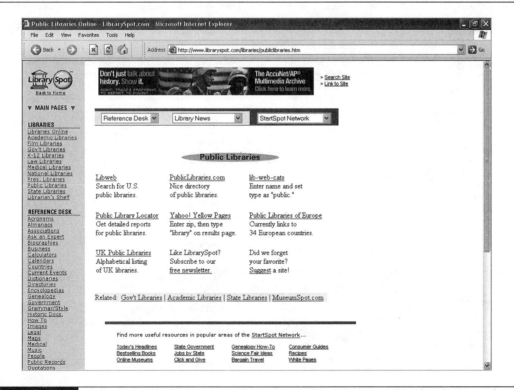

FIGURE 11-2   LibrarySpot.com is an excellent place to locate Internet sites for all types of libraries.

the United Kingdom, and in Europe. Similarly, to locate virtually any type of library, including public, academic, national, and special libraries across the United States, Canada, the United Kingdom, and in a number of countries around the world, look for the link labeled "lib-web-cats" and click on it. This will take you to the Web page shown in Figure 11-3, at **http://www.librarytechnology. org/libwebcats,** where you can search for libraries by type and country or, at the bottom of the Web page, select a location and browse the collection.

Alternatively, you can always use your favorite Internet search engine to quickly search for libraries' Web sites by typing the name of the location where you are going, followed by one or more words, as shown here:

> *[name of place you're going]* **library**
> *[name of place you're going]* **genealogy**
> *[name of place you're going]* **genealogy library**
> *[name of place you're going]* **"genealogy library"**

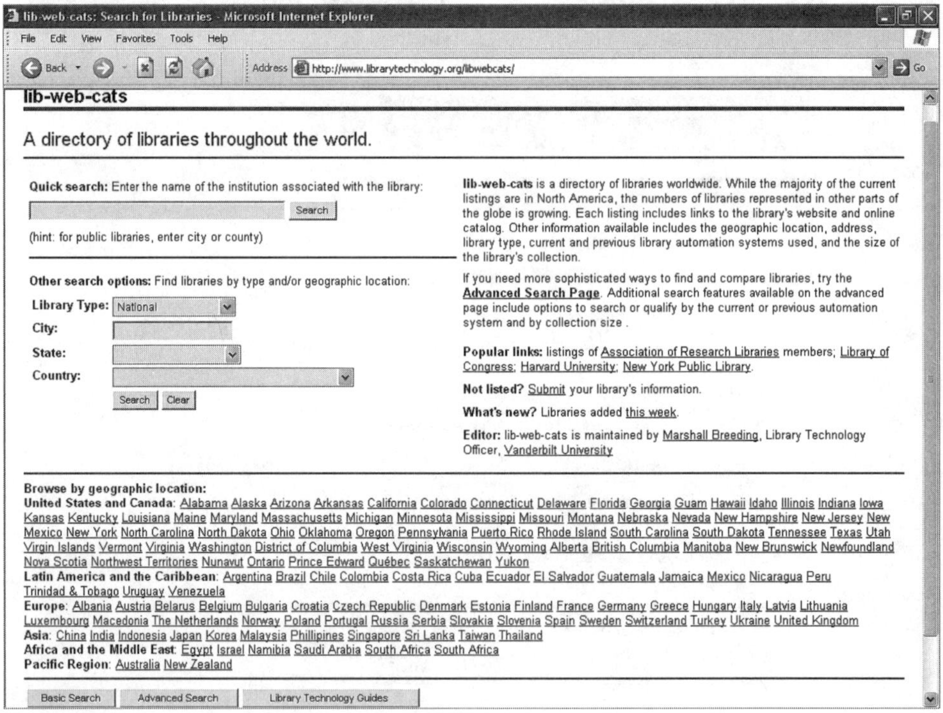

FIGURE 11-3   The lib-web-cats Web site provides searchable or browsable access to online library catalogs around the globe.

In the previous examples, you would omit the use of the square brackets and simply type the place name or, if the place name consists of more than one word or a hyphenated place name, enclose the place name in quotation marks to make it a phrase. You also may wish to specify the type of library by enclosing it in quotation marks as well. Here are some examples:

"fort worth" library
"richmond upon thames" library
"stoke-on-trent" "public library"

When you visit a library's or archive's Web site, there are a number of important things you can check online. These include the address and hours of operation. Often, you will find a map and/or driving directions at the site. Read the policies for the library to learn what to expect when you arrive. Some facilities may require you to use a researcher's card. If you have not visited the library before, you will need to complete a form and present identification on your arrival, and this process should be taken into consideration when planning your schedule there. Some libraries don't have open stacks, or shelves, of books for your access. You may have to fill out a call slip and a clerk will locate the item and bring it to you. In some repositories, you can only work with one or two items at a time, and this can be time-consuming to your schedule. By understanding the policies, you can anticipate how you will want to work at that library. Let me give you an example.

At the Library of Virginia, in Richmond, Virginia, you may not being any briefcases or bags into the genealogical and historical area, and you may only use a pad of paper and a pencil. You will complete a call slip for an item you wish to view, submit it at the reference desk, and a page is sent to retrieve it for you. You can only work with one item at a time. In order to work effectively in this environment, I did some preliminary research in the library's online catalog before I visited and compiled a list of items and their classification/call numbers in advance. Because I knew what materials I probably wanted to work with, and the sequence, the first thing I did was complete call slips for the first several items I wanted to use. I submitted the first one and, when that item arrived, I submitted the next one. The clerk could then retrieve that item while I worked with the first one. When I returned the first item, the second one was waiting for me and, at the same time, I submitted the slip for the third item.

If you know the facility also has microfilm and/or electronic materials you want to use, the library's policy will describe for you whether you need to sign up for time on a microfilm reader or computer, and the time allotted for each user. Costs will usually be listed for photocopies, printed images, and other services. Knowing these facts in advance can help you plan your time effectively. If I know I have to sign up for a microfilm reader/printer, I may plan to arrive early in the morning before there are large crowds and either complete my microfilm work first or sign up for time. Once signed up, I can use the waiting time to locate and work with other materials. The last thing any of us wants to do on site is sit around and wait.

Your use of the online catalog to plan your on-site use of the library or archive collection is very important. However, remember that not every single item in the collection is cataloged. Some loose documents may be filed in what librarians refer to as the "vertical files." This is simply another term for a file cabinet.

I often call the library when I am planning a research trip and ask to speak with the genealogy reference librarian. I introduce myself and tell the librarian that I am planning a visit, and that I have already spent time preparing by researching in the online catalog. I then indicate what it is that I plan to be researching, and ask if there are any items in the vertical files that may be of genealogical and historical significance that might help in my research. Whenever I arrive on site, I generally then ask for the librarian I spoke to, reintroduce myself, and ask for his or her help in locating and accessing those materials. The librarian will appreciate your thorough preparation and will generally give you excellent assistance. Be certain that you get the librarian's name and telephone number or e-mail address.

The library can be a base of operations for you when you are researching on site. I always check in at the library the first thing when I arrive in a place to do research. I meet and get to know library staff members who work with genealogical and historical materials, and spend time becoming familiar with the library's collection. By doing so, I will know when I'm visiting the area what materials they might have to help me overcome stumbling blocks. If I know what's there, I can make a quick reference trip to the library, get information I might need, and get back out to continue my research.

After you return home, it is an excellent idea to perhaps send a thank-you note for such great help. In addition, if you have questions after your trip and need follow-up information, you will have a ready-made contact person who will remember you and can help clarify any open item.

Search the Web for Government Offices and Departments

Government offices will be the repositories you will visit to obtain many of the official documents you will want to review and copy. A research trip may take you to a courthouse, a city or township hall, a public records office, the health department, the vital records bureau, a property and tax assessor's office, or any of dozens of other official agencies' offices. It is not unusual for government offices and departments to be geographically distributed in multiple locations. Sometimes they are logically arranged together or in close proximity based on function or responsibility. However, you can never rely on this.

Your work with telephone directories can help you tremendously. There is typically a central group of pages in the directory with all government operations and contact information listed. They are arranged by government level, such as town/township, parish, county, state, province, and national levels. Review each of these sets of listings for the area you plan to visit, especially in an area you have not visited before and/or if the governmental structure is different from yours at home or unfamiliar. Make note of department names, because the name may be different in one place than in another. For example, an agency responsible for maintaining death records may be called the "State Health Department" in one place, the "Office of Vital Statistics" in another, and the "Civil Registration Office" in yet a third location. And while their functions may be similar and each may maintain copies of death certificates and related records, the nominal difference may be enough to throw you off balance.

Once you have identified the applicable department name, invest some time in locating the government site on the Internet. Here you can verify the structure and departments, their current locations, their hours of operation, telephone and fax numbers, and the e-mail addresses. Read the office's mission statement and policies. Government Web sites also maintain Frequently Asked

The six Holder sisters in Rome, Georgia–1905 (From the author's collection)

Question (FAQ) collections with answers to the most common questions you might have. If you have other questions or want to obtain details about specific records, feel free to make telephone calls in advance to determine specifics.

Get the name and telephone number of each person you speak with, as well as where they are located. Let the person(s) know that you are planning a visit on particular dates and want to conduct family research for a specific family at a particular point in time. By communicating the time, the government representative can probably tell you what materials are and are not available, if any older records are stored off-site and how to gain access to them, and contact names and information for other persons who might be able to provide more information or assistance. You can then make additional contacts as needed.

Search Web for Genealogical and Historical Societies

As I've mentioned before, genealogical and historical societies are the keepers of sometimes amazing information and materials. They may have gathered and compiled data, documents, correspondence, photographs, and artifacts concerning people in their area. These collections usually are not on display or accessible to the public because these groups may not have the funding needed to provide such access. Most such societies are composed almost exclusively of volunteers and few have a dedicated office or staff. As a result, it is imperative that you make contact in advance to determine what materials or information they might be able to provide. Be sure to let them know you are planning to visit, who and what you are planning to research, and try to make an appointment with an appropriate society officer or member who might be able to help you with your specific research. Be aware that you may have to schedule an evening appointment in order to work around the person's schedule. The contact you make in this manner may be one of the most important you make on your trip, providing you with access to unique materials to help your personal research.

Contact Religious Institutions

One of the biggest challenges in researching some of our ancestors is locating the correct religious institution where their records may be located. The telephone directories, the business pages in particular, can be invaluable in locating congregations in the area. It really does behoove you to make telephone calls and write letters far in advance of your trip because you can expend a huge amount of time researching the wrong church. In addition, many churches do not have full-time personnel in their offices. You will therefore want to make contact in advance and, if you want to visit and examine records, it is important to set up an appointment to meet with someone there.

Locate the Cemeteries Where Ancestors May Be Interred

In Chapter 5 we discussed the importance of locating and delving into cemetery records. Cemeteries are among the most important and interesting places that we, as genealogists, can obtain information. Many researchers simply show up at a cemetery and wander about in search of grave markers in hopes of locating and transcribing the memorial inscriptions. Cemeteries may actually be a resource for much, much more information than what is on the tombstones. The cemetery's office may have detailed information about the cemetery lots and the persons interred there. I have had great success obtaining important documentary evidence by contacting the cemetery sexton, administrator, or caretaker responsible for a cemetery.

Your challenge is to locate the cemetery sexton, administrator, or caretaker responsible for the facility. A telephone directory listing for a cemetery whose name you already know may provide you with the contact you need. Check the business pages under the listings of "cemeteries" and "memorial gardens" if you don't know the name of the cemeteries you want to check. Don't overlook religious organizations that may own and operate their own graveyard. The county, parish, or municipal government may operate one or more cemeteries, in which case it should be comparatively simple to locate the responsible administrative office. Persons who served in a branch of the military service or their surviving family members may have requested military burial, military honors at a civilian interment, the payment of a military death benefit to help defer burial expenses, or placement of a military grave marker. If you know that a person was in the military at the time of death, or was a veteran, you may want to check with the respective branch and with the government office that handles military and/or veteran affairs for available information.

Be sure to seek information about local mortuaries, funeral homes, and funeral parlors. These companies are acquainted with many families in the community and are familiar with the public, ecclesiastical, and private family cemeteries in their area. They may be able to direct you to the sexton or administrative contact person for a specific cemetery or to someone else who can. They may even have files for the funeral and burial arrangements that they might share with you.

Contact Schools, Colleges, and Universities

Another resource for genealogical information may be the academic institutions in the area in which your ancestor or family members lived. The registrar's office, office of admissions, records offices, and so on, may still have the original records, microfilmed copies, or transcripts available. Often the older records are stored elsewhere, but if you make contact in advance of your visit, it is possible that the records you seek might be located and copied for you.

Use the Internet to locate public and private schools, academies, trade schools, colleges, and universities, and make contact with them to determine what they may have on file.

Mary Allen Morgan–circa 1907
(From the author's collection)

Make Appointments in Advance

You should have a good idea by now of the types of organizations at which or through which you might obtain information, copies of records, and referrals. While the telephone directories may be helpful in quickly locating all of these types of facilities, you may find more current, up-to-date information for them on the Internet. I therefore urge you to combine the use of your critical thinking skills and your proficiency at searching the Internet to locate as much quality information as you can well in advance of your research trip.

Your trip's success depends on your efforts to determine what organizations located in which places have the information you want to access. Obtain current address and contact information and then make contact *in advance* to set up appointments with organizations and specific, knowledgeable persons. Remember that no one is just sitting there waiting for you to show up. Offices and organizations that are not open and/or do not have personnel available all the time will need advance notice of your visit. While they are usually more than willing to help you, you must work around their schedule for availability.

Set Up a Schedule

If you selected the individuals you want to research, have defined what evidence it is that you want to discover, and have done all of your advance research and contacts, you should be ready now to put together your research schedule.

Earlier in this chapter, I discussed compiling a list of subjects and evidence. Consider again, now, the types of records and information you want and the places you have identified that possess (or probably possess) those materials. Add notations to the list you prepared earlier, this time indicating the name of the location, its address, and its telephone number. Continue the process until you have dealt with every item on your original list.

11

Samuel Goodloe Morgan–circa 1885
(From the author's collection)

At this juncture, your list may look pretty messy, but that won't last long. The next step is to rewrite your list, this time by location and address (and including telephone number). For each location, make a checklist of each person and piece of information that can or probably can be found at or through that location. Work your way through all the entries on your original list and make sure each one is listed under a location on your new list.

Your new list is now the research plan we talked about earlier in the chapter. Now you must consider timing and prepare a research schedule for yourself. Determine how long you have on site to perform research. Create a calendar for each day of your research trip and divide each day into one-hour blocks of time.

If some of the locations on your new list involve appointments you made in advance, enter those appointments in the appropriate time block on the calendar pages. These are fixed items. Make sure you have entered the name and telephone number for the person with whom you have an appointment so that, if you are running late, you can make a courtesy call and let the person know.

The next step is to consider the physical location of each of the places you want to visit to conduct research, and then how much time you expect to have to spend at each place. You probably already do this in your everyday life, scheduling your errands in a particular sequence based on where you have to stop, hours of operation, and other criteria. You are going to do the same thing with your research trip. Consider everything you have learned about these places already through your telephone calls or Internet research. Are some places only open certain hours? Do some of your tasks, such as visiting a cemetery, have to be done during daylight hours?

Use a map of the area and look at the locations again. Using all the information you have at hand, and recognizing how much time you have to spend researching on site, it is time to fill in the blanks on your schedule. You will work around the scheduled appointments, trying not to schedule an activity in advance that might overflow or conflict with an appointment. Be sure to include transit time between locations in your schedule, as well as time for meals and breaks. Don't expect to last 12 or 14 hours at a time. Your body and mind cannot take that much stress and abuse, and the last hours will not generate quality research.

Alvis Martin Weatherly–circa 1915
(From the author's collection)

Fill in the blanks on your calendar and then ask yourself if the schedule makes sense. If you are visiting a town in search of a variety of records, have you included a visit to the library at the beginning for orientation and a review of their collection? Does each location stop on your schedule help create a foundation for the next stop or another progression of research steps? Does your schedule include a lot of backtracking, crisscrossing, or redundancy of effort, time, or visits? Consider all of these factors as you review the schedule. When you are satisfied with the schedule, print it and consider it as "cast in" … well, pencil. You *will* have to maintain flexibility on site.

We'll talk about the on-site work shortly. However, since you have now developed a research plan and your schedule, let's consider the other activities associated with getting ready for your *very* successful research trip.

Take the Right Tools with You

Whenever I make a research trip of any kind, I always prepare a list of the items I need to take along. We've already discussed how to identify the person(s) and information you want to research. That's all part of defining the scope of the research trip. You also have produced a research plan and a schedule of places to go and materials to seek at each place. You've also compiled folders containing the pedigree charts, family group sheets, notes, and copies of documents you think may be important to have with you for reference on site. *And* you've prepared or updated your research calendar containing the places you've already researched and the source materials you've already examined and worked with, and this will help alleviate the possibility of duplicating previous research.

All of these things comprise your working research plan and immediate reference materials for the trip. However, in order to make sure you are prepared to capture and record information you acquire along the way, you need to determine the right set of tools to take along. This may be an easier task if you are driving a car and have unlimited space to carry lots of tools and supplies, rather than traveling by airplane where your space is limited. You may have to reduce the amount of tools you take, but that doesn't mean you can't be as effective a researcher. You just have to learn to "pack smart" and consider efficient and economical alternatives when you reach your destination. Let's examine some categories of materials to take with you on your research trip.

Pack the Right Clothing for the Activities

I'll tell you right away that a cocktail dress and spike heels are *not* the ideal choice of clothing for genealogical research, and especially not when combing through dusty files in a courthouse and emphatically not for research in a cemetery. Not only is this an uncomfortable outfit, those heels can be dangerous!

Consider the places you plan to visit, the time of year, the climate, and most of all your comfort. Casual clothes are always your best choice for personal research, and nothing can compare with having a comfortable pair of shoes when you will be on your feet for most of the day. If you have made appointments to meet with individuals, you may want to take some more "dressy casual clothes" for those situations. I would certainly never visit a church in a grubby pair of jeans and muddy shoes if I want to make a good impression and persuade the person I'm meeting that I am a serious professional researcher. You get the idea. Pack the right clothes for the occasions you expect to encounter.

Check the weather forecast for the place you plan to visit if you are not sure what conditions to expect. If you will be working somewhere where the weather is cold, consider taking and dressing in layers. You can always add and remove layers and maintain a good comfort level for yourself that way.

If you plan to be working in a cemetery or another outdoor area in the summertime, you need to be aware not only of the climate, but of the other "critters" you might encounter. Outdoor research forays, especially in wooded or overgrown areas, require attention to your comfort and safety with protective clothing. Long pants and a long-sleeve shirt are an excellent choice because they protect you from harmful sunlight and insects. I take rubber bands with me for my shirt cuffs and pants legs to keep insects from getting inside as well. Thick socks and high-top boots may be a better choice for walking in rugged or dense, weedy terrain. Hiking boots provide support for your ankles and protect against sharp objects hidden in deep grass or leaves. The socks and boots also are a preventative defense against snakes and other creatures.

A head covering is wise for all weather conditions. A straw hat or a lightweight cap with a visor will help protect you from the sun's heat and glare in summer and help keep your head warm in winter. Sunglasses are a requirement for outdoor work as well. Choose a pair that is comfortable and scratch-resistant, and invest in a cord so that the sunglasses can hang from your neck when you need to remove them for close examination. Likewise, if you wear glasses, consider another cord for those. You can wear both around your neck and alternate between them as necessary. Clip-on sunglasses are another option and the ones that attach to your regular glasses and flip up out of the way are simple to use and quite inexpensive.

Last but not least, take a couple of pairs of gloves with you. A pair of heavier garden gloves made of canvas or another durable material is excellent for pulling weeds, working with a trowel or cutters around gravestones, and for other chores that might injure your hands. A lighter weight pair that allows you more tactile use of your hands can also be handy to have along. I recommend rubber gloves because they are durable for less rugged chores and are also water-resistant.

Select Other Tools for Outdoor Work

Depending on where you will be working outdoors and the time of year, you may want to take insect repellent along. In addition, remember to take along and use sunscreen to protect your skin from harmful ultraviolet (UV) rays. Your sunscreen should have a Sun Protection Factor (SPF) rating of at least 15 or higher, depending on your skin type and susceptibility to burning. You do not have to, nor should you, apply insect repellent as frequently as sunscreen.

Choose Supplies for Recording Information

So much information, and so little time! Copying and transcribing as fast as you can to cover as many resources in a limited amount of time can be dangerous. We all make errors but, when we rush and don't take time to recheck our work, the potential for errors increases. Taking the right tools for recording the data we find can help reduce the possibility of making on-site errors. You have many choices of materials for "working smart" in this area on your trip. Let's examine them.

Select Tools for Writing

Give some consideration to the types of information you plan to locate and record, and then select a format for paper products for recording your research notes. A spiral-bound stenographer's notebook or composition book is a good, compact choice. If you are researching multiple families or, for whatever reason, want to create separate groups of notes, you might buy a composition book with dividers already included for multiple school subjects. Loose sheets of paper can be dropped, become shuffled out of order, or even blow away in a strong wind. A notebook is therefore a better option and has the capacity to help keep your notes organized for easy reference.

Some of these composition books come with storage pockets inside the front and back covers. These are convenient for tucking in photocopies and document copies as you acquire them on site.

You will want to take a collection of pencils, pens, and colored highlighters with you. Pencils are your best choice because you can erase and change information as necessary. You should also buy a small pencil sharpener, such as the one you had as a child, to slip into your pocket or purse for quick resharpening. Highlighter pens are good for highlighting information on your copies, but not on any records nor in any library's or archive's books, of course.

I always take a collection of different color 3M Post-It® self-adhesive tape flags with me and use them in different ways, depending on the need. I sometimes use them to quickly mark pages I plan to photocopy, although some libraries object to or ban their use, especially on older and more fragile materials. However, I use them all the time in the notes I take. For example, I used tape flags on one trip and applied different colored flags to document copies and notes to quickly distinguish which ones contained a specific surname. Red flags were for Morgan, green ones were for Wilson, blue ones were for Patterson, yellow ones were for Alexander, and so on. Some documents that had more than one of these surnames, such as a marriage certificate, had multiple tape flags, each of a different color, attached. You also can use tape flags to make impromptu tab dividers.

Post-It Notes are also a great tool for note-taking. I use them to remind myself of additional information I need to locate, to make a note of source citation information, and for a hundred other uses. Don't leave home without them!

You will want to take a small collection of basic office supplies with you. These include a small stapler, a supply of staples, and a staple remover. Paper clips of various sizes, rubber bands, some extra blank file folders, and extra large manila envelopes are useful to help organize and store loose papers. You can compile a small kit with some or all of these items, or you can purchase a ready-made travel kit at most office supply stores.

11

When traveling by car on what I believe will be an extensive research trip, I also take a cardboard box, a covered plastic file storage box, or an "egg crate" storage container with me to hold all the materials together. I can easily organize everything in one container, quickly locate what files I need, and can carry the entire collection into my hotel room for overnight review work.

Capture Fabulous Images

You are sure to want to take photographs of places you visit and, in some cases, to record information. Modern cameras provide exceedingly high quality images at a reasonable price and images can be processed into printed copies or into digitized format, which can be electronically stored, manipulated, enhanced, and then used in multiple ways. I used digitized images as documentation for genealogical facts, include them in my genealogical database, include them in written and printed materials, add them to family Web pages, and exchange them with other family members.

You have a number of image-capture options available to you. Let's discuss each one briefly.

- **Digital camera** A digital camera offers excellent images like the one shown in Figure 11-4 and control of the quality in a variety of lighting conditions. You can see the captured image right away to assess its potential quality, albeit in miniature format. You can even use some of the newer digital cameras to photograph document and book images, subject of course to obtaining the permission of the owner, library, archive, or other repository. The digital image can later be manipulated and enhanced using graphics and photo editing software.

- **35mm film camera** Modern 35mm cameras offer high-resolution images and more light-sensitive film choices than ever. They are often less expensive than a digital camera but do not give you the immediate feedback that the digital model provides. Photo processing options can include both print and digital images.

- **Disposable camera options** We seem to have traveled full-circle to George Eastman's original idea of taking film pictures and returning the entire camera for processing of the film. Today's disposable cameras capture remarkably great photographs and come in color, black-and-white, indoor, outdoor, indoor/outdoor, and built-in flash models. In addition, disposable panoramic cameras take magnificent photographs that can be used to place standard-size photographic subjects into a larger context. For example, I often use a panoramic camera to capture a wide-angle picture of a cemetery, such as the one in Figure 11-5. I also take standard-size photographs of individual gravestones and markers, and can cross-reference the images to one another. In the future, when I or another researcher visits the same cemetery and the landmark trees and plantings have changed, these panoramic pictures can help locate the family graves in relation to other markers and landmarks. Again, you can have prints and/or digital images made during the photo processing.

- **Video recorder** Camcorders have improved a great deal since their introduction. They are more compact, all-digital, and come with better image and sound quality than ever before. Rechargeable battery life is longer. Moreover, electronic USB interfaces to computers and software allow you to transfer video, reformat, edit, and enhance the original footage like never before.

■ **Portable scanner**   Prices on portable scanners have plummeted the last few years, and economical models can be purchased for less than $100 U.S./£65 U.K., and rebates sometimes reduce the price still further. Most libraries and archives allow you to bring your notebook computer and a scanner for use with many of their general collection materials, and some provide central desks with power sources for every seating position. You may be limited in using scanners with rare and fragile materials, but the ability to scan book and document pages saves photocopy expenses and can pay for the scanner in no time.

You also have audio options for your research trip. I purchased a small, handheld audiotape recorder for less than $30 U.S./£20 U.K. and take it with me. When working in a cemetery, I may take photographs but will also read tombstone inscriptions word for word, spelling and inserting punctuation as inscribed so that I can accurately record the information in my genealogical database program at home. In the event my photographic images don't come out as clearly and with as much visible detail as I need, I still have the information on audiotape. Oral dictation is much quicker than hand-writing the information. I also use the tape recorder in research facilities when I want to capture larger pieces of information without making photocopies or manually transcribing the material. The tape recorder also saves time recording source citation information. I can dictate the author name, publication, location, publisher, and date of a reference item on tape and, at the same time, add a simple note with the source name to a photocopy or document copy. I can later match the documentation and a source citation together and enter the full data and the citation into my genealogical database program.

For all of these electronic tools, be sure to take extra batteries, film, and/or tapes. You never want to be caught unprepared to capture that important image.

11

FIGURE 11-4   A digital camera can take high-quality photographs that can be manipulated and enhanced (From the author's collection).

FIGURE 11-5   A disposable panoramic camera can be used for wide-angle views of a larger area, with smaller pictures of component subjects (From the author's collection).

Consider Taking Some Additional Tools

There are other tools and materials you might consider taking on your trip as well. Some researchers are using portable handheld Global Positioning System (GPS) units, downloading national and local maps to the unit to help find and travel to specific locations. The GPS uses communications with multiple manmade satellites in geosynchronous orbits around the earth to calculate a very precise location at which the electronic GPS unit is located. Do you remember my mention of the Geographic Names Information System (GNIS) of the U.S. Geological Survey earlier in this chapter? I use that site to locate the latitude and longitude of a cemetery, church, or other feature and use my GPS unit to locate it on a map and chart a route there. Also, when I locate a piece of property, a family member's grave in a cemetery, church, family residence, or some other site important in my research, I make note of the GPS coordinates and add those to my database for future reference.

A cellular telephone is an absolute necessity for several reasons. First, it provides the ability to make calls while in transit between locations, and perhaps even call home for a check of reference materials you did not bring with you. More important, if you get into difficulty anywhere, you can always call for help.

Two-way, portable radios can be an excellent communication tool for pairs of researchers working together. These include "walkie-talkies" and FRS (Family Radio Service) models, which have a relatively short broadcasting range and are quite cheap to purchase. You can divide up in a cemetery to locate a particular grave and converse back and forth as you search, and use the radios to share information, ask questions, and call for assistance if needed. These units can be purchased in many department, hardware, and electronics stores, and on the Internet. Shop around for good deals on these very inexpensive units.

A visit to a cemetery might involve clearing overgrown grass, weeds, and brush from gravestones. You may want to take a pair of handheld garden trimmer shears and a small trowel with you. If you need these tools when you arrive at a site, never fear. Dollar stores and discount stores sell these

Sarah Edith Weatherly–1927
(From the author's collection)

at such cheap prices that you can almost afford to use them and discard them later. You may also take a few one-liter bottles of tap water with you to pour onto gravestones to darken them for photography purposes. Never use any chemicals or stiff brushes to scrub gravestones. Despite their permanent appearance, many older stone monuments and markers are actually quite fragile and may crumble when brushing or any other pressure is applied. Never use shaving cream or other chemicals to "clean" or to highlight inscriptions. If you want to provide contrast of the inscribed characters and images, consider taking a package of cornstarch or flour with you. Toss the material gently into the inscribed areas and then use a very soft brush or cloth to lightly dust off the excess. Take your photographs and then use the water to rinse the residue off the stone.

An extra-large aluminum cookie sheet makes a wonderful mirror, propped up with a pencil, pen, or stick, to catch sunlight and reflect it at an angle against gravestone inscriptions. This provides more contrast for a better photo.

To Rub or Not to Rub

A popular activity over the centuries has been to make a rubbing of the detail carved on a tombstone or marker. The process involves the use of a sheet of comparatively supple paper spread over the area to be captured. One then might use a crayon, chalk, charcoal, or some other material to press against the stone, rubbing back and forth, to produce a relief image.

While you may find this idea appealing, it is important to know that many, many municipal governments and individual cemeteries have banned the practice. That is because the practice of making a rubbing subjects the stone to pressure and stress and can seriously damage the marker. We think of tombstones and monuments as being permanent in nature; however, nothing could be farther from the truth. The extremes of heat and cold, expansion and contraction, and the effects of chemicals in the atmosphere cause these stones to erode and decompose. Marble, granite, and other types of stone used in the funerary markers can be chemically damaged and literally turn to sand. If you should attempt to make a rubbing on a stone already whose chemical composition and structural integrity has already been compromised, you could very well cause the stone to fracture, crumble, or collapse.

Samuel Goodloe Morgan–circa 1881
(From the author's collection)

Before taking the liberty of making a rubbing in a cemetery or in a cathedral, church, or chapel, always ask permission first. You may find that there are laws or regulations prohibiting making rubbings. In fact, I know of a woman visiting a cemetery in Ohio who decided to make a rubbing of a family member's gravestone. Imagine her surprise when a policeman arrived, pointed out a sign indicating that cemetery rubbings were against the law, and arrested her. She unfortunately learned that there was a $400 fine for this illegal activity.

Even if rubbings are permitted, make certain you know what you are doing. If there are any indications that the stone is not stable, walk away. One way to tell the status of a stone is to gently rub your hand against the surface. If your hand dislodges any granular, sandy residue, the stone is disintegrating. Any pressure you might apply while rubbing could damage the monument. Even natural veining in a stone can be the source of its destruction. If you notice any cracks or fissures whatsoever, don't even try to prepare a rubbing. And whatever you do, make sure that a stone marker is not going to topple and injure you or a companion.

A good photograph will serve your research purposes well, so you really do not need to make a rubbing after all.

Don't Forget the Money!

When you were doing your advance research on the Internet, you will have noted the prices of photocopies at libraries and archives, document copies at government offices, and the prices of other items. Also be sure you know whether the facility accepts credit cards, debit cards, personal checks, travelers' checks, or cash only, and be prepared with the right tender. I carry a small zipper pouch of coins with me for individual photocopies or, if I think I will make a lot of copies and the library offers the option, I may purchase a photocopying card for convenience and cash in the unused portion before I leave the facility.

Cover the On-site Territory Effectively

I talked earlier about the importance of preparing a research plan and a schedule of places to visit for research. It really is like running your personal errands on a Saturday morning, arranging them in a sequence in order to get everything done without having to backtrack. A professional researcher will do the same thing and, in addition, may try to do multiple things at once. Try to think creatively and do this yourself. Let me give you an example.

Earlier I told you that on one of my research trips I wanted to obtain death certificates for my grandmother's siblings—five sisters and six brothers. Having performed some research in advance and summarizing what I wanted, I prepared a list of the eleven people's names, their dates of birth, and the location and date of death of each person, as I thought it to be. I had contacted the county health department and verified that they maintained death certificates for the area and that the price of a certified copy would cost me $10 each. When I arrived in the town where I was to conduct my research, one of my scheduled stops was the health department. There I provided the same clerk I had spoken with by telephone the list I had prepared. She reviewed the list and told me to come back later. I paid her in advance for the copies and went on my way. Over the next four hours or so, I visited with the recorder of deeds' office in the courthouse and requested copies of specific land records and property tax records. I then had lunch, and visited the library to work with microfilmed newspapers to locate obituary records. When I returned to the health department, the clerk had located and issued certified copies of 10 of the 11 death certificates I had requested; the eleventh one was not on file in that office. She issued a $10 refund to me and I headed out with my copies. I then went to the recorder of deeds' office again, and paid for and collected the records I had ordered there.

What I accomplished was that I had two other people working on gathering together parts of my research material while I did other things elsewhere. You will want to consider how you can multitask in this way when you are on your own research trip. Now that is what I call "working smart!"

Remember to make careful note of names, addresses, telephone numbers, and e-mail addresses of people you talked to or worked with. You may want or need to follow up with them later with questions or requests for additional information. You also *will* want to send each person a thank-you note after you return home. You certainly will have appreciated their help, and they will appreciate your kindness. That one courtesy, too, may open doors for future communications with some of these people and they definitely will remember you!

Perform a Daily Reassessment

One of the greatest things about genealogical research is the feeling of accomplishment you get when you have completed a project or found something to further your work. When you locate new information and evidence of an ancestor or family member, it is a cause for personal celebration— what we call "the genealogy happy dance." However, even if you don't find what you wanted or expected to find, that is no reason to be glum or depressed. Actually, the fact that you conducted the research and found nothing also means that you have accomplished something important. You have investigated a research avenue and have eliminated it from the possibilities. Sometimes the absence of documentation, information, or other evidence is indicative that we must search in another direction. As a result, I can tell you that "the genealogy happy dance" has been done in my house (and hotel rooms) on any number of occasions when I *did* find nothing or when I *did* eliminate or disprove a hypothesis.

A vital part of each day of an on-site genealogical research trip should involve sitting back and reviewing what you have and have not found. Examine your research plan again and ask yourself what you accomplished. Mark those items off your list. Make notes on your research calendar or research log sheets to indicate what you have researched, the sources you used, and the outcome of each review. Evaluate all the material you acquired that day, organize it, and file it by individual in the research subject's folder that you brought along.

Now, compare what you did or didn't find with the information, documents, and data in each folder. Analyze what you think the next research step or alternative path might be. Prepare a list of your thoughts for each person. Once you've finished your review, you should have a strong feeling of accomplishment. And yes, you can do "the genealogy happy dance" too!

Based on your newly acquired knowledge, evidence, and experience, you should look at your schedule for the next day. Consider whether any of the places you plan to visit and records you planned to access might further extend your research for anyone whose information you acquired today. If so, add that to your list of things to research at that location. If not, consider what alternative research options you might have open to you, and what you might still be able to fit into your schedule.

Essentially what you are doing is performing a daily reassessment of your *actual* versus *planned* research schedule. Your review and analysis will help you regroup for the next day's research. Revise your schedule and alter your "to do" lists accordingly for the remainder of your on-site research. Always try to allow some extra time for the unexpected and extra things you discover. When I make a multiple-day research trip, I try to allow a final half-day for trying to resolve any loose ends I might have.

My last stop in town is usually the library or archive that I used as a home base. I can check any last-minute references I may have missed and explore ideas from the previous night's daily reassessment. And more important, I can personally thank the library or archive personnel again for all of their help.

A *very* successful genealogical research trip, as you can see, is not a haphazard, "pile-in-the-car-and-let's-go" affair. It involves some forethought, summarization of what you know, advance research, formulation of a research plan and a schedule, and a lot of organizational details. This is part of what you pay a professional genealogical researcher to do on your behalf. You may think now that hiring a researcher might just be a pretty good idea. Well, in some cases that may well be true. However, don't you want the thrill and enjoyment that a genealogical research trip can offer? And don't you want to be able to celebrate the discoveries yourself?

Method, planning, and organization are the keys to conducting a successful research trip, whether it's a trip to the nearby library, to another town, or halfway around the world. There is nothing like the thrill of a research trip and, with all you've learned so far in this book, you really are prepared to do it yourself!

Part III

Automate Your Genealogy with Hardware, Software, and Databases

Chapter 12

Select Hardware, Software, and Accessories to Aid Your Work

How to...

■ Identify the components of a computer system

■ Calculate how much computer you need

■ Assess your communications needs

■ Determine which printer, scanner, and photography equipment is right for you

■ Choose software products to help support your genealogical work

■ Integrate portable and handheld electronic equipment into your research

Most genealogists and family historians have made the move from permanently recording information on forms to maintaining their information on a computer. With so much information available on the Internet and on CD-ROMs, and with the availability of so many software application programs available, the choices you make in hardware, peripherals, portable equipment, and software can be mind-boggling.

This chapter focuses on the technical aspects of genealogical research, including the hardware and software options available to you. I don't intend to recommend one brand of computer or hardware over another. You will need to investigate the options you have, the type of activities you want to computerize, and the amount of money you have to invest. The Internet certainly allows you to research your options and comparison shop from the comfort of your home. However, use the critical thinking skills you've already learned in this book and apply them to your product research so that you can become a well-informed, savvy consumer.

Chapter 13 will discuss specific genealogical database software programs. However, I have taken the data and space requirements for those programs into consideration in the preparation of this chapter. I would recommend that you read both chapters and combine the information presented in both when making your choices.

Determine What You Will Be Doing with Your Genealogy

Part I of this book addressed the foundations of your genealogical research and discussed a broad selection of record types. Part II presented a number of methods and strategies that can be integrated into your work to help achieve success in your research. I believe that you will refer to the examples in Chapters 1 through 11 again and again to reinforce your knowledge of records research and your skills in accessing and locating them.

By this time, you should have a pretty good idea of what you want to do with your genealogical research. You should know what types of materials are available and how to critically evaluate your source materials. With this knowledge, you can now more accurately consider what you want and need in the way of the computer, peripheral devices, electronic tools, and software that can support your overall information processing needs, including your family history and genealogy work.

Let's begin by defining the hardware components of a strong home computer system and how they can be integrated together.

Caroline Alice Whitfield/Whitefield
Morgan (From the author's collection)

Identify the Components of a Strong Computer System

The vast majority of home computer users are using the IBM PC (personal computer), although there also are many users of the Apple Macintosh. When considering your computer choices, it is important to recognize that there are excellent general software packages for both types of computer for the basic, essential functions such as word processing, spreadsheets, personal publishing, Web browsing, and e-mail. There also are software packages for working with graphics and photographs for both systems. While the publishing industry continues to prefer the use of high-powered graphics software packages that run on the Mac OS, there also are excellent, powerful programs for the PC that perform just about every function the average home user will need. It is important to recognize, though, that there are many more choices of genealogical application software for the PC than for the Mac. These packages will be explored in more detail in the next chapter but be sure to consider this in your choice of computer systems.

When we think of a "computer," most of us think of a whole system of components. You really want to consider a computer as similar to a high-quality audio system. It should be a collection of integrated components that are electronically compatible and complementary to one another, and which interface to provide you with the optimum level of service for what you plan to do. Like an audio system, you can spend just about any amount of money you want on your computer system.

Remember the old adage that "you get what you pay for" and keep it in mind. That certainly applies to computer equipment, but it isn't always true. There are good choices at the lower end of the price spectrum and some not-so-wonderful choices at the top end of the line. Understanding your options makes you a savvy consumer, so let's break the basic PC computer system into components.

12

Understand What's "Inside the Box"

There is no real mystery to the "box" that sits on your desk or on the floor once you understand the components that are inside. Some people refer to the "box" as the CPU or the central processor unit. That is, however, a misnomer because the CPU is actually the processor chip that performs all the calculation functions and controls all the rest of the computer resources. Let's examine what is inside the box.

The Power Supply

Your computer needs electricity to operate. The cord you plug into the electrical outlet is connected at the back of the computer to a power supply box. The power supply's function is to act as a transformer. It transforms (converts) your standard electrical supply to lower and more appropriate voltages to power the components of your computer and some devices connected to it, such as the motherboard and the keyboard.

The Motherboard

The motherboard is nothing more than the largest circuit board in your computer. It is the base on which all of your computer's processor chips are installed and to which are attached a variety of components, either directly or through specialized circuit boards called "cards."

The Central Processing Unit (CPU)

The CPU is the heart of the computer and acts as an information clearinghouse for every piece of data that is processed in, out, and through the computer. It is plugged directly into a specific slot on the motherboard.

There are a number of choices of CPU chips. The two major manufacturers of CPU processor chips are the Intel Corporation (**http://www.intel.com**) and Advanced Micro Devices, Inc., also known as AMD (**http://www.amd.com**). While there are other manufacturers, approximately 98 percent of the world's CPU chips are made by Intel and AMD and their products are the best available.

There are various grades and speeds of CPU chips and, as the core of your computer's capabilities, this is your single most important decision to make. The Intel Pentium line of chips has been the leader in the marketplace over the years. The Pentium III and Pentium 4 processors have been standards in desktop computers for some time and are considered workhorses. Intel's economy processor chip is the Intel Celeron and, while it is a less expensive choice than the Pentium, it also is neither as powerful nor as reliable. When we talk later in the chapter about laptop computers, Intel sells both Pentium chips and its newer Centrino chips to manufacturers of notebook computers, and both of these are high-end, highly reliable processors.

AMD's Athlon processor chips have been touted as comparable and faster than the Pentium 4 chips because they require fewer internal instructions/commands to accomplish the same processing. AMD's economy processor is the Duron chip and is, again, less powerful than its Athlon counterpart.

The other consideration when selecting a computer and CPU is the processor speed. The processor speed refers to the rate at which the CPU chip executes instructions. Every processor contains an internal clock that regulates the rate at which instructions are executed. It is expressed in megahertz (abbreviated as MHz), which is 1 million cycles per second, or in gigahertz (abbreviated as GHz), which is 1 billion cycles per second.

Elizabeth Holder Weatherly–1908
(From the author's collection)

It is important to note that the rate at which data is actually processed in your computer will be a combined function of processor speed and the amount of memory, or RAM. In addition, a computer with a 3.2 GHz processor and 512 megabytes (MB) of RAM, connected to the Internet via a dial-up connection, will still not browse the Internet at any faster rate than one with a slower processor and 256 MB of RAM. That is because a dial-up connection is only so large a "pipeline" and only so much data can move through the connection at a time.

BIOS

The term BIOS is an acronym for Basic Input/Output System. It refers to software contained on a specific chip installed on the computer's motherboard, which stores the basic instructions that allow your computer to operate. The information is stored in Read-Only Memory, also referred to as ROM, and includes the system clock; information about the type and speed of the CPU; and other information about the computer's monitor, keyboard, disk drives, and the location of the operating system files. This information allows the computer to power up, recognize its essential hardware components, and to start the Windows operating system.

Memory/RAM

The second most important consideration for your computer is the amount of memory, or RAM, you have installed. Random Access Memory (RAM) refers to the fast but temporary data storage space that is used while your computer is doing its work. RAM allows you to open multiple application software programs and files at once, create and work with other documents and files, and display still other data, such as Web pages. The more memory, or RAM, you have installed on your computer, the more programs and files you can have open at once and the more things you can do simultaneously.

RAM consists of specific computer chips (memory chips) plugged into slots on the motherboard. These chips are measured in megabytes (MB), also called "meg," and each MB is the equivalent of 1,048,576 bytes of data. Think of a byte as the equivalent of a character. While one MB seems like a lot of information, it actually is very small when you consider that a single graphic on a Web page may consist of thousands of bytes of data by itself. It is important, therefore, to consider the *amount* of RAM you want on your computer. While 256 MB of RAM may be sufficient for running multiple programs at a time and achieving a good Internet experience, 512 MB is better. (Older versions of Windows and older motherboards may not be able to accommodate, much less use, more than 256 MB of RAM.)

Another consideration is that RAM comes in various forms in order to support the processing of different types of data. Here the technical definitions can get complicated. The contemporary

12

type of RAM is represented by the acronym, SDRAM. SDRAM refers to Synchronous Dynamic Random Access Memory and its purpose is to provide rapid movement of data into and out of the physical storage area on the RAM chip itself to speed processing. It uses what is referred to as a *synchronous interface,* or two-way communications, between the CPU and RAM chips. The essential SDRAM operation is a two-way communications operation known as *Single Data Rate (SDR),* which means that one chunk of data is processed at one time. There are SDR (Single Data Rate) SDRAM memory chips used to communicate like this. Another, more rapid chipset is *Double Data Rate (DDR)* SDRAM, which allows for two transfers for every one transfer with SDR SDRAM. In addition, Dual Channel DDR SDRAM transfers data four times for every one transfer with SDR SDRAM.

You will pay more for the higher transfer rate SDRAM. However, RAM as a commodity for your computer is comparatively inexpensive. You really can get a lot of RAM for your money, and RAM size really can make a difference in the quality of the operation of your computer.

Peripheral Cards and Slots

The devices that connect to your computer, such as the monitor, keyboard, mouse, audio speakers, microphone, headphones, printer, scanner, external disk drives and modem, and so forth, are referred to as *peripheral devices*. The keyboard and mouse usually plug into receptacles attached directly to the motherboard. The other devices typically are attached to the computer using cables that plug into receptacles on what are referred to as "peripheral cards." These cards are actually specialized circuit boards that are plugged into slots on the motherboard. They have a plate that lines up with the outside of the computer case and a receptacle to which the device can be attached using a cable of some sort.

The devices you select for your computer will determine what peripheral cards will need to be installed. At a minimum, you will need a graphics card to which your monitor will be attached, a card for connecting your printer, and a communications card of some sort. Other cards can be installed, particularly a sound card to accommodate attachment of audio speakers and perhaps a scanner interface card if you plan to use a scanner.

You must have a graphics card in order to attach and use a monitor. Graphics cards vary in type and capability. There are a number of options available to you. AGP (Advanced Graphics Port) cards allow for high-resolution video, and very high-resolution AGP cards allow users to enjoy three-dimensional (3-D) graphics for some of the intense computer games that are available. Unless you are a PC gaming enthusiast, one of these high-end cards may be overkill for you.

Sound cards are usually standard on computers these days to accommodate the connection of stereo speakers, headphones, and a microphone. Of course, there are high-end sound cards that will support enhanced sound systems that include stereophonic speakers, a subwoofer, and such features as Dolby, Dolby Pro Logic, Dolby Surround Sound, and other enhanced sound technologies.

You have options concerning data communications, as you will see a little later in this chapter. Depending on whether you decide to use a standard telephone line and dial out to access your Internet provider, use the services of a cable network utility, or subscribe to a DSL service, you will use one of two peripheral cards.

If you dial out using a telephone line, you will need a modem card. If you use a cable or DSL service provider, you will use a different type of card. In order to use these, you will need a specialized peripheral card referred to variously as a network card, a network interface card (NIC), or an Ethernet card. Your computer will need to have the network card installed, and it will be attached to a special type of communications modem "box" provided by your service provider.

Disk Drives

The primary storage of data on your computer will be on devices known as drives. It has been standard for many years for PCs to have at a minimum a hard disk (C:) and a floppy disk (A:) installed. CD-ROM drives began being added, and then Iomega Zip drives for specialized removable disks with high-volume data storage capacity were introduced and began being installed. Next came the CD drives with read-write capabilities and these have begun replacing the floppy drives on computers. CD/DVD drives are now highly popular for on-computer playing of DVD titles, such as movies and audio CD/movie combination disks.

Hard disks have become larger and less expensive. Hard disks as large as 200 gigabytes (GB) and more are available. With hard disks, invest in as large a unit as you can afford. You may not think so now, but you *will* use a lot of disk space over time!

Floppy disk drives are becoming less standard on new computers. They are being replaced by read-write-capable CD drives, Zip drives, and new miniature storage devices known as "flash drives." Flash drives are small, pen-sized removable data storage devices that interface with a computer by connecting through a USB port (see the next section), and are available in various capacities. Flash drives are therefore removable and very portable. Essentially, you could copy all of your genealogical materials onto a flash drive and take them with you for use on another computer using the same genealogical database software program.

USB Interfaces

In addition to all of the components covered above, another consideration for your computer is the type and number of external devices you can connect to your computer. The contemporary method of connecting other external equipment, such as modems, disk drives and storage devices, digital cameras and video camcorders, sound recorders, and more, is via a Universal Serial Bus (USB) connection. The "bus" we are discussing has nothing to do with your travel plans. Instead, a bus is simply a connection location or transmission path that allows the transfer of data. A USB port is a standard port (or connection receptacle) that enables you to connect external devices to Windows 98 and higher and Macintosh computers. The USB standard supports data transfer rates of 12 Mbps (million bits per second), a vast improvement over the serial port standard it is beginning to replace.

Devices equipped with USB connectivity can usually be attached to a computer without the necessity of the installation of a specific peripheral card. Instead, a USB cable connection is made and the Windows 98 or higher or Mac OS operating system searches its files for a piece of software known as a *driver*. The driver allows the computer and the device to recognize, communicate, and exchange data with one another. If the computer's operating system cannot locate a driver, it prompts you to locate or provide a disk/CD with the appropriate driver software for installation.

Some newer computers come with multiple additional USB ports that enable you to connect a USB device directly to the computer. At a minimum, you probably want a computer with two external USB ports. Even if you have a computer with only a couple of USB ports initially, you can purchase a USB hub device that acts like a "data extension cord" for your computer. The hub can plug into one USB port and then allow you to plug multiple USB devices into the hub.

12

Green Berry Holder (From the
author's collection)

All of the items I've described above are components that are enclosed inside "the box" and that interface and interact together to allow you to run a powerful and efficient personal data processing operation.

Assess Your Communications Needs

You will certainly want to use e-mail and the Internet in your research, and the resources available today are impressive. As mentioned earlier, you currently have three choices for the mode of communications.

- **Dial-up communications**   In this mode, you use a conventional telephone line and a dial-up modem. In this case, you would select a modem card for your computer.

- **Cable communications**   Commercial cable television providers have gotten into the business of providing data communications services and Internet connectivity over their existing cable network facilities.

- **DSL communications**   Many cable and telephone companies, as well as some specialized communications services provide high-speed connectivity using digital communications network facilities. DSL is an acronym for Digital Subscriber Line. DSL is really a method for moving data over regular phone lines. A DSL circuit is much faster than a regular phone connection, and the wires coming into the subscriber's premises are the same (copper) wires used for regular phone service. However, a DSL circuit must be specially configured to connect two specific locations: the provider and the specific customer. DSL is similar to dedicated, leased line connections used by a business, but is much less expensive.

Sarah Edith Weatherly and Nita Elizabeth Weatherly (From the author's collection)

There are many companies providing connectivity to the Internet for using e-mail and accessing the Web sites where you can conduct research. These types of companies are referred to as Internet Service Providers (ISPs). Regardless of whether you use dial-up, cable, or DSL type access, once you are connected, these service providers provide a threshold through which you will send and receive data. An ISP may only provide connectivity while another may provide content, such as news, weather, entertainment, and other services as well. America Online (AOL) and the Microsoft Network (MSN) are two of the largest of the services providing integrated content, e-mail, Internet search facilities, multimedia entertainment, news, weather, and many, many other materials.

If you are searching for the various communications options and ISPs in your area or elsewhere in the world, there is a Web site called "The List: The Definitive Internet Services Buyer's Guide" at **http://www.thelist.com.** You can search by telephone area code, by country and/or telephone code, and nationwide in the United States and Canada for ISPs. At a minimum, you will want the ability to connect to the Internet and to exchange e-mail. If you decide to publish your own Web page, you may want an ISP that provides Web hosting services. You will need to determine what services you require, and which ISPs serving your area provide those services with the options you want.

Determine Which Printer, Scanner, and Photography Equipment Is Right for You

It hasn't been that long ago that the only peripheral device most computer users had attached to their system was a printer. Things have certainly changed. Among the peripheral devices that many genealogists find indispensable are high-quality, multi-function printers, scanners, and digital photography equipment. Your decision will depend a great deal on what you plan to do with your computer, both for genealogy and for other applications. However, let's examine the types of equipment that are available in each category, and then you can begin your personal evaluation.

Evaluate Printer Options

Printers for home computer systems have evolved vastly in the last 20 years. Some of the early dot matrix printers were real workhorses, but these have been replaced by laser, inkjet, and bubble jet printers. As computer functionality and application software have become more sophisticated, the demands on printers have become greater. Your type of work, the software you plan to use, the quality of the materials you want to produce, and the ongoing expense of operating it should be the determining factors in selecting the printer you need.

There is no doubt that a home computer is an indispensable tool for all sorts of tasks, and not just for genealogy. If you plan to only produce documents printed in black and white, any printer will suffice. However, if you plan to work with any application in which color is used and the quality is important, a color printer is definitely the way to go. We will discuss the application software programs in some detail later in the chapter. However, for now, consider the fact that you may potentially be working with software to perform all kinds of tasks, and that most software will require you to be able to print output documents. This includes word processing of all sorts, creation of spreadsheets, e-mail, printing documents from your Web browser, manipulation of graphics and photographs, production of genealogy database reports and publishing, and more.

The quality of the output you produce will be important in many cases. If you plan to produce genealogy charts, reports, and other materials for inclusion in a published family history or in some other publication, you should know that a publisher will expect to receive high-quality, camera-ready materials. Printing photographs and graphics will require a printer that supports high-definition printing of many dots per inch (dpi) concentration, the use of archival quality inks, and the use of special photographic paper stock. The printer you select should be able to handle these demands if you plan to do anything with digitized photographs and other graphic images.

Generally speaking, a laser printer is more appropriate for an office or small business user rather than for a home user. A laser printer may handle a higher volume and print more rapidly (a higher page-per-minute rate) than an inkjet or bubble jet unit. However, a laser printer itself will be more expensive, the color toner cartridges are typically more expensive when considering the per-copy cost, and the quality of printed graphics images of laser units manufactured for home users are usually inferior to those produced with inkjet printers.

You may therefore want to consider the economics of purchasing more than one printer for your work. For example, you may select a relatively inexpensive color inkjet printer for printing ordinary documents on standard paper, and a photo printer specifically designed for work with photographs and other high dpi concentration images printed on special photo finish papers. In the long term, the investment in both printers may be offset by a lower overall per-document cost.

Some printers perform multiple functions, and we'll discuss that shortly. In the meantime, however, let's consider scanners.

Wilson brothers–Davidson College (From the author's collection)

Consider Adding a Scanner to Your System

I purchased my first scanner, a Hewlett-Packard color scanner, in January of 1995 after conducting an extensive comparison shop for the best possible price. I paid $995 U.S. at the time and suffered from "sticker shock" as though I had bought a new car. The scanner performed admirably for seven years until I replaced it with another unit, and I am still reluctant to get rid of it. Over the past decade, though, scanners have undergone great improvements and the prices have plummeted. In early 2003, for instance, I purchased a small, lightweight Canon scanner for the purpose of taking it with me on research trips. The price was $79.95 U.S./£45 U.K. and the retailer offered an on-site rebate of $20. In addition, I applied for and received a manufacturer's rebate of $40. In short, my final price was $19.95/£11.29! What's more, the scanner included software for manipulating images and OCR (optical character recognition) and it produces simple photocopies. The Canon scanner actually does a better job of scanning than my old Hewlett-Packard scanner at a fraction of the cost. This also is an example of the type of deal you can sometimes find among the competitive computer and electronics retailers.

At a minimum, you want a scanner that can produce a scanned image of up to 1200 dpi. Lower dot concentrations per inch produce a less crisp image resolution. A 300 dpi image, for instance, may be fine for digitizing a line drawing, but a photograph scanned at that resolution will appear grainy and fuzzy. There are top-of-the-line scanners available with resolutions of up to 3600 dpi. Scanners also produce digitized images in a variety of graphics format. The images you most often encounter on Web pages are .JPG and .GIF formats, and occasionally the larger Windows bitmap, .BMP, format. Most people's browser will not recognize other formats without setting it up to define a specific graphics software package to read the particular format. Most scanners will, by default, generate a digitized image in .TIF or .TIFF format. This format is the most data- and dot-intensive format and is great for high-quality, archival creation of scanned images. However, the scanner you purchase may or may not provide the ability to save to another format as the image is scanned. You may have to use a graphics software program to convert the .TIF image to .JPG, .GIF, or some other graphics format to use in another program. Most scanners today, though, include a graphics program of some sort on the disk that comes with the unit. It's a good idea to investigate the scanner's software in advance and its capabilities before you purchase, or else you may consider one of the full-featured graphics software packages discussed later in this chapter.

12

Some scanners offer attachments, either included with the unit or as add-on accessories, to scan strips/rolls of negatives and 35mm slides. If your family has a collection of these materials that you'd like to digitize, a scanner offering these accessories is important to you.

With scanner functionality so good and the prices so low, you can easily afford to add a scanner to your home computer configuration. In your genealogy work, you will find yourself wanting to make photocopies of photographs and documents all the time, and the convenience of doing so at home at any time for a tiny fraction of what photocopying costs somewhere else will more than pay for a scanner in a short time. The primary function of a scanner, though, is to digitize materials. I scan photographs and original source documents on a regular basis for inclusion in my genealogical database, and to print and mail or e-mail to family members and other researchers. I also embed scanned materials into documents I write and publish, and if you plan to produce a written family history, you are sure to want to do the same thing in your word processor documents.

Another option available is the combination printer/scanner/copier. These units have become increasingly popular and less expensive in the last several years. Some units also include a fax machine. If you have a physical space constraint in your home office, or if you want to minimize and consolidate your investment in peripheral equipment, you may want to consider one of these units. They come with a number of features, such as different page-per-minute printing speeds, multiple paper trays, envelope feeders, and other choices.

Evaluate and Comparison Shop Digital Still and Video Camera Equipment

Another consideration for your research is what kind of photographic equipment you want to use. The choices can be mind-boggling. In Chapter 11, we discussed using conventional, disposable, and digital cameras for your genealogical research trips. The fact that film used in the conventional and disposable cameras can be processed to produce digital images recorded onto photo CDs or e-mailed to you means that you can obtain high-quality digital versions of all of your photographs. You can then print them on your own printer or have your photo finishing service print copies for you. The limitations you face, however, are with the quality of the film used in the cameras themselves.

Digital cameras have become more sophisticated and less expensive in the last several years. Still, you can spend anything you like on a digital camera, depending on the features you want. The resolution of the images will be your primary concern in evaluating a digital camera because you will want the best resolution for the work you plan to do. Family photography and typical outdoor pictures are one thing. However, if you plan to use the camera for photographing documents in a library or making pictures of the family photographs that Aunt Lucy just won't let out of her sight, you will want a higher resolution image.

You will want to conduct some advance research into the models of digital cameras available, their image resolution specifications, the features they offer, and prices. An excellent guide to selecting and using a digital camera is Dave Johnson's book *How to Do Everything with Your Digital Camera* (McGraw-Hill/Osborne Media, 2003). I recommend reading this guide, followed by a fact-finding visit to a camera store or large electronics retailer. Consider, too, purchasing copies of some of the current photography magazines, such as *Popular Photography & Imaging* (printed for sale in the U.S. and on the Web at **http://www.popphoto.com**), *Digital Photographer* (printed for sale in the U.S. and on the Web at **http://www.digiphotomag.com**), and *Digital Photography Buyer & User* (printed for sale in the U.K. and Ireland and on the Web at **http://www.digitalphotouser.co.uk**). Gather as much information as you can and then conduct some research on the Internet. One Web site that can compare digital camera equipment based on features you specify is the comparison page at Digital Photography Review at **http://www.dpreview.com/reviews/compare.asp.** Another excellent place to obtain product information and compare prices online is at the CNET.com site at **http://www.cnet.com.** The site provides product reviews and, on its CNET Shopper.com page at **http://shopper.cnet.com,** you can compare features and prices.

Once you decide which digital camera you might want to purchase, you can search the Internet using brand and model number to locate merchants selling the camera. Comparison shopping for the best price is important because there is a great deal of competition on electronics equipment, and you can find some good deals.

Many genealogists are expanding their electronic recording of the interviews they conduct with family members, their research trips, and their family reunions and other events, using digital video cameras, also called digital camcorders. Video technology has improved a very great deal in the past several years and prices for video camcorders have dropped. What is important is that many video cameras come with a USB cable to facilitate connection to your computer and software to help get you started on transferring the video to your computer and, in some cases, to create CDs/ DVDs. If you are interested in learning how to use your digital video recorder, a great resource is *How to Do Everything with Digital Video* (McGraw-Hill/Osborne Media, 2002). The book discusses all the functions of a digital video camera, how to capture the best video images *and* sound, how to transfer data to your computer, and how to edit and enhance your video clips to produce highly professional-looking productions.

As with the digital camera, I recommend visiting a camera store or a large electronics retailer to do some fact-finding. Discuss how you plan to use the camera with salespeople, and let them tell you how they and other people have creatively used their digital video cameras. Gather brochures, price sheets, and any information you can obtain. Visit the manufacturers' Web sites to review product specifications. The CNET.com site at **http://www.cnet.com** and its CNET Shopper.com page at **http://shopper.cnet.com** again provide an excellent online forum for comparing features and prices.

Choose Other Software to Help Support Your Genealogical Work

By now, you must be reeling with the possibilities of using computers and electronic equipment. It is important to have strong application software packages to do the work on your computer to support what you plan to do with your genealogical research work.

We will discuss specific types of software and their application to your genealogy work, while reserving genealogical database software for Chapter 13. For now, though, let's concentrate of the types of application programs that you should consider and some of the functions they can perform for you.

Green Berry and Penelope Swords
Holder family–Rome, Georgia, 1905
(From the author's collection)

Anti-virus Software

The very first piece of software you should install on your computer after the operating system is an anti-virus program. If you are an experienced computer user, you will agree that this is imperative. It's a cruel Internet out there, for some reason, and there seem to be a lot of people creating software to wreak destruction on others. I refer to these people as "cyber-terrorists."

A virus is an executable computer program that alters another program running on a computer to either include a copy of the virus' code in its operation, or to reproduce and mutate the virus to elude detection and proliferate it to other computers. Some viruses do little or no damage, while others may delete, destroy, or corrupt other programs' files. In a worst-case scenario, a virus may reformat your computer's hard drive, deleting the operating system and files and rendering the computer completely inoperable. A complete reinstallation of your operating systems, programs, and files would be required.

A virus can be acquired in a number of ways. The most common method of delivering a virus to another computer is by piggybacking it with something else. Your computer can be infected by opening a Web page with an embedded program running in it. It can be attacked by opening an e-mail formatted in HTML format (Web page format) that has an embedded program in the text of the e-mail. Opening a file attached to an e-mail is always dangerous, especially if you don't know the sender, because the file could be an executable virus program. Another common method of transfer is by using a disk given to you by someone else whose computer is infected with a virus and who unknowingly has created a disk with an embedded or accompanying virus. Your computer can even be infected when you are exchanging instant messages over the Internet.

Once your computer is infected with a virus, you really have to do a lot of work to eliminate it and repair the damage it may have done. In some cases, you have to reinstall programs and restore backups of files. The best preventative measures you can take against viruses are the following:

- **Install and use an anti-virus software program.**   An anti-virus software program can identify known viruses and patterns in executable computer programs that seem to be performing functions identical or similar to known virus methods. The software can be configured at various security levels to detect, identify, stop, quarantine, and/or eradicate a virus program from your system. You can also specify when the anti-virus program runs: on demand, at start-up of your computer, at shut-down of your computer, whenever a new program starts to run, on receipt of certain types of files, on receipt of every file by your computer of any type, and/or combinations of these modes. Anti-virus programs provide a high degree of protection for your computer and a great deal of flexibility in how and when it runs. There are a number of excellent anti-virus software packages available. The most notable and impressive ones are McAfee VirusScan and Norton Anti-Virus, both of which I will talk about in more detail later.

- **Back up your important files on a regular basis.**   Make certain that you create backup copies of all of your important files on a regular basis. Not only can a virus infect your computer and destroy files, but your hard drive may experience a problem and data can be lost. Imagine a genealogist who has invested hundreds or thousands of hours inputting his or her genealogical information, source citations, notes, and scanning precious photographs, only to lose all the work because of a virus' activity, a hard disk crash, or an electrical power surge. It happens more often than you might think.

- **Know the sender of any e-mail and file attachments.**   Before you open any piece of e-mail, make sure you know who is sending it to you. There is a tremendous amount of spam mail that shows up in our e-mail boxes daily. You never know what is inside that e-mail, much less in an attached file. A good rule to follow is to either use your anti-virus software program to scan every e-mail message and file attachment before you open it, or don't open it at all.

12

McAfee VirusScan is an anti-virus software package that has been around for many years. It is a reliable product that performs an excellent job in protecting users' computers. The software is available for purchase on CD-ROM and enclosed in a box, through their Web site at **http://www. mcafee.com** as a download, or via an annual subscription. The company is continuously monitoring for new virus reports and regularly releases updates to its software to detect and eradicate new viruses. When you purchase the CD or download the software, you are entitled to connect to the McAfee Web site to obtain updates, and it is imperative that you do check for and download updates on a regular basis to maintain a high level of protection. Installation using the annual subscription program provides a version of the program that automatically checks the McAfee Web site for updates when you are connected to the Internet. The updates and any software version upgrades are automatically downloaded and installed on your computer without any effort on your part. I draw an analogy to having the computer doctor make house calls and give me preventive medicine while I sleep.

Norton AntiVirus is a program maintained by the Symantec Corporation. It is similar to the McAfee offering in that it has various security levels and scanning schedule options; checks files, e-mail messages, and instant messages; and quarantines or eradicates viruses found. You have the option of purchasing the software on a CD-ROM or downloading from the Norton site at **http://www.symantecstore.com.** Versions are available for both the PC and Mac OS operating systems and for a variety of handheld devices, and your purchase entitles you to free updates, just as McAfee does. There is not a subscription version of the Norton AntiVirus program at the time of this writing.

By the way, it is a fallacy to say that Apple Macintosh computers are immune to infection by a computer virus. While incidents are far less frequent than with other operating systems, there are still viruses that can infect a Mac.

Other anti-virus software programs are available for the PC and Macintosh. You can find trial versions, freeware, and shareware software at CNET's Download.com Web site at **http://www. download.com** and at Tucows.com at **http://www.tucows.com.**

Word Processors

Genealogists do a lot of word processing. We write letters requesting copies of documents from libraries, archives, courthouses, and other repositories. We address envelopes, create mailing lists, generate reports, create ancestor profiles, and produce all kinds of written materials. Some of us produce publication-quality family history manuscripts, biographical sketches, family newsletters, reunion announcements, family history questionnaires, and much more.

While every computer comes with some basic word processing software already installed, you will probably find that you'll want a full-function word processor. The most impressive of these for the PC are Microsoft Word and Corel WordPerfect, and AppleWorks for the Macintosh. You can learn more at their Web sites:

Microsoft Corporation	**http://www.microsoft.com**
Corel Corporation	**http://www.corel.com**
Apple Computer, Inc.	**http://www.apple.com**

Spreadsheets

Some genealogists use spreadsheet programs in their work. You may decide you want to create a correspondence log or your own custom research log using a spreadsheet. You might consider using separate columns for surname, forename, middle name, and other data, and then sort the data in different ways to produce different views and reports. There are many possibilities for the use of spreadsheets if you use your imagination. There are a number of choices. Microsoft Excel is a leading spreadsheet program for the PC. Look for information at the Microsoft Web site, and for other programs at Download.com and Tucows.com.

Ansibelle Penelope Swords
Holder (From the author's
collection)

Web Browsers

Your access to the Internet and the ability to work efficiently with Web pages are essential. That means that you need a full-function Web browser that processes Web pages with embedded graphics, video, audio, and other features. There are three major browsers at this writing that seem to be ruling the Internet browser world: Microsoft Internet Explorer, the Netscape Browser, and the Opera Web Browser.

The Microsoft Internet Explorer (IE) browser, shown in Figure 12-1, is by far the most-used browser today. It interfaces almost seamlessly with the other Microsoft products. There are versions available for Microsoft Windows 95/98/NT/2000/ME/XP, Mac OS, and Linux operating systems and the software download is free.

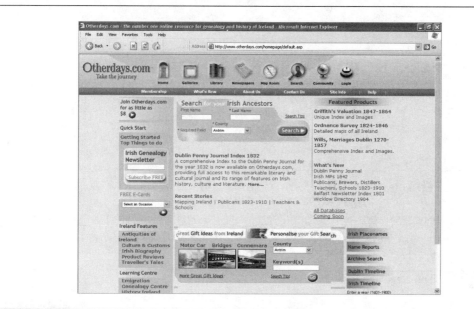

FIGURE 12-1   The Microsoft Internet Explorer browser

The Netscape Browser, shown in Figure 12-2, has lost ground in terms of number of users over the past few years to Internet Explorer. Still, it performs as a strong browser. It, too, is available for the Microsoft Windows and Mac OS operating systems, and the download is free.

Opera Software ASA is located in Oslo, Norway. The company has developed a robust browser touted by many users as being both faster and easier to use than Internet Explorer or Netscape. There are versions available for Windows, Macintosh, Linux, and several other operating systems. You can obtain and use a free download of the software from the Web site, shown in Figure 12-3, or you can purchase an Opera desktop license. The licensed version removes banner ads and provides some additional search options not available in the free version.

Visit the Web site for these browser providers, download the browsers, and decide which one(s) you like the best. Invest the time to read the Help text to become conversant with the functions and become an expert user.

Microsoft Corporation	**http://www.microsoft.com**
Netscape Communications Corporation	**http://www.netscape.com**
Opera Software ASA	**http://www.opera.com**

The world's leading online service, America Online, currently uses as its embedded browser an abbreviated version of Internet Explorer.

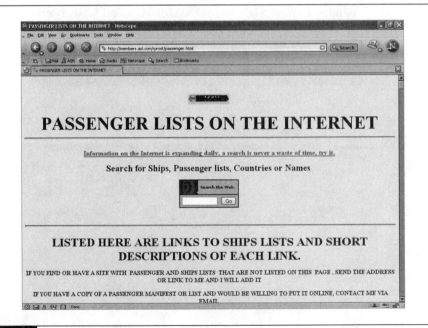

FIGURE 12-2   The Netscape Browser

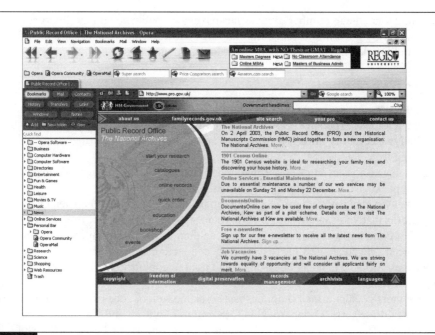

FIGURE 12-3   The Opera Browser

Adobe Acrobat

In the early days of personal computers, you either had to have a copy of the word processor software in which a document was created in order to open it and read it, or the document had to have been saved as a simple text (.TXT) file in order to read it. In addition, printers varied so much that a user often struggled to get his or her own printer to print a document that had been created on another computer.

One of the nicest developments in the past few years has been the development of a standardized format for text documents that is dependent on neither a specific word processor nor a particular printer in order to read and print documents. This was an absolute necessity in this "Internet Information Age," and the Adobe Corporation solved the problem. Adobe developed something called the Portable Document Format, a new format of document with which Internet users have become very familiar. These PDF files, as they are called because of the filename extension used on the documents, are created with a software package named Adobe Acrobat. In order to open, read, and print the PDF documents, you will need the Adobe Reader software, which is available as a free download for your computer from the Adobe Web site at **http://www.adobe.com.**

Unless you want to create your own PDF files, the only software you will need is the Adobe Reader. However, if you plan to publish PDF files, Adobe Acrobat can be purchased in retail stores and at the Adobe Web site and installed on your computer. Adobe also offers a subscription service at its Web site that allows you to create PDF files online. The subscription is available on a monthly or annual basis.

12

You will find that a huge number of materials have been published on the Internet in PDF format, particularly by government and corporate sites. However, more and more materials are being created in PDF documents, including genealogical materials.

E-mail Options

Electronic mail is a necessity for almost everyone these days. It is faster and more economical than postal mail and a lot less expensive. However, the two important bonuses are the ability to attach data files (which we certainly hope are virus-free) and the ability to subscribe to and participate in e-mail mailing lists.

There are many options available for e-mail today, and they can be broken into two categories: e-mail software packages and network-based e-mail.

There are many e-mail software packages that can be installed on your computer. One advantage for a dial-up user is that you can download all of your e-mail and disconnect from your ISP without incurring a lot of communications expenses. You can then read your e-mail, respond, delete what you no longer need, and create new messages before connecting to your ISP again. There also are software packages available that can be installed and used in conjunction with your e-mail software to filter out spam e-mail.

Among the most popular e-mail programs is Microsoft Outlook, one of the integrated programs in the Microsoft Office suite. Others include Qualcomm's Eudora and Netscape Messenger. Download.com and Tucows.com offer a number of free, shareware, and trial versions of other e-mail programs.

The network-based e-mail programs on the Internet allow you to access your e-mail from any computer that has access to the Web as long as you can access the site and enter your ID and password. America Online (AOL), the Microsoft Network (MSN), and other of the subscription ISPs provide e-mail as part of the subscription. However, there also are a number of e-mail service providers who do not charge for the use of their basic mailbox service. One of these is Yahoo! at **http://www.yahoo.com** in the U.S., an example of whose e-mailbox is shown in Figure 12-4. Yahoo! is accessible in other countries, and specifically at **http://ca.yahoo.com** in Canada, and at **http://uk.yahoo.com** in the U.K. and Ireland. Other free or low-cost e-mail providers include Excite at **http://www.excite.com,** Lycos at **http://www.lycos.com,** Juno at **http://www.juno.com,** and Mail.com at **http://www.mail.com.** There are many more to choose from.

Graphics Editing Software

It's one thing to take a photograph with a digital camera or scan an old family picture. It's quite a bit different working with a software program to manipulate the image. However, you may find yourself drawn to do all kinds of things with graphics. I enjoy scanning old photographs and working with the images in order to get a better picture. For example, I might crop the edges of a photo to remove indications of fraying or crop enough to improve the composition of the picture. I can change the size of the image and make it larger or smaller than the original. I've achieved some excellent results adjusting the brightness and contrast of an image to get a crisper picture and bring out the details. And in some cases, I use the software's tools to do restoration work. I'm improving my skill in matching colors or shades in surrounding areas so that I can cover or mask tears in the paper, stains, and other damage. There are some very sophisticated graphics software packages available

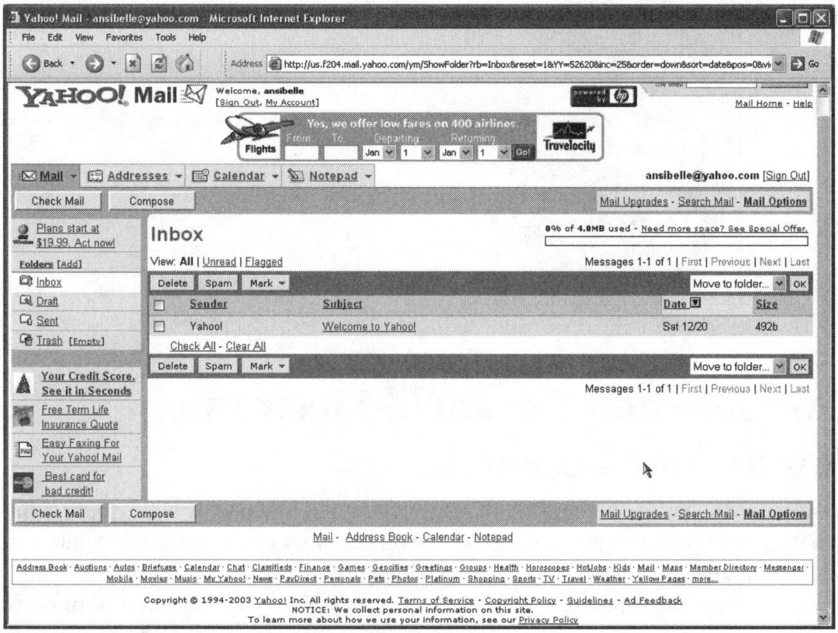

FIGURE 12-4   Yahoo! Mail offers a free e-mail account on the Internet

at quite reasonable prices that will assist you in photo editing and in creation of original graphics. Let's consider a few of these.

Windows users will find a copy of Microsoft Paint in the Accessories folder of the Start Programs menu. It is a simple program that does a small amount of editing work. It is fine for a quick touch-up but cannot achieve changes in contrast, brightness, and some of the other special effects you may want. It is, however, an excellent starter program to begin your learning process.

Jasc Software created Paint Shop Pro, an excellent, full-feature graphics editing program. You can edit any image you can open and save the image in more than a dozen formats. Whereas Paint only works with a few graphics formats, Paint Shop Pro allows you to work with all of the major formats and a few of the less familiar ones as well. The program also has a nice capture function you can use to capture an image of an entire screen, a window, or a specific area of a screen. This is a nice feature for acquiring some images you find online. Dave Huss has written a book titled *How to Do Everything with Paint Shop Pro 8* (McGraw-Hill/Osborne Media, 2003) that provides excellent instructions for using the program for photo editing.

Adobe Photoshop is undoubtedly the most comprehensive and feature-rich editing software available. Unless you are a graphics design professional, though, you will probably find this software package overly expensive at a recommended retail price of $649 U.S./£365 U.K.

There really are dozens of photo and image editing software packages from which to choose. I recommend a visit to Download.com or Tucows.com to see what freeware and shareware software is available. You also will find evaluation versions of both Paint Shop Pro and Adobe Photoshop at Download.com that you can try before you purchase.

12

Harriette Martin Weatherly
(From the author's collection)

Integrate Portable and Handheld Electronic Equipment into Your Research

Your home computer system is the nucleus of your genealogical work. It is the place where you enter, store, analyze, and publish genealogical data. You certainly can't take all that data with you when you make a genealogical research trip or visit the relatives, can you? Or can you? Well, actually the mobile computing options available to you today allow you a great deal of portability. There are electronic equipment choices available that allow you to take all or part of your genealogical data on the road with you, locate specific places, capture information on site, and print charts, forms, and reports for analysis while you're on the go.

The equipment and software choices discussed below are constantly evolving. As an experienced computer user and family history investigator, you are capable of conducting savvy consumer research to determine what models and features are available, and locate competitive pricing information. Let's discuss the portable and handheld electronic equipment options.

Notebooks, Scanners, Printers, and Data Communications

Mobile computing has certainly been around for years, but the computing and communications equipment choices are sensational. There are portable computers, scanners, printers, telephone and wireless modems, and network communications products available in all price ranges that can help take your computing on the road.

As with all other areas of the electronics marketplace, you really do need to be a well-educated consumer to wade through the options and select those that are right for you. Your Internet research abilities, coupled with those "critical thinking skills" I've been focusing your attention on throughout the book, will help you make informed decisions and stay within your budget. The first step, however, is to understand the options available to you.

Evaluate Your Notebook Computer Choices

The idea of a portable computer is nothing new. Everywhere you go businesspeople are taking computer cases with them. You see shoulder bags, backpacks, and computer cases on wheels. Inside those cases are high-powered computers and accessories. Genealogists, too, have entered the realm of computer-toting data processing professionals, and they have invaded the libraries, archives, courthouses, and all sorts of other research places with their portable computers.

The term "laptop" has really been supplanted by the use of the term "notebook." Yes, people still balance their computers on their knees in airport waiting areas, but "notebook" is actually more descriptive of the use of these computers.

My Sony VAIO notebook, now over two years old, has perhaps ten times the computing, data storage, and communications capabilities of the desktop computer I used a mere five years ago. I take it on business and personal trips, including genealogy research expeditions. My genealogical database is on the computer, as are software programs for word processing, spreadsheets, creating and delivering presentations, photographic and graphics editing, communications, Web browsing, e-mail, creating and reading PDF files, and a variety of other applications. I also invested in the lightweight portable scanner I mentioned earlier so that I can capture images, including photographs, documents, and printed materials, wherever I go. A portable printer allows printing of documents, invoices for my seminar business, pedigree charts, family group sheets, and reports from my genealogy database when I need them.

This gives you an idea of my own mobile computing hardware and software configuration at this time. Your own portable computing setup, like mine, will start with the selection of a notebook computer. There are lots of choices, but a key consideration must be compatibility with your home desktop computer. You can choose from those with PC operating systems, such as Microsoft Windows, or the Apple PowerBook with the Mac OS operating system.

The size of the unit, its display screen, and weight are physically obvious selling points. However, the amount of hard disk space and memory also should be part of your evaluation, just as with a desktop computer.

- All of the major desktop computer manufacturers are also manufacturing notebook computers. The majority of the brands are sold in retail stores or online at the company Web sites. Others, such as Dell notebooks, are available by ordering through the Internet (or at a few small kiosks in larger shopping malls).

- Another notebook option might be one with a desktop docking station. In effect, the notebook is your desktop computer but will dock with a unit on your desktop. The notebook's battery will recharge while docked. The notebook can be undocked and taken on a mobile excursion.

- Tablet PCs are a recent addition to the portable computer market. Tablets use a pen interface for inputting data. The screen is a data entry device, similar to a keyboard, except that you use a stylus (pen) and "write" on the screen. Your handwriting is recognized and converted into data. The primary advantage of a tablet PC is that it is extremely lightweight and portable. The screen can usually be detached from the rest of the computer unit and carried separately with just the stylus. (Actually, pen interface and handwriting recognition are nothing new. The technology has been around for more than a decade, first commercially introduced by the Apple Newton but discontinued in 1998. Handwriting recognition, though, has boomed with the explosive growth in the Personal Data Assistant (PDA) market in the last few years.)

A nice Web site that provides reviews of current notebooks, as well as of other computer hardware, software, and accessories, is IT Reviews at **http://www.itreviews.co.uk.** Reviews have been written by independent professional journalists who are experts in the computer field. You will want to use this site as one resource in your research into notebook computers.

Add a Portable Scanner

As I mentioned earlier in this chapter, scanner technology has improved and prices have dropped drastically in the last few years. A portable scanner is now within the financial reach of most users. Many libraries and archives allow the use of handheld and flatbed scanners, although it is always advisable to ask permission before setting up and starting to use one. You should consider whether and how you would use a scanner before leaping to buy one. Most scanners today support both color and grayscale image acquisition and resolution. Include this into your decision-making process. You really have three choices of types of scanners. Each will require installation of driver software to operate them and graphics editing and/or optical character recognition (OCR) software to process and manipulate the data acquired electronically from the source.

- A pen scanner is a small handheld device attached to your computer that acquires an image of data from another source. Pen scanners are designed primarily for use with text data. You attach the pen to your computer using a USB or serial cable. You will move the scanner over a piece of text to "read" it. The data image is acquired and temporarily stored in RAM while you use an OCR program to translate the image into text characters. One of the leaders in OCR technology, including both pens and software, is I.R.I.S., whose Web site is located at **http://www.irislink.com.** Their IRISPen is highly rated, as is the QuickLink scanner pen from WizCom Technologies, Inc., at **http://www.wizcomtech.com.**

- Handheld scanners are next in the hierarchy. These units are small, attach to your computer, and work in much the same way as a pen scanner. The difference is that a handheld scanner has a wider reader head. That head contains a light source and a platen that collects data in chunks, and then the chunks are assembled together as a unified composite before they are processed. An advantage of the handheld scanner over a pen unit is that the wider head accommodates the reading of a wider area and the processing of more data. The disadvantage is that the assembly of more than one scanned image into a single one can be awkward. Additionally, if you plan to scan graphics that are physically larger than the scanner head, the results may be less precise and pleasing than you might want.

- A color flatbed scanner can be an excellent choice for working with both text and graphics in both color and grayscale. The size of the scanning bed, the width of the scanning platen, and the resolution combine to provide the flexibility to generate and manipulate high-quality images of all sorts. A portable flatbed scanner also could act as your primary scanner for your desktop computer, and it could then be disconnected and taken with you on a research trip. The IT Reviews site at **http://www.itreviews.co.uk** again is a good place to learn more about available flatbed scanners, including portable units.

Take a Printer with You

Not everyone wants or needs to take a computer printer with them when they travel. There are, however, some times when it sure would be nice to be able to print from your notebook. I have a friend in the computer service business who takes a portable Canon bubble jet printer with him to print customer invoices on site. As a professional who builds and services all types of computers, he is pleased with the quality of his little printer but bemoans the fact that it is so "slow" in comparison to his office desktop printer. Once you recognize that there are not as many manufacturers and models available, and that a portable printer is inherently slower than a desktop unit, you can then begin to realistically evaluate the options you have.

Make Connections Electronically

You undoubtedly will want to be able to communicate while you are traveling. Your selection of an ISP is an especially important one if you plan to connect to the Internet and work on e-mail while away from home. Your ISP should have a local (non-long distance) telephone access number to allow you to make a dial-up connection from any hotel, motel, inn, lodge, bed and breakfast, or similar accommodation. More and more hotels, too, are providing high-speed communications via cable or DSL.

When deciding on communications equipment requirements, consider the fact that most notebook computers now include a built-in 56 Kbps dial-up modem as standard. This will provide you with good communications in most cases, although local telephone systems and some hotel systems can be a challenge when trying to establish and maintain a connection. The higher speed communications of cable and DSL will require you to have a network card, either installed inside the notebook computer or installed in a communications slot (COM1 or COM2 slot) on the outside of your computer. That network card can be one of two types: a wire/cable connection or a wireless connection.

A network card that connects via a cable to a high-speed network will use a separate apparatus referred to as a *dongle*. The dongle typically has a short wire that attaches to the network card in the COM1 or COM2 slot. The other end of that wire is a small box with a plug receptacle and a couple of lights. The plug accepts a network cable; the two lights, usually red and green, indicate that 1) connectivity with the network exists, and 2) data is actually being transferred over the connection.

A wireless network card uses radio frequency (RF) waves to communicate between the notebook and a central communications hub. The range varies but typically is about 800 feet/243.8 meters, through common walls and floors. Some libraries and archives have begun implementing wireless networks within their facilities. This allows them to offer Internet connectivity and access to their online catalog to people who bring their own notebook computers with them. This allows patrons to move about the library and enjoy flexible access to electronic resources in the facility without having to use and tie up dedicated Internet and/or catalog computers. These facilities' Web pages usually indicate the availability of wireless services on site, so be sure to look for that information when you do your advance research of the facility before your trip.

Global Positioning System

The Global Positioning System (GPS) is a precision navigation system originally established by the United States Department of Defense for military navigation, tracking, reconnaissance, and other applications. In the 1980s, the U.S. government made operational information available so that civilians could make use of the system.

The system is composed of 24 artificial satellites placed into precise orbits around the Earth. Each satellite transmits a specific unique identification signal to Earth. A GPS receiver detects the signals and uses triangulation to calculate its precise location using latitudinal, longitudinal, and altitudinal positioning. A GPS unit must be able to detect and receive signals from at least three satellites in order to calculate its latitude and longitude, and four or more in order to additionally

12

determine the altitude of the unit. However, GPS units typically detect, lock onto, and use these and other of the "visible" orbiting satellites in order to maintain a continuous tracking of location. Most GPS units use multiple communications channels in order to detect and lock onto the satellites. Some civilian GPS units employ as many as 12 channels to establish and maintain position.

From a genealogical perspective, GPS units can contribute a great deal to our research. I discussed the importance in Chapter 3 of using maps to find the *right* place to conduct your research. One of the resources I mentioned for locating places and features in North America was the United States Geological Survey Geographic Names Information System (also referred to as the USGS GNIS). The GNIS is a massive searchable database of United States national mapping information, and the online query form you can use to search the database is located at **http://geonames.usgs.gov/ pls/gnis/web_query.gnis_web_query_form.** A search produces a list of results, including their latitude and longitude, and you can further obtain a map from the U.S. Census Bureau's Tiger Map Server.

GPS units allow you to define the latitude and longitude of a specific location, such as the Saint Francis Xavier Cemetery in Red Lake County, Minnesota. The USGS GNIS search provided me with the latitude of 47°49'00"N and a longitude of 095°53'27"W. The map shows the cemetery to be southwest of the town of Oklee and east of the town of Brooks. The latitude and longitude, along with the map, are invaluable tools to help navigate your way to the exact location. However, the mapping software for a desktop computer that comes with the GPS unit, or a supplemental software package purchased from the GPS unit's manufacturer that includes that area, can be used to create a detailed map with driving directions that can be downloaded to the GPS unit. Further, by entering the latitude and longitude information in the GPS unit, it will help guide you precisely to that location.

Once you have identified or arrived at a precise location, you can record the latitude and longitude to add into your genealogical database. Then, the next time you or someone else wants to visit Aunt Neppie's grave in a specific cemetery, you have the precise coordinates to lead you to the spot.

There are a number of GPS manufacturers and software companies. Garmin, Ltd., at **http:// www.garmin.com,** is a leader in GPS technology. The company manufactures a wide range of GPS units for many price ranges. Their top-of-the-line model for use by motorists, the StreetPilot, can be mounted on the dashboard of your vehicle, operated using the touch screen or a remote control, and provides turn-by-turn directions and voice prompts. The company makes software for motor travel, hiking, and marine applications. Each of Garmin's units comes with a permanently installed non-alterable basemap, and updates are available for download from the company's Web site. In addition, there are maps for the Americas, Europe, Australia, and South Africa.

Thales Navigation, Inc., is the manufacturer of the other major GPS products, the Magellan GPS units and software. Like Garmin, there are a variety of Magellan GPS units, different travel applications, and software maps for various parts of the world.

DeLorme is another major player in the electronic cartographic community. The company produces printed maps and atlases, and has been involved in the GPS market. Their GPS unit can operate as a standalone unit or can connect to your notebook with an interface to their popular Street Atlas USA software.

GPS is an advanced function for your genealogical work but, having used a GPS unit for a while, I can tell you that it adds another dimension of fun and interest to the research.

Become Acquainted with Personal Data Assistants (PDAs)

Among the most popular personal computing devices around is the personal digital assistant, or PDA. A PDA is a handheld electronic device that can combine computing, networking, and communications capabilities. PDAs are also called by other names, such as palmtop, pocket computer, pocket PC, handheld computer, and personal communicator.

The most basic PDA can function as a personal organizer that incorporates a calendar, an address book, memo pad/"to-do" list, and a calculator. Most PDAs use some form of easy-to-learn handwriting recognition feature that allows you to make keystrokes on a screen to enter letters, numerals, and other characters. Some PDAs also incorporate voice-recognition features that can be "trained" to accept commands to perform certain functions.

Using software installed on your desktop computer, you can interface your PDA with the desktop to exchange data; to synchronize files such as the calendar and address book on both machines; and to download new programs, updates, news, and other data to your PDA. This, however, is just the beginning of the wonders of the PDA.

PDAs have become much more than "basic" and can be used for multiple purposes. The operating systems for PDAs have become more sophisticated and efficient and, coupled with more base memory and memory expansion options, will provide you with a tremendous amount of portable computing power. Screen resolutions have improved as well and almost all PDAs now use color rather than black-and-white displays, making them significantly easier to read.

Learn About the Operating Systems

Before we go into specifics about how a PDA can benefit your genealogical work, it is important to lay a little groundwork for you, especially if you haven't yet worked with a PDA. You need to understand something about the operating system (OS) choices you have with the PDAs you may consider. There are essentially two major operating systems for PDAs: the Palm OS and the Microsoft Windows Mobile OS (previously known as the Microsoft Windows CE OS). Both enjoy a sizeable following among the manufacturers of handheld computing devices and are comparable in operations.

The Palm OS is used by a number of leading PDA manufacturers in their units, including the Garmin iQue, palmOne Tungsten, Zire, and Treo units, and Sony CLIÉ . You can learn more about the Palm OS at the palmOne site at **http://www.palmone.com.**

PDA manufacturers using the Microsoft Windows Mobile OS in their PDAs include Dell Axim, Hewlett-Packard iPAQ, Toshiba Pocket PC, and ViewSonic Pocket PC. The Microsoft Windows Mobile site at **http://www.microsoft.com/windowsmobile** provides information about their OS.

The lists of manufacturers above are by no means complete. Please visit the Web sites of these and other PDA manufacturers and sellers to learn the details of the operating systems that they use on their units.

Be Aware of "Combination Devices"

Be aware, too, that there is a new generation of combination devices. You've undoubtedly seen cellular phones that incorporate a camera and can transmit the digital image to others whose telephone, computer e-mail, or PDA can receive and read the image. You therefore should not be surprised to know that there are cellular telephones that combine the functionality of a cell phone and a PDA in a single electronic unit. These "smart phones" incorporate communications and

12

data processing power to allow you to talk on the telephone, send and receive e-mail, instant messages, and pager messages, and to connect to the Internet. There are a number of these cellular smart phone units sold by a variety of companies. The OS of some use the Palm OS while others use the Microsoft Windows Mobile OS. The palmOne Treo mentioned earlier is one of the smart phones that uses the Palm OS; Microsoft and Motorola launched a joint venture using the Microsoft Windows Mobile OS.

The integration of multiple functions into a single device has been taking place in the PDA industry for some time. The Sony Corporation has been introducing accessories for its CLIÉ line to increase these units' functionality. These include a camera, a mini-keyboard, a game controller, an audio adapter, and a wireless LAN card, all of which attach or plug into the Memory Stick media card slot. Sony has continued to introduce additional PDAs with more multimedia and communications functions, including units that include wireless networking, a built-in keyboard, a built-in camera that can capture still pictures or video clips, and other features are on the way.

Finally, another unique combination device is the Garmin iQue. The iQue is touted as the first PDA to integrate GPS technology. It uses the Palm OS 5 and includes typical PDA functions such as calendaring, address book, and memo pad. In addition, however, the unit has integrated powerful GPS communications technology for mapping as well as turn-by-turn voice directions. While this unit is expensive, it provides a vast amount of functionality right out of the box. In the following sections, you'll see that any PDA can be upgraded with additional general software and genealogical research-specific programs.

Whichever PDA you decide to use, there are a number of good reference books available to help you become an expert user. The following list will give you an idea of the titles available from McGraw-Hill/Osborne Media, 2003:

- *How to Do Everything with Your Palm Handheld,* 4th ed., by Dave Johnson and Rick Broida
- *How to Do Everything with Your Pocket PC,* 3rd ed., by Frank McPherson
- *How to Do Everything with Your Sony CLIÉ,* by Rick Broida
- *How to Do Everything with Your Zire Handheld,* by Dave Johnson and Rick Broida
- *How to Do Everything with Your iPAQ Pocket PC,* 2nd ed., by Derek Ball and Barry Shilmover

These are among the best reference titles for PDAs and other electronic equipment.

Investigate General PDA Software Options

In addition to the sophisticated improvements in the PDA units themselves, an explosive growth in the choices of add-on hardware and the thousands of available specialized software programs have taken the PDA to new plateaus. PDA manufacturers are bundling more and more software onto their units. The award-winning Documents To Go software program from DataViz, Inc., for instance, is offered on some PDAs that use the Palm OS. Those software packages' components interface with the Microsoft Word, Excel, and Power Point programs on your desktop or notebook computer and allow you to convert and load word processor documents, spreadsheets, and presentations to your PDA.

Yes, there are a huge number of business and personal applications that can be purchased in retail stores and/or on the Internet. You simply download them to your desktop computer and schedule them to be installed on your PDA the next time you synchronize your desktop or notebook and the PDA.

A few of the important non-genealogical-specific applications you might consider include maps, language dictionaries, clocks, Internet browser software, an e-mail program, graphics/photograph viewer, and perhaps some games to pass the time on a long trip.

Consider Genealogical Software Programs for the PDA

Genealogists have not been left out of the explosive development of application software for the PDA. If you don't want to invest in a notebook to take your genealogical database along on your research trips to the local library or halfway around the world, a PDA may just be the answer for you. There are a number of programs available that allow you to download data extracted from your desktop-based genealogical database program to your PDA. (We will discuss the process of creating and working with a database extract file, known as a GEDCOM file, in detail in Chapter 13.) And while these programs don't necessarily accommodate data entry while you're on the road for upload back to your desktop database, just having your database on a tiny handheld device is a real boon. Let's briefly examine these programs, and then follow that with some other helpful and fun genealogy utility programs.

GedWise

The Battery Park Software Corporation has produced a genealogy database program for the PDA called GedWise. GedWise consists of two component application programs.

■ There is a program that is installed and runs on your desktop or notebook computer where your genealogy database program resides. This program runs on any PC using the Microsoft Windows 95, 98, ME, NT, 2000, or XP operating system, and it converts a GEDCOM file of data extracted from your genealogy database into a format that GedWise can read on the PDA. There is currently no conversion program for a Macintosh.

■ Another program, which will run on any PDA with the Palm OS 3.3 or higher, is installed on your PDA. This program accepts the converted file from your desktop or notebook computer and allows you to search the database and display information about any individual in a variety of formats, as well as create ancestor and descendant charts and other displays. Figure 12-5 shows the GedWise Individual Summary Screen for Louis Johnson, which also includes the Events List for his life and the first of his two wives, Eva Maria Valikangas.

You can purchase the GedWise software for $17.99 U.S. at the company's Web site, through the PalmGear.com Web site at **http://www.palmgear.com,** or at the Handango Web site at **http://www.handango.com.** (Links are provided at the Battery Park site to the order/shopping cart pages at each of these locations.)

12

Individual Summary Screen
with Events List

FIGURE 12-5 The GedWise Individual Summary Screen (Screenshot courtesy of the Battery Park Software Corporation)

For more information, you should visit the Battery Park Software Corporation's Web site at **http://www.batteryparksoftware.com.**

GedStar

GHCS Software offers GedStar, a genealogy data viewer that works on a PDA running the Palm OS 3.1 or higher. There actually are two versions of the program available: GedStar, which sells for $13.95, and GedStar-Plus, which sells for 19.95.

Like GedWise, GedStar uses a conversion program to convert a GEDCOM file extracted from your desktop- or notebook-based genealogy database running on any PC using the Microsoft Windows 98, ME, NT, 2000, or XP operating system to a format that can be read by a program on your PDA. GedStar boasts the fastest conversion of all the available PDA converters. There is no support for Windows 95 or for Macintosh at this time.

The difference between GedStar and GedStar-Plus is that the latter allows you to directly load data from the genealogical database software programs, Legacy Family Tree and The Master Genealogist, to your PDA without the need to run the conversion program.

Figure 12-6 shows an example of GedStar's Family View screen, on which are shown father Thomas Darnall, his wife Lucinda Jane Armstrong, their marriage date, and the beginning of the scrollable list of their ten children. Among the linked functions from this screen are the full list of individuals in the database, the search screen from which you can search for individuals, and source citation details.

More information about GedStar can be found by visiting the GHCS Software site at **http://www.ghcssoftware.com.**

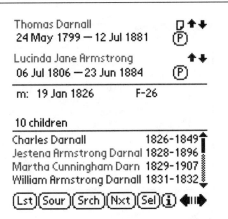

FIGURE 12-6   The Family View screen of GedStar (Screenshot courtesy of GHCS Software)

My Roots

Tapperware has created a powerful genealogy program called My Roots. The company's Web site at **http://www.tapperware.com** provides a thorough overview of the program, screenshots, the software manual, and a collection of FAQs. The company offers a trial version of the software at the Web site and also sells the program for $19.95 U.S./£12.04 U.K., and you can be billed in many international currencies. There also are versions of the software available in French and German. The program can be purchased on CD for an additional price. My Roots is a full-function application that allows you to search and locate individuals using filters for names, and display data in multiple formats on different interlinked screens: List of Individuals, Person Detail, Family Group Sheet, Ancestors, Descendants, and Events. Figure 12-7 shows the Descendants view screen for Thomas Lincoln, his three children, and the four grandchildren through his son, Abraham. From this screen, you can access the individual records of the father or mother and you can, alternatively, select to view Thomas Lincoln's ancestors.

My Roots will run on any PDA with the Palm OS 3.0 or higher. In order to convert your data from your desktop genealogical database so that it can be loaded onto the PDA, you will need the free conversion utility program available from the Tapperware site. That utility will run on any PC using the Microsoft Windows 95, 98, ME, NT, 2000, or XP operating system. In addition, there is a Macintosh conversion utility for Mac OS 8/9 and a native version for OS X.

For more information about My Roots, visit the Tapperware site at **http://www.tapperware.com.**

Pocket Genealogist

Users of PDAs running the Microsoft Windows Mobile OS (previously Microsoft Windows CE OS) will be pleased to know that a PDA software package is available for their use too. Northern Hills Software LLC offers a package called Pocket Genealogist that runs on PDAs with Microsoft Windows CE Version 2.11 or higher. There are two versions of Pocket Genealogist available: the Basic Version, which sells for $20 U.S., and the Advanced Version, which sells for $35 U.S. (A variety of payment options are available.)

12

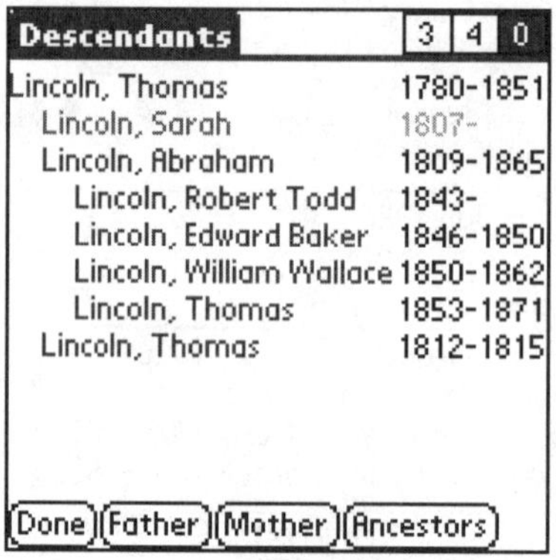

Descendants	3 4 0
Lincoln, Thomas	1780-1851
Lincoln, Sarah	1807-
Lincoln, Abraham	1809-1865
Lincoln, Robert Todd	1843-
Lincoln, Edward Baker	1846-1850
Lincoln, William Wallace	1850-1862
Lincoln, Thomas	1853-1871
Lincoln, Thomas	1812-1815

[Done] [Father] [Mother] [Ancestors]

FIGURE 12-7   The Descendants screen in My Roots (Screenshot courtesy of Tapperware)

The Basic Version of Pocket Genealogist supports most of the information found in major genealogy database programs and some data specific to the Personal Ancestral File (PAF) program offered by The Church of Jesus Christ of Latter-day Saints (LDS). This version does not allow you to do any "direct import" of data from any genealogy database program or enter any data into your PDA. It operates strictly as a data viewer with a variety of screens. This version might be fine for you if you only want to take a reference version of your genealogical database contents on a research trip.

The Advanced Version has all the functionality of the Basic Version, plus the ability to import data directly from the Legacy Family Tree and The Master Genealogist genealogy database programs. In addition, the Advanced Version allows you to enter data to add new individuals into or edit data about individuals already in your PDA. The display of data is elegantly done and easy to read, as illustrated by the Three Generation shown screen in Figure 12-8.

There are additional language packs available that can be downloaded and installed on your PDA after the initial files are installed. Languages supported by this program include Danish, Dutch, French, German, Norwegian, and Spanish.

Another add-on utility that can be purchased for $9.95 U.S. is the GenBridge for PAF Version 5.5, created by Wholly Genes Software (**http://www.whollygenes.com**) and available through the Northern Hills Software LLC. GenBridge works with both the Basic and Advanced Version of Pocket Genealogist and allows for the direct import of a PAF Version 5 database without requiring a GEDCOM conversion.

For more information about both versions of Pocket Genealogist and GenBridge, visit the Web site for Northern Hills Software LLC at **http://www.northernhillssoftware.com.**

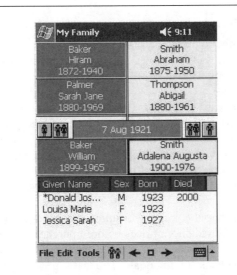

FIGURE 12-8   The Three Generation screen in Pocket Genealogist (Screenshot courtesy of Northern Hills Software)

Explore Other Genealogy Utility Programs for Your PDA

In addition to the programs discussed above, you will find that there are some interesting PDA utility programs for your genealogical research. Let me share these with you.

- **Cemetery** is a program developed by Donald Kieffer of John One One Graphics for the Palm OS. This little program is a nice utility to take with you on a cemetery trip. It allows you to enter the name of the person, the name and address of the cemetery, the type of burial (buried, entombed, or cremated), location in the cemetery of the burial site, space for entering the inscription on the marker, and information about a photo. A demonstration Version 1.0 of this software is available free in black-and-white at the Tucows Web site at **http://www.tucows.com.** A color-enabled Version 2.0 is available at Mr. Kieffer's Web site at **http://www.dkeiffer.homestead.com** for $10 U.S. Mr. Kieffer has other genealogy utilities at his site as well.

- **pSoundex** is a great little utility for your PDA that allows you to enter a surname and immediately calculate the Soundex code. This program is available for both the Palm and Pocket PC user from the developer's Web site at **http://home.comcast.net/~jimknopf6.**

In addition, as a new PDA user, you may want to stop at the newsstand to investigate magazines about PDAs and handheld computers and conduct searches on the Internet for new and existing genealogical software for your PDA.

12

Don't Be Overwhelmed!

Throughout this chapter, I've tried to provide a good overview of what options are available to you. Certainly, there are more choices in computer equipment, peripherals, software, communications, and PDAs than most of us can comprehend. However, you have the investigative skills to locate information on the Internet.

I also suggested fact-finding trips to retailers of electronic equipment and software, and this is an excellent way to obtain information in the form of brochures and face-to-face interviews with sales personnel. Don't overlook visiting the Web sites of companies in whose products you may be interested. There you will find pictures, lists of features, and other information about the products. Many also will have online versions of brochures and specification sheets, probably in PDF format, which you can print or download. These make side-by-side comparison of their products much simpler.

Don't forget to comparison shop the products features and prices on the Internet. I always —and I mean *always*—use the Web to check prices before I purchase computers, electronics, and software. I can enter the manufacturer's name and a model number and be rewarded with a search results list of sites where I can check for any deals. The last time I purchased a digital camera, I comparison-shopped on the Internet and literally found a difference between prices of more than $130 U.S./£73.75!

By now, you should have a better sense of what is and is not available in the way of hardware and software choices. The next step is to discuss genealogical database software programs, so let's move on to Chapter 13.

Chapter 13

Select and Use a Genealogical Database Program to Store Data

How to...

■ Learn the basics about genealogical database software programs

■ Find out what genealogical database programs are available

■ Determine which features you need

■ Exchange GEDCOM files with other researchers

■ Upload your GEDCOM file to an online database

■ Publish your family history in printed form

■ Publish your data on the Web

Find a Genealogical Database Program

You have learned about and seen examples throughout this book of many different types of resources. Many have been in the form of paper documents, and some have been published in or derived from books, indexes, journals, newspapers, and a wide range of periodicals. A growing body of high-quality information also is becoming available on the Internet in the form of digitized document images made available in indexed and searchable databases and catalogs. New details are discovered through your visits and research trips to sites where ancestors and family members lived, died, and are interred. And still more clues are revealed through interviews and family members.

The collection and analysis of the information and evidence you locate is a complicated process. The resources I just mentioned are only the beginning of the types of materials we gather and analyze, developing new hypotheses as we go along, following new avenues of research, and either proving or disproving our theories. You saw when we discussed developing an ancestor profile that placing information into a logical, chronological sequence and incorporating geographical, historical, and social events can provide keen new insights.

Organization of your information and source materials becomes more and more critical over time. Yes, it is important to organize and file your evidence using some method and medium that works and is most efficient for you. You may use binders and place the individual documents in acid-free, archival-safe, polypropylene sheet protectors to organize and preserve them. You might also use acid-free file folders and store your materials in a filing cabinet, using some organization scheme that facilitates your quick access and reference. You will, over time, devise a system that works best for you. I have organized my materials differently over time as my research evolved. I personally use a combination system that incorporates the binders and polypropylene sheet protectors for what I call "processed documents," those which I have analyzed and are satisfied with the content. I maintain file folders with the "unprocessed" materials that still need to be reviewed and analyzed, after which time they can be filed in the appropriate binder. I also keep ongoing folders of the "unknowns," those people who just might be related but whose information hasn't connected with my proven family lines. Photographs require different organization schemes and preservation/conservation techniques. I therefore organize and file these separately, sometimes making photocopies of one or two pictures to include in the binder files.

All of these different materials, different preservation requirements, and filing systems can present a considerable challenge on many levels. First, when you want to fully examine an individual's information and source materials, you may have to go into multiple filing systems in different places to access what you need. Then, if you want to expand your view to other family members, including ancestors and/or descendants, you will need to pull those documents as well. Finally, in order to really get a clear picture of the person and his or her place in the family, you may have to create a new set of family group sheets and pedigree charts. This can be a massive amount of work! Finally, there is no way to easily take all your genealogical materials with you on a research trip or to share information with other researchers.

Fortunately for us genealogists, there are a number of genealogical database software programs into which we can enter information, create source citations, make notes, and even incorporate digitized photographs, video clips, and sound files. There are some essential functions offered by genealogy software packages that you just cannot do without. Additional features can expand the amount of data you can include and structure the input in such a way that it can be sorted, analyzed, compared with other persons' information, and produce reports in many formats. I refer to this as "slice and dice" analysis, simply because you can manipulate the information in your database in different ways *and* do it quickly.

Your organizational system certainly will be influenced by the people you are researching, and perhaps by geographical area, ethnic or religious group, time period, or some other factor. These are part of your methodology but they also are goals. Your choice of genealogical software also will be influenced by a number of factors, most of all by what you want it to do for you.

The purpose of this chapter is to help you understand what functions and features are offered by the leading genealogical software programs. We will explore the basic functions first, followed by the more advanced and specialized features, and then take a tour of the major software programs. In the process, I will include addresses for those companies' Web sites and urge you to conduct your own research there, as well as read the message boards concerning software programs at Ancestry.com (**http://boards.ancestry.com**), Genealogy.com's GenForum (**http://genforum.com**), and at message boards in various other online venues.

New versions and upgrades of software are being released on a regular basis and, while I am including information about these programs that is current at the time I am writing this book, there are sure to be new features added that you will want to investigate. Unless otherwise noted, all of the programs listed here are for the Microsoft Windows operating system. Check the software companies' Web sites to determine if a specific program supports the version of Microsoft Windows you are running on your computer. Check for free trial versions that you can download and play with for a week or two. Look, also for online versions of user manuals because you will want to have well-written, understandable documentation, especially when you begin doing more complex reporting and publishing with the software.

13

Emma Dale Holder–circa 1902
(From the author's collection)

Learn the Basics About Genealogical Database Software Programs

You undoubtedly will hear other genealogists talk about their personal "genealogy software programs." That phrase really can encompass a number of types of software.

- **Personal genealogical database programs** are those software applications that are used to enter and store information we collect about our ancestors and family members for our personal use. That information will range from the most basic vital records or civil records of birth, marriage, and death, to records of religious ceremonies, military service and pension records, and many, many more. A genealogical database also provides space and, in most cases, a structure for entering source citation information and linking a source with a fact in evidence to create a citation. Further, a genealogical database will allow for on-screen display of search results and production of printed genealogical charts, sheets, and reports. Some databases facilitate the production of books, Web pages, and other formal documentary output. Almost every database allows for the export and import of data to and from other genealogy programs, using either a genealogical standard format referred to as a GEDCOM file and/or a proprietary database format from another program. (We will discuss the GEDCOM standard a little later in this chapter.)

- There also are online genealogical databases that are computer systems, usually on the Internet, to which genealogists upload copies of their databases and where other researchers may view and/or download the files. These online databases take two forms:

  - There are genealogy database systems to which researchers contribute copies of their database files, i.e., GEDCOMs, for the primary purpose of sharing their findings with other researchers working on the same lines. The hope is that another researcher will find your GEDCOM file at some Internet site such as MyFamily.com, the LDS FamilySearch.com, FamilyTreeMaker.com, or some other location in which an archive of GEDCOM files are stored. If he or she locates your file, examines its contents, downloads it, and discovers a connection, that person may contact you and you can perhaps begin to share additional information and collaborate.

■ Other Internet sites foster the use of online genealogical database software. Examples of these would include the Ancestry Family Tree (AFT) at **http://aft.ancestry.com** and the collaborative genealogical database facility incorporated in the MyFamily.com family sites available at **http://www.myfamily.com.** AFT allows you to input genealogical data and sources, or to import an entire database in the form of a GEDCOM file, from another genealogical database program. The information entered into your AFT database can then be matched against records in the immense collection of databases at Ancestry.com and GEDCOM files already uploaded to the Ancestry World Tree at the Ancestry.com site (**http://www.ancestry.com**).

■ Finally, in addition to the genealogical database software programs we will discuss later in this chapter are supplemental or genealogical utility programs. These typically perform a complementary function to assist your research efforts. An example of this type of program would be the AniMap software package from The Gold Bug, which provides extensive animated maps showing boundary changes in the 48 contiguous United States from the colonial era.

Before you can determine which genealogical database software program is right for you, it is important to understand the basic functions that are essential in the package you choose. Let's briefly investigate each of these.

Data Entry Capabilities

You might think that data entry is data entry, but you would be wrong. There are a number of options you will want to consider as you review and choose a genealogical database software program.

The name of each individual is the central piece of data you will want to enter. The person's full name is a key piece of data for your data entry because it, along with birth and death dates, can and will help you differentiate, say, John Pierpont Morgan from John Allen Morgan. In addition, your database should also be capable of storing a person's title, such as Dr., Col., or Rev., as well as any nickname or AKA (also known as) that could help to uniquely identify the individual.

Make sure your database can grow as large as you need it to grow. Some genealogical databases have had limitations on the number of individuals you could add. This was frustrating to those researchers who have been working for years and extending their knowledge about distant family lines. Imagine the dismay when the error message popped up on the screen to inform the user that he or she had reached the maximum number of individuals that could be entered!

Entering data into a genealogical database can be tedious and time-consuming, especially if you are entering the same data again and again. Consider, for example, entering the names, birth dates, and birth locations for a large family, all of whom were born in the same town. It would be awful to have to reenter a place name, such as Rock Creek, Cherokee County, Alabama, over and over. Some genealogy programs use a "smart entry" system that recognizes the first few characters you have typed into a given field and "suggests" the remainder of the field contents. The suggestion is based on another entry you have typed in before. This can save you copious amounts of time *and* can help prevent spelling errors, assuming you typed it correctly the first time around. If you are entering a similar but different entry, the next time you start entering the characters, the "smart entry" facility will read the characters you type and "suggest" the remainder only when you get past the characters the two previous entries have in common and enter a unique character it recognizes from a previous entry.

The entry of dates in a correct format is essential as well. Genealogical databases "assume" that you want to enter dates in the Day-Month-Year format that is most commonly used. Some programs allow you to enter abbreviated versions of the date and, when you press ENTER to leave the data field/box, converts and displays the date in the standard format. Let me give you three examples.

- **Example 1**   You enter 25 dec 1840 and the software formats the date for input into the database and displays it as 25 December 1840.

- **Example 2**   You want to enter the date of April 3rd, 1920. You know that the standard format of dates in your software is Day-Month-Year and so you enter 3/4/20. The database may prompt you to select the century and, when you have indicated the 1900s, it will format and display the information in the date field as 3 April 1920.

- **Example 3**   There was a change from the Julian calendar to the Gregorian calendar commencing in the 1600s in parts of Europe in order to correspond to the actual solar year. It finally was adopted in Great Britain in 1752. There, the day after 2 September 1752 became 14 September in order to align the calendar. The British also adopted 1 January as the day when a new year begins, as opposed to in March. Some dates from this period in Great Britain and the American colonies fall on the cusp of the change and are represented as 1752/53 or 1752/1753. Some genealogical database packages automatically handle this conversion function for you when it is appropriate.

Source citation information, which will be discussed a little later in this chapter, can also be extremely time-consuming to enter repeatedly. The use of a "smart entry" facility can save huge amounts of time and help alleviate data entry errors.

Vital Records Information

Every database will have data fields for birth, marriage, and death information that comprise the vital records. However, as you know, so-called "vital records" can include more than just these three types of documentation. Christening, baptism, confirmation, *bar mitzvah, bat mitzvah,* ordination records, divorce records and, in the Mormon faith, the "sealing" of a person to a spouse or a parent are some of the other life events that can be referred to under the designation of "vital records."

As you evaluate the genealogical database programs that are available to you, you should also consider the types of events that you want to include for your ancestors and family members. Make sure that the database software either includes these events as standard, nominated fields or allows you to create your own events. This is important because you will want to be able to enter and display these events in the database, and you will want to designate these fields and their contents for inclusion in reports such as pedigree charts, ancestor and descendant charts, and on family group sheets. You also can use such fields as filters to help you narrow and focus your queries when searching your databases.

Foster's Dry Goods Store in Rome, Georgia–Early 1900s (From the author's collection)

The designation of relationships between people in your database is another important consideration. Remember how great it was to find in some censuses the names of every member of a residence *and* their relationship to the head of that household? You will want to represent relationships as honestly as possible for your reference in your genealogical database. The better databases will provide flexibility in this area to accommodate a variety of circumstances. Remember that not every couple in your family tree will have solemnized their relationship with a marriage ceremony. Therefore, you might want a database that facilitates your ability to honestly represent the couple's status as married, friends, partners, or some other joining. The ending status of a marriage is another piece of information you may want to record, rather than just leave a relationship hanging as if it continued forever. Relationships end due to the death of a spouse, a separation, a divorce, or for some other reason, and you may want to be precise by including this relationship information.

Some persons were married more than once, and all of the genealogical databases will have the ability to allow more than one spouse to be linked to an individual. For reporting purposes, you will want the ability to designate one spouse as the "primary" or "preferred" spouse. By that I mean that the spouse designated in such a way will be the one whose name and information appears on certain printed reports, such as an ancestor or descendant report. You already know that each marriage or similar relationship is to be treated as a separate entity and that children of that relationship are to be designated as the issue of that pairing. When you enter data into the database, you will create a family unit by indicating the "husband" and "wife" or "father and mother" on a screen and then you will input each of their children's information. They will therefore be grouped together into a family unit and can therefore be represented that way when you print a family group record from the database for them.

Relationships of children to adults likewise may be represented as natural, adopted, foster, step, unknown, family member, or some other designation. When marriages and other similar relationships dissolve or are terminated, children may be relocated, like my great-grandmother, Caroline Alice Whitefield, to live with another family unit. In her case, she became the ward of her older half-brother but she went to live with her mother's sister, Emily, and Emily's husband, Dolphin Villines. So, in that instance, Caroline's relationship to Emily and Dolphin Villines could be represented as "family member," and not as "adoptee."

Weatherly family baseball team–circa 1910 (From the author's collection)

Support for Many Types of Facts and Events

When you stop to consider the many different types of events that we ourselves experience and take part in throughout our own lives, and that also may be recorded in some way, you get a pretty good idea of the range of event types that could and should be supported in a genealogical database. All the major genealogical databases come with a standard group of "fact" or event names. Every family is unique and there is a vast potential that there are going to be unique "facts" or events that you will want to document. These fact or event labels can be used in multiple ways in your database. First, a label of "Scholarship" attached to a date of 10 May 1970 and a description of "scholarship received at graduation ceremony" looks a lot better than "Fact 16" when displayed on the database screen. It is easier to recognize and locate on the computer screen and on reports you may print. It also serves to make that fact or event unique so that it may be used as a sorting filter.

There are several databases that allow for an unlimited number of facts/events to be entered, and many allow you to create your own. While not all databases will allow user-created events to be used for filtering searches, the ability to create your own fact or event labels makes your work appear very professional.

Master Sources and Source Citations

You have learned in this book and in talking with other genealogists that you should always be taking a scholarly approach to all your research work. When you take the time to locate high-quality, authoritative evidence and include it in your database, the inclusion of the source citation is almost as important as the data itself. Source citations provide details about the provenance of the evidence you are citing. Good citations will always help you and other researchers retrace a research path, locate the source material, and personally analyze it in order to develop their own hypotheses and reach their own conclusions.

The genealogical database software developers have, since the early 1990s, strived to create user-friendly methods for the entry and attachment of source records to individual data fields

Sydney Warren–circa 1914 (From the author's collection)

in their databases. Some have done a better job than others but it is hard to be too critical of any shortcomings. After all, there are literally hundreds of different types of source materials we may use and the formats of the citation will vary from source to source. As you've seen, for instance, the citation for a book is different from that of a newspaper obituary, which differs from that of microfilm, which is different from that of an embroidered sampler.

Because the entry of source citations can be so time-consuming and prone to data entry errors, it is nice to have a genealogical database package that "helps" you in as many ways as possible. Here are some features to look for when considering a database for your own genealogical research work.

- The more sophisticated databases will use a "master source file" in which source materials are entered, either directly or during the process of creating or adding a new source citation for a particular piece of data/data field.

- A source can be easily called up when you want to add a source citation by opening the master source file and locating the record you want. Locating that source record may be done by scrolling through a list or by using "smart input" of characters that will jump to and display matching entries. The master source record's information is automatically loaded into a template for the citation, and you can then type in additional information, such as a page number, library call number, microfilm publication identifier and roll number, or some other distinct identifying reference.

- In addition to being able to invoke the master source file, you should be able to open a source citation box directly from the field that you are documenting and be able to type directly into that template box. "Smart input" will allow you to enter characters and the software will "suggest" matches that you can accept or override. You should be able to create a new source citation from this template that not only will be used for this fact or event, but which also will become one of the master source records in the database.

An optimum method of handling a source that potentially may be used in a citation for more than one person's data or for more than one fact or event is to first enter it directly into the master source file. Then, for every place that you need to create a citation using that source, invoke the master record for that source and, if appropriate, add a page number, etc., to make the source accurate. As an example, you might use a family Bible as a source for birth, marriage, and death information for a family group. You would first input a master bibliographic source record with the name of the book, its publication location, publisher, and publication date. For each person whose birth date is recorded in the family Bible, add a source citation using the master record you just built

13

Caroline Alice Whitfield
Morgan–circa 1894 (From
the author's collection)

and add a notation concerning where in the Bible the birth information was located (the "Births"
section in center pages, inside the front cover, on the end pages, etc.).

Physical and Medical Data

Medical genealogy and the use of DNA to genetically connect people have become more popular
since the mid-1990s. Most genealogical databases provide some data fields to enter some of an
individual's physical attributes, such as height and weight. Others may provide fields for hair color,
eye color, complexion type, cause of death, and space for additional medical text notes. Genealogical
databases are not yet incorporating much in the way of genetic data, but there are other software
programs that can be used to gather, process, and produce reports such as a genetic pedigree chart
and genogram. A genogram is simply a chart that graphically represents relationships between
individuals and can be used to represent medical history. Two of these software packages are
Geneweaver, a product from Genes & Things, Inc., at **http://www.geneweaveronline.com;** Relativity
by WonderWare, Inc., at **http://www.interpersonaluniverse.net/wware.html;** and SmartDraw by
SmartDraw.com at **http://www.smartdraw.com/specials/genealogy.asp?id=39025.**

Notes

You will find that the notes section of your genealogical database is an invaluable tool. Here you
will enter the information that cannot be entered elsewhere, especially the textual materials you
discover. Some of the individuals in your database may not have much, if anything, in the notes
section, while others may have page after page of text data. You therefore want to make sure
there are no constraints on the amount of space that is available for the notes you may want to
enter here.

I use the notes section of my database for every single person almost like an ancestor profile.
Figure 13-1 shows a small section of the notes from my genealogical database for one of my
great-grandfathers, Green Berry Holder.

You can use the notes section of your database any way you want, just so long as it is effective
and efficient in supporting your research. Here is a detailed example of what is contained in the notes
section of the database for my great-great-great-great-grandfather, John Swords, who was born in
York County, South Carolina, on 19 March 1755 and died in Anderson, Anderson County, South
Carolina, on 28 September 1834.

The following was found among family papers. It is a copy of a document addressed to the Camp No. 368, U.C.V. (United Confederate Veterans).

Rome Ga. Aug. 29, 1914

To Camp No. 368, U.C.V.

Your Committee appointed to write a few lines in memory of a member of this Camp submit the following: There is a last roll call which is being answered by those who wore the grey and also those who wore the blue. Comrade Green B. Holder is no more with us, he answered the last call June 18, 1914. With folded arms he bid comrades, friends and loved ones adieu. Comrade Holder was born at Lawrenceville, Georgia [sic], December 22, 1845. What we gather concerning his war record is the following:
Comrade Holder in March 1862 was mustered Into the Confererate [sic] Army in Capt, T..M. Peeples Company "D" with Battalion Light Artillery at Bristol, Tennessee, said Battalion was in many engagements in East Tennessee and West Virginia. After the fight at Wythville, Va. in the spring of 1864 they campaigned down the Shanandoah [sic] Valley to Winchester, then under orders from Richmond they turned over their guns at Waynes Gap and went to Richmond where they were put in heavy Artillery. During the seige [sic] of Richmond and Petersburg, July 1864 to 1865 they manded [sic manned] the guns in forts [sic] Gilmer and Hoke. On April 2, 1865 when the Confederates could no longer hold the forts they spiked their seige [sic] guns and blew up their magazine and marched out with Lee's Army to or near Appomattox. On the evening before the surrender Comrade was wounded In the wrist.   Comrade Holder was parolled [sic] with Lee's Army. He reached his Georgia home on the 29th of April. In December following he moved to Floyd County. For a time he engaged in merchandising,, afterwards in real estate. One of your Committee by his vote elected Comrade a member of the Board of County Commissioners and he made an acceptable member. Afterwards he served two years in the General Assembly of Georgia.   Comrade Holder was President of the Rome Mercantile Company and other industries. He was a good neighbor, good business man and a true friend to both white and colored. He was a great lover of old sacred harp songs. His life long Consort recorded him only a few months to the haven of rest. They left with their friends and comrades to mourn their passing away twelve children, six sons and six daughters. We extend the bereaved ones sincere sympathy. We respectfully ask that a page in our Minute Book be ascribed to the memory of comrade G.B. Holder, and we further ask that our Adj. Send a copy to either Miss Emma or Miss Ida Holder.

                                                                                   Respectfully submitted,

                                        W.L. Selman, }
                                        H.C. Jennings, } Committee.
                                        H.C. Hones   }

FIGURE 13-1   Transcription of a document in the author's genealogical database for his great-grandfather

- John Swords, Sr., was a soldier in the Revolutionary War, serving in the 1st Regiment (Harris') of the Georgia Militia commanded by Lt. Col. Walton HARRIS.

- "He enlisted while residing in York District and was in the Snow Campaign. During the spring of 1777, he served under Capt. George Warley and Col. Sumter. He was on the Florida Expedition and in the battles at Beaufort and Stono. He was in the siege of Savannah under Capt. Boyce. After being taken prisoner at the Siege of Savannah, he was held two weeks before he escaped. Next, he was under Colonel Bratton, and was in the battles at Rocky Mount, Hanging Rock and Eutaw Springs." (Source: Moss, Bobby Gilmer. "Roster of South Carolina Patriots in the American Revolution." Baltimore, MD: Genealogical Publishing Company, Inc., 1985.)

- Information about bounty land warrant issued to John SWORDS for partial service in the Continental Army during the American Revolution (Source citation included)

- Information about specific land purchases and sales (Source citations included)

- 1790 and 1800 U.S. federal census entry information for him in York County, South Carolina (Source citations for microfilm included)

- More land and property transactions (Source citations included)

- 1810 and 1820 U.S. federal census entry information for him in the Pendleton District of South Carolina (Source citations for microfilm and online databases included)

13

■ Description of American Revolutionary War Service and Pension records received from NARA and selected transcriptions of data obtained in them, including application, sworn affidavit of service, family Bible pages, and pension payment stubs (Source citations included)

■ Transcription of federal document discontinuing John Swords federal military pension in 1819 (Source citation included)

■ Note to myself indicating that I want to determine why John Swords' pension was discontinued

■ E-mail correspondence with two individuals regarding the military service of John SWORDS. (Each citation includes correspondent's name, e-mail address, date, subject, text, and notations.)

■ Description of Revolutionary War Pension records, including his petition for a pension made to the South Carolina legislature in 1826, sworn affidavits (different from NARA documents), and correspondence received from South Carolina State Archive and selected transcriptions of data obtained in them (Source citations included)

■ Index of deed book entries in Pendleton District of South Carolina from 1822 and 1824 (Source citations included)

■ 1830 U.S. federal census for Anderson County, South Carolina, for John SWORDS and women in his household (Source citations for microfilm and online database included)

■ 1834 petition by widow Eleanor Swancey Swords to South Carolina legislature for continuation of the pension, obtained from the South Carolina State Archive and selected transcriptions of data obtained in them (Source citation included)

■ John Swords, Sr. died on 28 September 1834. His will was dated 15 January 1834 and was recorded in Will Book A, Page 498 on 14 October 1834. It was also proved on 14 October 1834. (Source citations of copies obtained from Anderson County probate court records included)

■ Additional correspondence between the heirs of John and Eleanor Swords and the South Carolina government dating from 1834 to 1836. These were obtained from the South Carolina State Archive and provide documentation of Eleanor's death on 3 May 1841 and concern the settlement of pension payment claims to her estate and heirs. (Source citation included)

As you can see, the information here is very extensive. In addition to the materials I listed above, I also have notations concerning evidence and hypotheses that I have not yet proved and notes to myself regarding additional research required. I will also include information obtained via postal mail and e-mail, along with citations of those exchanges. Information that is not proved needs to be notated as such so that I don't make any erroneous assumptions based on possible inaccurate data, and so that any other researcher with whom I am collaborating or sharing data likewise will not draw any conclusions on evidence I have not verified.

Some genealogical databases include a spell checker built into the software. This can be a great help, especially in the notes section. If the database doesn't include it, never fear. You can always copy-and-paste all of the text into a word processor that does include a spell checker. Perform your spell check there, make your corrections, and then you can copy and paste the entire set of notes back into the database, replacing the previous set of notes.

Multimedia Capabilities

Most genealogical database programs now include the ability to include photographs and other graphics. The graphics are typically stored in another directory on your computer and are linked to by the database. You may or may not initially want to incorporate photographs into your genealogical database work, but I can guarantee you that it won't be long before you realize how great that will be. Remember that photographs are visual evidence as well, and that they provide data for your documentation *and* graphical interest to the database on the computer and on printed charts and reports.

Some database developers are beginning to support video and sound clips in their products as well. Again, these are supplemental files stored elsewhere on the computer and linked to by the database. While these types of files aren't useful on printed reports, they can be incorporated into multimedia publications you might create, such as a family history CD-ROM or a genealogical Web site.

Search and Filter Results

The genealogical database software packages currently available are much more than just spreadsheets or word processing documents. They are sophisticated applications that store an individual's data in pieces. Each piece contains a similar data key that allows everything for an individual to be pulled together to present what appears to us as a single cohesive record. By the same token, that facility also means that a single piece of data need only be entered once, and then it can be used in multiple screens on the computer, on multiple pages of a printed document or on a Web page you create, *and* in performing searches of the database.

The genealogical databases typically can present you with an alphabetical list, or roster, of all the individuals in the database. You can scroll through the list to locate the person whose record you want to see or, with databases using "smart input" capabilities, you can type a few letters of the surname and the display will jump to that part of the list. The more characters you type, the closer you get to the exact record you want to access. In addition, most allow you to perform a simple search by opening a Find window and typing in a keyword. This is a quick way to home in on an individual with a unique name on the list.

Some of the databases allow you to sort the list in different ways. For example, Family Tree Maker allows you to sort the list in alphabetical sequence by last name in ascending order (A to Z) or descending order (Z to A), and by birth date in ascending order (oldest first) or descending order (youngest first). It also allows you to use an AKA (nickname) if it is available, using it as an additional entry and after the middle name (if any). You also can specify that the list use married names of females in order to cluster them with the family surname into which they married.

This leads us right into reporting, which is a vital function to support your research.

Reporting Capabilities

You will want to consider the types of reports you might want to use for your genealogical research. Every genealogical database will be able to manipulate the data to produce standard reports for you

May Wrenn Morgan–circa 1928
(From the author's collection)

such as pedigree charts, family group sheets, ancestor tree charts, descendant tree charts, and simple descendant reports, and outline descendant reports in which the members of each generation are numbered and indented. The database you select should provide you the ability to specify how many generations to include in the report, as well as which fields to include. These reports are first created and displayed on the computer, and you then have the option to save them to disk, print them, or process them in some other way.

Don't underestimate the importance of being able to produce custom reports. For example, before I plan a research trip, I will generate custom reports of the surnames of the people in the area that I plan to visit or research. I can specify that I want to see the dates and birth location, marriage location, and death location of each one. I can include a cemetery name and even perform a search for that name. As I said earlier, I ultimately will have "sliced and diced" the information stored in my database so that I have fine-tuned my lists of the who, what, and where I want to research, and the types of records I want to locate. Custom reports can be among your best research tools.

A few of the databases have integrated maps into their programs. These can be used to produce helpful reports. For example, based on the information you enter concerning place names of facts and events, your database can prepare a display on your screen of a specific geographic area and a complementary listing of all the persons in your database who are documented for that area. The listing is dependent, too, on individual persons and data fields you select to include both on the map and in the listing.

When considering the reporting capabilities of the genealogical databases, remember that it is usually better to have more options than less.

Import and Export of GEDCOMs and Other Files

An important facility of any genealogical database software package is its ability to create and work with GEDCOM files. I can already hear you saying, "What the heck is a GEDCOM file?" GEDCOM is an acronym that stands for GEnealogical Data COMmunications. It is a data format standard that allows data from one genealogy computer program to be shared with and read by another genealogy computer program. Computer application programs typically use their own organizational structure and format for the data they create, process, and store. In order to facilitate the exchange of data between researchers using different genealogical database programs, a standard was created that programmers could use to write programs to extract and export data from their database application and format into another file format, the GEDCOM. The GEDCOM file could then be given or sent to another researcher, and he or she could then import the file into their database.

The GEDCOM is really just a series of records, each in a particular location in the file itself and labeled with numbers and text codes to help a receiving genealogical database program identify what data is contained there and where it should place the data in its own file format. Figure 13-2

```
0 @I0001@ INDI
1 NAME Samuel Thomas /Morgan/
1 SEX M
1 BIRT
2 DATE 18 DEC 1909
2 PLAC Mebane (Alamance) NC
2 SOUR Birth Certificate (delayed issue - 5 October 1971)
3 CONT Genealogy Binder - Ref # M-13
1 DEAT
2 DATE 2 MAY 1980
2 PLAC Reidsville (Rockingham) NC
2 SOUR Death Certificate
3 CONT Genealogy Binder - Reference # M-4
2 CAUS Stroke
```

FIGURE 13-2   Portion of a GEDCOM file showing birth and death information

shows a small portion of a GEDCOM file I created, and this sample shows the records that contain the birth and death information for my father. The GEDCOM file is read by the receiving database program, recognized as a GEDCOM, and is then reformatted into a file that it could then open. The GEDCOM file format is, in effect, the lowest common denominator between genealogical database application programs.

More recently, some genealogy software packages have been produced that can read what is known as "native" format data. What that means is that the proprietary format of the file used by one genealogical database program can be imported in its "native" state by the other program without the first program's data being formatted into the GEDCOM format.

Later in this chapter, we'll discuss the process of creating and sharing GEDCOM files with other researchers. However, you will remember our discussion of PDAs in Chapter 12 and the fact that there are genealogical software packages for them. The PDA software packages we discussed there accept GEDCOM files or go through a free conversion program to convert GEDCOM data into a file format that the PDA can read and use.

Publishing Functions

Many genealogists and family historians, after they've gathered a substantial amount of information, feel compelled to produce some kind of durable documentation. Many produce a printed family history, filled with genealogical evidence, photographs, lineage charts, and lots of biographical information. Others write biographies of individual ancestors or family members. Others publish information electronically onto heirloom family CDs and/or to Web sites.

Many of the genealogical databases currently available possess the ability to produce professional-looking publication materials that can be readied for printing. These can be formatted to include a cover, a table of contents, individual sections and chapters, embedded photographs,

13

Charles Warner Holder–1905
(From the author's collection)

charts, and maps, source citations, footnotes and endnotes, appendices, a bibliography, and an index. All or most of this can be derived or extracted from your genealogical database and supplemented with other materials during the editing process.

Some produce PDF files that can be printed, attached to e-mail messages, or made available through family Web sites. Some can even produce HTML output, which are the formatted documents used to produce Web pages.

If you never plan to publish a printed or Web-based family history, you may never need these functions. Remember, you can always generate reports from your database and save them as text files that can be opened in or copied-and-pasted into a document in a word processor. However, if you are interested in publishing functions, investigate the options described at the respective software companies' Web sites and look for reviews from other users.

Find Out What Genealogical Database Programs Are Available

You have many choices of genealogical database programs. The prices range from free to $100 U.S./£56 U.K. The old adage "You get what you pay for" doesn't always hold true with genealogy programs. For example, both the Legacy Standard Edition and Personal Ancestral File are free database programs and both are feature-rich and robust in both operation and output. Conversely, some software packages, such as Generations Grande Suite 8.0, Generations Liberty Edition, and Generations Deluxe DVD Edition, come with bundles of CD-ROMs, some or all of which may be outdated and/or completely useless to your research. It is important to comparison-shop the features and evaluate what is and is not included in a specific genealogical database.

Some beginning researchers start with a free genealogy database and gain some experience with the data entry facilities and with the charts and reports functions. They may later decide to upgrade to a more robust edition of the same software with more features and functions, or they may decide to move to another database altogether. Migration does not mean having to input all your data again. You usually can extract a GEDCOM file and import it to the new program, and some programs will accommodate opening the file format from another database without having to take the intermediary step of creating a GEDCOM file.

The software packages described below do not comprise a full list of the available genealogical databases. However, these are the major players in the database marketplace today.

Ancestral Quest

Ancestral Quest is a product of Incline Software, LC, and runs on computers running Microsoft Windows 98 or later. More details are available at the Ancestral Quest Web site at **http://www. ancquest.com.** The database is simple and intuitive software to learn and to use. Its graphical views of an Individual's Record shows his or her parents, spouse, and children in a clear-cut view and you can add photographs and other graphics. The Pedigree View displays up to five generations at a time, allowing you to easily go farther back. Clicking on a name in the Pedigree View expands a box to display an individual's birth, marriage, and death details. A detailed data entry screen allows you to enter event details for each individual and includes a source citation for each.

The software uses a sophisticated yet simple citation management system called CitePro that allows you to enter, administer, and attach source citations to a whole event or simply to a date or a location. Source citations can be set to print once on reports and be referenced for additional occurrences in the same report as footnote numbers.

Advanced searching of your database is available using a technology named FilterPro. This facility allows you to use combinations of user-defined criteria to fine-tune your searches and focus in on specific persons, places, events, and other data.

Progeny Software, Inc., has produced Ancestral Quest Charting Companion, which is compatible with Ancestral Quest Version 3.0, 10 (AQ 2002) and 11 (when using the .aq database type). It allows you to produce a variety of customizable charts and reports that can print in portrait or landscape orientation on any paper size. They also can be produced in PDF format. Learn more about it at the Ancestral Quest Charting Companion at **http://www.ancquest.com/aqchartcompanion/ aqchartingcompanion.html.**

Brother's Keeper

Brother's Keeper is a shareware genealogy program created by John Steed for Microsoft Windows users. The full version with manual sells for $45 U.S./£25 U.K., and upgrades are available for users of previous versions at less than half that price ($20 U.S./£11.30 U.K.). You may visit the Brother's Keeper Web site at **http://ourworld.compuserve.com/homepages/Brothers_Keeper** to read about and download the software.

Family Historian

Family Historian is published by Calico Pie, Ltd., in England, and offers a full-feature genealogical database for users of Microsoft Windows 98 and subsequent operating systems. The software offers an intuitive graphical interface that is at once both engaging and simple to use. Four diagram-icon buttons open the Diagram Window to show different views: an Ancestor diagram, a Descendants diagram, and Ancestors *and* Descendants diagram, and an All Relatives diagram. Data entry is easy and intuitive, with strong support for source citations. Among all the genealogy programs, its support for the entry, linking, and labeling of photographs is perhaps the most comprehensive and elegant. Standard reports can be customized and can be saved in simple text format (TXT); Rich Text Format (RFT), which can then be opened by any word processor; and in HTML format for use in building your family history Web site. The software also offers a merge-and-compare files function

13

Joseph Patterson Wilson and wife,
Frances Lamb Mimms Wilson–1912
(From the author's collection)

and backup and restore functions to help safeguard your genealogical data. Visit the Web site at **http://www.family-historian.co.uk** for a comprehensive tour of the software and details about its features and functions.

Family Tree Maker

The Family Tree Maker database software, also known as FTM, has been around a long time and Version 11 was released in 2003. The software was originally developed and marketed by Broderbund and its ownership has passed through several companies. It became part of the MyFamily.com, Inc., companies when it purchased Genealogy.com. The Web site for the product is **http://www. familytreemaker.com.**

FTM has grown in functionality over the years and includes all the standard data entry and reporting functions you might expect. It now supports opening two database files simultaneously and cutting-and-pasting individuals and data between files. The package supports a scrapbook function that allows you to add photographs and graphics from files, photo CDs, and other sources, and the option to include or exclude the graphic from a scrapbook or slide show. A single graphics file of a photograph, digitized document, or some other image can be linked to multiple individuals' scrapbooks with different descriptive text added to that person's scrapbook record.

The software provides a strong source citation function in which you may enter a Master Source and later, with only a few keystrokes in a citation field, invoke that source and add unique information for the citation, such as a page number, microfilm reel number, or other reference. Embedded, too, are maps that can be used to visually show the locations where ancestors and family members lived, along with textual details that you can customize.

The package connects to the Web locations to search predefined databases, particularly at the FamilyTreeMaker.com online site. The FamilyFinder facility helps you locate information by connecting with Genealogy.com's databases and the GenForum message boards, allows searches of Family Tree Maker CD-ROM products, and enables you to learn about and access other resources.

Reports can be produced in standard formats and using filters that you define for individuals and data fields to include/exclude. You can create custom reports as well focus on the people whose history you want to investigate on a research trip.

The FTM Publishing Center is an easy place to produce an heirloom quality book of your family history research, complete with table of contents, index, bibliography, and detailed source citations, and incorporating text and graphics. The construction and editing processes can be done with the use of prompted guides. In addition to producing a printed publication, you can create a family Web site at **http://www.familytreemaker.com** in either PDF or HTML or both formats. Data files are created, saved to your hard disk, and then automatically uploaded to the Family Tree Maker Web site. Photographs and graphics linked to the database also can be published to the Internet.

An excellent book by Rhonda R. McClure, *The Official Guide to Family Tree Maker 11,* published by MyFamily.com, provides the definitive handbook for users of FTM at all levels. The book is filled with step-by-step instructions and hundreds of screen illustrations and is the perfect companion to the software.

HEREDIS

HEREDIS is a product offered by the French company, BSD Concept. It is available at **http://www. myheredis.com** for both Microsoft Windows and Apple Macintosh OS X users. The HEREDIS Standard Edition for Windows is free, and the HEREDIS Premium Edition for Windows and the HEREDIS Mac X are available for purchase. (A free Mac demo version is available for download.) The software boasts an unlimited number of individuals, generations, events, data, and notes. All of the functions can be displayed simultaneously on a single screen, making this a truly multitasking genealogical database. The Premium and Mac Editions incorporate a significant number of additional report functions and formats, among other bonuses. The graphical 3-D family tree is a compelling, innovative approach to displaying relationships and data, and both the database filtered search and source citation facilities are reported to be strong in all the packages.

Legacy Family Tree

The Millennia Corporation's Legacy Family Tree (**http://www.legacyfamilytree.com**) is a full-feature genealogy database program for Microsoft Windows available in two versions. The Standard Edition allows you to input data and source citations, add notes, produce reports, merge files, import and export data, and all the other standard functions. It has a great deal of power and flexibility *and* it is free. The Deluxe Edition includes a large number of additional functions and warrants the price if these look like useful features for your research. These include: language support for Dutch, French, German, Norwegian, and Spanish; additional views, including a report of multiple lines of descent; the Geo Location Database, a searchable compilation of more than three million current locations; mapping functions; Web page creation; and many more. You may want to download the Standard Version, try it, and consider upgrading to the Deluxe Edition to obtain the other features.

The Master Genealogist

The Master Genealogist, also known as TMG, is a feature-rich genealogical software package offered by Wholly Genes Software for Microsoft Windows 98 and higher version users. It comes in two editions, Gold and Silver. The Silver Edition has all the data entry and some of the reporting functions. The Gold Edition, however, has enhanced and expanded search, view, and reporting functions. Integrated Web support is included for searching at a number of specific

13

sites, including Ancestry.com, the LDS FamilySearch.com, RootsWeb.com, and other sites. Reporting options are extensive, including the ability to export data directly into word processing and spreadsheet applications and embedded production of PDF files. TMG allows you to customize your working environment, and set up user-defined life events for entry, tracking, and reporting, making for a product that can be used by beginners and advanced researchers alike. TMG also facilitates sophisticated book publishing, complete with table of contents, embedded graphics and photographs, footnotes, multiple indexes, and bibliography. Direct import of data from a number of the other major databases is supported without having to use intermediate GEDCOM files.

A companion book, *Getting the Most out of The Master Genealogist,* edited by Lee Hoffman, is available from the Wholly Genes Web site at **http://www.whollygenes.com.**

Personal Ancestral File

Personal Ancestral File, or PAF as it is known in the genealogy community, is a free product of The Church of Jesus Christ of Latter-day Saints. Family history research is an essential part of the Mormon faith and, in order to facilitate this work, the LDS created a software program to collect, organize, and document family history. The software has been around for many years and each new version or release is robust. The software is available for free download at the FamilySearch Web site at **http://www.familysearch.org.** When you arrive at the main screen, click on the link labeled Order/Download Products and, on the next screen, click on the link labeled Software Downloads-Free. Here you will find the current version of the software, which supports multiple languages, and the user's guide in English, French, German, Portuguese, and Spanish. In addition, the Hope Foundation has written the *Personal Ancestral File User's Guide* for Version 4.0 of the software, and published by Ancestry.com, Incorporated. While there is a more recent version of the software available from the LDS, you will find the content quite satisfactory for quickly becoming an expert with the new version.

PAF is an excellent package with full support for data entry, most types of life events, detailed source citations, sorting, producing a full range of reports, and creation of Web pages. There are versions available for both the Microsoft Windows and Apple Macintosh operating systems.

Reunion

Reunion, by Leister Productions, Inc. (**http://www.leisterpro.com**), is the one of the few full-feature genealogical database programs currently available for the Macintosh operating system. It records names, dates, locations, source citations, and notes. It also supports photographs, graphics, sound files, and video clips. It displays family relationships in a graphic form. Objects in charts can be selected, grouped, and easily aligned. Photographs can be placed inside individuals' information boxes, and display and print report formats can be changed and combined to provide an easily customized look. Reunion 8 is the most recent release at the time of this writing, and this came with two identical versions of the software: one for native Apple Macintosh OS X and another for native OS 8.5 to 9.2.

RootsMagic

FormalSoft, Inc., is the company that developed the Family Origins genealogy software program, which has been discontinued. Its successor is RootsMagic, a robust software package that works with Microsoft Windows 95 and above operating systems. There are three navigation view levels: pedigree, family (shown in Figure 13-3), and descendants. You can open multiple databases at once and can drag-and-drop to move and copy persons and their information between databases. Each database can contain an unlimited number of individuals with names, dates, locations, source citations, and notes. The software supports 60 predefined fact types and you can create your own.

RootsMagic is strong in its publishing abilities. It allows you to create complete books from your database, complete with charts, photographs, notes, citations, photographs, a bibliography, table of contents, and index. You can print to a printer or to an Adobe Acrobat PDF document, or to export text in Rich Text Format (RTF) to a word processor.

Standard output reports include pedigree charts, family group sheets, and ancestor and descendant reports. You can use the preformatted reports create or customize your own, create calendars, mailing labels, and other lists. The software can create and export GEDCOM files, as well as produce sophisticated Web pages.

Detailed information can be found at the RootsMagic Web site at **http://www.rootsmagic.com.**

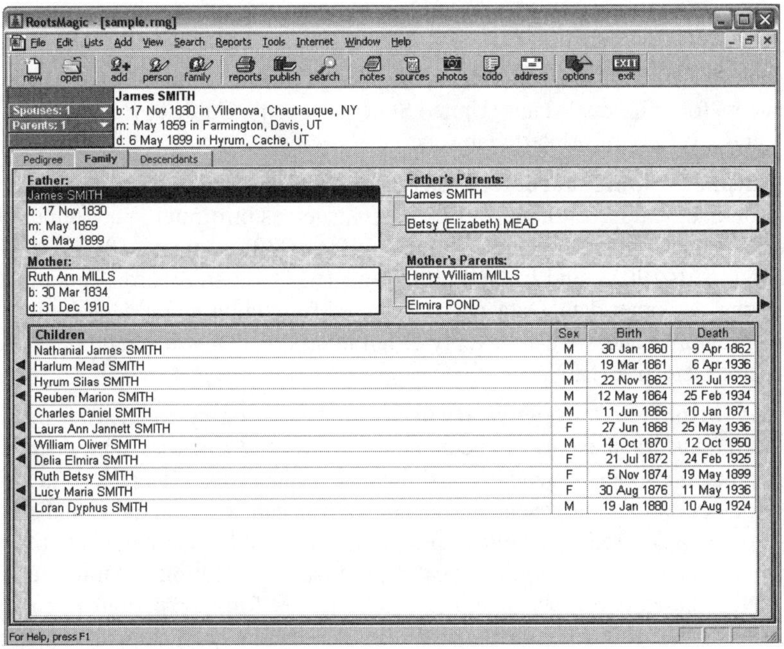

FIGURE 13-3   The RootsMagic Family View screen (Courtesy of FormalSoft, Inc.)

13

Other Genealogy Database Software

There are a number of other less prominent genealogy database packages you might also consider. Most are shareware packages, and this means that you may be able to download and work with the software for free for some period. Then, if you like the software, you can purchase it.

- **BirthWrite (http://www.birthwrite.com)**   Shareware software package with no date timeout for trial use. Registration is $30 U.S./£16.96 U.K.

- **Cumberland Family Tree (http://www.cf-software.com)**   Trial version available for 45 days. Program costs $45 U.S./£25 U.K. Supplemental downloadable files available, including support for other languages: Afrikaans, Czech, Danish, Dutch, Finnish, French, German (Austria), German (Standard), Hungarian, Italian, Norwegian (Bokmål), Norwegian (Nynorsk), Polish, Portuguese (Brazil), Portuguese (Standard), Serbian, Slovak, Slovenian, Spanish, Swedish.

Supplemental Genealogical Programs

In addition to the genealogical database software packages, there are specific applications and utilities you may find useful.

- **AniMap (http://goldbug.com)**   AniMap Plus is a product of The Gold Bug. It contains more than 2,300 maps showing boundaries and changes for the 48 contiguous United States since colonial times. The company also sells historic maps and gazetteers on CD-ROM of England, Wales, Scotland, and Ireland, the World Gazetteers for 1859 and 1895, a variety of gazetteers for individual states (United States), Lovell's Guide to British North America (1895), and a variety of printed map sets.

- **Clooz (http://www.ancestordetective.com)**   An electronic filing cabinet that can be used to file data you have found over the years, such as information about people, city directories, censuses for the United States (1790–1930), Canada (1852–1901), United Kingdom (1841–1901), and Ireland (1901 and 1911), death records, funeral records, photographs, and other data. Data can be exported from eight major genealogical database software programs, and there are twenty different reports that you can produce. Published by Ancestor Detective, LLC.

- **Genelines (http://www.progenysoftware.com)**   Developing an ancestor profile and incorporating historical events can be complex. However, Genelines, a product of Progeny Software, Inc., is a sophisticated historical timeline package that offers the ability to produce a variety of reports for your genealogical analysis. You can create an individual biographical timeline or an age-based comparative biographical chart that compares the life events of two or more individuals. The program also produces a collection of family relationship charts that graphically display timelines in a variety of formats: pedigree chart, family group chart, a direct line of descent chart, a full descendant chart showing all generations, and a timeline fan chart. The program also produces textual biographical charts showing begin and end dates for a life event, the location, and notes or source information.

■ **World Place Advisor**   Another product offered by Progeny Software, Inc. (**http://www. progenysoftware.com**). It is designed to work with a number of the Microsoft Windows–based genealogical database application packages, and is used to check more than 3.3 million place names to verify that places included in your database exist, are spelled correctly, and are associated with counties and countries. Its primary limitation is that it uses current geographical information, associating place names with the current county, parish, country, rather than the geopolitical relationships that existed at the time of the event you have recorded. Progeny Software has stated that it plans to include that facility in future releases of the software. Still, the software provides an easy way to update your incomplete location entries in your database if you omitted them when you originally input them or have been procrastinating on doing that task.

These are just a few of the better known supplemental genealogy software programs for the Microsoft Windows operating system. You can learn more about these and other programs at Cyndi's List at **http://www.cyndislist.com.**

Determine Which Features You Need

Now that we've discussed the functions of genealogical software packages and introduced a collection of available genealogical databases and supplemental utility packages, you may feel a bit overwhelmed. That is not uncommon when you have so many options from which to choose. I recommend taking a methodical approach to the evaluation and selection of genealogical software.

1. Prepare a list of the genealogical research you are conducting or plan to undertake. Consider the geographical locations where your ancestors and family members lived, the types of records created in those locations at those times, the types of facts and events you will be documenting, the sources you will be using, and the types of reports you are likely to use most often.

2. Consider what your publishing plans might include over time.

3. Visit the Web sites of the genealogical software companies and learn as much as you can about each software package. Compare the lists of features to the list you prepared in Step 1.

4. Look at the screenshots that the software companies have placed on their Web sites. Consider the types of information you want to input to your database, whether the software supports that, and how user-friendly the data entry screens seem to be.

5. Send any questions you have about the database packages in an e-mail to the technical support address. They can and will answer your questions and, in the process, you will learn how good or bad the company's support staff's performance might be.

6. Visit message boards and locate the ones that address and discuss genealogical software packages. Search the current message board postings and the archives for users' discussions of the pros and cons of the software packages. Post messages with questions that you have and check back regularly to read and respond.

13

7. Search the Internet for reviews of the current version of each software package you are considering. Enter the name of the software package in quotes, followed by the keyword "review." This may give you additional information to digest.

8. Visit Web sites where the software is sold and read the users' reviews. These can provide additional insights into the features that people really like and any problems that others have encountered.

9. Visit the library or a bookstore to locate genealogy magazines that may contain reviews of genealogical database packages. (*Genealogical Computing,* a quarterly publication of Ancestry.com, Incorporated, regularly reviews genealogical software of all types. Visit the Shops at Ancestry.com at **http://www.ancestry.com** to learn more about this publication. Other genealogical magazines also review software.)

This approach will give you a great deal of perspective from many angles to help in your decision-making process. By the end of your review, you should have a good idea of what you want. The last step is to be a savvy consumer and to use your Internet research skills to comparison shop for the best deal on the software. You're on your way!

Exchange GEDCOMs with Other Researchers

I always tell people that, for me, genealogy is much more than just locating a document or filling in a blank on a form or in a database. It is the thrill of the chase, the research, and learning experiences that challenge my interest.

One of the most rewarding things about genealogical research, however, is making contact with other researchers and sharing information. Genealogists are undoubtedly some of the nicest, most generous people I've ever met and you will find that too. Strike up a conversation with another researcher in the genealogy and local history area of your local public library or at a genealogy society meeting. It's probable that you will soon begin discussing your ancestors and their lives, sharing your research experiences and anecdotes, and exchanging advice about different record types and resources that may help one another get around those inevitable brick walls.

You already know from our discussions in Chapter 9 that you can and will discover important leads through your research on the Internet. Message boards and mailing lists are excellent communication venues for making contact with other researchers working on the same lines that you are investigating. Once you find the common thread between you, it is likely that you will begin exchanging information in some form or another. I often find myself engaged initially in the exchange of small groups of names and facts via e-mail and that establishes the first level of communication and collaboration. The exchanges increase with perhaps reports extracted from our database; digitized images of family photographs; lists of publications that contain important information; and the addresses of libraries, archives, courthouses, and other facilities at which documents and other evidence may be found. Addresses of helpful Web sites and online databases can be shared as well.

You may become so well acquainted with and trusting of another researcher that you may decide to share detailed information from your database. Whereas before you may have extracted data in report format and may have e-mailed it to the other person, you may now want to provide more detail. And that is where GEDCOM files can really be extremely helpful.

All genealogical database software programs can produce files. Your actual database's content is a specific application file. In Family Tree Maker, for example, the active file you work with has a file extension of .FTW (Family Tree for Windows). Every time you open the database to work with it, that file is opened. When you close the program, the entire database is saved to an .FTW file.

If you want to share the contents of all or part of your database with another researcher, you must first determine what database package they are using. If, by chance, he or she is using the same database that you use, you should be able to simply provide a copy of your database file. However, if the person is using a different genealogical database, it is important to ask whether it can accept the "native" file that is produced and used by your database or whether the person needs a GEDCOM file. Based on the reply you receive, you can determine what you want to produce.

Next, decide what it is you want to share with the other researcher. Do you want to share your entire database or only information on specific individuals, such as one branch of your family tree? Do you want to share only information on deceased individuals and preserve the privacy of living persons? Who knew there were so many options?

While you want to expand the amount and quality of your family tree by sharing and collaborating with other researchers, common courtesy usually dictates that you will preserve the privacy of living persons whenever you share your database. An exception, however, might be made when sharing data with another close family member. However, always use good judgment to protect the confidence and privacy of family members who may have shared information with you on a strictly *entre nous* basis. You can preserve the privacy of living persons in your file by "privatizing" the file. Privatization is a common feature in genealogical database software that removes all information about a person except the relationship of the person. For example, you might want to suppress sharing any information about your parents and siblings who are still living. The privatization process reads the database and looks for persons who were born within the last 100 years and/or for whom there are no death dates. If no death date has been entered, these people's records are masked. The GEDCOM file may simply show the person as "LIVING" or "LIVING Smith" and no other information. Consult the Help file of your database software to learn how to privatize your database. After you have finished generating the GEDCOM or native file you plan to share, you can go back and un-privatize the file. This will allow you to again see and work with all the data for living individuals.

Once the privatization is complete, you can determine how to create the appropriate file for another researcher. If you are providing your entire database, you should be able to go to the database's menu and select the File option. There will probably be an option shown on the drop-down or pull-down menu that is labeled Copy, Export, or Copy/Export. Click on that option and you should be presented with a standard Save File window. Click on the arrow at the right side of the Save as Type field. If you are creating a GEDCOM, you should see an option labeled "GEDCOM (*.GED)" and should select that. (All GEDCOM files use the file extension .GED.) Supply a unique filename for your GEDCOM file. I always use a filename that includes a date so that I can easily recognize different versions of a similar file. For example, I have a file named Morgan_010204.GED that is a GEDCOM file of my entire genealogy database that I created on January 2, 2004.

You may decide you want to create a GEDCOM file for only a specific group of individuals or a branch line. In that case, you will want to refer to the Help file of your database software for details about how to do this. You may have to create a report, an ancestor tree, a descendant tree, an outline descendant tree, or some other report that contains the group of individuals that you want to include in the GEDCOM file. You may also specify what data fields to include and exclude. When you are ready to create your GEDCOM file, open your database program. Go to the menu bar at the top and click on the File option, and then on Copy, Export, or Copy/Export option. Your database will display the Save File window I described above. Choose a name for the file and, in the Save as Type field, select the GEDCOM (*.GED) option. Click on the Save button and the file should be created.

Once you have created the GEDCOM file, open it in your database program to make certain it contains the individuals you wanted included. You can open the file by selecting the File option in the database software's menu bar and, in the drop-down window, choosing the Open File option. You can then locate the GEDCOM file you just created, click on it to select it, and click on the Open button. Your database will then try to open the file and may prompt you to indicate in what new native file format the new file should be saved. (Remember that a GEDCOM file must be converted to the file format your database uses.)

Always refer to the Help file for your genealogical database program for detailed instructions about how to create, export, and open GEDCOM files. Not all programs work alike and the process I have presented may differ from that used by the database you are using.

There are multiple ways to provide the GEDCOM or native file to your fellow researcher. You might save it to a floppy disk. Your GEDCOM file may, however, be too large to fit onto a standard 3.5-inch floppy disk. It also is possible that your researcher friend may have a newer computer on which a 3.5-inch floppy disk drive was not standard, in which case he or she would require another format. You might then consider using a Zip disk or burning the file onto a CD. These physical media can then be given to or mailed to your researcher. A storage media-independent option, though, would be to send the file as an attachment to an e-mail message. Make sure, of course, that you have scanned the file with your anti-virus software package to ensure that it is virus-free.

If you are the recipient of a GEDCOM file from another researcher, the first thing you should do is scan it for viruses. Once you know it is virus-free, you can start your genealogical database program and then open the file. With a new file and new clues, let the research fun begin!

Upload Your GEDCOM File to an Online Database

One way to extend your research reach is to let other people know who you are researching and what you have found. Message boards or mailing lists are excellent places to publicize your interest in locating information about specific lines, surnames, and individuals. However, another way to expand your contact range is to upload your database to one of the online database sites. There other people can see what you have found, download and review the file, and make contact with you.

Some genealogists express concern that if they upload their data to such an online site, someone will steal "their research." Certainly there are researchers who do not have the knowledge or experience to know better than to simply download a file and accept what they have downloaded as fact. You know that before you can accept anything as fact, you should retrace the research path, personally examine the evidence, and form your own educated conclusions based on all the evidence you can locate and apply. If you are going to fret over what someone else might do with the information you worked so hard to compile, you shouldn't upload or share any data with anyone else. However, if you are interested in making contact with other researchers, placing your data and your contact information out on the Internet for others to access is definitely a way to proceed.

Before you upload anything, you will go through the process of privatizing your database. Once that is complete, create a GEDCOM file of what you want to upload and share. After the GEDCOM file has been generated, you can go back into your database and un-privatize the database so that you can see and work with the data in its entirety again.

There are a number of online databases to which you can upload your GEDCOM file. You will encounter them in various places on the Internet. However, perhaps the largest and best known is the Ancestry World Tree at Ancestry.com (**http://www.ancestry.com/trees/awt**) with more than 200 million persons' records already uploaded. When you upload your GEDCOM file, you will be asked to supply a name for the file and an e-mail address. People can then browse the data in your GEDCOM file in a pedigree file format or they can download the full GEDCOM file. With your e-mail address available, people can then contact you with questions, comments, suggestions, and requests to collaborate. Likewise, you can visit the Ancestry World Tree, search for individuals, locate GEDCOM databases, and contact other researchers.

Publish Your Family History in Printed Form

Publication of a family history is an intensive undertaking. The research you perform should be crisp and well documented, your materials logically organized, and the writing clear and succinct. It also should include a table of contents and a detailed index of names, places, and major events. Appendices with lists of accurate sources, citations, footnotes, endnotes, maps, a glossary of unfamiliar terms, and other reference information can be compiled and included. Your family history should strive to be an accurate and authoritative work. It should be edited for grammar, spelling, transpositions of dates and numbers, and to ensure factual content. If this sounds intimidating, well it should be. The work you do to produce a scholarly publication is important in order to provide an accurate heirloom-quality document for your family and contemporaries. However, you also want to leave an excellent historical and genealogical reference work for use by other researchers.

Many of the genealogical database software programs discussed in this chapter can be used to produce a well-organized, professional-looking manuscript with all of the component parts I've mentioned. Other software programs can be used to prepare other materials for inclusion in your publication.

Understand Copyright and Trademark Laws

A major consideration in any publishing venture is copyright and trademark law. If you have any questions about whether to use something written or created by another person or a company, be sure to obtain written permission to include it. That includes output from some programs. Read the license agreements that came with your genealogical database and other software program with regards to the use of their materials. Make sure you understand what you can and cannot use.

Whenever you use a trademarked name, take the time to investigate the way the trademark is represented. In the United States, for instance, an item might be trademarked and that product is represented with a "TM" designation in superscript following the name, such as Ancestral Quest[TM],

13

which is a trademarked product of Incline Software, LC. Other products are listed as registered trademarks. These are represented with the letter "R" enclosed in a circle in superscript following the name. A good example of that would be the Windows® operating system, which is a product of the Microsoft Corporation. It is possible to have a multiple-trademark listing, as in the example of Microsoft® Windows® 98. A similar protection for a unique service name is the service mark, which is represented by the letters "SM" in superscript following the name. A good example of this for genealogy is shown at the Buffalo.com Web site on its Family and Genealogy page at **http://www.buffalo.com/Family/Genealogy_204.asp.** Both the Buffalo.com[SM] logo and Everything Buffalo[SM] name carry service marks.

Consult an attorney or solicitor for assistance in determining whether you need to take any extraordinary precautions to protect yourself from legal complications.

Publish Your Data on the Web

Another way to extend your genealogical research reach and to attract other researchers' interest is to publish your genealogy on the Internet. An excellent place to learn more about the process of setting up a Web site is Cyndi's Genealogy Home Page Construction Kit at **http://www.cyndislist. com/construc.htm.** Written by Cyndi Howells, whose Cyndi's List Web site at **http://www. cyndislist.com** has become an Internet reference focal point for genealogical researchers around the world, this compilation of information and links to other Web resources is your authoritative guide.

A number of the genealogical database programs described earlier can generate HTML documents that will be Web pages. Many can produce PDF documents, which also can be used as Web-accessible documents included in a Web site. Even if the database program you select now doesn't produce HTML documents for Web pages, there are conversion programs that can take your GEDCOM file and generate a series of Web pages.

Keep on Researching!

We have covered a tremendous amount of territory in this book, from a definition of genealogy through working with documents, out onto the Internet, through hardware and software evaluation and selection, to finally putting your *own* genealogical research on the Internet in files and on Web pages. What a wonderful beginning for an adventure!

"A beginning?" you ask. Yes indeed! With the knowledge and skills you have gained in this book, you should feel well-prepared to get out in the world and pursue your genealogical research. Your genealogy is an exciting adventure of discovery. You will meet wonderful people, visit fascinating and unusual places, handle and examine fascinating documents and artifacts, and make a lot of new friends along the way. Among those friends will be your ancestors and family members from the past, and you will build and strengthen friendships with your contemporary family members as well. I'll venture to suggest, too, that your genealogical adventure will lead you on an adventure of self-discovery as well. We are, after all, the result of our ancestors on a great many levels. So, as you explore the past, explore the present and plant the seeds for your descendants in the future!

Happy hunting!

Index

INTERNATIONAL CONTACT INFORMATION

AUSTRALIA
McGraw-Hill Book Company
Australia Pty. Ltd.
TEL +61-2-9900-1800
FAX +61-2-9878-8881
http://www.mcgraw-hill.com.au
books-it_sydney@mcgraw-hill.com

CANADA
McGraw-Hill Ryerson Ltd.
TEL +905-430-5000
FAX +905-430-5020
http://www.mcgraw-hill.ca

**GREECE, MIDDLE EAST, & AFRICA
(Excluding South Africa)**
McGraw-Hill Hellas
TEL +30-210-6560-990
TEL +30-210-6560-993
TEL +30-210-6560-994
FAX +30-210-6545-525

MEXICO (Also serving Latin America)
McGraw-Hill Interamericana Editores
S.A. de C.V.
TEL +525-1500-5108
FAX +525-117-1589
http://www.mcgraw-hill.com.mx
carlos_ruiz@mcgraw-hill.com

SINGAPORE (Serving Asia)
McGraw-Hill Book Company
TEL +65-6863-1580
FAX +65-6862-3354
http://www.mcgraw-hill.com.sg
mghasia@mcgraw-hill.com

SOUTH AFRICA
McGraw-Hill South Africa
TEL +27-11-622-7512
FAX +27-11-622-9045
robyn_swanepoel@mcgraw-hill.com

SPAIN
McGraw-Hill/
Interamericana de España, S.A.U.
TEL +34-91-180-3000
FAX +34-91-372-8513
http://www.mcgraw-hill.es
professional@mcgraw-hill.es

**UNITED KINGDOM, NORTHERN,
EASTERN, & CENTRAL EUROPE**
McGraw-Hill Education Europe
TEL +44-1-628-502500
FAX +44-1-628-770224
http://www.mcgraw-hill.co.uk
emea_queries@mcgraw-hill.com

ALL OTHER INQUIRIES Contact:
McGraw-Hill/Osborne
TEL +1-510-420-7700
FAX +1-510-420-7703
http://www.osborne.com
omg_international@mcgraw-hill.com

Sound Off!

Visit us at **www.osborne.com/bookregistration** and let us know what you thought of this book. While you're online you'll have the opportunity to register for newsletters and special offers from McGraw-Hill/Osborne.

We want to hear from you!

Sneak Peek

Visit us today at **www.betabooks.com** and see what's coming from McGraw-Hill/Osborne tomorrow!

Based on the successful software paradigm, Bet@Books™ allows computing professionals to view partial and sometimes complete text versions of selected titles online. Bet@Books™ viewing is free, invites comments and feedback, and allows you to "test drive" books in progress on the subjects that interest you the most.

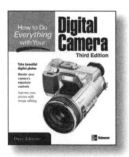
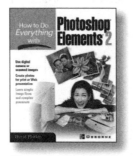

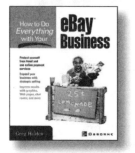